Vegas Pro 11 Editing Workshop

Douglas Spotted Eagle

Routledge
Taylor & Francis Group

LONDON AND NEW YORK

Supplementary Resources Disclaimer

Additional resources were previously made available for this title on DVD. However, as DVD has become a less accessible format, all resources have been moved to a more convenient online download option.

You can find these resources available here: www.routledge.com/9781138419544

Please note: Where this title mentions the associated disc, please use the downloadable resources instead.

First published 2012

This edition published 2015 by Focal Press

Published 2017 by Routledge
2 Park Square, Milton Park, Abingdon, Oxon OX14 4RN
711 Third Avenue, New York, NY 10017, USA

Routledge is an imprint of the Taylor & Francis Group, an informa business

Library of Congress Cataloging-in-Publication Data
Spotted Eagle, Douglas.
    Vegas pro 11 editing workshop / Douglas Spotted Eagle.
        p. cm.
    ISBN 978-0-240-82369-0
    1. Vegas (Electronic resource) 2. Digital video–Editing. I. Title.
    TK6680.5.S6743 2012
    006.6'96–dc23
                                                    2012001153

British Library Cataloguing-in-Publication Data
A catalogue record for this book is available from the British Library.

ISBN 13: 978-1-138-41954-4 (hbk)
ISBN 13: 978-0-240-82369-0 (pbk)

This book is dedicated to those who create and inspire beauty through their actions and effort.

Hoo'zoo n'aan' taa' (Fly in Beauty)
I miss you, Joshua

Contents

Part Two: Turning Up: Going Deeper into Sony Vegas

Part Three: " ... This One Goes to 11 ... "

Foreword

Anyone who is still wondering when the tipping point of the HD revolution will happen is either living in a cave or simply refusing to look at the realities of modern motion-picture production and the current state of digital technology. Every six months we see more and more advantages and advances, further improving and streamlining workflow and production. If you consider yourself part of the many who feel left behind, this book is a great place to get caught up and discover what is possible.

My own adventure with HD began in 2004, with my first all HD production of a movie for television called *The Librarian* for TNT. Although I had many years of experience with digital special effects, I had never shot with digital cameras. Everything I had heard about the technology warned me that it wasn't quite ready yet. Still, I felt compelled to try. We all knew it was coming, so why not get on the bandwagon early and begin to learn the new tools?

I had been told that HD never looks quite as good as film. I had been told that it was good for interiors or low-light conditions, but shooting in the sun or making any quick camera movements would quickly reveal the limitations of the medium.

In our first week of production, our initial fears were realized. Shooting in the jungles of Mexico, the bright light breaking through the foliage caused bright white hotspots in our images, a telltale sign of video. When we asked our HD technician for help, he shrugged his shoulders and said, "That's HD."

After a few days of shooting, another HD tech arrived to help out on our second unit. Keith Collea had worked with us for years in video assist, but in the months leading up to our production he had become a leading technician in HD cinematography. When he arrived on set, he noticed the hotspots in our images and asked us why we didn't fix it. We said we didn't think it was possible. Keith quickly made some adjustments to our cameras and the hotspots vanished.

Alan Caso, our excellent director of photography, quickly asked Keith, "What else can you do with that camera setup?" Keith replied, "What would you like?" Alan asked, "Can you give me grain?" to which Keith responded, "How much would you like?" With a few adjustments we were suddenly giving a grainy film look to our image.

Needless to say, Keith moved over to our first unit and suddenly our limitations vanished. We learned that it wasn't the medium that had limitations, it was our knowledge of how to use the medium that needed expanding.

Though back in 2004 we did have to work hard to make sure our images were as good looking as film, in today's world it's much harder to get *film* to look as good as the HD images we create. Whether working with arguably the best digital camera today, Panavision's Genesis, in full 4.4.4 color space, or working in the lowest-end HDV recording, world-class motion-picture creation can be accomplished with greater ease and versatility than ever before.

I first met Douglas Spotted Eagle after I finished making a feature film called *Flyboys*. It was one of the first films to ever use the Genesis camera, and I had fallen madly in love with the process. It created a hunger in me to learn more about what's possible in the world of HD.

It was then that I discovered the SonyV1U prosumer camera that recorded in the HDV format. Though completely on the opposite end of the HD spectrum from the Genesis, this was an intriguing format. What was different about this camera from all other HDV cameras was the claim that it could create 24p, 1080i images. Other HDV cameras recorded in a lower resolution, then "rezzed up" to 1080i. I was anxious to put the camera to the test.

However, once I got my hands on the camera, no one could quite figure out how to get it to actually live up to its claim. We called everyone we could think of, each of whom was sure he or she had the answer. Each of them was mistaken and our tests failed miserably. In my desperation to find a solution, the kind people at Sony suggested I meet Douglas Spotted Eagle. Of course, he was the only person with not only a sensible solution but a full grasp of the format.

It was Douglas who suggested I use the Sony Vegas editing software to get me to the finish line. At first glance, Vegas didn't appear to be professional editing software. I thought it was something more like an advanced consumer product. But after a few lessons from Douglas, I discovered that this was an amazingly powerful tool, deceptively simple but with enormous depth in terms of what you could accomplish with it.

I ended up getting his DVD series on how to use the software and was frankly shocked at what you could do. Just on my laptop alone I was able to create a completely professional edit, with credible sound mixing and color correction. It was stunning.

Since then Douglas has become the person I most rely on for the cutting-edge information on what is happening in world of digital technology. With his guidance I was able to integrate HDV with high-end Genesis HD material in my new *Leverage* television production, seamlessly and effortlessly. His broad knowledge of the state of technocracy is tempered by his easy manner and ability to explain, in simple language, complex technical information that would otherwise make your head spin.

So sit back and enjoy his book. I'm sure you'll be surprised at what you'll learn. There's no one better to take you on this digital journey.

Dean Devlin
Electric Entertainment

Editor's Note

Well, here we are again. This is the third Vegas book I've edited for Spot, and you would think it gets easier each time. It does not. Each outing presents its own set of challenges and opportunities. But this one was different. This one was a near-total rewrite from the ground up. The focus as I see it was not on creating a Vegas reference that details exactly what each menu item does. You have the program's help for that. Instead, you get more of the experience of attending one of Spot's workshops. A really, really, long workshop where you get to pick the teacher's brain and ask all sorts of questions. Want to know Spot's exact rendering template for the Web? It's in here. We made sure that the book is full of nuggets like that.

If you're a more casual user of Vegas Movie Studio, Section One is for you. It's a FASST start to get you up and going. Once you've mastered the basics, move on to Section Two for a deeper understanding.

Editing a tome of this size is an unbelievably tedious process. I'm very thankful to have had lots of help, including my wife and partner Christie, as well as Leila, Randy, Dave, and Mannie doing the lion's share of screencaps over many late nights. This can't be anyone's idea of a good time, yet somehow we seemed to enjoy it.

We've worked hard to bring you the most up-to-date and error-free information possible. But on my best day I'm human and have a hard time pronouncing *Bezier*, or for that matter *Favre*. If you do find mistakes in the book, please let us know via email or on the forums and we'll do our best to provide explanations or corrections as needed. In addition, there are bonus chapters that could not be included due to publishing constraints. Refer to the DVD that accompanies the book and the author's Website at www.vasst.com.

You hold in your hand the bible when it comes to learning Sony Vegas. But more than that, this book provides a solid foundation of audio and video production techniques, image compositing, and camera technology, regardless of which NLE you're using. I urge you to absorb this book in small bites, and I challenge you to take the time you can to learn it all. Douglas is a fantastic teacher for any level of user, from novice to expert, as well as a great friend. Poring over the manuscripts for this book once again has made me a better media professional, and I know it can do the same for you.

David McKnight
December 2011

Acknowledgments

It seems like only yesterday that I authored the *Vegas 3 Companion* booklet; now here we are at Sony Vegas 11 Pro and Vegas Movie Studio 11. The stack of Vegas books and guides that have sprung forth form a huge stack of books at this point, and with every book, I feel as though I'm "worded out." I also swear I'll never do another book again.

The *Vegas 4 Editing Workshop* book was a great springboard, and much of that early writing laid the foundation for the subsequent books. Over time, I've become dissatisfied with the foundation and felt it was time to start anew.

Vegas Pro 11 Editing Workshop is a new effort, written from the ground up. It was a monumental task that was begun long before Vegas Pro 11 was released, ending around Christmas 2011.

All the words in this book are mine, and I am responsible for them and any inaccuracies. However, to say that I wrote this book entirely in a vacuum would be the greatest inaccuracy of all. Many people are deserving of mention. I'm sure I'll forget someone (I always do), but it's an error of memory and not one of respect.

The first person to thank is you, the reader. Without your interest in the software and the book, there would be no purpose in writing it.

Above anyone else, I need to recognize and express gratitude and appreciation for my best friend, my business partner of many years, and the guy that keeps me grounded. Mannie, thank you so much for your patience with me as my writings and skydiving keep me in the air so much. I'm proud to wear "VASST" on my tailwing and have you as my wingman for so many years.

David McKnight produced this book. Although he is credited as only a technical editor, he served to push me harder, questioned every comment and tutorial in the book, and provided a great deal of guidance for tips, notes, and "Spot Sez." David, words cannot well enough express my gratitude. If it weren't for you and Christie helping with screenshots late into the night, we'd still be producing this book on the delivery date. Randy Stewart, thank you for your tremendous help in tech edits and correcting less than perfect grammar.

Ray Schlogel, Underground Planet, and the band AlphaRev: Ray, Casey, I'm grateful, as are the readers of this book. I hope this book helps propel "Black Sky" to the heavens. David Paul, thank you for the "Spot Sez" icon! Donald Schultz, thank you for the sweetness you've added to this one!

John "Hammo" Hamilton, Laurent "Lob" Lobjoit, Karl Gulledge, and the gang at Skydive Elsinore, thank you so much for the air support, opportunities to test Vegas in a same-hour-edit setting. We done good, and this book wouldn't exist were it not for you. Thank you for the beautiful backdrop on the cover of this book. Jose contributed to the cover of the book; muchas gracias to you and Alvaro Barros at CreativeBasic.com for the unusual, exciting cover imagery.

Randy, Leila, Dave, of the VASST team, thank you for helping deep into the night with screenshots and DVD matter. JR Rofrano, thank you for your untiring efforts with the Media Manager chapter, help in the FX section, and the awesome plug-ins we create together!

Darren, Joel, Linda, Lisa, Michele, Lelo, Tom, Matt, Andreea, Ke, Shane, Shellie: Much gratitude to you all for your faces, videos, writing environment, support, and can-do attitudes. Julie, Peggy, Artbeats: You guys rock as always (bad beer choices and all). No one has stock media like Artbeats.

Jarno, thank you for the 3D help and the 3D models of myself found in this book. You're not just a great creative, you're also a great friend.

And of course, to the people at Sony Creative Software: Dave Chaimson, thank you for helping me fly. Thank you, Sony, for the great tools you offer editors around the world.

Fly in beauty!

Introduction

I'd never intended to be a writer. I'm still not a writer; I'm merely a musician and multimedia producer who happens to write about multimedia. Multimedia is an articulate beast; anything combining the eye and ear is bound to sorely display any errors, whether you or others discover them. Hopefully this book will teach you to avoid some of the pitfalls that you otherwise might step into.

One of my favorite sayings is, "I've screwed up more times than most people attempt to try." And I feel this is true. I've perhaps made every mistake that can be made in audio and video, multiple times. This book is a result of the knowledge that I've gleaned in the process of discovery. It's not a book of articulated mathematical expression of the editing process, it's a book of my experiences and my love for the craft. The sands of our industry are constantly shifting, and one must constantly be on a journey, attending to the forks in the road and the whimsy of technology.

When I wrote the Vegas 2 users' guide and, later, the much bigger *Vegas 3 Companion*, we were struggling with this new format called DV, and delivery to a DVD was far and away too expensive and unreachable for the average small business. Today DVD is nearly dead, the Internet is the primary delivery mechanism, and we're delivering to cell phones, tablet computers, and wireless distribution devices. We've moved from DV to HD, and from 2D to 3D. And still Vegas continues to stay ahead of the game. Vegas has been a part of every production I've been involved in since 1998, including Emmy and Grammy-winning productions and recordings, and has been used to deliver for feature film, broadcast television in SD/HD, and virtually any kind of device one can imagine. Most people would be surprised to learn that the most profitable film in the history of Hollywood was edited, color corrected, and pulled down in Sony Vegas using VASST Ultimate S plug-ins.

If this book seems too technical, I'd ask that you go back and reread the passage. I've done my best to keep descriptions and explanations as simple as possible in this book for the purpose of getting information across, not to demonstrate my technical skills (or lack thereof).

David McKnight, John Rofrano, and I have labored to share our knowledge with you throughout this book; we're competent in Vegas, but we're creative first and editor/recording engineers and producers second.

As you read through the book, I'd urge you to take the initiative to go beyond the projects laid out for you. They are merely springboards, places from which your flight of fantasy takes off, not where it lands. Vegas is merely a tool to bring life to your imagination and your message.

It's not difficult to reach the point of intuitive harmony with Vegas. When this happens, cutting the story takes focus as the technology fades into the background in the creative process, and that's what it's truly about. Telling stories, using technology as the vehicle.

It is my hope that if and when you, the reader, and I meet at a video, audio, or skydiving event, you'll have a story to tell me about a dog-eared book that rarely sits on the shelf due to the number of times you've pulled it down and referenced it. I'm honored and grateful to be on your shelf.

Thank you,
~Douglas

PART ONE

Plugging In

THE FASST START GUIDE:
Introduction and Importing Video

In this first section, we're going to go through a speed-session on using Sony Vegas. Only basic information relevant to setting up Vegas, importing media to Vegas and the timeline, basic editing features, and output will be covered. If you're an experienced Vegas user, you may wish to skip forward to "Turning Up" (Going Deeper in Sony Vegas).

This chapter assumes that Vegas is already loaded on the computer, either by the user or as an included application in a software bundle. If Vegas isn't installed, install Vegas and DVD Architect now.

Let's get started!

Open Vegas for the first time, and you'll note that there are three predominant areas in the graphical user interface (GUI): the Docking windows, the Preview window, and the Trackspace/Timeline.

> Vegas Movie Studio Users will see a pop-up window suggesting different methods of using the software. For this exercise, please select "Start using Vegas Movie Studio."

The Docking windows are where the Vegas Explorer, access to FX, Transitions, and other editing tools may be found. These windows are called "Docking windows" because they are moveable and user-definable as to how they are laid out. See the "Turning Up" section for more information on how Docking windows may be configured for user-defined layouts.

The Preview window is where Events on the timeline will be viewed in their current state. This is where you'll visualize the finished video as it is being edited. There are several controls in this window. For purposes of getting started in Vegas, please choose the Preview Quality of "Preview (Auto)" in the drop-down menu. Learn more about Preview window settings in the "Turning Up" section of this book.

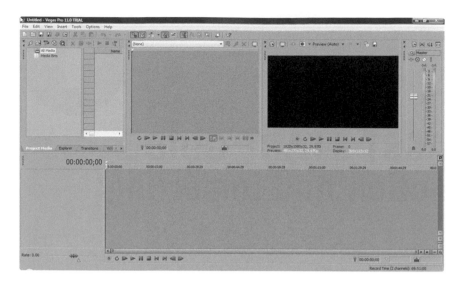

Figure 1.1

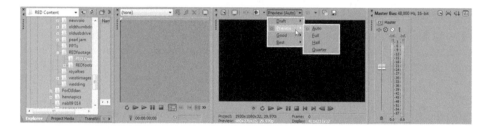

Figure 1.2

Figure 1.3

You'll get the best editing performance if you set the properties of your project to match the media contained in the project. In the upper left corner of the Preview window, there is a small white box. Click this box to open Project Properties. Project Properties is where you'll find settings to best match your media. If your media comes from a typical HD camcorder, you'll want to set the Properties to match this screenshot.

Figure 1.4

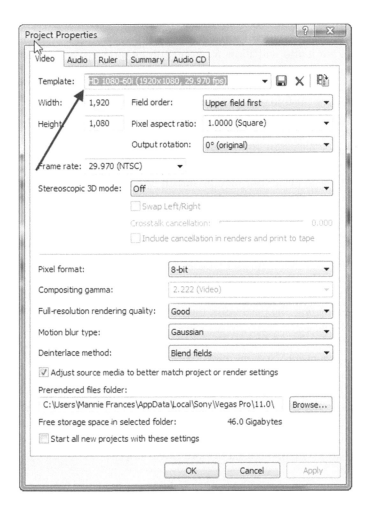

HD camcorders can only shoot either 1280 x 720 (less common), 1440 x 1080 (somewhat common), or "Full HD," 1920 x 1080. However, regardless of what kind of camera was used, Vegas will create the correct project settings when the "Adjust Source Media to better match Project or Render Settings" tickbox is checked.

With these settings out of the way, now we can bring media into the application. This assumes you are using a file-based camcorder (one that records to HDD, Flash media, or DVD). If you are using a tape-based camcorder, please see the section at the end of this chapter.

If actual camera media is not available, you can use files found on the DVD contained in the back of this book. The files on the DVD are in numerical order, and should be imported in ascending order for the best editing experience.

Media may be imported to Vegas using a variety of methods; we're going to demonstrate the simplest one in this FASST Start Guide. File-based video cameras do not require files to be transferred to a computer hard drive when working with Vegas, yet it's always a good idea to transfer files from the camcorder device to a hard drive prior to editing. Not only does this generate an archive/copy of the files, but it also will allow for faster editing, preview, and render of a finished project.

If your camcorder is a file-based device, find the device in your Windows Explorer. Traverse down the folder hierarchy and open the folder that contains the actual video files (often in a folder called "Streams, DCIM, or MP_Root) and select all the files you'd like to copy by holding the CTRL key and clicking on each file to be transferred. Another method is to select the first file, hold SHIFT, and select the last file. Doing so will select all files in between the first selected and last selected files. (These are standard Windows conventions.) Use CTRL+C for "copy" and then browse to the directory in which you'd like to place your files. Be sure to properly name file folders with a name, date, or other indicator related to the media being transferred. This makes it easier to locate media later in the editing process. In a file-based workflow, it's easy to lose track of files when they're named "001.mts," etc.

As mentioned, you don't have to transfer files in order to work with them. Vegas allows you to edit files directly off the camcorder. For dailies, for quick views, or for files that aren't life-death-of-production critical, editing directly off the camera is certainly acceptable. In other chapters of this book, we'll discuss how to save a project edited straight from a camcorder, saving either entire files used in the project, or saving only the portions of files used in the finished edit. For now, we'll discuss a basic edit right off the card.

In the upper left corner of the Vegas GUI, there is a tab labeled "Explorer." Select this tab. If for some reason the tab is not visible, use the keyboard shortcut ALT+1, or navigate to VIEW | Explorer to open the Vegas Explorer window.

This window acts exactly like the Windows Explorer, allowing users to find and select media files for use in the Vegas project. In this window, find the Auto-Preview button. When enabled, this feature allows users to select a file in the Vegas Explorer window and the file will auto-play, demonstrating what file has been selected. This is a very efficient means of finding files that are created in a file-based workflow (usually with numeric names and extension, such as 0001.mts). Enable Auto-Preview for this exercise.

Starting with My Computer, browse to a video file in the Vegas Explorer. Select the file. Double-clicking the file will insert the file to the timeline; if your intent is to merely select or preview the file, do not double-click, only select/single click the file.

In the bottom area of the Vegas Explorer, Vegas will provide vital information about the file. Notice that a selected file displays file resolution, frame rate, length of file, codec, audio format, stereo/mono, and audio compression format information. This is a very fast method of determining the properties of a media file without actually opening a File Properties dialog. As you become more familiar with Vegas and various workflows, this information may aid you in setting up Vegas projects.

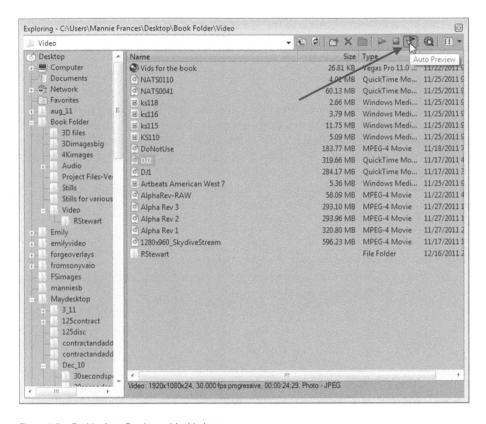

Figure 1.5   Enable Auto-Preview with this button.

Video: 1920x1080x24, 30.000 fps progressive, 00:00:24;29, Photo - JPEG

Figure 1.6   File Properties are displayed for any file selected. Selecting multiple files of varied formats/resolutions will display as blank.

Capture the Flag

More Capture Topics in Sony Vegas

The concept of "capture" in digital video is a nomenclature predominantly left over from days gone by. "Capture" or "digitizing" is actually done at the camera when dealing with digital formats such as DV, HDV, XDCAM, and advanced video codec–high definition (AVCHD). As you've seen above, transferring media from the camcorder to the computer is simply a data transfer. The media does not change; it is bit-for-bit the same. Compression has already occurred in the camcorder/recording device stage, whereas in the analog video past, a camera captured uncompressed images and the capture card would compress the video into a data stream that the computer could manage.

Importing AVCHD/AVC

Advanced video codec–high definition is a fairly new format in the video industry, and Vegas is capable of importing AVCHD and AVC content. These highly compressed formats have several codecs that various manufacturers may use; at the time of this writing, Vegas imports AVCHD from all Sony and Panasonic camcorders, and AVC from Canon camcorders, HDSLR devices and most small-format cameras, and allows for native editing of these files.

AVCHD/AVC media may be recorded on an HDD unit, DVD-based camcorder, or some form of static memory such as the Sony Memory Stick, Compact Flash, or SDHC.

 Tip_____
Although possible (and demonstrated above), it is recommended that users in a production or critical environment never attempt to edit video directly from the card. The editing experience will be much better from a hard drive due to the highly compressed format's CPU requirements and transfer ratio.

Figure 1.7

Depending on the camcorder, users may or may not have to use an import application. For example, all Sony video cameras using AVCHD or MPEG 2 are bundled with Picture Motion Browser for import of video/stills, yet users of Vegas will not need this additional software. The camcorder may be connected directly to the computer via USB, or the card may be inserted into a card reader, and then viewed through the Vegas Explorer or Device Manager. Select the files individually or as a group in the Vegas Explorer, and drag and drop them to a location where you'd like the files to be stored. The dragged/dropped files will not appear in the Project Media window, however. Once these files are added to the Vegas Timeline, they will appear in the Project Media window. Using the Device Manager will import these files to the Project Media window.

Be sure to set Vegas to the file properties closest to the output of the AVCHD camcorder. Most AVCHD camcorders are 1920 x 1080, which means that the HD 1920 x 1080 project preset should be selected.

Figure 1.8 This is the template to be used for AVCHD camcorders recording Full HD at 24p.

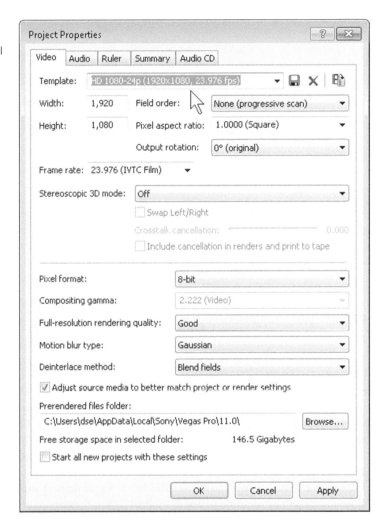

AVCHD/AVC is highly compressed. The CPU is going to be working quite hard to decode the video information and display it in the Preview window.

Only the very fastest, most optimized computer systems will be able to preview AVCHD/AVC at full frame rates. As computers grow faster and applications are better optimized to deal with AVCHD/AVC, preview speeds will improve. In the meantime, there are tools such as VASST Ultimate S or NewBlueFX's UpShift which may be used to convert the AVCHD/AVC files to a more efficient intermediate file format such as HDV or Cineform codecs.

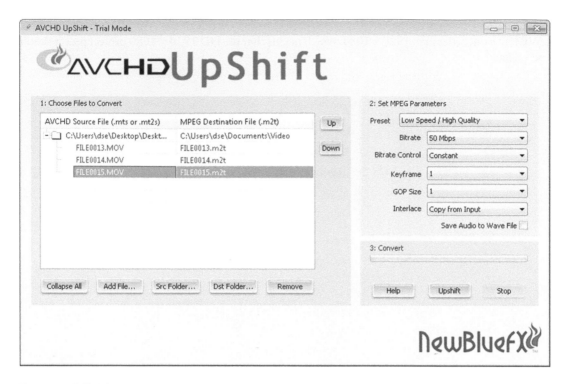

Figure 1.9   UpShift from NewBlueFX

AVCHD/AVC comes in multiple flavors, or "profiles." There are two profiles used in consumer AVCHD camcorders. The first is the "Main Profile" and this is used predominantly by Sony camcorders. The bitrate is variable up to 24 Mbps (18 for DVD -recorded media) and accommodates up to 1920 x 1080 resolutions. Some Main Profile camcorders record a 1440 x 1080 resolution image with a Pixel Aspect Ratio (PAR) of 1.333, just as HDV does. AVC is not standardized so quality and resolutions may vary.

High Profile camcorders allow for a maximum bitrate of up to 24 Mbps, and resolutions of 1920 x 1080.

Panasonic has a format known as AVC-Intra. Vegas doesn't support this codec; a converting software utility will be required just as DVCProHD requires a conversion utility such as Raylight™. For competitive reasons, Panasonic has indicated they will not license Sony Creative Software to access their proprietary codecs. Users may also encounter a codec known as AVCCAM. This is merely Panasonic re-branding standard AVCHD High Profile; it is the same video format as any High Profile camcorder, regardless of branding.

Importing Media from a DVD Drive

Camcorders that record to DVD are very common, and Vegas is capable of importing most types of DVD-based recording formats.

Figure 1.10   DVD camcorders allow you to shoot video directly onto recordable DVD media and can be useful when little or no editing is required.

 Tip_____
Any disc from a DVD camera to be imported to Vegas needs to be finalized in the camera prior to import.

Connect the Camcorder to the USB port on the computer and a file import dialog box will open. Browse to File I Import I DVD Camcorder Disc. (The disc could also be in the computer DVD drive.) Vegas will import the video and stereo or 5.1 surround information. If installed, be sure to uninstall the Sony Handycam USB driver from your Add/Remove Programs prior to attempting to import media via the Vegas import tools. The Sony Handycam driver may prevent Vegas from recognizing any brand of DVD camcorder. If the disc to be imported contains 5.1 surround audio, set up a 5.1 surround Vegas project prior to import. Vegas will then properly import the six channels of audio to corresponding surround tracks. The 5.1 audio imported to a stereo project (Vegas default) will be down-mixed to a two-channel mix.

Figure 1.11

Project properties are accessed via File/Project Properties or by selecting the Project Video Properties button found in the upper-left corner of the Preview window. Once the import begins, Vegas will ask for a location where the video should be stored. It is not practical to attempt to edit footage directly from the DVD.

Once the media is imported, it is automatically added to the Project Media window in Vegas. From here, you may drag the media files directly to the timeline or open them in the Vegas Trimmer prior to adding to the timeline. Files may also be previewed in this window by pressing Play or selecting the Auto-Preview option.

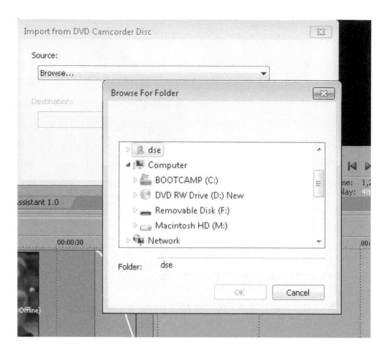

Figure 1.12

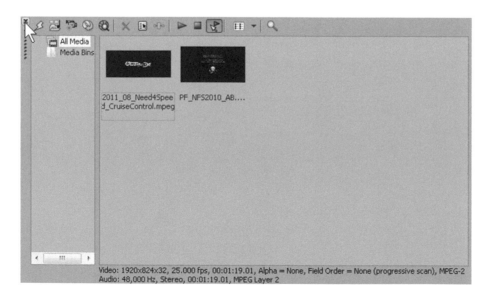

Figure 1.13   The Project Media window displays all media used in the project.

Importing Media from a Hard Disk Drive Recorder

Hard disk drive (HDD) recorders such as the Sony DR60 are very popular, as they reduce the importance of tape as a recording medium and allow for fast transfer of files, saving tremendous amounts of capture time. A 60-minute tape requires 60 minutes of transfer time (realtime), whereas 60 minutes of recorded media on a HDD unit takes approximately 15 minutes. It's not difficult to see the benefits of a tapeless workflow.

Connect the HDD unit to the computer via Firewire interface (also known as IEEE 1394). The computer should recognize the HDD unit as a drive. In Vegas, browse to FILE | IMPORT | MEDIA.

Vegas will ask where you'd like to transfer files from the HDD unit. Specify a location.

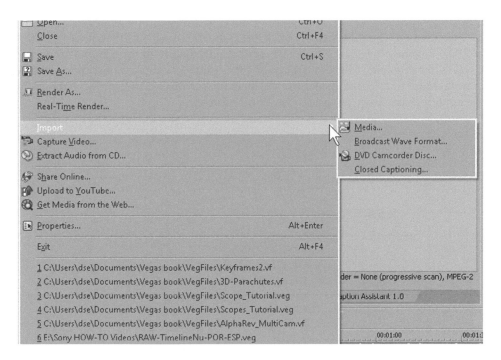

Figure 1.14

A dialog will open. This dialog determines where HDD content will be stored once it has been transferred. It is highly recommended that a location separate from the operating system/application drive be chosen. Once the files are transferred, they are found in the Project Media window.

It is possible to edit files directly from some HDD recorder devices; generally this is not the most efficient means of editing. Be sure to set the HDD unit to record AVI Type 2 files for best results when working with DV. Although Vegas may import other formats, this is the best DV format for Vegas to work with. HDV file format should be .m2t.

When transferring media from an HDD device to a FAT32 drive, Vegas will import/copy the files exactly as they are found on the HDD device. When importing to an NTFS drive (recommended), Vegas will create a single AVI Type 2 file from any smaller AVI files created as a long file. Similarly,

Vegas will generate a single .m2t/HDV file from smaller files created as a result of the FAT32 limitations found on HDD recording units.

Vegas uses the Index (idx) file on your HDD device to ensure that transferred files are not retransferred.

Device Explorer in Vegas Software

At first glance, the Device Explorer is really nothing special, but what makes it unique is the ability to look inside the storage systems of several different device types.

Even as recently as a couple years ago, most video was DV or 10-bit BetaCam, and everything was stored on tape, thus requiring that a Capture Utility be used to ingest media (as described later in this chapter).

Today, media is stored on CF cards, Memory Stick Pro Duo, SDHC, HDD, DVD, internal RAM, and external HDD systems, and some NLE's have difficulty reading from the panopoly of device types. Some NLE's, for example, require that the camcorder itself be used as a transfer device. Some NLE's are incapable of transferring media from a memory card-based camcorder without the camcorder being in its base device plugged in via USB or Firewire.

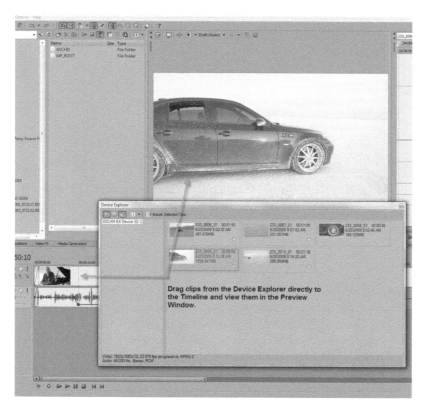

Figure 1.15   Access the Device Explorer via the shortcut keys CTRL + ALT+7. This window allows for import of AVCHD, XDCAM EX, and other file-based media.

Vegas offers a "Device Explorer" that can be accessed via the shortcut keys (CTRL+ALT+7) and allows users to access multiple devices either via the camera, card reader, USB reader, or other device. For example, an SxS card from an XDCAM EX cam will open up in the Device Explorer complete with thumbnails from all files found in each folder on the card. The files may be selected individually, selectively by holding CTRL + individual files, or all files (CTRL + A), and then imported to a selected hard drive, and the new project.

The Device Explorer will also allow users to re-import already imported clips, import only new clips, or all clips.

To change the import location in the Device Explorer, right-click in the left side of the window, and choose "Browse." To change the import location, right-click the import device and choose Properties.

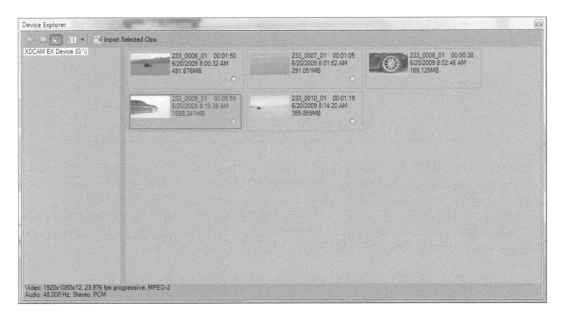

Figure 1.16   The Device Explorer allows import from USB or HDD drive devices, providing thumbnails or list views.

XDCAM and Sony Vegas Pro Software *(XDCAM Support Not Available in Vegas Movie Studio)*

Sony Vegas Pro editing software offers in-depth XDCAM support, along with an XDCAM browser that displays and sorts with XDCAM SD, XDCAM HD, and XDCAM EX formats.

The workflows for XDCAM are varied, but will be similar to the following:

Use the Import XDCAM Disc button in the XDCAM Explorer to import clips. Proxies, full-resolution clips, or both sets of clips together may be imported. Once imported, the clips appear as thumbnails in the XDCAM Explorer. Edit your project using the proxy files.

Figure 1.17

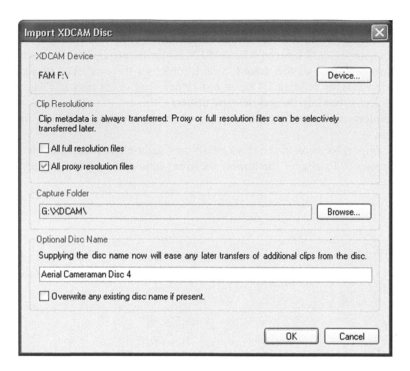

This is an XDCAM Proxy timeline. Proxy media may be shifted once the project is complete.

Using the Conform XDCAM Media in Current Project button in the XDCAM Explorer, conform the edited project to full resolution. If you're using legacy Sony Vegas Pro, version 7d software will conform the full-length file, regardless of edited length on the timeline. New versions of Vegas Pro will conform the full-resolution files to the trimmed length of the proxies, thus saving storage space and potentially reducing the conform time.

Figure 1.18

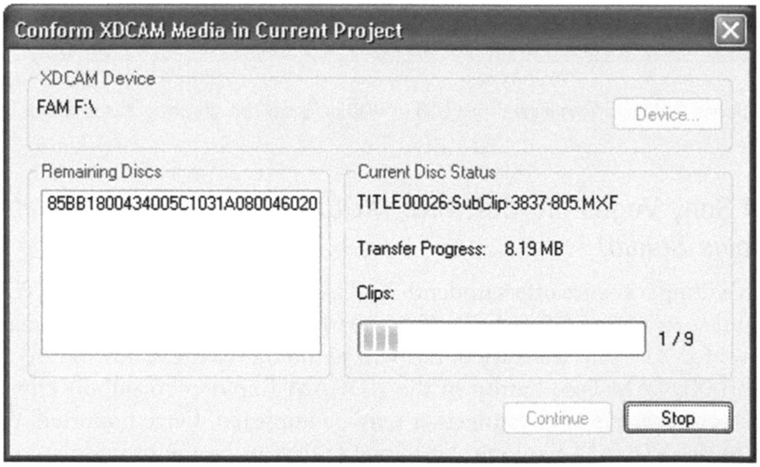

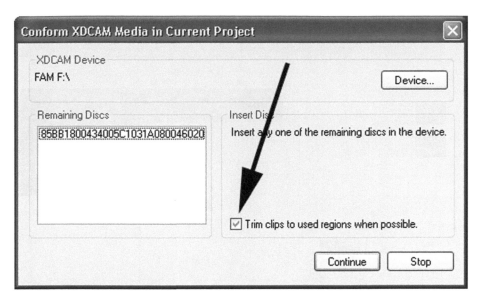

Figure 1.19

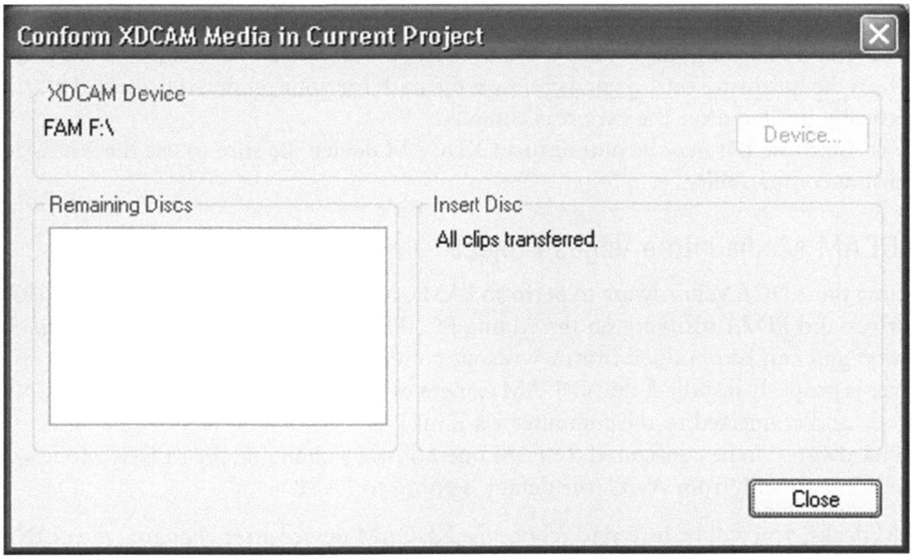

Figure 1.20

Conforming the timeline will replace all Proxies with full-resolution XDCAM files.

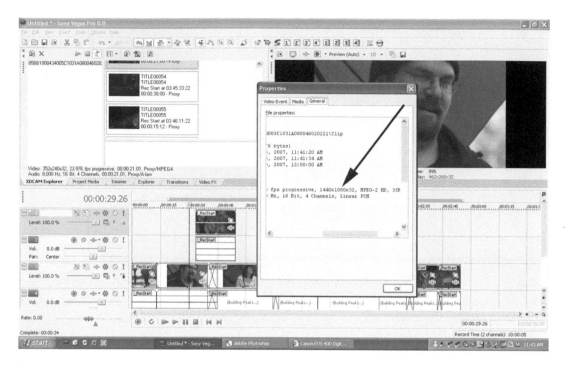

Figure 1.21

Output your project by clicking the Export Video to Sony XDCAM Disc button in the XDCAM Explorer. Confirm the hardware settings and choose a file path for your rendered project. This file can be automatically deleted after the export is complete.

Once the file is conformed, it may be output to an XDCAM device. Be sure to use the XDCAM templates to ensure compatibility.

Importing XDCAM Media into a Vegas Project

Before connecting the XDCAM hardware to perform FAM operations, install the ProDisc PC Utility software driver and PDZ1 software on the editing PC. The driver is *not part of the standard Vegas installation* and can be obtained from www.sony.com/xdcam.

Once the driver is properly installed, the XDCAM camera or deck needs to be switched to i.LINK File Access Mode and connected to the computer via iLink.

All XDCAM hardware can be configured for FAM operations by changing the i.LINK Mode setting in the operational menu from AV/C (the default setting) to FAM.

- On XDCAM decks, you will be forced to reboot the XDCAM device after changing the i.LINK Mode setting. On XDCAM camcorders, you need to power the deck off and back on for the mode change to take effect, but this can be done at your convenience.

- Connect the i.LINK cable after switching the i.LINK Mode. When XDCAM devices are set to File Access Mode and connected to a computer, "PC REMOTE" is displayed on the LCD/View-finder, the hardware controls (with the exception of the Eject button) are disabled, and there are no linear VTR, output, display, or menu functions available to the operator.

A few things to remember when working with XDCAM hardware:

- To terminate File Access Mode safely—for example, if you need front panel or menu control—use the Safely Remove Hardware button on the Windows taskbar, browse to the XDCAM device, and remove it from the system. The camera/deck will now function normally.

- To re-enable File Access Mode, cycle power on the XDCAM device or disconnect and then reconnect the i.LINK cable.

- Until a disc is inserted, the FAM-enabled XDCAM device will not be assigned a drive letter or path and will not appear in the Windows Computer Explorer.

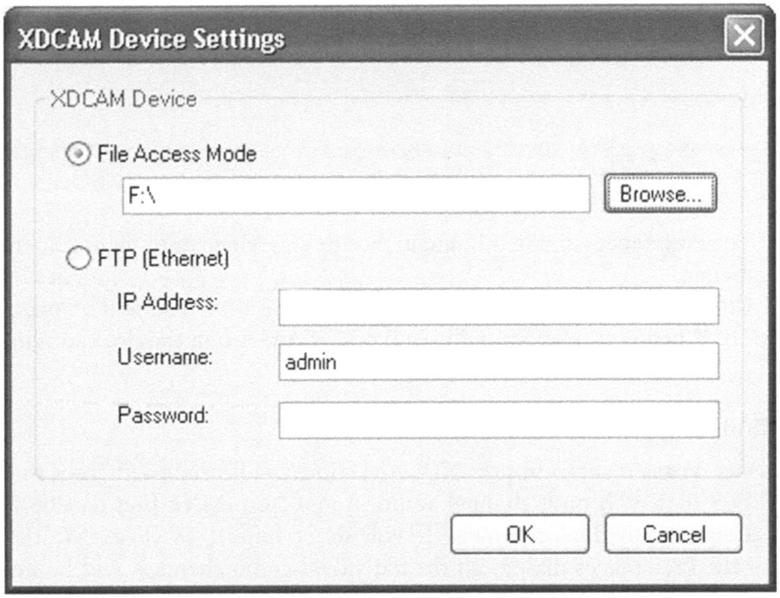

Figure 1.22 This is the directory that will open when the XDCAM disc is registered/mounted.

If Windows preferences are not set to display new Explorer windows when a drive is detected, wait a few seconds and then click on the My Computer icon to verify that the XDCAM device is properly mapped and available.

Enabling the XDCAM Explorer

Vegas is unique in that it provides a built-in XDCAM browser and workspace, the XDCAM Disc Explorer. Because this tab is not needed for all Vegas workflows, it may be disabled/enabled in the application preferences to conserve processing power, memory, and screen space. The first time Vegas Pro is launched, this option is disabled.

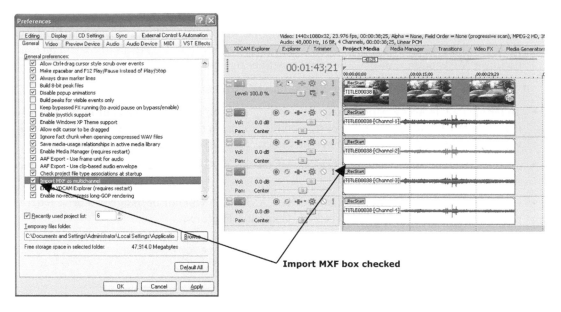

Figure 1.23   Enable the XDCAM Explorer by navigating to the General tab of the Preferences window and checking the "Enable XDCAM Explorer" box found at the bottom of the Preferences options.

The Preferences dialog is found in the Options Menu or by right-clicking in any unused area on the timeline.

Click the Apply button after making your selection. You will be prompted to restart the application. When you return, you'll see the XDCAM tab in the docked windows area.

Enabling Multichannel Audio Import

Once Vegas is set to import XDCAM clips, you'll need to instruct the application how to handle MXF files with multichannel audio. Audio from MXF files can be imported in stereo or as up to eight individual channels. If you select Import MXF as Multichannel in the General tab of the Preferences dialog, all the individual audio channels will be automatically available when the clip is placed on the timeline.

If you leave this selection unchecked, the audio will be brought in as stereo and will enable one stereo track when the clip is placed on the timeline. If audio is imported in this manner, the additional channels may still be accessed and assigned to their own tracks at a later point (after locking and conforming the video, for example) by right-clicking on an audio Event and selecting Channels in the context menu.

With the XDCAM deck, camcorder, or drive unit connected and set to i.LINK FAM, click on the Import XDCAM Disc button to open the Device dialog. This will enable browsing of the XDCAM device.

Click the Device button to browse to the XDCAM hardware. This will open a dialog box that you'll use to select either FAM or FTP import and then browse to the appropriate device.

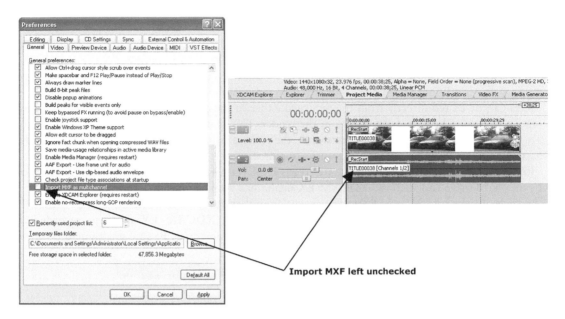

Figure 1.24   Enable multichannel audio in the Vegas Preferences.

Check the box next to File Access Mode and click the Browse button. This opens a browser window.

You should see the XDCAM device followed by the drive letter it has been assigned. In this case the deck appears as the F: drive. If the disc has a name, the name will also appear. Highlight the XDCAM device and click OK. Be sure to select the Root Directory or up-permost level of the XDCAM device and not any of the folders contained inside. This will return to the Device Settings dialog box, which should now display the drive location of the XDCAM hardware. Select OK.

This will return you to the Import XDCAM Disc dialog. The XDCAM device is now online and can set the res-olution required for capture as well as the location in which to store your imported material.

Figure 1.25   Importing XDCAM discs.

Sony XDCAM EX and Sony Vegas Pro

Users of previous versions of Sony Vegas Pro software needed to install/load a Sony clip browser and preview software to convert XDCAM EX files from the PMW-EX1 and PMW-EX3 camcorders to an .mxf wrapper that Vegas could properly read. Vegas Pro users need only install the SxS card driver software (Express card driver software, downloadable from www.sony.com/xdcam).

Files can be edited directly from the SxS card either in the camera, or if you have an SxS card reader, files may be edited directly from the reader. This is not optimal, but if rushes or dailies are needed, or instant review is needed while the camera is in use, reading/cutting files from the card is certainly possible even while transferring media.

Import the media to the project using the Vegas Explorer whether importing from an SxS card or from a hard drive to which the XDCAM EX media has been imported.

Project settings for XDCAM EX media are different than for XDCAM HD media. XDCAM HD media records at 1440 x 1080 with varying framerates. XDCAM EX media is recorded as 1920 x 1080 or 1280 x 720 frame resolution with varying framerates. Be sure the framerate you've recorded matches the framerate of the project. You can instruct Vegas to automatically optimize the media settings to the project settings, if you wish. This will optimize the system for your primary media format, and help speed processing when mixing media formats. This is done by checking the "Adjust source media to better match project or render settings" check box found in the Project Properties dialog box.

The reverse is also possible; Project Properties can be automatically set based on the properties of a media file. To accomplish this:

1. Open a new project.

2. In the Video tab, on the far right of the Template options, there is a folder icon. Hover the cursor over this icon and the description will read "Match Media Settings."

3. Selecting this icon will open a browser window. Whatever media file is chosen will determine the project settings. This is handy if you're not certain what the project settings should be and want the optimal editing experience.

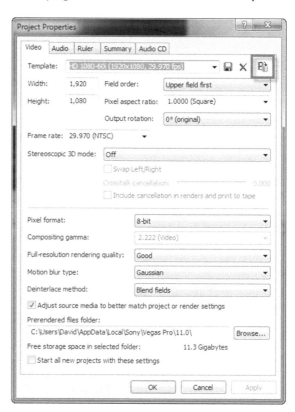

Figure 1.26   Selecting this icon will match the project settings to whatever media file is chosen in the Explorer window. This is perfect for assuring correct project settings for the media type selected.

In all cases, regardless of whether the media being edited is DV, AVCHD, HDV, XDCAM, XDCAM EX, RED ONE, or any other format, the best user experience can typically be found by right clicking right on the Preview window, and selecting "Adjust Size and Quality for Optimal Playback" in the submenu. This allows Vegas to best work with the media while providing the best possible playback experience.

Capturing DV

Vegas automatically senses the frame rate, image size, and any other information that might be part of the DV stream. No special settings are required for capturing video from a Firewire-equipped camera via an OHCI card. Whether the media is PAL, NTSC, 24p, 16:9 anamorphic, or another supported format, it is captured, or transferred, from the camera with those attributes recognized.

DV, HDV, and XDCAM all use the Firewire standard for transferring video data. AVCHD and some consumer camcorders use USB2 as a transfer protocol.

Manually Capturing DV

Connect the camera to the Firewire port of the computer. Open Vegas and select FILE | CAPTURE VIDEO, which opens the Vegas Video Capture utility. The capture utility may also be opened from the Project Media by clicking the Capture Video button.

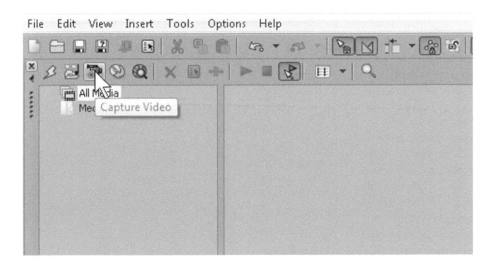

Figure 1.27   Opening the Video Capture utility.

When Video Capture launches, select OPTIONS | PREFERENCES. Select the Disk Management tab. The default capture location for captured files is C:\Documents and Settings\username\ documents.

If the camera is turned off, Video Capture will prompt you to turn it on. When the camera is turned on, Windows will automatically open screens asking what it should do with the camera.

Cancel the Windows screens, as Video Capture is already open. If you select anything else, it may override the Video Capture drivers, and then you'll need to start again by shutting down the newly launched application and recycling the camera power.

You may want to place the capture tool icon on the main Vegas toolbar if you need to regularly access Capture. This is accomplished via the Customize Toolbar function.

If a capture drive has not been specified, Video Capture will ask for a drive to be specified. Unless necessary, never capture media to the same hard drive as the operating system. Specify a hard drive and specify a disk overflow size that is at least 3 percent less than the overall drive size. This option will allow room for defragging drives and will prevent a drive from filling to total capacity, possibly rendering the drive incapable of being recovered in the event of a drive or system crash.

Video Capture will prompt for a tape name with the Verify Tape Name dialog. This step is the first in proficient media asset management or digital asset management.

Enter the name of the tape you

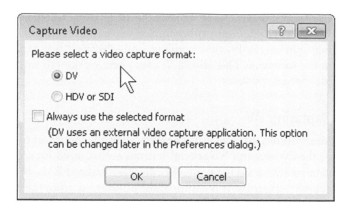

Figure 1.28   First capture window when the utility opens.

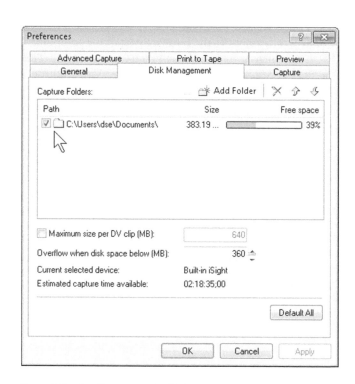

Figure 1.29   Specify capture drive. Notice that Vegas indicates capture time available based on free drive space.

wish to capture. This tape name will be appended to filenames as they are captured, so be sure it's correct. You will have one more opportunity to correct this easily later on. This process is known as logging.

Tip_____

Enter the name of the tape exactly as it's written on the tape spine in the event that you want go back and recapture the media. This process avoids errors in logging and locating tape.

The Verify Tape Name dialog also provides the following choices:

- Don't capture any clips right now.
- Start capturing all clips from the current tape position.
- Start capturing all clips from the beginning of the tape.

For the moment, select "Don't capture any clips right now" and click OK. Video Capture is now ready to capture video. Clicking the Play button or pressing the spacebar causes the camera to begin playing.

Video is not captured until you click the Capture Video button or press Ctrl+R. Video Capture can capture video from the camera/tape in several ways, including:

- Manual capture by starting and stopping (labor/time intensive)
- Capture from a specific location and detect or not detect scenes, starting and stopping with the control (user's preference, can be labor/time intensive)
- Capture entire tape with scene detection (little effort)
- Batch capture logged clips (fair amount of effort to log clips; time saving/disk space saving in end view)

Scene Detection is a feature in which Video Capture sees breaks in the date and time stamps created when the camera is started and stopped during the recording process. Each time the camera is stopped, Video Capture sees the change in the date and time stamp and starts a new file. So if you've started and stopped the camera 10 times while videotaping at an event and then connected the camera to the computer and opened Video Capture, Video Capture creates 10 files in the Project Media when it is activated. (Files are stored in the folder/drive specified in Disk Management. Project Media creates a pointer to that file; files are not actually stored in Project Media.)

 Tip_____

When using DV tape, be certain that the timecode isn't broken on the tape. Broken timecode often happens when reusing old videotape or when cameras aren't allowed to run for a moment following shooting. This problem also occurs when tape is viewed in the field and allowed to play past the end of timecode. Avoid this problem by:

1. Always recording blank time completely over previously used videotape by recording with the lens cap on for the length of the tape;

2. Allowing 5–10 seconds of tape to roll by when recording in the field, if you know you will be reviewing tape in the field;

3. Using Last Scene Preview, on many camcorders available today.

Video Capture is capable of batch capturing an entire tape while left unattended. Click the Capture Entire Tape button. Video Capture will rewind the tape to its beginning/top and then start to capture the tape to the folders/drives specified in the Disk Management preferences. If the specified hard drive does not have enough space to store an entire tape, be certain to specify more than one drive. Video Capture will automatically roll files over to the next specified drive.

Begin capturing tape by either pressing Ctrl+R or clicking the Capture button in the capture tool. Video Capture will start capturing from the moment you click the button. If the camera or tape deck is OHCI/1394 standard, the device will start playing and transferring media from the tape to the hard drive. Clicking the Capture Entire Tape button instructs Video Capture to rewind to the beginning of the tape and start recording. Video Capture will auto-detect scenes in the tape and create new files for each scene. (Enable Scene Detection is enabled by default in the OPTIONS | PREFERENCES | CAPTURE dialog.)

 Tip_____

Hard drives formatted as FAT 32 drives do not allow files larger than 4 GB, or about 18 minutes in tape time. Video Capture will automatically find the best point at which to divide files in the event of FAT 32 drives. NTFS drives have a file size limitation of 4 TB, which is roughly 330 hours of DV.

In the analog tape world, such as a VHS or Betacam SP, a digital video converter (DVC) is required to convert analog to DV. Several converters are available on the market today, from the very high-end Convergent Design SD to the Canopus ADVC 1394 card. YUV input, composite input, and S-Video input are all common input features, making it fairly simple to find a converter that meets your specifications.

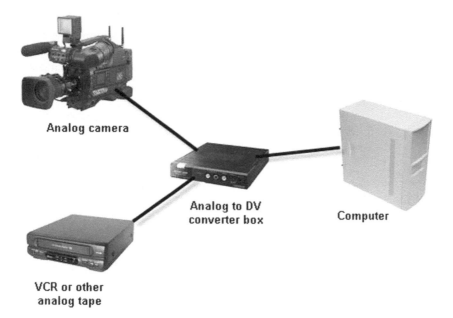

Figure 1.30   An analog camera or video deck, such as a VHS or BetaSP machine, uses composite S-Video or component video output to a DVC, which converts the analog video to digital video so that the computer can see the video signal as data.

If an analog machine is used with a converter or analog card, the machine must be turned on and Play enabled before capturing video. Scene detection does not take place with analog tape machines passed through a converter. Machine control is not possible with analog machines, with the exception of some high-end converters that read DV control signals and translate them to RS-422 control signals, to which some analog decks will respond. DV control can be disabled in the OPTIONS | PREFERENCES | GENERAL dialog. Typically, leaving DV control enabled does not affect a DV capture but can create some confusion if shifting between DV and non-DV sources.

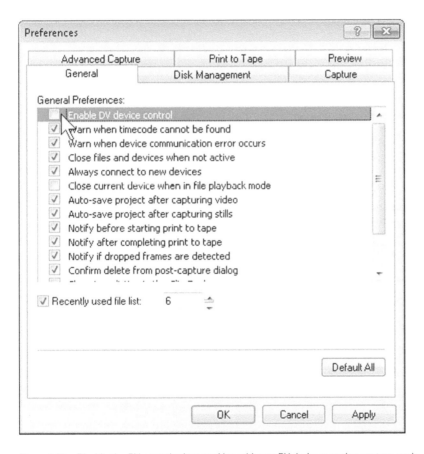

Figure 1.31   Disable the DV control when working with non-DV decks or analog capture cards.

In the Video Capture OPTIONS | PREFERENCES | CAPTURE tab, set the minimum clip length to 5 or 10 seconds. This instructs Video Capture to ignore the OOPS!-type of files, in which a camera was inadvertently started and stopped, leaving small video clips on the tape. Of course, if working with animations or other projects that require short shots, you might wish to leave this set unchecked, which is the default setting.

Animation-type capture is also possible by selecting a maximum capture length of only one or two frames. Experiment with clay models or action figures to get the hang of editing this type of captured media.

When Video Capture has captured the entire tape or when you have manually captured all clips desired from the tape, Video Capture will prompt you to save the capture session. This feature is useful if there is any possibility that you will be going back to the tape to recapture at some future point.

Lost video, accidentally deleted video, and failed hard drives are all reasons to recapture tape, so it is generally good practice to save the capture session.

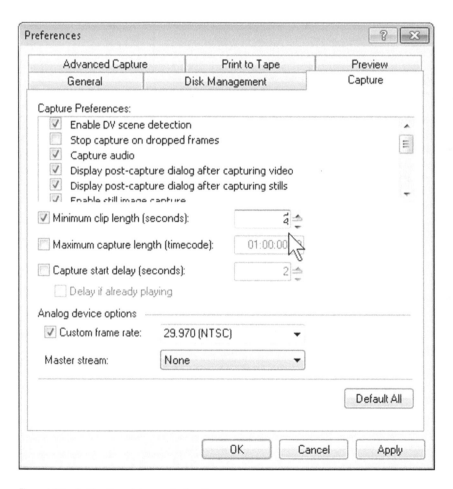

Figure 1.32   Setting the minimum clip length.

Store the capture session if any likelihood exists that the same tape will need to be recaptured later or if the session needs to be shared on a network.

After capturing video and closing the Video Capture application, the captured media will appear in the Project Media.

Video Capture has other tools available for logging and capturing in Vegas. Click the Advanced Capture tab. This tab opens a different view of Video Capture. Comments, ratings, length of clip, and in/out information can all be logged and added in this view. Use this feature to keep track of media and how it appears for rapid editing decisions later in the editing process. These comments appear in the Project Media and can assist in making editing choices.

Advanced Capture Tools

The Advanced Capture tab has dialogs that allow for more advanced file management. Open the Advanced Capture tab at the upper left of the capture utility. Detailed capture logging tools are located on the right side of the capture screen.

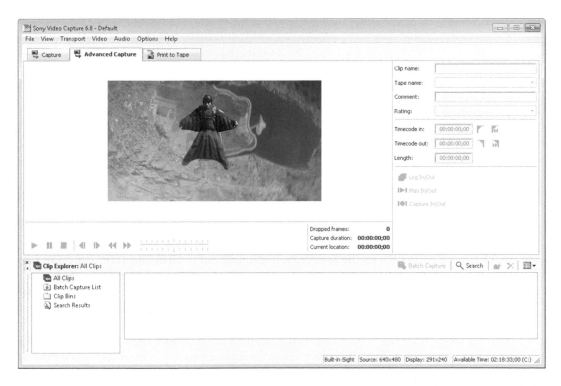

Figure 1.33   Advanced Capture tools offer efficient capture logging and automated capture tools, saving tremendous time in the editing/ capturing process, in addition to saving disk space.

The Capture and Advanced Capture dialogs provide the ability to create and use Clip Bins. Each master tape or B roll might have its own bin, and clips can be sorted in any fashion that makes sense to the project editor or producer. Remember how Radar O'Reilly stored the maps to the minefields on *M*A*S*H* under "B" for "BOOM"? Each person has their own method of sorting and storing files. Media bins accommodate this. Right-click the Clip Bins folder, select Create New Bin, and name the bin with the filename information that relates to the part that the clips will play in the project. If the "Add Clips to Media Bin" checkbox is selected in the postcapture dialog, clips are auto-added to the Project Media bins in Vegas, and bins from Video Capture may be dragged to the Project Media in Vegas as well.

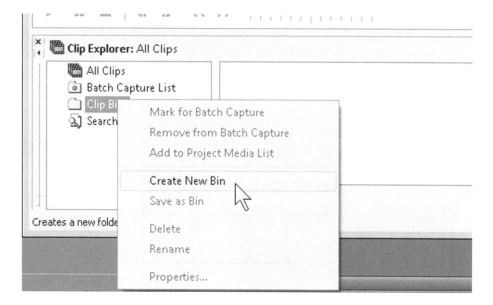

Figure 1.34   Right-click the Media bin to create a new bin to aid in locating, managing, and logging media.

Bins from the Video Capture utility can be imported to the Project Media in Vegas by creating the bin in Vegas before capturing media.

In the NLE world, if a clip is on the hard drive, it is considered to be online. If the clip disappears from the hard drive but is part of a project, it is considered to be offline, and Vegas shows the file as offline in the Project Media, shown as grayed out or missing media with the text "Offline Media" in the lower-left corner of the Project Media. Vegas provides the opportunity to recapture offline media by right-clicking the offline media and selecting "Recapture Offline DV Media."

Recapturing media from the Project Media launches the Video Capture application automatically, and you will be prompted to place the correct tape in the deck/camera if you have not already done so.

This is a point at which careful logging/labeling is invaluable. Video Capture will seek out the timecode related to the clip that is marked for recapture and start the capture process with no assistance. The recaptured media will need to be directed to a folder on one of the drives.

Capturing Stills with Video Capture

The Video Capture tool allows stills to be captured and cataloged during the capture process. To capture stills, click the Capture Still button. Still images by default are stored as JPEG files unless otherwise specified in the OPTIONS | PREFERENCES | CAPTURE dialog. In this same dialog, Video Capture can be instructed to deinterlace video images and to apply the correct aspect ratio to still images. If the "Saved Captured Stills as JPEG" box is left unchecked, images are stored as uncompressed bitmaps.

Stills captured to the clipboard can be opened in any photo editor for color correction, image correction, resizing, or other manipulation.

Many video cameras have the ability to capture stills as well.

Still images are generally captured to videotape and can be narrated during the still capture on the video camera. Video Capture treats these still images as video because the tape is moving and the still image generation is created by the video camera. Default still-image length on most DV cameras is five seconds. If Scene Detection is enabled, Video Capture creates a new file for each still photo taken with the camera.

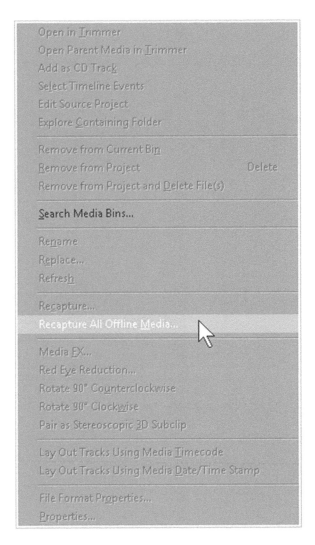

Figure 1.35 To recapture DV media with Video Capture, right-click in the Project Media in Vegas and select "Recapture All Offline Media."

Capturing/Transferring HDV

HDV uses a different capture application than the standard DV capture application. Batch capture tools are not available in the HDV capture application. To access the HDV capture application, go to File/Capture Video. The Capture Video dialog box will open.

Choose "HDV or SDI" in this dialog. This will open the HDV capture utility. Notice that this application has far fewer options than the DV capture application.

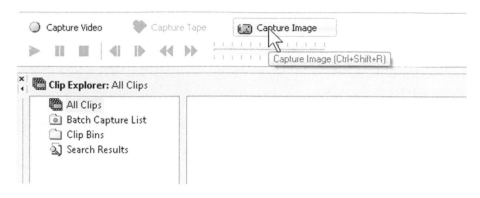

Figure 1.36   Still images can be captured directly with Video Capture.

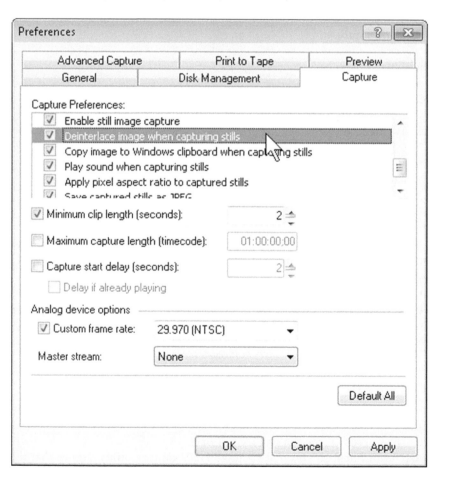

Figure 1.37   Specify preferences for managing still images in Video Capture and for viewing formats.

In the Capture dialog, choose Preferences in the upper-lefthand corner. This will allow the choice of 1394 connection or AJA SDI (serial digital interface) connection (if an AJA or BMD SDI card is present).

For HDV, choose the IEEE 1394 MPEG2/TS device. If the HDV camera/deck is connected, Vegas will display the status of the deck in the Capture Preview window.

One of the most common errors when capturing HDV in Vegas is that the camcorder is not set up for HDV capture. If the HDV capture

Figure 1.38   Capture choice dialog box.

utility is opened and configured, and the dialog reports that the camcorder/deck is not available, yet all connections are made, the camcorder/deck is turned to VCR mode, and a tape is inserted in the deck, it's quite likely the camcorder/deck is in DV down-convert mode instead of HDV mode. Open the camcorder/deck menu in VCR mode and be certain the camcorder indicates it is outputting HDV. Most of the HDV devices will specify output resolution in the display window.

The device may now be controlled via the capture utility. Start/stop, Rewind, Fast-forward, Capture are all enabled, so that the camcorder/deck does not require any local control.

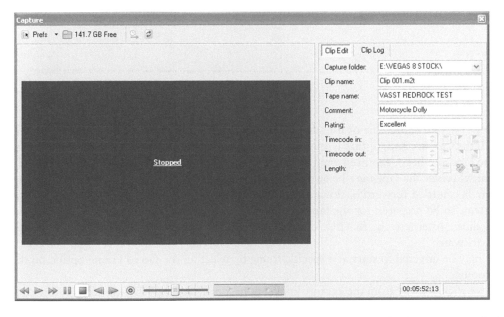

Figure 1.39   Note that in this dialog, the device is stopped and is ready for control via the Vegas capture application.

Prior to transfer of the HDV stream to a hard drive, it's important to specify the location to which the video stream will be stored on the computer.

It is highly recommended that the storage location not be the C: drive location. As mentioned previously, it's best to store video (and audio) on a drive separate from the OS and application drive.

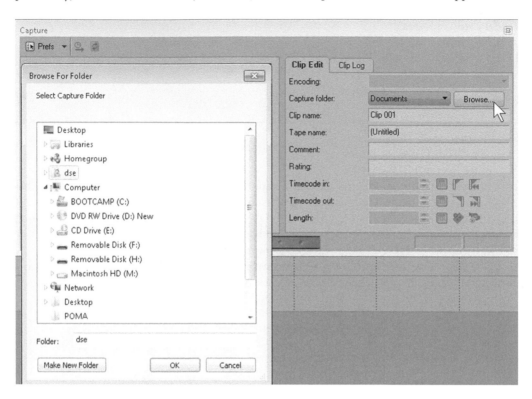

Figure 1.40

Capturing either an entire tape or user-defined start points are the two capture options available for HDV. If the Capture Tape option is selected, Vegas will instruct the HDV device to rewind to the start of the tape and begin capture from that point. If the Capture button is selected, capture will begin from wherever the tape may be at that moment in time.

Tape may be shuttled forward/backward via the shuttle option in the capture tool; this tool is slightly latent, so be prepared for the tape mechanism to be slightly slow in responding to input from this slider. Alternatively, the JKL shuttle keyboard shortcuts may be used to shuttle tape forward/backward.

Capture may be directed to start at a specific frame by selecting the Go to Frame option on the Capture toolbar.

If you have clicked away from the capture application, sometimes the HDV device will lose connection with the capture application. If this occurs, select the Reconnect to Current Device option on the toolbar.

The capture device is started via the Capture button and may be stopped by either selecting the Stop button or simply hitting the spacebar. Vegas will then open a dialog asking users to keep the current capture session as a file or not.

Figure 1.41

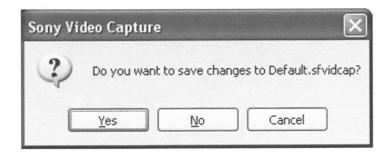

It's not necessary to save this capture session information; the Project Media feature in Vegas keeps tabs on this same information, making it very easy to recapture media. It should be noted, however, that frame-accurate recapturing of HDV is not always possible; all efforts to keep media available via archive are a very good practice.

Vegas will offer an opportunity to save a capture session. Generally this is not necessary, as batch capture/recapture of HDV is not frame-accurate.

Sometimes, various HDV devices might not be seen immediately. You may need to cycle the device on/off/on for Vegas's video capture application to see it correctly.

1.   In the Control Panel, choose System, click the Hardware tab, and click Device Manager.

2.   Click on the AVC devices, where you'll see a connected device.

3.   Right-click and choose Update Driver. You want to search manually for the new driver.

4.   Browse to Sound, Video, Game Controllers; you want the SONY folder.

5.   In the Sony folder, specify the DVHS driver.

6.   Reboot the camera or HDV deck.

The other option in the setup of the HDV/SDI capture utility is to choose where you'll store files. When you select this option, a dialog will open up providing additional Preference choices.

On the General tab, there are four choices. If the computer being used to capture HDV is a slower machine (Single proc, or slower), it's a good idea to disable all but the last choice in the dialog. This will task the machine with less processing horsepower, even though these preferences may not seem to be significant.

Hardware Cards and Vegas Pro (Not Available in Vegas Movie Studio)

Vegas Pro also offers support for AJA Kona LH-series and BlackMagic Design Decklink/Intensity hardware cards. These cards offer 10-bit ingest/output via component input connections to camcorders that offer component output. Using these cards requires a fast computer and large RAID and will use the Sony YUV codec instead of using the MPEG2 codec from HDV and XDCAM camcorders or the DV codec output from DV camcorders.

Figure 1.42   The KONA LHi
card from AJA.

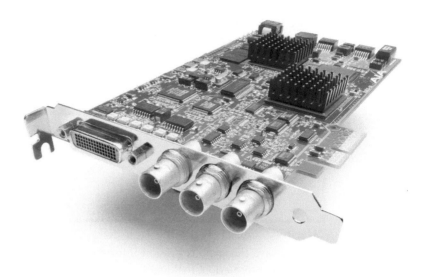

Some users feel that access to the 10-bit codec does offer a better image. It's true that chroma smoothing is managed differently via the analog input/output mode of the camcorders and the digitizing of the footage using the YUV codec, but the image source is still whatever the image source is. In other words, don't expect HDCAM-like output from an HDV camcorder simply because the footage is captured via a 10-bit card and analog output. The 10 bit media may be pushed more deeply for color and post-processing, however.

Be certain the latest AJA Kona Windows or BlackMagic Design Decklink/Intensity 32- or 64-bit driver is installed.

Figure 1.43   Black Magic
makes the
Intensity card for
HDMI input/
capture and
monitoring.

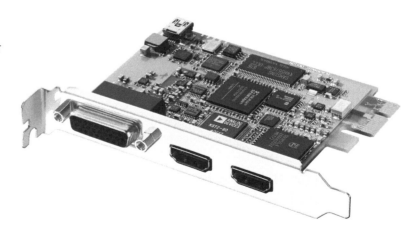

One benefit of these systems is in live studio work, in which the camera head is used and no recording system other than direct capture is part of the workflow. In this case, the camera is used to acquire the image, and the live video stream is output from the camera as a 4:2:2 uncompressed image and digitized by the hardware card as a 4:2:2, 10-bit stream straight to the computer hard drive. In this environment, the image quality is limited only by the glass and sensors in the camera. Extremely high quality footage is possible, as the compression stage in the camera is bypassed.

The AJA Kona or BlackMagic Design Decklink/Intensity is a great choice for 10-bit, uncompressed capture in Sony Vegas Pro software. Capture via this card is accomplished using the same capture tool as used for HDV. Only the capture device needs to be changed. In the Preferences dialog, select the AJA Video or BlackMagic Design Decklink/Intensity Device. This will prepare the hardware card for capture, and the Details dialog will open, displaying information about the device.

It's best to select the Conform Output to the Following Format option. This means that no matter what is on the timeline, output will be configured to match your preview monitor. There are two options: Always and Only When the Project Does Not Match Any Available Format. "Always" means that regardless of project settings, output to monitor will conform to the preview monitor settings. An example of using this option might be if you've got PAL footage but are previewing on an NTSC monitor. Otherwise, choose the Only When the Project Does Not Match Any Available Format option. This will instruct Vegas to conform output when the project settings don't match standard formats.

Other options in the Preferences include setting Progressive Segmented frames and Timecode. Use the PsF option if the project properties are for a progressive format, such as 24p, 25p, and 30p formats. The Timecode offset is used in the event that the captures are not frame-accurate. Use the slider to offset as compensation adjustment.

The Audio format option allows for multichannel format if your playback device supports multichannel output. Otherwise, *leave this set to two channels.*

The 10-bit option is for capturing 10-bit files. If this option is used, *be sure to set the Project Properties to 32-bit floating point.* If the 10-bit option is not selected, then video will be captured with 8-bit accuracy. Bear in mind that using this option will require a large RAID array and RAID controller for capture without dropped frames.

In the Disk Management tabs of both capture utilities, the only option available is to select a specific disk that you'd like to capture media to. The primary consideration here is to be certain that you're never capturing to your system disk. This is particularly important with HDV or SDI capture, as dropped frames would be a virtual certainty if media is captured to the system drive. For adequate SDI capture, you'll need a RAID 0 configuration. The RAID could be either eSATA or SCSI, although SCSI is generally preferable, and a minimum of four drives, although a RAID of eight drives (10k speed) or more is a good idea. Blackmagic Design suggests you could possibly squeak by with only six 10k drives, but they don't recommend it. Hardware controllers for the SATA RAID are highly recommended, although there may be a software RAID controller available that will provide the necessary throughput. SDI and HD require a fairly significant amount of bandwidth, and so the drive array will need to be up to speed. One benefit of working with uncompressed media is that it actually requires less processor power than DV or transport streams require, as there is no compression taking place. The challenge in working with uncompressed files lies with throughput, not with processor speed. If you visit the www.blackmagic-design.com web site, you'll find a speed test utility that will let you know if your system is ready for processing uncompressed SD and uncompressed HD files. For SD file transfer and storage, 30 MB per second is a safe benchmark data rate.

You'll need approximately 180 GB of storage per hour of SD video. HD (without audio) is approximately 170 MB per second, or roughly 600 GB per hour of uncompressed HD storage. 1280 x 720p files require slightly less bandwidth and storage than 1920 x 1080 files, asking for an average of around 170 MB per second. When working with uncompressed files on a marginal system, consider 24p as your frame rate, as this can significantly reduce throughput requirements, dropping the required data rate to just under 150 MB per second. As you can see from these data rate requirements, you'll not be able to get into uncompressed SD or HD very inexpensively. Check the Blackmagic Design web site for additional details on supported and recommended motherboards, processors, and RAM configurations. Finally, on the Device tab, you'll specify the default for capture, whether it's a DeckLink card or an HDV device captured via 1394.

If you plan on using one of the Blackmagic Design or AJA cards, you'll need the following:

- A fast RAID array
- RAID controller card/system

You will also need to speed test the system prior to capturing/ingesting video. You can download the system speed test software from the Blackmagic Design web site.

The Blackmagic Design and AJA hardware cards supported in Vegas provide users with some options that previously weren't very easy to work into the Vegas workflow. Most importantly, rather than working with DV, users can work with 4:2:2 uncompressed footage on the timeline in Sony Vegas Pro. Previously, to import uncompressed to the Vegas Pro Timeline required capturing with a third-party application, importing to Vegas Pro, rendering to the desired codec, and then outputting via the third-party application. With the Kona and DeckLink cards, you can import analog media or SDI media as uncompressed media. This means a deeper, richer picture, fewer artifacts, better color-correction processing, and a higher-quality output, depending on the originating camera or format.

Another benefit, especially for footage destined for broadcast, is that the signal can be transferred via SDI, or serial digital interface. Coupled with a device like the Convergent Design SD Connect or HDV Connect, users can import uncompressed video directly from a BetaSP or HDCAM system and output back to that same device via SDI.

If you aren't using BetaSP, SX, or HDCAM in your workflow and are primarily working with DV, HDV, or AVCHD, you likely will find an SDI card to be unnecessary. If your only output format is MPEG-2 for DVD, SDI is of even lesser importance to most editors.

SDI requires a completely different setup on the equipment side compared to DV. For instance, most professional monitors don't come with SDI input and output, so you may need to purchase an SDI plug-in card for the monitor. Any switchers you might use also require SDI input and output. SDI-capable equipment isn't inexpensive and is really necessary for only a few areas of the video industry.

THE FASST START GUIDE:
Video Editing in Vegas Pro and Vegas Movie Studio

Although there are many workflows for editing video, for purposes of this chapter we're going to follow a Timeline Edit workflow, where media is edited directly on the timeline instead of using the Trimmer tool (explained later in this book).

Drag media from the Vegas Explorer to the Timeline area. Video will go to a video track, audio will go to an audio track.

Vegas Movie Studio opens with three video and three audio tracks. It will auto-route files to their correct track format. Vegas Pro will auto-generate video/audio tracks when the first media clip/event is needed.

In "Vegas-Speak," video clips, audio clips, graphic files, and anything else that may go on the timeline are referred to as *Events*. This is because Vegas treats all "Events" on the timeline with equality. There is no unique workflow for audio vs. video, titles, graphic files, or generated media. All are edited identically and treated equally across the timeline.

Once the first piece of media is on the timeline, bring other pieces of media to the timeline. Don't worry about gaps between media; those can be dealt with later. Arranging the media on the timeline isn't terribly important right now either because it can be arranged at any point in the editing process. Some editors like to edit as they bring media to the timeline, and this is a very efficient technique. Get all the media that is an initial part of the edit onto the Vegas Timeline, and we'll begin the process of *rough editing*.

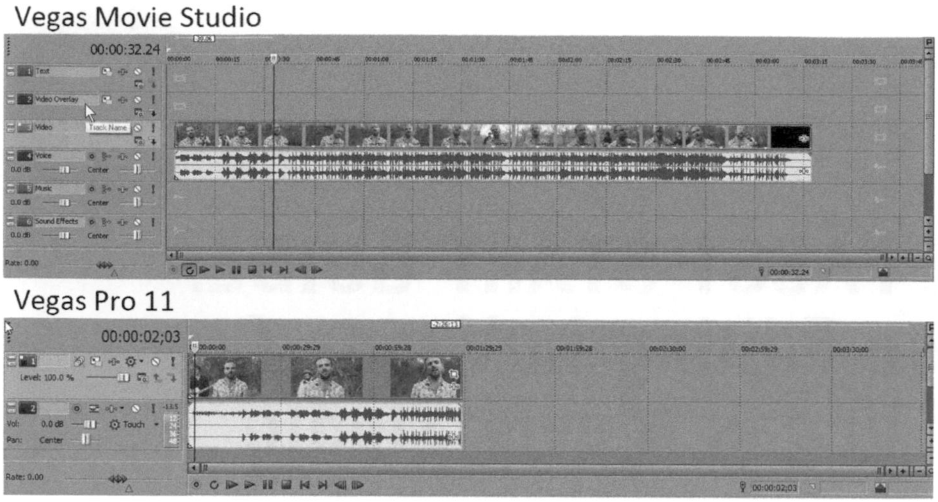

Vegas Movie Studio

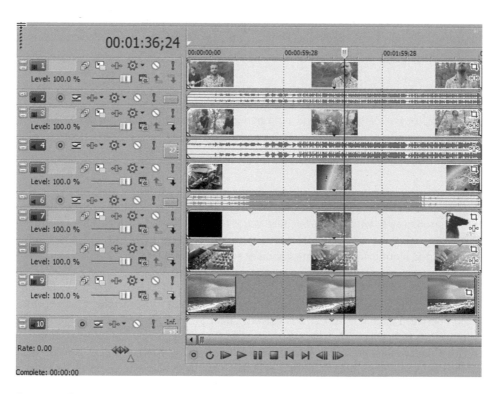

Vegas Pro 11

Figure 2.1   The image on the top shows how media will appear on the Vegas Movie Studio Timeline. In the bottom image, this is how media will appear on the Vegas Pro Timeline.

Figure 2.2   Once all the files are on the Vegas Timeline, we'll begin the process of rough editing.

Before beginning the editing process, let's mouse around a bit. Click on various parts of the video Events and notice how the Preview Window displays the frames of the video. Play around with the cursor a bit to become familiar with how the media displays and how Vegas "feels."

To play the media, press the **Spacebar** or click on the **Play** button in the transport. You can also use the transport keys **J**, **K**, and **L** to rewind, stop, and play, respectively, on the timeline.

Figure 2.3   The Transport buttons may be used to play, fast forward, or rewind media, but shortcut keys are much faster and efficient.

Tip _____

Clicking J or L multiple times will increase the speed at which the timeline plays, either forward or in reverse.

The first step in rough editing is to trim the media so that only the parts we want to use are left on the timeline. For example, many camera shots begin with shaky camera movements due to the camera's Record button being pressed; sometimes shots begin aimed at the sky or the ground. We'll definitely want to trim those sections out. We're going to learn two trimming techniques in this section.

The first method is to use the **Split** command. Play back the media using **Spacebar** or the transport buttons. You'll quickly find the point at which the video should actually start. Press the **Spacebar** again to stop when you've found that point. We're going to place the timeline place indicator (also known as the *Playhead* or *Current Time Indicator,* or CTI) at this point in time. Note that you can click the mouse to the approximate location and use your left-arrow and right-arrow keys to fine-tune where you want the starting frame to be. Press the **S** key to split or scissor the media into two pieces. The piece of media or Event on the right side will be selected/highlighted.

A different Event may be selected simply by clicking on it. Press the **Delete** key to delete unwanted media. **Ctrl + X** may also be used; this will place the deleted Event on the Windows Clipboard. We'll look at using **Ctrl + X** in a later chapter; it is a great tool in the speed-editing workflow.

The **S** key isn't the only method for splitting or deleting media from the Vegas Timeline. Users may also trim the edges of the Event simply by placing the cursor at the left or right edge of the Event, clicking, and dragging to the left or right. Place the mouse cursor at the leftmost edge of the first Event on the timeline and notice how the cursor changes to a box with an arrow. The box surrounding the arrow indicates which Event is going to be trimmed. This feature allows users to edit an Event without first selecting it, thus significantly speeding the editing process.

Once all the Events are trimmed via either the Split/Scissor method or the edge-trimming method, there are likely some gaps in the timeline.

This is also a good time to save a project. To save the project, use the shortcut keys **Ctrl + S** or browse to **File** (Project in VMS) | **Save.** Give the file a unique name so that you can find it easily later. Vegas also auto-saves by default (files are saved by a different name in a default directory); locating auto-saves is discussed elsewhere in this book.

Figure 2.4   The box on the edge of an Event indicates which Event is being edited. Events do not have to be selected prior to using edge trimming.

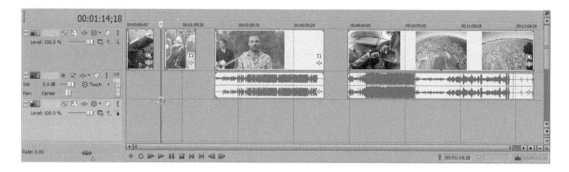

Figure 2.5   The gaps between media will be blank or black areas in the video. These gaps must be removed prior to finishing the video.

Ripple Editing

Now we'll use a method known as *ripple editing* to close any open gaps on the timeline and ensure that all Events are properly butted against other Events so that there are no blank or black spots in the finished project.

Ripple editing is something of an advanced process and is discussed in detail later in this book. Vegas Pro users will benefit greatly from the VASST Production Assistant plug-in for Vegas, which can make the ripple-editing process a single-click experience and ensures that all the pieces fall into their proper place. For now, we're going to use a simple form of ripple editing to close any timeline gaps.

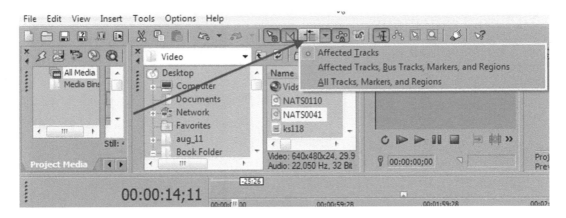

Figure 2.6   There are three Ripple modes; for this exercise, it does not matter which mode is currently active.

You can enable ripple editing by pressing **Ctrl+L** or navigating to the Toolbar and selecting the **Ripple Edit** button. Next to the Ripple Edit button is a drop-down arrow. In this drop-down dialog box, we'll set the behavior of a ripple edit, but since the current project only has one video and one audio track, we do not need to be concerned with which Ripple mode is enabled.

Double-click in any gap between Events. Use **Ctrl+X** or **Delete** to remove the gap. The media on the right will slide to the left, butted perfectly and framed accurately against the next Event. Continue this process until every gap on the timeline has been deleted. When every gap has been deleted, disable the Ripple tool using either the **Ctrl+L** shortcut or by clicking on the **Ripple Tool** button on the Vegas Toolbar. The timeline should be cleaned up, looking much like the image you see here.

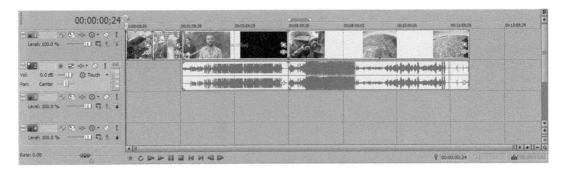

Figure 2.7   This is a post-Ripple timeline. All Events are next to each other, with no gaps present.

Once the files are rippled together, it's time to begin the first-pass edit. In this pass, we'll be looking at fading in/out media, transitions, and titles. We'll also be adding some FX and filters to some of the Events on the timeline.

Adding Transitions

Begin by creating a fade on the first Event. This is achieved by placing the mouse cursor in the upper-left corner of the first Event.

Figure 2.8   The cursor changes from an arrow to a quarter-circle icon. This indicates that a fade will be created when the cursor is dragged right or left.

Click and drag the cursor to the right. This will create a small curved line in the Event, indicating a fade-in. Place the Playhead/CTI to the left of the Event and press the **Spacebar** or click the **Play** button in the Transport. The Preview Window will play back the video and the fade-in will be displayed.

This fade curve offers more than just a plain old fade-in; a fade is nothing more than a transition, and the fade we just created may also be referred to as a *transitional point*. A fade from black is a transition from no Event to an Event.

We'll now use this same fade point to create a different kind of transition. Browse to the **Transition** window in the Docking Windows. If the Transitions window is not visible, use the key command **ALT + 7**. This will open the Transitions window.

In the Transitions window, various transitions are animated, and you can see their behavior by hovering the cursor over the transitional element. Try it, and find a transition that will be good for opening the video project. Cross Effect, Flash, Iris, and Portals are all good tools to open a

Figure 2.9   This curve indicates that a fade has been placed on an Event.

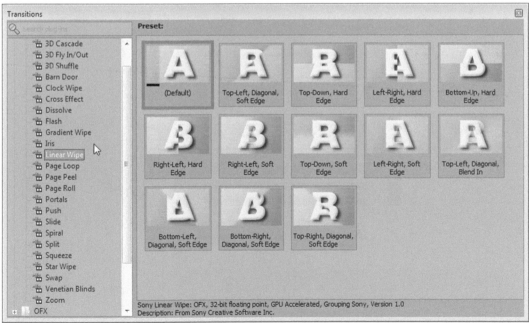

Figure 2.10   The Transitions window is where various transitional elements are selected and inserted into edit points.

presentation. Click-drag one of these transitions to the part of the video that contains the curved line of our fade and drop it in. A **Transition** dialog box will open. (Vegas will not allow the transition to be dropped anywhere but on the curved portion of the Event.)

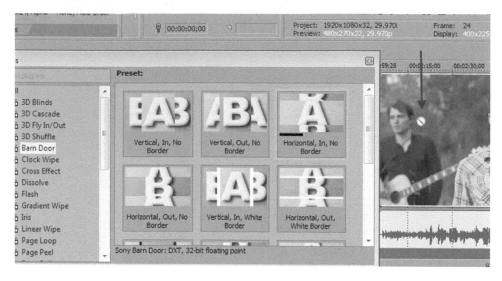

Figure 2.11 Vegas will not allow transitions to be dropped on an Event unless a transitional point has been established first.

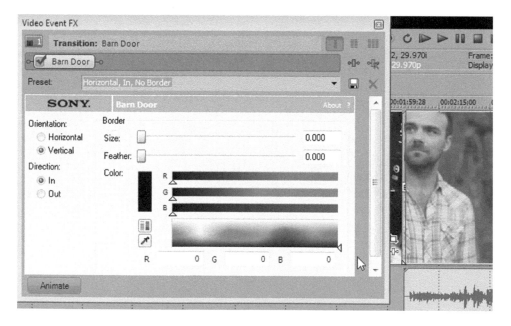

Figure 2.12 Vegas will open a Transition Parameter dialog box whenever a transition is dropped onto a transitional point. Parameters of the transition may now be adjusted to the user's preference.

Tip

Double-clicking the Event creates a *selection*. Press the **Q** key to make the selection loop. (The gray selection indicator in the top of the timeline will change to blue.) Press **Spacebar** to begin playback. As the transitional parameters are adjusted, changes will be seen in real time in the Preview window.

Once a Transition has been created, we can move on to create cross-fades and more transitional elements of a slightly different sort. We're going to once again turn to the Ripple tool to keep our timeline sequence intact while making some adjustments to the Events.

Enable ripple editing by using the keyboard shortcut of **CTRL + L** or by enabling **Ripple** on the Vegas Toolbar.

In this next exercise, we'll be moving Events to the left to create cross-fades.

Click and drag the second Event on the timeline to the left so that it overlaps the right edge of the first Event on the timeline. This will generate a small X between the two Events, indicating the length of the overlap. A small time indicator will show in the upper-right corner of the X. This demonstrates the length of the overlap in minutes, seconds, and frames. Create a seven-frame overlap, indicated in time by 0.07 in the time indicator.

Figure 2.13 Time of transitional length/overlap length displays as seen earlier. In this example, an overlap of seven frames is indicated.

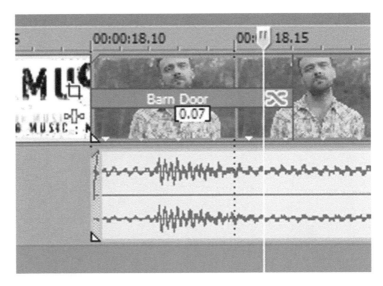

If getting the Transition length to seven frames proves challenging, it's because the timeline might be zoomed in too deeply. Using the **Up/Down Arrows** on the keyboard, zoom in more deeply with the Playhead/Current Time Indicator at the Transition point. The timeline will stay centered around the Playhead/CTI position.

Computer mice that have a scroll wheel may be used to zoom in and out of the timeline. Simply scroll the wheel upward to zoom in, downward to zoom out. This is a significant time saver for the Vegas professional.

Double-click the **X** overlap indication between the two Events. This will create a selection. If the Loop feature was left enabled, a blue line will be indicated in the top of the timeline; if looping is disabled, a gray bar will appear in the top of the timeline. Be sure that looping is enabled (blue indicator). The **Q** key or looping button in the Transport bar will enable/disable looping.

Press the **Spacebar** or **Play** button in the Vegas Transport bar. The selection will begin to play, and the cross-fade transition between the two Events will be shown. Expand the Selection by click-dragging the yellow indicators on both sides of the Selection indicator.

Figure 2.14   These small triangles indicate Selection in/out points. They may be click-dragged to expand or reduce timeline selections. They'll be fairly important later on in this book, so it's best to become familiar with them early in the learning process.

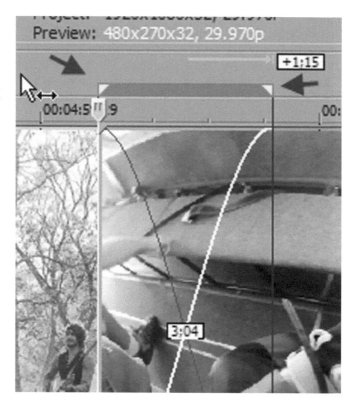

Allow the cross-fade to play through a few times. This accomplishes two things: If the processor is slow, older, or heavily taxed, the cross-fade (or any other transition) may not play through cleanly. Repeated play allows the cross-fade to render itself in system RAM so that it ultimately plays through cleanly. It also allows the eye a few moments to decide whether the timing of the cross-fade is correct or needs adjustment. Keep the cross-fade looping, even if the decision is made to adjust the length of the cross-fade/overlap. Moving the Event on the left or right of the cross-fade will increase or decrease the length of the cross-fade.

*Tip*_____

If the PC keyboard has a numeric keypad (the 10 number keys typically grouped on the right side of the keyboard, *not* the numbers across the QWERTY keys), the **3** key or the **6** key may be used to nudge selected Events to the right or left. The amount of movement is determined by how deeply the user has zoomed into the timeline. Use the **Up** and **Down Arrows** to zoom in and out of the timeline.

Vegas should still be playing the cross-fade due to the Looping feature. Choose **Click/Drag a Transition** from the Transition window and drop it onto the **X** overlap indicator between the two Events. The transition should be immediately displayed in the Preview window. As before, a **Transition** dialog box will appear.

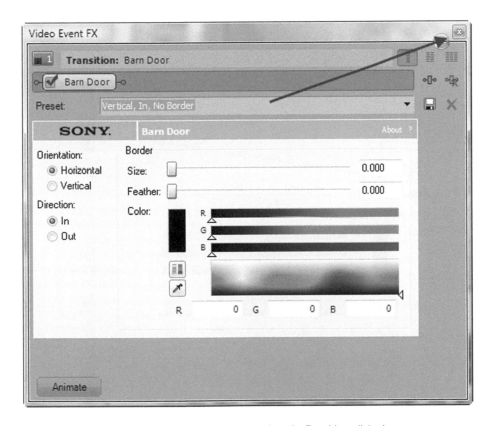

Figure 2.15   Click the red X in the upper-right corner to close the Transitions dialog box.

Adjust the transition until you're satisfied with how it appears. During these adjustments, the video should be looping in the Preview window. This is one of Vegas's main strengths—the way it adjusts in real time, all the while utilizing system RAM to create instant Preview.

*Tip*_____

Holding the **Shift** key when dragging or dropping transitions into the Transition/Overlap space will prevent the Transition dialog box from opening. This is a time saver if a transition preset is dragged and dropped. Users may create and save their own presets.

Let's create a transition preset now. Open the **Transition** dialog box of your choice. Adjust any of the Transition parameters and click the **Preset** box in the **Transition parameter** dialog box. Give the transition a unique name and click the **Save Preset** icon (which looks like a small floppy disk). That's all there is to it! You'll use this technique any time you want to create presets for any of Vegas's effects.

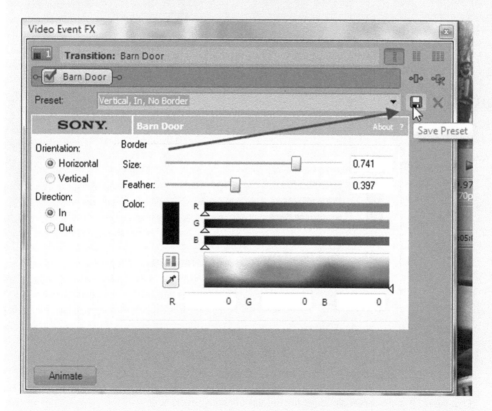

Figure 2.16   Users may create and save Transition parameters by choosing and clicking the **Save Preset** button in the Transition parameter dialog box.

Now we're going to add some FX to the Events on the timeline.

Adding FX

FX, effects, or filters (all these names work) can be used most effectively to bring out the best in video, audio, or graphic Events. FX can be used for color correction or special effects or to give a unique style to a production.

FX are added the same way as transitions: by selecting a specific FX from the Vegas FX library and dropping it onto an Event. (Vegas has other methods of implementing FX; for this particular chapter, dragging and dropping is the method we'll use. Other methods are explored in other chapters of this book.)

Place the **Playhead** over any Event in the timeline; the current frame should be displayed in the Preview window. Moving to the **Video FX** tab in the Docking Windows area, browse to the FX labeled **Color Curves** and click on the words **Color Curves** in the Video FX library. If the Video FX tab or window is not visible in the Docking Windows area, use the keyboard shortcut **Alt + 8** to bring up the Video FX window.

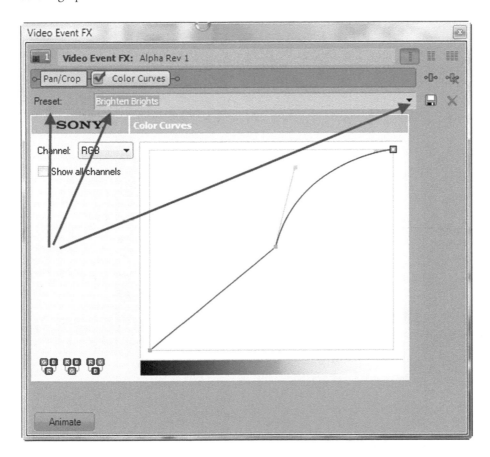

Figure 2.17   The presets displayed on the right side of the FX/filter may be dragged and dropped directly onto an Event, thus changing the way it appears.

On the right side of the FX library you'll see several icons, just as they appear in the Transitions window. These are presets for the various FX available in Vegas. Choose the Color Curves preset labeled **Warm Colors** and drag/drop this preset on to the video Event displayed in the Preview window. Notice that the display in the Preview window immediately changes to a warmer tone. Vegas does not need to render this filter so that its impact may be seen; the effect is immediate. Also note that Vegas opens up an FX dialog box in the same place, size, and manner as the Transitions dialog box when it opened. This allows users to not only adjust the parameters of the FX but also to store FX presets in exactly the same manner as with Transition. Set **parameters** to desired settings, fill in the **Naming** field, and click the **Save Preset** (floppy disk) icon. The preset will be stored.

Close the Event FX dialog box by clicking the red **X** in the upper-right corner of the FX dialog box.

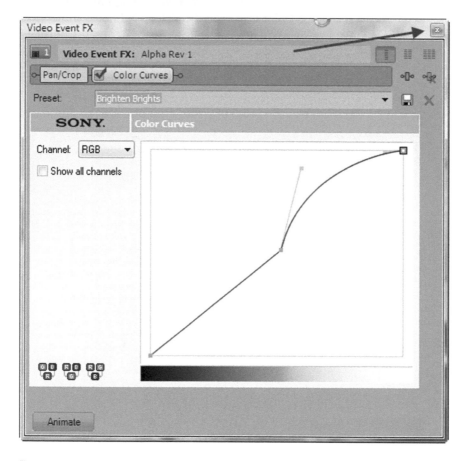

Figure 2.18   Click the red **X** in the upper-right corner to close an FX dialog box.

What if this preset isn't the right one? It's very easy to alter or delete FX after they've been applied to an Event. There are two methods to easily access FX that have been applied to an Event. On each Event (by Vegas defaults), there is a small button on its right side.

Figure 2.19   Each Event has an FX button. If the button is
gray, it means that no FX have been applied to
that Event. If the button is green, it indicates
that FX have been added to that Event. Click this
button to access the FX parameters.

The button may be gray or green; gray indicates that no FX have been applied to that specific Event, and green indicates the Event has one or more FX applied to it. Click this button to reopen the FX dialog box and edit FX parameters to their desired settings.

 Tip_____
Keep the timeline running with the **Looping** tool (select an area and press the Q key) while adjusting FX parameters. Not only does this save time; doing so will allow for immediate feedback on FX settings. Another benefit is that this utilizes system RAM for the Preview.

Apply FX across the project as needed. For this exercise, it's recommended that you apply simple FX such as the White Balance, Color Curves, Color Balance, and the like to the Events. Once FX are applied to all desired Events, we'll move on to adding simple titles.

Basic Audio Tools and Functions

Audio is 70% of what the audience "sees." No, this isn't a typo, it's something I've been preaching for nearly 30 years. Viewers determine the quality of what they're watching based in great part on what they're *hearing*. Poor sound quality equals poor visual experiences.

With that in mind, this next section addresses a few basic yet important audio tools found in Vegas Pro and Vegas Movie Studio.

Remember how we created a fade on the video Events earlier in this chapter? Placing the mouse cursor over the upper-left or upper-right corner of a video Event changes the cursor to a quarter-circle icon, allowing users to click-drag left or right. This method works exactly the same way with audio; place the mouse cursor over the left or right corner of an audio Event and drag to the right or to the left.

Figure 2.20   Inserting fade in/out on audio Events is identical to fades on video Events.

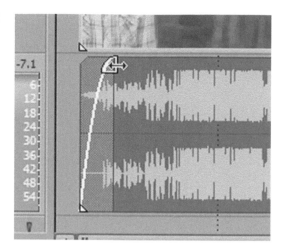

Each audio Event in Vegas may be independently adjusted for volume and gain. This is one of the super-fast benefits of editing audio in Vegas. To access Event gain control, place the mouse cursor at the top of an audio Event. The cursor will change to a finger point; this indicates that the audio Event may be click-dragged downward, reducing the gain of that particular Event. This is a terrific technique for leveling audio across the audio track.

Figure 2.21   When the cursor displays this icon, the gain may be reduced on an audio Event. The negative numbers displayed next to the cursor indicate the amount of gain reduction.

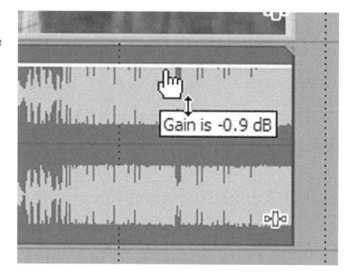

Selecting an audio track and pressing the **V** key (or browsing through **Insert | Audio Envelope | Volume Envelope**) will insert a *volume envelope* that allows users to set nodes or points of volume change. This is also referred to as *rubber-band audio* in some nonlinear applications. The volume envelope will display as a blue line; double-clicking it will insert audio control points, allowing for volume to be raised or lowered at any point in the timeline. Other methods of inserting volume control points or nodes are discussed in later chapters of this book.

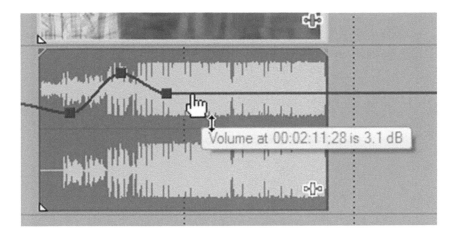

Figure 2.22   The volume envelope may have as many volume control points as needed. To be certain that distortion is not introduced at the Master Output, use caution when raising levels.

Each audio track header has a **Track FX** control button. This button looks exactly the same as the FX button on each Video/Graphic Event.

Figure 2.23   This FX button allows access to inserted audio FX, just as a similar button is found on Video Events and Tracks.

Audio Events also have an Event FX button; these will be discussed in detail later in this book.

Clicking the **Audio FX** button in the track header opens a Track FX dialog box that contains three FX: a noise gate, an EQ, and a compressor. These may be used to clean up or enhance audio. Click the **EQ** effect, choose the **Boost frequencies above 7 kHz** preset, and start playback. Notice how you can hear the change immediately.

Feel free to play around with the parameters, but we'll save the finer details of how to use these tools for a later chapter. It's worth noting that audio FX may be adjusted in real time just as the video FX are adjusted: Set Vegas to loop using the **Q** key and adjust **audio FX** parameters to suit personal tastes.

Tip_____

All audio tracks in Vegas Pro and Vegas Movie Studio (by default) have the same three audio FX inserted. Default FX may be set to user preference.

Adding Titles

Titles are an important part of any production, whether they are static titles, lower thirds with a name board, station ID bugs, text interpretations of dialogue, credit rolls, or actual messages. Vegas Pro offers a few different titling options; Vegas Movie Studio has one titling option.

For this section, we'll be working with the basic Text Media Generator found in both versions of Vegas.

Place the Playhead/CTI at the beginning of the project and be sure there is a blank track for titles. Vegas Movie Studio users already have a Title track; Vegas Pro users will need to insert a new track. Use **Ctrl + Shift + Q** or **Insert | Video track** to create a new video track.

Titles may be inserted via more than one method; a preferred method is to right-click inside the new video track boundaries and choose **Insert Text Media** from the menu that appears. Another method is to browse to **Insert | Text Media** from the Insert menu. Either method will open a Text Media Generator dialog box.

Figure 2.24 The Text Media dialog box will open with the words *SAMPLE TEXT*. Highlight these words to replace them with your own text.

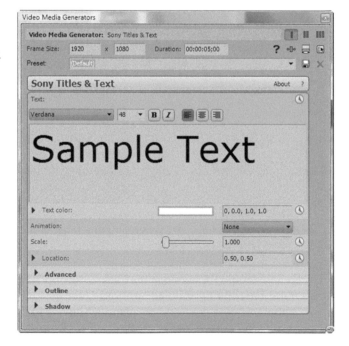

The Text Media generator will open with the words *SAMPLE TEXT* already in the box. Select these words with the mouse cursor by click-dragging over them, and then type in your own words.

You can choose fonts and font sizes in this dialog box as well. Select **Impact,** for example. Pressing the **I** key with the **Font** drop-down menu active will immediately bring up the Impact font (assuming that Impact is the first font beginning with the letter *I* in the menu). Fonts that do not have serifs are generally preferred for video production because the small, fine lines of serif fonts can be problematic on interlaced televisions or small displays.

Figure 2.25 Fonts may be selected in the drop-down box. Using a key for the first letter of a named font provides a shortcut access to a group of fonts.

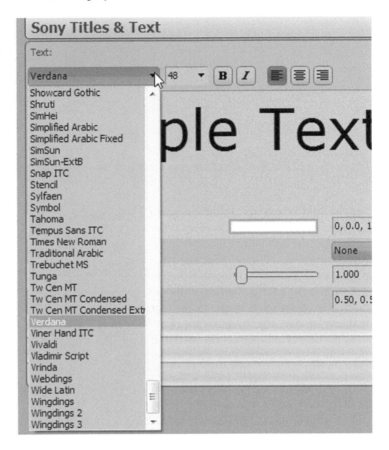

Choose a font size via the **Font Size** drop-down menu. The default font size is 72. Fonts smaller than 12 points might look great on a full-screen computer view, but bear in mind that when viewers are seeing your video project on the Web or a screen smaller than the screen being used for editing, smaller fonts could make for difficult reading.

Title positioning may also be determined in this dialog box. There are four tabs in the Text Media dialog box. The first is the **Edit** tab, where font, size, and text content are determined. The next tab is the **Placement** tab. In this tab, users can select preset positions such as Center, Upper Right, Lower Left, and so on. Text may also be free-form placed by clicking the **Text** box in the Placement window and dragging text to the desired position.

Figure 2.26 Text may be positioned using Vegas presets or manually dragged to preferred positions.

In the **Text Properties** tab there are two color selection options. The Text color option on the left colors the text itself, determining the color of character display. The Text color option on the right determines the background color. By default, this is set to Transparent so that text can lay over the top of video. However, if a title card is being generated or if there are specific effects you want to create, a color may be added in this box. Any color generated in this option will be full-screen color and may not be cut out without using additional filters, masks, or FX.

The **Text Effects** tab allows users to outline, shadow, or deform text. The **Outlines** and **Shadows** options allow users to choose the colors of the outlines and shadows. The **Deform** function allows users to shear, bend, or curve text with varying degrees of deformity. These tools may be used to animate text; we'll discuss how in the section on keyframing.

Figure 2.27 The color selection on the left controls color of text fonts and characters. The color selection on the right controls the background color behind the text fonts and characters. By default, the color selector on the right is set to 100% transparent, allowing titles to be laid over video.

Figure 2.28   Shadows and outlines can help text stand out in a video presentation. Text may also be deformed or distorted via this dialog box.

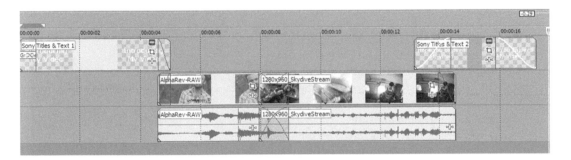

Figure 2.29

Create two title Events for the beginning and ending of the project (right-click on the track where you want the titles to go, then choose **Insert Text Media**). Once the titles are inserted, they can be made more interesting by using transitions and FX. Change the text of the first title to "Introducing My Video" and the text of the second title to "Hope You Enjoyed My Video." On the first title, create a fade-in by putting the cursor on the upper-left corner of the incoming title. Make this fade-in 10 to 12 frames in length. Create a fade-out on this title that is the same length. Browse to the Transitions tab in the Docking window area and locate the Gradient Wipe transition. The reason this transition is suggested is that it offers many user-defined parameters and it's a great choice for introducing a production. Drag this transition to the Bezier curve you created with the fade-in on the first title. (Bezier is the actual name of the curved line introduced earlier in this chapter and seen in Event fades and transitions. It will be used frequently in this book.)

With the DVD found in this book in your computer's DVD drive, click the **Browse** button in the Gradient Wipe Transition dialog box and browse for the **GRIDMETAL** image in the Graphics folder. This will display the .jpg in the Gradient Wipe Transition dialog preview window. Set a selection to loop using the **Q** key as we did before and begin playback by pressing the **Spacebar** or using the **Play** button in the Vegas Transport bar. While this is looping, experiment with the Threshold Blend, Gradient Blur, and Reverse options, which will provide a variety of styles. Any image may be used for this process, but images that have varying shades of white to black make for the easiest-to-use transitional elements.

Choose a second transition to exit the title from the screen. A fade works well, of course. If you desire, slide the title to the right so that it is above part of the first Event on the video track. This will put the title as an overlay to the video. Note that the title background is transparent, so only letters are overlaying the video. This is where adding a shadow on the text media could come in handy.

Clicking the green **Edit Generated Media** button on the text media will open the Text Media generator, allowing for text to be edited, including color, shadow, outline, and so on.

Get creative with the ending title, tweak it to a desired state, and we'll move on to outputting the file to a variety of formats.

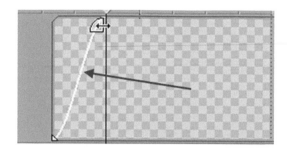

Figure 2.30 Dropping a transition on this fade-in point allows text to be more dynamic and eye-catching.

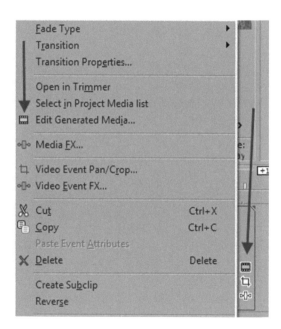

Figure 2.31 Text may be edited at a later time. Access the Text Media dialog box by clicking the **Edit Generated Media** button found on each text Event.

THE FASST START GUIDE:
Outputting a Project in Vegas Pro and Vegas Movie Studio

You'll want to Preview your project a few times before rendering and finishing it. *Rendering* is the process of assembling all the file and generated media elements of the timeline into one finished file. Rendering is much like baking a cake. Eggs, flour, sugar, milk, and butter are all elements of the cake; they're mixed together and then baked. Once the cake is baked, it's impossible to remove individual elements from it. Rendering a video file is the same way. Once the file is rendered, the elements may no longer be separated. Of course, the project can always be rerendered using the original "ingredients" in the event of an error or desired change.

We're going to look at outputting to both the Internet and DVD. The Internet settings we'll use are the same for mobile devices such as a Droid, iPhone, iPad, and the like.

Before beginning the last steps to output a file, it's a good idea to create a *render region*. This will come in handy should a file need to be reedited. Click-drag across the top of the timeline to create a selection that incorporates the entire project from beginning to end. Press the **R** key (for Region) on the keyboard, and in the name field that will open, type **Render Region**. This identifies the render area and length of project and provides a return point should the project require rerendering. Regions are defined by the green marker points found on the timeline.

This is also a good time to save a project. To save the project, use the shortcut keys **Ctrl+S** or browse to **File** (Project in VMS) | **Save**.

Output to the Internet and Personal Devices

The Web is a great way to distribute video, so we're going to output our timeline in a format that is compatible with YouTube, Vimeo, Facebook, and Blogger. These same settings will work well with most mobile and personal devices.

Although Vegas Movie Studio and Vegas Pro both have templates designed specifically for these sites, we will not be using them as delivered. Modifying the Sony templates will provide for a better end-user experience and a much higher-quality output.

Figure 3.1   The process of rendering for mobile and personal devices uses the same settings as rendering for Internet/streaming delivery over most user-generated content (UGC) sites.

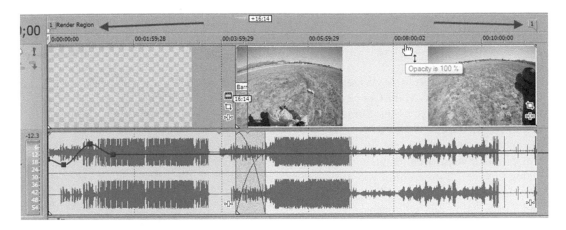

Figure 3.2   Creating a render region is not required, but it is good practice when finishing a project. It provides a point of reference, develops a range for the batch-processing technique, and helps with housekeeping of your projects.

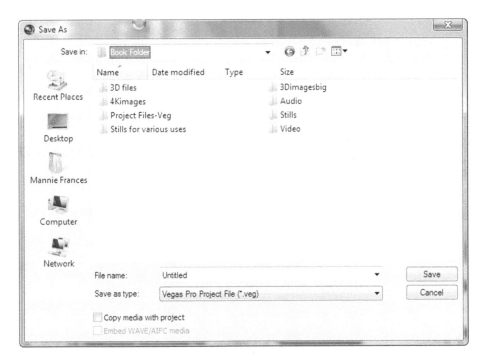

Figure 3.3   Save your project often. Although Vegas automatically generates backup copies of projects, it's a good plan to save frequently. **Ctrl + S** opens the save dialog box when you're saving for the first time. After the file has been saved once, the dialog box will not open; saved files will be updated.

Vegas Movie Studio users may use the Make Movie option if speed is an issue, but quality will suffer. In these next steps, Vegas Pro and Vegas Movie Studio users will follow the same steps.

Browse to **File** (Project for VMS users) | **Render As**. In this dialog box, select the **Main Concept** AVC/AAC format. Click the triangle next to the format, and a drop-down of choices will open.

Browse down to the Apple iPad/iPhone 720p30 Video template and select this template. On the sidebar of the dialog box, scroll down until you can see the **Customize Template** button. Click the **Customize Template** button, and a new dialog box will open.

In this dialog box, we'll alter some of the factory settings to a more pleasing output quality. This process might create some instability with older personal devices, but is perfect for Web and newer personal device delivery.

In the dialog box, uncheck the **Allow Source To Adjust Frame Rate** check box. Check the **Use Deblocking Filter** box, and scroll down to the **Variable Bit Rate** box. By default, this is set to 4Mbps. Click in this box and set a value of **6,500,000**.

Figure 3.4 Vegas provides outputs to all the popular social media, video distribution, and other UGC sites.

Figure 3.5 Render templates are selected in this dialog box. Note the stars on the side of each template; these allow users to set Favorite Render templates.

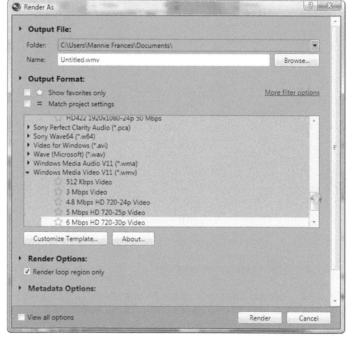

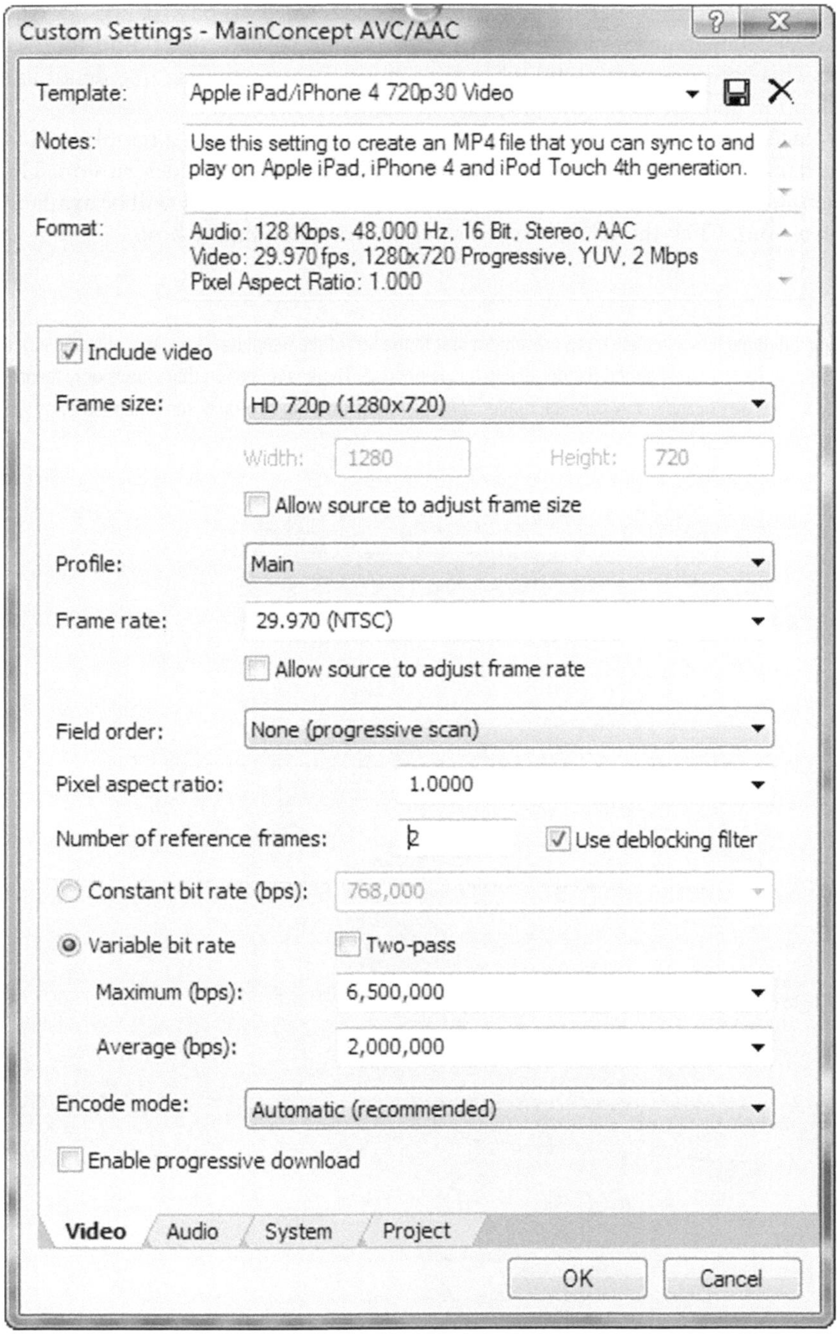

Figure 3.6   Render settings for UGC sites and mobile or personal devices should match these settings.

To the right of the Variable Bitrate option is a check box labeled **Two-pass**. Checking this box allows the Vegas encoding/compression tool to prescan a file to help determine the best compression settings. This option is very useful when time is not as important as fine detail in a video file. Leave the option unchecked for the purposes of this exercise.

With all settings in place, at the top of the **Render** dialog box is a place to name a template. Give the template a unique name. Fill in the **description** box with the 720p30 6.5Mbps description. This will allow the same template to be used later (and for Vegas Pro users, this template will be available for batch rendering later on). Click the **OK** button to close the template dialog box.

 *Tip*_____

Before proceeding, notice that the new template has a grayed-out star to the left of the template name. This allows users to create favorite templates, to be shown when the Render dialog box is opened. There is an option that shows only favorite render settings. This is a good way to show only common render settings rather than the several dozen render settings that Vegas offers.

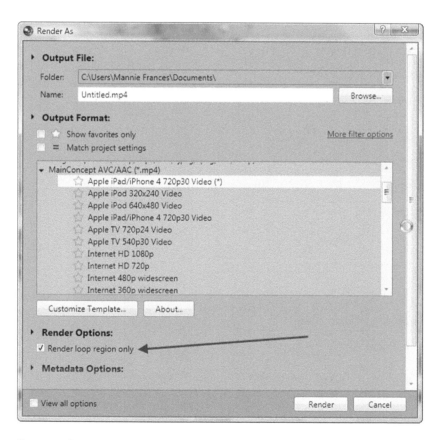

Figure 3.7   By selecting **Render Loop Region Only**, this assures that the render region will be the only area rendered. This is a good practice for quality assurance.

In the Render dialog box, scroll further down and check the box labeled **Render Loop Region Only**. This will instruct Vegas to render/assemble all the Events found within the green render region created earlier. Scroll up to the top of the **Render** dialog box and give the file a unique name, and if the render location is different from the default (Vegas defaults to a Documents folder), point the Render dialog box to a new file location.

Now the file is ready to be rendered/assembled. Click the **Render** button. This process may take a moment or two, depending on CPU speed and other variables based on each computer's different hardware and software configurations. It's often a good time to stand up, stretch, and give the eyes a rest from the computer screen.

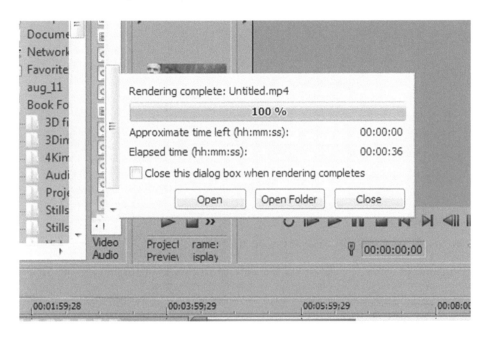

Figure 3.8   When the render is complete, this dialog box will open. It's good practice to open the file location and review the finished file before uploading to the Web or to mobile devices.

When the file has completed the rendering process, it will provide a window that shows it is complete and gives the user an option to open the file folder containing the new video file. This is a good time to view the file in Windows Media Player or other playback software outside the Vegas Timeline. If any corrections are necessary, go back into the Vegas Timeline and adjust accordingly.

Output to DVD

Vegas offers the ability to burn DVDs straight from the timeline. Vegas Pro and Vegas Movie Studio users will each have a slightly different experience. In either case, Vegas has rendering templates for DVD output built in. Later in the book we will alter these for maximum quality but they are fine as-is for this exercise.

Vegas Pro Users

In the **Tools** menu there is a **Burn Disc | Burn DVD** option. Select this option to burn a DVD from the timeline. Vegas will auto-format the Picture Aspect Ratio/PAR (4:3 or Widescreen) based on project settings. Press **OK** and let the disc encode and burn.

This is all that needs to be done. If no disc is present in the DVD burner, follow the prompts to put a disc in the burner and click **OK** again.

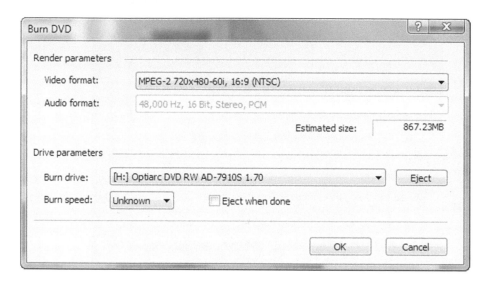

Figure 3.9   Vegas Pro can deliver DVDs straight from the timeline. These are not DVDs with menus but are great for sharing projects or previewing projects that do not require an authored DVD with menus.

Creating DVD files for authoring DVDs is discussed in Chapter 13, "Rendering and Output."

Vegas Movie Studio Users

Vegas Movie Studio users will click the **Make Movie** template in the Toolbar at the top of the screen. Next, choose **Burn Blu-ray or DVD disc** from the second menu. Then choose **Burn DVD** from the third menu option. Again, burning DVDs for authoring (with menus) is discussed later in this book. Choose **Next** in the bottom of the Render menu dialog box. A new dialog box opens with a choice of DVD render options. Leave the default options as they are, click **OK**, and let Vegas create the new file and burn to disc. If no disc is present in the DVD burner, follow the prompts to put a disc in the burner and click **OK** again.

Figure 3.10 Vegas Movie Studio users have a very simple dialog box and flow to follow. Vegas Movie Studio will automatically downconvert HD media to SD widescreen when delivering to DVD.

In this FASST section we've looked at:

- Understanding the Vegas Graphic User Interface (GUI)
- Setting basic preferences
- Preview settings
- Importing and locating media and video files
- Getting content to the timeline
- Splitting/trimming Events
- Fades and transitions
- Adding FX
- Basic audio features
- Adding basic titles
- Exporting for various mobile devices, the Internet, and DVD

Congratulations! With an understanding of these basic tasks, you should now be ready to Turn Up ... and Go Deeper into Sony Vegas Pro and Vegas Movie Studio software.

PART TWO

Turning Up: Going Deeper into Sony Vegas

Preferences: Settings for the Best Vegas Experience

Vegas Pro and Vegas Movie Studio are both applications that can satisfy the needs of a professional video editor in a broadcast, religious, educational, or hobbyist environment. With this in mind, different needs may call for different approaches to setting up the editing system and editing environment.

Establishing proper setup of the editing system in advance will save a great deal of time when the editing process begins.

The next section of this book offers suggestions in how to best set up the editing environment for both professional and hobbyist needs.

Dual-monitor setups are highly desired in a professional environment; not only do they allow for more application viewing space, they also allow for easier multitasking. The greater real estate offered with dual monitors also allows for full-screen preview of the editing project (although a single monitor may also be used) while viewing the Vegas Timeline.

Figure 4.1   Screenshot of Vegas on dual monitors.

Dual monitors are helpful for performing screen-intensive tasks such as color correction, compositing, or audio mixing. Due to the Open CL GPU acceleration found in the NVIDIA GeForce GT2XXX and ATI Radeon HD 57xx (or newer) video cards, dual head, accelerated monitoring/rendering can really be powerful and fun while doubling as gaming display systems.

In addition to faster speeds found on Open CL cards, there are also hardware cards available from AJA and Black Magic Design that offer alternatives for ingest and playback monitoring over Serial Digital Interface (SDI) and High-Definition Multimedia Interface (HDMI). These hardware cards do not assist in rendering speeds.

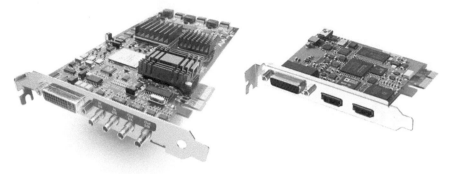

Figure 4.2   AJA Kona Series (above left) and Black Magic Intensity (above right) allow for capture over HMI or SDI. Vegas Movie Studio does not support the use of hardware cards from BMD or AJA.

Hardware cards such as the AJA Kona Series and the Black Magic Intensity allow for capture over HDMI or SDI, requisite for most broadcast facilities. However, capturing over HDMI or SDI eliminates the speed of file-based formats, since capture is a real-time process. The benefits of this capture process are that time may be saved when intermediaries or transcoding are part of the workflow or when live capture is required. Live-capture systems bypass the compression systems of whatever camera is being used and provide an uncompressed, pristine image in most conditions. File sizes are significantly larger; depending on bit rate, approximately one hour of AVCHD = 6 GB of storage, one hour of HDV = 13 GB of storage, one hour of average intermediary (compressed) is approximately 60 GB per hour, and one hour of uncompressed = approximately 600 GB, assuming an 8 bit video stream. A quad-core system with plenty of RAM is highly recommended for working with these file types.

Figure 4.3   Audio cards may connect via USB, Firewire, or PCI card. There is a significant difference in both playback and recording quality/options between a standard sound card and a professional grade audio card.

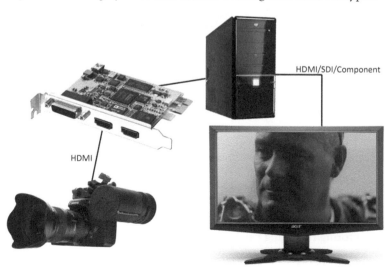

Audio cards are another piece of the puzzle; most sound cards built into a computer do not offer multiple channels of input, although most allow for external monitoring of 5.1 or 7.1 Surround Sound. Cards from Mark of the Unicorn (MOTU), M-Audio, Echo, and other manufacturers of pro audio cards may be used in serious hobby systems or for professional editing setups. These cards are essential for professional-grade mixing of 5.1 or 7.1 Surround Sound or for professional-grade multitrack recording.

Figure 4.4   Audio cards may connect via USB, Firewire, or PCI card. There is a significant difference in both playback and recording quality/options between a standard sound card and a professional-grade audio card.

A high-end audio card will call for higher-end speakers/amplification, so bear in mind that moving to a professional-grade audio card will bring additional costs.

Figure 4.5   Although these sorts of monitors are more expensive, the listening experience for critical monitoring is significantly better with them. Mixing, noise reduction, and critical audio editing will require higher-grade monitors such as these.

Editing keyboards, like those offered by Bella USA, are terrific add-ons for any Vegas-based editing system. Not only do they offer many shortcut keys that will speed the editing process, plus a jog/shuttle wheel for dialing around the timeline with speed; they also simply add a professional flair to the editing suite/system.

Avoid keyboards with stick-on keys that quickly fall apart and are a bigger headache than any benefit they may offer in the short run. Of course, a standard keyboard will suffice for editing; colored keys found on systems such as the Bella USA keyboards simply help remind users of valuable keyboard shortcuts in addition to the shuttles and the memory keys.

Figure 4.6   Editing keyboards can make editing a bit faster, and they offer a professional feel to the editing room.

Setting Preferences in Vegas

The user preferences are a great place to start in setting up Vegas and Vegas Movie Studio for the best possible experience. Although Sony provides very good settings straight out of the box, there are some improvements that you can make to the preferences for faster, more efficient use of the software. Remember, video editing is about getting the story finished, not about stumbling through software menus and processes.

Access the User Preferences either by browsing to **Options** | **Preferences** or right-clicking in a blank area in the track header window.

Figure 4.7   Right-click in a *blank* area of the track header section to access user preferences, or browse to **Options** | **Preferences**.

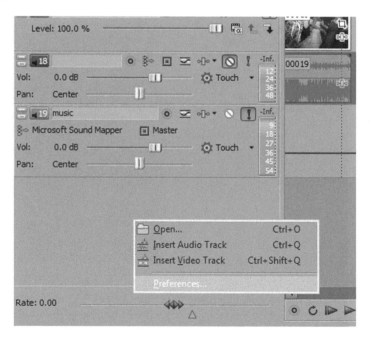

The Preferences dialog window will open. You'll see several tabs; we'll look at them one at a time.

The General Tab

Figure 4.8   Although most of the tabs are identical in both Vegas Movie Studio and Vegas Pro, there are fewer tabs in the Vegas Movie Studio application.

Note in the screenshot shown here that additional checkboxes have been ticked. Start by matching your own preferences to the preferences you see in this screenshot.

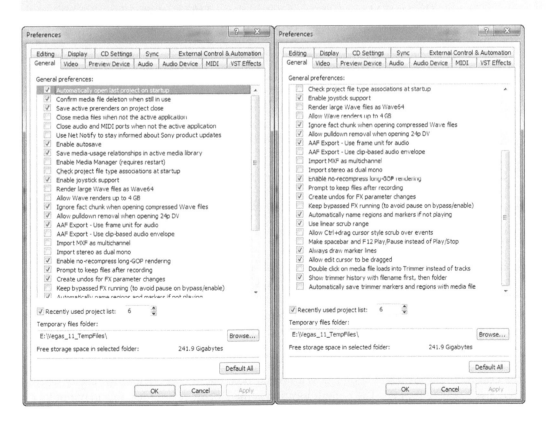

Figure 4.9

This section does not examine every single aspect of the Preferences dialog box, but we will take a closer look at the more important settings that will have an impact on editing speed and preserve system resources.

Close Media Files When Not The Active Application is an option that allows other applications to access the files while Vegas is still open but not active. This prevents the files from being modified while on the Vegas Timeline.

Close Audio and MIDI Ports When Not the Active Application allows Vegas to reduce demanding priority from the PC's resources. However, if you're shuffling back and forth between other applications not related to the editing application, it's a good idea to uncheck this box so that Vegas does not have to request the port each time it becomes the active application.

Disabling **Use NetNotify** prevents Vegas from "phoning home" to see what new versions of the application are available. This will speed up the Vegas boot process.

Be sure **Enable Auto-Save** is checked. There will come a time when Vegas will crash, a hard drive will disconnect, or a power failure will sabotage a project, and Auto-Save will be there to save the day. If a project fails, the next time Vegas is opened it will ask if the auto-saved project should be opened.

Import Stereo As Dual Mono is a terrific feature if the camera is used for interviews, dialogue recorded on channel one, and nats recorded to channel two, or if separate dialogues are recorded as separate inputs. The Dual Mono feature separates the right/left information into two mono tracks, making the editing process faster and easier.

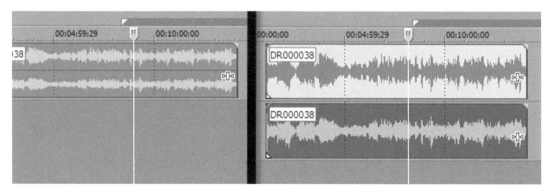

Figure 4.10

Double-Click On Media Opens In Trimmer is a valuable resource, especially when long clips are to be edited on the timeline. This feature allows clips to be opened in the Vegas Trimmer, where markers or regions may be added to the file or sections of the longer-form clip can be chopped out and dropped on the timeline. Checking **Automatically Save Trimmer Markers and Regions With Media File** enables markers to not only be saved with media but for markers to be visible on the Vegas Timeline. These marker views may be invaluable in working on any kind of project, especially when perfect timing and speed are part of the editing challenge.

At the bottom of the General dialog box is a **Browse** box that allows the user to specify where a "scratch disk" will be located. The default location is the Documents folder; this may not be the ideal location, especially for projects that could be moved around on external hard drives. Use the Browse button to select a more suitable location.

Other Tabs

Next up is the **Video** tab. Set the RAM Preview value to half of whatever the machine RAM offers, and no more. This is particularly important when you're working with large stills or graphics on the Vegas Timeline.

> Your system may be a combination of 32 bit Windows/32 bit Vegas or 64 bit Windows/64 bit or 32 bit Vegas. All 64 bit versions of Windows can address more RAM than 32 bit versions of Windows, and if you are using 64 bit Windows and Vegas Pro it is beneficial to load your motherboard with 6–8 GB or RAM or more.

Set the maximum number of rendering threads to 4, 8, or 16. This number will vary from machine to machine and depends on the number of cores of your CPU. Vegas will default this value, but you can experiment with different settings to see different levels of performance. The GPU Acceleration drop-down box will not be available or will offer no choices if there is no graphic acceleration available on the editing machine.

Vegas users producing video depositions may find the **Display Timecode** option a valuable feature; most users will find it annoying and distracting. Selections in the **Thumbnail** options allow users to determine the way that thumbnails are seen on the timeline. Older or less powerful computers will perform best if this option is set to **None** or **Head**. Faster computers will be great with **Head/Center/Tail** selected, and the fastest computers will smoothly play **All** frames. This is an option so that Vegas may be optimized for the fastest or slowest machines.

The **Use External Application** allows users to choose another capturing application for capturing tape-based, SDI, or HDMI-based capture. The Vegas capture tool works well for most users, but a third-party application may be specified in this window.

Leaving **Display at Project Size** unchecked is desirable unless a second monitor is dedicated as an external monitor. Otherwise, the monitor will get in the way during simple edits. However, the **Simulate Device Aspect Ratio** option should be checked. Otherwise, square and nonsquare pixel aspect ratio sources may cause some confusion in editing.

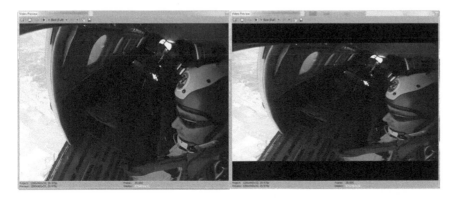

Figure 4.11   This media is a nonsquare pixel format displayed as square. Checking the **Simulate Device Aspect Ratio** option ensures that it will properly display as widescreen media, as intended.

The other Default settings in the Video Preferences tab should be left as they are for the time being. However, 3D or multicam editing may call for changes to these settings at a later point.

The Preview Device Tab

This tab is related to the preview device, not to be confused with the Preview window. Preferences related to the specific preview device and video card are selected in this tab.

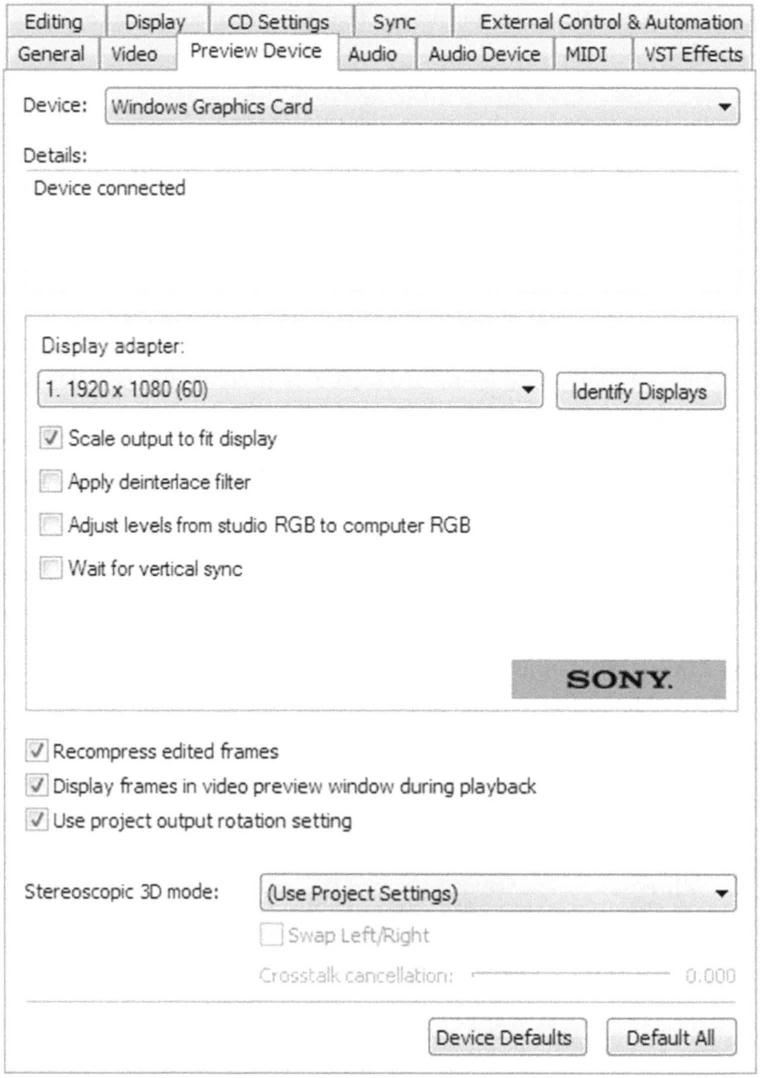

Figure 4.12

This is where you select preferences relating to display of video external to the computer preview window. First, select the video card or device. Most computers will use the Windows Graphics card unless one of the AJA, Black Magic Design, or 1394 cards have been set up for external preview. If one of these devices has been selected, it's likely that the external display is an interlaced display, and so the **Apply De-interlace Filter** should *not* be checked.

If the external display is a computer monitor, then the **De-interlace Filter** option should be checked. Using this option will reduce the artifacts that appear on the edges of interlaced video source material when it's displayed on a progressive monitor. The Apply De-interlace filter check box will be unavailable if your video adapter does not support pixel shading.

All computer monitors are progressive scan monitors and should benefit from this feature being enabled. Most flat-panel displays today are also progressive scan, although some are interlaced. You'll need to test television and HDTV displays to see how the feature affects the image. If ghosting appears on motion frames, this setting should be enabled.

CRT monitors are interlaced. If you use a CRT monitor, leave this setting disabled.

Adjust levels from Studio RGB to Computer RGB will assure that the broadcast standard of 7.5 IRE to 100IRE are managed properly (when this option is left unticked). If a computer monitor is used for display, then this box should be ticked. Leave the **Wait for Vertical Sync** option unchecked unless tearing or smearing issues are seen on the display.

The Audio Tab

As computers have gotten faster, there is little necessity to change many of the settings in this tab in any version of Sony Vegas. Slower computers may benefit from not drawing all waveforms, yet most computers will have no trouble displaying all audio waveforms. Waveforms are drawn as graphic files; this is why Vegas allows for sample-level audio editing. Some older or much slower computers struggled with drawing multiple waveforms for audio files.

Broadcast .wav files are the same file format as any other .wav file and so may be played on any player that allows for .wav file playback. What makes Broadcast waves (.bwf) different is that a Broadcast .wav file allows for additional metadata chunks to be embedded with the audio file, giving users greater options for managing the .wav file.

Import Audio At Project Tempo serves only one function: It allows Vegas to read metadata found in ACID™ loops. Vegas may be used for casual composing, such as using ACID loops in a project. However, this setting may also have a negative impact on importing MP3 or .wav files to the timeline, and audio may be sped up or slowed down, depending on the Tempo settings defined in the Project Properties (120 bpm by default). Uncheck this option if you aren't using ACID loops in the project.

If Vegas is being used for Automated Dialogue Replacement (ADR) or as a recording studio application, **Send Listen to Mute** is most likely a preference to be checked. This will mute all pre-fade audio from the master bus (and any assigned buses). Leave the **Legacy Track Gain** option unchecked unless you're opening older veg files (Vegas 7 and older).

The **Preferred Audio Editor** option is used when an external audio editor for Vegas is called for. Many Vegas users have also installed Sound Forge, Audition, Sound Booth, or a similar application. By setting a default application in this preference, users may right-click an audio file on the Vegas

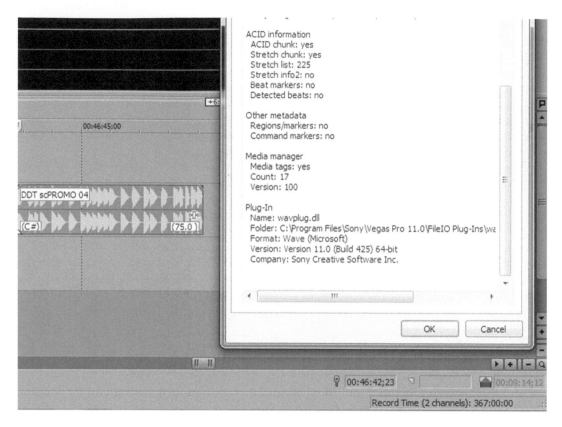

Figure 4.13   Notice the additional metadata found in this loop? Users may choose to have Vegas ignore or recognize this metadata.

Timeline and open that file directly into the preferred audio editor. This is a huge timesaver and allows for direct "round tripping" of audio files while keeping the original file intact. This is a highly recommended feature when an external audio editor is available. Browse to the executable of the preferred default audio editor and click on the .exe file. This will instruct Vegas to use that specific editor.

Video editors will likely not find much value in the built-in metronome, yet musicians will find it tremendously useful as a click-track tool or for keeping a base time on a project. Users may use the default metronome click or specify a unique sound for the metronome. There are many metronome sounds downloadable on the Web, but a snare drum rim shot, hi-hat, or other short-length, percussive sound is very common.

The Audio Device Tab

The Audio Device tab is where audio hardware will be selected. By default, the Microsoft Sound Mapper is designated, yet most users will find benefit in selecting the Windows Classic Wave Driver instead. Doing so will open surround sound options and reduce latency.

This tab is where the default recording device will be selected. If any microphone is connected to the computer, Vegas will find it. If any mic or device is preferred as a default, choose that microphone or device in the drop-down options for default recording devices.

The MIDI Tab

MIDI, or Musical Instrument Digital Interface, is a protocol that allows Sony Vegas to control MIDI-equipped devices. This is useful for control surfaces, musical instrument control via Vegas, starting and stopping external hardware devices used for recording, and other MIDI-related functions.

The VST Tab

VST, or Virtual Studio Technology, are instruments and effects that may be loaded in Vegas. Many free VST reverbs, compressors, delays, and the like can be found on the Web. Vegas allows for two types of FX plug-in: Direct X (DX) and VST. VST and Direct X are simply methods of interacting with an interface. VST was developed by a music-industry company; the Direct X standard was developed by Microsoft. There are no advantages of one over the other; it boils down to which standard the programmer chooses to use when it comes to writing a plug-in for the audio application. Many plug-in developers write code for both standards.

Figure 4.14   Many free VST plug-ins are available on the Internet.

For best use of the VST features, download and install any VST tools into a folder on the root drive, then point the VST Search option to that folder. Vegas will find these VST plug-ins and decide which may or may not be used. VST plug-ins are terrific options, even for video editors. Download a few tools from Websites such as FREEVST.com and play around with the sound-shaping tools available to editors.

The Editing Tab

The defaults in the **Editing** tab are pretty good. The first two boxes should absolutely be checked in a video environment; musicians may want to disable looping and pitch preservation. Vegas has tools for audio stretching that no other video editor offers and, given the quality of the Elastique feature, stretching audio while preserving pitch is just short of amazing.

Cut/copy/delete grouped events is an option that allows users to delete individual events that have been grouped or have Vegas delete all events within a group. Most users will want to delete all events within a group, yet this allows users flexibility.

Do Not Quantize Audio to Frames should be checked when audio-only edits are expected. Nonquantized cuts for audio is useful for creating J or L cuts, so it's recommended that this option be checked for the most flexible audio options.

Setting the **JKL** preference from the default **Medium** to **Fast** is a personal preference. Most editors will want this option set to Fast, but if micro-editing is the method, perhaps a setting of **Slow** is best. JKL editing is a standard in all editing applications as a means of shuttling through a timeline. Tapping the J or L key up to four times will provide for 4x playback in forward or reverse modes.

Setting the **Still Image Length** value assigns a default length to stills dropped on the Vegas Timeline. This setting also affects the default length of all generated media such as titles, solid colors, gradients, and more.

If keyboard shortcut editing—that is, 10-key editing—is to be part of the workflow, it's recommended to change the value of the Cursor Preview to a length of at least 4 seconds. When the 0 key is pressed on the 10-key, Vegas will play 2 seconds pre- and post-cursor position. This feature is very useful when you're testing transitions or intensive keyframes.

Automatic overlapping allows users to drag multiple clips to the timeline as one action; Vegas will automatically create cross-fades between clips. The value set in this preference will determine the length of the automatic cross-fade. Of course, the user can adjust these cross-fades at any time. The same holds true for the **Cut-to-overlap conversion**; in a 10-key edit, the / key may be used to create cross-fades from cuts, and preferences set here will determine the length of the cross-fade created at a cut point. A setting of .25 is equal to 7 frames of overlap, a common length found in broadcast media.

Vegas also allows for auto-cropping of stills added to the timeline; this is a valuable feature when you're using many stills and when no scripting application such as Ultimate S® or Production Assistant® is available to auto-crop or pan images. Images will typically need to be moved around, yet this timesaving feature is quite valuable for editing with stills or odd-sized graphics on the Vegas Timeline. Customize cropping by opening the **Pan/Crop** function and moving the crop area to the desired location.

The Display Tab

In the **Display** tab, users may set default colors for tracks, envelopes, and snap lines. In the drop-down menus for each function, a separate color may be selected for each function. Personally, I find many of the default colors are too dim and faded for most uses and so have defined stronger colors, particularly for snap points of Events and Envelopes.

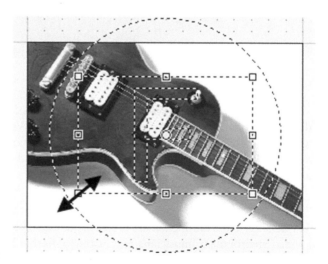

Figure 4.15 The pan/crop tool is used to move cropping around still images.

The default colors of Vegas may be turned off in favor of a Windows theme simply by unchecking the **Use Vegas Colors** option. Windows themes are available for purchase or for free all over the Web. Windows themes allow users to customize their system colors, fonts, cursors, and more. As a Vegas user you might find these desirable so that you can set up a custom editing suite. The color schemes found in Vegas 10 and newer versions are from a user-designed schema.

Audio users may find the **Hide Docking Area** preference a useful tool. It is also useful when you're using multiple monitors and the video workflow is cuts-only. This tool provides greater screen real estate for large projects. Users may also put the timeline at the top of the window, which is useful for situations in which external monitors are present. Previewing monitors at the top of the screen helps prevent neck and eye stress; placing the timeline at the top of a dual-monitor system when external monitors are used may provide the same sort of relief. In this same vein, users may place tabs in the docking windows at the top of the docking area.

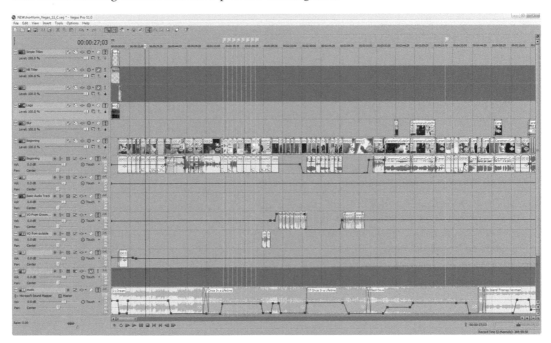

Figure 4.16   When the docking area is hidden, it leaves more room for track visibility.

The CD Settings Tab

Vegas has been used for over a decade as a Redbook-compliant CD authoring application. This tab allows you to set CD Authoring preferences. By default there are few settings, since Redbook authoring is very specific. However, users of older legacy systems that have wide SCSI devices attached may want to seek SCSI drives at startup. Autodetecting drive capabilities on startup is another available option; this choice will slightly slow Vegas as it loads.

SPTI, or SCSI Pass-Through Interface, is another legacy option; users of newer computers will not need to select this option (nor the legacy driver option).

Sync and External Control Tabs

The **Sync** tab allows users with a MIDI-capable sound card to control external devices or allow external devices to control Vegas. The Sony Virtual Midi Router (available from SonyCreativeSoftware.com) may be used as a software routing system to allow other recording or midi software to control Vegas (or be controlled by Vegas). This same routing system may be used with external controller devices such as the Mackie Control, Frontier Tranzport, or Presonus FaderPort hardware devices. These devices allow for external mixing/color correction/transport control of Vegas. The drop-down menus in the External Controller interface dialog box allow users to set the preferences for envelopes and keyframes created in Vegas via the external control device. Changing these settings does not affect the control of Vegas keyframes and envelopes from within Vegas with a keyboard/mouse combination; these are relevant only to external hardware device controls.

Internal Preferences

*Warning: Before accessing internal preferences, please read this disclaimer. Vegas has hidden preferences. You are on your own when you're working with these settings! They are hidden for a reason. It is fairly easy to "break" Vegas Pro and Vegas Movie Studio if settings are not correct. In the event that the changing of internal preferences "breaks" Vegas, hold **Ctrl** + **Shift** as Vegas is booting. This will reset all preferences to the default and all user-specified preferences will be lost.*

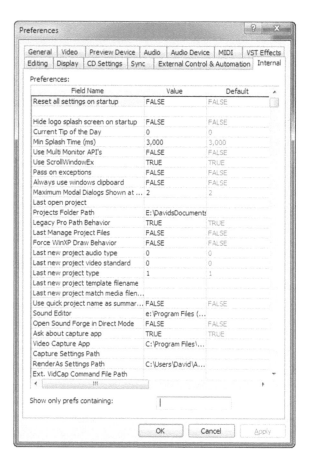

To access internal preferences, hold the **Shift** key while selecting **Options | Preferences** or right-clicking a blank space on the track header. A new tab labeled **Internal** will appear in the **Preferences** dialog box. In this tab, many user preferences may be set to numeric values or to True/False. Default values are seen next to the changeable value in the Internal Preferences window.

Figure 4.17 Proceed with caution if the internal preferences are accessed. It is somewhat easy to "break" Vegas, which will require a reset of all user preferences.

Preview Window Settings

The **Preview** window is the "WYSIWYG" window, where all elements of the timeline are combined to display final output. The settings in this window greatly affect playback speed and quality of media, and these settings are directly related to the horsepower of the computer on which Vegas has been installed.

Figure 4.18   Frame rate and quality of picture are the two determinate factors in this window. Faster computers may be able to play back multiple streams at the highest quality with full frame rate. The **Preview** screen may be "torn off" the Docking windows (by grabbing the "handle" at the upper left) and floated over the timeline, on a second monitor, or anywhere the user specifies. Hold the **Ctrl** key while floating the window so that it does not snap back to the docking area.

Figure 4.19   The size of the Preview window will affect playback quality, so be sure to size appropriately for the computer screen display. This size will vary depending on resolution capabilities of the computer screen.

Tip_____

To increase the frame rate and overall performance, reduce the size of the Preview window.

In the upper left of the Preview window is the **Project Properties** icon. Clicking this icon (or keying **Alt + Enter**) opens the **Project Properties** window. This window allows users to set the project properties. Generally, project properties are best left set to match the majority of the media on the timeline; that is, if the majority of the project is 1920 x 1080 60i AVCHD, then the project properties should be set to match those source settings. Even if the final output of the project is 1280 x 720 or 720 x 480 (DVD), users will generally enjoy a better experience, better-quality view, and faster processing if the project properties match the properties of the source media. Setting project properties to values different from the source properties requires Vegas to scale (and perhaps other processes) video on the fly, and this may slow playback.

Figure 4.20

Figure 4.21

To the right of the Project Properties icon is the **External Preview** icon. Selecting this option will shift preview from the Vegas Preview window to either an external monitor or a full-screen view on a single-monitor system. This option may be accessed via keyboard shortcut of **Alt + Shift + 4**. The keyboard shortcut may be best assigned to a single key on a Bella keyboard (www.bella-usa.com) or multimedia keyboard for ease of use. In the **Options | Preferences | Preview Device** tab there is a checkable option for **Display frames in Preview Window During Playback**. This allows Vegas to draw frames both on an external monitor and in the Vegas Preview window during playback. In other words, playback will be seen in two places. This is useful when you're using a client monitor feed or a video village or for comparing what is seen externally to what is being seen in the Vegas window. However, this will draw on system resources, so if the computer is not fairly fast, playback may be jerky or of lower quality on both internal and external monitors.

Vegas allows the user to drop filters/FX on the master output of a video project. This is useful when you want to create a finished look to an entire project, master a project for broadcast, or use other project-wide FX. Selecting this button will open an FX dialog box that allows users to choose FX to be placed on the Master video output. When FX are inserted into the Master output stream, this icon will change from gray to green, indicating that FX are inserted. Use this feature with caution because inserting FX at the master stream may significantly impact playback speed and quality prior to render.

Figure 4.22   Use this option to display video on both external monitors and in the Vegas Preview window at the same time. Set Preview video quality to Preview/ Auto in most playback circumstances for optimal playback of unrendered projects.

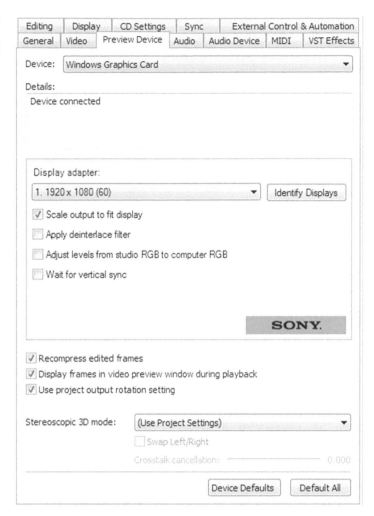

Vegas Pro allows users to bypass all FX, compare the before and after view of FX, or view contents of the Clipboard.

Selecting this icon in its default state allows for all FX to be bypassed. This is useful when FX are slowing down playback and editing, as opposed to when FX adjustments are called for. In other words, when you're editing, lower resolution is useful for speed.

Figure 4.23

Bypassing all FX is an efficient means of speeding up preview without changing resolution (this feature is not available in Vegas Movie Studio).

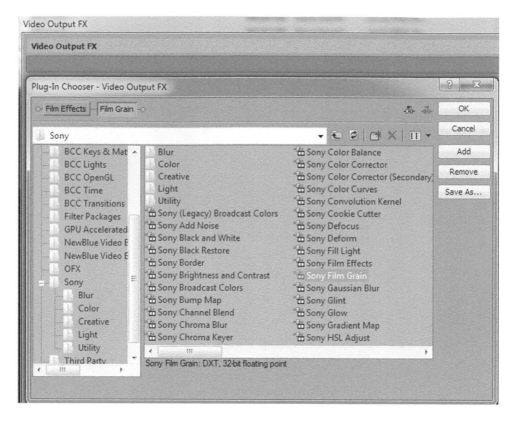

Figure 4.24   This dialog box will open when the **Preview Window FX** button is selected. The button will change from gray to green when FX are inserted into the master output process (project-wide FX).

In the drop-down menu at the right of the **Split Screen** icon, users may select **Clipboard, Select Right/Left Half**. The "half" selections aren't necessary at all. When this feature is enabled, users may left-click and "draw" a square or rectangle in the Preview window. When this is done, either the Clipboard or pre/post FX can be seen. This feature is invaluable when you're

Figure 4.25

doing color matching or color corrections to compare original clips to processed clips. For example, a subject's face may be the target of color correction from two cameras. Copying a frame from one camera to the Clipboard, placing the cursor or playhead over the same face from another camera, selecting the **Split Screen** option, and drawing a square or rectangle over half the subject's face will provide a way to perfectly match the second camera to the first camera.

Figure 4.26   The **Split Screen** function is very useful for color matching or pre-/post-FX monitoring. Pre-/post-FX monitoring occurs with live video. Using the Clipboard results in one portion of the screen being static/nonmotion (similar to a still image on the timeline) while the other portion may be live video.

Preview Settings

Preview settings are perhaps the most important feature in the Preview window. There are four options:

- Draft
- Preview
- Good
- Best

Each of these options offers four subchoices:

- Auto
- Full
- Half
- Quarter

  Preview/Auto is a standard default setting and should be used for most editing functions where frame rate or story flow is the priority. However, color correction and compositing call for higher resolutions and frame rate is not critical. Compositing should always be performed at Best/Full resolution, regardless of frame rate, in order to see critical details. Color correction also benefits from the higher resolution. However, Best/Full may weigh very heavily on a CPU, and some systems may become unstable if enough resources are being called on. Users of less than optimal systems may find that settings of Good/Auto or Good/Full are sufficient.

Most modern computers will play out media that matches project settings when set to Best/Full. However, the addition of FX, titles, multiple streams, or multi-cam may call for preview settings to be reduced to Preview/Auto. If the frame rate does not remain constant (as shown in the lower-right corner of the Preview window), reducing resolution via one of the Preview choices is likely the best option when constant frame rate and smooth playback are priorities.

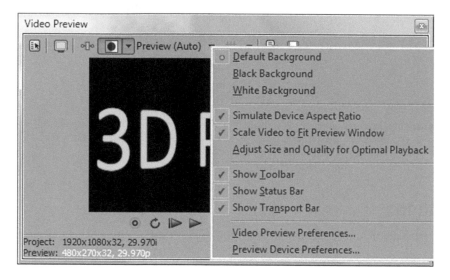

Figure 4.27   Choosing **Scale Video to fit Preview Window** will scale video up or down. Depending on the Preview window size, this may result in pixelated, low-resolution video. Choosing **Adjust size and quality for Optimal Playback** will allow Vegas to make choices for you. If this is the choice, setting the Preview window to **Best/Full** will allow Vegas to manage scaling and frame rate. I recommend using this option for best experiences.

Next to the Quality icon is the **Overlay** icon. Vegas Pro and Vegas Movie Studio offer several different overlays.

Grids may be overlaid for line/height specific placement of graphics, titles, or other elements that benefit from vertical or horizontal mark points. Enable the grid to overlay the vertical/horizontal overlay. Grid settings may be adjusted in the **Options | Video** Preferences tab. Users may choose more or fewer grid lines, depending on the amount of desired detail.

The **Title safe** area is not terribly important for videos going to the Web, where there is no over-scan area to concern editors, yet if the project is going to DVD or broadcast, it is very important to observe title-safe areas. These assure that overscan and television display bezels will not cut off portions of titles.

Figure 4.28

Figure 4.29

Vegas Preview Window, outside the Title Safe Area   Extends beyond TV bezel

The outer ring in the **Safe Areas** overlay is for Action-safe areas. No significant action should occur outside this boundary in the video display. This is more important for compositing, graphic overlay, or recomposing a frame (such as with the Pan/Crop tool).

Vegas Pro allows Closed Captioning (C/C) information to be seen in the video preview prior to rendering for C/C. (This feature is not available in Vegas Movie Studio.) Closed Captioning is discussed later in this book.

Video may be isolated by individual channel in this same drop-down; Red, Green, or Blue channel-only may be specified. This is useful for compositing masks or checking color correction. Alpha

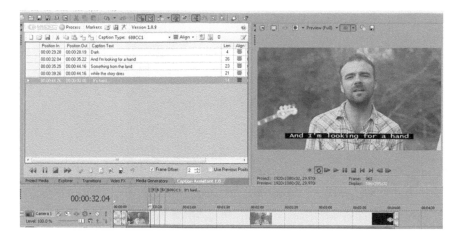

Figure 4.30   Vegas Pro users are able to observe Section 508 Closed Captioning laws via either the VASST Caption Assistant plug-in or, if using XDCAM, the built-in Vegas Closed Captioning tools.

channels may also be viewed as grayscale. Use this when adjusting masks for compositing or for checking how alpha channels have been selected in the properties of a 32 bit clip.

Copy Snapshot to Clipboard is a feature that allows Vegas users to capture a frame-grab to the clipboard. This is quite useful for color correction (discussed later in this book), and it is useful for a frame-grab to be sent to a photo editor such as PhotoGo, Photoshop, or the like.

Figure 4.31   The **Save Snapshot to File** option allows users to capture a still frame and store it as a .jpg or .png file. These files will be available in the Project Media folder as well as in the folder specified in the saving process.

When the **Save Snapshot to File** option is selected, a snapshot of the current frame is captured at the project resolution/setting. For the highest-quality image, set the preview quality to Best/Full prior to capturing a snapshot. Tools such as Ultimate S will auto-set the Preview Quality properly prior to capturing any screenshots.

Vegas Pro and Vegas Movie Studio also have "hidden" menu items in the Preview window. Right-click the Preview window to access these preferences.

Figure 4.32   These options are available via a right-click of the Preview window.

Personal preference has all options excepting the Transport bar selected, using a black background. The gray background may confuse users when they're dealing with various pixel aspect ratios (PAR), whereas black or white shows the frame in its original size, with unused areas filled in black. White is a good option but is hard on the eyes in long editing sessions. The Transport bar is available as a keyboard shortcut (advanced users will typically use keyboard shortcuts) or via the separate Transport bar found on the timeline or on user-specified custom Toolbar icons. The Status bar allows users to see project size, playback size, frame number, and the rate of actual playback (frame rate). The status bar may be important to users shuffling back and forth between codecs, color correction, compositing, or other CPU-intensive tasks.

For best experience, I recommend enabling these options:

- Black Background
- Simulate Device Aspect Ratio
- Scale Video to fit Preview Window
- Adjust Size/Quality for Optimal Playback

- Show Toolbar
- Show Status Bar

There is no value in placing the Preview window on a secondary monitor and sizing to full screen resolution. This will slow playback due to scaling. A better option is to designate a second monitor as a secondary monitor in the **Options | Preferences | Preview Device** dialog box, and select **Scale Output to Fit Display**.

Menus and Docking Windows

Menus

Figure 5.1

There are several menu options across the top of the Vegas application; many of them are recognizable as standard Windows functions. File, Edit, View, Insert, Tools, Options, and Help are not unique to Vegas. Many of the menu functions are duplicated on the Toolbar, right-click context menus, or buttons found on Events. In this section we'll cover the more important items in each menu. Some are self-explanatory; others are not.

In this section, keyboard shortcuts are provided. These keyboard shortcuts offer faster editing techniques in that they require less mouse movement and provide direct access to common functions. Learning and using the keyboard shortcuts not only saves time; many keyboard shortcuts translate directly to other applications and overall make for a better editor.

The FILE Menu

When Vegas opens for the first time, it will open with a new, blank project. If default settings have been kept, Vegas will open the second time with the last project opened. Opening a new project may be accomplished by using the **File | Open New** option or the **Ctrl + N** shortcut. **Ctrl + O** will open the last folder used, or the **File | Open** option may be used.

Ctrl + S will save a project; it is unique from the Save-As option. The Save-As selection does not offer a shortcut.

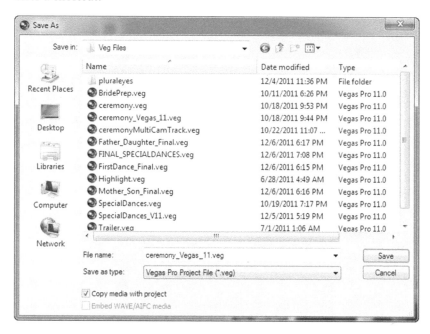

Figure 5.2 The Save-As dialog box allows users to package a project for transport to another computer or for archiving.

Using Save-As, note the checkbox at the bottom of the Save-As dialog, labeled **Copy Media with Project**. If this option is checked, a second dialog box opens, asking users to determine whether all original media should be copied or only the trimmed media as it appears on the timeline is copied. If the trimmed option is chosen, users may also determine how the media should be saved. Exact copies of trimmed media may be saved, or heads/tails may be saved. As a general rule, it is recommended to save at least 2 seconds of head and tail media in the event that the project will be repurposed later on. If the project is being saved with media as a package to be transported to another computer or archived, it is a good idea to save original media rather than trimmed media. This will save to a user-determined folder that may be burned to a disc (Blu-ray discs are good for this purpose), saved to a network drive, or archived to a removable disk system. Many editing houses not only store/archive the final project but also archive masters, Web versions, and thumbnail versions with text files for faster searches.

Vegas 10 and newer versions offer an Import option that is different than older versions (previously labeled **Import Media**). The newer option assists in importing Media, .bwf (Broadcast Wave), DVD-recorded media (this feature will not rip a commercial DVD), and closed captions.

When **Import** is selected, Vegas will open a dialog box relevant to the type of import specified. Import Media will open up a Windows Explorer to be browsed and files located. Import Broadcast Wave (not available in Vegas Movie Studio) will do the same but will offer some sorting options.

Figure 5.3

If **Import DVD Camcorder Disc** is selected, Vegas will first seek out a drive. If media is found on a drive, Vegas will attempt to open it. (*Warning:* Discs recorded with copy protection may cause Vegas to lock up and require a restart.) If no disc is found, Vegas will open a dialog box that allows users to specify which drive should be used. Copies of DVD camcorder discs previously transferred to an HDD may also be located via this disc browser. If DVD camcorder disc content is to be transferred to HDD, it's only necessary to copy the Stream folder.

Figure 5.4

Tip

Some DVDs do not import well into Vegas (or any other program). If you experience problems importing a DVD, try opening the IFO file. First, copy the contents of the DVD to your hard drive. Then, click **File | Open** and navigate to the **VIDEO_TS** folder. Choose the **VTS_01_0.IFO** file and Vegas should import the entire collection of .VOB files for audio and video.

Vegas is capable of importing several types of closed caption file extensions (not available in Vegas Movie Studio). The most common in the Sony world is the .sub extension from DVD Architect (subtitles). However, Vegas will also import .scc (Scenarist Closed Captioning), .rt (RealPlayer captions), .srt (Subrip subtitles), .smi (Windows Media Player Captioning), .mcc (CPCMacCaptioning), and .txt (Quicktime/transcript) files.

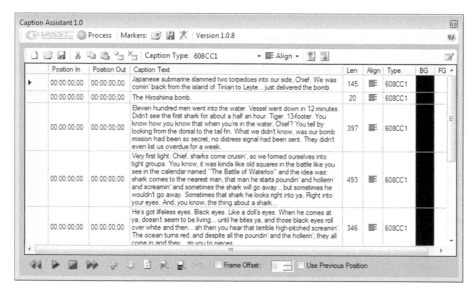

Figure 5.5   Vegas is a powerful tool for closed captioning. Vegas will read most C/C format files and, with VASST Caption Assistant, may output captions for YouTube, DVD, XDCAM masters for broadcast, and Windows Media virtually everywhere captions may be viewed. Note that Vegas has an internal captioning tool for broadcast users; Caption Assistant is not necessary but is quite a bit faster.

Video capture is nearly a practice of the past; *capture* refers exclusively to tape-based acquisition and recording systems. Vegas will capture video over SDI in both SD and HD and over 1394/Firewire (DV/HDV). There are some older capture cards that use analog converters to convert analog tape (Beta SP, VHS/C, and so on) to digital; these converters also use SDI or 1394 as the input system (SDI capture not available in Vegas Movie Studio). While some USB systems occasionally cooperate with Vegas, USB capture is not supported, since USB shares bus resources and Vegas cannot guarantee capture with no dropped frames. See the section on capturing video for more information.

Both Vegas Pro and Vegas Movie Studio offer the capability to rip CDs for use in a video or audio project. Extract Audio From CD allows users to place a CD in the DVD burner/player and extract entire discs, regions of discs, or single songs/files. This is especially useful when sound effects CDs are being used for video projects; many are delivered in CDA format rather than the more easily accessed .wav or .mp3 format.

Figure 5.6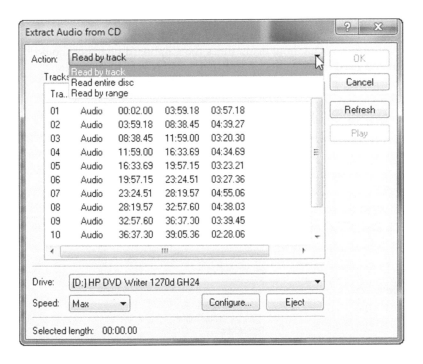

Share Online is a newer feature in Vegas. This feature helps users choose online delivery providers or UGC site providers and upload directly to those sites from the Vegas Timeline or application. This option is separate from the Upload to YouTube feature found directly below it.

As the feature implies, **Upload to YouTube** assists users in uploading files directly to YouTube. Vegas Pro and Vegas Movie Studio will ask users for their password and username to YouTube, and they provide tools to add keywords, choose quality of file, category, and so on. This is a significant timesaver.

When uploading videos to the Web, create a region around the project (create a selection and press the **R** key). Save the project, and tick **Render and upload loop region only**. This provides a backstop against accidentally uploading black before or after the project begins or ends. It also provides a later reference to what parts of the file were actually rendered and uploaded.

Get Media From the Web is a direct link to a Sony media marketing and sales page at the same location as the Get Media From the Web icons and links found in the Vegas Explorer/Project Media windows.

Project Properties, mentioned in the first chapter, set the properties of the project. This information may be accessed from the **File** menu, shortcut **Alt+Enter**, or from the **Properties** icon in the Video Preview or Audio mixer windows.

The EDIT Menu

All the standard Edit menu options (Cut, Copy, Paste, Undo, Redo) are found at the top of the **Edit** menu. Contents of the Clipboard may be pasted multiple times using **Ctrl+B** or **Paste Repeat**. A dialog box will open, asking how many times the Clipboard contents should be pasted. This is helpful when you need many copies of an Event, such as generated media.

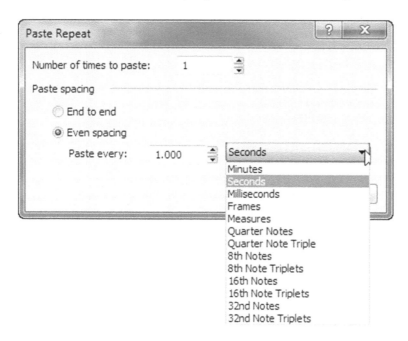

Figure 5.7   Files may be pasted end to end (butted against each other) or spaced over user-determined time. This is a very useful tool for musicians and video editors. If the tempo of a piece of music is known, Vegas assists in pasting on time or on musical beats from the cursor point. This same feature may be used in the video world to create stingers at X points throughout a video or to match cuts and transitions. With the current trend in video being repeat/overlay cuts, this feature is a great timesaver.

Trim/CTRL+T will cut any video outside of a selected area. Make a selection, choose **Edit | Trim**, and any media outside the selected area will be cut from the project.

Split (shortcut **S** key) is the same as any other application's Razor tool (shortcut **C** for Cut in Adobe Premiere). The Split tool has a unique use in Vegas; like the Trim feature, the Split command may occur on an In and Out point, but the Split key will not delete any clips within or outside a region. Being able to Split both in/out points at the same time is sweet.

Note that the next three editing tools all have shortcuts. It is highly recommended that you learn them. They are so common that using a mouse could become very repetitive and time-consuming, whereas a shortcut workflow saves a lot of time, frustration, and potential mistakes due to a misaimed cursor.

The post-edit ripple function (shortcut **F**) is a common tool in all editing applications. Make a cut/deletion in an Event, press the **F** key, and the Event on the right will slide left to butt against the out point of the newly edited Event. This will affect only the single track being edited. This is known as a *ripple edit*.

Ctrl+F will ripple all Events, regions, and markers relevant to an edited Event on a specific track or relevant tracks.

Shift+Ctrl+F will ripple all Events/regions/markers, regardless of what tracks are selected or being edited.

⏱ Speed Tutorial

1. Place three clips or Events on the Vegas Timeline, all on the same track, so that all three are butted against each other (no gaps).

2. Place the cursor in the middle of the second Event and press the **S** key to split it. The right side of the Event will be highlighted.

3. Use **Ctrl+X** to cut the highlighted media. This will leave a hole or blank space in the timeline.

4. Now press the **F** key to ripple the remaining Events so that they are butted up against each other, as they were before a section was cut. You've just learned a faster way to cut and align Events! Learn more about ripple editing elsewhere in this book.

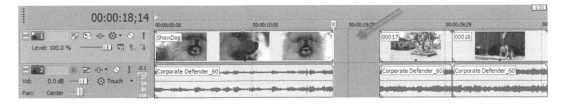

Figure 5.8   This blank area or hole will disappear when a post-edit ripple is applied. Events on the right will move to the left, butting up against the newly edited Event.

The Select option also assists users in selecting Events. **Ctrl+A** selects all media on the timeline. With a specific track selected, you can select the beginning of an Event by pressing the 7 key on a 10-key pad. (This does not work on a laptop that does not have a 10-key pad. Power users may wish to purchase a USB 10-key if editing speed is a need.)

Figure 5.9   A USB 10-key is useful for editing in high-speed, high-turnaround situations. The 10 keys in Vegas are essentially the same as those found in other editing applications such as AVID.

In the old days of video, prior to the advent of the mouse, video programs were edited entirely via 10 keys and shortcut keys. Many of these shortcut keys are similar in Vegas, making it easy for editors to jump from older newsdesk applications to Sony Vegas. Even Vegas Movie Studio has 10-key shortcuts!

The **D** key in Vegas functions the same as the **V** key in other applications; pressing this key shifts between common editing tools such as edit, envelope, selection, and zoom.

To zoom in on an Event or area of the timeline, press the **D** key until the Magnifying Glass/Zoom icon replaces the Editing icon. Click/drag over the portion of the timeline to be zoomed.

Zoom out using the **Up/Down Arrows** on the keyboard.

Pressing the **D** key again will refocus the editing cursor. The **Envelope** editor function edits, inserts, and deletes envelope points but will not move Events on the timeline. This is perfect for a locked-picture, where moving Events would be problematic. The **Selection Edit** tool allows Events to be selected across tracks in any direction. This is useful for selecting all Events within a specific timeframe for grouping, deleting, copying, or moving on the timeline.

Vegas does not require refocusing the cursor to the edit tool after making splits or other simple edits. This is by design; saving keystrokes and mouse moves are all part of what makes Vegas so fast.

The **Edit | Extensions** option will display any installed extensions such as the VASST plug-in tools or other extensions that load when Vegas boots up. Extensions may also be loaded as shortcut icons on the Vegas Toolbar (discussed later in this chapter).

Edit | Switches is an active menu item; either video or audio must be selected before any of the switch functions may be selected. Video selections open up Mute, Lock, Loop, Maintain Aspect Ratio, Reduce Interlace Flicker, and Resample functions:

- *Mute.* Blanks the video (Event goes dark).

- *Lock.* Event may not be moved, and although FX may be added, they may not be reopened and edited without first unlocking.

- *Loop.* When the Event reaches the out point, the Event will loop at the in point. This is a default setting. If Loop is disabled, the last video frame in the clip will freeze and may be stretched to desired length. This feature is very useful for ending a production and fading over time (assuming there is no action in the last frame). Be aware that while video looping is disabled, audio looping may not be (it's a separate switch), so audio may loop while video locks on the last frame in the stream.

- *Maintain Aspect Ratio.* Enabled by default, this option prevents Vegas from stretching media to fit project properties. For example, many small-format cameras shoot a 1280 x 960 image. If this switch is disabled, Vegas will attempt to fill a 1280 x 720 frame with the 1280 x 960 image, and the image will be distorted. Sometimes this distortion is acceptable.

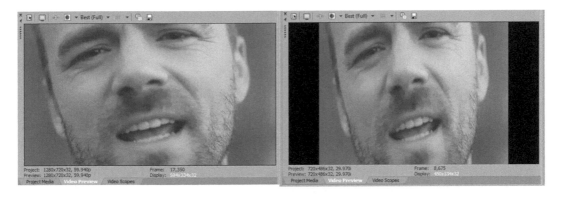

Figure 5.10   Here is an image for which Maintain Aspect Ratio is enabled. The distorted image is the result of disabling the Maintain Aspect Ratio switch.

Tip

All the switches found in the **Edit | Switches** menu may also be found via a right-click of any Event on the timeline.

Reduce Interlace Flicker is a setting primarily used for media that is not sourced from video. Photos and generated media particularly benefit from this switch. Sometimes fine horizontal detail on interlaced video source being displayed on and rendered to progressive formats can benefit from this setting, although its primary purpose is to reduce crawling or flickering in nonvideo sources.

Resampling video was originally intended as a means of resampling video content whose source frame rate is less than the project frame rate; for example, a camera shoots at 15fps and the project frame rate is 29.97. Vegas will resample the frames, blending newly created frames into existing frames to create smooth motion in the upsample. However, this feature is also useful for doing time-shifting or warping, like slow motion.

There are three settings for resampling video:

- *Smart Resample*. Vegas will only resample the frame rate when the source frame rate is less than the project frame rate and the project frame rate is greater than 24fps. Vegas is aware of velocity envelopes, Events that are slowed or sped up, and any undersampling.

- *Force Resample*. If this switch is engaged, the Event will always be resampled, regardless of project frame rate. This setting is useful for Events that have had velocity envelopes inserted, playback changes, or undersampling. Using Force Resampling may slow rendering on switched Events.

- *Disable Resample*. Any resampling is disabled. Use this for animations or masking if ghosting should appear.

Remember in Hollywood films, a production assistant might call out, "Scene four, take five"? Vegas allows "takes" of media (alternative views) to be laid on top of one another, much like layers, with only the top layer visible. This assists users in editing, since alternate takes of a scene may be viewed at track level without inserting additional video tracks as some other applications do. It not only saves screen real estate; it also allows takes to be cycled through on the fly so that edit decisions can be made quickly. This feature is similar to building alternate edits in other applications, the difference being that using takes doesn't require additional tracks.

Grouping Events locks them together so that whenever one Event is moved, so are all other Events grouped with that Event. Selecting multiple files on the timeline and pressing the **G** key will group these Events. This essentially creates a single Event from multiple Events (although FX and processes still occur at the individual Event level). Vegas allows multiple groups on a timeline, but it does not permit any Event to be part of multiple groups. To remove an Event from a group, select the Event and press the **U** key (or use the **Edit | Groups** function).

The **Streams** switch provides an option to select any other streams embedded within a file.

Most camcorders record audio as a stereo file when what is often wanted are discreet Channel 1/Left, Channel 2/Right streams. The **Channels** switch in the Edit menu assists users in choosing which audio streams are to be used or combining channels if the source should be mono but was recorded in stereo. Professional users never have need for stereo audio; rather, most typically record dialogue on Channel 1 and nats (natural sound) on Channel 2. In Vegas Preferences, users may choose to import stereo audio as dual mono. If this preference isn't selected yet streams need to be separated, the Channels function is used to separate audio streams.

 Tip_____

Given that digital audio is cumulative, audio that is destined to be mono but recorded in stereo may be combined using the **Edit | Channels | Combine** option. The two stereo channels will be combined and output level will increase. This is a useful feature when audio has been recorded at low levels.

Undo All is identical to the Revert function in other applications. It will undo all edits performed in the session.

Clear Edit History is useful on long-form projects when the system becomes unstable. Vegas stores the last 100 edit points, making it easy to step back to a given action in a session. Use this feature with caution if there is any doubt about the state of the edit.

To revert to a specific point in the edit, click the drop-down arrow next to the Undo button on the Vegas Toolbar.

Figure 5.11 Vegas stores the last 100 edit points in a session. The **Undo** button allows stepping back to a user-specified point in an edit session.

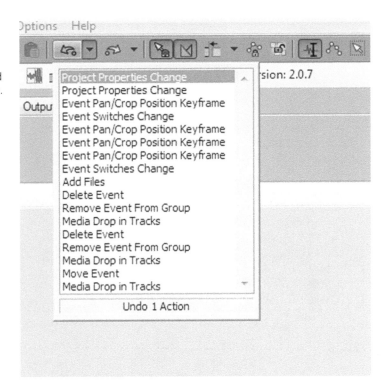

The View Menu

The majority of the **View** menu options are docking windows and their functions are explained later in this chapter.

 Tip_____

If you ever can't find a window or a button that you know used to be there, check the **View** menu. It might have been set to "hide" by mistake.

If the Auto-Preview function was enabled in Explorer, Project Media, Device Explorer, XDCAM Explorer, or Media Manager, files will play back with audio at full level (based on the Windows system level) as opposed to any mix levels that may be set in Vegas. This is not only annoying, but it could be problematic in quiet environments. The **Preview Fader** enables users to preset the level of playback from the various Explorer windows.

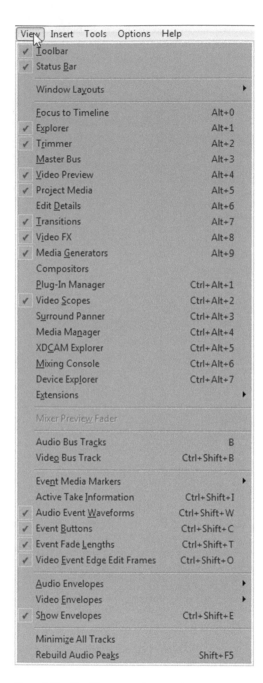

Figure 5.12   The **View** menu is extensive and provides many options; most of them are Docking windows or available via shortcuts.

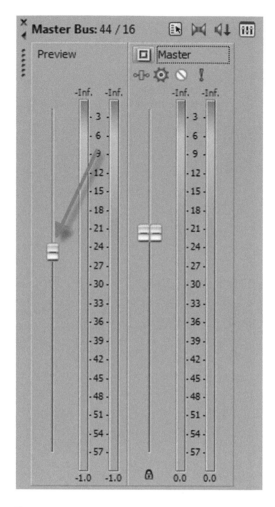

Figure 5.13   Enabling the **Mixer Preview Fader** controls levels of auto-preview audio. This feature may save your ears and perhaps a relationship with the neighbors.

View | **Audio Bus Tracks,** when enabled, creates a bus track for every bus inserted into the mixer. If no bus tracks are inserted, only a master bus (master output) track will be created. Envelopes may be inserted into the master bus and any other bus tracks, generating user-controlled level automation (automation is discussed in detail in the Audio chapter).

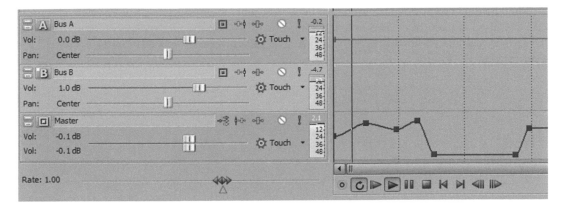

Figure 5.14   This is the master bus track. The envelope points are automation control for entire groups of tracks.

Bus tracks are a means of grouping dialogue, music, and effects (DME) for separate control. For example, there might be five dialogue tracks, each with its own level controls. Perhaps there are two music tracks and a dozen effects tracks, each track with its own level of volume control. During the mix, it is discovered that the dialogue levels are higher than they should be for the mix, yet they all fit together very well relating to each other. By assigning the output of each of the dialogue mixes to a bus, the bus level may be lowered, leaving the relative levels of the dialogue exactly the same but letting the dialogue sit more appropriately in the master mix.

This is also a useful way to output stems for broadcast mixes or translation. Surround Sound mixing is simply another way of describing a system with five buses that do not feed a master mix.

The video bus track is similar to the audio bus tracks. What makes it different (and unique to Vegas) is that it controls the master video output. Processes such as super sampling, motion blur, muting/blanking, and fades may be inserted. Imagine a project that has 20 video tracks and at the end a fade to black is desired. In other applications, each track must be faded to black, all fades beginning and ending at exactly the same I/O point. In Vegas, a video bus track is used to fade all 20 tracks simultaneously, without requiring work on the individual tracks or Events.

Show Event Media Markers displays markers and regions embedded in video streams. This switch does not affect timeline markers; it only shows or hides markers inserted in the Trimmer. In this same dialog box is the ability to show or hide marker labels. Markers inserted in the Trimmer may be labeled, and these labels may be shown or hidden independently of the markers themselves. If "notes" have been inserted in these labels and there are several markers in an Event or clip, it may be desirable to turn off the labels to keep the track clutter-free.

When media is transferred, captured, or imported, most users will provide filenames relevant to the files used in the project. These filenames may be viewed on the timeline for reference or hidden to reduce timeline clutter. Using the **View | Active Take Information** (**Ctrl + Shift + I**) switch, you can toggle the filename to show or hide filenames.

Figure 5.15   Show or hide filenames on the timeline via the **Ctrl + Shift +** *I* shortcut. Short clips or Events on the timeline will greatly benefit from hiding filenames and reducing clutter on the timeline.

Audio waveforms may be shown or hidden. This is a feature from legacy versions of Vegas back in the day when computers were slower and displaying a large number of waveforms weighed heavily on the CPU. However, some users still prefer the look of a clean timeline, without audio waveforms displayed. Therefore, this feature is still available. Show or hide audio waveforms via **Ctrl + Shift + W** or via the **View** menu.

Figure 5.16   Audio waveforms may be turned off. Some users may prefer the clean, waveformless timeline.

Every Event on the Vegas Timeline displays Event Buttons by default. Video Events offer Pan/Crop and FX buttons by default, and Generated Media offers Pan/Crop, FX, and Edit Generated Media buttons. These buttons are shortcuts to their respective processes. However, these may be hidden if a clean interface is preferred. All switches and processes are available via a right-click on the Event. Show and hide Event buttons via the **View** menu or the **Ctrl + Shift + C** shortcut.

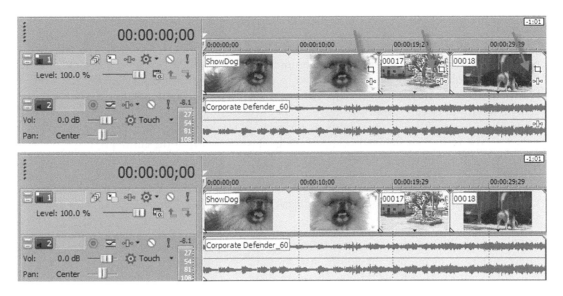

Figure 5.17   On the left, Event buttons are visible. In the image on the right, Event buttons have been hidden. This is a user preference that does not affect the speed of Vegas.

Transitions and fades on the timeline may be displayed one of two ways. The first (default) is that Vegas will display the number of frames, seconds, or minutes of a transition or fade as a numeric value inside the frame. As the fade or transition is created, Vegas will always provide a live display of its length. If the **Event Fade Lengths** option is enabled, the length of a fade or transition will display in the middle of the Event. If this option is disabled, the fade or transition is visible, but the length is not. You'll have to click on the transition or fade to see the actual length. Again, this is a means of keeping the timeline clean and free of clutter, if that's the user preference.

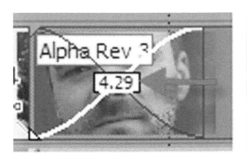 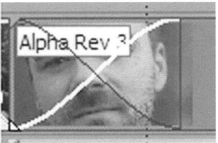

Figure 5.18   Event fade lengths may be shown or hidden at the user's pleasure.

When trimming Events or clips, it's valuable to see the new in or out point of a clip when the edge is trimmed. Users may toggle this feature on and off. If snap editing to embedded markers or using the 10-key editing system, this may be beneficial to disable. By default, it is enabled and there are few reasons to disable it. It can be confusing for all but extreme power users of Vegas if this Event is disabled.

The **View | Audio/Video Envelopes** switch in the View menu is there more for display than actual use. These features are much, much easier to insert or view via their keyboard shortcuts of **P** (for Pan), **V** (for Volume), and **Z** (for Mute) than to use a mouse and scroll through the View menu. However, the option is available for users who prefer a mouse. All envelopes may be shown or hidden via the shortcut **Ctrl+Shift+E**.

A hidden feature of Vegas is the ability to minimize all tracks via the ∼ key. Pressing this key will reduce all tracks to their minimal size, providing a fast overview of the entire project.

 Tip_____

Double-click the horizontal or vertical scrollbar at the bottom or side of the timeline to minimize the entire project, forcing it to fit inside the width of the timeline or monitor. Use this as a high-level view of the entire project.

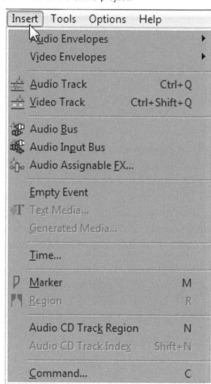

Video and audio envelopes may be inserted via the **Insert** menu; as mentioned previously, use shortcut keys for the most efficient workflow. There are three audio envelopes and there are three video envelopes that can be inserted using the Insert menu. For all practicality, they are identical:

- Mute (Audio) = Mute/Blank (Video).

- Volume Envelope (Audio) is the same as Composite Level (Video).

- Pan (Audio) is similar to Track fade (fades to "one side" of Black or White, depending on Preferences).

Insert Audio Track may be accomplished via the Insert function, right-clicking a track, and choosing **Insert Audio Track** from the submenu, or using the keyboard shortcut **Ctrl+Q**.

Insert Video Track may be accomplished via the Insert function, right-clicking a track, and choosing **Insert Video Track** from the submenu, or using the keyboard shortcut **Ctrl+Shift+Q**.

Audio buses (not available in Vegas Movie Studio) may be inserted via the Insert menu, as can audio input buses. Use an audio input bus when you're making a recording that will also record FX such as reverb or compression. FX may be recorded directly (baked in)

Figure 5.19 The **Insert** menu enables insertion of key functions, most of which are available either via right-clicks on the timeline or via key shortcuts.

to the audio stream or simply set up and monitored so that the recording is unaffected yet always routed to a particular FX and adjustable at any point in time. The difference between the two methods boils down to horsepower and desire for ability to adjust FX at a later point in time. My personal preference is to never bake in FX, since a cake can't be "unbaked." Mixing the ingredients right up to the point of putting the cake in the oven (rendering) is a more flexible workflow.

Audio FX may be inserted via the **Insert** menu, by right-clicking a track header and choosing **Insert Audio FX**, or by choosing an **audio FX** button on a track header, on an audio Event, or in the Project Media window (with an audio Event selected).

Empty Events are similar to slugs. They may be used to mark a point in time or for specific FX. For example, perhaps timecode is needed over a particular area of the timeline that spans several Events, and continuous timecode is needed for only the specific area of the timeline. The only way to accomplish this is with an empty Event.

⏱ Speed Tutorial

1. Generate a new video track (**Ctrl + Shift + Q**). Create a selection on the timeline.

2. Right-click the selection and choose **Insert Empty Event** (or use the **Insert** menu). This will generate a white block/empty Event on the timeline.

3. Browse to the **FX** tab and locate the Timecode FX. Drag the **Timecode FX** from the FX preview window and drop it on the empty Event.

4. Timecode will now appear over all video tracks beneath the empty Event.

5. *Bonus credit!* Place the cursor at the top of the Event. The cursor will change from an arrow to a pointing finger. Click this pointing finger, and drag the finger down. This will reduce the opacity of the timecode seen in the empty Event.

6. *Extra bonus credit!* Browse to the FX window and locate the Mask Generator. Drag the Default preset of the Mask Generator FX to the empty Event the same way that the Timecode FX was dropped onto the empty Event.

7. Watch the black background of the Timecode display change to a transparent background, laying only the timecode (T/C) over top of the Events beneath. If you're new to compositing, congratulations, you've just created a basic composite!

Speaking of compositing: Titles are also basic composites, and the next item in the Insert menu is **Text Media (Titles)**. Vegas Pro 11 has a very new Titling tool called **Text Media** in the application Help menu. Titles may be more efficiently inserted by creating a selection on the timeline, right-clicking, and choosing **Insert Text Media** (or **Generated Media**, if the ProType titler is to be used). This will create a title that fills the selection. In **Options | Preferences | Editing**, remember where the default length of still images was set? This is the same setting for default titles. By using the method outlined previously, titles will be the length of the selection rather than the default title length.

The Generated Media window is explained in detail in the Docking Windows section later in this chapter. Note that Generated Media may also be placed on the timeline via the Insert menu or by creating a selection and right-clicking, then choosing **Insert Generated Media** from the submenu.

Vegas Movie Studio users have an option to insert slideshows (not available in Vegas Pro). Slideshows have no default length; length is determined by number of still images used to generate the slideshow.

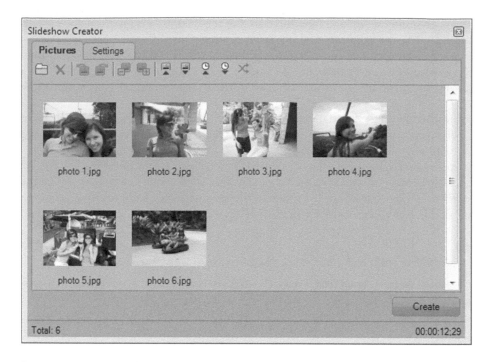

Figure 5.20   Vegas Movie Studio users have the ability to insert slideshows to the timeline. Slideshows may be created from popular still-image formats. This feature is not available in Sony Vegas Pro; using a plug-in like Ultimate S Pro or Production Assistant from VASST.com provide very powerful slideshow capabilities in Vegas Pro.

Sometimes it's necessary to add time to a project, either to make way for media at the head of a project or to set timecode to a specific value. The **Insert | Time** feature allows users to specify a time value, and all Events on the Vegas Pro or Vegas Movie Studio Timeline will be rippled downstream.

Tip_____

If your project is destined for DVD or Blu-ray, consider having 1 to 2 seconds of nothing prior to the start. This should allow for any lag time present in older or cheaper disc players.

Markers and regions are essential tools in any editing workflow. Markers and regions are mentioned several times throughout this book because they are important tools. The **Insert** menu is available for the insertion of markers and regions, but shortcut keys (**M** for Marker, **R** for Regions) is much more efficient and intuitive. Markers and regions may be named as notes or labels.

Audio CD track regions are identifiers for unique files or starting points of a selection on an audio CD. These are used for mastering CDs for replication. The shortcut key for audio CD regions is the **N** key. Index markers (start points) maybe inserted via the **Insert** menu or via **Shift + N**.

Figure 5.21

Command markers are active markers in Vegas. Although they may be used as a different color marker, command markers may also function as "action" markers in a rendered video stream.

Figure 5.22 Command markers may be used to direct viewers to a Web page (auto-opening a browser), subtitles, captions, embedded copyright information, author information, Scott/SS32 (radio broadcast) information, and more. They also may be left empty as uniquely colored markers on the timeline.

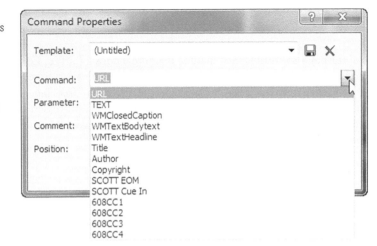

Command markers are predominantly used for closed captions (for broadcast, YouTube, or Windows Media Player) or URL redirection. However, since command markers are a different color, they also may be used as unique markers that are notably different than the orange timeline markers and green region markers.

The Tools Menu

Most of the items found in the **Tools** menu are not available via keyboard shortcuts but may be added to the Vegas Toolbar as shortcuts.

Audio/video tools include opening audio in an external editor. In the **Preferences | Audio** tab, an external audio editor may have been configured, and this is where Vegas will open an audio file in an external audio editor. **Ctrl + E** will open an audio file in an external editor. If no external audio editor has been specified, Vegas will pop up a warning that no external editor has been configured. It's very common to configure Sony Sound Forge Pro in Vegas Pro and Sound Forge Audio Studio in Vegas Movie Studio, but you can assign any audio editing utility you have.

Figure 5.23

I'd recommend opening copies of files in an external audio editor as an alternative to opening source files in the audio editor. The former action protects the original file, and saving a copy of a file will result in an audio take on the Vegas Timeline, allowing users to reference either edited audio (the take) or source audio.

External audio tools also include opening a copy of a file. For the most flexible workflow, open copies of files, not original source files, in an external audio editor.

Render to new track is a feature that is identical to "freezing" content in other applications. This will render all content to user-defined formats (uncompressed is common if rendering to collapse content or to delete files for space saving, but the new track will be rendered again as part of an overall project).

 *Tip*_____

Do not render compressed formats to a new track if the new track is part of an incomplete project that has not yet been mastered. Each rendering results in quality loss; rendering to an uncompressed format may take longer and result in larger file sizes, yet the maintained quality will be appreciated when the master file is created.

Selective PreRendering is a feature that goes back to the days of DV. Vegas will prerender any areas of the timeline that require compression for preview purposes. Most applications use this same function but indicate areas that require rendering in red or yellow on a timeline. This feature is used less in modern workflows because of the many variations in output potential, and timelines serve as masters for HD broadcast, Web, DVD, and mobile delivery platforms. A fast computer should not require prerendering processes for most project settings.

Figure 5.24   Prerendered files can take up a lot of disk space without the editor being aware that they are being stored. If prerendering compressed areas are used, it's a good idea to clean up the Prerendered folder from time to time. (This folder is set in Project Properties.) Some editors place prerendered files in the same folders where they store project media.

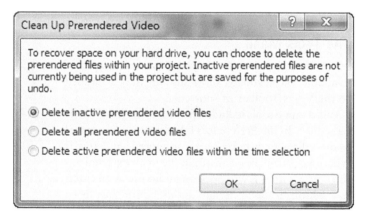

Dynamic RAM Previews are a different animal than prerendered files. Dynamic Ram Previews are RAM renders much like After Effects and other applications use. This feature allows users to render selections to RAM instead of actually creating a file. I personally find this feature indispensable. It is great for rendering composites, titles, transitions that are slow/choppy, or critical color correction areas for preview when the video will not play back smoothly due to loads on the CPU. RAM renders are entirely based on selection length and preview quality. If the RAM render cannot render an entire selection, either increase the amount of Dynamic RAM available in the **Options | Preferences | Video** tab or decrease the quality of view by setting the Preview window to **Preview/Auto.** In most situations, this will free up more RAM and allow for longer RAM Preview renders.

 *Tip*_____
Use **Shift+B** for RAM renders. This is a shortcut every Vegas editor should know.

Print Video to Tape is exactly as its label implies: print to DV tape or to SDI output for tape. This feature is used for printing DV, SD-SDI, and HD-SDI. It is not used for HDV.

Print Video to HDV Tape is used exclusively for HDV print to tape. If you do not have an HDV camcorder or deck, you might not use this feature.

Export Video to XDCAM Disc is a file transfer protocol for XDCAM Professional Optical Discs. Using this function will require installation of the FAM drivers found at www.sony.com/xdcam (not available in Vegas Movie Studio).

The Layout Audio CD from Events option assists editors in creating Redbook CD master files. Vegas will scan the project for audio Events and layout CD markers for these Events.

Figure 5.25

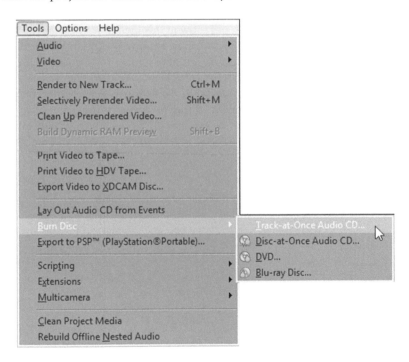

The Burn Disc menu option allows for several types of discs to be burned directly from the Vegas Timeline. This feature is useful for sharing rushes, for archiving master content, or for quick output of DVDs that don't require menus or authoring.

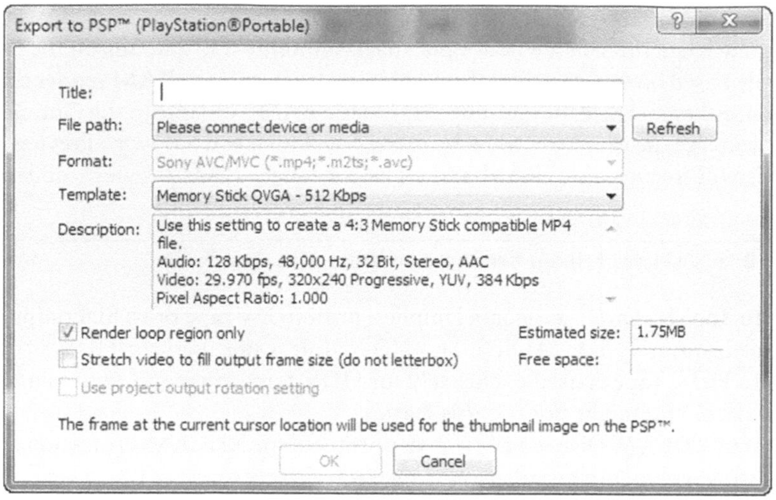

Figure 5.26

Export to PSP™ (PlayStation®Portable)

Title:

File path: Please connect device or media ▼ Refresh

Format: Sony AVC/MVC (*.mp4;*.m2ts;*.avc) ▼

Template: Memory Stick QVGA - 512 Kbps ▼

Description: Use this setting to create a 4:3 Memory Stick compatible MP4 file.
Audio: 128 Kbps, 48,000 Hz, 32 Bit, Stereo, AAC
Video: 29.970 fps, 320x240 Progressive, YUV, 384 Kbps
Pixel Aspect Ratio: 1.000

☑ Render loop region only Estimated size: 1.75MB

☐ Stretch video to fill output frame size (do not letterbox) Free space:

☐ Use project output rotation setting

The frame at the current cursor location will be used for the thumbnail image on the PSP™.

OK   Cancel

A Sony PSP™ must be connected to the computer to access the **Export to PSPdialog** option. There are several specific presets and paths for exporting to PSP.

The **Tools | Scripting** function allows users to see all scripts installed to the Sony scripting folder. There may be other scripts available that do not show in this menu. Sony includes some very useful scripts with the application (not available in Vegas Movie Studio). Scripts are powerful tools that save editors tremendous amounts of time. For example, all stereo tracks in an entire project may be combined to mono with one click on a script. All scripts may be placed as shortcuts on the Vegas Toolbar.

Multicamera editing functions are accessed via the **Tools** menu as well (not available in Vegas Movie Studio). See the section on multicamera editing for more information.

Figure 5.27   Vegas was one of the first editors to offer multicamera editing and is a very efficient multicamera application. Multicam may be edited with camera audio or with a master track (or both). It is fast and intuitive and works much like a production switcher in selecting takes or active cameras.

Vegas Pro and Movie Studio have a feature called **Clean Project Media.** This feature is the same as the lightning bolt found in the Project Media window; it cleans unused media from the project. Use this feature before archiving a project or before saving a project in its final state.

The OPTIONS Menu

The first two options in the **Options** menu might seem confusing to video editors. **Quantize to Frames** is a feature unique to Sony Vegas. It allows users to keep video locked so that the smallest movement in time is a single frame. Vegas began life as an audio editor, and frames-only quantization is not at all adequate. Files must be moveable at sample levels, and Sony Vegas is the only video-editing application that offers this functionality. Disabling Quantize to Frames will allow for audio and video to be adjusted at a mind-boggling 32,000 points per second vs. 29.97 frames per second when it is enabled. Video editors may or may not find this useful. By default, Quantize to Frames is enabled, and I recommend that video editors leave it enabled. Audio-only editors should not have it enabled. For audio-only edits, disable Quantize to Frames (**Alt + F8**).

Snapping allows Events to snap to each other or to the playhead, markers, regions, or selection points. This helps ensure that there are no blank edit points in a timeline (one-frame blanks). Snapping may be temporarily disabled by holding the **Shift** key while moving Events around. Snapping to vertical gridlines is also possible (disabled by default). Gridline values are set in the **Options | Grid Spacing** menu choice. Snapping to markers or regions may be disabled in the Options menu as well.

Automatic cross-fades are enabled by default; most users will appreciate this feature. If it is disabled, whenever Events overlap a butt-cut will be created instead of a cross-fade.

Figure 5.28

Quick-fade audio edits should always be enabled for video editing. Audio editors may have cause to disable this feature. Disabling this feature may lead to truncated audio that clicks or pops. A 10ms fade (at minimum) is recommended for all audio fades. This value may be set in **Preferences | Editing.**

Figure 5.29   Video, music, or time values may be used for grid spacing on the Vegas Timeline. This feature is very useful if specific snap values are required. However, **Snap to Grid** is not enabled by default, to better allow users to control snap points. On a long-form video with many edits, having Snap to Grid enabled may allow blank spots to appear by mistake.

When you're moving Events around on the timeline, any inserted envelopes may be locked to Events (very handy when Events are copied) or left on the timeline in place, regardless of how Events move around the envelope points. **Lock Envelopes to Events** may be enabled or disabled via the Toolbar or in the Options menu.

Ignore Event Grouping is disabled by default, as Vegas always wants to keep audio/video locked

Figure 5.30   Auto-ripple is a terrific feature when used properly. If it's not understood, however, it can have disastrous results on a project. Understand the use of ripple before using it in an auto mode. Rippling may be done on a per-edit basis using the **F** key or the **Shift + F** key combination.

together. However, when creating J or L cuts or when you want to extend audio or video past an edit point, this feature is very useful. **Ignore Event Grouping** may be enabled or disabled via the Toolbar, Options menu, or **Ctrl + Shift + U** key shortcut.

 Tip_____

J cuts and L cuts are specialized cuts often found in narrative projects and are effective transitional devices. With a J cut, you will hear the audio of the new Event before you see the video of the new Event. The reverse is true of an L cut. The name comes from their appearance on the timeline.

⏱ *Speed Tutorial*

1. Create a new video track (**Ctrl + Shift + Q**). Drag two different pieces of media to the track and butt them together. (An audio track will be created if one does not already exist.)

2. Click **Ctrl + Shift + U** to enable Ignore Event Grouping.

3. Click and drag the audio from the left Event to the left about 2 seconds.

4. Click and drag the audio of the right Event to the left until it snaps against the audio from the left Event.

5. When you play back the two Events you will hear the audio of the new Event/scene for a couple of seconds while viewing the video of the first Event. This technique should be used only when no critical audio is taking place in the first Event or scene.

Don't forget to disable **Ignore Event Grouping** when you're done!

Somewhat related to Event grouping is the **Slip All Takes** option. If alternate Events have been layered as takes, and an Event is slipped or rolled in an edit, be sure that Slip All Takes is also enabled so that all takes in the Event are slipped or rolled with the active/visible Event.

Figure 5.31   In this image, the left side has looping disabled; the right side shows looping enabled. This is one of my most favorite features in Vegas. When an Event is looping, all FX controls may be adjusted, transitions may be adjusted, and all edits/FX/transitions within the selection will play in real time. Enabling looping allows for fine tweaking of FX or transition settings without having to hit the Spacebar to audition changes. This is a super-timesaver (and will help prevent wearing out a hole in the Spacebar).

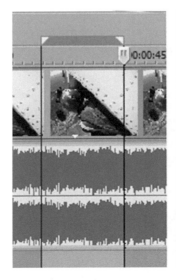
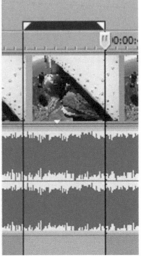

Looping is a valuable feature and is in my personal top-10 favorite Vegas features. Looping instructs Vegas to play a selection in a loop, allowing for real-time auditions of FX settings, transition parameters, and any other functions. The **Q** key is the most efficient way to enable and disable looping. When looping is enabled, a blue bar appears at the top of the selected area. When looping is disabled, a gray bar will show in the selected area.

Vegas offers a metronome that is invaluable to musicians. It also serves as a click-track for creating ACID™ loop sequences on the timeline. The metronome sound may be changed in Preferences. Tempo of the metronome is controlled in the **Project Properties | Ruler** tab.

Bypass all audio FX may be toggled on/off in the **Options** menu. If multiple FX have been laid into a mix and the mix is weighing heavily on the CPU, toggling FX on and off is valuable for listening to the mix prior to render. Additionally, it is often desirable to listen to the mix without FX enabled.

The **Timecode** option is related exclusively to Vegas and acts as a MIDI trigger or slave. The External Control toggle empowers Vegas users with external hardware to disable/enable external control. Disabling external control will have no impact on a mix; all automation elements in a mix are stored in Vegas. The external control is merely an interface.

Figure 5.32   The Vegas Toolbar may be loaded with icons for common functions. In this image, several scripts and other shortcuts have been added to the Vegas Toolbar.

The Vegas Toolbar is horizontally quite long, and many icons may be added to it for custom access, depending on user preference.

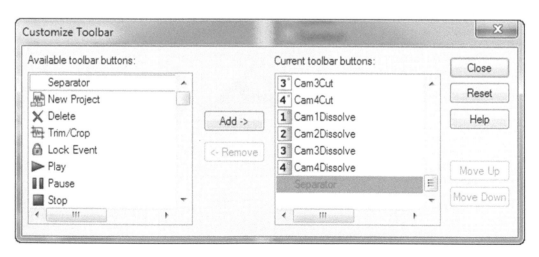

Figure 5.33   Double-clicking any icon on the left side of the **Customize** dialog box will insert the shortcut to the Vegas Toolbar.

Notice the separator icon; it allows users to separate customized icons with a small vertical bar.

Keyboard shortcuts may be customized as well. Users coming from Avid or FCP may want to customize the Vegas shortcut keys for familiarity; keyboard shortcuts may be saved and transported from machine to machine. Copy keyboard shortcuts to and from C:\Users\< username >\AppData \Roaming\Sony\ Vegas Pro\ 11.0. The keyboard shortcuts will then appear in the **Customize Keyboard** menu found under Options and can be imported to any Vegas machine.

It's worth noting that the Help feature in Vegas has a searchable window. This may be accessed by pressing **F1** or, if help with a specific feature is needed, by pressing **Shift + F1**. This will open an interactive Help icon. Click on the feature you want to better understand, and Vegas will provide more information about that feature. These are called *Interactive Tutorials* in Vegas Pro and *Show Me How* in Vegas Movie Studio.

There is a keyboard shortcut map in the Help menu. With the number of keyboard shortcuts available, searching through this part of the application is a way to find useful information about keyboard shortcuts and keymappings.

Also in the Help option is the version number you're using. In the Preferences, NetNotify may have been disabled. Without NetNotify enabled, it will be useful to know the build number in the Event that upgrades are available. Choose **About Vegas Pro** or **About Movie Studio** for information about version or build number.

Docking Windows

The Docking window area is the most-used area in Sony Vegas Pro and Vegas Movie Studio outside the Timeline and Preview windows. Docking windows may be viewed, hidden, and rearranged to user preference. Some Docking windows are already in place when Vegas loads. Others are available in the **View** menu. Since not all Docking windows are necessary for all projects, users are encouraged to determine which Docking windows should be used for particular projects and purposes. Docking window layouts may be saved as a user preference and recalled at any time (as can any Vegas project window layout; see the section "Saving Windows Layouts" for more information on saving and recalling layouts).

Figure 5.34   This is the Docking windows section of Vegas. FX, transitions, Project Media, the Vegas Explorer, and other often-used tools are found in the Docking windows section of Vegas. These windows may be arranged and viewed according to user preference.

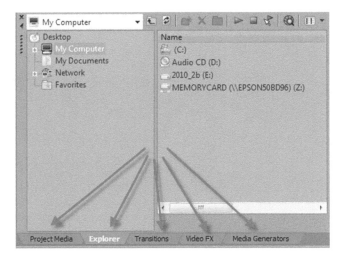

On the upper-left corner of every docking window are six small dots that represent a "grip" or "handle." Clicking, holding, and dragging this point of the window allows a window to be removed or "torn" from the docking area and dropped into another docking area or floated over any portion of the Vegas interface. Docking windows may be floated over other Docking windows by grabbing and dragging while holding the **Ctrl** key.

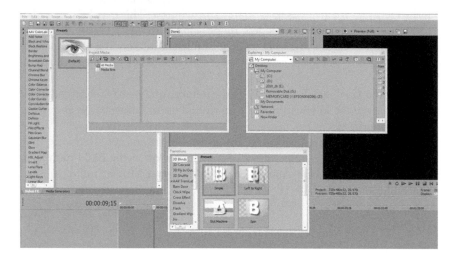

Figure 5.35

By default, there are several Docking windows already placed in Vegas, and other windows may be added. Also by default, the entire upper section of Vegas is a Docking window and may be segmented according to user preference. Docking windows may be placed to the left or right of any other Docking window. For example, here is a screenshot of my personal laptop setup. Note that Vegas Explorer is placed to the right of the Preview window.

Figure 5.36   Docking windows may be placed on either side of the Preview window. Windows that are used most often are typically placed to the left, whereas lesser-used windows are placed on the right.

The Vegas Trimmer

All pro NLE applications offer a Trimmer; some even require a Trimmer's use for chopping clips to put them on the timeline. Vegas does not require that the Trimmer be used, and in today's file-based workflows, it may prove to be superfluous. However, many users of other applications will appreciate the Vegas Trimmer and how it works because it resembles a familiar workflow. For cutting clips from long-form recordings, the Trimmer is invaluable.

Figure 5.37   The Trimmer may be dragged off the Docking window area by "grabbing" (clicking and holding) the handle on the upper left of the Trimmer window. Drag it to any area on the screen. If the Trimmer wants to snap back to the Docking window, hold the **Ctrl** key while dragging. This prevents the Trimmer (and all other Docking windows) from redocking and allows very fine user control over window placement.

The Trimmer is a valuable tool not only for chopping long-form recordings into manageable chunks but also to mark and recall regions, set in/out points, create subclips, restore removed audio/video from a clip, and recall used sections of media. It may be used as a logging tool and in/out points later exported to an edit decision list (EDL) or Excel file sheet.

Use the Vegas Explorer to browse to a video folder. Right-click any video file in the folder and in the submenu select **Open in Trimmer**. The file will open in the Vegas Trimmer. Depending on the file length, Vegas may take a few moments to draw the waveforms, indicated by the message "Building

Peaks" in the Trimmer's audio view. Long files may take some time to build peaks, and Vegas generally only needs to do this once.

Vegas uses graphics to draw audio, and these graphic files are stored as .sfk files. The .sfk files serve no other purpose beyond being the graphical representation for audio. Occasionally, users might want to sweep their systems for .sfk files not related to current projects and delete them. The VASST Ultimate S application has a feature that will delete .sfk files that are not in use. Although the files are quite small, they'll build up over time. We jokingly refer to them as "mouse droppings" as they build up inside the hard drive.

Once the peaks are built, the video and audio are visible in the Trimmer. Now the video file may be sorted. As a matter of practice, I generally play through files in the Trimmer at high speed, stopping to mark usable regions. The high-speed preview is accomplished by tapping the **L** key two or three times for 2x/3x playback. When the playhead/cursor arrives at a desirable point, playback is paused by pressing the **K** key. Pressing the **I** key will mark an in point, and pressing the **O** key will mark an out point. When in and out points have been selected, a gray or blue bar will be seen in the Trimmer timeline. The gray and blue area marks a region. The region may be stored (permanently with the file if this option was selected in **Options | Preferences | General | Automatically Store Trimmer Markers/Regions with Media file**) with the file and recalled later. This is a fast form of logging, or choosing shots to be later inserted to the timeline.

Tip_____
Using the **JKL** keys with one hand and a mouse in the other hand makes for speedy editing.

Sometimes markers as notes may be inserted in the Trimmer as an alternative to inserting regions. Just as the **R** key inserts regions, the **M** key inserts markers. Markers are auto-numbered (depending on user preferences in the **Options | Preferences | General** settings) and are visible in the video file, whether it's on the Vegas Timeline or viewed in the Trimmer.

Depending on the workflow, inserting regions to the timeline as they're selected may be all that is required to build the project timeline. Regions may be inserted to the timeline by pressing the **A** (for Add) key. In/out points in the Trimmer will insert after the playhead point (from the cursor) and move the playhead to the end of the newly inserted clip/Event. Clips and media may be added to the timeline before the playhead by pressing the combination **Shift + A**, which will add media up to cursor. This is a great method for filling in gaps in a timeline.

Other functions of the Trimmer allow for enabling overwrite on a timeline (similar to Avid **Shift + B**) and creating subclips.

To overwrite a video file on the timeline, first place the playhead/cursor at the in point on the Vegas Timeline. In the Trimmer, select the in/out points. Be certain that the track to be written to on the timeline is highlighted and selected. Otherwise, the insert will go to either a new track or to any selected track. Press the **A** key to insert the media you selected to overwrite existing media.

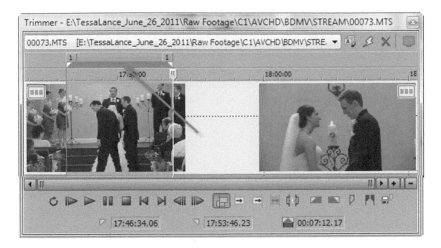

Figure 5.38   Pressing the **R** key will provide users with the ability to mark and store selected regions. Regions prove invaluable throughout the editing process. The region may also be given a user-specified name. These regions will be indicated by a green line embedded in the video stream, both on the timeline and in the Trimmer.

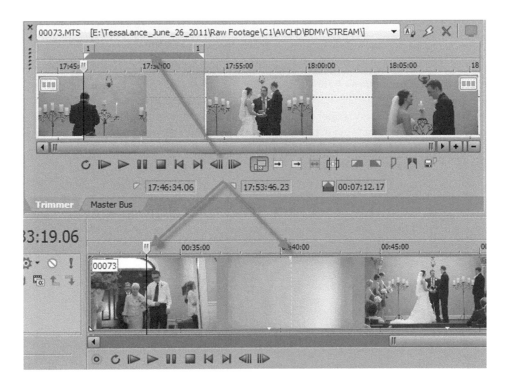

Figure 5.39   The region in the Trimmer window will overwrite existing media on the Vegas Timeline. Note that the playhead is at the insert point, the track to be written to is selected, and the region is identified and marked in the Trimmer window.

Tip_____

Media may be inserted with the **Overwrite** option disabled; this will leave existing media as it is and merely overlay the "new" media on top of the original media. No cuts to the original media will occur. In the event of an overwrite, media in the place of the inserted media are removed from the timeline. Therefore, if the overwritten media are also deleted, a blank space will remain where the original media were originally placed. In short, Overwrite mode deletes and replaces media. Without Overwrite mode, media simply "lay over" original media on the timeline. Non-overwrite editing may lead to confusion if users are coming from other NLE application workflows.

Subclips

Subclips are mostly a media management tool in Vegas and Vegas Movie Studio. They are handy for finding selects and for repeating media. Subclips also make for more efficient views and searches in the Project Media window. Subclips are also used for making sections of video play in reverse and for stabilizing segments of longer video files. (Vegas does render subclips in the event of video stabilization.)

To create a subclip: Select media in the Trimmer, defining the in/out points to be used in the subclip. Right-click the selection and choose **Create Subclip** in the submenu that opens. Another option is to select the in/out points and press the **Create Subclip** icon in the Trimmer toolbar. Either method creates the same file references. Vegas will open a Save dialog box where the subclip may be given a unique name. There is also a checkbox that will reverse the subclip (so that an entire video Event will not require reversal). This saves CPU cycles when this option is used to reverse a video file.

> Subclips in Vegas are not physical subclips. They are virtual representations of original media. Users of other applications such as AVID or Final Cut are familiar with the application actually rendering a physical subclip. Vegas simply creates a reference to the existing original source media. This feature is very fast and super for time saving. However, if the original source media is deleted from the hard drive or moved from its original location, the subclip will not be able to locate its reference source. Since subclips do not use any disk space, there is no reason to delete the master or original source file.

In the event that automatic saving of regions and markers has not been enabled in the Preferences dialog box, users may manually save regions and markers by selecting the **Save Markers** button in the lower right of the Trimmer.

Figure 5.40   Low-resolution computer monitors or tightly crowded Docking windows may have hidden this button. Either expand the right side of the Trimmer Docking window or select the **Down Arrow** in the lower right of the Trimmer window to see More Buttons options. Alternatively, pressing the **S** key while the Trimmer window is active will save regions and markers with the file.

At the top of the Trimmer window is a small menu bar. File addresses are stored in this bar for fast recall of the most recently used files in the Trimmer window. Next to this drop-down location bar is a small button for sorting recently used files. This allows users to sort them in order of filename versus order of use.

The "lightning bolt" icon is used in the Trimmer much the same way it is used in the Project Media window: it clears the recent history. Finally, next to the lightning bolt is a red X. This will clear the current file used from the Trimmer history. This feature might be used for one of those "feet shots" where the camera was being tested or, if there are alternate takes that should not be reaccessed, this will clear the file until it is accessed in the Trimmer again.

Selecting Audio and/or Video in the Trimmer

Sometimes just the audio portion or video portion of a file is preferred. Vegas allows audio-only, video-only, or both to be selected in the Trimmer. The **Tab** key will cycle through these options, indicated in the left side by a film frame icon, audio waveform icon, or both icons, indicating both are selected.

Figure 5.41   In this screenshot, only video is selected in the Vegas Trimmer. Audio will not go to the timeline with selected video. Pressing the **Tab** key will select audio-only; pressing **Tab** a third time will cause both audio and video to be selected to go to the timeline. Alternatively, selecting **Shift + Tab** will select audio-only.

Right-Click Access in the Trimmer

All commands for the Trimmer are also found in a right-click submenu. Editing with a mouse, users may find this submenu more intuitive than will power users who use the shortcut key commands.

Figure 5.42   The right-click
submenu found by
right-clicking in the
Trimmer area will call
up this submenu. All
icons are found as
submenu options.

A Quick Trimmer Exercise/Workflow

I frequently use the Trimmer to sort media and quickly get it to a timeline. In my Preferences, I have set a double-click to open a file in the Trimmer. Once the file is open, I make my selection and press the **A** key to add the selection to the timeline. I repeat the process until I've reached the end of a specific piece of media. I'll load a new piece of media into the Trimmer and repeat. Essentially it comes down to:

- Double-click media to load in Trimmer.

- Use **JKL** keys to speed through the Trimmer at 2x.

- Find in/out points of select.

- Press **R** to create a region. (This step is not required, but it does make it easier to revisit the media later on and know if I've used a segment of a piece of media. I'll also often use the region naming to insert notes for an editor who may follow me in the project. This is also useful for broadcast houses for marking and logging media.)

- Press **A** to add the region to the timeline.

Lather, rinse, repeat. In other words, continue this process until all raw media have been viewed and "logged."

When all the selects are on the timeline, editing can begin. This shortens the logging/EDL process and provides a head start on building the story. When shipping a segment or package to broadcast, this workflow is very, very fast because it allows the story to build in a linear fashion, allows the B-roll to be quickly identified and labeled and SOTS, nats, M&E to be added as needed and output. (If you're outputting over SDI, it ships immediately to the network storage system for immediate access for broadcast.)

The Project Media Window

Projects will always run more smoothly if a library is built in advance and when libraries are properly maintained with all related media to a project. The **Project Media window** is a repository of all media files used, whether audio, video, graphic, or nested project/veg files. This window is different in Vegas from other editing applications; copies of media are not recreated for each time they're used in various media bins. Vegas projects do not contain media but merely references to media locations. The Project Media window collects and manages all media found on the timeline and allows users to add media FX, create bins for more efficient project management, configure pull-down removal, pair media files for 3D, search media, and much more.

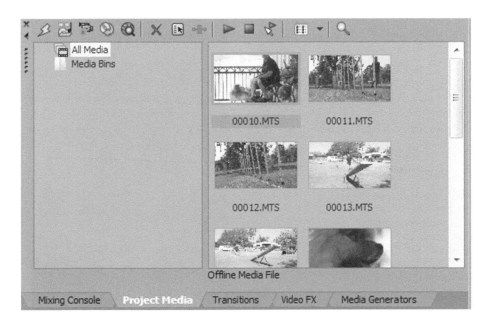

Figure 5.43

Moving aside from the Project Media toolbar for the time being, create a new bin. Right-click the **Media Bins** in the Bin window and choose **Create New Bin** or press the **N** key with the Media Bin selected. A new bin will open, ready to be named. Bins may be created for different types of media such as B-Roll, audio, transitionals, selects, primary, and so on.

Import media to selected bins by either dragging media from the Vegas Explorer and dropping them into a specific bin or by selecting the **Import Media** icon in the Project Media toolbar while a bin is active. Media may also be selected in the Vegas Explorer, right-clicked, and choose **Add to Project Media List** in the newly opened submenu. When this method is used, files are added to whichever media bin happens to be open, so be sure of which folder is open before using the right-click/add method. Dragging and dropping is the fastest, most accurate method of building a library. This will require undocking and floating the Explorer window; hold **Ctrl** to float the Vegas Explorer outside the docking area.

Bins may also include sub-bins. For example, a bin for all audio may be made, with sub-bins made for MP3, .wav, stingers, transitions, stock music, sound FX, and so on. The more complete and specific the bin structure, the faster media may be located in the project.

 *Tip*_____

Files may be dragged from Windows Explorer straight to the Vegas Timeline, to the Vegas Trimmer, or to the Project Media Bins.

Whether placed in a media bin or not, any media added to the timeline will be automatically added to the Project Media list. Media that are added to the timeline and later deleted from the timeline will still be seen in the Project Media list. Project Media lists may need to be swept from time to time to reduce the amount of information processing load placed on the CPU.

Large projects or projects using large files may benefit from being swept clean from time to time. Select and click the lightning bolt icon in the Project Media window. This will clear files that are not present on the timeline and open more memory allocation. If Vegas becomes sluggish or unstable, clearing the Project Media list should be considered as a first step.

Figure 5.44   Use this button to Remove All Unused Media From Project. This will also sweep media from bins, so this step should be taken near the end of a project or when Vegas becomes unstable.

Bins may be copied from one project to another. If a project bin is to be used for multiple projects, it's a good idea to keep media in a library bin. Open two copies of Vegas, and drag media bins from the old instance to the new instance. This is the only way to share bins across instances of Vegas. For consistency, another method is to keep a hard library (media actually stored in Windows folders) that can be dragged and imported into new projects as a bin.

Figure 5.45 Vegas Project Media offers many options for searches, including metadata fields. Phrases, portions of filenames, or exclusions of filenames/phrases may be used (chosen in the **Conditions** drop-down menu). This function may also be accessed via the magnifying glass icon in the Project Media window toolbar.

To search for specific media in a project, right-click anywhere in the **Project Media** window. The **Search** dialog box offers many unique fields and metadata options for the search.

Media may be captured directly into a Media Bin. Use the **Capture Media** button at the top of the Project Media window to open the default capture application.

Next in the toolbar is an **Extract Audio from CD** icon. Clicking this button will open a CD extraction dialog box where specific songs may be extracted from an audio CD.

Figure 5.46

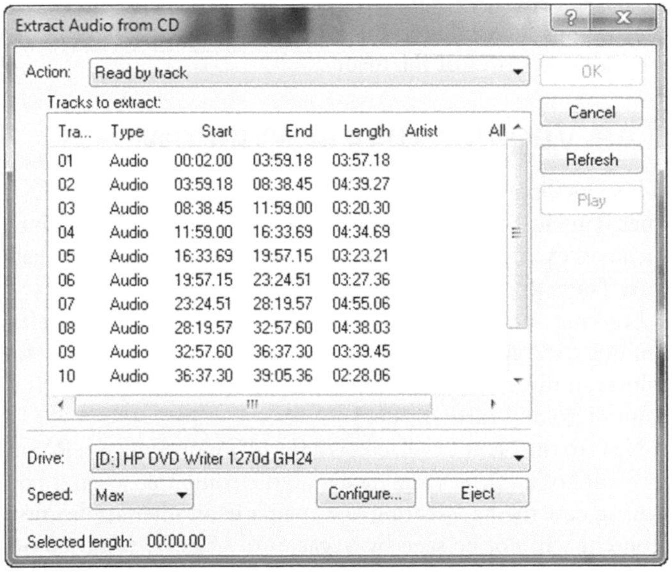

Figure 5.47 In this dialog box, Vegas will extract audio from a CD. Users may select the files to be extracted and where they will be stored once extracted.

Next in the toolbar is the **Get Media From the Web** icon. This will launch a Web page at sony-creativesoftware.com that gives users access to various ACID loops, stock video media, and other tools for Vegas users.

Remove Selected Media from Project is the next button in the toolbar; it merely deletes media from the Project Media list. It does not delete media from the storage system. The **Media Properties** button found to the right of the Remove Selected Media button will open the Media Properties dialog box just the same as right-clicking media on the timeline and selecting **Properties** from the submenu. This dialog box provides all available information about the video file.

The Media FX button is one of four places that FX may be added to media and the only place that FX may not be dragged to. This FX access allows for FX to be inserted into an entire media stream, no matter how many times the media has been edited in the Trimmer or timeline. For example, say that a 30-minute recording has been split into 20 sections at various locations on the timeline, and it is later discovered that the source media was not white balanced. It would be very laborious to insert the FX 20 times across the timeline, and it is more CPU intensive to process each clip. A better option would be to insert the White Balance or Color Correction FX at the Project Media level only one time, and all clips cut from the original 30-minute source would be corrected. This also ensures that all clips are matched in process. This feature is very useful in multicam situations where multiple camera sources must be matched.

The next three buttons are control buttons and are self-explanatory. Take note of the icon that is a "play" icon with a cursor symbol next to it. This is the auto-preview option and is, by default, not selected. Selecting this option will begin playback of any media selected in the Project Media window. This same function exists in the Vegas Explorer and is selected by default on all of my editing systems.

The **Views** button allows users to select the sort of views they prefer. Thumbnails are often the fastest means of recognizing media but they are also the most CPU intensive. If the computer system is slow or balking at loading large projects, it may be best to set this option to **List**. The **Details** option allows users to see how many times a clip has been used in the project, any added comments to the clip, timecode I/O (in/out), what media FX have been inserted to a clip (if any), tape name, and all properties of the media.

The Vegas Explorer Window

This Docking window is where users may locate media files and from here send them to the Trimmer, Timeline, or Project Media windows or bins. For all intents and purposes, the Vegas Explorer behaves exactly like Windows Explorer. Files are sorted, displayed, and accessed in the same manner. There are, however, a few differences.

Looking at the top of the Vegas Explorer window from left to right, you'll see a few icons that are unique to Vegas Explorer. The **Up One Level** button is the same as a Back button in Windows Explorer; it directs users to the next level up in a folder tree. If the file is at the root of a hard drive, it cannot go any further "up."

Next to the Next Level icon is a fairly important icon: **Refresh**. When Vegas loads, the application is aware of all drives and media on the computer when it boots up. Adding a new hard drive, capturing new media, creating new media in another application, creating graphics, or any other new content will not be seen by Vegas until Vegas is restarted or until the Refresh button is selected.

The **Refresh** button is used for refreshing the Vegas Explorer so that any new drives connected to the system or any new media that have been generated or stored may be seen in the Vegas Explorer.

The Vegas Explorer allows users to delete folders or media files from within the Explorer; this is helpful for when those "accidental records" occur or for simply getting rid of files that are no longer needed.

Users of older versions of Vegas will appreciate a new feature found in Vegas 11: the ability to "favorite" a folder. This allows commonly accessed files to be favorited and so found very quickly. In the drop-down address box at the top of the Explorer, there is a choice labeled **My Favorites**. Selecting **My Favorites** in the address box will instruct Vegas to display only favorited folders in the right side of the Explorer dialog box. This feature is a terrific shortcut for finding commonly used media folders. I use this feature to access lower thirds, stinger audio, and templates that are often used for nested veg files.

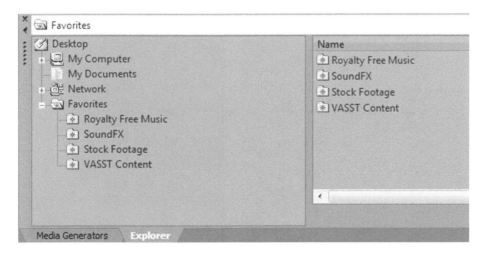

Figure 5.48   Folders or files that have been added to **My Favorites** may be quickly located. For episodic or common-use media files and folders, this feature is a great timesaver.

The transport bar in the Vegas Explorer window function is similar to the transport bar found in the Project Media window. Media may be played or stopped in this window. The **Auto-Preview** selection allows users to auto-preview/auto-play any selected file. This is another timesaving feature, allowing users to cycle through video files using the Up/Down Arrow keys, previewing media on the fly. This feature, coupled with **Double-click files to open in Trimmer,** allows for very rapid preview and timeline population. High-speed/SDE environments will benefit from this feature because it allows extremely efficient file navigation.

Get Media From the Web is indicated in the globe/magnifying glass icon. This is a direct link to Sony's media Website, where users may download stock audio and video to be used in commercial projects.

The **Views** icon provides users options as to how the Vegas Explorer will display files. Files may be displayed with details, in trees (most common), and with or without summaries. Take note of the Region view; this is not seen in the Windows Explorer. The **Region** view shows users what regions have been saved (if any) in a video file. Regions must be created in the Vegas Trimmer. If no regions have been assigned to a file in the Vegas Trimmer, this view is not of any use. Long-form projects where the Trimmer has been utilized for regions/markers will allow users to quickly locate and identify media and related regions or clips within that media. Clicking on a region in the Region view will auto-play if the Auto-Preview feature in the Explorer is enabled. Otherwise, users will need to manually click the **Play** icon found in the Vegas Explorer toolbar.

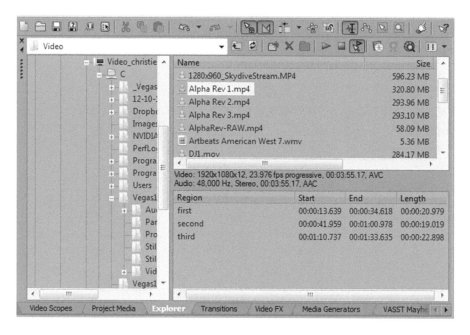

Figure 5.49   If regions have been added to a file in the Vegas Trimmer, these regions will be displayed in the Vegas Explorer. Clicking on a region allows it to be manually played, or if the Auto-Preview feature has been selected, the region will auto-play. This is a terrific tool for auditioning regions before adding them to the Vegas Timeline.

 Tip_____

On occasion, docking windows will seemingly disappear. The windows are still there; they've just become hidden behind the Windows taskbar or behind other windows. The easiest way to find windows hidden beneath the Windows taskbar is to go to the Windows Taskbar Properties and Unlock the taskbar. Let it slide down, place Vegas to full screen, and the "hidden" window will be found. If the window has docked itself behind other windows and the tab cannot be seen, simply start closing down docked windows until the "missing" window is found.

Other Docking Windows

Default installs of Vegas Pro and Vegas Movie Studio will display transitions, Video FX, and Media Generators. Transitions and FX are discussed at a later point in this book. Many other windows may be added to the Vegas Docking Windows schemes; we'll briefly look at each window in this section.

Media Generators are tools that can create media to be used on a Vegas Timeline. Solid colors, gradients, stripes, blocks, checkerboards, credit rolls, and titles are all part of the Media Generators (earlier versions of Vegas named this feature *Generated Media*).

All media created with the Media Generators is always at project size, uncompressed, and 4:4:4 color space. Media Generators are commonly used for compositing, overlays, lower thirds, slugs, and title cards, among other uses. Titles also fall into the category of Media Generators.

⏱ *Speed Tutorial*

1. Open a new Vegas project with the settings of 1280 x 720, 30p.

2. In Vegas Explorer, locate the still image named **Audio_sees.jpg**.

3. Drag and drop this file on the Vegas Timeline. It should be the default 5 seconds in length (unless still image length was changed in the **Options | Preferences | Editing** dialog box).

4. Press **Ctrl + Shift + Q**. This will insert a new video track.

5. Click on the **Media Generators** tab and browse to Checkerboard. In the Checkerboard settings, find a Generated Media style labeled **Ridges**. Drag and drop the Ridges generator so that it sits above the .jpg file inserted on the lower track.

6. A Media Generator dialog box will open. Adjust the opacity of the **Black** (color 2) color in the Media Generator to suit personal preference. This should provide an image that appears similar to this one.

7. Save this project so that you can use it later. Name the file **Moving Eyes** in a location where it may be readily found. The fastest way to save a project is to press **Ctrl + S** (for Save) and a **Save** dialog box will open. Alternatively, go to **File | Save** and follow the dialog box prompts to store the project in a user-preferred folder.

This provides just one idea of how Media Generators may be used. Add the TV Simulator FX (default setting) to the Media Generator and watch the static file come to life.

Credit rolls may be inserted with the Media Generators as well. Text may be copied from an Excel, Word, or Google Spreadsheet document directly into columns of the Credit Roll Generator.

Insert a credit roll to the timeline by dragging a Credit Roll Preset from the Media Generators window to the Vegas Timeline. The credit roll dialog box will open, allowing characters and text to be typed or pasted in place. Double-click the Event to create a selection, and press the **Spacebar** to play it. The credit roll will play in the Vegas Preview window.

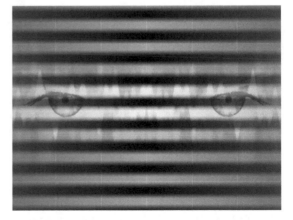

Figure 5.50

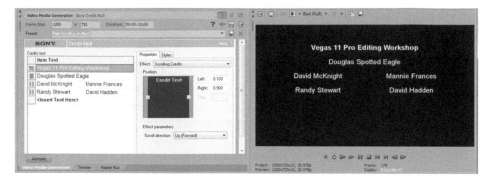

Figure 5.51   Inserting credit rolls is very fast and easy in Sony Vegas. Drag a credit roll preset to the timeline, input desired text, and close the dialog box. Use the **Spacebar** to play out the credit roll.

> Vegas and the Vegas manuals refer to all media on the timeline as an *Event* versus the industry-standard term *clip*. This is because Vegas treats video, audio, graphics, nested projects, and comps with equal control and does not require users to use different workflows for audio, video, and the like. It's a simple nomenclature for the application itself; most users still refer to media on the timeline as *audio clips, video clips*, and so on.

If additional text needs to be added to the credit roll, edits are easily made by first clicking the **Generated Media** icon found in the upper-right of the credit roll Event.

Figure 5.52   Click this icon to reopen the Credit Roll Generator. This will allow text to be added, deleted, or edited. This icon is found on all forms of Generated Media.

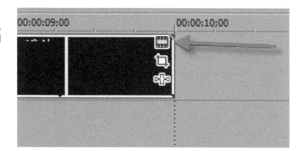

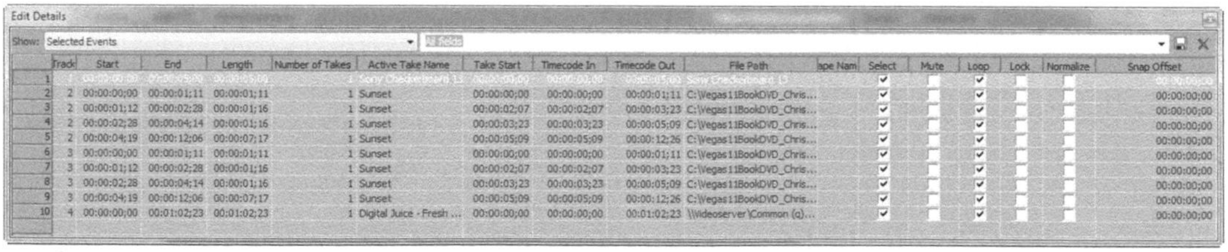

Figure 5.53   Be sure to do this from a reasonably populated timeline, and spread it out wide so that Normalize, etc. are visible. (Edit Details is not available in Vegas Movie Studio.)

The **View | Edit Details** window is terrific for exporting Edit Decision Lists (EDLs), viewing the project as an EDL, seeing processes applied to Events, or applying limited processes to an Event. EDL values may be exported directly to an Excel or Google Spreadsheet, used to generate metadata, store asset recall, or share with other editors as a list of processes applied. Comments related to Events may be inserted here and viewed in other windows of Vegas (Project Media Window) and shared with other editors. This is a valuable tool in workflows where multiple editors will be working on a project at different times or in different studios. The Comments field may be used much like sticky notes. (VASST also offers the freeware NotePad that allows for "sticky notes" to be applied to projects and Events; see the DVD included with this book.)

The Compositors Window

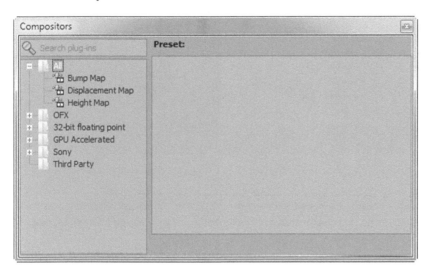

Figure 5.54

The Compositors window (not available in Vegas Movie Studio) is new to users of older versions of Vegas; these tools were originally found in track headers under Compositing Modes. If compositing modes are track-accessed, the Compositors window will open as either a floating window or a docked window, depending on how the user's machine has been configured.

Compositing tools found in Vegas are:

- Bump Map
- Height Map
- Displacement Map

Of these three compositing modes, only the Bump Map is OFX (Open FX). These compositing modes may be dragged to a track header and used for creating unique composited effects on frames. More on compositing is covered later in this book.

⏱ *Speed Tutorial*

1. Open the **Moving Eyes** project created earlier in this chapter.

2. Open the **Compositors** window.

3. Drag the Bump Map compositor **Default Preset** to the track header of the track containing the generated media (the Event with the lines in it). The **Bump Map** dialog box will open.

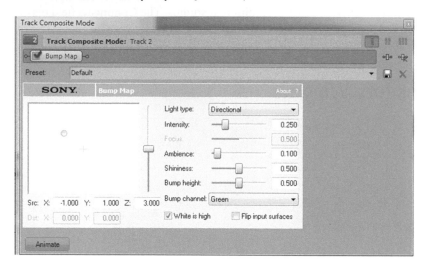

Figure 5.55

4. If the **Bump Map** dialog box is covering the Preview window, click and hold at the top of the dialog box and drag it to the side so that both the dialog box and the **Preview** window are visible. Notice that the lighting of the eyes has changed in the Preview window.

5. In the **Bump Map** dialog box, move the **Intensity** slider from the left to the right. Notice how the lighting changes and the Generated Media seem to almost disappear.

6. Now adjust the **Ambience** slider back and forth; experiment a bit. Note that the **Focus** slider is grayed out; this is because the default lighting in the Bump Map is directional.

7. In the **Light Type** drop-down menu, change the light type from Directional to **Spotlight**. Notice the change in the **Preview** window, and now the **Focus** value may be changed as well.

8. Finally, note the small triangle in the left of the **Bump Map** dialog box, next to the word **Location**. Click this triangle and a pair of values will open. Click the triangle next to **Source**. In the **Source** window, move the **Source** target point from right to left and see how it affects the frame in the **Preview** window.

9. Save this file as **Moving Eyes-Bumped**. We'll be reopening this file later in the book.

🖊 *Tip*

Double-clicking an Event creates a selection, indicated by a gray bar at the top of the timeline. Pressing the **Q** key enables a loop. Playing a loop allows the Event to be edited while the loop is playing, providing instant feedback to the user. No rendering is required. Looping while editing is a super-fast way to fine-tune composites, FX, transitions—virtually anything!

The Plug-in Manager

The Plug-in Manager (not available in Vegas Movie Studio) is a legacy docking window that helps users manage plug-ins. Users of older versions of Vegas may appreciate this feature, yet the newer Docking windows for transitions, FX, and compositors make this window somewhat superfluous (audio editors will still appreciate the plug-in manager). The new folder structure and search window in the Transitions, FX, and Compositor windows effectively replace the Plug-in Manager for speed and access to favorite video plug-in tools.

Video Scopes

Correcting colors, matching colors, and meeting broadcast standards are more easily accomplished using Video Scopes (not available in Vegas Movie Studio). Histograms, waveform monitors, Vectorscope, and RGB Parade monitors are available in Vegas as a Docking window. Vegas allows for live monitoring or static monitoring on a single frame. See the section on "Color Correction" for more information on Video Scopes and how to use them.

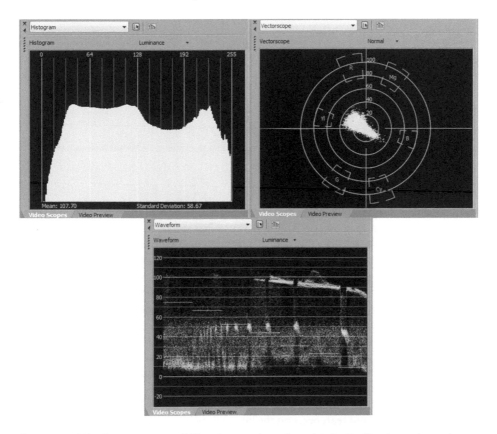

Figure 5.56   Video Scopes are very useful for color correction and ensuring that legal broadcast color requirements are being met.

Surround Panner

Many of today's mixes are in 5.1 Surround Sound. Vegas is not only up to the task; it has been an industry-standard application for mixing Surround for over a decade. The Surround Panner window will not display any information unless a 5.1 project has been created in the Project Properties Audio tab.
See the audio chapter for more information on Surround Sound and the Surround Panner.

Media Manager

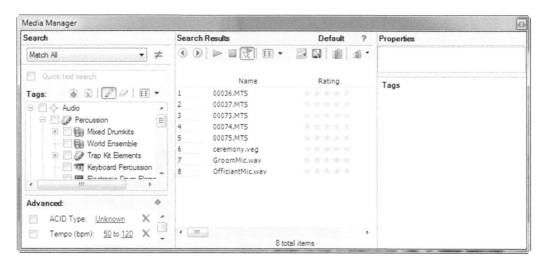

Figure 5.57

The Sony Media Manager (not available in Vegas Movie Studio) is a deep, tremendously powerful tool. It is a separate application that functions within Vegas Pro software. For working with file-based workflows, the Media Manager is a must-have, although using the application/tool requires some discipline. Media will never again be lost and may be searched via commonly defined and user-defined parameters. If the Media Manager has not been installed, the system will display the message "Media Manager Not Installed" if a user attempts to open it in a dock. Visit www.sonycreativesoftware.com to download the 69 MB Media Manager. Microsoft C++ and Microsoft SQL might need to be installed before the Media Manager can be configured.

This application is a separate install that many Vegas users unfortunately miss. They have no idea what they're missing, since this application is very useful. Other NLE systems charge thousands of dollars for this functionality. Early versions of the Media Manager were not stable; since the days of Vegas Pro 8, the Media Manager has been very stable and optimized to operate more smoothly within the Windows environment. Clips and media can be tagged (think "Like" in Facebook terms) and rated, keywords added for rapid searches, and the libraries may be transferred with hard drives, so no matter where the work is being done, it is quite easy to find files in a project. It is a powerful media database tool. For long-form editors, the Media Manager is a must-use. See the chapter on the Media Manager for in-depth information on installing and using this great tool.

XDCAM Explorer

XDCAM is a broadcast-standard camera format. These cameras use Professional Optical Discs for media storage, and as a file-based format in professional broadcast and production environments, these cameras use a unique format for file access. The format also provides for proxy-based editing of HD content so that stories can be cut on low-resolution files and replaced with high-resolution files transferred over hard line, satellite, or physical transport. The XDCAM Explorer should not be confused with EX-series camcorders; the formats are similar, yet the file structure is very different. If the XDCAM Explorer is being used with FAM modes of XDCAM products, there are additional drivers to be installed that are available at www.sony.com/xdcam. These drivers are also included with the cameras at purchase.

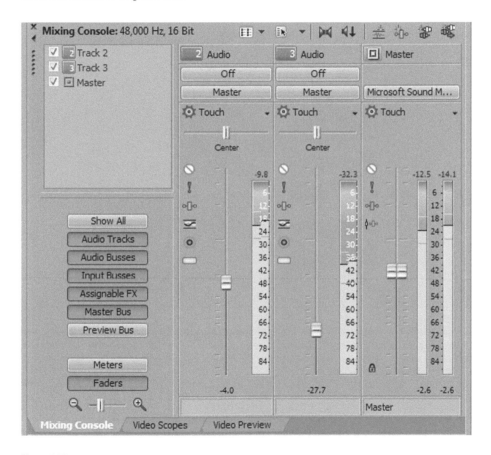

Figure 5.58

Mixing Console

Vegas began life as an audio application and digital audio workstation (DAW), and of course mixing audio is a primary function of a DAW application. The mixing console has evolved several times in the Vegas world; the latest version of Vegas brings forward a very powerful mixing console that can create automated mixes on its own or be controlled by outside hardware, such as the Frontier Tranzport or Mackie Control surfaces.

The mixer is where all FX, buses, rerouting audio, Surround Sound channels, master output controls, monitoring for a recording studio, envelopes, downmixes, and levels are controlled. Mixes may be manually configured in real time or fully automated and stored. Projects containing numerous channels and audio Events will benefit from docking the mixer across the entire Docking window area or stripped out to a secondary monitor.

See the audio chapter for more information on using the mixer and other audio features in the Vegas application.

Device Explorer

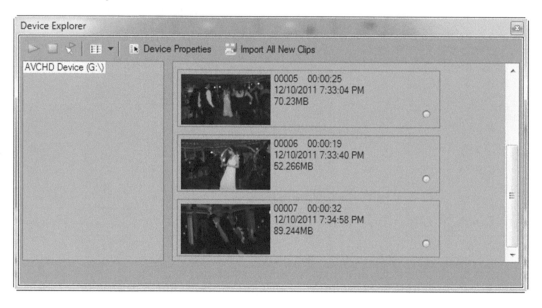

Figure 5.59   The Device Explorer is designed to make ingest from file-based camcorders faster and more efficient, allowing users to preview and mark files prior to import. Files may be simply imported, or they can be opened in the Trimmer and dropped on the timeline, no transfer or import required. This is a feature somewhat unique to Vegas; files do not need to be transferred prior to editing.

Devices not supported by the Device Explorer may still be seen in the Vegas Explorer window, and files may be edited directly from the device. For example, the Sony Bloggie camcorder is not supported by the Device Explorer. However, the Bloggie will show in the Vegas Explorer, and files may be transferred or edited directly from the Vegas Explorer.

File-based workflows are the future; tape is effectively dead (it just doesn't know it yet). Previewing media before import not only speeds the transfer process; it allows the beginning of logging and

Figure 5.60   Third-party plug-ins may also show up as Docking windows, seen in the Extensions menu of the Docking Window options.

file management. Device Explorer currently supports AVCHD, XDCAM EX, NXCAM, HVR-MRC1, DR60 units, RED ONE, and EPIC devices. Other devices will be made available in future updates.

Several third parties have made their products as Docking windows. Having these applications as windows allows fast access to the applications and functions.

⏱ *Speed Tutorial*
Saving Window Layouts in Vegas

Vegas allows for new layouts to be created and preserved, permitting users to create their own layouts for single-, dual-, or even triple-head monitor configurations. Up to 10 different templates may be restored and saved in Vegas for each editor's profile, or perhaps for each task. Each time Vegas opens, the saved layout will open as it was saved. Moreover, a template for each type of project may be created and opened, saving the user time. If various users are accessing Vegas on the same computer, each user is capable of having his or her own personal layout template. To save a layout, create the layout appearance and save the template via **Ctrl + Alt + D** and then number keystrokes. This even allows for templates to be shifted during the editing process.

To save a workspace template in Vegas:

1. Lay out the workspace the way you'd like to have it look and feel.

2. Press and hold **Ctrl + Alt + D**, and then press a number key that you'd like to assign the layout to.

3. Repeat up to 10 times, saving up to 10 layout templates.

4. Recall layout templates by pressing **Alt + D +** [*number assigned to desired template*].

With multiple windows floating at various locations on the screen, setting up a template is always useful if Vegas should open with the same views each time. Consider having a template layout for times when audio editing instead of video editing is the focus or for times when deep composites and track views require more screen space, or even when using a template during rough cutting and another template for finishing work. Out of the box, Vegas includes three layouts: the default layout as well as layouts designed for audio mixing and video color correction. These specialized layouts bring up windows specific to their tasks and are a great starting point for creating your own custom layouts. You can switch to these layouts at any time by pressing **Alt + D + D** for default, **Alt + D + A** for audio mixing, and **Alt + D + C** for the color correction layout.

Editing Techniques

In this chapter we're going to look at some editing tools and techniques to make the process of editing as efficient as it can be.

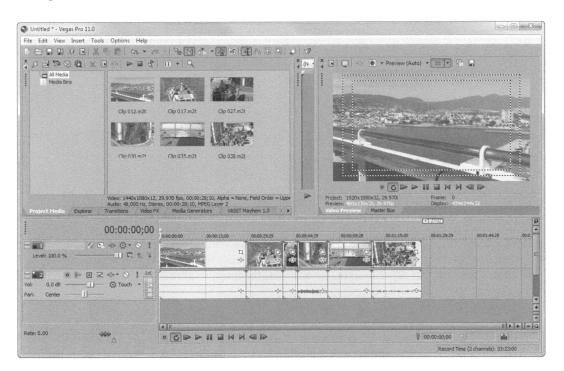

Figure 6.1   Editing with precision is very important, but precision does not have to be a slow process. Vegas has many power tools for editors that speed the editing process without compromising precision.

In Section One we looked at how to simply bring Events and clips to the timeline. Now we'll look at some different methods of editing them.

Editing Events

Put a video Event or clip on the timeline. Place the cursor next to the Event and the cursor will change to an arrow and box, as pictured here.

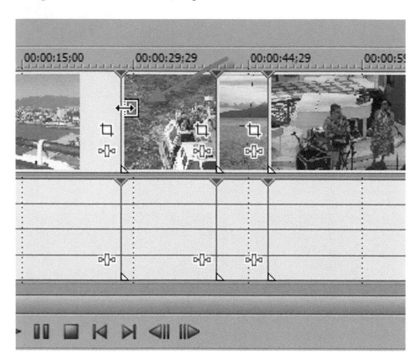

Figure 6.2   Notice the double-headed arrow pointing toward a box? The box indicates which edge is being trimmed.

Clicking and dragging on the edge of an Event or clip allows the Event to be trimmed. If you select the right edge of an Event and the Event is already at its out/end point, Vegas will treat the Event in one of two ways: it will either loop the Event (from the beginning) or lock the Event, allowing the last frame of the Event to be dragged out.

 Tip_____

Locking Events and dragging out end frames is a useful way to create a longer fade-out on a frame. Of course, this will depend on the composition of the frame. Editors who become camera operators quickly learn to hold the camera steady at the end of a scene.

Access locking and looping by right-clicking any Event, choose Switches, and choose Lock or Loop from the submenu. Looping is enabled by default.

If the right side of a file is grabbed and dragged to the left, it will trim; if dragged to the right, it will either loop or lock. If the left edge is grabbed and dragged to the right, the Event will be trimmed. If the Event is dragged to the left on the left edge, the Event will loop from the end of the video. If Lock has been enabled, the left edge will not move.

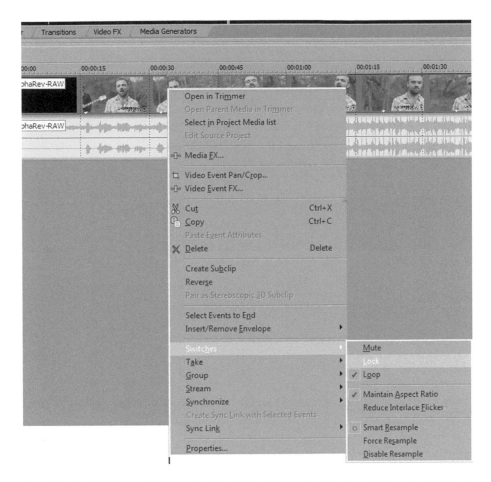

Figure 6.3   Locked Events will repeatedly display the last frame of an Event, much like a still-photo image.

The mouse method of edge trimming may be the most common mode of editing, but it is by far not the only way to edit Events on the timeline.

Rolling edits are performed using shortcut keys. A *rolling edit* is when you move an edit point without changing the length of the timeline. The first (outgoing) Event becomes shorter as the second (incoming) Event is made longer by the same amount, or vice versa. The overall length of the project is not altered.

Most applications require dropping a standard edit tool to get to a rolling edit tool. Vegas does not. In Vegas, simply hold the **Ctrl** and **Alt** keys at the same time, with the cursor positioned at a transition or cut point. When the **Ctrl+Alt** keys are held at the same time, the cursor becomes a solid box with a double-sided arrow inside and the Vegas Preview window will become a split screen. The left side of the Preview window shows the out point of the outgoing Event and the in point of the incoming Event. Moving the cursor back and forth will "roll" the edit points.

Figure 6.4   Rolling edits change the in/out points of two contiguous Events without changing the combined length of the two Events.

Slip/sliding trim edits are somewhat similar; they allow in/out points of an Event to be slipped forward and backward. These are quite useful for setting new in/out points without altering the duration of an Event. Holding down the **Alt** key will toggle the **Slip Edit** trim tool when an Event is selected. The cursor becomes a film frame (sprockets on the side) with the Double Arrow inside. The Vegas preview will split into two halves; the left half shows the new in point, the right half shows the new out point.

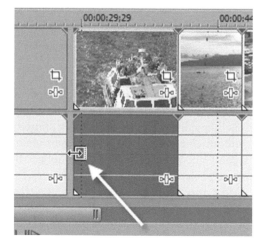

Figure 6.5   Holding the **Alt** key while hovering over a selected Event will enable the Slip/Slide edit tool.

Splitting/Cutting/Copying/Pasting

Events may be split on the timeline using the **S** (Split) key. This is similar to using a razor tool in other applications, except Vegas does not require refocusing on the timeline or editing tool.

Cutting Events from the timeline may be accomplished via the **Delete** key or **Ctrl + X**. Both are standard Windows function keys. Anything cut from the timeline lands on the Windows Clipboard and therefore may be pasted via **Ctrl + V** (standard Windows convention). Events may be grouped (G key) and copy/pasted as groups. The U key ungroups; click on one or more Events in a group and press U to ungroup that Event (audio, video, or both) from the group.

Copying in Vegas is the same as copying in any other Windows application. **Ctrl + C** will copy any selected Events. What makes copying somewhat different in Vegas is that an Event with any FX, Pan/Crop, or reverse applied may be copied and the properties pasted to other Events. For example, say that an Event has color correction applied to it, and the color correction needs to be applied to other Events. Perhaps this same Event has some cropping applied to remove edge distortion from a lens. Copy the Event (**Ctrl + C**) and select all other Events that should receive this treatment. Right-click one of the selected Events and choose **Paste Event Attributes**. This will paste the attributes of the originally selected Event or clip to all selected Events and clips in one paste, saving editing time.

Ten-Key Editing

Trimming may be accomplished via a 10-key pad (sometimes referred to as a *micro keyboard*). This method is a holdover from the early days of editing, long before the invention of the mouse. But 10-key editing is not intuitive until the method is learned, and then it quickly becomes second nature. Because it involves less hand movement, it is by far faster than using a mouse for basic edits.

The computer must have a 10-key device on the keyboard. Laptops that have 10-key settings via a numpad feature can work, but it's very clumsy and gets in the way of other editing shortcuts and functions.

The 10 keys enable editors to jump around the timeline from track to track, Event to Event, to trim edges, shift time, preview cuts, insert transitions, and more. If you're a serious editor, someone doing same-day edits (SDEs), then this workflow should be very appealing.

First, be sure **Event Edge Trimming** is enabled (**Ctrl + Shift + O** or **View | Video Event Edge Edit Frames**). Enter Edge trimming mode by pressing the 7 or] key.

Use the **Up/Down Arrow** keys on the keypad or keyboard to shuffle through selected tracks. Press the **7** or **9** key to shuttle between in/out points of Events. Keys **1** and **4** will trim an edge to the right, keys **3** and **6** will trim Event edges to the left. The 1/3 key will trim Events by one frame to the left or right. The 4/6 keys will trim by one pixel to the left or right. Zooming into the timeline will allow for greater trim values using the 4/6 keys.

Press the **0** key to preview an edge trim edit. The 0 key will play X seconds before and after the cursor/playhead position. The amount of time previewed is determined by settings in the **Options | Preferences | Editing | Cursor Preview Duration**. The default preview is two seconds (one second before, one second after playhead position). I feel this generally isn't enough. My preview selection is four seconds (two prior/post playhead position).

 Tip _____

If editing on a laptop, consider purchasing a USB Numeric Keypad for faster, more productive editing sessions.

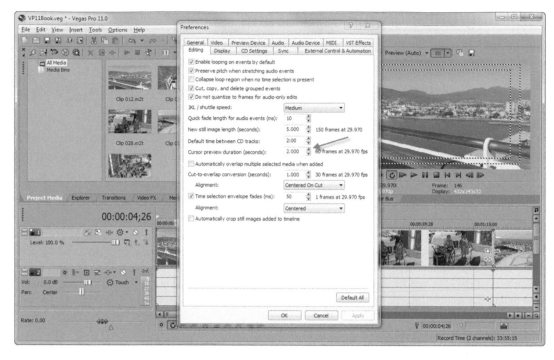

Figure 6.6

Figure 6.7 Using the **0** key as
a selection play
back will play the
timeline before
and after the
cursor/playhead
position.

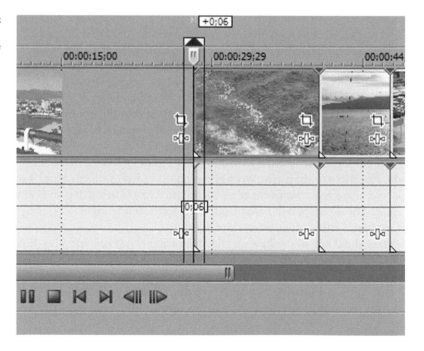

Cross-fades may be inserted at an edit point by pressing the **/** key on the 10-key (this doesn't work with the keyboard **/** key, typically found with the question mark (**?**) character). A linear wipe may be inserted by pressing the **–** (minus) key, and a dissolve by pressing the ***** key. All of these are numpad/10-key shortcuts, not standard keyboard shortcuts. Pressing the **–** or ***** key on the numpad will open the **Wipe** and **Dissolve** dialog windows. No dialog window will open for the cross-fade.

Cross-fade length is determined in the **Preferences | Editing | Crossfade length** dialog box. The default length is one second; my personal preference is seven frames/.25 sec to match standard broadcast lengths for cross-fades.

Exit Edge trimming mode by pressing the 5 key. Outside of Edge trimming mode, selected Events may be moved forward and backward on the timeline. Large moves are performed using the 4/6 keys; fine-tuning moves are made with the 1/3 keys.

Entire rough cuts may be assembled without touching the mouse, and once you're even marginally fluent in this technique, editing is fast and accurate.

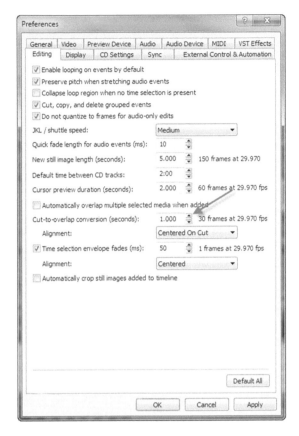

Figure 6.8 The default preference length for cross-fades is a bit too long for most types of editing. Change the value in Vegas Preferences.

 Tip_____
Using a hybrid of mouse and keyboard editing is very efficient and works well in today's mouse-centric workflows.

Other Timeline Navigation Tools

Holding the **Ctrl** key while pressing the **Left/Right Arrow** keys on the keyboard will jump the playhead to/from the start of the timeline to each marker or region point on the timeline and to the end of the project. Holding **Shift** while keying the **Right/Left Arrow** keys will create a selection on the timeline, just as though click/drag were being used in an empty track area. This method works very well for creating time-precise selections for selecting areas in Events, creating selections for titles or generated media, or for creating region points. This technique functions in both the Trimmer and the Vegas Timeline.

Holding **Ctrl + Shift** while keying the **Arrow** keys will jump the playhead from Event to Event, much like the 7/9 keys do in a 10-key edit workflow.

Figure 6.9   The Track Indicator will blink to call attention to which track is active. Tracks may be named by double-clicking in the scribble strip.

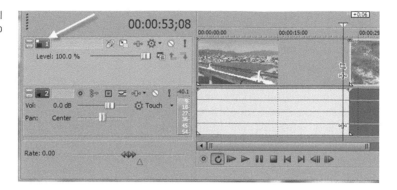

Use the **Tab** key to jump from timeline to Track focus. This enables users to switch from focus on the timeline to focus on the track header so that you can switch tracks quickly using the keyboard. Not only will the track header highlight, the track header indicator will blink to show it's the active track. The track may be named by double-clicking in the scribble strip (or pressing **F2** with a track selected). Audio track names will be duplicated in the Mixer. For audio-intensive projects, it's a good idea to name the track (and buses) so that the track is readily identifiable in the mixer when the final mix is created. Track headers and track features are discussed in more depth later in this book.

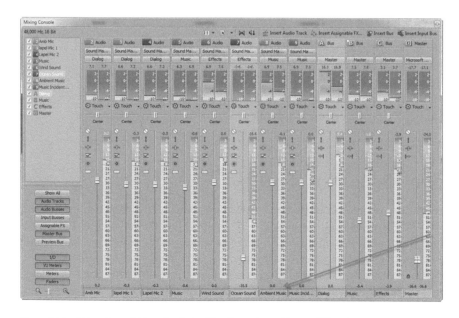

Figure 6.10   Using the scribble strips helps identify tracks and buses. This will also help with routing and separation when it comes time to output stems for DME. (Buses are not available in Vegas Movie Studio.)

Multipoint Split

Vegas allows for two-point splitting and deleting. This feature is exceptionally useful when culling content from a long Event. Create a selection on the timeline, marking the in point and out point of the area of the Event to be kept. Press the **S** key, and two splits will appear in the Event. The right side of the selected area will be highlighted so that it may be deleted with the **Delete** key or the **Ctrl + X** command. However, if media is being culled from a longer Event, it's likely not desirable to delete all remaining media until all of the Event has been previewed.

Another method of cutting content from longer files is to make the same selection of the in/out points of an Event and cut everything outside the selection. **Ctrl + T** will delete all media outside the selected area.

Ripple Editing

Ripple editing enables users to cut Events and clips from the timeline without leaving holes behind. This is a very useful function, but in the hands of new users or those unfamiliar with rippling, it can also create headaches.

Rippling may be automatic or manual and may be set to affect related Events while leaving markers and regions intact, related Events and moving markers and regions, or shifting an entire project/all tracks while moving markers/regions (everything on the timeline moves).

Auto-rippling is the fastest method of rippling, yet it might not be the most efficient method and is potentially dangerous. Auto-rippling is enabled via the shortcut **Ctrl + L** or the **Toolbar** button for **Auto-ripple**.

Figure 6.11   Auto-rippling has three options: Affected Tracks/Affected Tracks, Markers, Regions, and All Tracks, Markers, Regions.

Enabling auto-rippling means exactly what its name implies: Vegas will ripple Events on the timeline based on deleted or inserted media.

It is possible that ripples can occur far down a timeline without the user being aware of whether the timeline stretches beyond the length of the screen. Also, auto-ripple only permits one mode at any given moment. For this reason, I'm an advocate of manual-ripple edits for projects of any complexity. Auto-ripple modes are terrific for whittling down a two-track timeline or creating a rough cut, yet without the user having some practice and solid understanding, an auto-ripple may create

Figure 6.12   The top image (1) shows the original edit and placement of Events. The second Event in this timeline is what we want to delete; the Event to the far right should move to the left and take its place. The middle image (2) shows how a ripple may incorrectly affect an edit. Notice that all Events have moved to the left; even the closing region marker has moved. The bottom image (3) demonstrates correctly rippled Events.

problems in the long-form edit that the editor is not aware of until later down the line, especially where locked or grouped Events are present.

Post-edit ripples are another option and best used for long-form editing (in my opinion) because they allow for three choices at the point of edit, compared to an auto-ripple using a default setting. Post edit ripples involve an additional keystroke, but they also allow for a pause to consider which type of ripple should be implemented.

Post-edit ripples are accomplished via either the **Edit | Post Edit Ripple** option or via the more efficient shortcut keys of:

- **F**=Affected Tracks

- **Ctrl+F**=Affected Tracks, Bus Tracks, Markers, Regions

- **Ctrl+Shift+F**=All Tracks, Bus Tracks, Markers, Regions

Here's how it works: make an edit, either lengthening or shortening an Event on the timeline. Use the **F** key and watch related Events shift down the timeline. Key **Ctrl+Z** to Undo the action, and key Ctrl+F to see Events with markers/regions moving. Key **Ctrl+Z** to undo the action, key **Ctrl+Shift+F** to move everything on the timeline relevant to the modified Event (even across tracks).

Markers/Regions/Command Markers

A lot has already been said about the value of markers and regions; here we'll look at how to manage them. Markers and regions are different from each other; markers define a specific point in time, whereas regions define two specific points in time, often viewed as in/out points. Regions may be used to specify areas to be rendered (in/out points) or marking areas for specific editing focus. Both markers and regions may be named and can be used as notation tools for editors.

Markers are inserted via the **M** key. Regions are inserted by selecting a region and pressing the **R** key. Command markers are inserted by pressing the **C** key. Markers and command markers may be inserted on the fly, while the playhead is playing. Regions require stopping playback. Creating a region on the fly will stop playback and cause playback to focus on the selected area.

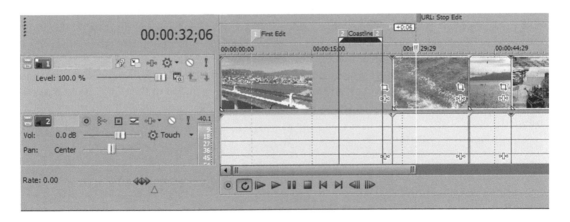

Figure 6.13 Markers are displayed in orange, regions are green, and command markers are blue.

Tip_____

Markers are very useful during audio playback to mark beats in music, key points where transitions should occur, or any other audio-based edit. These may be used with the Trimmer to insert on-beat cuts or accessed from third-party applications such as Ultimate S Pro or Production Assistant from VASST.com.

When a project is complete on the timeline, it's a personal habit to mark out the in/out points of the entire project and use the **R** key to insert a region. This region is then named "Render Region" so that if the region must be rendered for multiple uses, the same in/out points are defined for each render. If the Vegas or VASST Batch Render tool is to be used, the region is required so that the applications know where to begin and end the render process.

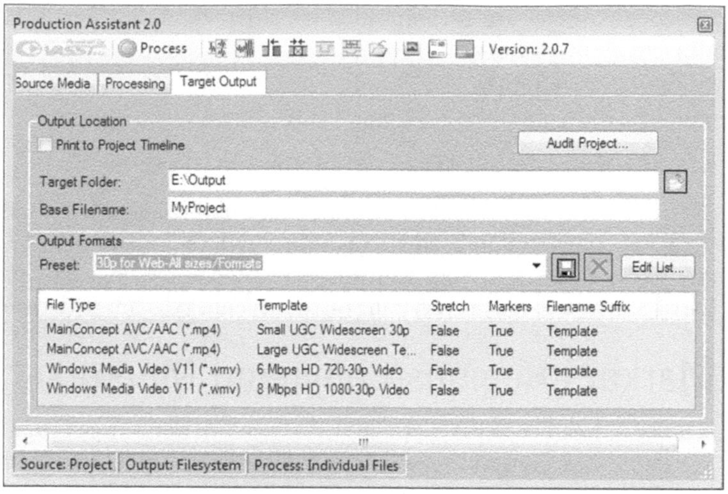

Once markers or regions have been inserted, there are two points in time where they can be named. As a marker is inserted, a dialog box next to the Marker flag opens and text may be entered. If no text is entered, a number will be assigned to the marker. Markers will vertically draw across all tracks unless **Always Draw Markers** has been disabled in the Vegas **Preferences | General** tab. If this function is disabled, markers will only draw when **Snapping** is enabled (use **F8** to enable/disable; use **Shift** to temporarily override).

Markers may be managed in groups by pressing the **Marker** tool in the upper right of the timeline. Click a marker, hold **Shift,** and click on the last marker to be included in the range. Now markers may be moved as a group within the Marker bar or deleted. Markers will highlight when they're selected.

Figure 6.14   Sony Production Assistant has a batch-render module that will output multiple file types from a single or multiple file source. This is useful in today's environments where video goes to broadcast, the Web, mobile devices, and DVDs from a single source, yet all delivery mechanisms require different codecs, resolutions, and bitrates.

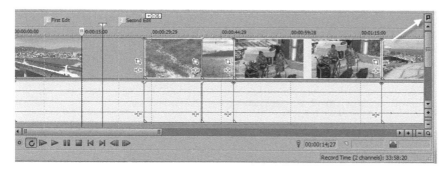

Figure 6.15   The **Marker** tool allows multiple markers to be selected in a range or selection, moved with separation intact, or deleted.

Regions contain both the in and out points of a selection. Regions may overlap, allowing for cross-regions when creating render points or selective areas. Double-clicking a region's in or out point will select the entire region. If there are markers or other regions between region in/out points, the region in/out point must be clicked or Vegas will only select the time between the marker and the region in/out marker. Regions are great for naming scenes or, if nested veg files are used, regions are terrific for marking where each veg lies within a master timeline.

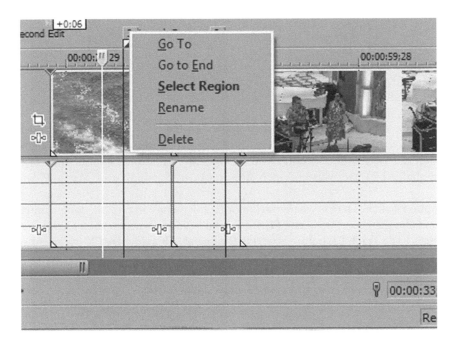

Figure 6.16   Similar to markers, regions may be named. Right-click the in point of a region and choose **Rename** from the submenu.

Markers and regions may be deleted by selecting a range in the **Marker** toolbar, right-clicking, and choosing **Markers/Regions** and **Delete All** (or **Delete All in Selection**).

Track Headers

Track headers are where all track controls are found. Track headers may be expanded as long or as wide as a user would like or completely hidden if a more broad view of the timeline is preferred.

Track headers are the area on the left side of the application. There are track headers for video and audio; these are preassigned a size, setting, and FX. Track defaults may be modified to user preferences.

Video Track Headers

By default, every video track is pre-sized. This size may be changed by grabbing the bar at the bottom of the track header and dragging upward or downward. While you're becoming familiar with the video track header, it may be beneficial to drag the header downward so it becomes taller.

Figure 6.17

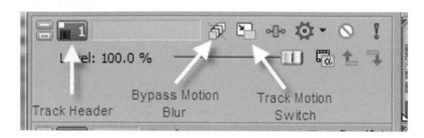

On the left side of the header, the small button with the video frame inside indicates a video header. If the track is active, the small white box at the top of the button will blink and light up. Next to this button is a bypass motion-blur switch. This is an important switch in the Event that motion blur is enabled in the Master Video Bus track (not available in Vegas Movie Studio).

Next is the track motion switch. Here is where track motion for picture in picture, compositing, image resizing, and matching aspect ratio occur. (There are multiple methods for matching aspect ratio; this is one of them.) The Track FX button is next in the lineup. This is where FX for an entire track may be added, controlled, edited, or removed.

Track Automation is represented with the small "cog/gears" wheel seen in the track header (not available in Vegas Movie Studio). Fade to color (set in **Preferences | Video**), mute, or track level (opacity) may be automated and envelopes drawn on the fly or during playback using either a mouse or hardware device.

⏱ *Speed Tutorial*

1. To use the Automation, first put the track in **Automation Write/Touch** mode by clicking the "cog/gears" icon. Now right-click the track header and choose **Insert Envelope/Composite Level** from the submenu.

2. Rewind the playhead to the beginning of the project/timeline using either the **Transport** rewind button or pressing **W** to rewind. Hover the cursor over the **Level** slider, and press the **Spacebar** to begin playback.

3. While the project is playing back, move the **Level** slider back and forth; watch the automation nodes write as the timeline plays back.

4. While Vegas is recording these automated movements, dozens of small nodes and envelopes will be written. When playback stops, Vegas will interpret these nodes and thin them out so that the load on the CPU is minimal. Node points may be adjusted by hand or rerecorded.

5. When the track mix is complete, place the track in **Automation Read** mode and Vegas will continue to read the automation during subsequent playbacks.

Track automation may be disabled at any time by pressing the **Automation** button on the track header.

Track automation may also be written by hand via the mouse or external hardware device such as the Mackie Control. To write the automation by hand, hold the **Shift** key while the mouse hovers over the video envelope inserted via the right-click/submenu. Start playback and the cursor will transform into a pencil, allowing the track automation to be written.

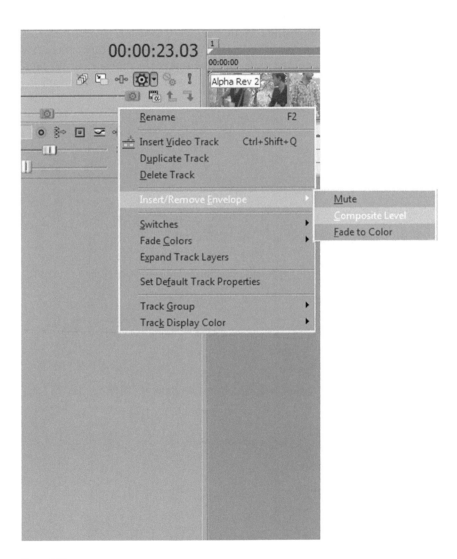

Figure 6.18

The **Mute** button next to the Automation button is another automatable feature, or it may be used in static mode. This button allows a video track to be muted or hidden during playback. The **Exclamation point** next to the mute button allows a track to be solo'd (all other tracks hidden, only the track selected will be visible). Multiple selected tracks may be muted by keying **Z** and solo'd by keying **X**. Automation will continue to run (invisibly) on a muted or solo'd track.

If automation is disabled, the track header will show only the **Level** slider. This controls overall track opacity. If automation is enabled, the **Fade to color** slider is visible; this allows an envelope to fade a track to the default colors of black/white (or whatever has been set in Preferences).

Next to the track level control is the **Compositing Mode** button. This is a powerful feature; it enables editors to do basic composites directly on the Vegas Timeline. Compositing is the art of taking two or more layers of imagery and mixing them into one image. Composites or "comps" may be as simple as a title or dozens of layers of complexity to create deep cinematic effects.

Figure 6.19

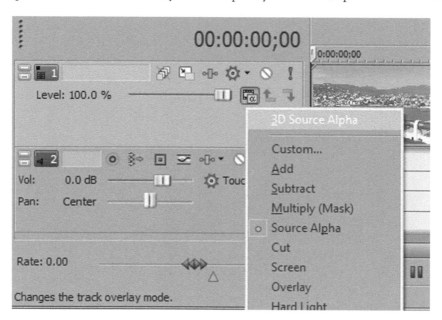

Compositing modes include:

- 3D Source Alpha (not available in Vegas Movie Studio)

- Custom (not available in Vegas Movie Studio)

- Add (not available in Vegas Movie Studio)

- Subtract (not available in Vegas Movie Studio)

- Multiply/Mask

- Source Alpha (default)

- Cut (not available in Vegas Movie Studio)

- Screen (not available in Vegas Movie Studio)

- Overlay (not available in Vegas Movie Studio)
- Hard Light (not available in Vegas Movie Studio)
- Dodge (not available in Vegas Movie Studio)
- Burn (not available in Vegas Movie Studio)
- Darken (not available in Vegas Movie Studio)
- Lighten (not available in Vegas Movie Studio)
- Difference (not available in Vegas Movie Studio)
- Difference Squared (not available in Vegas Movie Studio)

Along with the Compositing modes, the two buttons found to their right are **Parent/Child** buttons. Parent/Child modes enable tracks to control or be controlled by other tracks above or below them. More on Compositing modes and how to use them, as well as Parent/Child functions, may be found in the chapter on compositing.

Right-clicking a video track opens a submenu with several options.

Figure 6.20　Duplicating tracks, inserting new tracks, and deleting tracks are all common actions using right-click. As we learned in the Speed Tutorial, automation envelopes may be inserted. Envelopes do not require automation; envelopes may be inserted and manually controlled via inserting keyframe nodes.

Expand Track Layers is an unusual feature, unique to Vegas. When two Events on the timeline are crossfaded, Vegas displays one track, yet in reality, the two Events are two tracks collapsed. Expanding the timeline allows the two tracks to be separated. This is not beneficial for anything except seeing transitional layers between A/B rolls on a single track. No editing is possible in the A/B rolls that offers any superior method to working with collapsed tracks.

Default track properties may be set by first setting up a track so that it meets user preferences. This includes track height, composite modes, automation modes, and user-preferred FX inserted to the track. Once these values and parameters are set, right-click and choose **Set Default Track Properties**. All new video tracks will appear and contain these properties. For example, if all acquired footage is from low-grade AVCHD camcorders, a color-correction FX might be good to insert as a default with presets for gamma control.

In the lower-left corner of the video track is a small diamond icon. This diamond expands and collapses keyframes associated at the track level. If FX have been inserted to the track, then keyframes related to inserted FX are visible and may be modified at the track level. Some users demand this level of view; others prefer the clean, sleek look of Vegas.

Keyframes are discussed in great detail in the keyframes chapter.

Figure 6.21   Keyframes are kept hidden until a user prefers to see them. This enables the timeline to appear very clean without restricting user control. With multiple plug-ins inserted at the track level, this display may appear to become complex.

Audio Tracks

Audio tracks are identical to video tracks in the left screen corner: You'll see a track height button, an active track indicator, and scribble strip. Next to the scribble strip is the **Record Enable** button. This arms an audio track for recording a new file. When the **Record** button is enabled, Vegas will open a dialog box asking for the location to which the new file should be recorded. The Windows Documents folder is the default; users should create a new folder where project-specific folders are the destination.

The **Phase Invert** button allows users to invert the phase of audio. This feature may be used to create a stereo "widening" in the audio mix, monitor small changes between two audio tracks, or simply repair a misphased recording.

Next in line is the **Track FX** button. By default, every track has a Noise Gate, Equalizer, and Compressor inserted into the signal chain. Some FX may be automated, and the three default FX inserted are all automation-capable. The small **Down Arrow** next to the FX button enables you to choose which FX functions should be automated.

The **Mute** and **Solo** switches next to the FX button are identical to video tracks; if the track is selected, keying **Z** for mute and **X** for solo will mute or solo tracks.

Level sliders are for adjusting audio levels much in the same way as opacity of a video track is adjusted, and panning the timeline enables audio to be panned right/left in a mix. Both levels and panning may be automated. Muting envelopes may also be applied to entire tracks.

Right-clicking an audio track header offers many submenu choices, which are discussed in depth in the audio chapter.

Hiding/Revealing Track Headers

On the right side of the Track header is a vertical bar that separates the headers from the Vegas Timeline. Double-clicking this vertical bar will hide the header windows, providing for more space on the timeline. This is a very useful option when the project is locked and being mixed or color corrected for final output. Double-clicking the same vertical bar will restore the header window to view.

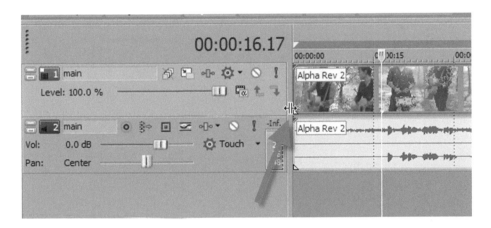

Figure 6.22   Double-click this bar to hide or reveal the Track header window.

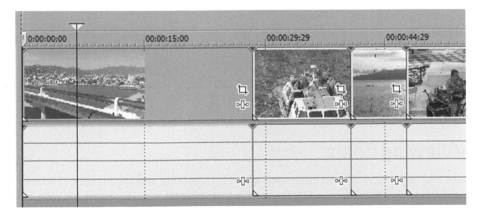

Figure 6.23   Hiding the header bar provides more timeline viewing area. Once a project is locked and ready for mixing audio or color correction, hiding the track header may provide a more simple view.

My personal preference is to hide the header bar when mixing audio; having two VU meters going at the same time (one in the mixer, one at the track) might look cool, but it's distracting and potentially confusing.

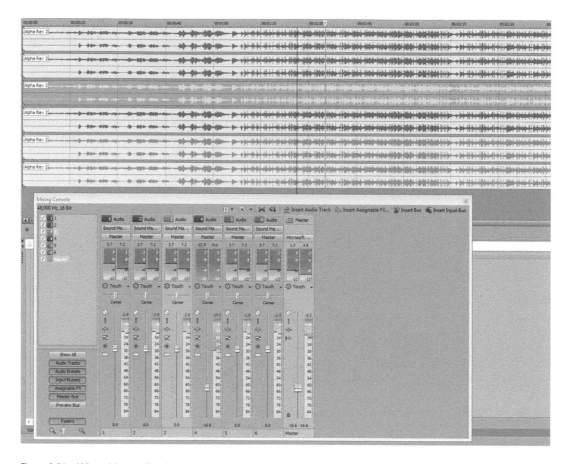

Figure 6.24   When doing audio mixes, sometimes it's easier if the mixer is at the bottom of the screen, similar to the way a traditional mixer might be placed.

 Tip_____

You can choose whether the docking windows are at the top or the bottom of the screen in the **Options | Preferences | Display** section.

Zooming/Viewing Tools

Previously mentioned in Chapter 1, the editing tools allow for zooming into the timeline. There are other methods for zooming. Clicking the **Up/Down Arrows** on a keyboard is the most common method (while the Event is selected). However, clicking the horizontal +/- keys in the lower-right corner of the application will zoom or reduce the timeline centered around the playhead/cursor. Clicking the vertical +/– keys will horizontally expand or reduce tracks.

At the bottom and right side of the timeline are zoom/view bars. Double-clicking these bars will zoom the timeline so that an entire project may be viewed.

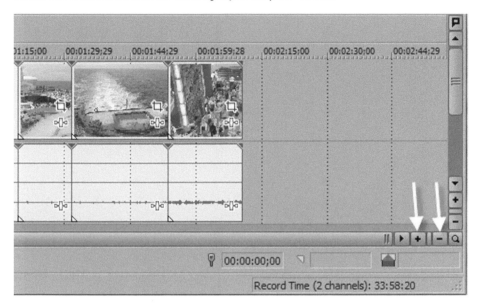

Figure 6.25   Double-clicking either of these bars will zoom the timeline so that an entire project may be viewed within the timeline window. Grabbing either edge and dragging will zoom to user-defined view/zoom depth.

Alternate methods of zooming on the timeline include pressing the **D** key until the Magnifying glass icon replaces the standard editing icon. Draw a rectangle around the area to be zoomed and the magnifying glass will zoom in to the area of focus. Use the minus (–) key to zoom out.

The tilde key (~) will minimize all tracks, and keying ~ again will restore the tracks to their last height.

While looking at the lower-right corner, take note of the three time views near the +/– buttons. These windows display information about the position of the playhead and/or any selected area.

The window on the far left displays an in point (where a selection starts), the middle window displays the out point (end of any selection), and the window on the far right displays the total length of a selection. Double-clicking in any of the windows allows for manual time input so that specific in/out points may be navigated, and the selection window allows for very specific selection lengths to be created.

Figure 6.26

Multicam Functions in Vegas Pro
Not Available in Vegas Movie Studio

Shooting with multiple cameras is more common now than ever before due to the low cost of cameras and acquisition sources. Vegas Pro allows for a couple of different ways to edit multicam, either through third-party plug-in tools such as Ultimate S, infinitiCam, or DuoCam (free) or via the installed multicamera functions. This chapter discusses only the functions built into Vegas Pro.

Open the AlphaRev_MultiCam.vf project. (This project is in .vf format so that Vegas Movie Studio users can play along at the end of the tutorial.) Even though Vegas Movie Studio doesn't offer multicam tools, there are ways to get around the feature and do multicamera work in Vegas Movie Studio.

Figure 7.1   These tools are not available in Vegas Movie Studio. However, the end of this section will show a way to mark and edit for multicamera functionality in Vegas Movie Studio.

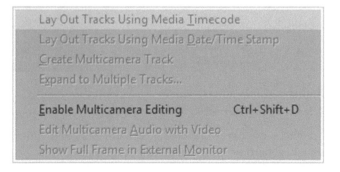

In the AlphaRev_MultiCam.vf project, find three video tracks (cameras 1-3) and four audio tracks (cameras 1-3, plus Master Audio track). For purposes of expediency, I've already aligned audio/video for these three tracks and master audio; cameras and master audio MUST be sync'd prior to collapsing tracks for multicamera editing.

Do not color correct or add any FX to a camera video track. When using the Multicamera editing tools, all FX, blurs, and other track processes are disabled to preserve frame rate. The best place to color correct for multiple cameras is in the Project Media windows, although these, too, are disabled during multicamera editing processes. Color matching may be done pre- or post-multicamera editing processes.

Enable Multicamera Editing via the keyboard shortcut **Ctrl + Shift + D** or **Tools | Multicamera | Enable Multicamera Editing**.

Select all three camera tracks by holding the **Ctrl** key while selecting tracks, or select the first track, hold **Shift**, and select the third track. With all three tracks selected, choose **Tools | Multicamera | Create Multicamera Tracks**.

The three tracks will be collapsed to one track as layered takes. The Preview window will show the three takes/cameras, with track labels.

Figure 7.2

Switching between cameras and takes is very easy and can be done with either a numpad or time-line keyboard or by clicking in the Preview window.

It's usually a good idea to become as familiar as possible with the project prior to cutting so that various takes are not surprises and so that any audio cues may be prepped for.

Begin playback from the beginning titles (rewind by pressing the **W** key). Click on any of the three available cameras and the active take will highlight. As the timeline plays back, switch from camera to camera by clicking in the window, then pressing the **1-3** keys on the numpad or numbers **1-3** at the top of the keyboard. Vegas will generate cuts between the switch points.

*Tip*_____

Hold the **Shift** key while selecting takes to create cross-fades between cameras. The cross-fade length is determined in **Preferences | Editing | Cut to Overlap Conversion**. My preference is set to 0.250 or 7 frames. Generally speaking, shorter cross-fades are better. Cross-fades may be converted to other transitions later in the editing process. Use Ultimate S Pro to convert all cross-fades to a user-selected transition as a one-pass function.

Once the first rough pass is completed and selects are made, it's common practice to do another pass. My personal workflow is to go through a no-cut pass and make either paper or mental EDL that helps me know where to be looking. The rough cut is the first pass, the second pass is for fine cuts, and the third pass is for finish cuts (as far as selects are concerned).

After selects are finished, disable Multicamera editing by keying **Ctrl + Shift + D** or **Tools | Multicamera | Enable Multicamera Editing** (uncheck the tick box).

That's it. We're done with the Multicamera pass/process in Vegas Pro. The timeline is ready to be rendered from these cuts or more finely tuned and finished.

Tracks may be expanded back to individual tracks if there is a need to do so: **Tools | Multicamera | Expand to Multiple Tracks**.

More on Multicamera Editing in Vegas Pro

Once you understand the process, it's time to look a little more deeply at the features and functions of the multicamera tool.

In the **Tools | Multicamera** submenu there are a few additional options for multiple camera functionality.

Synchronizing Video/Audio for Multicamera Editing

There are three ways to sync audio/video and multiple video tracks. The first is common in the professional world where timecode is part of the workflow. No consumer camera offers timecode generation/gen-lock, so this is rarely a perfect option. However, some of the Sony and Canon cameras offer users the opportunity to time-sync multiple cameras on a shoot. See your camera manual for how this is done. Matching cameras are usually required. Vegas will lay out Events based on T/C and timestamps. In this tutorial, the AlphaRev files were rendered out for watermarking, thus stripping all camera T/C from the stream.

Even if different camera models are used for multicam work, they still may be closely sync'd. Set the date and time in each camera. The closer these are, the more accurate the *approximate* layout. Even when using a master timecode source, set the date/time as a backup. Before or after each scene, record a sync point. It is traditional to use a video slate board for this purpose, but a loud and visible hand clap will suffice. Be aware that in distant shots, audio captured by a camera's microphone will be delayed 1 frame for every 11.5 meters from the video. You can also use a photo flash recorded by all cameras as a sync point.

In the Vegas Timeline, lay out all cameras on individual tracks. Select the track header for all included tracks and enable multiple camera editing (**Ctrl + Shift + D**). Select the multicam track and choose **Tools | Multicamera | Layout Tracks Using Media Timecode Or Layout Tracks Using Media Date/Timestamp.** If there is no T/C from the camera or if TC is dramatically different per camera, use the **Date/Timestamp.** Events on tracks will be laid out as closely as possible. Camera starts and stops will generate new Event points.

 Tip_____

PluralEyes and similar tools will often be able to automatically sync all video tracks/audio tracks very quickly. If matching multiple cameras is a common need, look at this fantastic plug-in for Sony Vegas Pro (not available in Sony Vegas Movie Studio); visit www.singularsoftware.com for more info.

The next method to lay out tracks is to use audio. This is the most common method in today's prosumer camera workflow. At the start of each scene, generate a common sound (usually a clap or slateboard) that all cameras and audio devices can see and/or hear. This will create an audio spike, allowing the spike to be most easily synchronized with other tracks. With Vegas's ability to zoom into sample-level audio, getting this sync is perfect, easy, and very fast (it takes less than five seconds when sync pulses are very close to each other).

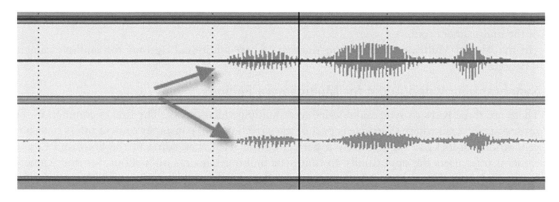

Figure 7.3   Find a percussive point in the audio and drop a marker. Disable **Quantize to frames** and slide the audio to match the marker point. If there is a suitable point at the head of the program material, it should be very fast to sync.

 Tip_____

When syncing with audio, do so two tracks at a time. Use headphones and pan one track to the left and one track to the right. Line the tracks up by nudging a frame at a time (1 and 3 keys on the numpad). When the sound seems to blend into one source in the middle of your head, you are lined up perfectly.

Line up files for sync as a first step. Lay out all files in the project before cutting, to save time. My personal workflow is to lay out the entire program, select areas to be deleted by selecting across all tracks, **Ctrl+X** to cut, **F** key to post-edit ripple, and repeat until all the undesired parts of the timeline are gone. Multicam is then generated.

Figure 7.4   Vegas does not have to work from a master audio track; dialogue tracks may travel with selected video, although it is often more efficient to create a master dialogue track prior to multicamera editing.

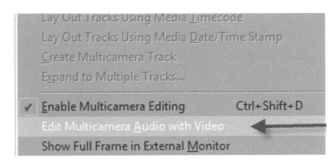

One other method that uses audio or video is to set markers in the Trimmer.

Be sure that markers are enabled in **Preferences | General | Automatically save Trimmer markers and regions with media file**. Load camera tracks in the Trimmer, locate a readily identifiable sync point or Event (such as the clap or clicker seen by all cameras), and drop a marker by pressing the **M** key or using the **Trimmer marker** insert. Be sure **Always Draw Marker Lines** is enabled in the Preferences.

Drag each camera's media to a new track. The marker inserted in the Trimmer will be seen on the timeline. Enable snapping (**F8** key) and drop a marker on the master timeline. From here, it's a very simple matter to move and snap all the camera views to the single timeline marker, prepping the project for multicamera editing.

Vegas allows for toggling back and forth between external and Vegas monitoring while in multi-camera mode. If the External preview is engaged, Vegas will display the active take as a full-screen view and will not display multiple cameras (this saves on resources, and it is not possible to click on an external monitor). If full screen with clickable control is wanted (from a producer's desk, for example), tear the Preview monitor from the Docking windows and place on a secondary monitor, then stretch to fill the secondary monitor. Cameras or active takes may still be clicked or controlled via a remote numpad or keyboard.

Multiple Cameras in Vegas Movie Studio

Vegas Movie Studio is a consumer-level application, although it is more powerful than the most powerful NLEs were just a few years ago.

Multicamera editing is not part of the Vegas Movie Studio tool set, but it is still quite easy to perform multicamera edits. Open the AlphaRev_Multicam.vf project. Right-click each track and insert a **Composite Level envelope**.

One method is to play back the project/timeline and make a mental or paper edit decision list (EDL). Play back each track at least once; multiple passes are preferable. Getting familiar with the assets before editing goes a long way when it comes to determining the content and feel of a project. Once the file has been played back a few times, begin playback from the beginning, and drop markers at the preferred edit points (press the M key).

Zoom into the timeline so that the Composite Level envelope is easily double-clicked and dragged. This will create fades into each Event or camera view.

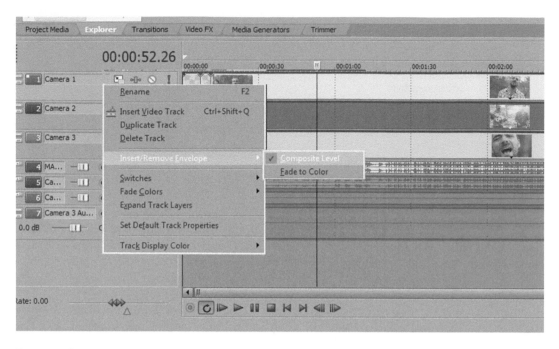

Figure 7.5   Composite Level envelopes may be used to create multicam edits.

Another method (the one I use in Vegas Movie Studio) is to select cut points, press the **S** key to split, and then, using the Event opacity controls, set the unwanted Events to **100%** transparency. When the timeline passes are done, unwanted Events are deleted, the "wanted" or 100% opaque Events are moved to a master timeline inserted above the work tracks (using the **8** key on a numpad to prevent vertical movement), and the timeline is assembled and fine cut from that point.

Although this is an old-school way of cutting multicam in the NLE world, it still functions very well, even if it's not as efficient as having multiple camera options immediately available.

Time Shifting, Transitions, and FX

Time Shifting

Time shifting refers to any instance where video or audio is played back faster or slower than normal. Vegas offers users several different methods of shifting time or time warping. In this section we'll look at a few of those ways.

Open the TimeShift.vf file. Vegas may have to search for the 1280 x 960 video file. As mentioned on the disc and elsewhere in this book, files should be transferred from the DVD to an HDD location for best experience.

The first method used for timeshifting will lengthen a video file, but it is also the easiest method of stretching time. In the first region, place the cursor at the right end of the first Event and hold the **Ctrl** key. The cursor will change to a squiggly line, indicating a time shift. Drag the file to the right while still holding the **Ctrl** key, and drag to the marker on the timeline. This will slow the video by almost 50%.

Loop the video (select the Event and press the **Q** key) to let it render to RAM.

 Tip_____

If you observe ghosting with interlaced source footage, right-click the Event on the timeline, choose **Switches** from the submenu, and choose **Force Resample** from the sub-submenu. This will force Vegas to resample the image in the same way it resamples media for transitions and other temporal processes.

Figure 8.1

This is the simplest way to create a slo-mo effect. Sometimes it is desirable to run the timeline at normal speed, slow down for motion effect, and return to normal speed. Let's do this in the second region of the timeline.

Split the Event at the first marker indicating **Split here**. Repeat at the second marker. You've now created three Events out of the original one Event. Move the third Event/clip to the marker labeled **Drag event to here**.

While holding **Ctrl**, click on the right edge of the second Event, and drag to fill the hole left behind when the third Event was dragged to the marker. Play the sequence and notice how the normal speed moves to slow motion that then goes back to fast motion without skipping a frame. This technique is a great way to match frames when Velocity envelopes are not available. (Velocity envelopes are available in Vegas Pro but not in Vegas Movie Studio.)

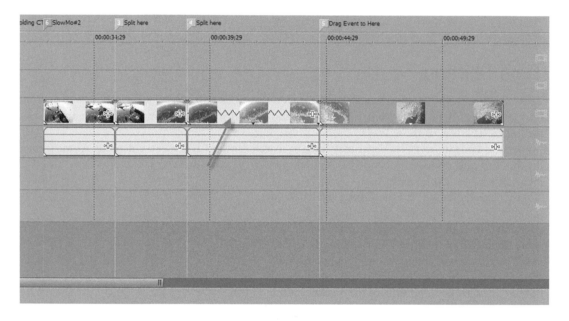

Figure 8.2   The corrugated/squiggly line indicates a time-shift.

The third region labeled SloMo#3 is a unique method of timeshifting. The bottom Event is stretched to the preferred time/slow-motion value. The Event is then copied to another track above. (Click **Ctrl** and drag the Event to copy it to a new track.) Disabling **Quantize to Frames** (under the **Options** menu) allows the upper Event to be moved one-half frame forward or backward on the timeline. The Event is then set to **50%** opacity. Both Events are set to **Force Resample**. This technique works well when you're slowing clips more than 50% speed and plug-ins such as Twixtor are not available. Tools like Twixtor will always provide smoother, better interpolation of slowed frames, but the price of the plug-in may be more than a hobbyist will want to spend, and this method works as a "poor man's time shift" effect. If the source is 24p, this method does offer some slight improvements; 24p is not at all a good source for slow motion, ever.

Tip_____
Experiment with this technique where the top layer of video is shifted two frames or more for a dreamy, trippy effect.

Region #4 has no slow motion, but we're going to look at another method of shifting time in both Vegas Pro and Vegas Movie Studio. Right-click the Event and select **Properties** from the submenu.

Figure 8.3   Enter the desired playback rate in this field. A setting of .750, for instance, slows playback by 25%. A value of half-speed would be .500. Vegas does not do well with values less than .400, and tools like Twixtor should be a consideration if extreme slow motion is part of the workflow.

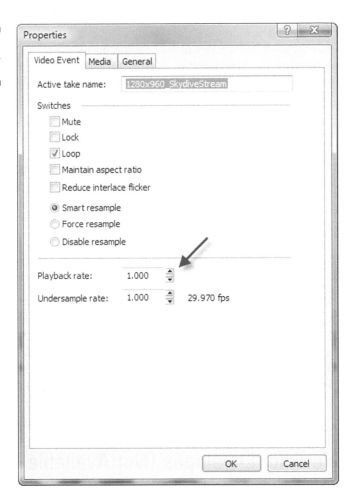

In the **Properties** submenu, enter a value of **.6**. Vegas will properly interpret this as .600. Close the **Properties** box and play through the Event. Notice the slow speed? Forced resampling may be necessary, depending on the speed/variable. If you see ghosting, consider duplicating the Event and offsetting by half a frame on the upper track, varying the amount of opacity of that track.

Increasing the Speed of Events

Just as speed may be decreased, so may it be increased. Vegas Movie Studio may speed Events by up to 400%, and Vegas Pro can be used to speed Events by up to 1200% without rendering to a new file or stacking nested .veg files.

Using the same method as stretching the Event while holding **Ctrl**, the same Event may be compressed or shrunk. This will speed the Event. In Region #9 on the Timeshift.vf project, hold the **Ctrl** key while clicking and dragging the right edge of the Event to the left. Snap the right edge to the marker placed there for you.

Alternatively, right-click the Event and enter a value of 4.00. This will have the same effect, with the exception that a hole will not be left in the timeline. Vegas will simply fill in the shrunk area with downstream media. However, if the media isn't long enough to fill the empty section, the Event will be forced to loop (if looping is enabled for the Event/default setting in Vegas). If looping is disabled, Vegas will freeze on the last frame.

 Tip_____

Time lapse, or showing the change of something over time, is an effective tool for some video productions but must be planned in advance. Lock down your camera's focus and allow for exposure; some situations may require using auto-exposure. Record for at least 10 minutes and up to an hour or more. Then in Vegas use the previously described techniques to increase the velocity as much as possible for a video where the original Event lasted 20 minutes (or however long it was), but the final result is just a few seconds.

Reversing Events

Events may be played backward or reversed in both Vegas Pro and Vegas Movie Studio. Right-click any Event and choose **Reverse** from the submenu. On the Timeshift.vf timeline, locate Region #11, labeled **Reverse**. Right-click and choose **Reverse** from the submenu, and use **Shift+B** to render this Event to RAM, allowing for smooth playback. If this Event is to be used more than once or if the same media is used elsewhere in the timeline, it might be worth creating a subclip of this Event.

Velocity Envelopes (Not Available in Vegas Movie Studio)

Velocity envelopes are a feature that enables time to be shifted via ramping. Vegas Pro users may open up the TimeShift.vf file and in the last region, right-click the Event (region 12) and choose **Insert/Remove Envelope, Velocity**. A green envelope will be inserted to the Event. Zoom in on the Event for precise control.

⏱ *Speed Tutorial*

1. Put the playhead/cursor at **00:02:48;15** and double-click the **green envelope** to insert a keyframe/node.

2. Jump forward five frames (**00:02:48;20**), double-click to insert another keyframe.

3. Right-click the keyframe, choose **Set To**, and enter a value of **40%**. This will ramp down the speed to 40% of original speed. This is different from the Event Properties window where Vegas interpolates input values to percentage. A percentage value is required for the Velocity envelope in Vegas Pro.

4. Move the cursor/playhead to **00:02:55;00** and double-click to insert another keyframe.

5. Arrow down a few frames and double-click to insert another keyframe, then double-click the keyframe to set it to **0**.

For playback:

1. As with other keyframes, right-click to set keyframe interpolations. Keyframe points may also be flipped via the right-click, inverting the envelope.

2. Remove the envelope by right-clicking and choosing **Insert/Remove Envelope** from the submenu.

Ultra-Speeds (Not Available in Vegas Movie Studio)

There is no real limit to how many speed increases may be created in Vegas Pro. Events may be stacked as nested .veg files and Vegas will treat them as video clips. Right-click an Event, set the playback speed to **4.00**. Close the **Properties** dialog box and insert a **Velocity** envelope set to **300%**. This will cumulatively speed Events by 1200%, or 12x original speed. Should additional speeds be required, a sped-up file may be stored as a .veg file; then, drop the saved .veg file on a new instance of Vegas Pro as a nested .veg file, where an additional 400% and 300% speed increase may be added to the original file. Files may also be rendered to a new track and sped up in the new track (useful for long-form videos on older systems that have limited CPU resources).

Changing the Speed of Audio

Vegas has a unique time-compression/expansion feature called Elastique that is a resampling feature in newer versions of Vegas. It is tremendously useful in any type of workflow. This feature is regularly used in broadcast as a means of forcing a package into a specific time slot. Open the project file **Elastique.vf** and note the three Events on the timeline. The first is original speed, the second is dramatically slowed, and the third is sped up. Note the audio quality. Elastique also works very well on spoken word/dialogue.

To access Elastique, right-click an audio Event and choose **Properties**. In the Properties window is a drop-down menu labeled **Time Pitch/Shift**. In the **Method** drop-down, choose **Elastique**. More fields open. In the **Stretch Attributes** drop-down, chose **Pro** for stereo audio. **Efficient** is the default. For voice-only, choose **Soloist/Speech**; for a singing voice, select **Soloist/Monophonic**.

Pro uses more CPU and RAM than the other options, so be aware that when stacking many retimed audio Events using Elastique, it's quite possible to overburden the CPU and playback will begin to stutter. In this Event, "freeze" tracks by rendering the processed audio to a new track and deleting the original time-shifted audio Event.

Figure 8.4 Elastique provides a great way to increase or decrease the speed of audio without seriously compromising audio quality.

Ctrl-Stretch Events

Like video Events, audio Events may be time-stretched by holding the **Ctrl** key and clicking and dragging the edge of the Event to desired length. Elastique may be invoked in the same manner: right-click and choose **Properties**. Time/length values may be entered in the appropriate fields in this same dialog box.

> Many of today's audio and video sources are compressed formats such as .mp3 or .aac. None of the compressed formats will stretch as well as uncompressed formats such as .wav. Use .wav files whenever possible. This translates to AVCHD and HDV audio, which use highly compressed audio formats. Neither is a great candidate for any kind of time shifting compared to uncompressed audio.

Transitions and FX

A transition in Vegas happens anytime you move or change from one piece of media or Event to another. Transitions may be very simple, or they can have flair and style. In this section we'll discuss most of the transition options.

In the Docking windows are two tabs: Transitions and Video FX. In this section, we'll examine how to most efficiently use these functions.

Before we can create cross-fades, let's first begin by creating a fade (two fades into each other are known as a *cross-fade*). Open the Vegas Explorer, browse for a video file, and place it on the timeline.

Put the cursor near the upper-right corner of the Event and the cursor will change from an arrow to a quarter circle.

When the cursor becomes a quarter circle, click and drag to the left. This will create a curving line leading from the top of the Event to the bottom right of it. Now preview the edit. Double-click the curve area, and it will create an auto-selection, or press the 0 key on the numpad to preview (be sure the playhead is over the newly created curve). This curving line is a fade. The video should fade out to black as it plays in the Preview window.

Now place the cursor at the upper left of the Event and repeat the process to create a fade-in.

Place a second piece of media to the right of the first one. If two Events are selected from the Explorer and dragged and dropped on the timeline, these two Events should be butted against each

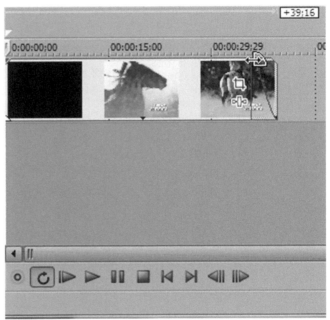

Figure 8.5

other. This type of transition between Events is called a *jump-cut* or a *butt-cut*, depending on where you're working.

With the cursor between the two Events, press the **/** key on your numpad/10-key. This should automatically insert a cross-fade between the two Events. Depending on the zoom level of the timeline, you may need to zoom in to clearly view the transition. Zoom in by pressing the **Up Arrow** key or by clicking the plus sign (+) in the lower-right corner of the application. This will zoom the timeline.

The 10-key is a great way to auto-insert cross-fades, but they can also be inserted by simply dragging an Event on top of another. Cross-fades are indicated by the X between the two Events.

Cross-fades are displayed with an *X* in between Events or clips. If this *X* is not seen, be sure that Automatic Cross-fades are enabled on the Vegas toolbar, or key **Ctrl + Shift + X**.

The cross-fade is the default transition in Vegas. Make a selection over the cross-fade (or double-click inside the cross-fade to auto-create a selection) and press the **Spacebar**. This will play through the transition, and the cross-fade may be previewed.

Press the **Q** key to loop the video, and the cross-fade will play repeatedly. Looping is one of my favorite features in Vegas. Even if the media source isn't playing back smoothly, Vegas will write the transition into RAM, and after one or two loops the transition will play smoothly and cleanly when written to RAM.

Add at least one or two seconds of selection before and after the cross-fade for this next step.

Figure 8.6 The cross-fade is the default transition in Vegas, indicated here by the *X*. The selection in this image has pre- and post-roll so that the cross-fade can be auditioned in context.

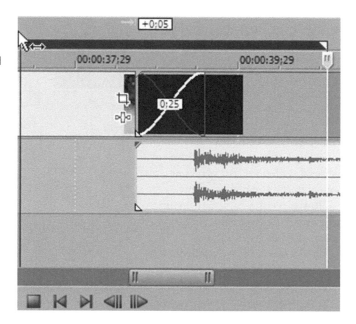

In the cross-fade window, there is a small time indicator that displays the length of the cross-fade in minutes, seconds, and frames.

Think carefully about using long cross-fades (longer than 12 frames) in professional workflows. Although they are romantic and easy, long cross-fades are often a typical sign of unprofessional work.

Inserting a Transition

With the cross-fade created and looping, click on the **Transition** tab in the Docking windows. If no transition folders are expanded, six folders should be seen:

- All
- OFX/Open FX
- 32-bit floating point
- GPU Accelerated
- Sony (contains all of the preceding transitions)
- Third Party (this is where you'll find transitional plug-ins from New Blue, Genarts, Pixelan, etc.—any transition packages you have installed that did not come with Vegas)

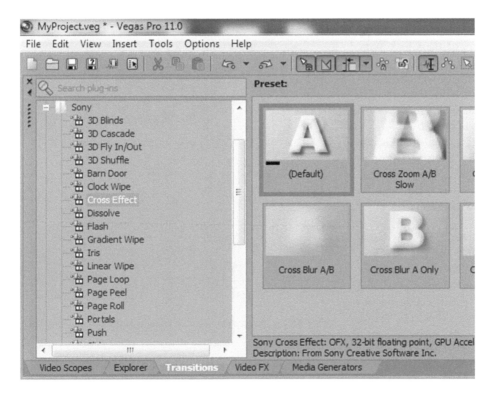

Figure 8.7 In this window you can see all of the Vegas transitions.

Click the **ALL** folder to expand the folder and show all transitions. The Vegas Timeline should still be looping and playing back.

Select the **Clock Wipe** transition (a standard in broadcast work) in the left side of the Transition window. In the right side of the Transition window you can see presets for the Clock Wipe transition. Click and drag the **Clockwise/Soft Edge** transition from the preset window and drop it on the X of the cross-fade that is currently looping. A dialog box will open allowing fine-tuning of the Cross Wipe transition. For this exercise, close the dialog box by clicking the red X at the top right of the Transition dialog box.

The Clock Wipe transition has replaced the cross-fade, and the transition overlap (the X between Events) will now show a thin line that shows that the Clock Wipe transition is in place.

> If Event Names are enabled and the track height is small, Active Take Information may prevent the transition name from being seen in the Event overlap. Disable **Active Take Information** by keying **Ctrl + Shift + I**.

With Vegas still looping, adjust the parameters of the Clock Wipe transition. The dialog box that allowed for fine-tuning the transition was closed when the transition was dropped in place, so we'll need to reopen the dialog box.

Click the transition name in the overlap, at the **Transition Properties** icon. This will open the **Transition Properties** dialog box and the transition may be adjusted to user preference.

If the Transition Properties dialog box covers the Preview window, simply click the header/top of the **Transition Properties** dialog box and move the dialog box to one side or the other. The dialog box may also be resized. Some-times the dialog box will want

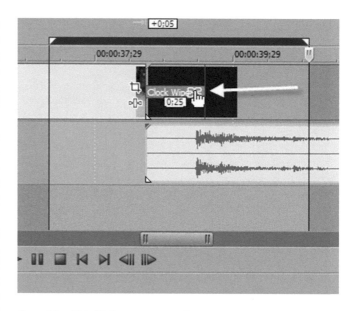

Figure 8.8   Click this icon to open the **Transition Properties** dialog box.

to dock as it is being moved around the Vegas interface. Holding down the **Ctrl** key while moving the box around will prevent the window from docking and will keep it floating on the interface.

Notice that changes to the direction of the Clock Wipe or adjustments to the Feather Angle display in real time while the preview is looping? This is another feature unique to Vegas—the ability to play back in real time while adjusting parameters, with no render required. If the computer system is slower or the project is complex, the preview may not be smooth or full frame rate as the preview plays through. Let the preview loop a couple of times, or use the RAM render command (**Shift + B**) to render the looped selection to RAM.

Insert a different transition to the Vegas Timeline to replace the Clock Wipe. In the **Transitions** window, click on the **Flash** transition. By default, Flash has four presets. Click and drag the **Soft Flash** preset to the same place as the Clock Wipe transition was dragged. Notice that Vegas immediately previews this transition, even as it is being dropped on the overlap. As with the Clock Wipe, close the **Flash** properties dialog box (unless you'd like to tweak the values of the Flash Transition).

In the Flash transition, a color tint may be applied to the flash (alternative to the default white). Stop playback by pressing the **Spacebar**. Use the **Arrow** keys to find a frame that has colors that you'd like to use as a tint in the Flash dialog box. Click the **Tint** box in the Flash transition properties window and a color palette will open up. Select the **eyedropper** in this palette, and click on the color range that is desired as a Flash tint.

 *Tip*_____

Much of the time when you use an eyedropper in Vegas to sample a color, you can click and drag the eyedropper over a range of colors to get an average color—for instance, if your source is skin tone where the light source provides a shadowing with darker and lighter tones. This feature provides more flexibility than just clicking on one pixel in a frame of video.

On the far right side of the transition is a keyframe switch. This switch allows various transition parameters to be keyframed. Keyframes and keyframing are discussed in greater detail later in this book.

All of the transitions in Vegas are useful and have their place in various types of productions, but some are more commonplace or have more options/parameter adjustments than others. We won't look at all the transitions here, but I'd like to point out some of the more complex options available.

First and foremost, limiting transitions to "traditional" Digital Video Effects (DVE) transitions is a fairly safe approach. Nothing screams amateur more loudly than spinning cubes, rainbows, and other specialty transitions. Traditional DVEs include short cross-fades, linear wipes, clock wipes, and dissolves. Watch any long-form documentary, film, or television show and notice that all transitions are essentially the same. Rarely do fancy transitions fall into traditional programming. So why does Vegas offer all these options? They fit really well into composites, title sequences, or for the nonprofessional editor who is doing work for a church, school, or corporate facility where a little extra "pizzazz" is acceptable. Remember, however, that all the fancy transitions in the world can't fix a boring production.

The 3D transitions work really well for titles and graphics that are being flown in, and they are terrific for pulling on/off supers or lower thirds. One of my favorite nontraditional transitions is the cross effect. This is a great effect for demonstrating passage of time or change of location in some of the high-action personal videos we edit (like skydiving videos).

Figure 8.9   There are many parameters in the Cross Effect dialog box for both 2D and 3D editing; the effect settings drop-down must be clicked to view the additional options.

The Flash effect is a terrific transition to focus the viewer's eye on a new scene, to shift or go back in time, or to provide an instant replay. Use the color selector to choose the predominant color found in the background as a Flash color. It makes a huge difference.

The Gradient Wipe is a recent addition to Vegas. The transition can use built-in graphics, or users may substitute their own. Open the **Lower Thirds** project from the DVD, delete the two yellow slugs/blanks, and drop a video file on the background as a replacement. The text that appears uses the Gradient Wipe and the 3D Blinds to bring text on/off the screen. Replace the wipe graphic with one of the graphics in the **Stills** folder that came with this book and watch some magic happen!

A *lower third* is a graphic, text, or combination of the two that is laid over the bottom "third" of the screen. Usually it is informative or supportive in nature.

Note that the "fancy" transitions are being recommended as a way to spice up titles and graphics versus being used for video effects. Hopefully you're reading this book because you want to be a more proficient and professional video editor, and one of the first things I recommend to new editors is to try to avoid "cool" transitions out of the box so that the story speaks for itself. Be sure to ask yourself, "What does this transition bring to the story?" The number-one transition in the film and video world is still the jump or butt cut.

There are also many third-party transition plug-ins that bring a lot to the table; the same applies to other transition plug-ins. Avoid overuse of "specialty plug-ins." NewBlue, Genarts, Boris FX, Prodad, and other plug-in developers offer some terrific transitional elements for Sony Vegas and Vegas Movie Studio.

Adding FX

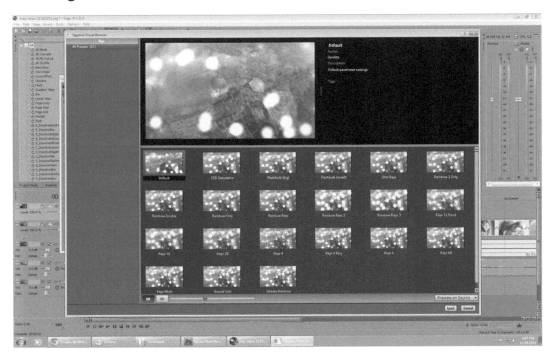

Figure 8.10　Genarts Sapphire offers previews of FX before they are applied, much like the VASST film looks do.

Adding FX works exactly the same way as adding transitions: you drag them from the FX tab to any Event. Vegas offers users the option of adding FX at multiple points in the process. FX may be added:

- To individual Events (affects only the specific Event on the timeline, regardless of original source)
- To individual tracks (affecting all Events on the track)
- To the master output (affects all Events, all tracks)
- To an entire piece of source media in the Project Media folder; this is where color correction for multicam or sources trimmed into multiple Events is best performed

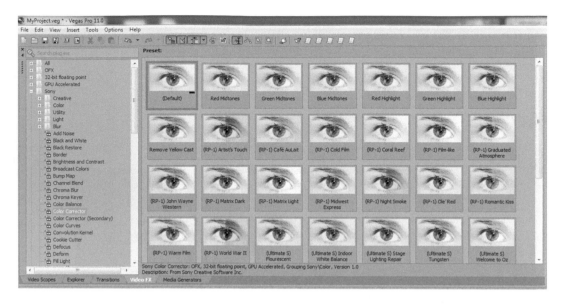

Figure 8.11   FX, or *effects*, are part of the DVE portion of Sony Vegas. Vegas Pro offers a few more FX than does Vegas Movie Studio. FX include repair tools to fix video that wasn't shot properly, to create a specific ambience, to enhance images, to shift reality or create alternate realities, to create transitions, to set moods, or to refocus the viewer.

For this section, we'll be using the **AlphaRev-FX.vf** project file found on the DVD included in this book. Open this project in either Vegas Pro or Vegas Movie Studio. (Vegas Pro can open Vegas Movie Studio files; Vegas Movie Studio cannot open Vegas Pro files.)

In this project I have created some FX settings to be previewed. Set the Preview Monitor to **Preview/Auto** for smoothest playback. Double-click the **Timeline** bar to fit the entire project in a single view.

The full-length clip has been split into individual Events and unique FX applied to each split or Event. Note that each split is labeled with a region marker for reference.

Rewind the project to the start (press the **W** key) and press the **Spacebar** to begin playback.

The first Event you'll see is the original, unaltered footage. The second Event has been re-white balanced to give the footage a less emotional feel. In the second Event, click the **FX** button. Note that it is colored green. This is an indicator that FX have been dropped on the Event. The first Event's FX button is gray, indicating that it has no FX on the Event.

This Event or clip is already white-balanced; however, we're going to re-white balance the clip. In the **White Balance** dialog box, choose the preset **Reset to none** in the drop-down. This resets the white balance to null. Now select the **eyedropper** tool and **Select White Color** button. With the eyedropper tool enabled, click on the keys of the accordion player (it's safe to assume that these keys are white). The white keys will act as a reference to let Vegas know what white point it should

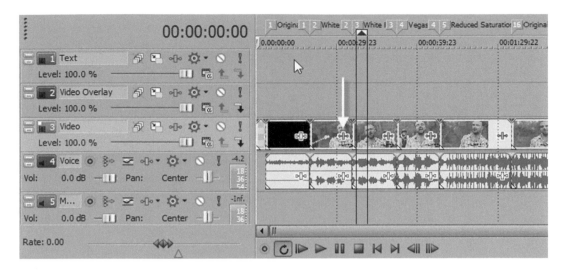

Figure 8.12   Click this button to open the FX properties dialog box. The **White Balance** dialog box will open.

reference. Note the change in the preview window. The color will shift from (intentionally cold) blue to a more natural color cast.

Let's match the first Event to the second Event. Place the playhead over the first Event so that the first Event is seen in the preview window. In the **FX** tab, browse to the **White Balance** FX. Click and drag it to the first Event, and the **FX** properties dialog box will open. Click the **Select White Color** icon (eyedropper) and the cursor will change to an eyedropper. Click on one of the white squares in the vocalist's shirt. The preview window will show the change. Adjust the brightness, and move the correction amount slider back and forth to get a feel for how this works. Play the timeline from the middle of the first Event to the middle of the second Event. The two Events will be nearly identical in color cast and white balance (they will not be exact).

It's important to understand that when it comes to white balancing (and similar color functions), it's rarely best performed at the Event level rather than the clip or source level. We'll look at how to do that in a few moments.

Removing FX

For purposes of this tutorial, remove the **White Balance** filter from the chain from the first Event in the timeline. Select the **FX** properties button in the first Event, and the **FX** dialog box opens. In the upper right of the **FX** dialog box there are two small buttons; one adds more FX to the chain and the other removes FX from the chain.

Select and click the **Remove** button and the FX will be removed from the Event. Close the **FX** properties dialog window and note that the FX button on the Event has turned gray.

Add as many FX as desired to any Event. A collection of FX can be grouped together and saved as a chain. This may be desirable as a "library" for projects or consistency across projects.

Figure 8.13

⏱ *Speed Tutorial*

1. Drop the **Sepia** FX on the first Event in the **AlphaRev_Raw** timeline. Using the drop-down, select the preset **Warm**. Now drag the **Glow FX** to the same Event or to the FX properties dialog box.

2. Select the **White Highlights** preset. Note in the **FX** Properties dialog box that both Sepia and Glow are seen in a "chain" or "package."

3. Now select and click the **Plugin Chain** button. This will open the FX chooser.

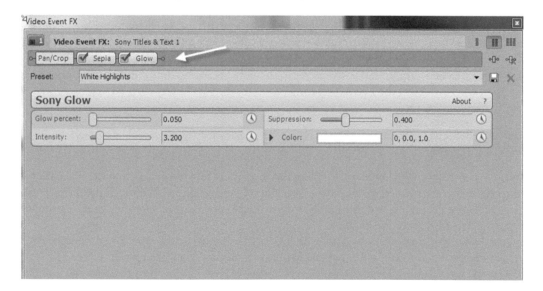

Figure 8.14

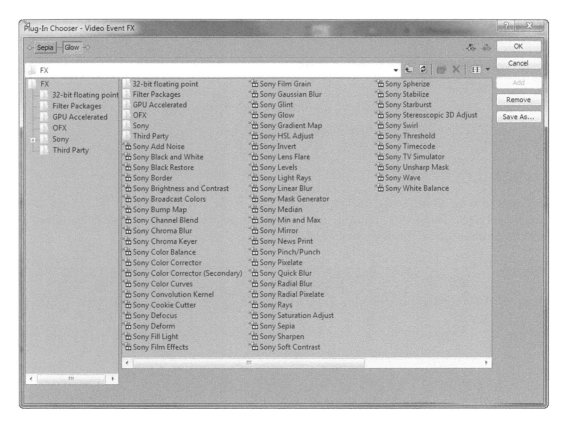

Figure 8.15   The FX chooser displays all installed FX that Vegas has registered.

4. On the right side of the chooser there is a button labeled **Save As**. Click this button and a **Save Plugin Package** dialog box will open. Name this chain **Sepia Glow**.

5. Now close the chooser, and in the **FX** Properties dialog box remove both FX from the Event. The **FX** dialog window will close when the second FX is removed, and the FX button on the Event should be gray.

6. We're going to illustrate adding a chain of FX all at once. Reclick the gray button, and the FX chooser will appear (showing all available FX, just as before). On the left side of the chooser, notice the **FX/Filter Packages** folder. Open this folder and the package/chain created a few clicks ago is seen as **Sepia Glow**.

7. Click the **Sepia Glow** package (on the left) and the **Add** button on the right side of the plug-in chooser. Double-clicking the Sepia Glow package will also insert the package to the Event. Click and select **OK** in the chooser, and close the **FX** dialog box (click the red **X** in the upper-right corner).

Now the FX chain/package has been applied to the first Event on the timeline.

Play through the AlphaRev_FX timeline to see the different types of FX that have been inserted. Most of them are color FX, although a few special FX and timecodes have been inserted. These are in place to demonstrate some of the different plug-ins and how they may be used.

These are all *Event-level* FX. To summarize, all FX added to individual Events are added by one of these methods:

1. Dragging and dropping FX onto an Event

2. Selecting the FX button found on each Event

3. Right-clicking an Event and selecting **Video Event FX** from the submenu

FX added at the Event level affect only individual Events.

Track-Level FX

FX may also be added at the track level. FX added at the track level affect all Events on an individual track. Track-level FX are good for fixing a single source where all sources are identical, creating composites, auditioning looks, and more.

Figure 8.16

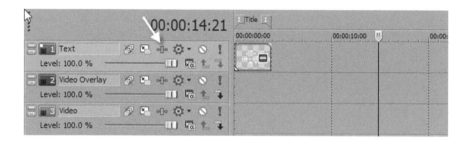

On every video track header there is an FX button just like the one found on Events. Inserting FX at the track level is identical to inserting FX at the Event level; FX may be dragged and dropped on the track header, or the **FX** button may be selected and FX are selected from the FX chooser.

Open the **AlphaRev_FX** project used in the previous tutorial. If it is still open, close it (be sure to *not save*), and reopen the project file.

Sony Vegas Pro users: Drag the **Soft Contrast FX** to the track labeled **Video** (not available in Sony Vegas Movie Studio).

Sony Vegas Movie Studio users: Drag the **Film Effects FX** to the track labeled **Video**.

Notice the change in the output of the video. All Events on the track are now processed with the same filter, and even though there are many changes to the way the video FX are placed on the individual Events, notice that the track-level FX tie the various Events together by creating a common look within the project. Once this is accomplished, remove any FX from the track header, since we'll be visiting this project again. Alternatively, close the project without saving.

 *Tip*_____

One of my common workflows is to place FX chains on several blank tracks (I even have created and saved off a blank project for purposes of auditioning) and then I drop a clip on one of the tracks. Double-click the Event or clip to create a selection. Play the selection, and enable looping (press the **Q** key). With the Event looping, I use the **8** key on the numpad to move the Event or clip up to the next track with a different FX chain. This is a very fast way to audition FX settings or A/B FX settings on the same clip. Another quick tip is to capture the original to the clipboard (press the **Copy to Clipboard** button in the preview window) and let the clipboard fill half the Preview window while you audition clips in the other half of the preview window.

Track-based FX will be used for compositing as well.

Project-Level FX

Vegas enables users to place FX at the project level, affecting everything on a project timeline. Titles, graphics, video will all be affected by project-level FX. This is particularly useful for broadcast-filters and overall color correction, vignettes, or applying a "looks" filter to tie all Events/clips into a particular style, creating continuity. This can be less intensive on the CPU than putting the same effect on every Event or track.

Figure 8.17

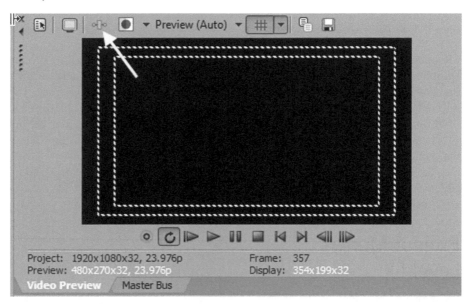

FX are inserted at the project level using the same methods as Events and tracks. In the Preview window, there is a **Video Output Effects** button. Selecting this button will open the FX chooser, just as it did with the Event and track FX buttons. FX may also be dragged and dropped on the Preview window.

For those sending SD video to broadcast, one application of the Video Output Effects feature is the Broadcast Colors plug-in. This FX module provides users with a guarantee that the video project will meet Rec. ITU-R BT.601 broadcast standards.

 Tip_____

Broadcasters such as PBS have exceptionally stringent standards as to what they will and will not accept for broadcast, and inserting the Broadcast Colors FX to the master output of the Vegas project using the Conservative-7.5 Setup preset will assure that the project is within standards. More on the Rec. ITU-R BT.601 standard may be found at www.itu.int.

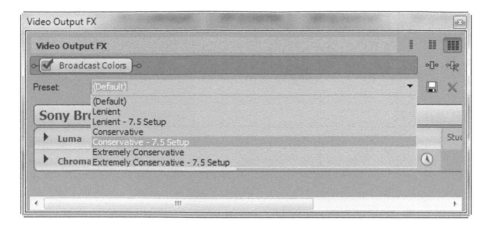

Figure 8.18   For SD broadcast, this FX tool assures users that their projects will meet broadcast standards for color.

Reopen the **AlphaRev_FX** project. In the track above the video, we're going to place a new title. Double-click on the Event above the video track at **Region 13** (there is already an empty Event in the Video Overlay track). In the blank area above the Video Overlay track, right-click in the selected area and choose **Insert Text Media** from the submenu. Type **AlphaRev** in the text box.

Now locate the **TV Simulator** FX in the FX window and drag and drop it on the preview window. The default FX is the TV Look preset. Note that the TV look covers the title and all video in the window. Dropping certain FX on the master output/video output effects is a quick and easy way to create continuity in a project.

Project Media-Level FX

FX may also be added at the project media level. This technique serves one primary purpose: to process or enhance an entire media file so that Event-level processing and enhancing is not necessary later on.

For example, perhaps there are three cameras on a production, and one of them wasn't white balanced and one of them simply has a blue color cast. The third camera is essentially perfect. There are two options at this point; the first is to create a track

Figure 8.19

for each camera and color correct at the track level while hoping that the track layers work out. When you're using the built-in Vegas multicam function, this method will not work well.

The other option is to correct each camera in the Project Media window. Every time a clip is taken from one of the "bad" cameras, it is precorrected so that nothing further will need to be done to the clip.

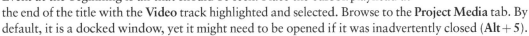

Open the **AlphaRev_NoFX** project. No clips should be on the timeline; a Title Event at the beginning is all that should be seen. Place the cursor/playhead at the end of the title with the **Video** track highlighted and selected. Browse to the **Project Media** tab. By default, it is a docked window, yet it might need to be opened if it was inadvertently closed (**Alt + 5**).

Select the **AlphaRev_RAW** media in the Project Media window and then select the **Media FX** button just below the top row of icons. The FX chooser will open. Choose the **Gradient Map** FX, click **OK** in the chooser, and in the **Gradient Map** window that opens, choose the **Warm** preset. Close the **FX** properties window.

Right-click the **AlphaRev_RAW** file in the Project Media window and select **Open in Trimmer**. The file will open in the Trimmer. Expand or undock the Trimmer if necessary, since we'll be grabbing selects from this window.

Play the file in the Trimmer, and put the cursor or playhead at **00:00:16:02**. Press the **I** key to mark an in point. Now move the playhead to **00:00:47:02** and press the **O** key to mark an out point. The Trimmer will create a selection from the in/out points. Press the **R** key to create a region. Name it if you'd like. Press the **A** key to add the clip to the timeline.

Figure 8.20   Note that the video in the Trimmer does not show the FX invoked in the Project Media window. This is because the Trimmer always displays the source file as it exists on the HDD and does not display any FX or other processes. This is what the Preview window is for. This exactly mimics the linear editing world where source is clean, pre-DVE in the Source/Trimmer monitor.

Notice that the video in the Preview window is processed, while the video in the Trimmer window is the actual source.

In this section, we've looked at how to add video FX to Events, tracks, project, and source media in the Project Media window. Audio FX are also a big part of the editing process in Vegas Pro and Vegas Movie Studio.

Adding Audio FX

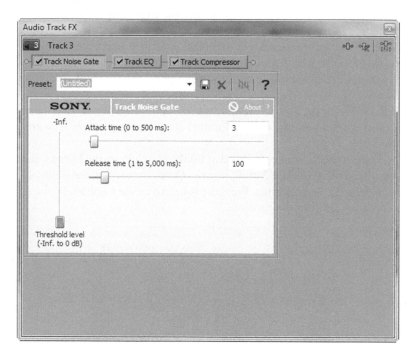

Figure 8.21   Audio tracks in Vegas have a default Noise Gate, Equalizer, and Compressor inserted to the audio chain. All parameters are currently set to null (no effect).

Vegas began life as a Digital Audio Workstation (DAW) and has only grown to be more powerful in the audio world.

By default, every audio track in Vegas has three inserted FX: Noise Gate, Equalizer, and Compressor. View them by clicking the **Track FX** button on the **Voice** track header (track 3 in the **AlphaRev_Raw** file). The FX dialog box will open.

Rewind the playhead to the beginning of the timeline (press the **W** key). Begin playback. While the file is playing, click on the **Equalizer** in the audio FX chain.

Click the **#2** node in the Equalizer (EQ) and push it up by a few dB. The effect is immediately heard. The effect may be "swept" by moving the node back and forth across the spectrum; be cautious if your speakers are turned up loud. It's possible to blow out a speaker and the sound may become obnoxious.

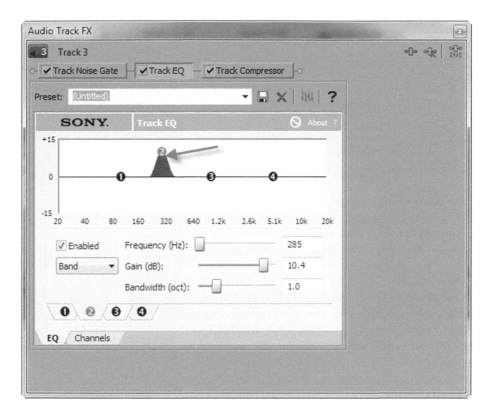

Figure 8.22

Once you've swept the EQ a couple of times to become familiar with how it functions, look below the node window. There are fields where values may be manually input. In the first (**Frequency**) field, enter a value of **90** (this is 90 Hz). In the **Gain** field, enter a value of **4.5 dB**. In the **Rolloff/Bandwidth** field, enter a value of **1.5**.

The audio changes should be immediately heard. Do not change the master volume output in the Vegas mixer if the audio is too loud. Reduce volume at the Windows mixer or on the speakers themselves. Reducing the volume in the Vegas mixer may create problems in a final render. We'll discuss this more in the audio chapter.

The FX inserted are at the track level. The Master Output may also have FX inserted. In this project, your Mixer levels should be peaking red and clipping, with an over of approximately 6.5 dB. We can correct this at the track, yet for this exercise we'll fix it at the output point of the audio chain. In the Master Bus (Mixer), select the **Master FX** button.

The FX chooser/plug-in chooser will open. Select **Wave Hammer Surround** and click **OK** in the chooser window. The Wave Hammer properties dialog box will open. In the drop-down menu, select the **Master for 16bit** preset and close the Properties window. The meters in the Master Output/mixer should no longer be clipping or showing red at the top.

The Wave Hammer is an excellent way to quickly bring levels under control, yet if the mix is clipping from too much input, it's quite possible that the Wave Hammer only brings the output level under control but does not remove or reduce distortion. If the mix is clipping, we'll need to process it at the track level. See the audio chapter for more information.

Click the Master FX button again and the Wave Hammer dialog box will open. Remove the WaveHammer plug-in from the Master Output by selecting and clicking the **Remove Selected Plugin** button.

Vegas allows for video FX to be applied at the Event/clip level; it does not offer quite the same functionality on the audio side because there is no Audio FX view window. However, just as there is an FX button on each video Event, so there is on each audio Event.

Select and click the **audio FX** button to open the Audio FX chooser. Open the **Sony** folder in the Plugin chooser. Choose **Express FX Equalization** and click **OK**. The equalizer will open. The three-band EQ is very simple yet effective. If frequencies are pushed upward, distortion will be heard in the monitors and seen in the mixer output. Adding audio FX is often a "subtractive" action whereby frequencies are reduced rather than added. If an audio clip sounds too bass-heavy, instead of boosting high-end frequencies, try reducing low-end frequencies to minimize the possibility of distortion. Think of it in terms of the old sculptor's expression, "I don't know what's inside the stone, I just carve away anything that doesn't look the way I think it should."

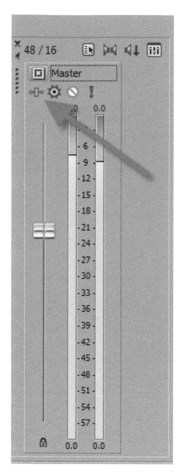

Figure 8.23

Figure 8.24

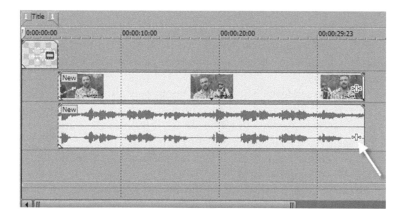

Color Correction Tools in Vegas Movie Studio and Vegas Pro

Vegas Pro and Vegas Movie Studio both have huge arsenals when it comes to color correction weapons. Both are more than adequate tools for features, documentaries, television projects, or commercial projects destined for television, mobile devices, or the Web.

Before we get into the color correction tools, there are a couple of points worth making to improve and enhance your color correction experience.

The primary reason that color is seen as a challenging, mythical experience in the "getting it right" realm is because most editors don't have rooms properly set up for color correction any more than they're likely to have a room set up for audio mastering. Such a room takes some prep, and in these next few paragraphs I'd like to offer some suggestions that make for an easier and better color correction output and experience.

Prep the Room

Buy an 18% gray card from any camera supply house. You should have one anyway for white balancing the camera. Stare at the gray card for a few minutes before any color correction session. If you can't immediately find an 18% gray card, then find any neutral-colored card and use it to "reset" your eyes.

> Start every shoot with an 18% gray card in the foreground; it provides a white/neutral/black point for color correction. Seriously. Even after white-balancing the camera, you'll thank me for this tip later in the editing process.

- Be sure your monitor is out of the path of any direct lighting sources, especially sunlight. As fun as it may be to sit in front of a big picture window and enjoy beautiful views while you edit, it will not help with the color correction process.
- Lose or hide any colorful objects near your computer screen. This includes that really cool Intel™ doll/action figure and that silly robot with the red top. If the monitor is reflective, hide any

colorful objects that are behind you as well. These things only serve to confuse the eye when it should only be seeing neutral.

• Keep your monitor clean. Use a dust-free cloth and cleaning solution to keep the monitor screen (and your eyeglasses) clean before any editing session.

If budget and space aren't too big an issue, paint a back wall a flat, nongloss neutral gray. Munsell N7 or N8 are common paints. B&H sells them as GTI/gray neutral. Failing that, take the 18% gray card to the local home improvement store. They'll easily be able to match it and provide a flat, durable paint. You'll also find that gray rooms are less fatiguing, if not exciting to work in. I took this step in our studio a few years back and find it to be quite relaxing, along with recessed, directional lighting.

OK, all that aside, let's dig into the color correction tools found in the Vegas family. Note that in this chapter we are only dealing with FX/plug-ins that come standard with Vegas Pro or Vegas Movie Studio. All the tool names are prefaced with "Sony" in the software, but we have omitted that in this text for clarity.

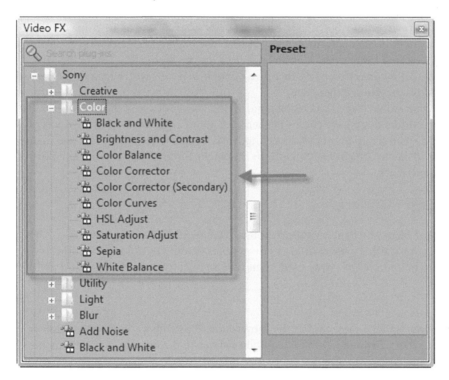

Figure 9.1 Vegas offers a plethora of color correction tools. Sometimes it's difficult to know just which one to use.

• Black and White
• Brightness and Contrast
• Chroma Blur
• Color Balance

- Color Corrector
- Color Corrector/Secondary
- Color Curves
- HSL Adjust
- Saturation Adjust
- Sepia
- White Balance

These are all the tools Sony lists in its Color Correction arsenal. However, my personal workflow adds a few more tools:

- Bezier Mask
- Cookie Cutter
- Levels (really a utility, but necessary in the color correction world)

These are all tools we'll be using. We'll also become familiar with the Video Scopes (**View | Video Scopes**). (Video Scopes are not available in Vegas Movie Studio.)

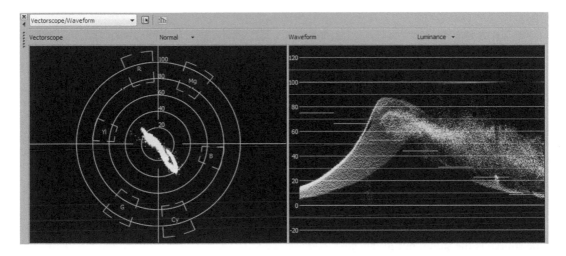

Figure 9.2   These scopes are very useful for assuring color match, checking output levels, identifying clipping colors, and more.

Let's start with a new project. Open the **Color Correction-MovieStudio.vf** or **ColorCorrection-Vegas.veg** file found in the projects included with this book. (Vegas Pro users may open either file; the ColorCorrection-Vegas.veg file has some other tweaks not available to Vegas Movie Studio users.)

This is the same AlphaRev video we've worked on in other sections of the book. Notice that this particular piece is very cool; it was balanced to a green card (for intentional coolness). The first thing we'll do is re-white-balance the shot.

Tip_____

You can create completely different looks by white-balancing your camera to something other than a standard white card. White-balancing to a very light baby-blue color is a common trick to warm up the footage right out of the camera before any color grading is done in post.

Put the playhead **to 00:00:13;00** (13 seconds). Browse to the **FX** tab and locate the **White Balance FX**. Drag and drop it on this first Event. The **FX** dialog box opens, and we'll use **Select White Color** and the **eyedropper** to choose white. In the 00:00:13;00 frame, then choose the white fret marker on the neck of the bass instrument. The image will instantly warm up and lean to green in color.

Figure 9.3   Although the image appears to have shifted to green, note the skin tones. The image has simply been balanced out, with a very slight lean toward red.

Now we'll white-balance again. It's not a great idea to white-balance from Event to Event when the source is the same, but in this next exercise, we'll be adding other tools to the FX chain.

Put the playhead on **00:00:43;27**. Drag and drop the **White Balance** tool on this Event, this time balancing on the white keys of the accordion. If Video Scopes aren't visible, open them and enable the **Vectorscopes** and **Waveform** view. Vectorscopes, Waveform, or Histogram will work equally well. In the Waveform monitor, select **Luminance** from the drop-down menu. The White Balance dialog box should still be open.

Locate the **Color Curves** FX in the FX browser window and drag and drop it on either the second Event or the White Balance dialog box you just worked with. This will insert a Color Curves FX to the processing chain. The curves are capable of processing a single channel or all three channels in one action. We'll be using only the **RGB** channels. Create a gentle *S* curve in the **Curves** tool. Vegas Pro users will notice the change in the scope and the broadening of the color range.

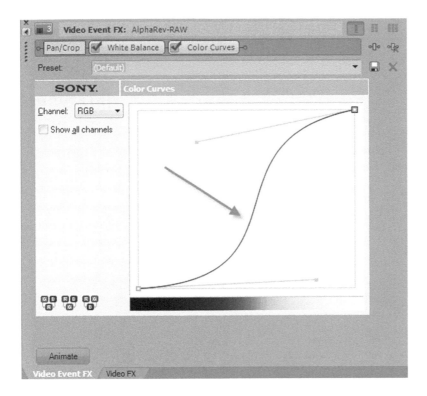

Figure 9.4

Figure 9.5   The split screen feature enables us to see original image and altered image compared side by side.

For the third region, set the playhead to **00:00:51;00**. Drag and drop the **Color Correction** FX/plugin to the Event. The Color Correction dialog box opens. We're going to set this image to a neutral color.

At the top of the dialog box is a **Parameter/Custom** tab option. Select **Custom**. Starting with the **High** corrector, click the – button, or the **Complementary Color** button. Click this white/high eyedropper on a white portion of the singer's shirt. The accordion keys are also white. Move to the **Low** complementary eyedropper (the – eyedropper). Click this on the black of the accordion bezel/body. This is the blackest part of the image outside of the watermark. Finally, select the **Mid** complementary eyedropper and click

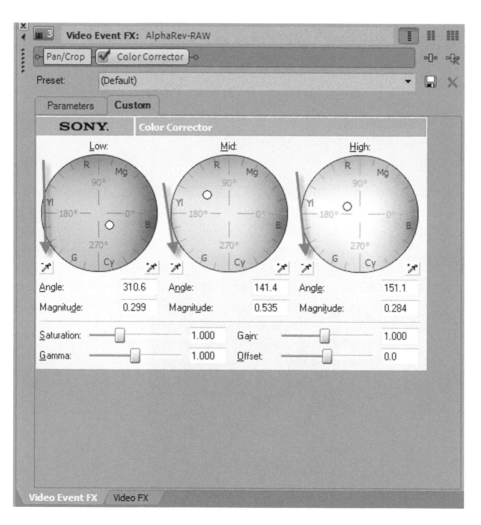

Figure 9.6   The Custom tab, which shows the legacy horizontal view of the color wheels.

on either the accordion player's hat or a tree limb that is gray (we want a neutral color for this process). The image is now neutral. Vegas Pro users will notice the "centered mass" in the Vectorscope.

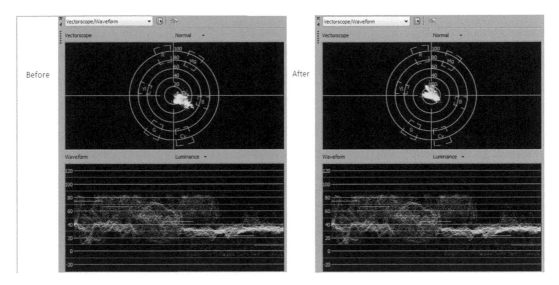

Before   After

Figure 9.7   Although Vectorscopes might be intimidating to some, the process becomes fairly self-explanatory with a little use. In these images, we can see the color balance leaning more to blue in the preprocess image on the left and balanced to neutral in the image on the right.

The three-wheel color corrector is the most visible color correction tool in the NLE world simply because of the "cool" factor. It allows for tremendous flexibility in correcting color, yet it is also often used simply because users don't know any better. Sometimes using the three-wheel color corrector is like bringing a bazooka to a slingshot fight; it's overkill. Used improperly, it may cause huge headaches. In my workflow it's often the last tool I turn to.

There are two eyedroppers for each wheel; the complementary color will adjust color 180° from the color selected. Select a blue hue and its opposite color will be added. Adjustment color works on the actual color selected. Complementary colors are often used instead of adjustment colors, since the color being selected often is the one needing correction, and complementary colors allow for precise (computed) response to that specific hue and saturation value.

The Primary Color Corrector tool works much like an equalizer in an audio system. The three wheels control lows (blacks), mids (largest range of color information), and highs (whites). Thinking in this mode may help some editors work with the colors more comprehensively.

Continued

The three-wheel corrector is a terrific tool, but it's often not needed for basic corrections due to the most common problems associated with not white-balancing a camera, exposure problems, or bright hues in a scene.

VASST.com also offers an in-depth DVD on the subject of color correction in Vegas.

Figure 9.8   Shadows and contrasts fall into the category of black/low. Facial colors, clothing, paints, and predominantly everything focused on in a frame all fall into the midrange color category. Whites/high are the sparkle and the high end of various hues of color, providing detail in most instances. Dulling the high end, as in audio, generally results in less clarity of a picture image. Sometimes illegal colors, however, function much like distortion and need to be reduced to bring colors to a more reasonable and appreciable level. Depending on how the image was captured or acquired and with what, resolution levels might not allow colors to be intensified without seriously degrading the image.

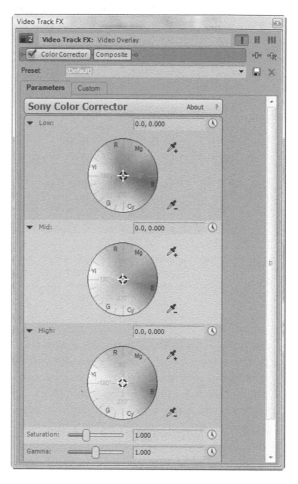

In the fourth region, notice that there is a copy of part of the file on the upper track in both Vegas and Movie Studio versions of this project. In Vegas Pro, I've used the Bezier Mask to cut out the area around the vocalist's eyes so that they can be highlighted. In Vegas Movie Studio, I've used a Cookie Cutter FX to cut a round portion of the vocalist's face for the same reason. Vegas Pro allows greater precision, yet this technique may be applied in Vegas Movie Studio with some limitations to the complexity of the masking.

The upper track is masked, and a Color Curves FX is applied to it. Because of the feathering in the Bezier mask, the color curve is smoothly integrated into the lower track image, giving the illusion of the vocalist's eyes being lit with an eye-light. In this tutorial (both Vegas Pro and Vegas Movie Studio), I've provided keyframes only up to a certain point; when the keyframes end, it's quite obvious since the mask is no longer subtle and does not move with the vocalist's face.

This is a simple example of how a compositing mask and color correction may work together to repair or enhance an image.

In this next exercise, we're going to use a different kind of masking. The Secondary Color Correction FX may be used as a mask. Move down the timeline to the fourth Event, marked as Region # 6.

In this order, add the following FX to the Event:

- Color Corrector

- Color Corrector (Secondary)

- ChromaBlur

The playhead/cursor should park at **00:02:10;22**. The ChromaBlur FX is the visible FX in the FX dialog box; at the top of the dialog box, click the **Color Correction FX**. There is a **Parameter/ Custom** tab option. Select **Custom**. Starting with the **High** corrector, select and click the – button, or the **Complementary Color** button. Click this white/high eyedropper on a "white" portion of the singer's shirt. Click the **Low** complementary color button and sample the bottom of the drummer's hat brim in the far right corner. Select the **Mid** complementary color button and select a tree trunk as the neutral/gray point.

In the slider parameters are below the color wheels, set the **Saturation** value to **.695**. Vegas Pro users may want to view Video Scopes during this process to gain greater understanding of how saturation and desaturation display in the Vectorscope.

Figure 9.9 Select these areas for best color sample results.

Now click over to the **Secondary Color Corrector,** click the **Parameters** tab, and click **Select Effect Range.** Using the eyedropper tool, draw a square in the lit and shaded portions of the vocalist's neck area. This will tell Vegas the color range it should be limiting itself to, thereby ignoring any colors outside the skin-tone range (there will be some spill, but not enough to worry about). These next steps will help define the range of colors with greater accuracy.

Enable the **Show Mask** checkbox in the **Secondary Color Correction** FX. This will turn the preview monitor to black and white. Select the drop-down/expand arrow in the **Limit Hue** section of the Secondary Color Correction tool. Hold down **Ctrl** while adjusting the **Center** parameter. The goal in this part of the exercise is to turn all skin areas to mostly white and everything else to mostly black in the mask seen in the Preview window. Once the skin area is mostly white, work the width of the **Hue,** and fine-tune as necessary. **Smooth** the edges of the color selection.

Enable the **Limit Luminance** checkbox. Expand the **HIGH** value and observe how the **Limit Luminance** values reduce the visibility of the trees in the background. Smoothness should be set to **0.**

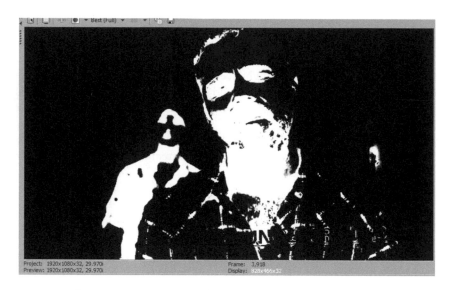

Figure 9.10   Your preview screen should appear similar to this screenshot.

Click on **ChromaBlur,** and set both horizontal and vertical to **2.0.** Nothing should change in the Preview monitor when this is done. Why? Because the ChromaBlur tool isn't seeing any color. It's a black-and-white image. So why is the ChromaBlur the last FX dragged to the chain? To illustrate a point that the order of FX is very important. Click and drag the **ChromaBlur** to the second position in the FX package/chain. The image will immediately soften the lines. For this image, it's quite possible that you'll be setting the blur all the way to 4.00 or the maximum value. The goal in this step is to smooth the transition from white to black where possible.

Click back to the **Secondary Color Corrector.** Disable the mask by unchecking the **Mask** box. The color will be restored. In the **Secondary Color Correction** wheel, click the **center** target to move the color. Move the target toward the **R** (for Red). This will affect the skin tones only, because we used the **Select Effect Range** feature to limit the bandwidth of color that Vegas is allowed to control or affect. For some fun, run the target around the color wheel and watch the skin change from red to green to blue to magenta. That's a drastic effect. Keep this technique in mind for when colors need to be replaced. Double-click on the **Color Corrector (Secondary)** to reset the wheel and your screen should look like this (split screen view).

Figure 9.11 Here is a desaturated effect with a fairly warm skin tone to create a nice effect. This is a chain of FX that can be saved and used on other clips and projects.

If the image appears to be too dark, drag down a Color Curves FX and add some brightness.

Tip_____

You can reset almost any control in any FX or plug-in by double-clicking it. Sliders, color wheels, knobs—it works on almost anything. Try it!

Tip_____

When images are too dark and are highly compressed formats, use Color Curves to brighten the image. *Never* use Brightness/Contrast, as this will also raise the light and related noise, making grain in the frame more apparent.

Single Color Pass

Place the cursor/playhead at **00:02:27;19.** Remove any FX that might be on the Event. White-balance the image. Drop the **Secondary Color Corrector** on the Event. When it opens, **Select Event Range.** Enable the mask. Use the eyedropper to select a range around the vocalist's neck/skin tone.

At the bottom of the tool, click the expander for **Limit Hue.** Narrow the width until the singer's outline is mostly black and the rest of the preview is mostly white. The goal in this session is to get the vocalist's skin as white as possible and the rest of the screen as black as possible.

(Remember, we're looking at the mask.) Hold down the **Ctrl** key to fine-tune the smoothness. It won't take much to adjust more of the background to black.

Expand **Limit Saturation** and hold down the **Ctrl** key as the **Highs** are adjusted to the left/reducing the high range. Smooth the saturation.

Expand the **Limit Luminance** menu. Move the **Highs** to the far right until the background starts to go white, then back off until it remains black. Depending on all previous selections, you may be all the way to the right or at full value.

Disable the **Show mask** checkbox. The preview will appear as though nothing has been done with the image. Click the **Invert mask** checkbox. In the middle section of the **Secondary Color Corrector**, find the **Saturation** adjustment and move it to the far left/no saturation point. The background will turn grayscale. Depending on how cleanly the mask was made, there may or may not be a small amount of red in the background. We'll look at how to get rid of this in the compositing chapter. Note that by checking or unchecking the **Invert mask** box you can choose whether the background or the singer's skin is in black and white.

Figure 9.12

Inserting or replacing colors that aren't part of the original shot is fast and easy with Vegas. Using the Secondary Color Corrector tool, you can selectively replace, grade, or enhance colors.

As an example, the movie *Pleasantville*, along with various commercials on television, has made the all-black-and-white-except-one-color look very popular. This type of work is nearly impossible to create with only a camera without doing lots of preproduction work. In Vegas, it's a few steps to create this look cleanly and quickly.

⏱ *Speed Tutorial*

Using the Secondary Color Correction tool, Vegas users have been able to create easily the *Pleasantville* look that is so very popular, particularly with wedding videographers and editors. Vegas 6 and later versions make this even easier by adding an Invert Mask to the Secondary Color Corrector, making this effect possible without using a copy of the same Event as a mask.

Pleasantville/Single Color Pass Look

Open the Single-Color_Pleasantville.vf project file.

1. Open the **Secondary Color Correction** tool and apply it to the Event on the timeline, then select the blue of the shirt. Enable the **Mask** mode and fine-tune the mask.

2. Set **Luminance Low** to **0, High** to **255**.

3. Click the **Limit Saturation** drop arrow and set **Low** to **0** and **High** to the far right max.

4. In the **Chrominance** section, slide the **Saturation** control completely to the left, or to none.

5. Select the **Invert mask** tick box and uncheck **Show mask**. Notice that the image is now black and white and desaturated, but the selected blue color selected is allowed to pass through.

This Invert Mask option makes for very easy creation of the *Pleasantville* look. This is particularly effective in wedding videos (though now a bit dated), used to pass only red found in bouquets or perhaps the white found in the bride's dress. Multiple instances of the Secondary Color Corrector may be used as well, allowing for two or more colors to pass.

Using the Gradient Map for Effect/Correction

Sometimes color cannot be smoothly corrected using the color corrector tools. Inserting a gradient map may be used for effect. In Region #8 (place the cursor/playhead at **00:03:06;00**), drag and drop the **Gradient Map** FX to the Event. We're going to warm up the shot while leaving the vocalist somewhat cool.

When the Gradient Map opens, click the **#1** target in the **Gradient Map** and then select the eyedropper tool. Click on the vocalist's neck. This will turn the scene very blue. Since the opposite of blue on a color wheel is yellow, move the color target in the gradient palette to a yellow hue (you'll be sliding the target to the left).

Figure 9.13   Place the target somewhere in this range to set the gradient to yellow. Vegas may display a small exclamation point over a target color. This means the color is out of range for NTSC SD broadcast. If the warning displays a *P*, this means it is out of range for PAL broadcast (in SD).

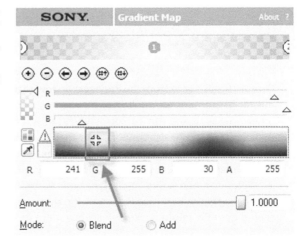

The entire scene will now appear to be blown-out yellow. No worries! Now blend the gradient with the scene by moving the **Blend** slider to the left. A value of approximately **.200** is appropriate. Set the color values to:

R-255

G-177

B-0

Alpha-255

Now set **Blend** to approximately **.200**; this should suffice to warm up the scene while leaving the vocalist fairly cool and desaturated. It's a smooth transition because we're overlaying color to the entire scene.

Select the **Add** radio button and watch the scene slightly change. Now adjust the **Blend** slider and the scene will overexpose but still have an interesting look that may be appropriate in some settings. Check your work by enabling the half-screen FX bypass view.

Figure 9.14 Use the Split Screen/FX bypass often to check work and be sure that the color correction is still within the range of the desired look as compared to the original scene.

Capture a still frame from the Preview window to the clipboard. This snapshot should be from a master or primary scene. It may be used as a reference point for color correcting/matching other scenes. Place the cursor/playhead in a different scene, and enable the **Split Screen/ Bypass** FX. In the drop-down next to the Split Screen button, click the **Clipboard** option. The screen will display the snapshot on one half and the current time frame on the other half. The snapshot may be used for color sampling or matching the two disparate images. This is useful for correcting multiple cameras or for matching a single camera in different lighting situations. It also is useful for checking color alterations for aesthetic effect or for seeing how FX might make two scenes more or less compatible.

Figure 9.15 Often overlooked, the Split Screen view is very useful for comparing frames, including before and after. Projects may even be rendered with split screen if that effect is desired.

Black/White and Mixing

Desaturated color, either partially or to complete black and white, comes and goes as a fad in the video production world. We've already looked at some different methods of achieving this effect, but sometimes we'll want to do this fast and dirty. Here is a quick method.

In Region #9 of the **Color Correction.vf** project, drop on the **Black/White** filter. Set the value of the Black and White mix to **75%/.75**. Now drop on the **Saturation Adjust** FX, and set the **Amount** to **Full**. Set the **Center** to the left, or approximately.**10**. Adjust other settings to desired appearance. This provides a quick-and-dirty process that also renders quite fast.

Figure 9.16

Adjusting Levels Using Scopes (Not Available in Vegas Movie Studio)

The Video Scopes in Vegas Pro provide a means of measuring and analyzing video output levels to ensure that they meet legal broadcast standards for SD. The easy explanation of scopes is to think of Vectorscopes as being used for measuring color and saturation (chroma), whereas waveform monitors are used to measure light (luma). The Vectorscope's graticule roughly represents saturation as distance from the center of the circle, whereas hue is represented by the angle away from center. The Waveform monitor displays video signals to help us ensure that neither the color gamut nor the analog transmission limits are violated.

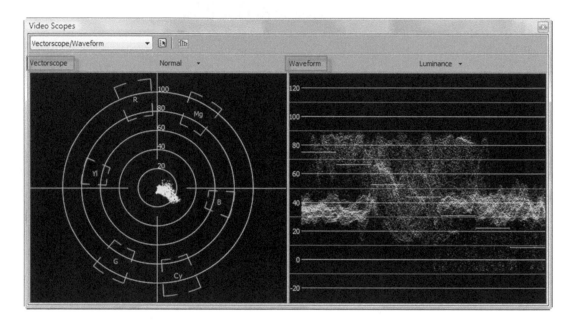

Figure 9.17

Illegal colors are colors that are not compliant with NTSC standards. Illegal colors overmodulate the broadcast signal, causing distortion of video and audio. No one will put you in jail for using illegal colors, but the strain on the eyes and ears, in most instances, will drive viewers crazy. If you've ever seen a low-budget car-lot advertisement on television with buzzing audio and distortion on the announcer's sibilants, chances are great that the commercial contains illegal colors, most likely the whites used in titles. (Distortion is actually across the entire audio signal but seems more apparent with an overmodulated color signal.)

Color value in the NTSC world is measured in IRE. Color value in the RGB world is measured in RGB component values. For example, in the IRE world, extreme black is 7.5 IRE. Extreme black in the IRE world, however, is really just a very dark gray, measuring at 16.5 in the RGB world. Extreme white in the IRE world is 100 IRE. Again, this is really just very bright gray, measuring at 234 in the RGB world. RGB extreme black is 0, whereas extreme white is 255. Any color value in the RGB world that goes below 16 or above 234 is illegal by NTSC broadcast standards. Any color value in the IRE scale that goes below 7.5 IRE or above 100 IRE is also illegal.

Legal colors are related to NTSC broadcasting. Most video equipment in the NTSC realm is calibrated or manufactured to the same specification. Practicing legal color on DVDs, videotapes, and hard drives is always a good habit to practice. The Internet currently has no color limits. Many MPEG-2 files delivered on DVD are also presented with "super black," or black values extending to 0 RGB.

Vegas also includes *histograms*, which can be used to measure the exposure of an image in post. With a histogram, we can see, from left to right/dark to light, what values are in a scene, and use various FX tools to bring the shot to a balanced point using just the display.

All these are tools designed to aid in adhering to standards, but as we're working in post, they're predominantly tools designed to give us confirmation of what our eyes see. Assuming that monitors are calibrated, trust what the eye sees rather than the scopes say.

The biggest relationship that we'll want to understand is one of levels and scopes. Open the **Scopes_Tutorial.veg** file. Place the cursor/playhead at the marker indicated, where we see the skydiver exiting the aircraft. Enable Video Scopes if they're not already open (**View | Video Scopes**).

Set the scopes to either **Vectorscope/Waveform Monitor** or just the **Waveform** monitor. See how the display lines go well above 100 IRE, and the blacks just barely reach 0 IRE? This is the measurement we'll want to view when aligning our video for proper output. There are other aspects we'll monitor along with the levels.

Set the preview window to **Best/Full**.

Drag the **Levels** FX to the Event/clip on the timeline. Seeing the preview window isn't terribly important, so if the FX dialog box covers it, that's okay. We'll start by adjusting the gamma of this clip to .850 to compensate for how this particular camera has distributed color. The scope will show the redistribution of Luma in the Waveform monitor. The Chroma component may be added to the Luma display by changing the Waveform monitor to **Composite** mode, but for what we're looking at in this section, viewing **Luma** only will work best.

Many of the small-format AVC and AVCHD camcorders use auto-modes for exposure, and often these encode with a lean toward overexposure. Using the Levels tool to shift the gamma and reexpose the scene will yield richer, more pleasing (if not color-accurate) results. The micro cameras seem to have a reduction in blue and a gain in yellow, so adding blue and reducing yellows often smoothes the image very nicely.

Hold the **Ctrl** key for fine-tuning, and click and drag the **Output End** slider. Move it toward the left until the Waveform monitor displays the high whites down to a value of **100**. The top line of the Luma display should barely be touching the 100 line in the Waveform monitor.

Figure 9.18

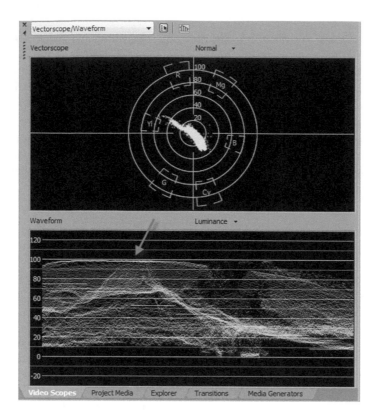

Select the **Input Start** slider, using **Ctrl** for fine control. Slide to the right until the bottom waves are just at 0. Use the **Enable/Disable** check box at the top of the FX dialog box to create a before/after view. Note that colors are deeper and richer and the image is more properly exposed.

Tip_____

The parade display in Vegas shows which colors are within individual limits. It also demonstrates the level of the total video output.

This valuable tool can help you discover color distortion at output. A standard parade display shows level information on RGB instead of showing the total level of the modulated video output.

The parade display can be updated by enabling the **Update scopes while playing** button. Leaving this enabled will take a hit on your CPU. (If your playback seems choppy, it might be a good idea to open the scopes and check that the Update Scopes option is *not* enabled.) Place the cursor over the highest part of a color display in the parade scope to display the RGB value of that color point.

Now we'll complicate matters by adding a Color Curves FX to the stream. By default a newly added FX always shows up as the last FX in the chain, on the far right. However, the Levels tool needs to be the last value in the chain; pull the **Color Curves** FX ahead of the **Levels** FX in the stream. In the **Curves** FX, choose the **Blue Channel** from the Channels drop-down menu. Use the **Curves** tool to bring up the blue in the image.

Figure 9.19

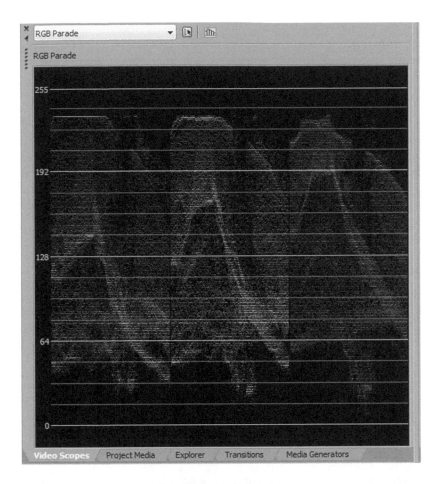

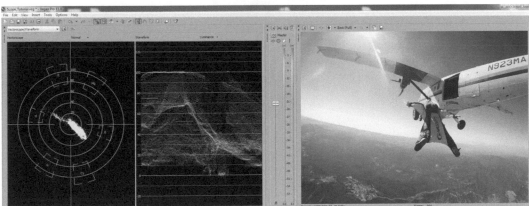

Figure 9.20   Your image and scopes should look similar to this image.

*Tip*_____

Right-click the **Tangent** anchor in the Curves tool, and disable the **Lock Tangent** option. This will allow the tangent to be moved up and down the scale, offering more flexibility.

 *Tip*_____

As a general rule, when using the Levels FX always place it last in the FX chain.

Do I Use Levels or Color Curves?

Levels are used to bring colors into legal range, but also to limit (or expand) the allowed dynamic range in a frame. The Levels tool may be used to brighten or darken media, yet this is not what it is intended for, and it could create other issues down the line. I use Color Curves in most situations to raise or lower apparent Luma in media, and I use Levels to adjust gamma and bring levels to a desired range.

Broadcast Levels FX

The Broadcast Levels FX is there to ensure that colors don't exceed standards for broadcast. Dropping this FX on the preview window (so that it filters the entire timeline) will ensure that legal colors for broadcast are not exceeded. Use this FX plug-in in conjunction with Scopes to better understand what the FX is doing to the picture. The Conservative settings act as a guarantee that video will meet stringent standards such as those required by PBS and other broadcasters.

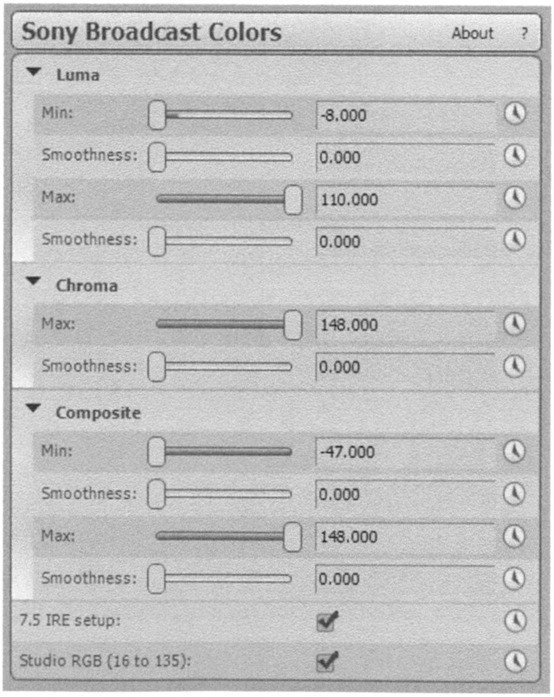

Figure 9.21   Even though the Internet does not have color limitations, inserting a Broadcast Color, Black Restore, or Levels filter on Events can indeed benefit video streams over the Web. Encoding is an art form, have no doubt. The fewer color variations in a stream, the better the stream. Redundant frames are the key to good streams. The Levels plug-in can limit colors. This process would not be useful if the HSL and Restore Black filters were used to crush blacks and reduce color saturation. Be aware, however, that the Broadcast Colors plug-in will not ever add anything to colors but will only ensure that colors are within legal ranges.

Making Digital Video Look Film-like

Notice that this section heading says "film-like" and not "like film." Video cannot look just like film. It's a different medium. Video can be made softer, with adjusted gamma, grain, and color saturation, but it still will not look the same as 16 or 35 mm film. I'll preface this section by saying that if you are interested in shooting only media that looks like it was shot on film, shoot on film. If you are interested in exploring how to make video more palatable to the eye, read on.

Making video look more film-like requires starting at the lens and the shooting aspects of the production. Using nothing but prime lenses, using dolly shots rather than lens zooms, and shooting with lighting intended for film are all part of the process. Shooting through filters, such as the Tiffen Black Mist series, helps warm the image as well. Practice shooting in a progressive scan or frame-based mode rather than shooting interlaced images, and, if the camera allows, shoot at 24p or 25p (NTSC or PAL) and learn how to operate the camera properly in progressive scan mode. In progressive scan mode, the camera must be handled differently from shooting in interlaced modes. Pans can easily become mush and blur in the hands of the inexperienced user. Handheld shots become a wash of colors in those same hands. Managing the camera correctly is half the battle in getting a good film-like appearance from the digital information.

Interlaced or Not?

One of the first exercises in the process of making video look film-like is to *deinterlace*. We discussed interlacing elsewhere in the book, but to revisit, interlacing is the process in which lines, known as *fields*, are drawn for every frame of video. NTSC DV and 60i HD have a frame rate of 30 or 29.97 fps. PAL DV and 50i HD has a frame rate of 25 fps. This information means that NTSC and 60i HD have 30 half-frames of lower fields/lines and 30 half-frames of upper fields/lines. PAL and 50iHD have 25 half-frames of upper fields/lines and 25 half-frames of lower fields/lines. These lines generally should be removed or blended to gain the smooth look of film. Video shot in progressive scan mode does not have these temporally offset fields. Be certain that when editing progressive scan footage in Vegas the project properties are set for Progressive Scan. If the setting is not correct, Vegas may insert the fields in transitions or other generated media.

Removing interlacing can be done within the project itself by setting Vegas to the project settings of progressive scan versus interlaced. Several ways to accomplish a properly deinterlaced image are available. The first and fastest way is to set the project properties to Progressive Scan. To do so, open the **File | Properties** dialog box, and in the **Video** tab, select **Blend Fields for Deinterlace** method and **None** (progressive scan) for the Field Order. This method is fast and easy and ensures continuity.

Another way, or "look," is to blend fields manually. This process creates a slightly softer image and may be preferable to your eye. When manually deinterlacing, create a new project. Set the Project Properties to **Progressive Scan**, and insert a new video track (**Ctrl + Shift + Q**). Place Events on the timeline. To deinterlace for a film-like appearance, duplicate the video track. Select an Event on the top track, right-click, and then select **Properties | Media | Field Order | Upper Field First**. Using the **Track Opacity/Level** slider on track 1, set opacity to **50** percent. On track 2, be certain that Events are lower-field first. This process deinterlaces the footage by drawing all parts of the frame rather than drawing only half the frame.

Gamma

Another big difference between video and film is the gamma curve. In Vegas, the gamma can be reduced using a color-correction tool. Increasing saturation is also good practice for obtaining a more film-like look. Using tools like the Red Giant Magic Bullet, Genarts Sapphire Edge, or New Blue color tools are all powerful options. The VASST REELPaks offer similar looks as well, with faster render times due to the looks being native to Vegas rather than external plug-ins.

Shooting Video for the Large Screen

You need to know a few things about shooting for a film-like appearance. First, if the video will ever be transferred to film, do not shoot with filters such as the Black Mist 2 from Tiffen. Shoot clean and with clarity. The same goes for using film-look plug-ins, such as grain. The digitally created film look is created in the transfer from video to film. You need to understand going in that video-to-film transfers are exceptionally expensive. An average 90-minute project will cost a minimum of $30,000 to transfer from video to film; www.dvfilm.com has lots of information on how to make this happen if this is your end goal. If video will be shown on a large screen, digitally projected, test the footage before sending out the entire project as an uncompressed file. Projection can create problems, such as pixelation or overblown colors, so the entire project should be checked over before public viewing. Rendering uncompressed footage, which is generally advisable for large-screen projections, can take a long time, particularly when motion blurs and supersampling are applied. Be sure to have everything checked out before starting this process, to avoid long periods wasted because of haste in the post-production process.

Audio Tools in Sony Vegas

Recording Audio in Vegas

Vegas Pro was one of the early multitrack editors available for the PC before the advent of Vegas Pro Video was born. Having set the standard for audio on the PC with Sound Forge several years previously, a multitrack tool was a logical step, and like Forge it became a standard for the Windows environment.

Vegas Pro is used for basic voiceover-only setups or as the heart of a full-blown multitrack studio setup for recording live bands, film scoring, television production work, or other professional audio requisite. Some users feel video is more difficult to edit than audio. Perhaps so, but audio has the greater importance of the two media forms. Those who would argue the point might want to take any movie, turn the sound off, and see how enjoyable the film is. Even in the days of silent film, a musical score accompanied the film, and most theaters had a piano or organ player who performed the score live along with the silent film. In current times, audio and video artists and engineers are crossing formerly strongly drawn lines in the authoring of various forms of media.

Vegas manages media at three levels:

- Event
- Track
- Project

(Some media management occurs in the Project Manager, but it is not controllable as in Event, track, and project levels.)

Events contain graphic, video, text, or audio information. Events can be individually edited and have effects added, processed, and controlled. Events live on tracks.

Tracks contain multiple Events. Tracks can control, process, and add effects to all Events on the individual track.

Projects contain a single track or multiple tracks. All Events contained in all tracks can be controlled, processed, and finished. (Effects may be added in the Project Media as well; however, this is not a timeline management of media/filters.)

Basic Setup

To record audio from a microphone plugged into the computer, a microphone and sound card are needed. Plug the microphone into the soundcard's microphone input and open Vegas.

The timeline/workspace will open with no audio or video control panes in Pro, and with the default tracks in Movie Studio. If an audio track needs to be inserted, do so by pressing **Ctrl + Q** or by selecting **Insert | Audio Track**.

Click the **Record** button on the control pane of the new track. Vegas displays a dialog box asking for the location to which audio files are to be recorded.

Figure 10.1   Clicking the **Record** button will call up a dialog box asking for the destination of audio.

 *Tip*_____

Recording to a second hard drive is highly recommended for purposes of keeping audio files off the system drive. This process allows input and output to run more efficiently and helps ensure flawless recording.

Audio is now ready to be recorded. Click the **Record** button on the transport control to begin recording.

Click the **Stop** button on the transport control to stop recording. You won't believe how many people will not think of that! This is all there is to recording basic audio in Vegas. From here, much, much more can be done.

When the **Record** button is armed (clicked), an icon that looks like two speakers is located in the Track Control pane next to the Record button. If a multichannel card is installed on the system, a number will appear instead of the dual-speaker icon. Clicking the speaker or number icon allows audio input to be converted from stereo to mono or a unique input channel to be selected on the multichannel device. If voice or a single instrument is all that needs to be recorded, it's good practice to use a mono input. Mono cuts required disk space by half.

The **Input Monitor** option also appears in the same menu as the stereo/mono inputs. Vegas allows inputs to be monitored with effects/processing as it's recording. For musicians, this feature is

Figure 10.2   Click the **Record** button on the transport control to begin recording.

fantastic; it allows you to monitor a reverb with compression added during the performance. The reverb/compression/other processing is not recorded to the track—it is there only to assist the vocalist or musician in getting the best performance possible. This feature gives Vegas the ability to be a multitrack recording system with no additional hardware whatsoever. The ability to monitor inputs with processing is entirely dependent on processing speed and system ability. FX Automation envelopes are bypassed during monitored recording.

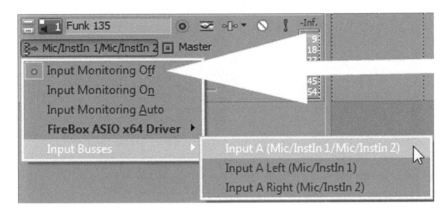

Figure 10.3   Audio may be recorded in stereo or mono and may be live-monitored in Vegas Pro.

Figure 10.4   Monitoring the recording.

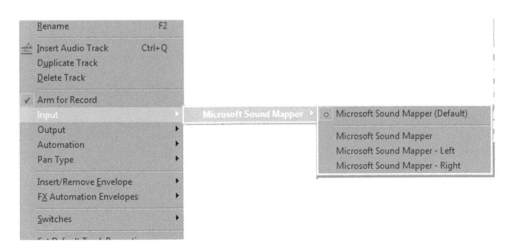

Figure 10.5   Selecting the Recording Inputs.

Checking the **Input Monitor** box enables processing to be heard through the output specified in the output/bus assignment dialog box. To assign outputs other than the default soundcard outputs, select **Options | Preferences | Audio** and specify input/output settings. If only a two-channel soundcard/Blaster-type card is present, nothing more can be set, since there is nothing for audio to be assigned to.

If a multichannel soundcard is available, such as an Echo Audio Layla, M-Audio Delta, or other similar card, up to 26 input/outputs can be specified. Multichannel cards are required for mixing 4.1, 5.1, or 7.1 Surround Sound.

Figure 10.6   Echo Audio Layla.

To use multichannel audio cards, select **Options | Preferences | Audio** and choose Windows-Classic Wave Driver or ASIO Driver in the Audio Device Type list box; otherwise, multichannel cards will not be properly accessed.

In general, multichannel soundcards do not have microphone preamplifiers (preamps) in them; however, a few models do. In the event that your multichannel card does not have a preamp built in, you will need one to properly drive channel input levels. If you don't have one, audio will be very noisy and not very loud. Separate preamps are typically better. However, many of the built-in preamps, such as the M-Audio Quattro and PreSonus FIREstation, are excellent and, for the investment, a terrific value.

Additionally, Vegas Pro is capable of working with multiple soundcards. Consult your soundcard manual for information on configuring more than one soundcard.

The volume control found in the Track Control pane is for playback volume only. Adjusting this setting during the recording process does not affect the recording process at all. Output from the soundcard, soundcard mixer, preamp, or other external input device determines the level of incoming audio.

To adjust the volume of incoming audio when you're not using a soundcard mixer, select **Start | Programs | Accessories | Multimedia | Volume Control**. Select **Options | Properties** and click the button to adjust the volume for recording. In the **Record Control** window that is displayed, recording input volume can be increased/reduced.

Recording audio in the digital realm can be tricky, particularly if one is familiar with analog techniques and practices. In the analog realm, it's acceptable to hit 0 dB and sometimes go slightly past

Figure 10.7   Setting preferences for a multichannel soundcard.

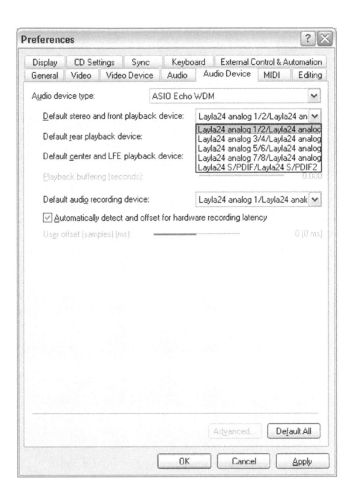

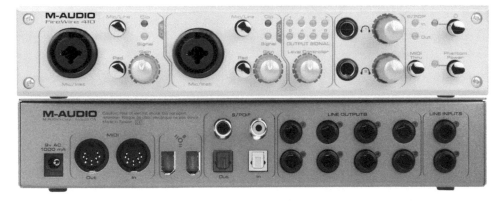

Figure 10.8   M-Audio Quattro.

Figure 10.9   PreSonus FIREstation.

0 dB. Tape has a saturation level that digital does not offer. Record audio in the digital realm with peaks hitting at not more than –3 dBFS and averages at around –15 dBFS. Because of the low-noise/no-noise digital signal-to-noise ratio, it is also easier to expand audio levels later in the editing/recording process. Bear in mind that digital 0 and analog 0 are –20 dB apart based on the Advanced Television Standards Committee (ATSC) standards (www.atsc.org). When using analog meters to view digital information, be sure that tones are used to match up analog meters to digital output. When you're working with audio for video broadcast, the analog broadcast standard is +4 dB into a source impedance of 600 ohms. Traditionally house reference meters are set to 0 VU based on the +4 dB level. A good maximum level to target is –3 dB for maximum levels at input.

Figure 10.10   Levels peaking at approximately –6 dB. The instrument is an acoustic guitar with no compression and is prone to unexpected peaks. Therefore, levels are marginally lower than they might otherwise be.

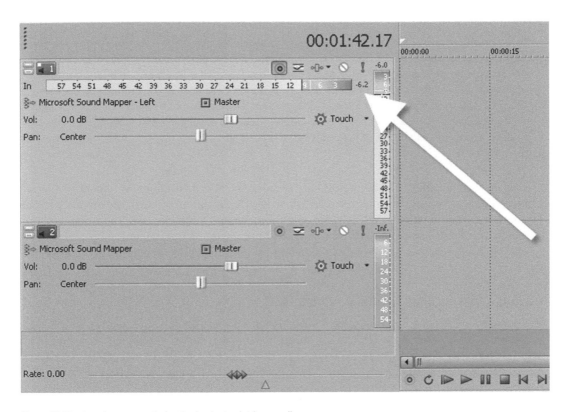

Figure 10.11   Level set correctly for the loudest point in recording.

Vegas Movie Studio is limited to 10 audio tracks. Vegas Pro allows for an unlimited number of audio (and video) tracks, dependent on the capabilities of your PC.

Recording Multiple Tracks

Multitracking is what Vegas is all about. The ability to monitor tracks while recording is critical. Vegas provides this ability with most low-end soundcards and with nearly any multichannel card. Recording and monitoring tracks is fairly fast and self-evident. Start by inserting a second audio track (**Shift + Q**) and assigning its inputs as you did for the original mono track. If the second audio track is to be mono, set it up this way now. Track 1 will play back through whatever soundcard is assigned. Track 2 will play back through the default assigned soundcard as well. Depending on the soundcard, this process can demonstrate latency during the recording process. This process is also one in which a professional soundcard is invaluable. Professional soundcards use ASIO drivers, which dramatically reduce latency in the hardware/software relationship.

In a computer audio system, *latency* means any delay or wait time that increases real or perceived response time beyond the response time desired. More specifically, latency is the time between sound being input to Vegas, processed, and returned to headphones or speakers. A contributor to computer latency includes mismatches in data speed between the CPU and input/output devices and slow buffers. Drivers and buffers can be set in Vegas to reduce latency. Small buffers reduce latency but increase the risk of dropouts. Larger buffers lessen the likelihood of dropouts but increase latency.

Vegas Pro has the ability to access ASIO drivers used by most professional soundcards. Latency can be reduced to as little as 2 milliseconds, which is virtually indiscernible to the human ear. This idea means that although the CPU is processing the incoming, outgoing, and affected audio information, the ear will hear audio playback in correct time.

Clicking the **Record** button (**Ctrl + R**) on the Transport bar starts the recording process while at the same time audio is playing back through the soundcard.

Advanced Recording Techniques and Tools

Vegas Pro and Vegas Movie Studio have many advanced tools for recording audio. Both offer a metronome for monitoring a click track during recording sessions. (This feature requires that Vegas's properties be set for beats and tempos.) Although this feature doesn't affect playback or recording speed from the timeline, it does affect the tempo at which the metronome is heard. Metronomes are useful for video editors as well because they can help set a cadence at which video may be edited.

 Tip_____

Ask the scorist for the video for a tempo map, and Vegas may be mapped out accordingly so that when the score is complete, the audio is dropped into place if tempo-based editing is the goal. The metronome will speed up and slow down according to the tempo map created in the production stages.

Tempos cannot be adjusted over time; they are fixed in the setting specified in the **Audio | Options** dialog box. Although Vegas Pro can't change tempos without an ACID loop acting as the driving click track, true tempo maps may be created in Vegas Pro by using an ACID loop as a click track, shifting tempo over time.

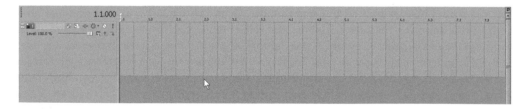

Figure 10.12   Setting a tempo grid in Vegas Pro.

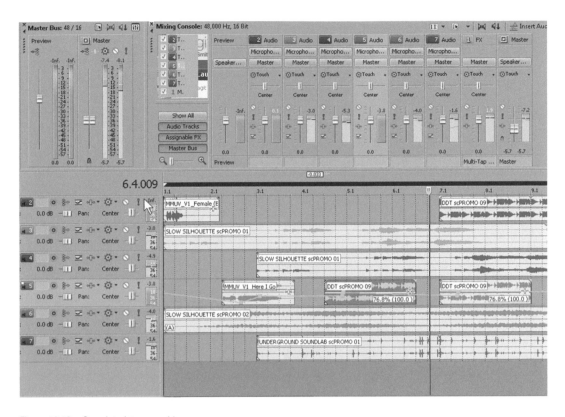

Figure 10.13   Completed tempo grid.

Recording with Takes

Rarely is a performance perfect every time; consequently, Vegas allows for takes to be recorded, just like in the movies when you hear "Take 1, take 2." In Vegas, takes may be recorded in a number of different ways; the number of takes is limited only by hard drive space.

Setting up a loop over the area where multiple performances are wanted instructs Vegas to continually loop over the area. If the area that requires multiple takes is a single Event, double-click the **Event**, which will set up the loop. Press **Q** or click the **Loop** button on the Transport bar. Click the **Record** button on the Transport bar, and Vegas begins recording. To stop recording, press the **Spacebar** or click the **Record** button again. A new take will appear on the timeline, layered over the old audio. The old audio is still there, it is merely hidden beneath the most recent recording. Pressing **T** or right-clicking and selecting the appropriate menu item toggles back and forth between the various takes. Takes can also be directly monitored by stopping playback, right-clicking, selecting **Choose Active**, and then clicking **Play** in the dialog box.

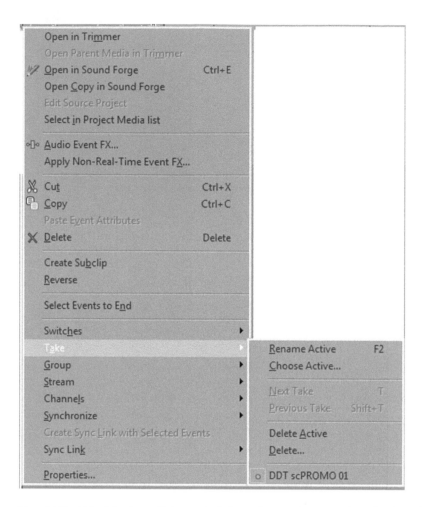

Figure 10.14   Using takes is an efficient method of recording a section over and over, keeping only the best performance. Takes may be split out and comps built from the various takes to create the best performance word by word or note by note.

Takes may be renamed to help identify them. Takes can also be opened in a specified audio editor for further editing and then saved as a new take or saved as the name of the take opened in the audio editor. Takes may be deleted from an Event as well, leaving only the desired audio in the Event.

Takes can also be added to the timeline in yet another fashion, albeit not necessarily in time. Right-click and select multiple audio clips in the Explorer or Project Media, drop them on the timeline, and, when the menu is displayed, select **Add as Takes** to put all files into one take. Takes can then be selected either using the right-click method or by scrolling through takes by pressing **T** or **Shift + T**. This method is handy for just about anything because it allows for toggling back and forth.

Takes are very handy for cutting together the best performance and for having the performer re-cord the same piece several times and then cutting the unwanted parts of a take. Press **S** to split takes and then choose the best of each line. This process is known in the industry as *comping*. With digital audio workstation/nonlinear editor software, comping is easy and fast. In the past, engineers had to take several tracks and, using mute buttons and fader moves, comp parts of several similar performances together to a new track. With Vegas, it's all done on one track with no difficulty, as there was in the analog world where it needed either loads of hands on the mixer or good automation.

Pre- and post-roll settings are available in Vegas Pro. Pre- and post-roll also act as punch-in/punch-out settings and may be combined with takes. To create a pre- or post-roll in a single Event, split the Event where the record in/out points are desired. Then create a loop or selection that begins before the split point and ends after the split point. Use the **Loop** tool if multiple takes are desired, and use a time selection only if a single punch-in/out is desired.

Next, click the **Record** button (**Ctrl + R**), and Vegas begins playing at the beginning of the time selection, begins recording at the split point in the Event, ends recording at the split point at the end of the Event, and stops or loops at the end of the time selection or loop point.

Recording actually occurs through the entire selection. This process allows you to expand the Event out in either direction if you need to get a pickup note.

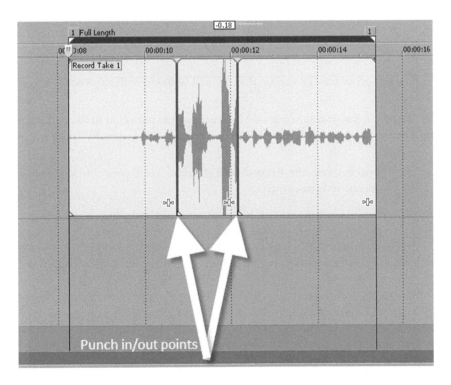

Figure 10.15   Defining pre- and post-roll on a single Event.

How About a Flyin' Smooth Punch?

Punch-ins have long been challenging for digital audio workstations like Vegas because of the digital look-ahead required to make punches smooth and clean. However, Vegas has conquered the punch-in problem and given it a total K.O.

A punch-in takes place when audio that has been previously recorded is monitored during playback, and Vegas is put into Record mode during the playback process, allowing a new section to be rerecorded. For example, perhaps a voiceover (VO) has been recorded and only one word is problematic. The VO is monitored during playback, and when it comes time to replace the bad word, a punch-in takes place that allows only the bad word to be replaced. Once Vegas has gone past the punch-in region, it disengages Record mode and continues in Playback mode.

Figure 10.16   The **Record** button can be punched in manually in Vegas, glitch-free.

To accomplish a punch-in:

1. Record a track. Assuming the track has errors, position the cursor prior to an error in the existing recorded track.

2. Locate the flawed section and, using the **S** key, split the recorded file section prior to the error, and split again at the end of the flawed area. Create a time selection with a few seconds prior to the split, extending slightly past the split. Looping may or may not be enabled.

3. Arm the existing audio track for recording by pressing the **Record Enable** button found on the track header.

4. Start playback of the project or file. The original audio will be heard until the **Record** button is pressed.

5. Press the **Record** button on the transport bar or hardware device connected to the computer. Vegas will begin recording at that point. If Input Monitoring is enabled, the new audio will be heard.

6. To stop the recording process, press the **Record** button again. Vegas will continue rolling (post-roll) for a few moments and then stop.

Vegas will also allow you to record multiple takes if looping is enabled. Press the **Looping** button or the **Q** shortcut key and Vegas will create a new take each time the loop repeats. This provides multiple choices of various performances, allowing you to choose the best one. Vegas will actually create regions with each take. These regions will not be part of the project but will be displayed in the Trimmer.

If you have multiple punch-in sections, you can select each one by holding **Ctrl** and clicking on each split-out section. Vegas will automatically punch in and out at these sections, allowing multiple retakes to be created over the length of the entire file. Prior to the recording process, a file location should have been specified in the **Project Properties** dialog box. If one has not been selected, Vegas will prompt for the file to be named and saved. If the track was named prior to the recording process, Vegas will automatically select the track name as the filename. The file may be renamed in the Post-record dialog box.

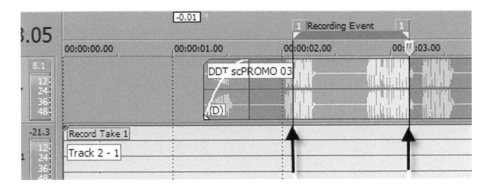

Figure 10.17 Illustration of trimmed section with pre-/post-roll.

Figure 10.18 The Post-record
dialog box.

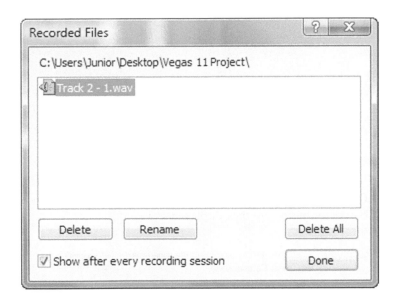

Assigning Buses (Not Available in Vegas Movie Studio)

Buses can be used to route audio to anywhere it must go. A bus can feed another bus, creating virtually limitless routing if necessary.

Vegas Pro is capable of handling up to 26 simultaneous buses, corresponding to the letters of the English alphabet. This means that up to 26 channels of audio can be streaming out of the computer at once if enough hardware devices are connected. It takes four to eight channel converters to meet this output and to leave six output channels empty. The norm is to have 24 channels of output.

This feature does not mean that Vegas Pro is limited to 24 channels of audio; not at all. Vegas Pro is limited to up to 26 channels of audio busing, but the number of audio *tracks* is limited only by the processing power of the computer.

If several tracks are on the timeline, insert buses into the mixer by clicking the **Insert bus** button.

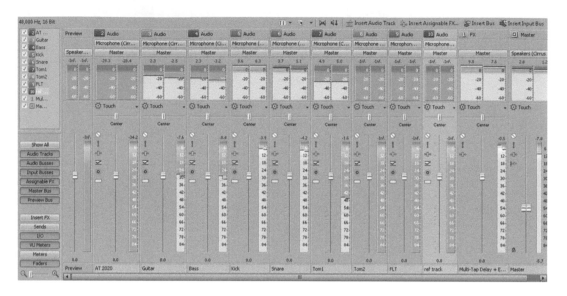

Figure 10.19   Adding a bus to the mixer.

On the **Track Control** pane, click the small square that appeared when the first bus was inserted. Choices for busing are then displayed.

Figure 10.20   Select bus routing by clicking the square on the **Track Control** pane.

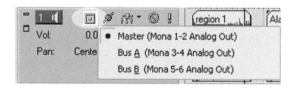

Select bus **A**. Audio on that track is now sent to the bus A mixer section. For example, bus A could be sent to the normal right/left outputs of a mix, or it could feed a rear channel of a Surround system. Alternatively, it might feed a signal processor, such as a flanger, reverb, or delay; perhaps it's a submix that eventually routes back to the master output.

Assign the bus outputs in the **Mixer** window in the same manner. Click the small square that appears on the bus control. On track 2, assign the track to the same bus **A** output. This step routes tracks 1 and 2 through the bus A outputs.

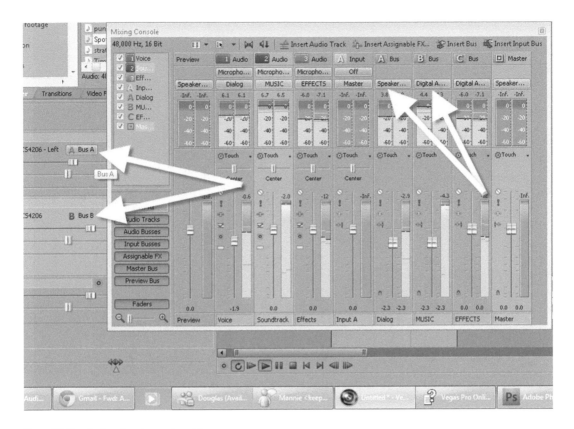

Figure 10.21   Assigned and unassigned buses.

Buses are often used for submixing, such as all drums going through one submix, all keyboards through another submix, and all rhythm instruments through yet another submix. This feature is of value because then all drums can be pulled down or up in volume without affecting the mix levels of each instrument/track or all keyboards can be raised or lowered. Signal processing is less taxing on the CPU if processing is done at the bus level as well. Putting six compressors on a drum kit is much more processor-intensive than putting one compressor on a drum submix. Generally, kick and snare drums are left out of submixes, as are lead vocals. These primary instruments/tracks are typically controlled individually.

 Tip_____

In the video world, buses may be used for DM&E, or *dialogue, music, and effects*. Dialogue feeds channels 1/2, music feeds channels 3/4, and effects feed channels 5/6. In the pre-stereo days, DM&E were mixed to mono tracks so that if dialogue (or music or effects) needed to be changed out for voice dubbing for foreign languages or other changes, only the dialogue track was affected. It is still done much the same way in today's digital workflows.

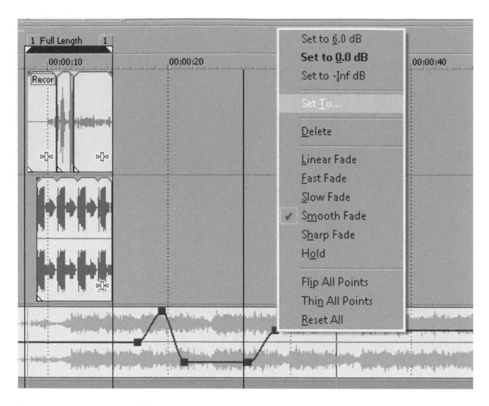

Figure 10.22 Inputting specific values available via right-click.

Using Buses for Routing Effects

Buses may also be used to route effects. Effects can be placed on individual tracks, but as the number of tracks grows, the load on the processor increases. It's therefore a good idea to place effects on buses to affect several tracks at once. In other words, instead of having 10 tracks, each with their own individual reverb, a single reverb might be applied via a bus and 10 tracks feed the single reverb, thus saving a lot of CPU cycles.

This process can be done using direct track assignment, the multipurpose fader, or through assignable FX envelopes. Envelopes can be used to automate effect levels, sends, and returns.

In the **Mixer** window, click the **Insert FX** button, choose a delay effect, and set the effect to the parameters you'd like to hear. Now right-click in the **Track Control** pane and choose the bus to which you assigned the delay. An envelope is displayed in the track timeline. This is the Send-to for the specified bus. Raising the line will increase the amount of audio sent to the delay and lowering it will decrease the amount of it. Double-clicking the envelope places a handle/node on the envelope, allowing for automatic send changes. If a delay is needed only on a specific phrase or moment in an Event contained in the track, the envelope can be pulled all the way down until that moment when the envelope will be raised to the desired level. Handles or nodes can be right-clicked, and the Set-to percentage or volume can be specified that way as well. Additionally, holding Shift while hovering over an inserted envelope allows envelope points to be drawn, just as they're created by a HUI device such as the Mackie Control Universal.

> FX can be set as pre- or post-faders in Vegas Pro. This option is found on nearly all mixing consoles and is important, particularly for sound designers. This option allows audio to be sent to the processor before the fader, so regardless of where the track fader is set, even if it's off, FX receives an audio signal. Post-fader is the way most processing is done; reducing the output volume of a track also reduces the send to the FX. As an envelope fades on the track, the send to the FX fades as well. Bus sends are post-fader by default. To change them to pre-fader, right-click the **Bus Send** to change it to post from the submenu that appears. You can also right-click a bus output fader in the mixer section, or select **Pre/Post** in the Mixing Console view (**Ctrl+Alt+6**).

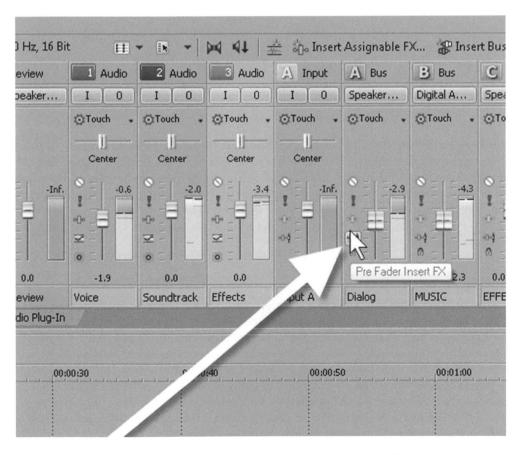

Figure 10.23   Right-click the **FX Send** on a track to select pre- or post-fader send to the FX.

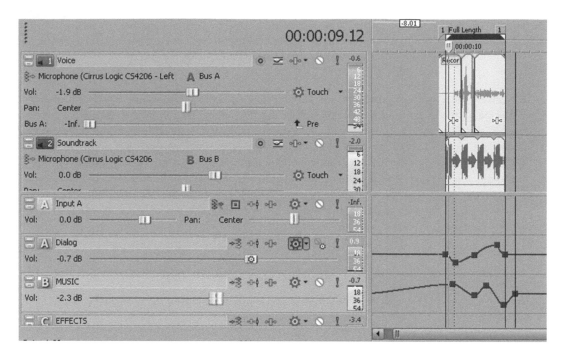

Figure 10.24   Vegas Pro bus assignment.

Buses may be viewed as tracks for automation. Bus outputs/returns can be automated for much greater mixing power, for example, if there were several tracks with background vocals, all vocals needed to be raised in volume at once, and all required a reverb to rise with the volume. The vocals could be sent to one bus, with the reverb sent to another bus. The reverb is controlled by an inserted bus send, and the vocal levels are controlled by an envelope assigned to another bus, just like a bus routing on a typical mixing board. With busing and automation, mixes are capable of being very deep and exacting.

Could I Get a Transfer Please?

Buses are used to route audio from place to place, being used for submixes or effects send and return. However, Vegas Pro provides the option of routing buses to buses. This allows for much easier patching of submixes. One use of this feature is to patch separate mixes to two different locations, such as sending one mix to a hardware device or external mixer while sending the other to a master bus. Buses may be used in a recording studio to set up master mixes while also having a headphone mix for the talent to listen to. Artists usually like to hear their performance with a little more reverb than the producer might like to hear, or perhaps they need a little more of this or that in their mix that is different from what is being heard in the control room monitors. Buses can provide all of that.

The bus panel indicates where audio is being routed to. If the [icon] is shown, then the audio is being routed to a hardware device. If the [icon] is shown, then audio is being routed to the master, and if the [A] is shown, audio is being routed to another bus. Up to 27 buses (letters A–Z plus the master) are available.

Vegas Pro also has a wonderful fail-safe capability that prevents a bus from being routed back to itself. If you have two buses in your project and the first bus is routed to the second bus, the second bus may be routed only to the master output or a hardware device. This prevents feedback loops from occurring.

Audio Mixer (Not Available in Vegas Movie Studio)

The audio mixer in Vegas Pro is an emulation of an analog mixer in a recording studio. Editors and producers can see exactly what is incoming here and outgoing there; all buses, FX sends, channels, levels, automation, soundcards, tracks, and more are visible in this one view, and it is viewed with a layout immediately identifiable to anyone who is working or has worked in a recording studio or live-sound environment. The mixer can be docked across multiscreen monitoring systems in the Docking window or be made to go full screen on all monitors once recording is complete.

One of the primary benefits of the audio mixer is the routing system. Older versions of Vegas Pro could not route buses to individual audio FX. In the mixer, each channel strip will display any audio FX inserted into the channel. Inserted buses will also display any audio FX inserted into the channel, as will the master output channel.

Automation may be controlled from either the track header or the audio mixer. I believe most users will find the audio mixer to be more intuitive. Another major benefit of the audio mixer is that track headers may be minimized completely, with all track media being viewed on one screen, with the audio mixer viewed full screen on a second screen. Double-click the bar on the right side of the track headers to minimize all track headers. Place the audio mixer on the second computer screen, and in this manner a much more comprehensive view of the project is possible.

In prior versions of Vegas Pro, audio weighting was managed differently. In the Options | Preferences, **Use Legacy Track Gain** has been added. If Add Channels (the default) or the Balance 0 dB pan modes are used, there is no difference when this preference is invoked. For the other pan modes that cut the signal when the pan is set to center, there is a decrease in the level (depending on which pan mode is used). When working on legacy projects (projects begun in versions of Vegas Pro prior to 8), it's best to use the legacy track gain function. New projects moving forward will work best if this option is left unchecked.

Notice the differences when working with panning/track modes in Vegas Pro:

- Add Channels (no cut)
- Balance 0 dB (no cut)
- Balance –3 dB, constant power, film (3 dB cut)
- Balance –6 dB (6 dB cut)

Audio FX panning may also be performed. If this is the goal, right-click the **FX Send/Fader** in the track header and choose **Link to Main** in the menu.

FX Packaging

Creating FX chains is an important aspect in Vegas Pro. Often, default presets in FX are simply not enough. If multiple FX chained together with specific presets are needed, Vegas can save a chain of FX with presets. For instance, an equalizer (EQ), a compressor, and a chorus might be used for vocal processing, with each of the individual FX having its own presets. Rather than having to insert and choose presets for each effect manually on each track or Event, all three may be saved as a chain or package complete with presets.

To create a package, perform the following steps:

1. Click the **Insert FX** button in the Bus, Mixer, or Track Control windows, which opens the Plug-In Chooser.

2. Choose the plug-ins you want to use.

3. Arrange the plug-ins in any manner, either by dragging a plug-in before another or by using the **Shift Plug-In Left/Right** buttons found in the upper-right corner.

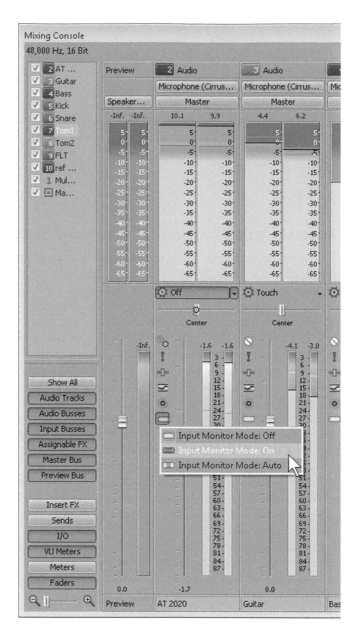

Figure 10.25   The audio mixer found in Vegas Pro provides a graphical interface familiar to audio editors and live-sound engineers.

4. Click the **Save As** button and name the chain, which will now be stored as a package in the Plug-In Packages folder.

5. Click **OK**. Your preset is now stored and can be recalled at any time.

FX to Go, Please?

Moving FX settings from one computer to another has long been a challenge for users of most any nonlinear editing (NLE) system. Vegas Pro has a feature that allows FX folders to be moved from system to system, permitting users to share FX chains and presets. Using the Preset Manager (available at www.sonycreativesoftware.com/download/utilities/), you can back up and share your chains and presets across multiple installations of Vegas Pro. This tool is especially useful when you have developed a chain of FX that you want to share with multiple editors or workstations.

This feature works the same as all the other plug-in explorer folders, but now it also works for audio FX packages, video FX packages, transition packages, and media generator packages. Newly created packages go in the appropriate top-level package folder. (You'll need to close and reopen the plug-in explorer to see the new order of FX packages.)

Using the Preset Manager to move packages from one computer system to another is simple; save the Filter Package as a **.sfpreset** file, then copy that file and paste it to the new computer system via a network, USB drive, hard drive, or other means. Then open the **sfpreset** file with the Preset Manager on the target system and save the FX chain. The FX package will reside on the new system.

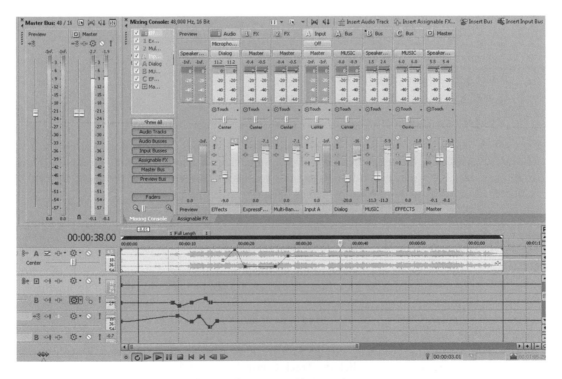

Figure 10.26   A single track feeding four buses and two auxes with automation.

Inserting Effects without Using a Bus (Not Available in Vegas Movie Studio)

Effects can be directly routed and controlled in Vegas Pro without inserting a bus. This process is similar to an aux send that doesn't return to a bus on an analog mixer.

Click the **Insert FX** button in the Mixer window, which calls the Plug-In Chooser dialog box. Plug-ins can be viewed by All, Chains, Automatable, Sony, Third-party, or Optimized. **All** shows every available plug-in installed in the system.

Choose the FX desired. If multiple FX are desired, press and hold down **Ctrl** while selecting FX. They will all be placed in the mixer as a series. FX selected this way cannot be individually controlled, since they all share the same send and are chained together.

FX can also be inserted individually. Every FX plug-in that is inserted in the Mixer window is also available to every track or bus. Keep in mind that this process can be very processor-intensive during preview, although it will not affect the final render.

Use FX assigned to buses, as opposed to individual tracks when several tracks need the same effect. For example, a group of tom-toms, cymbals, and percussion might be able to share a reverb or delay. Rather than insert a reverb and delay on every track, send all related tracks to a bus and insert the FX, controlled by the bus.

To route multiple tracks to the same effect, perform the following steps:

1. **Insert FX.**

2. Insert a **bus**.

3. Assign all desired tracks to the bus.

4. Select **View | Show Bus Tracks.**

5. Right-click the **bus** track and insert an **FX envelope**.

6. Set envelope as desired.

Now all tracks have the necessary FX, with automation to those FX controlled from the bus. Choruses, verses, fills, bridges, other sections of a song, or sound design for a movie can be unique in the way that FX are heard and managed as a result of this method, yet processor and RAM resources have been spared the heavy load of having many plug-ins active.

Using Track FX

Every audio track in Vegas has a chain of FX installed on it already. A noise gate, EQ, and compressor are found by clicking the **FX** button on each audio track. They can be heard during recording by using input monitoring, they can be removed from the track, or they can be appended to or replaced all together. These FX are optimized to keep processor resources at their peak, but they still place a load on the processor.

Set the default track properties by setting up the track the way you'd like it to default to. Set up an FX chain for the track FX, right-click the **Track Control** pane, and select **Set Default Track Properties**. Checking the boxes in the dialog box that opens will cause the current track settings to become the default settings for future tracks inserted into the current project. Now every time Vegas opens, these track settings become the default, saving time and preventing the user from having to remember how the last mix was set up before beginning.

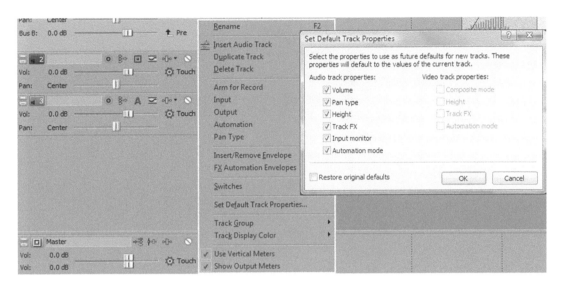

Figure 10.27a   Set the track defaults before recording so that all audio tracks have the same settings when they're inserted.

 Tip_____

Set up a blank project with all track settings in place so that when a project is started, a template of several tracks is already built. Starting with 8 to 16 tracks, complete with commonly used compressor, EQ, and reverb settings, not only saves time but also impresses clients when they hear how quickly a tight sound can be dialed in. On the DVD enclosed with this book, you will find a recording interface with tracks in place that can be used as a starting point for your preferences.

Tempo-Based FX

ACID Pro offers a feature that allows users to tempo-map certain audio effects, and this feature has been incorporated into Vegas. It's a creative tool that allows a delay, chorus, or other time-based effect to read the tempo of the project and match the tempo when the delay is played out. This is somewhat useful for dialogue only, but if music has been inserted into the timeline or if ACID loops or other files containing tempo metadata are being used, they will significantly benefit from this feature. For example, perhaps there is a cadence to a song that has been used for editing. When the song ends, a delay that matches the beat of the song might be effective in smoothing out the decay of the song. Tempo-based audio FX might be very effective in filling out a thin audio track or powering up SFX.

Figure 10.27b   In this window, set the project tempo as the Beats per minute value.

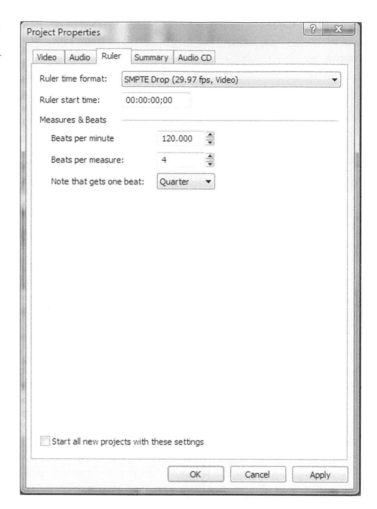

All versions of Vegas Pro have offered a Project tempo setting, found in the Project Properties. This is where you'll set the tempo of the project. When you are working with VASST TrakPaks, ACID loops, or other meta-rich audio, the audio's metadata will indicate the native tempo of the audio in the Explorer Summary. This is the tempo that should be set in the Project Properties.

To use the tempo-based FX, insert a time-based effect such as a Sony Reverb, Delay, Chorus, or Simple Delay. When the effect dialog box opens, there will be a checkbox labeled **Tempo Sync Delay**. Checking this box locks the delay to the timing of the project tempo. In the drop-down box below the checkbox, timing locks to specific musical note values may be chosen, ranging from dotted half-notes to 64th triplets, dotted half-notes being the slowest value. If **Multiple Delays** are chosen in the dialog box, then **Tempo Sync Decay** lights up. Note that the same sync values apply, with the addition of syncing to measures. This will be the slowest repeat of decay available.

When using ACIDized loops, the loops will not conform to the tempo settings of the project unless the **Import Audio at Project Tempo** checkbox is selected in the **Options** | **Preferences** | **Audio** dialog box. Although it is very easy to set and forget this preference, some MP3 media or other non-ACIDized audio files may not play back properly. If this occurs, uncheck the **Audio at Project Tempo** preference.

Virtual Sound Technology

VST[†] is a plug-in format that often runs a little more smoothly than DirectX plug-ins but also offers a very wide array of access to various audio plug-ins that will benefit the audio user. In fact, a very large number of free VST plug-ins are available on the Web. I like the Kjaerhus audio plug-ins; they've got a Classic Series that is free, and they sound great.

To access the VST plugs, download or install them to a directory on your preferred hard drive. I install all my VST plug-ins to a folder on my C: drive labeled **VST** and that's it.

Figure 10.27c   Virtual Sound Technology, or VST, is a competing plug-in format to Direct-X.

Figure 10.27d   The free versions of the Kjaerhus audio plug-ins may be found on the DVD included with this book.

[†]VST is a trademark of Steinberg Media Technologies GmbH.

Vegas searches for a default directory of C:\ Program Files\Vstplugins\, so this is where you might prefer to install them. This directory may be shared by other applications.

Now open Vegas, go to **Options | Preferences,** and click the **VST Effects** tab. Point the **Default VST** search folder to the folder you've installed or downloaded the files to, if it's a location other than the default location indicated previously, and then click the **Refresh** button. This will instruct Vegas to search for whatever plug-ins you've installed, and they'll show up in your Vegas Audio FX options in the folder marked **VST.** This search could take a while if you've got a fair number of plug-ins installed. If you'd like to have alternative VST plug-ins, perhaps in the event that you'd like to sort them by manufacturer, Vegas allows for up to two separate, alternative locations for search for FX. VST plug-ins (in the Windows format) are dynamic link libraries (DLL), and the free versions of most VST plug-ins do not have an installer but rather a Zip file containing the DLL. As mentioned, you'll want to copy or install these DLL files to the C:\Program Files\Vstplugins\ location or a different location of your choice. Find free VST plug-ins on the DVD that accompanies this book, along with demo versions of other VST plug-ins.

You'll apply VST FX just as you would other plug-ins. Double-click and click **OK,** or single-click and select **Add** and then **OK.** Then adjust the parameters of the plug-in just as you would with any other plug-in. You can chain VST plug-ins right alongside DirectX plug-ins, and there are many automatable VST plug-ins available if you need to automate certain FX on the timeline. Storing

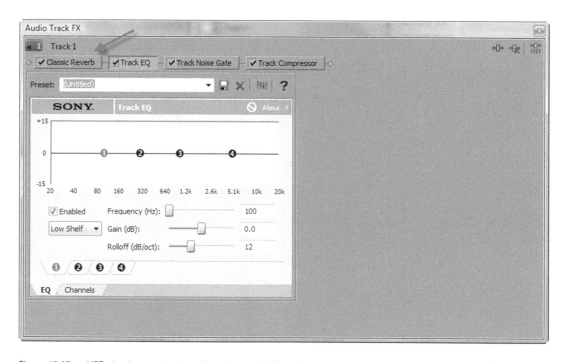

Figure 10.27e   VST plug-ins can be placed in a chain with DirectX plug-ins, and they operate the same way a DirectX plug-in does.

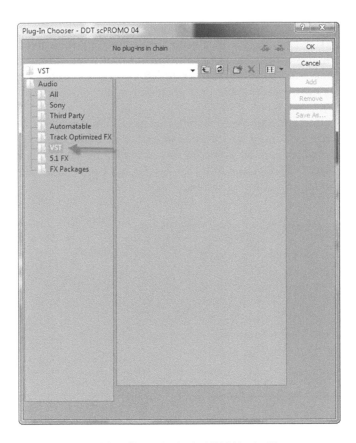

Figure 10.27f   Find the VST plug-ins in the VST folder for FX.

presets for VST plug-ins will be somewhat different, and these presets cannot be exported in the same manner as presets that are exported using the Preset Manager.

One thing to note about VST plug-ins: If a manufacturer offers both VST and DirectX installations of their plug-ins (many do), then you should install both. The reason is that some DirectX plug-ins occasionally cause audio to drift, whereas the same application in VST form might not. The opposite may also apply; a VST plug-in may incur drift, whereas its DirectX counterpart might not. VST and DirectX plug-ins aren't really different except for how they're wrapped and how much attention was paid to optimizing the code that runs the plug-in.

Recording Multiple Tracks

When you're working with a band or ensemble, several tracks might need to be recorded at one time. A multichannel soundcard is best used in this situation. If a two-channel soundcard is used, only stereo information will be recorded, and an analog mixer will be required to manage all of the microphones. With multichannel cards, an unlimited number of microphones can be input directly to

Vegas, depending on the number of cards used. (Many manufacturers of hardware cards have limits as to how many cards can be stacked.) These can be individually controlled without using an external mixing device. To select multiple inputs with an individual microphone routed to each input, assign the input of each track as mono and select either the right or the left input of the soundcard.

Remember, if your soundcard does not have preamps built in, a preamplifier is needed for every input channel to be used simultaneously.

Select a channel input for each microphone, and with every channel that has an input assigned, be sure the channel is armed. Click the **Record** button (**Ctrl + R**), and all tracks that are armed will record in sync. Enable input monitoring where necessary—the more tracks that are set for input monitoring, the heavier the processor load. Without using ASIO drivers, latency can be unreasonably high. Use ASIO drivers for input monitoring for best results.

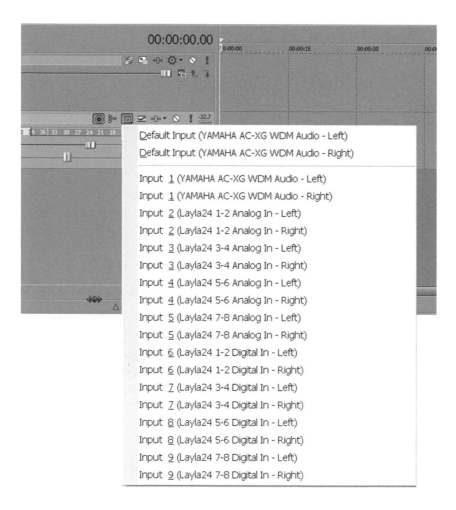

Figure 10.28   The Echo Layla has multiple analog and digital inputs.

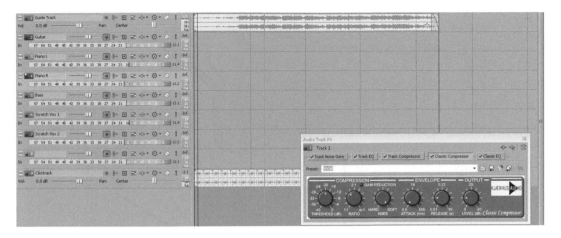

Figure 10.29   Typical session armed for recording. Double-click the right side of the track header bar to show or hide track headers.

Vegas has the ability to support ASIO drivers, found in most professional soundcards.

 *Tip*_____

Pressing **Ctrl + A** selects all tracks at one time, and clicking the **Record** button on one track simultaneously arms all tracks. Clicking the **Record** button again after the recording is finished disarms all tracks. Use this same technique to insert volume, pan, bus, or FX envelopes on every track.

Synchronizing Vegas Pro to External Devices (Not Available in Vegas Movie Studio)

Some studio setups can call for a multitrack tape machine, sequencer, or other external device to control Vegas Pro, or conversely, Vegas Pro can be the master device controlling external equipment if the proper hardware is in place. To do this, a device that can convert SMPTE to MIDI timecode (MTC) is required.

Most MIDI distribution devices are capable of converting incoming MIDI timecode to SMPTE or outgoing SMPTE timecode to MIDI timecode. Most tape machines will accept either MTC or SMPTE. Some accept both.

If Vegas Pro is to be the master device, Vegas Pro needs to generate timecode. Set this up in the **Options | Preferences | Sync** dialog box.

Figure 10.30   Setup of a timecode device to connect Vegas Pro and external recording devices.

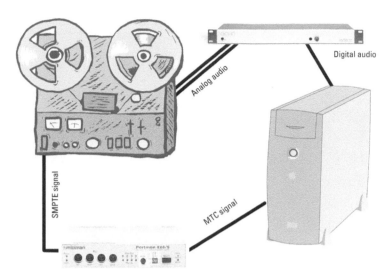

If you click **Play** in Vegas and it starts or stops an external device, Vegas is known as the *master*. If starting and stopping the hardware starts and stops Vegas Pro, Vegas is the *slave*.

To generate a timecode that an external device can read, have the owner's manual of the external device handy so you can learn the incoming timecode specs that it requires. Most devices default to 30 frames per second, whereas other devices call for 29.97 nondrop. The standard for most professional audio equipment is 30 fps. DV has a different standard, based on U.S. television standards.

Vegas generates timecode that is sent to the conversion device, by which it is distributed to whatever external devices Vegas needs to control. Timecode connection is necessary if Vegas will be used to edit external media that will be returned to the external recording device after edits are completed.

In the **Options** | **Preferences** | **Sync** dialog box, Vegas has an option to use either an internal clock from the CPU clock or the clock generated by the soundcard. Most instances will call for the clock to come from the soundcard. Vegas also has the ability to send full-frame messaging to external devices. Full-frame information can speed up location in some external tape machines. Not all devices can respond to full frames, and some devices can become confused. Check the documentation that came with the device that Vegas is controlling.

If Vegas is to be a slave to timecode generated by an external device, Vegas must be set to trigger from timecode. In the **Options** | **Preferences** | **Sync** dialog box, set the trigger from the device sending timecode into the computer. Be certain that Vegas Pro's frame-rate setting matches the frame rate being sent from the external master device. Otherwise, audio will drift ahead or behind the master when Vegas is played in time with the external master. For Vegas to operate consistently with a word clock connection, trigger must be used. *Trigger* refers to Vegas seeing a point in timecode, at which point it will begin to play. It is not locked to the timecode specifically. Chasing timecode means that

Vegas remains synchronized with incoming timecode and follows the timecode as best as possible. Vegas has a Freewheel mode that allows it to continue to play for a period of time even if timecode input is occasionally lost, playing until it sees timecode again that it should be synchronized to. If timecode is consistently lost, check the hardware or signal flow from the master device.

Sync is set up in the Preferences dialog box but must be enabled in the Options menu (**Ctrl+F7**).

Still using tape? Use Vegas to edit audio from a tape machine and apply EQ, noise reduction, and processing. This process saves buses on an external machine, frees up reverbs and other processing hardware during a mix, and generally affords an opportunity to give a smaller studio the capabilities and power of a much larger recording facility.

To view incoming or outgoing timecode, right-click the time display, which defaults to the upper-left corner of the timeline. Choose which timecode you want to display: time at cursor, incoming timecode, or outgoing timecode.

The timecode window is docked by default but can be moved to a convenient space on the timeline or wherever it is most visible. It cannot be completely removed from the workspace.

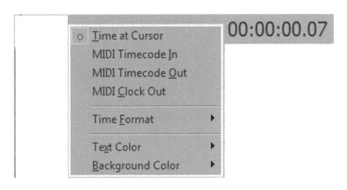

Figure 10.31 Select the timecode you want to view.

Editing Audio in Vegas

The audio-editing tools found in Vegas Pro are among the best in the world. Moreover, the audio tools in Vegas Pro are superior to any audio tools found in any NLE system. Playback and recording tracks are limited only by the amount of available CPU, hard disk space, and RAM. Vegas Movie Studio is only slightly less capable.

Placing Audio on the Timeline

Audio recorded is immediately found on the timeline and is also found in the Project Media bin. However, it's often necessary to place audio on the timeline that might be a take, from a stock music collection, an ACID loop, sound FX, or other stored audio file.

To do this, open the Explorer in Vegas and find an audio file to place on the timeline. Double-clicking the file inserts the file directly on the timeline. Right-clicking a file opens several options, such as opening the file directly in the Trimmer, which allows audio sections to be trimmed before putting media on the timeline. After audio is placed on the timeline, it becomes an Event.

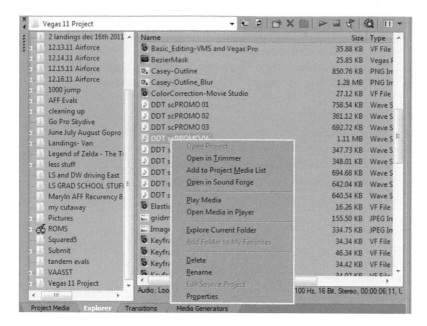

Figure 10.32   The Explorer in Vegas Pro looks similar to Windows Explorer.

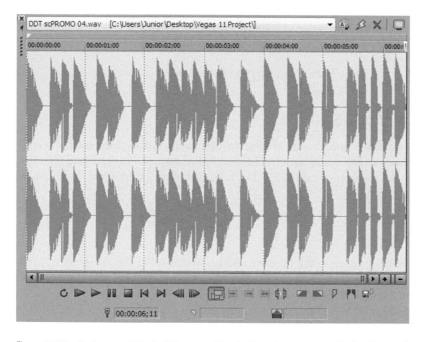

Figure 10.33   Audio opened in the Trimmer, with selections chosen to be added to the timeline. Regions for insertion may be
specified and saved in the Trimmer just as video regions may be saved.

Right-clicking also offers the option of placing the audio in the Media Pool or opening the file for editing in a third-party audio editor or in Sound Forge, depending on settings in the **Options | Preferences | Audio** dialog box. Opening the file in the Trimmer is a simple workflow that allows phrases or sections to be marked and added to the timeline.

After making a selection in the Trimmer, press the **R** key. This creates a nameable region in the Trimmer that stays with the audio and will be shown any time the audio is opened in the Trimmer. After creating the region, place the cursor on the **Timeline** where the audio is desired and press **A**. This step adds the media to the timeline, where it now is an Event on a track. Selected audio can also be dragged to the timeline from the Trimmer. Do whichever is comfortable for you.

Audio in the Trimmer can also be inserted in Ripple mode (see "Using Ripple Editing" later in this chapter for more details) by copying the audio in the Trimmer and enabling **Ripple** or by copying and pressing **Shift + Ctrl + V**. The audio is pasted as an Event at the cursor, and subsequent Events ripple down the timeline for the length of time equal to the size of the pasted Event.

Extracting Audio from CDs

Both versions of Vegas provide tools to allow audio to be extracted from CDs. Whereas a single track will play back from a CD, multiple tracks or clips from a sample library that are scattered all over a CD might not play back so well due to the limited speed of a CD or CD-R.

There are two menu areas in which Vegas can be instructed to extract audio. The first is the Media Pool. Clicking the **Extract Audio from CD** button opens a dialog box in which users are asked to choose which tracks are to be extracted. Audio can be extracted three ways:

- By track (individual indexes can be selected)

- By time selection (a range of time for extraction can be specified)

- By the entire CD (the entire CD is extracted to the hard drive as one large file)

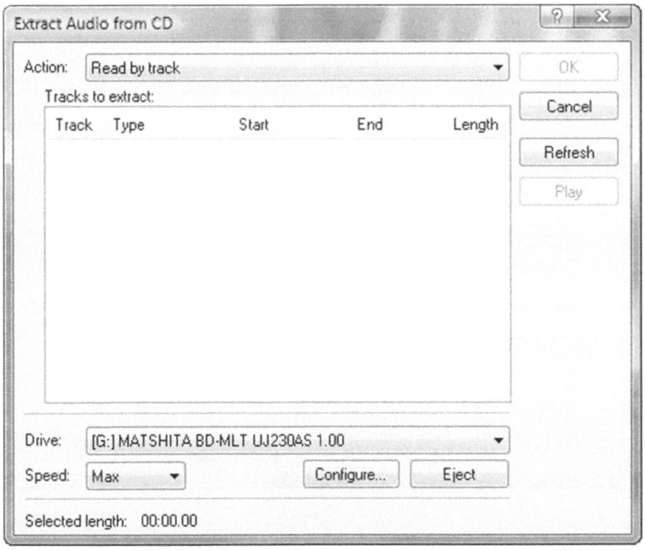

Figure 10.34 Clicking the **Extract Audio from CD** button calls up a dialog box requesting information as to where files should be extracted from.

When placing any media on the timeline, it's easy to lose focus on what the media is or where it came from. Selecting **Options | Preferences | General** and checking **Show active take names in events** places the name of the take on each Event, whether graphic, video, or audio in nature.

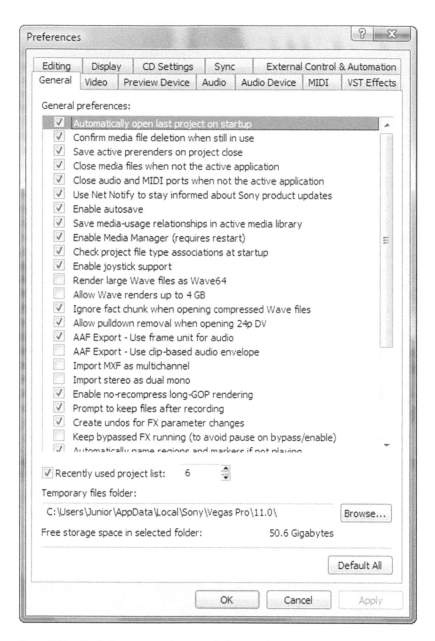

Figure 10.35   The Preferences menu has many choices to make editing in Vegas Pro/Vegas Movie Studio easier and more personal.

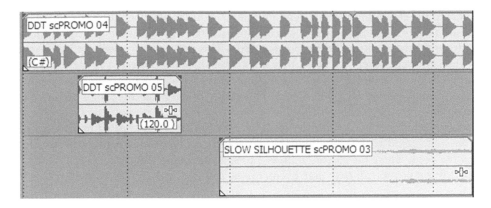

Figure 10.36   Active take names help identify Events.

With audio on the timeline as Events, it is ready to be edited. Basic edits include cutting, copying, pasting, fading audio in and out, cross-fading, splitting, and moving a file.

Cutting, copying, and pasting are handled in Vegas as in most applications. To cut an Event, select the Event and press **Ctrl+X** or select **Edit | Cut** after selecting the Event. Events that are cut are available from the clipboard. To copy an Event, select the Event and press **Ctrl+C** or select **Edit | Copy** after selecting the Event. To paste an Event, first cut or copy the Event and then place the cursor where you want the Event to go. Pressing **Ctrl+V** pastes the Event(s) to the timeline wherever the cursor is located. Cut, Copy, and Paste commands are also accessible by right-clicking any file and choosing one of the commands from the context menu.

Vegas also has a **Paste Repeat** command that allows Events to be pasted multiple times. Events can be pasted end to end the number of times specified in the dialog box or can be spaced at intervals defined in the menu.

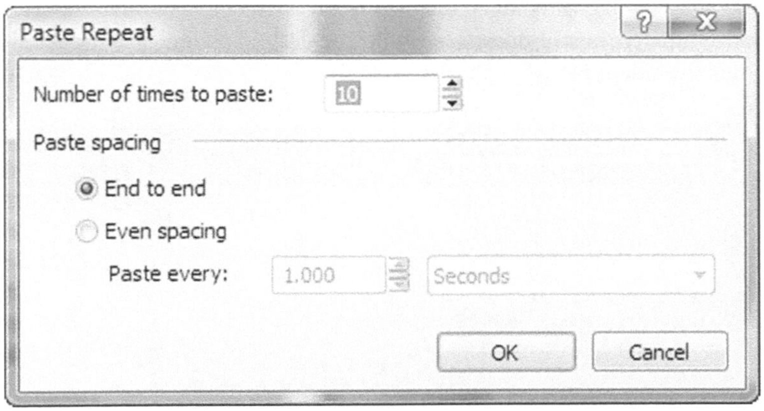

Paste Repeat

| ? | X |

Number of times to paste: 10

Paste spacing

◉ End to end

○ Even spacing

Paste every: 1.000   Seconds

OK   Cancel

Figure 10.37   Pasting multiple instances of an audio Event.

Selecting Events to the end of the timeline is an option when all Events need to be moved up or down the timeline as a group. Rather than Shift-clicking each file, right-click only the first file in the series, and from the menu choose **Select Events to End**. This process will go all the way to the end of the timeline and select every Event on that track after the cursor/selected Event.

To fade an audio Event in or out, it's as easy as clicking and grabbing the upper corner on either end of the Event. A small quarter-circle will appear. This circle indicates that the tool is prepared to fade audio in or out.

Splitting an Event or series of Events that are on different tracks is accomplished by placing the cursor where the split should occur. If no single Event is selected, all vertical Events on the timeline will be split on the point where the cursor is. Press **S** to split the audio files.

If an individual Event is selected, only that Event will be split.

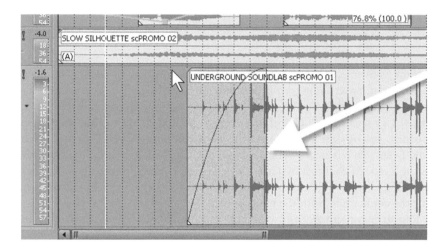

Figure 10.38   Creating a fade-in.

Fades can be customized by right-clicking the fade and choosing from the menu of five different types of fades. If one of the five fade types still doesn't provide the desired sound, use the **Audio Envelope** tool to create the desired fade type.

Figure 10.39   Different fade types available in Vegas.

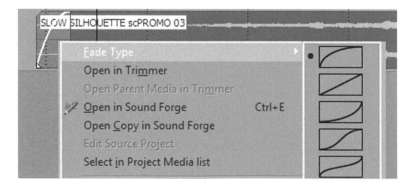

Creating a cross-fade, in which two audio Events overlap each other and one fades out as the other fades in, is achieved by sliding the two Events over the top of each other for the desired length of fade. Automatic cross-fades must be enabled on the toolbar. Although defaulted to Enabled, check to be certain that the button shown in the figure is pressed:

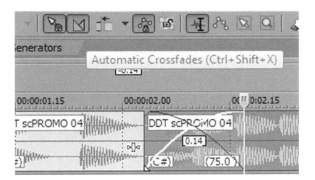

Figure 10.40

Vegas has the ability to create auto-cross-fades of a preset length. In the **Options** | **Preferences** | **Editing** dialog box, cross-fade times can be preset. Set the desired length for cross-fades by time or by frames and select multiple files in the Explorer by pressing and holding **Ctrl** and selecting media by clicking them. Drag them to the timeline, and the media will drop in as automatically cross-faded Events. This same behavior applies to video files.

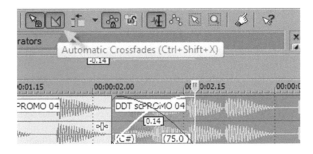

Figure 10.41   Ensure that this button is pressed to enable automatic cross-fades.

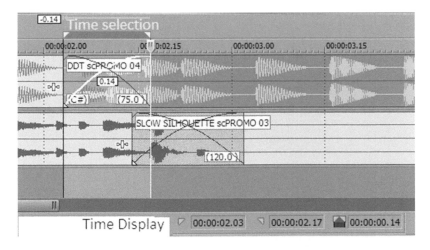

Figure 10.42   Double-click a cross-fade to make a selection. The length of the cross-fade is displayed in the Time Display window.

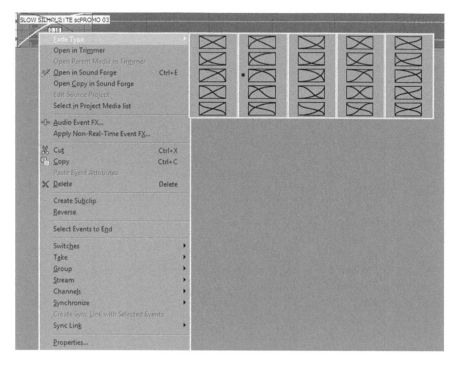

Figure 10.43   Vegas has many cross-fade choices available. Right-click the cross-fade to call up the Fade Type menu. Properties of a cross-fade can be adjusted by inserting a volume envelope (V) over a cross-fade.

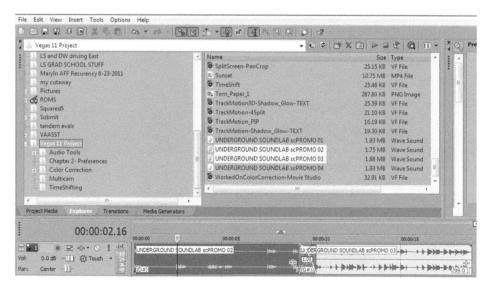

Figure 10.44   Several files can be dragged to the timeline and automatically cross-faded by selecting several files in the Explorer.

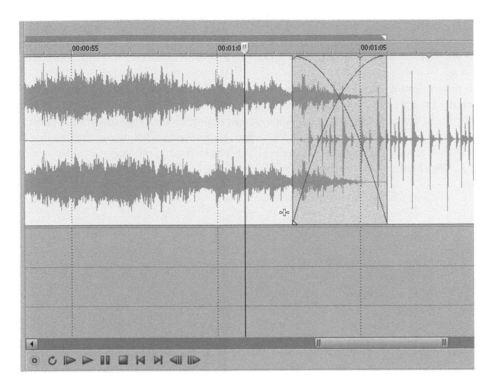

Figure 10.45   A mono Event faded into a stereo Event.

When interviewing with a camera and using one mic for the interviewee and one for the interviewer or another interviewee, the two channels are captured as one audio file with right and left information. With most NLE systems, separating channels requires editing in a separate sound editor. Vegas Pro allows stereo audio to be imported from the camera as dual mono tracks. **Options** | **Preferences** | **Import Stereo as Dual Mono** will bring in two mono tracks of audio from the stereo camera.

In Vegas Movie Studio, place the two-channel audio on a timeline. Duplicate the track by right-clicking the **Track Control** pane and selecting **Duplicate Track**. Click the upper of the two identical tracks. Right-click the audio in the upper track and select **Channels** | **Left Only**. Right-click the lower track and select **Channels** | **Right Only**. There are now two tracks of mono audio on the timeline that are capable of being edited and processed separately. This method is a fast means of accomplishing two tracks with separate control.

All tracks added to the timeline are stereo. Only Events are either mono or stereo. A mono signal, however, will remain mono when dragged to the timeline. Mono and stereo signals can occupy the same track, and a mono Event can be cross-faded over a stereo Event on the timeline.

Audio that is stereo but should be mono can be quickly converted by right-clicking a stereo file and choosing **Combine** from the popup menu. Files that have been combined can be restored by selecting **Both**. Audio can also be selected as Right Only or Left Only, and channels can be switched by selecting **Swap**.

Audio that is not at nominal level can be normalized nondestructively by right-clicking an audio Event and selecting **Properties**. Check the **Normalize** box, which will bring audio to a level normalized as specified in the **Options | Preferences | Audio Event** dialog box. On the disc in this book, a JavaScript is found that can be run as a script in Vegas Pro, normalizing all audio on the timeline as a script rather than normalizing all audio manually. The file is located in the \scripts\ folder as normalizeall.js. Sony Production Assistant and VASST Ultimate S also offer this as one of hundreds of other processes.

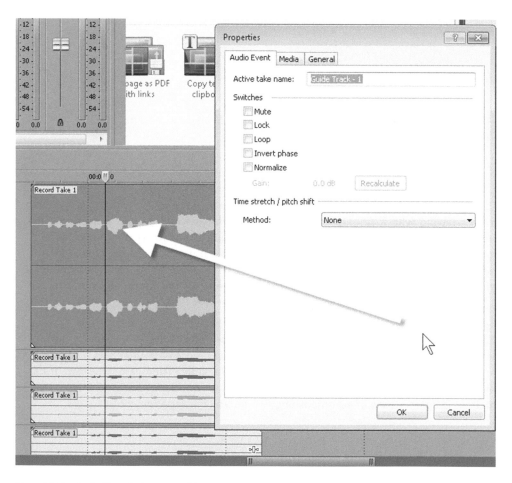

Figure 10.46   Audio Event before normalizing.

🗿 *Tip*_____
Normalize in Sony Sound Forge as opposed to Vegas, so you can normalize on the RMS value as opposed to the peak value.

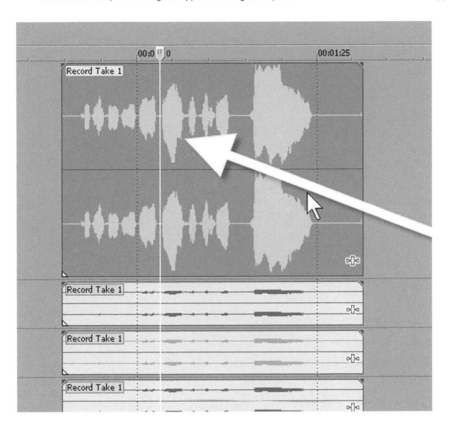

Figure 10.47   Audio Event after normalizing, a 4.1 dB increase in gain. Normalizing an entire project may also be accomplished with scripting tools available for free at vasst.com.

Audio Events have an individual gain reduction on each Event as well. Place the cursor at the top of the audio Event and watch for the cursor to turn into a hand icon. Then click and hold, dragging the hand icon downward. Vegas indicates the gain-level reduction as the gain line is pulled downward.

Right-clicking an audio Event calls up several menu options. One of them is the ability to loop an Event, which is different from setting up a play-back loop for previews.

Right-click an Event, choose **Switches**, and check the **Loop** box. This step allows the audio Event to be dragged out infinitely, and the audio will constantly loop. Vegas inserts an indicator that looks like a

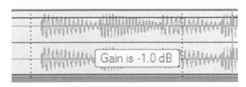

Figure 10.48   Reducing the gain of an audio Event on the timeline.

small divot or carrot in the Event at the point of the end/beginning of a loop. Looping is terrific for repeating sounds that might fade together or for using an ACID loop that should repeat. Looping is set to **On** by default.

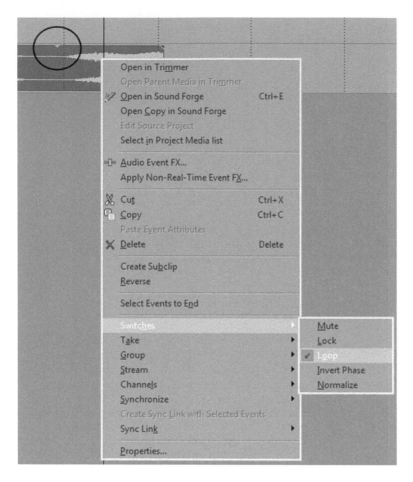

Figure 10.49   Setting an Event for looped playback.

Looping is helpful in most situations; however, it can also work against a mix in some instances. If a reverb or delay is desired to continue reflection for a long time after an audio Event ends, looping must be disabled and the file dragged out for the length of time that the reverb/delay is desired. Otherwise, the plug-in sees the end of the audio Event and thinks it needs to shut off if the end of the project is reached. Dragging out an empty portion of the Event with looping turned off allows the reverb or delay to continue to be audible.

Figure 10.50   Event dragged out with looping off. Because looping is disabled and the audio has ended, Vegas treats the stretched Event like empty media.

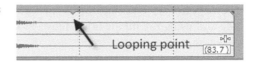

Get ACIDized!

Speaking of loops, ACID has long been recognized as one of the most valuable creative tools for composing royalty-free music for video and recorded productions. ACID uses prerecorded loops, recorded by some of the finest musicians in the world. Imagine having Mick Fleetwood playing drums for you, Rudy Sarzo on bass, Ken Jordan from Crystal Method on keys and sound design, and some of the world's best-known R&B vocalists all performing on your video soundtrack! With ACID loops and Vegas's ability to take advantage of ACID metadata, you can have these great performers and more. Visit www.acidplanet.com and download some of the free eight-packs of loops. Unzip them and start creating music in Vegas.

ACID files are .wav files containing metadata that informs Vegas Pro and Vegas Movie Studio of the tempo, key, and length of the audio file. Vegas will take recordings of disparate tempos and lock them up to whatever tempo is set in the Project Properties. Using the **Pitch Shift** functions, you can shift loop pitches up or down to make them harmonically acceptable.

One of the caveats about using ACID loops is that Vegas, unlike Sony's ACID application, cannot shift tempo on the fly by using tempo markers. This doesn't mean that soundtracks or underscores can't change in tempo, however. This merely means you need to work around the limitations.

In Vegas, whatever the project tempo may be, it determines the tempo of the loop. Therefore, if the project tempo is left to the default value of 120 beats per minute (bpm), any loops dropped on the timeline will conform to the 120 bpm tempo. However, the project tempo may be changed downstream/later in the project, and any loops dropped on the timeline prior to the tempo change will retain their tempo of 120 bpm, whereas any loop dropped on the timeline after the project tempo is changed will retain the new tempo value. Put another way, if you drop loops on the Vegas Timeline with the tempo at 120, any loop you drop at any point will always be at the 120 tempo. If you shift tempo later and attempt to place loops on the timeline in sync with the earlier inserted loops, the loops will not synchronize correctly. So be sure to get your compositions correctly assembled prior to changing any project tempo in Vegas. It's also handy to save various versions of your project if you expect to be changing tempos or creating mapped tempos later on.

Vegas does not indicate the current tempo, so it's a good practice to create markers on the timeline to indicate where tempo changes are occurring.

Another workaround is to create your project the way you want it to sound in Vegas, create a tempo change, and then reload the loops after the tempo change has occurred, loading them from the Project Media. The loops originally dropped on the timeline will retain their original tempo information, and the loops inserted from the Project Media will exist at the new tempo.

Key changes are not possible as a global function in Vegas. Individual loops may be pitch-shifted to create key changes, but this is done only on an Event-by-Event basis. Vegas will not recognize the actual key of a loop, but loops may be tuned by using the pitch-shift capability found in Vegas. If **Show Active Take Name** is selected in the **Options | Preferences** dialog box, Vegas will display the original pitch or key of the loop. (Drum loops rarely contain pitch data and so will be blank.)

A workaround to the lack of global pitch shift is to select all loops to be shifted by holding the **Ctrl** key and using the minus (–) or plus (+) keys to shift them up or down the desired amount.

Shifting loops in amounts of 2 semitones, 5 semitones, and 7 semitones will follow the average pop song format. There are 12 semitones in an octave. Music today is often written in what is called I, IV, V or 1, 4, 5 format. This means that the chord or pitch changes will reflect a shift up by a fourth or a shift up by a fifth. An interval of a fourth is equal to 5 semitones, and an interval of a fifth is equal to 7 semitones. To shift a pitch down to the fifth the downward value would be –5 from the original pitch and to shift down to the fourth, the value would be 7 semitones down. It's rarely a good idea to shift a loop more than 12 semitones up or down unless a specific sound or effect is being sought. Loops in higher octaves will display less of a negative effect than a lower octave loop because of the distance between frequency amplitude. Don't expect to shift a bass guitar loop by more than a couple of semitones without damaging the integrity of the loop.

If you have two loops of disparate or dissonant pitch, select the loop that is different from other loops or lower in pitch overall from the opposing loop. Using the hyphen or equals key, pitch the loop up or down until it is harmonically acceptable or in the same pitch as the other loops on the timeline.

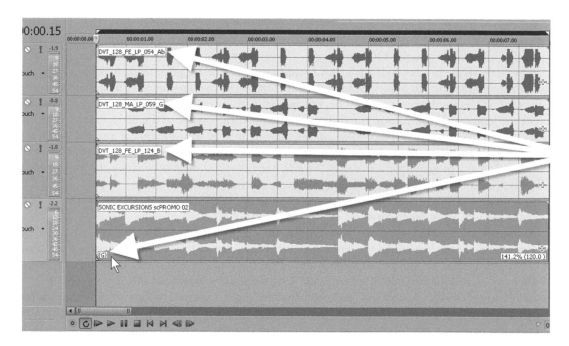

Figure 10.51   Notice that the pitches do not match. This generally will mean that the audio will be discordant and not sound correct.

Using ACID loops in Vegas Pro and Vegas Movie Studio is a powerful addition to the creative palette for musicians and video editors. This allows video editors to create rudimentary beds or sound design tools. If greater or more powerful music creation tools are required, I recommend that readers check out ACID, another of Sony's desktop media applications.

And There Goes the Pitch! (Vegas Still Hits a Home Run)

Vegas Pro has always had amazing audio manipulation tools since the inception of version 1. Vegas Pro 5 brought some new audio tools to the game, and one of them involved pitch-shifting on the fly. This feature is simply amazing. A weak voiceover, a music bed that conflicts with dialogue, an unintelligible word or two can all be improved or even repaired just by using this feature.

To shift pitch in Vegas Pro or Vegas Movie Studio, make a selection of an audio Event. If only a single word or section needs to be shifted, use the **S** key to split the audio Event, singling out the area to be shifted. Create a time selection above the selected Event, and press the **Q** key to enable looping. Start **playback**. During playback use the plus and minus keys (+ and –) to shift the pitch up or down. Pitch may be shifted up or down as much as two full octaves or as much as 24 semitones in either direction. By holding down the **Ctrl** key while shifting pitch, you can make changes by cents rather than semitones, giving very tight control to critical pitch shifts. Use this feature to correct an out-of-tune vocal or to thicken a doubled/duplicated track.

Any shift greater than approximately 5 semitones in either direction may have adverse effects on the quality of the audio, depending on content. Entire music beds may be shifted up or down as much as a fifth or plus or minus 7 semitones to complement dialog or make way for other audio Events, whereas stingers or other special effects Events might be shifted very low or high for maximum impact.

Try inserting a cymbal or other hard attack and long-sustain sound and pitch it down to –24. You might find it very powerful as an introductory sound or perfect accompaniment to a fly-in transition or graphic object. Coupling this with the real-time reverse found in Vegas makes for a wonderful effect in some circumstances. Experiment with different sounds to learn how this effect might best suit your workflow and creative opportunity.

Open the dropped pitch.veg file on the DVD in the back of this book and experiment with how these audio-processing tools function.

Shifting stock music or other music found in the project down or up by a pitch or two will have a tremendous impact on the feel and texture of a scene and usually will clear the frequency range for a better dialog track. Experiment with this feature, and it may well become your favorite tool in Vegas. It's definitely in the top two or three favorite audio features in Vegas for me.

Get the Mark Up

Vegas has a logical managing of markers; it allows numbering of up to 99 markers that are auto-numbered when they're inserted into the timeline. Of course, all markers may be renamed and renumbered to user preference, but just having the ability to insert more than 10 markers and have the numbers stay sequential is a great thing.

Clicking the Marker indicator in the upper-right corner of the workspace causes the Marker bar or timeline to take focus from the rest of the application. This allows the arrow keys to be used to jump from marker to marker. The left-arrow key moves cursor and playhead to the previous marker, and the right-arrow key moves cursor and playhead to the next marker. Markers also move with media when a multiple selection is created and moved. Markers may be deleted individually or in groups in addition to being able to be selectively deleted. When focus is shifted away from the Marker timeline, the Marker tools are disabled.

To get familiar with the Marker timeline, click the **Marker** tool button in the upper-right corner of the window. Now click on any marker. (Insert a few markers if you don't have any. To insert a marker, press the **M** key.) Notice that when the marker is clicked, it becomes selected with its number highlighted in the marker box. Click **Delete** to remove the marker, left-arrow to move to the previous marker, or right-arrow to move to the next marker. You may select multiple markers by holding down **Ctrl** as each marker is selected. Markers may be moved in tandem when multiple selections occur, or multiple markers may be deleted at one time by selecting each marker while holding down the **Ctrl** button. If you have a number of markers to be deleted, click on the first marker, hold **Shift**, and click on the last marker. All markers in between the first and the last marker will be selected and may be deleted with the **Delete** key.

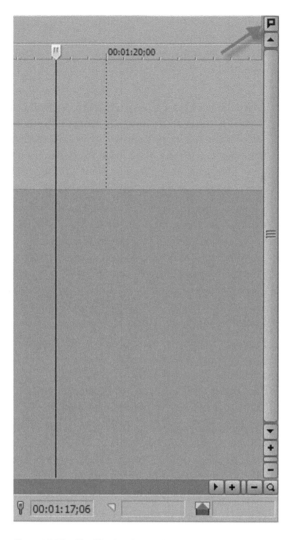

Figure 10.52   The **Marker** button lets Vegas focus on the Marker timeline, providing users with several options.

Inserting Markers

Markers are often needed to indicate a specific point on the timeline that requires an edit, to serve as a cue, to insert metadata, and for many other helpful uses. Vegas allows for three different types of markers:

* *Markers*. Reference points to be returned to later, which identify timing or act as a reminder for later edits. Markers can be inserted on the timeline or in the Trimmer. Markers can be named at any time.

- *Regions.* Defined sections on the timeline. Regions can behave as permanent indicators of a selection either in the Trimmer or on the timeline. Regions can act as reminders of specific sections to be returned to later or can act as edit-length indicators in the Trimmer. Regions can be named at any point in time. All training materials on the DVD contained in this book are built with regions.

- *Command markers.* Used to insert metadata in streaming media files. Text data, such as lyrics, promotional information, URL locations, and closed captions, can be embedded with command markers.

Markers and regions can remain with the audio file when inserted in the Trimmer tool. The **Options** | **Preferences** | **General** dialog box has a checkbox to save markers and regions automatically in the Trimmer tool.

To insert a marker, place the cursor where the marker location is desired. Press **M**, right-click the **Marker** bar, or select **Insert** | **Marker**. This step places a marker on the timeline. Markers can be deleted by right-clicking the individual marker or by right-clicking in the **Marker** bar and choosing **Delete All Markers**. A group of markers can be deleted by making a selection on the timeline that contains the markers to be deleted, right-clicking in the **Marker** bar, and selecting the menu option **Delete All in Selection**. Markers can be named when inserted or later by right-clicking a marker and selecting **Rename**. Pressing **Enter** or clicking out of the box on the timeline sets the marker's name.

Markers can be navigated by pressing **Ctrl + Left** or **Right Arrow**. This step will jump the cursor from marker to marker.

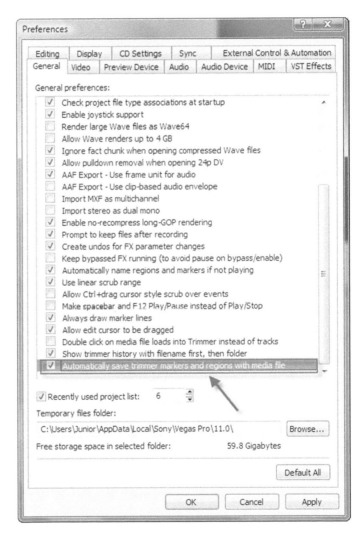

Figure 10.53 Be certain that the checkbox for **Automatically save trimmer markers and regions with media file** is checked to save the indicators in the Trimmer.

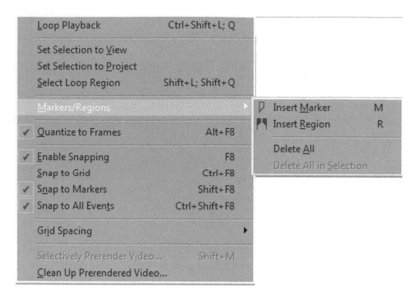

Figure 10.54   Inserting, deleting, or editing markers can be done by right-clicking the **Marker** bar.

Regions are defined by creating a selection on the timeline and pressing **R** or by selecting **Insert | Region**. Double-clicking an Event creates an automatic selection for the length of the Event. The region can be named in any way that you choose. Regions can be renamed at any point.

Figure 10.55   Cursor behaviors inside a region can be selected by right-clicking a **Region** marker.

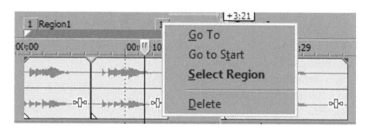

Use regions to indicate miniprojects or minisections, such as a verse, chorus, or bridge. This option makes it easier to find full sections or loop full sections during the recording session. It also makes it easy to fly in a repeat chorus or bridge later on if necessary.

Regions can be navigated or toggled. Regions can be navigated by selecting a corresponding number on the keyboard (not the numeric keypad) or by pressing **Ctrl + Left/Right Arrow**. This step allows rapid navigation within Vegas of various regions on the timeline.

Command markers are created when the cursor is placed at the desired point for a metadata Event to occur, and **C** is pressed or **Insert | Command** is selected. This step calls the **Command Properties** dialog box, in which the desired type of metadata is selected.

Metadata allows for media to become rich media or media that is more than just audio.

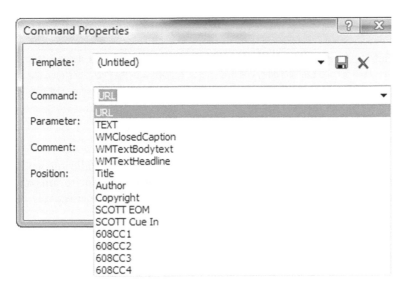

Figure 10.56   Different types of metadata that can be inserted.

The command marker can have a name different from the properties associated with the marker. Right-clicking the command marker provides a menu for renaming the file. Command markers can be deleted individually by right-clicking the marker and selecting **Delete**. Right-clicking in the Marker bar and selecting Delete All does not affect command markers.

Rubber Audio

Vegas has a feature known as *rubber audio*. Audio can be stretched by grabbing the right side of an audio Event, pressing and holding down **Ctrl**, and dragging the Event to the right. This option is useful to correct a slightly off-sync voice or to expand or compress an audio Event to make it fit within a specified period. Audio that is expanded or stretched much more than 10%, however, will sound very strange indeed. Perhaps long stretches are valuable for a specific effect; however, the audio is quickly recognized as affected after it has gone past the 10–15% stretch point. Use the Rubber/Time Stretch feature only as a means of achieving sync on an out of sync and time format Event or as a special effect.

RubberAudio.veg is a project on the DVD that allows you to hear what rubber audio/stretched audio sounds like at various speeds and pitches.

Time stretch can also be accomplished by right-clicking the audio Event, selecting **Properties**, and adjusting the length of the file. Audio pitch/tuning can also be adjusted in this same dialog box.

Use **Semitones** to move pitch in musical half-steps and use the **Cents** dialog box to change by hundredths of semitones. For example, a pitch shift of −7 semitones is equal to a fifth interval down from the tonic or original pitch. Shifting a pitch by +4 is a minor third up from the tonic or original pitch.

Tip_____

Sound designers will find the Pitch Shift/Time Stretch tool invaluable. Using household sounds, such as blenders, flushing commodes, gelatin being slowly sucked out of a can, and other creative sounds, coupled with the Pitch Shift/Time Stretch feature yields usable sounds for any kind of video or audio production. Adding reverbs, delays, flanges, and panning information to these sounds further enhances value and realism.

Elastique

Elastique is a newer feature in Vegas Pro and Vegas Movie Studio that takes rubber audio into a new dimension. Using proprietary algorithms, music or dialogue may be stretched out to amazing lengths without shifting pitch or speed. Elastique preserves audio formants, which effectively re-serves the audio integrity.

Where Elastique comes in handy (aside from the musical value) is that it allows producers/editors to make audio fit within a specified timeframe. Imagine being assigned to fill a two minute package and the edit runs to 115 seconds or perhaps 215 seconds. With Elastique, it doesn't matter whether the package is dialog-only, or contains music, the audio/video may be sped up or slowed down to meet the slot requirement. Holding the CTRL key, drag the right edge of the audio Event to the right. Right-click the audio Event and select Properties. In the Properties dialog, there is a drop-down box for Time Stretch/Pitch Shift. In this drop-down, select Elastique. Another drop-down box will open. Select the appropriate stretch attribute. See the Timeshifting section for more information on Elastique.

Variable-Speed Audio in Vegas

Currently, Vegas does not have the ability to gradually speed up, reverse, or slow down sound on the timeline. If audio speed must be gradually reversed or slowed down, the file must be opened in either Sound Forge or another audio-editing application. If a multichannel soundcard is available on the system, however, there is another option.

Create a new bus and route the audio to be sped, altered, or reversed to this bus. Create a new track and select the output of the new bus to feed the new track. Click **Record** and adjust the **Playback Rate** control in Vegas. This process is a lot more accurate and fun than using the J, K, or L keys or a Contour ShuttlePRO/SpaceStation AV. The altered playback shows up on the new track on which it can now be filtered, EQ'd, or otherwise processed.

This process can also be accomplished with the Windows Media Recorder by selecting the inputs from the Windows Media Mixer.

To reverse audio with no gradation in speed, right-click the audio Event and choose **Reverse** from the submenu options. This is a real-time process, so you'll see the audio Event reverse itself and redraw its waveform.

Reverse Decisions

Ever wanted to reverse an audio or video clip? In the past, video could be reversed by using the Velocity envelope set to a value of –100% and video would be easily reversed. To reverse a file, right-click and select the **Reverse** option from the submenu that pops up. The beauty is that this reverses video, too, if video is selected. Any audio can be reversed, whether it's tied to a video Event or not.

Any time audio is reversed, a subclip is created that will be found in the Project Media. This subclip may be placed on the timeline as a separate Event. A creative use of the Reverse tool is to apply it to a cymbal that has a strong attack and a light decay. Reversing this provides a great opportunity to create a stinger or audio Event that can lead up to and impact a particular scene or action in a video. The Beatles were the first to take great advantage of reversed audio, but one of the best examples is when Roy Thomas Baker used reversed tape on a piano for the "We Will Rock You" and "Bohemian Rhapsody" songs recorded by Queen. Try this on a variety of instruments, combined with the pitch-shifting tools found in Vegas. You'll be surprised at the creative inspiration you'll find. For even greater effect in dialogue, try placing a duplicate of a dialogue track and reversing one of the two tracks. It creates a mess, but where the two tracks converge, it's a very interesting effect. You might want to split out one section of the dialogue and do this. Alfred Hitchcock used this technique in *Psycho* to create a sense of babbling and underlying confusion, and it certainly worked well. It might just make your production take on a whole new meaning.

Snapping Audio Events

Vegas can snap audio Events to a marker, region, grid indicator, or a butting Event.

Two Events on the same track always snap together if snapping is enabled. Two Events can also be snapped together on different tracks, however. To do this, follow these steps:

1. Double-click the Event to which you want the next Event to snap. This step creates a time selection.

2. On the track that holds the Event to which the selected Event should be snapped, move the Event toward the front or back of the region or selected Event. Vegas autosnaps the moved Event to the first Event that is selected, regardless of tracks. Several Events can be snapped at once.

Events can also be snapped to a grid line. Pressing **F8** enables snapping, and pressing it again disables snapping. If snapping is not enabled, timing grids are not visible. To snap an Event to the grid, press **Ctrl + F8**. To snap an Event to a marker, press **Shift + F8**.

Trimming Events on the Timeline

Events can be trimmed in the Trimmer window before being placed on the timeline. They can be edited for length directly on the timeline as well. Position the cursor over the start or end of an Event, and the cursor changes to the trim cursor.

Grab either the start or the end of an Event by clicking and holding, and drag the end of the Event to the left or the start of an Event to the right. The Event shortens as it is dragged or trimmed.

If Auto-Ripple (**Ctrl + L**) is enabled, any trimming on the timeline will result in Events following the trim filling the space/hole left behind because of the trim.

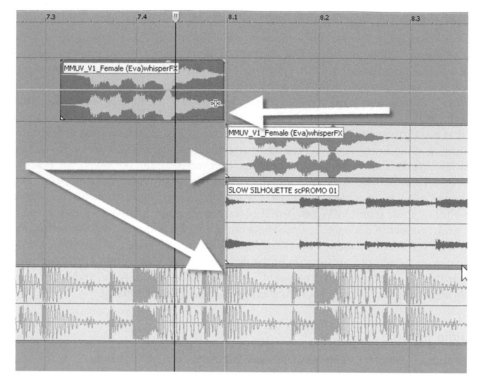

Figure 10.57 Snapping several Events to a selected track Event.

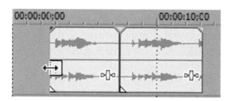

Figure 10.58 Before trimming on the timeline.

Figure 10.59 After trimming on the timeline.

Figure 10.60 Hold down the **Alt** key while click-dragging within the audio Event to move audio within the same time space.

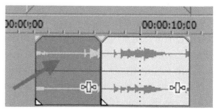

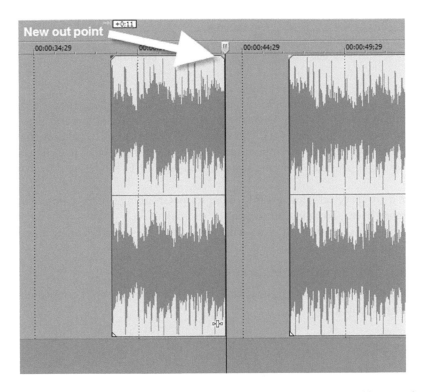

Figure 10.61   Rippled on the timeline, media following trim filled in time vacated because of trimming on the timeline.

Another option to trimming on the timeline is to slip or shift the contents of an Event. By pressing and holding down **Alt** and dragging right or left inside an Event, audio may be slipped forward or backward in time without moving the actual Event. This feature is great for moving audio within a specified time space without having to be concerned about losing space in time. The Event remains a placeholder while audio can be fine-tuned. This feature is also useful for fitting audio in a stipulated time space when time is specified but the contents can be determined later.

Deleting Events from the Timeline

Selecting Events by clicking them and then pressing **Delete** removes them from the timeline. Multiple Events can be selected by pressing and holding down **Shift** and clicking Events to be deleted. Deleting Events removes them from the timeline but does not eliminate the empty space that remains unless **Auto-Ripple** is enabled (**Ctrl+L**). If an entire space in time across multiple tracks is to be deleted, make a selection on the timeline. Select **Delete** (**Ctrl+X**). (Selecting **Delete** does not place deleted media on the clipboard.) If **Ripple** is enabled (or if a post-edit ripple is used), all Events remaining on the timeline shift to fill the empty space; otherwise, the time selection remains behind and is left empty. Events or time can also be deleted by selecting **Edit | Delete**.

Tip_____

If in the process of deleting Events for which ripple is needed but not enabled, use a post-edit ripple to close deleted areas. Post-edit ripple behaviors are selected in the **Edit** menu or by pressing **F**, **Ctrl + F**, or **Ctrl + Shift + F**.

Grouping

At times, it's helpful for entire sections or types of Events to be grouped or locked together so that when one is moved, all of them move. Grouping Events is quick and easy in Vegas Pro and Vegas Movie Studio. Select a number of Events and press **G**. This step ties all of the Events together so that when one is moved, all the others move with it. For instance, perhaps all Events related to a chorus, bridge, or verse might be grouped so that when one section is moved, all Events related to that group are moved with it.

To remove an Event from a group, select it and press **U** to ungroup. Grouping can be temporarily ignored by clicking the **Ignore Event Grouping** button on the toolbar.

Groups are great for applying edits to multiple Events at one time. To apply an edit to all members of a group, perform the following steps:

1. Press **Shift + G** or right-click one member of the group.

2. Select **Group | Select All**. You can cut, copy, or paste edits to the entire group. Grouped but unselected Events are not edited together.

Figure 10.62   Grouping can be temporarily ignored.

Events can belong to only one group at a time. Adding an Event to a group essentially dissolves the existing group and creates a new one. As many groups as needed can be created, yet no two groups can contain the same Event.

Working with Audio Plug-ins

Vegas Pro has a tremendous assortment of plug-ins that come with the application and that provide massive mixing and editing power. Particularly necessary in the digital audio world, these plug-ins include multiple types of compressors and equalizers, plus reverbs, delays, flangers, noise gates, resonators, and more. As a result of the open DirectX platform, plug-ins from companies such as WAVES, Ozone, and dozens of other manufacturers can be used in Vegas Pro.

Sony was the first adopter of what was once called Active Movie, which later became ActiveX, which then once again changed names to DirectX. Sony supported Active Movie in its 4.0a version of Sound Forge. Because of Sony's pioneering work in the plug-in interface market, most every video-editing application, as well as every audio application, supports the DirectX audio platform.

Plug-ins, such as compressors, reverbs, delays, and noise reduction, all take the place of hardware counterparts in the analog world. In fact, many software plug-ins look just like their hardware counterparts, and, in some cases such as WAVES, the software tools were so popular that the company followed up the software tools with hardware tools for the nondigital environment!

Sony offers over 40 plug-ins with Vegas Pro. Rather than examine each of them, we'll look at what each family of plug-ins does.

Dynamic-range plug-ins offer the ability to ensure that audio doesn't exceed the dynamic-range capabilities of digital audio. This includes compressors, limiters, and combinations thereof, such as Wave Hammer, Sony's final-step plug-in.

Although digital audio has an extreme dynamic range, it is also less forgiving than its analog counterpart in that the zero point in the digital world is cold, harsh, and unforgiving. In the analog world, the dynamic range is fairly limited by any comparison, ranging in the upper 60 dB area depending on the quality of equipment used. Twenty-four-bit digital recordings have a dynamic range of 138 dB, or more than double the dynamic of analog. Dynamic-range plug-ins help reduce dynamic range while maintaining most of the nuances of a fairly dynamic performance. They could be considered automatic volume controls. By limiting, or subtly compressing, the exceptionally loud portions of a performance, the performance still maintains its soft to loud moments but at the same time doesn't exceed the preset point. More on dynamic-range control is found under "Mixing Techniques" in this chapter.

Sony Dynamic plug-ins include:

- Express FX Dynamics
- Track Compressor
- Graphic Dynamics
- Vinyl Restoration
- Multi-band Dynamics
- Wave Hammer

Frequency-based plug-ins/FX function by varying the amount of volume of a given frequency or group of frequencies to change the way a recording sounds. Equalizers, wah-wahs, phasers, and similar tools work on either moving a frequency's amplitude up or down to change the audio's sound or timbre. Wah-wah and phaser sounds sweep/shift the amplitude and frequency over time, giving the sound of motion, similar to the concept of a Doppler effect. In fact, some plug-ins are written to simulate the Doppler effect.

Frequency-based plugs include:

- Wah-wah
- Graphic EQ
- Paragraphic EQ

Continued

- Smooth/Enhance

- Track EQ

The Doppler effect, discovered in about 1845 by Christian Doppler, an Austrian mathematician, demonstrates that shifts in frequency occur as the article generating the sound moves. This effect is how our ears perceive sounds coming toward us and moving away from us. Listen to a train as it approaches. The frequencies contained in the sound that the train makes shift as the train moves toward you or away. The shifting frequencies result in shifting pitch as the object moves in either direction.

Time-based plug-ins/FX are based on just that: time. Delays, reverb, chorus, and flangers are all based on delaying, recombining, and/or reflecting a moment in time. When a sound originates, roughly 40% of its sound that we perceive is based on reflection of sound in a given space. In other words, singing in the shower is so much more fun than singing in a closet because the reflections of the voice in the shower hit the ear much more quickly than the reflections in a closet do. Some types of music are predominantly based on reverbs and delays, used to create emotional expression and to fill holes in a song. Without long delays and reverbs, many of the ballads and arena anthem rock songs would sound empty and powerless because the lead vocal and chorus vocals would lose their presence and power through the absence of filled time and massive reflection. Time-based effects are used more than any other effect to create emotional responses. Dripping water combined with huge reverb settings is part and parcel of nearly every horror movie ever made, and the simulated sounds of space (space has no air and therefore sound cannot pass) also include reverbs and delays.

Time-based plug-ins include:
- Flange/Phase
- Multitap delay
- Reverb
- Simple delay
- Acoustic Mirror*
- ExpressFX Chorus
- ExpressFX Delay
- ExpressFX Flange
- ExpressFX Reverb

On the DVD that accompanies this book, you will find demonstration plug-ins from several manufacturers. A wide variety of plug-ins are available for you to experiment with and enjoy.

*Optional FX from Sony

Automating FX in Vegas Pro

One of the most exciting tools in Vegas Pro is the ability to automate FX. Many of the DirectX plug-in tools can be automated. EQ settings, delay times, reverb decays, and much more can now be controlled by Vegas Pro's automation envelopes. Many of the high-tech sounds demanded by production music today require either several hands at the mix console or automated FX control.

For instance, if a vocal line reaches a break just before a chorus and a long delay is needed, automated FX can change the length of the delay time as opposed to using another FX send just for the vocal breaks. Perhaps an EQ sweep, just as a car passes from right to left, creating the illusion of a Doppler effect, would make the sound more believable. Frequency sweeps added to drum mixes or to a main instrument sound become part of the instrument itself, creating an unmatchable identity. Remember "Axel F," the theme song from Beverly Hills Cop? The sweeps heard on the bass lines in that song were created by synthesis, but the sound itself was a huge part of the song. Techno music is nearly always automation-dependent because of the repetitive nature of the music.

To hear an example of automation, open the FX Automation project on the DVD. On track 1, you can observe an inserted automation envelope by right-clicking the **Control** pane and choosing **FX Automation Envelopes.** Notice in the Track EQ settings that the **Band3 Gain** and **Band3 Bandwidth** boxes are checked. Click **OK.**

Figure 10.63   Select the boxes related to the automation parameters you want to control.

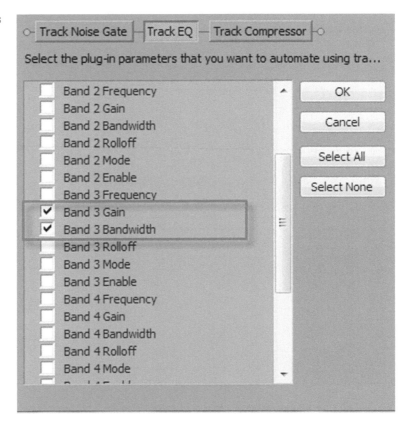

A pair of dark-colored envelopes are on the track in the timeline. These are the bandwidth and gain controls for the EQ that you have set for automation.

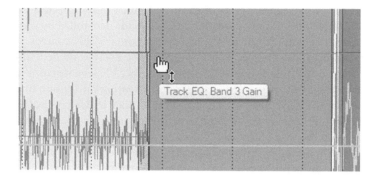

Figure 10.64 Automation envelopes appear when **Automation** parameters are selected.

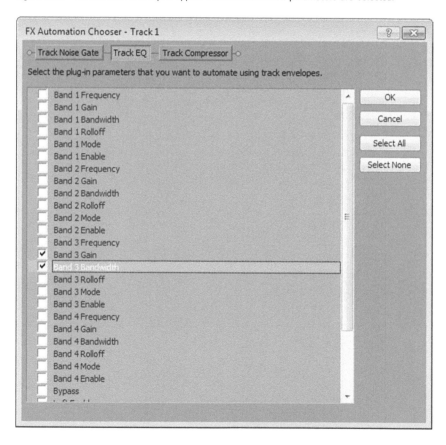

Figure 10.65 The **FX Automation** button opens a dialog box in which tool automation features can be viewed and selected.

Every 2 seconds, insert a handle on the Band3 Gain envelope or the envelope that appears in the middle of the track. (The project grid is laid out in seconds.) In between the handles on the Band3 Gain envelope, handles are already inserted on the Band3 Bandwidth envelope. Now drag every other handle of the Band3 Gain handles down to the bottom of the track, or –15 dB worth of adjustment. Experiment with the type of fade by right-clicking the handle and selecting different fade types. You'll be astounded at the degree of control this offers the sound.

Not all DirectX plug-ins have the ability to be controlled by automation envelopes. iZotope, NewBlue, Sonic Timeworks, WAVES, Wave Arts, and the plug-ins found in the Automated plug-ins folder are all examples of automatable plug-ins. If a plug-in is capable of automation, a selection button will appear in the upper-right corner of the plug-in. When the button is clicked, the parameters available for automation will appear.

Some plug-ins have to be added to a chain at least once before they are recognized as automatable. Don't be alarmed if you don't see them in the automatable folder right away.

Working with Other Types of Plug-ins

Noise Reduction

In 1995, Sony released a product called Noise Reduction 1.0. This new tool revolutionized the music industry. In the past, only very expensive hardware tools or the Digidesign Intelligent Noise Reduction tools found in ProTools or No Noise from Sonic Solutions were available. One was too expensive and only occasionally effective, the other not satisfactory in extremely noisy circumstances. Sony's Noise Reduction tool gave working musicians the ability to clean up poor-sounding rooms or environments.

Noise Reduction uses an algorithm known as Fast Fourier Transform (FFT) as part of the power behind its functionality. This algorithm is large, requiring millions of calculations based on information selected in the noisy portion of the file. A basic explanation is that when noise is present in a sound file, the noise can be isolated in sections between words, between instrument attacks, or in heads or tails of a file. The noise is then sampled, and the algorithm is applied to the rest of the audio file, removing the sampled sounds but leaving behind the original sound. Sometimes if the sample is too large or contains too much information (sounds other than noise) or if the noise sample is frequency unstable (sound is moving), the process can remove some of the original, pre-noisy sound, resulting in artifacts. These artifacts often resemble the sound of rushing water or a waterfall. At other times they have a metallic, robotic sound. In fact, some films have used this extreme noise reduction technique to create alien sounds. In this section, however, we're interested in removing noise to make a file sound cleaner.

In short, Noise Reduction is similar to a frequency-dependent noise gate that is divided into several hundred bands. The noiseprint determines the threshold or open level of each gate, and any time the volume of a frequency is below that threshold, it is suppressed or silenced.

Noise reduction is particularly effective when you're trying to remove a constant noise source, such as an air conditioner, refrigerator, or AC hum. It is least effective on moving sources, such as constantly passing traffic, running water, or varying wind noise.

A trial version of Noise Reduction is located on the DVD that accompanies this book. Install it now if it has not already been installed (this demo will only function in 32 bit Vegas and Vegas

Movie Studio). To apply Noise Reduction to a file using a standalone audio-editing tool such as Sony Sound Forge, first open the file in a DirectX-capable audio editor by right-clicking in **Vegas Pro** and choosing **Open copy in (audio editing application)**. This option should already be configured if you followed the steps in Chapter 1. If you have not done so, select **Options | Preferences | Audio** and use the **Browse** button to locate the executable for your favorite audio editor. It is located in the C:\Program Files directory in most instances. In our examples here we will always refer to Sony Sound Forge when referring to an external audio editor.

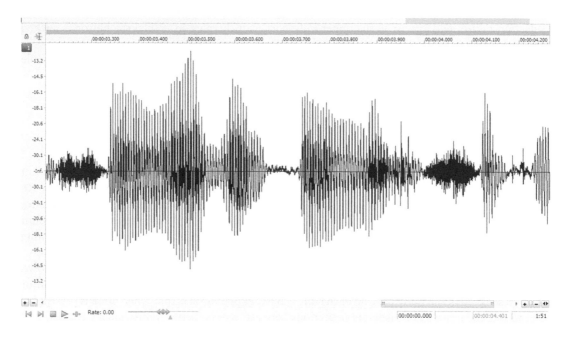

Figure 10.66   When the file opens in the sound editor, it looks something like this. Notice the noise between spoken words.

On the audio file, select a very small slice of audio that contains only the noise that needs to be removed. When you're selecting a noise sample, less is more. Fewer frequencies in the sample make for a more accurate reduction in those frequencies.

Now open Noise Reduction from the DirectX plug-in host (for Sound Forge it is **Tools | Noise Reduction**), and the screen shown in Figure 10.68 will be displayed.

Check the **Capture noiseprint** box and click the **Preview** button. This step allows you to hear what section has been selected. At the same time, a noiseprint has been captured. Click the **Noiseprint** tab if you want to see what the noiseprint looks like. Thousands of handles are on the noiseprint so that custom or exceptionally accurate control of the noiseprint may be achieved. It is generally best to allow the plug-in to function automatically, however. Playing with these handles does offer the opportunity to create some fairly inventive and radical sounds.

After the noiseprint has been captured, the area that the filter should be run on must be selected. Noise Reduction allows for selectable time spans, entire files, regions, or specific areas to be

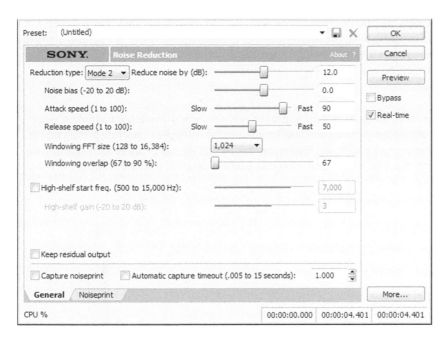

Figure 10.67   This is the main window for Noise Reduction, where all control of noise removal takes place.

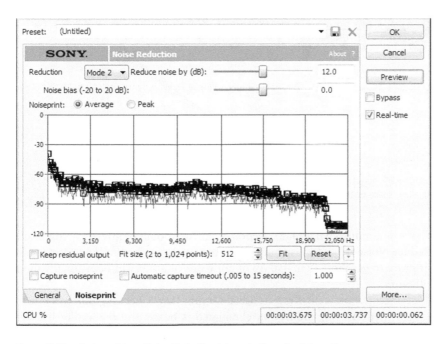

Figure 10.68   A view of how Noise Reduction interprets the noise information.

processed. Generally, files will be the entire area, but you can specify an area if you desire. Generally, choose the entire audio file, because if noise is present in one area, it's typically present in the entire file. (Other host applications can operate differently.) In Sound Forge, click **More** to select the start and end points for applying noise reduction.

> Trying to use large noise samples is counterproductive, damaging wanted information while possibly ignoring unwanted information. Use small samples multiple times rather than trying to use a larger sample one time. Noise Reduction can be run as many times as necessary to remove noise from the file, and using small selections usually has little impact on the desired sounds.

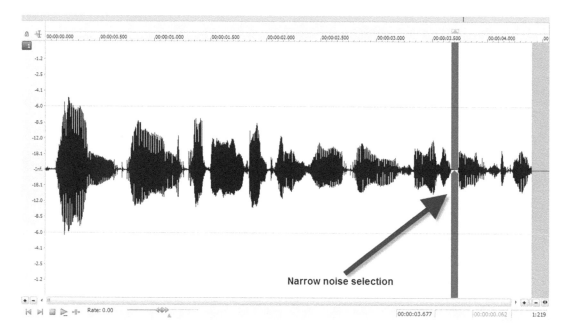

Figure 10.69   Select the smallest space possible for a noise sample.

Click OK when you have determined what time selection of the file should be affected. Now you'll be able to move the **Reduce Noise By** slider, listening in real time as Noise Reduction processes the noise out. Typically, it's rare to get more than –50 dB of noise out of a file, but occasionally more aggressive settings will work.

A useful feature in Noise Reduction is the **Keep Residual Output** box. Checking this box inverts the signal so that the information being reduced or eliminated is heard and the audio that will be kept is masked. This process allows you to hear if too much of the original signal is being affected.

After the desired level of noise is reduced or eliminated, click **OK**. The Noise Reduction plug-in will process the file. Closing the file in Sound Forge will prompt you to save the file. Save the file, and it will be deposited on the timeline in Vegas Pro in the exact place that it came from, but it is now named the original filename with *Take (number)* in the filename. It can be toggled back and forth from the original audio file for comparison.

Some files require multiple passes of Noise Reduction to obtain the best results without affecting the original or desired audio.

The DVD included with this book includes a project called **Noise Reduction Project**. Open this file. You will see two video files; the first has had no noise reduction on it, the second has been noise reduced. If you monitor the project through a good set of speakers or through any headphones, the hum in the background is very clear. The noise source is a refrigerator, three rooms away from where the interview was being conducted. In the case of the second file, −70 dB of noise was taken out, without creating artifacts in the desired audio file. Even if you don't have speakers that can accurately reproduce the noise, pay particular attention to the master meters.

Practice on the first file. If you don't capture a small enough segment for your noise file, you'll most likely create artifacts in the speech. FFT processing doesn't require a large slice; use a 100 millisecond slice of noise at most for your sample.

> Noise Reduction can be used for other purposes, such as creating unique sounds over a drum loop, voice, or sound effect. Experiment with it and find what works creatively for you. Drastically removing the high end by sampling the decay of a high hat or snare can give unique personality to the sound of any drum loop. Try using Noise Reduction on a heavily compressed speech file and make any human sound become more robotic.

Fingertip Mixing: Using the Mackie Control (and Other Control Devices in Vegas Pro) (Not Available in Vegas Movie Studio)

A significant barrier to using Vegas Pro in the all-digital recording studio was that until version 5, Vegas Pro was incapable of working with any hardware device except the Contour ShuttlePRO, which offered no mixing capabilities whatsoever. Since Vegas Pro 5, Sony has provided direct access to external surface control with the Mackie Control and Frontier Tranzport devices and with generic controllers that can be programmed to work with Vegas Pro. For instance, for fading and panning, no mouse is needed; simply use the Mackie Control in the same manner as you'd mix with any mixer. Accessing all parameters of FX such as compressors and EQs is very simple and intuitive with the control. Any generic device such as the M-Audio Oxygen keyboard or a Tascam 424 can be set up to function with Vegas Pro as well. Once you've mixed with a mixer, mixing with a mouse becomes extremely irritating and almost painful.

Figure 10.70 The Mackie Expanders and Control together make a very powerful control for Vegas Pro as well as many other audio applications. The console housing for the Mackie Control was built by Omnirax and contains many racks for external audio gear.

To set up a Mackie Control within Vegas Pro, you'll need:

- A Mackie Control.
- A MIDI interface device (many soundcards can manage this).
- A Mackie Extender. This is a nice addition, but not necessary. The Extender expands the capabilities of the Control so that the Control, for instance, manages channels 1 through 8, and the Extender manages channels 9 through 16. However, the Mackie Control can manage up to 128 channels of audio at a time. Switching from one channel set to another is a minor inconvenience; the video editor might not find it cumbersome nor inefficient in the same manner that an audio engineer or mix engineer might.

Connect the MIDI input of the Mackie Control to the Output MIDI connector of your soundcard or MIDI input/output (I/O) device. Connect the MIDI output of the Mackie Control to the MIDI Input of your soundcard or MIDI I/O device.

Select **Options** | **Preferences** | **External Control and Automation**. This opens the dialog box of the external control parameters. This is where Vegas Pro will be instructed to access the Mackie Control hardware interface.

In this dialog box, select the **Available Devices** drop-down menu and choose the **Mackie Control** from the

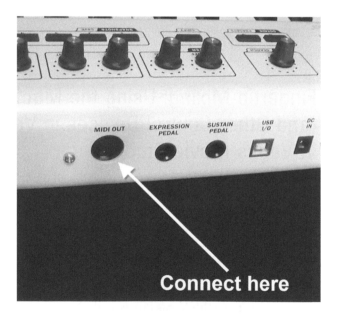

Figure 10.71 Connect the Mackie Control to the MIDI interface device.

dialog box. Then click **Add** to add the Control to the Active Control Devices dialog box. This should cause the Mackie faders to move to indicate that the device is communicating with Vegas Pro. (If it doesn't respond, don't be concerned. The next step will determine communication.) When the device shows up in the dialog box, double-click the box containing the Mackie Control. This opens up the **Configuration** dialog box, which allows Vegas Pro and the Mackie to be set up not only to be compatible but also to be as efficient and powerful as you'd like it to be.

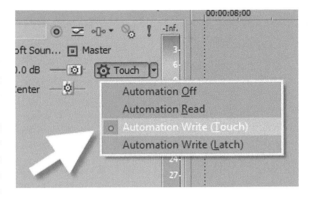

Figure 10.72 This dialog box, found in the track header, is used to tell Vegas Pro how to read or write any automation or level settings from the Mackie Control.

Click **Scan** in the Configuration dialog box. This will instruct Vegas Pro to scan the MIDI connections to see what is connected to the ports. If you have Mackie Extender devices attached to the MIDI interface, they'll show up here as well. Each device must be configured separately, but the engineers at Sony and Vegas Pro have done most of the work for you. However, you'll need to instruct the Configuration dialog box to set up the channels on the various devices. For instance, if the system is set up for one Expander and one Control, the Control can be set up to be channels 1–8, or 9–16, and the Expander can be set to control whatever channels the Control is not controlling. Since I'm right-handed and find my need to access the Control more imperative than reaching the Expanders, I set my system up as follows:

- Expander 1: Channels 1 through 8
- Expander 2: Channels 9 through 16
- Expander 3: Channels 17 through 24
- Mackie Control: Channels 25 through 32

After clicking **Scan** and setting up each device for its controlled channels, click **OK**. Now click the **Apply** button in the External Control and automation dialog box. All is set for Vegas Pro to know what to do, except one last detail.

Close the **Preferences** dialog box and go to **Options | External Control**, and click on **External Control**. This will place a small check mark next to the External Control words. This tells Vegas Pro that you'd like to control the application externally. Of course you'll still be able to operate Vegas Pro via the keyboard and mouse, but this tells Vegas Pro to accept information from the Mackie Control.

Vegas Pro will automatically be mapped to all the knobs on the Mackie Control, so nothing more is needed. The Mackie Console should have come with a Lexan overlay that you can stick to the surface of the control. The Lexan overlay is specific to Vegas Pro, indicating how each push button relates to Vegas Pro and what it controls. As mentioned earlier, you may customize the key mapping to set any button to perform a specific task in Vegas Pro.

Figure 10.73 Set up Vegas Pro and the
Mackie Control to behave
exactly as you'd like them
to behave in the
Configuration dialog box.

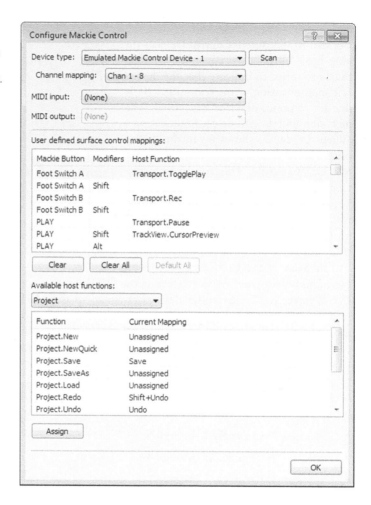

A single Mackie Control may be set up to operate as many as 128 channels at a time on a single device, but this does require a lot of paging through various views to look at each channel past the eight that are automatically displayed. Because most of my audio mixes require me to have immediate access to all channels, I find it more efficient to use a series of extenders and controls. One powerful side benefit of the Mackie Universal Control (and any other controlling device) is that the device may be used as a video switcher as well, providing access to color-correction plug-ins and other plug-ins found in the Vegas Pro filter set.

Other Controlling Devices

Any MIDI control device may be set up to control Vegas Pro. For example, the M-Audio Oxygen keyboard has eight generic control knobs that may be accessed within Vegas Pro and may be used like a mixer via generic surface control. Some MIDI devices, such as the Oxygen, won't use a MIDI connection. Control data is passed back and forth via the USB connection.

To use generic surface controls, the setup is very similar to the Mackie Control setup. First install the device drivers and connect the device to be used as a generic surface control. Open the **Options | Preferences | Midi** dialog box. The generic device should appear in the dialog box. Tick the boxes related to the connected device, telling Vegas Pro which devices you'd like to use as a control surfaces.

Click **External Control and Automation** and select **Generic Control** from the drop-down in the Available Devices dialog box. The dialog box will display the generic devices. Right-click or double-click the **Generic Control** and open the **Configuration** dialog box. Here you'll need to map the keys and controllers to specific functions within Vegas Pro. Some devices may be ready to roll with Default Mapping. Devices such as the Tascam 424 and the eVolution U Controller should link up fairly quickly, although no mapping has been created for the device. You can locate the files for surface controllers in the **C:\Program Files\Sony \< Vegas Pro Dir >\External Control Drivers\Generic Control Maps** folder.

Locate the **Quikmap.xml** file on the vasst.com Website, which will set up all automation needs for the M-Audio Oxygen. You will also find other controller parameters on the VASST site.

Figure 10.74   Enable External Control from the **Options | External Control** dialog box.

Figure 10.75   The eight knobs on the Oxygen may be assigned as controlling devices for Vegas Pro.

Audiomation?

Even if you don't have HUI devices connected to Vegas Pro, you can still take advantage of the automation in Vegas Pro. Each audio track header's automation button contains several options. Right-click the **Automation** button to view the options.

The Automated Mute feature allows audio to be muted during the recording of automation during playback of a file. To insert an automatic mute into your project, place an audio file on the timeline. Click the **Automation** button and select **Show Automation Controls** from the submenu. This will insert the **Automated Mute** button into the track header. Click the **Automation** button again and choose **Write (Latch)** or **Write (Touch)** from the submenu.

Begin playback, and while the playhead is moving down the timeline, press the **Automated Mute** button. Vegas Pro will insert an automated mute point into the timeline, and each time the playhead crosses this point the audio will be muted. Press the **Automated Mute** button again and the audio will be unmuted.

Audio may also be mixed on the fly with Vegas Pro using a mouse, clicking on the track and inserting envelope points during playback. Choose a track header, press V to insert a volume envelope or P to insert a pan envelope. During playback, click the volume or panning envelope. This will insert an envelope point or handle into the timeline. Moving this envelope point or handle will modify the volume or pan position of the track. All movements of the volume or panning envelope will be remembered and recalled automatically for future mixing. Setting up a time selection and loop will allow mix points to be tweaked on the fly.

Training Vegas

Vegas can be trained to work with most standard controller devices. To train Vegas to accept input from your MIDI Controller device, open the **Options | Preferences | External Control and Automation** tab. Choose **Generic Controller** from the drop-down and click **Add**. The Configuration dialog box will open. In the **Configure** dialog box, click on the parameter you want to control.

Touch any controlling device button, slider, or knob. This will cause the **Learn** button in the dialog box to light up. Tick the **Learn** box and turn, slide, or press the parameter knob, fader, or button to instruct Vegas to link it to the specific parameter. Repeat this step for each parameter you want to control. Be certain you save the map so that it's available for your next session. (Maps are saved as XML files.)

Figure 10.76a   Select the parameter that you'd like to control by clicking on it and then moving, sliding, or pressing the controlling device, knob, slider, or button. You'll need to tick the **Learn** box.

Every Breath You Take, Every Move You Make!

Automation is the act of the host application remembering every move made on the external control device. In past versions of Vegas Pro, automation was entirely controlled by a mouse. Although intuitive and functional, it is certainly nearly impossible to generate an inspired mix with a mouse. Music is supposed to be inspired by the whim of the moment, and sometimes generating mixes by hand at random moments will spark the most amazing muse and mixes. Moreover, being able to recall random mixes at will and create multiple mixes to play back for a director or producer is a wonderful thing.

Nearly all parameters of Vegas Pro's functions may be automated and recalled. With a higher-end controller such as the Mackie Control, you can access parameters of all effects, bus sends, auxiliary sends and returns, reverbs, and compressors.

Automation in Vegas Pro is a wonderful thing to experience because of its simplicity with underlying complexity. To automate, even a small Griffen knob can be used. It's a little challenging to set up, but once the controller is set up, here are the steps to automate a mix:

1. On the track to be automated, click the **Automation settings** button.

2. Choose **Automation Write** in one of the two modes offered, **Touch** or **Latch**.

3. Click **Play** or press the **Spacebar**, and start to twist knobs, slide sliders, or push buttons.

4. Stop playback. If you are pleased with the mix, it may be put into **Automation Read** mode, in which no movement will be taught to the application; it merely will read the moves previously input with the controlling device.

 Tip_____

If you are an experienced audio engineer, you can mix all tracks live just as you would with an analog mixer. Select all tracks in Vegas Pro before putting a track in automation mode, so when one track is placed in automation record mode, all tracks are put into automation record mode. You can always go back and overwrite all fader moves quickly on individual tracks if necessary. If you have a hardware device such as the Mackie Universal Control, it's fast and easy to write a full mix and then go back and tweak later. If you have more audio tracks than you have fader control over, enable automation only for the tracks you have faders for, then switch the faders to the remaining tracks, writing automation and tweaking as you go. Remember, you can always reorder tracks in Vegas Pro by dragging tracks to where they are most convenient in layout and priority.

Touch Me, Latch Me! Automation Modes

There are two forms of writing automation. One is Latch mode, the other is Touch mode. Each has its benefits, and each is fairly common to automated studios. Generally the workflow between the two processes is managed in a specific order. For most recording scenarios, you'll be working with Vegas Pro by starting in one mode and finishing in another.

For a fresh mix with no automation moves inserted, start in **Latch** mode. Play the mix by pressing the **Spacebar** or clicking **Play** or by pressing the **Play** button on your controlling device. Move knobs or faders during the playback on however many tracks you have in automation mode. This creates a "rough mix," as it's called in the industry. Now Vegas Pro will remember all movements you made, regardless of whether they are volumes, pans, or FX automation movements. This is usually done with all tracks in record mode, but just because it's usually done this way doesn't mean you have to do it this way.

Figure 10.76b

Continued

Latch mode will continue writing settings regardless of whether you are making fader movements or not and will overwrite any existing movements that you may have created earlier, making Latch mode excellent for writing over an entire mix or an entire track if you are dissatisfied with the mix or want to create an alternative mix.

Following the mix setup or rough mix, the mix can be either fine-tuned by individual track or tweaked with all tracks still in automation mode. However, switching tracks over to **Touch** mode is best. In Touch mode, keyframes and control points are created only when you are touching or adjusting the parameters of the track. As soon as you stop moving sliders or knobs, Vegas Pro quits writing movements, and the already existing movements you inserted in Latch mode or the first write of automation take over again. This is why Touch mode is best for tweaking a mix.

On each track header, there is an **Automation** icon. You can see it next to the Mute and Track FX button. Click it and a submenu appears.

Automation is found on all track headers and may be set up for all tracks at once or set for individual tracks.

In the submenu, you can select **Show Automation Controls**, and this will cause the Automation icon to display the mode that the specific track is in. This is handy if you find yourself wondering why a specific track is behaving in a particular way.

Mutes may now be automated, too. A device like the Mackie Control or the eVolution 33 has Mute buttons on it. Mutes may also be inserted by clicking on the **Mute** button on the track header or by pressing the **Mute** button on the controlling device. Automated muting is very handy for music or dialogue composites, in which various sections and takes are on multiple tracks and you want to comp together all the acceptable parts of different tracks to create one final track.

Figure 10.77 The four icons that indicate track status are Off, Read, Touch, and Latch. Notice that Read and Touch are very similar. The Read icon is green and the Write icon is red.

Feeling Fat? Get Thin!

Automation will write literally thousands of nodes, also known as *handles* or *keyframes*, during a write. This can be exceptionally tasking on the CPU if left on its own. However, Vegas Pro has a feature known as *thinning* by which the number of nodes and keyframes can be thinned out, controlled by the user. In the **Options | Preferences | External Control and Automation** dialog box, there is a checkbox for **thinning**. Thinning will be necessary on slower machines that are used for large mixes. Otherwise, the thousands of envelope points generated by fader motion will be more than the processor can handle.

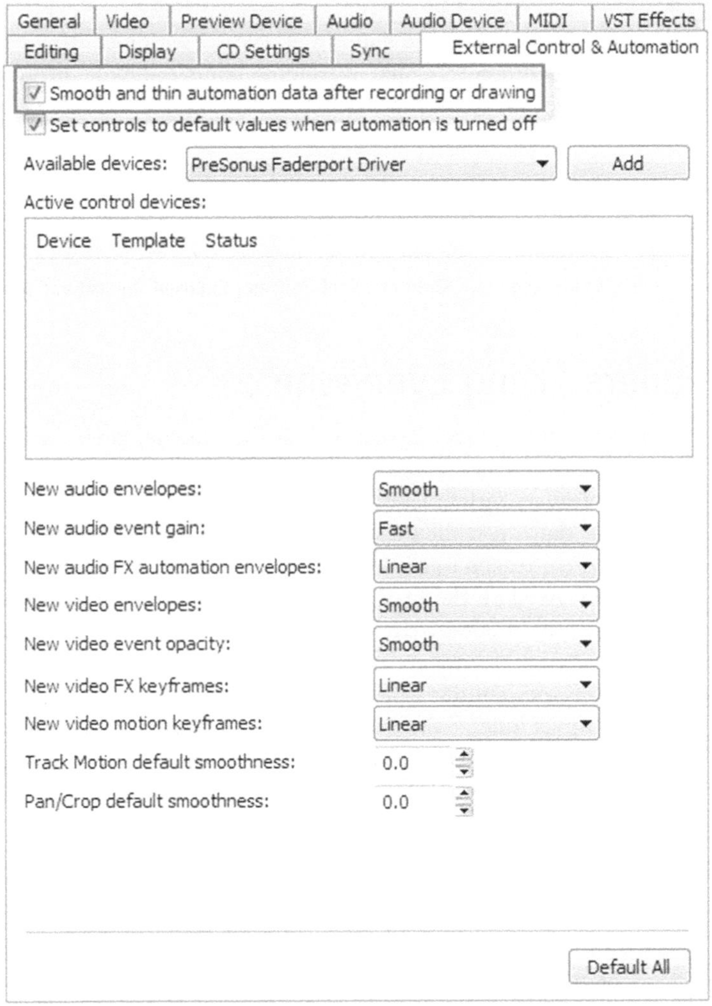

Figure 10.78 Use this menu to reduce or increase the amount of thinning of keyframes and handles found in a mix.

| General | Video | Preview Device | Audio | Audio Device | MIDI | VST Effects |
| Editing | Display | CD Settings | Sync | External Control & Automation |

☑ Smooth and thin automation data after recording or drawing
☑ Set controls to default values when automation is turned off

Available devices: PreSonus Faderport Driver ▼ [Add]

Active control devices:

Device   Template   Status

New audio envelopes: Smooth ▼
New audio event gain: Fast ▼
New audio FX automation envelopes: Linear ▼
New video envelopes: Smooth ▼
New video event opacity: Smooth ▼
New video FX keyframes: Linear ▼
New video motion keyframes: Linear ▼
Track Motion default smoothness: 0.0
Pan/Crop default smoothness: 0.0

[Default All]

Video editors may or may not find the nuances of thinning necessary to control. Musicians will demand as much control as possible and so will want to set this to their preference. If you still feel that thinning is missing or hitting an area that doesn't feel just right, you can always manually adjust handles by using a mouse and clicking and moving the node or envelope point until it is sitting just right in the mix. One suggested workflow is that the mix be created in Latch mode with Thinning enabled. Turn Thinning off, and tweak or fine-tune the mix using Touch mode. Use Touch mode only on the areas that need fine-tuning or you may end up rendering the earlier-thinned sections moot.

Though it may seem odd, various controllers may send differing amounts of information and some may insert far more values or fewer values than necessary. Experiment with your controller device to determine whether thinning is necessary for your mix.

The small marks inserted either manually or with a controlling device may be called nodes, handles, keyframes, grips, envelope points, and/or rubber band markers by various applications. All of these names mean the same thing. Sony calls them envelope points.

Tip_____

If you need extreme control over complex mix sections, do a rough mix and get things as close to finished as possible, then turn off **Thinning** in the **Options | Preferences | External Control and Automation** dialog box.

Faders Flying Everywhere

If you have a flying fader device such as the Mackie, faders will move on the device regardless of whether the screen is drawing the movement or not. This is a very sexy and impressive event for those not familiar with fader movement. Watching faders move, meters bouncing, and all functions doing what they do while the user is hands off is quite exciting.

Another great reason to use a device like the Mackie for an external control surface is that metering can be viewed on the LCD screen of the Mackie Control. Sony has made this work in such a manner that you don't have to look constantly at the computer monitor while setting up a mix on the Mackie, since the meters are very accurate and are laid out above each channel strip, making it easy to see and familiar to audio engineers used to viewing metering on the console. The meters will show up as long as the Mackie is in I/O mode, found on the console view section. Also, the Mixing Console view in Vegas Pro is adjustable as to the level of detail you'd like to observe in the meters.

Mixing Audio in Vegas Pro

Mixing audio is a practice based entirely on personal preference, but some standards and techniques are used by most engineers and producers to achieve mixes that meet with industry expectations. Each person's ears are different; this is what makes one producer more popular for various kinds of music than another. Mutt Lange, a very well-known producer of heavy metal, pop rock, and country, is one of the few to jump from one musical style to another. Peter Gabriel is renowned for his production of world-pop music, just as William Aura is known for his adult contemporary work. Alan Parsons, Tom Lord-Alge, Ross Collum, and Danial Lanois are all unique and well-known producers/mix engineers. All of them credit their years working with the equipment and producers in the studios they cut their teeth in as third engineers, janitors, or receptionists. All of these producers got to where they are not only because of their inspired sense of what people want to hear and how to bring an artist's talents to the fore but also because they knew the basic principles and practices of mixing audio. Knowledge and a practiced ear are the two most important things to creating a great mix. Knowledge is easily found. Having a practiced ear can take years. The basic principles of understanding a mix are fairly simple; from there, it simply becomes a matter of expanding on experience.

Mixing Techniques

Setting up a mix is entirely dependent on the contents of the track, whether it's instrumentation, bed music with a voiceover, Foley, sound design, or full-blown orchestra. Bass frequencies tend to be more centered in a mix than are high frequencies, in which a right-to-left spread is more evidently heard. Bass frequencies below 250 Hz aren't really very directional but rather omnidirectional. Higher frequencies are very directional, which is why bass drums and bass guitars/synth bass are generally mixed to the center of a mix and higher frequency sounds are spaced throughout the right-to-left areas of a mix. An easier way to think of it is to look at a photo of a beautiful mountain vista. The mountains form the base of the image, and the eye is drawn to the bugling elk in the forefront, slightly off center. You notice the green trees and the stream or brook flowing through the picture. The primary subject of the picture is the elk in the foreground, but without the surrounding beauty, the elk looks rather stark. Creating a good mix is just like that: lots of individual elements that draw the ear to a primary element. Try to picture a mix visually with the score or performance in your mind's eye, which will help achieve the end goal.

> Fine-tune mixes by holding down the left mouse button and use the 2 or 8 key on the numeric keypad to fine-tune any envelope up or down. The 4 or 6 key moves a node forward or backward on the timeline. The amount of control is determined by the depth of track focus. With maximum zoom, superfine envelope increments are possible. The **Quantize to Frames** (**F8**) option might need to be disabled to have accurate access at maximum zoom.
>
> The same keyboard trim features affecting the video timeline are also found in the audio toolset. Use the 7 or 9 key on the numeric keypad to select an Event edge; use the 1 or 3 key to edit longer or shorter by samples. The depth of track focus determines how fine the keyboard edits are made. Zooming in deep on a track causes up to sample-by-sample edits; zooming out on the track edits larger sections of audio. (See the "Editing" section for more information on keyboard-based editing.)

Some mixes are built from the bottom-end elements first, finishing with the primary element, and other mixes are built starting with the primary element and the other sounds are built around it.

For working with a dialog-based mix for film or video, this is a good way to start, getting the voice to a level that is comfortable. It should be loud but never crossing the −6 dB mark so that room exists for other elements to maintain their dynamic expression. Adding a compressor to the primary element is fairly standard practice. If the primary is a voice, start with light compression settings of 1.5:1, or 2:1, working with the threshold to suit the mix. Be cautious of squashing the sound too much, as this element is the most out-front part of the mix.

Next, begin to place the foundation elements, such as static walla, traffic, or background noise. In a musical context, these elements would be the kick drum, bass guitar, or other bottom-end elements. If the bottom sound is muddy or tubby, remove some of the frequencies in the 300 Hz region. In a musical mix, add a little 1.5 kHz for some snap in the kick drum and bass guitar. In a mix for video with dialogue, leave out some of the upper frequencies, perhaps even dampen them a bit, so as not to fight with the frequencies in the primary element/front voice. Use a compressor, starting with a basic setting of 3:1 or 4:1, and work with the settings from there to keep the mix from becoming too dynamic in the low frequencies. Send all the bottom/foundation elements to one sub-mix/bus, with an additional compressor if necessary on the bus.

> The term *walla* stems from the early days of radio, when extras were brought in for a radio or film show, and actors would say "Walla-walla-walla" over and over, with just a few people saying the words out of sync with each other to create the sound of a murmuring crowd. No individual "real" words were spoken at all. To this day, background dialogue is called *walla*, but actors no longer use the fixed-word format.

Sound design comes into the mix next, with motion and depth filling the speakers with moving elements that can be musical or not. Either way, the sound should be a filling sound that underlies the other pieces of the mix. In a music-oriented mix, this is the rhythmic element. Try to avoid panning this sound hard right or left if possible. More of a 9 o'clock and 3 o'clock is the ticket, washed wide rather than being too loud, so as to take away focus from the aural subject. Guitars, synths, and background vocals all fit into this space, too. Be cautious of wanting too much sparkle or bottom end in these elements and leave room for the primary sounds and foundation sounds. Use reverbs or delays to wash these sounds across the sonic canvas, rather than increasing the volume of an individual instrument. These sounds contribute a sense of color or timbre of the musical element. If everything were taken away except this element and the lead element, there would still be something worth listening to. If inconsistent sounds are in this element, try to bring them in and out gently rather than with surprise. Otherwise, they'll detract from the front elements.

Next placed are the special FX or signature sounds of a piece. In the musical context, this is the moving sounds of a synth that has a signature to mark the song, rather than a synth that is emulating a traditional keyboard. In a video context, these sounds are the cannon fire, bullets flying, spaceships, aircraft swoops, or other action sounds. These should be placed to move right to left or front to back in a surround mix. These are the exciting elements of a stereo or surround mix.

Remember, these tips are mere rudiments. From here, the mix can be tweaked according to the individual ear.

Compression

One might say that it is simply impossible to do a good digital mix without compression, yet compression is one of the most misunderstood parts of the mix and audio process. First, it's important to understand the difference between a compressor and a limiter.

A *limiter* prevents audio from passing at a predetermined volume. Any audio that attempts to pass the preset level is squashed to fit the preset level. Limiters are generally not good for music or audio for video mixes but are more suited to situations in which not all elements of the media can be controlled.

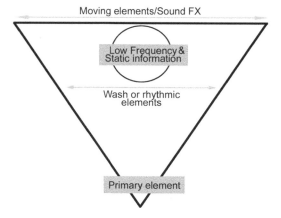

Figure 10.79   An overhead view of mix elements.

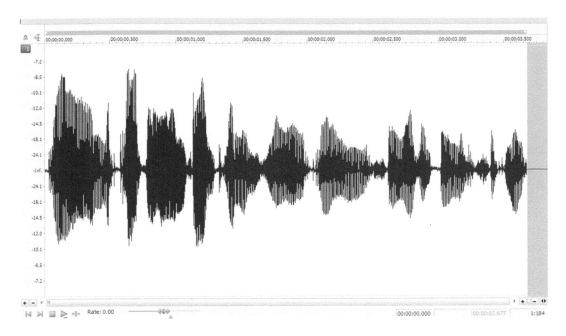

Figure 10.80   Audio before being limited.

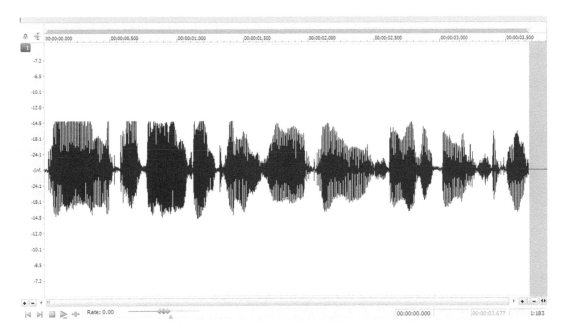

Figure 10.81   Audio after being hard-limited.

There are hard limiters and soft limiters. The difference is how much of a dynamic the limiter might be set at before the hard limit point. In other words, a limiter might be preset to ensure that nothing greater than –3 dB is allowed to pass, but the majority of the audio information is at –5 dB with lots of dynamic that wants to go much louder than the –3 dB allowable maximum. Using a setting that instructs the limiter to start reducing levels at –9 dB allows some dynamic feel to remain in the audio track. Limiters often squeeze the high end and life out of a mix, making it dull and boring. Television commercials are often hard limited and compressed to give maximum volume (one of the annoying things about the overall volume of a television commercial).

The term *soft limiter* is really just drawing a comparison to a hard compressor. Most compressors also have limiting ability built in.

Compressors operate a little differently compared to a compressor limiter; they are more elastic or malleable only in the way they control dynamics on release. A limiter is a compressor with a ratio of 10:1 or greater but usually with fewer adjustable attributes than a compressor. Compressors can make audio louder while at the same time making sure that the dynamic range is reduced. Generally, a compressor is used to keep dynamics as accurate as possible while at the same time preventing audio from crossing a chosen threshold. This feature makes it easier to get an Event/signal louder in a mix, while still maintaining control over the apparent signal.

For example, compression might be required for a singer or voiceover artist in the studio who moves toward and back from the microphone. Recorded levels are not consistent. Perhaps the same vocal artist has very quiet to very loud passages in their speech. A compressor evens out the differences between the two sections.

A compressor is used by guitar players and bass players to maintain the sustain of a plucked or strummed note/chord. A compressor smoothes down the attack on the strings and then opens up/releases gradually by allowing the note/chord to appear as though it is going on longer than it would have otherwise been heard.

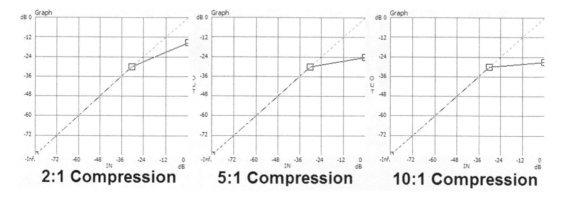

Figure 10.82   Threshold set at –30 dB, with variable compression ratios: 2:1, 5:1, 10:1. Notice the compression curve at the different settings.

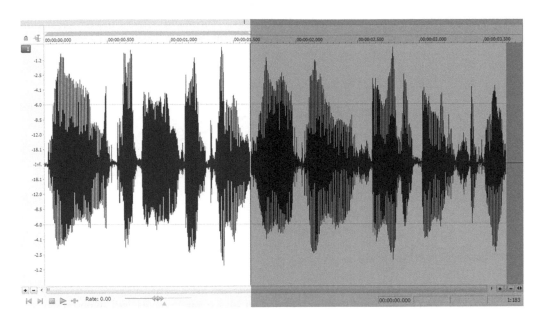

Figure 10.83 Mastering level compression at 2:1, with threshold at −8 dB, allows the signal to be louder overall because of the reduced dynamic range.

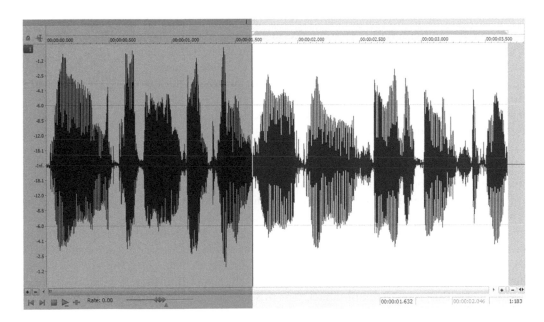

Figure 10.84 Compression applied at 2:1, with threshold at −24 dB. Beginning the attack earlier in the signal with a lower threshold makes a huge difference in the behavior of the compressor.

Here's how a compressor works. Comprehending the ratio, threshold, attack, and release are the most important pieces to understanding compression.

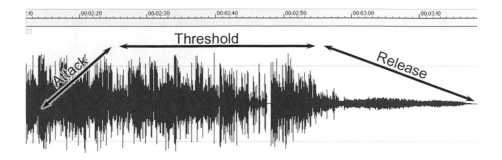

Figure 10.85   Attack, threshold, and release.

Vocals generally won't sound right with compression of greater than 6:1. All dynamics of the voice will be squashed to the point of having no performance or nuance left in the audio.

On the DVD included in this book are five demonstrations of audio and audio for video. Listen to the differences in how the audio cuts through on the repaired sections.

Sony provides a multiband dynamics processor in their plug-in arsenal. This multiband tool is a combination of four compressors with frequency-dependent settings. Rather than compressing an overall instrument or mix, individual facets of the audio can be affected while leaving other portions alone. For example, a snare drum might be exactly the sound you want but is too loud at one particular frequency or range of frequencies. The multiband dynamics plug-in, or EQ-based compressor, gives the ability to compress only the offending frequency or range of frequencies without affecting the rest of the audio information.

De-essing

A component of both spoken and sung word is *sibilance*. Sibilance is the hissing sound made when a person speaks or sings *S* or *SH*. Difficult to repair, this issue, known as *essing*, creates distortion or apparent distortion on cheap speakers and high-end systems alike, regardless of how much compression or EQ is applied. In fact, EQ is the last resort to repair essing, and compressors are only one step ahead of EQ when it comes to de-essing sound. A *de-esser* is just a band-specific compressor.

When sibilance from *Ss* gets in the way of the mix, open the Sony Multiband Dynamic plug-in and start with the **De-Ess** preset. Reset the attack time to **5** milliseconds. Reset the decay time to **40** or **50** milliseconds for a male voice, set the frequency center to **5** kHz, and for female vocals, set the frequency center to **6.5**. True sibilance is usually centered between 8 and 10 kHz. Both of these settings are starting points. It might be that further adjustment is required.

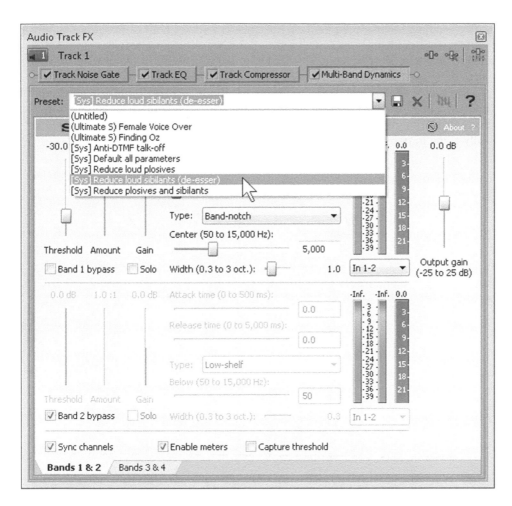

Figure 10.86   Saving the **De-Ess** preset setting preserves it for another session or for other de-essing in the same project.

The compression ratio should be set at 30:1 to start with, and the threshold set at –30 dB. Now start a loop over a section where sibilance is present and adjust the multiband settings as the loop is heard. Be cautious of applying too much of a ratio; a singer or voice-over can quickly gain a lisp if it's set too high. Sometimes as little as 6:1 is enough. Experiment with raising the threshold and reducing the ratio until the desired fix is found. Save this setting as a preset by typing a preset name in the Preset box and pressing the icon that looks like a floppy disk. This preset is now part of your toolbox.

Using Equalization

Equalizers, also known as *EQs*, are one of the most oft-turned-to tools in the plug-in arsenal. EQs are used to cut frequencies of fat sounds that occupy space in the audio spectrum that other sounds can also occupy, creating confusion about what the ear is hearing. EQs are also used to correct problems with a tracking room or poor frequency balance in a microphone or sometimes simply to enhance a performance or characteristic of an audio Event. Invented initially to flatten sound over the telephone, today's EQs are predominantly used to unflatten sound, and so in jest, some engineers call these tools *unequalizers*.

The use of an EQ must be judicious. Too much boost of any frequency can cause overload of the outputs, can cause a compressor to work harder than it needs to because of excess volume boost, or can even create distortion in the harmonics related to a sound.

EQs typically come in two formats: graphic and parametric.

Figure 10.87   Graphic equalizers set at octaves.

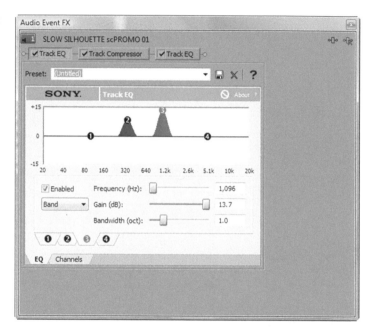

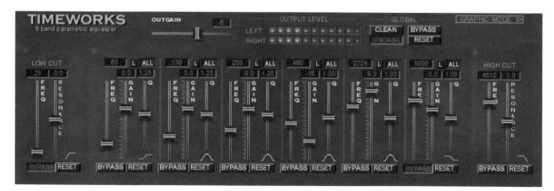

Figure 10.88   The Timeworks parametric EQ resembles a graphic EQ. However, frequencies can be selected, and the bandwidth or Q of the frequencies can be defined.

With graphic EQs, frequencies are preset, and only the gain of specific frequencies can be increased or reduced. It is found in octave, half-octave, and one-third octave in most instances. An octave is determined by a frequency multiplied by 2. The octave of 125 Hz is 250 Hz, the next octave being 500 Hz, and so forth. Frequency centers are set by the International Standards Organization (ISO).

Vegas Pro has four different graphic EQs available as plug-ins.

With parametric EQs, users can select a specific frequency center, select the amount of bandwidth that the frequency has control over, and control the gain or reduction of that same frequency band. Usually parametric EQs allow several frequencies to be specified and controlled.

A derivative of both graphic and

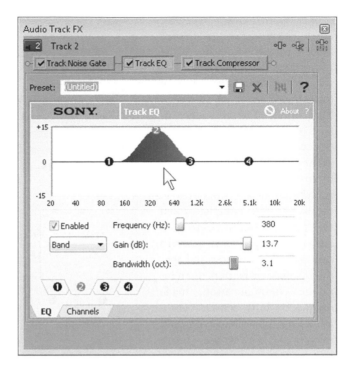

Figure 10.89   The Q is fairly wide, affecting frequencies on either side of its center.

parametric EQs, paragraphic EQs are mixed-mode equalizers that generally have fixed frequencies for the bottom and top frequency spectra and midrange frequencies that can be shifted. This type is rarely seen in software-only forms.

Tight Q is useful for cutting out a specific frequency that can be a hum, distortion, or simply a problem frequency. Tight Q is also valuable for enhancing specific frequencies, such as boosting presence in a vocal to give an airy quality to obtain the pop vocal sound that is popular today.

Tip_____

On the DVD, open the Equalization Demonstration project. The file contains the same Event in duplicate. The first version is the broadcast version; the second has presence and compression added to it using a parametric EQ with a boost at 4.1 kHz. Notice the difference between the two. Either of these two mixes is acceptable for final output, but a difference exists in how the two are perceived.

Using Reverb

Reverb can be used for any kind of audio mix, whether for video or audio, spoken word or music. It is also one of the most overused effects in the palette of tools available. Reverb is used to reproduce various room environments artificially. In the past, music had to be recorded in large chambers or in rooms with large reflective areas. The reverb created in such large rooms helped blend sounds together, creating a cohesive yet individual expression of instruments or vocal authority. Ever notice how the voice of God in film or recording always is accompanied by a large reverb? As technology and creativity grew in the music industry, reverberation was emulated in tubes, springs, complex room systems, eventually electronics, and now in software. Reverb can express a vastness and spatial distance or be part of an intimate communication, made unique by how certain consonants, syllables, or instrumental inflections sound within a reverberant sound. Every environment common to the world has a sound. What makes up this sound are the reflections within that environment. Singing in

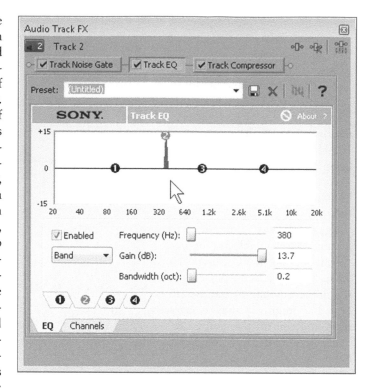

Figure 10.90   The Q is very narrow, affecting only the immediate frequency selected.

the shower makes even a poor voice sound rich, whereas that same voice singing in a closet sounds dull and lifeless. The shower is full of hard surfaces, while the closet is full of soft surfaces. The hard surfaces effectively create a doubled voice sound that the ear hears immediately, whereas the soft surfaces absorb nearly all sounds, preventing almost all reflections and making the sound harder to hear. Large rooms with reflective surfaces, such as cathedrals, auditoriums, and long hallways, not only reflect the sound, but reflect it repeatedly, expanding and elongating the sound, all the while softening the sound, giving an illusion of infinity.

Somewhere between the sound of a closet and that of a cathedral, there are reverb settings useful to nearly every situation. Vegas Pro has lots of great reverbs built in, and incredible software reverbs are available from several third-party manufacturers, such as PSP Audio software, WAVES, iZotope, and more. Several reverbs are included on the DVD with this book.

 Tip_____

Overused or overly loud reverb can wash over too much of the audio spectrum, making the audio sound muddy and without clarity. Use reverb carefully.

Consider using reverb in very short, quiet settings for interviews that might be too dry from being in a very tight, quiet room or that might have some ambient noise that can't be washed with other sounds or beds. Reverb is also useful for making a mono audio signal appear to be stereo by creating artificial reflections that reach the ear at different times. Feed a mono voice or instrument into a bus or FX send that is only the reverb and then route back to the master output. Make sure the reverb is fairly short and has very little predelay. Panning the reverb/sending the reverb to the same location as the dry sound also is a great technique for keeping the sound large but located. Pan the original signal to where it sounds right in the mix before adding reverb. Use an FX send to route the dry sound to the reverb. Pan the reverb to the same space. This technique works well with vocals mixed with a music bed, as well as with single-instrument sounds, such as guitars, snare drums, keyboards, and other single-point-source instruments.

Be cautious about reverb sounds that are too bright. Although they usually warm up a voice, bright reverbs also tend to elaborate sibilance and can easily create distortion in the high end. Use a de-esser or EQ before the reverb if this problem occurs.

When you're mixing audio, sometimes a need arises to lower the audio volume quickly, whether for a phone call or visitor or because it's too loud for a conversation. Vegas Pro provides a **Dim** button that dims audio by 20 dB. This option ensures immediate volume reduction without changing the audio output level sliders and without affecting render output. The Dim button is found just above the Master Volume slider or can be enabled by pressing **Ctrl+Shift+F12**. Of course, with Vegas Pro's key-mapping feature, you can map the Dim button to be any key setting you'd prefer.

Mixing for 5.1 Surround Sound (Not Available in Vegas Movie Studio)

Surround Sound mixing brings an entirely different perspective in prepping and setting up a mix. Rather than being concerned with just two speakers in a stereo field, you now have six speakers, all individually controlled. The term *5.1* is derived from there being a right and a left speaker for the front and the rear, a center channel, and a subwoofer (the .1 of 5.1). Each speaker has its own input, and setting the mix for each speaker can quickly become a challenge, as the stereo field all of a sudden becomes small. Moreover, having extra sound points excites most any engineer who hasn't had experience in the Surround realm, and it's very easy to create an over-the-top mix, which, while sounding exciting in the control room, loses its excitement in the listening environment. Sometimes mixes don't even make sense to the ear when taken in the context of a nonvisual setting. In short, it's easy to overemphasize the rear channel speakers simply out of the novelty of having them.

Vegas Pro has the ability to do 5.1 channel Surround mixing. This type is the standard for most DVDs, and many music recordings are moving into the realm of 5.1 Surround. The Eagles' *Hell Freezes Over* CD was one of the first immersed-experience CDs on the market and is an excellent example of a 5.1 Surround Sound audio recording.

The room must be set up correctly for mixing in 5.1 Surround. Having a 5.1 sound system from the local office supply and a 5.1 Surround card is barely going to suffice and will not suffice at all if the room is not set up correctly.

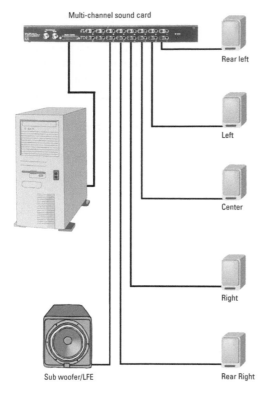

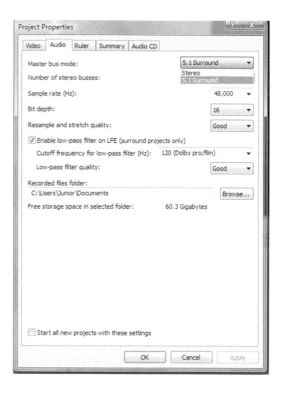

Figure 10.91   Wiring the Surround system properly is important. Use high-quality cables to connect speakers to a soundcard.

Figure 10.92   Select the Surround setting to create buses for the surround mix.

On the DVD contained in this book is a test clip that allows audio to be tested on the output of all speakers in the room. It's critical that they all be equal in volume to achieve a balanced mix. Use these tones to test the output.

Do this process by placing the tone as an Event on the timeline of Vegas Pro and then open the **File | Properties** dialog box. Select the **Audio** tab, and, in the **Master Bus Mode** drop-down list, select **5.1 surround.**

This process automatically inserts buses in the Mixer Docking window to allow for mixing levels to front, rear, and center speakers, plus a low-frequency enclosure (LFE) control. It also adds a Surround panner to each audio track on the timeline.

Set levels on the soundcard's mixer at 0 dB to ensure that Vegas Pro is the only mixing device being used to control levels. Otherwise, it's possible that rendered files will not be accurate to what is being heard. Having unequal soundcard mixer settings guarantees an unbalanced mix.

Figure 10.93　Some soundcard mixer control levels outside of Vegas Pro. Check this carefully for accuracy in the mix.

This panner control is how Vegas Pro maneuvers audio around the audio space. Notice that five speakers are in the panner. Clicking the **LFE** button in the upper-right corner of the panner control sends the channel only to the LFE output.

Audio is panned from front to rear and from right to left using keyframes. Vegas Pro uses keyframes in the audio tools slightly different from how it uses keyframes in the video tools. Automatic mixing makes this very effective and powerful; rather than using hardware to set up the mix, audio positioning can be exactly keyframed and edited at any point in the mix, with Vegas Pro graphically showing the placement of audio at any point.

After opening the **Surround Panner,** right-click the **Track Control** pane associated with the open Surround Panner. Select **Insert/Remove Envelope (Shift + P)** from the menu and then **Surround Pan Keyframes** from the submenu. This process allows keyframes to be placed on the timeline, instructing audio to pan to wherever you want it to be, at any point on the timeline.

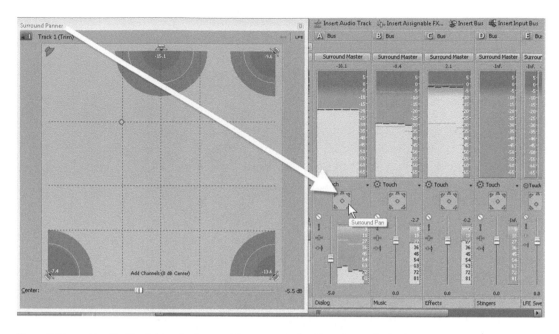

Figure 10.94a and b   Double-clicking the Surround Panner on the Bus Control or audio Track pane splits it off as a movable window, making panning easier to define and control.

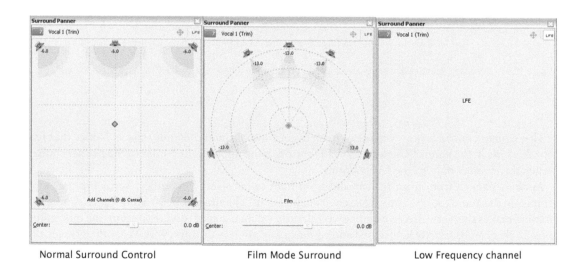

Normal Surround Control   Film Mode Surround   Low Frequency channel

Figure 10.95   These are the three Surround pan modes in Vegas Pro. Right-clicking the first/default pan mode allows selection of film style or LFE control, shown to the right. Selecting the LFE button sends audio only to the LFE channel output.

With the Surround Panner open, follow these steps to move audio in the listening space: Place the cursor where movement should occur or should finish, if the location is different from the default front-center position.

Move the orange dot found in the **Surround Panning** box to where the audio should be at that moment. Audio will slowly pan to this point from where it originated at the first keyframe. Notice that the reference position is followed by small dots, indicating how the audio will move.

Place the cursor on the next time point to which audio should be moved.

Move the reference position in the **Surround Panner** to the desired point.

Repeat until all panning is complete for the project on that track. Keyframes/audio position can be edited later.

When you're panning stereo signals, moving right to left can create problems when audio becomes louder on one side than on the other side when audio is off balance during a pan. **Add Channels**, the default setting, can easily create distortion. The **Constant Power** setting moves audio around the audio spectrum at equal volume with no change in volume at any point. Notice that Vegas Pro displays the relative volume for each channel in the Surround Panner tool. Experiment with various settings during panning operation if audio seems to jump in volume during a pan.

Vegas Pro has separate control of the center channel per track rather than assigning it to a bus as some 5.1 systems do.

Right-clicking keyframes in the Surround Pan timeline opens a menu, which shows choices for the velocity attributes of how the keyframe will move sound. **Hold** freezes audio until the next keyframe. **Smooth** gently speeds up as it leaves the keyframe and slows down as it approaches the next keyframe. **Fast** ramps the audio quickly to its next keyframe. **Slow** ramps the audio to the next keyframe fairly slowly. **Linear** provides a straight movement. This is the default keyframe setting in Vegas Pro.

Figure 10.96 Linear movement may be locked in the Surround panner.

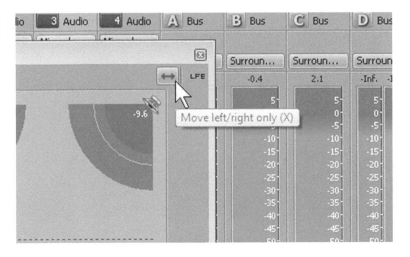

The center channel is at zero volume by default. As the volume is increased in the Surround Panner window, however, notice that the sound grid draws backward as the power/volume increases in the center channel.

Vegas Pro has surround modes that may be accessed by right-clicking the Surround Panner and choosing Film from the submenu that appears. The Film panner mode more closely simulates the theater environment for more accurate mixing of surround. Notice that the center channel is now defaulting to 0 dB rather than the -Inf. position that it defaulted to in earlier versions of Vegas Pro. This will have an impact on currently existing projects, so monitor carefully, as your monitoring environment may not have changed, but you may not have had an accurate mix.

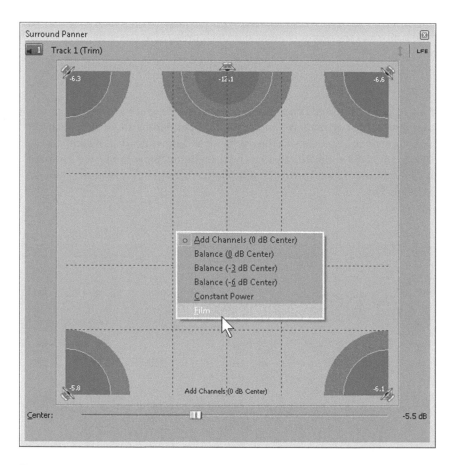

Figure 10.97 Film panning more closely resembles a theater sound system, and you may find it easier to mix in this mode.

When using motion in the center channel, experiment with the Smoothness setting. If dialogue or center audio is fairly transient in nature, such as intense dialogue, fast-attack guitar playing, or other sharp sounds, and the smoothness is set too high, the audio will sound very slow moving from center channel to the left or right. If set too low, audio will appear to "jerk" into other speaker fields. This issue varies with the listening environment, which again demonstrates the necessity of having a good monitoring system.

 Tip_____

In earlier versions of Vegas Pro, audio weighting was managed differently. In **Options | Preferences**, **Use Legacy Track Send Gain** has been added. If **Add Channels** (the default) or the **Balance 0 dB** pan mode is used, there is no difference. For the other pan modes that cut the signal when the pan is set to center, there is a decrease in the level (depending on which pan mode is used). When working on legacy projects (projects begun in versions of Vegas Pro prior to 8), it's best to use the legacy track gain function. New projects moving forward (post Vegas Pro 8) will be best if this is left unchecked.

Notice the differences when working with panning/track modes in Vegas Pro:

- Add Channels (no cut)
- Balance 0 dB (no cut)
- Balance –3 dB, constant power, film (3 dB cut)
- Balance –6 dB (6 dB cut)

If you prefer the older format, or are working with legacy audio projects, in **Options | Preferences | Audio,** check the **Use Legacy Track Send Gain** tick box.

The room should be set up with equal distances between audio speakers (audio monitors), and it should also be damped and have reflective surfaces minimized. Monitors should be equidistant to the listening space, measured from where you'll be sitting.

Try to set the room up similar to a home listening environment, since this environment is how most recordings will be heard.

It is possible to mix through a typical home stereo system, if the receiver allows for separate audio channel inputs. Vegas Pro does not send a decoded AC-3 stream, so you'll need to have connections that allow for line input. Many receivers/amplifiers today do. Run cable from each output on the soundcard to the inputs on the receiver back. Using high-quality cable is critical if radio frequencies and other noise in the room is to be avoided. Mix in the room, perhaps referencing a favorite or similar DVD.

Additionally, many professional soundcards have TOSLINK outputs/optical outputs that can feed consumer receiver/amplifiers for monitoring over home theater systems. This process is not advised, as home theater systems are anything but flat, and it is very difficult to create a quality mix on anything but reasonably flat speakers.

The primary elements of a surround mix are:

- Dialogue
- Music
- Sound design
- Effects

Dialogue is obviously the most important consideration in most situations. Typically, it is in the center channel and should receive attention first. When setting up the mix, find the peak point of the dialogue and then lower the dialog by −6 dB relative to the peak. This process allows for headroom/increase in the dialogue channel, as it usually is needed after the final mix is prepared. If the peak is lower than −3 dB, consider normalizing that Event or perhaps raising the level at the track.

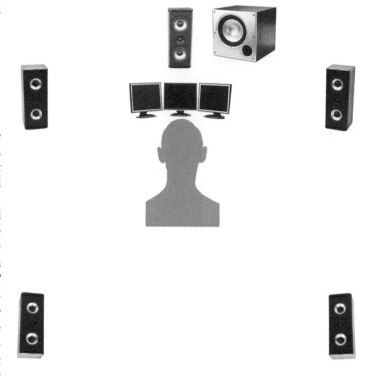

Figure 10.98a   Monitors should be equidistant from the listening space, measured from the listening position.

Conversational dialogue or direct dialogue belongs in the center channel in most instances. Working with the center channel presents some challenges, particularly in music mixes. If sound isn't properly handled in the center channel, listeners on a stereo system or a four-channel system missing the center speaker will hear strange artifacts in sounds mixed for the center channel. Adding a slight reverb to the center channel is always good practice, even if it's merely a small room bounce with no predelay. Walla or background conversation goes in the left/right or rear left/right, so it won't be brought into the mix at this point.

The next element is music in most instances. Music typically is placed in the front right/left monitors, with some elements moving to the rear speakers, depending on the point of view or movement of the camera, the sound design, or moving dialogue.

This point is where the actual mixing starts. Bring the music up to the level that it should be, monitor at a comfortable level. Listening too quietly makes the mix out of balance in both levels and equalization. Listening too loudly means your ears fatigue fairly quickly. Low-quality speakers also tire the ear, so use the best monitors that you can afford. Active monitors are typically cleaner, flatter, and easier to work with in a surround environment.

Begin bringing in any sound design underneath the music, leaving the dialogue channels alone for the time being. Mix the music and the sound design, working the sound design to the rear channels. Be cautious of too much movement in the rear channels as it quickly becomes distracting to the ear.

As an example of a mix, we'll take a cityscape shot with a dialogue in the foreground and examine some of the aural potential, as shown:

- *Center speaker.* Contains dialogue between two people. Low frequencies rolled off/high passed from 120 Hz and above.

- *Left/right front speakers.* Contain traffic, walla, moving audio, bed music, and sound design. Low frequencies rolled off/low passed from 120 Hz and above.

- *Left/right rear speakers.* 20-30% sound design, 10-20% bed music, traffic noise panning from front at camera movement or when dialogue permits. Motion front to back related to transitions in video. Music moves to rear speakers during dialogue as scene elements require.

- *Subwoofer/LFE.* Contains dialogue elements, bed music elements, and sound design. High passed at 120 Hz by default in Vegas Pro's Surround setup and as ISO. Although this is a standard, experience suggests that a high-pass filter, rolled off at 24 dB per octave, starting at 80 Hz, be inserted in the LFE channel.

Be cautious of moving audio into rear speakers during dialogue.

In this scenario, when dialogue is the focus but music is required along with traffic and walla, move the music to the rear before moving traffic and walla to the rear. Cut midrange in walla and traffic to make room for dialogue. With dialogue taking place, the cut frequencies are not noticeable unless the midcuts are too drastic.

Use smooth keyframes for sound design and music that is moving to the rear. Don't be afraid to use hard keyframing/abrupt shifts in audio placement, based on hard cut editing. Smooth visual transitions call for smooth aural transitioning. Hard visual transitions can use either hard aural transitions or smooth transitions, based on what is happening on-screen.

Overall, do not tread on the dialogue mix. As keyframes start to fly bed/design/FX audio right to left or front to rear, it's easy for the dialogue to get lost. This point is when the extra 6 dB of headroom left in the early stages of the mix is invaluable. If you find that 6 dB isn't enough, something is not correct in the other audio mixes.

View buses as tracks in Vegas Pro. Doing so provides automated mixing of the buses, offers easier surround control, and is visually more comprehensive to follow. Assign dialogue, bed music, FX, and sound design to separate buses. If a single track doesn't provide enough control of a sound/ series of events, duplicate a track and keep the volume out of the track until it's called for in two aural locations. At that point, raise the duplicate track volume assigned to the correct bus.

When planning a project that will include a surround mix, camera shots can be a consideration as well. Panning the lens toward and away from a scene makes an easy transition both visually and aurally. Dollying into a scene makes a wonderful rear-to-front transition. Panning from the bottom of a scene with upward motion or panning down from above a scene into the subject makes a wonderful visual transition that sound readily enhances.

Do not remove all low end from the right/left/center/rear mixes. If there is no bass in these mixes, listeners in a collapsed environment (stereo only) will hear no low end. Most everything in the mix goes into the LFE mix anyway, but if there are exceptionally important low-frequency elements, such as gunfire, cannons, and extremely low end in sound design, it's advisable to duplicate those tracks, roll the low end out of one copy of the tracks, and roll the high end off of the other copy. Send the copy that has high end removed to the LFE channel to supplement the bottom, while not distorting the other surround speakers and ensuring that audio collapses properly in a stereo listening situation.

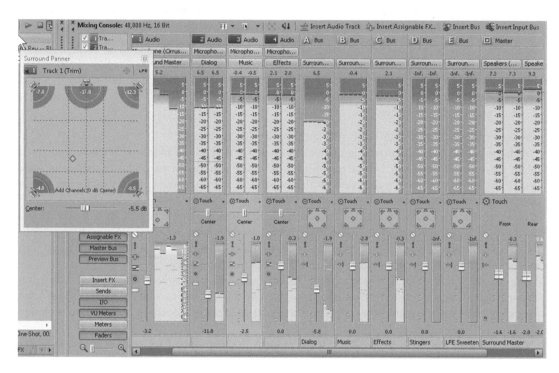

Figure 10.98b   Viewing buses as tracks offers tremendous control. Notice each bus in the mixer and that the left/right speakers are disabled in the dialogue bus.

Surrounded by FX: Surround Plug-ins

Yet another feature of Vegas Pro is to bring specific plug-ins to the Surround Sound toolset. Digital audio requires very tight control of outputs. The Sony Wave Hammer Surround 5.1 plug-in allows users to control the output levels on all buses in the Surround environment, preventing distortion on any output and making it easier for editors to create a robust, yet clean, Surround audio signal. The Wave Hammer plug-in may be enabled or disabled per channel of audio by checking or unchecking the checkbox found in the Routing tab of the 5.1 Wave Hammer.

There are three components to the Wave Hammer 5.1 plug-in tool. First is a compressor. The compressor can be used to smooth out dynamics and add power to the overall mix. Used improperly, it can also create a somewhat warm distortion in the signal, but this is rarely desired in a Surround mix. Wave Hammer's presets are set up quite well for most video-mix situations, but you may want to experiment with the settings to find what works best for you. Particularly in a Surround mix, be sure to keep the threshold set fairly high and the overall compression levels set low. Using a fair amount of compression starting at low trigger levels will nearly always create distortion. Particularly for video-output mixes, leave the **Auto Gain Compensate** checkbox unchecked. This will nearly always result in distorted signals that will be obvious with dialog.

Wave Hammer allows for either peaks or RMS levels to be scanned for processing. Either scanning method works fine, but be aware that setting this to RMS may allow fast transients such as gunshots or other fast and hard sounds to escape processing, creating distortion that you may not be able to hear easily but that clip beyond the output level of 0 dBFS.

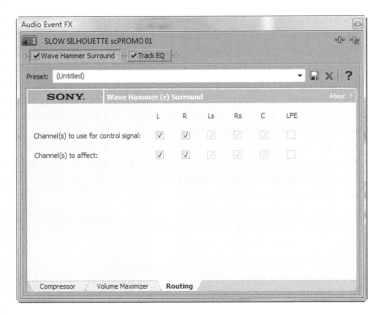

Figure 10.99 Enable/disable the Wave Hammer on individual Surround channels by checking or unchecking these boxes.

If very light compression is used, it's a good idea to turn on **Use Longer Look Ahead** for best results. This allows the plug-in to scan audio farther ahead in the file for information, usually creating a smoother attack when slow attack times are used. However, if a large transient is encountered it can sometimes create a fade-out or breathing or pumping effect just before the transient, so monitor transients carefully if the Longer Look Ahead is used.

Next is the **Volume Maximizer,** found in the second tab of the Wave Hammer plug-in. This could easily be one of the most important plug-in tools for any broadcast-destined audio for video mix. The Volume Maximizer works exactly as its name implies. It maximizes volume of an audio track or bus without creating clipping on output. When using the Volume Maximizer, any levels that go beyond the threshold are limited to whatever level the threshold is set to. Audio not crossing the threshold is managed and increased in overall level. Because digital audio does not have the flexibility for going beyond zero in the same manner analog does, this is a terrific means of maintaining maximum output while ensuring that at no point will audio exceed the output level. More importantly, using the Wave Hammer tool provides the ability to have a house-standard level of output as part of a final render process. If files are destined for AC-3 output, this also ensures that the AC-3 encoder receives maximum information for the best possible encode. I recommend using the Wave Hammer set to the **Master for 16 bit** preset on virtually all audio for video mixes. In the absence of my favorite WAVES Ultramaximizer plug-in, this is the next best thing and is the only plug-in available for a 5.1 Surround output.

The **Routing** tab is next in line on the Wave Hammer plug-in. Although this seems to be a simple row of checkboxes, it's much more than it appears to be. For example, a setting that instructs the Wave Hammer to begin compression on the surround speakers when the center/dialogue channel reaches a specific point might save an otherwise muddy or loud mix. Any one of the 5.1 output channels may be used to determine the point at which other channels will be ducked or compressed.

Also available as a 5.1 Surround plug-in are the Track EQ and Dither tools. EQ is important as it allows editors to fine-tune the EQ of individual surround buses as opposed to inserting EQs on the individual tracks or mix buses. This not only saves processor power but also prevents EQ settings that may conflict with one another. Track EQ does not provide a specific EQ for each bus, but rather provides a master EQ that affects all buses. You may enable or disable the track EQ from affecting a specific bus or buses.

Use the Track EQ settings to create a tighter mix signal in your Surround, repair muddy or weak areas, or balance the overall signal. Automation may be applied to Track EQ found on the surround bus, including the enabling and disabling of the EQ on specific buses. Therefore, if you have an EQ setting in place that should affect only a specific portion of a mix on a specific bus, you may enable the EQ on that bus only via automation. The 5.1 EQ is the only automated 5.1 effect that Vegas Pro has available.

Generally you'll want to have the EQ precede the Wave Hammer in a final output or mix. Otherwise, the Wave Hammer will not have the equalized signal information and won't be able to react appropriately. This could easily lead to distortion as well, if the Volume Maximizer is used prior to the EQ and the EQ is being used to boost any frequencies in the audio signal.

Dithering is the process of adding noise to an audio signal to mask or hide quantization noise. With surround, this is particularly useful on mixes that contain a lot of high-frequency information to keep the information clean in fade-outs.

Figure 10.100   Track EQs can be automated while in 5.1 format in Vegas Pro. By selecting or deselecting these checkboxes, individual buses may or may not be affected by EQ settings.

See the Dithering guide on the DVD found in this book for more information. In most instances, however, you'll be using a Rectangular or Triangular dithering shape.

Mixing Surround or DVD Audio

Musical DVD is an entirely new soundstage with Surround Sound, offering musicians, producers, and engineers entirely new methods of presenting their art. The quality of digital versatile disc-audio (DVDA) finally goes past the consumer-hype words of "CD quality." CDs are 16 bit/44.1 kHz, whereas DVDA is 24 bit/48 kHz.

Mixing audio only for Surround presents new opportunities while also presenting new challenges. Caution must be taken with placement, EQ, and sonic spacing to keep the mix cohesive and credible. One major advantage of surround is that it requires far less compression as currently called for in a stereo-only environment.

In a recording of a vocal-based group, the lead vocal takes center space. It's very important, however, that the lead vocal not be assigned exclusively to the center channel, or collapsed listening environments (stereo only) will hear artifacts and ghosting of the vocal. Using a slight reverb on the vocal helps dilute this phenomenon, if the reverb is added to the right/left mixes.

Percussion, acoustic guitars, and ethnic instruments all share the listening space of left/center right/center quite well, which opens up more frequency space for vocals or lead instruments.

Picturing the soundstage as it would appear to a concert-goer helps build the mix. Drawing the mix in advance can't hurt and often provides a great visual reference for an engineer.

Consider pairing left/center and right/center, rather than thinking of left/right as separate elements. Treat the rear speakers predominantly as assignments of the reverbs, delays, and audience responses. Audience members don't often sit in the middle of a stage, so placing much musical information in the rear speakers is not often a good practice. Placing the audience, however, where a lead vocalist might stand is a wonderful place to be. Save the rear surrounds for effects and aural surprises.

Mix the bass guitar/bass synth to all speakers, without regard for the LFE. If more low-end punch is needed, bus the bass and any other low-frequency information to a separate output, feeding the LFE. Whereas the bass channel in a surround system has 12 dB more headroom than the remainder of a surround system, few consumer-grade subwoofers are able to handle the extreme volumes of low end, so be mindful of your listening audience. Save the LFE for exceptional low end, such as the five-string bass or synthesizer that really needs the punch. Kick drums should be sent to the LFE with caution.

Feed reverb returns to the rear speakers, along with any vocal or instrumental effects. Sending the vocal to two reverbs or delays with similar settings allows for separate control to front and rear speakers, giving listeners a more intimate seat in the listening experience.

Use the rear channels for any audience information, such as applause and walla. Don't forget to feed a little to the front speakers as well, or stereo-only listeners will hear odd anomalies at the end of songs in a live environment. Panning reverbs and delays to the rear as part of an effect makes the rear speakers become part of the art of the mix. Keeping the rear speakers at full volume, full of a Surround element can quickly dilute the value of a surround mix. Use the rear speakers as a paintbrush, not as a canvas.

Always check a Surround mix in a stereo-only environment as well to ensure that it is collapsing correctly. Headphones are great for checking this out. (Remember never to mix in headphones.)

Surround Sound is part of the future, and eventually nearly every facet of video production will call for it. Artists like Surround productions because they are harder to pirate. Consumers enjoy 5.1 because it's a sweeter entertainment experience. Engineers with Surround chops will find their talents more and more in demand.

I'm All Mixed ... Down! Down-mixing in Vegas Pro

Mixes on DVDs are often 5.1 these days, yet many viewers of DVDs don't own speaker systems or receivers capable of playing 5.1 Surround Sound. Furthermore, some viewers have only mono televisions. Most systems have a feature in them that allows for audio to be down-mixed so that the viewer is capable of watching the show even though it's not being heard in the original mixed format of 5.1 or stereo. However, whether the mix is down-mixed correctly is the responsibility of the editor and engineer. No playback system can repair a bad mix when the six channels are collapsed to be heard over stereo speakers or even a mono speaker. Even the small DVD players that are used for flying or automobile viewing can't accurately play back 5.1 mixes that are not correctly assembled.

Figure 10.101a   Vegas Pro provides a tool allowing editors and engineers to monitor their mixes for all playback situations: mono, stereo, or 5.1.

Down-mixing is not an arbitrary process; it is controlled by information embedded in a metadata stream contained in the AC-3 file. This metadata is present in all AC-3 bitstreams. For example, the dialog channel sets the normal information for the stream. This is what tells the program how loudly it should be played by way of the information being received by the Dolby Decoder in the system. In a down-mix to stereo or mono, this information is combined and modulated to allow it to be heard on a standard stereo or mono system.

Needless to say, if the mix isn't correct, or if there are parameters out of whack in the 5.1 mix, the down-mix at the viewer's end will also be strange and could mask dialog, lose bottom end entirely, or create an overburden of bottom end. Other information may be either lost or overbearing, depending on the way the mix was managed in the authoring stages.

To allow Vegas Pro users to combat this issue or at the least address it, Vegas Pro provides a **Down-Mix** button that allows users to hear what their mixes sound like in stereo or mono and compensate for those scenarios during their 5.1 mix session. Users of earlier versions of Vegas Pro will need to convert their mixes to mono or stereo by changing the project properties, but this won't provide the same sort of information.

To use the DownMix feature, click the **DownMix** button, found on the master bus in Vegas Pro.

Broadcast Wave Format

Vegas Pro supports BWF files, or Broadcast Wave files. These are used as a packaging format by various recording devices such as the Studio Devices and Edirol recording products, among others.

Although the average user might not find these valuable, filmmakers, radio stations, television broadcasters, and users of high-end recording devices will appreciate this feature. The Broadcast Wave file format was developed to foster a format of audio interchangeability by the EBU Project Group P/DAPA (Digital Audio Production and Archiving), with significant input from the audio industry. An easy way to think about BWF files is as standard wave files with a metadata layer.

The BWF file metadata contains several parts not found as part of the standard wave file format. Included are:

- Broadcast Extension Chunk
- Compulsory Chunk defined by Microsoft
- The Broadcast Wave file
- Audio Data

Broadcast Wave files are the same as WAV formats, which you're likely already familiar with, except that a BWF file can contain metadata about the file, such as the author, the length of the file, and logging information that will allow the file to be logged for broadcast and copyright or performance royalty needs. It also allows for time-stamped files to be laid onto a timeline in exact position. To add all this data to the file format, a new chunk, or layer of information, is added to the wave file. BWF files also support the MPEG audio format, and an additional layer of information is added to the MPEG file where the BWF metadata resides. Only linear PCM and MPEG audio files may become BWF files. If the file is a not a PCM file, an additional chunk, known as a "fact chunk" will reside with the file.

The Broadcast Extension Chunk may contain:

Description	Title information
Originator	Name of the author or producer
Reference	A reference number issued by the author or recordist
Date and Time	When the file was created
Coding History	A record of the signal coding, e.g., linear PCM or MPEG.

If you have BWF files, you can import them several different ways. Import them in alphabetical order, import them by time stamp, import files as a single timeline track, or create a new track for each file imported. The latter is critical if you've got multitrack projects from recording devices that generate BWF files. You can find demo BWF files for import on the DVD in the back of this book.

To import a BWF file:

1.   Choose **File | Import | Broadcast Wave**.

2.   Browse to the device containing the Broadcast Wave or to the location at which the Broadcast Wave is stored.

3.   Determine whether you want to add the file across tracks or across time.

4.   Determine whether you want to order tracks by timestamp or filename. (This applies only when you are adding across tracks, not adding across time.)

5.   Determine whether you'd like to place the file based on where your cursor currently is placed or based on Ruler time.

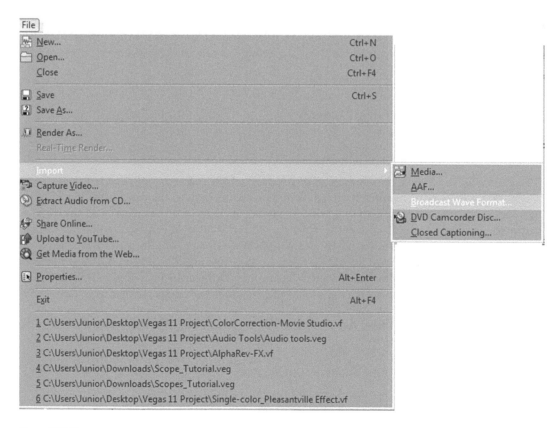

Figure 10.101b

Encoding Audio to AC-3

Encoding audio to AC-3 is included in both versions of Vegas. AC-3 is a compressed audio format that allows audio for DVD or DVDA. DVDA typically doesn't use AC-3; it uses meridian lossless packing. The whole point of the separate format is to allow ultrahigh-quality audio to be compressed to fit up to six channels of information onto a DVD for video or audio. This process allows for greater bitrates of video on a DVD and allows for higher sampling rates for audio on a DVDA. AC-3 stands for Audio Coding–Third Generation. AC-3 is licensed from Dolby and follows their specifications. Sony became one of the first licensees in the PC environment with their Soft Encode product in 1996.

After a mix is finished in Vegas Pro, it's a simple matter to select the AC-3 encoding option in the **File | Render As** dialog box. Audio is output that is then imported to a DVD authoring application. If you are working with Sony's companion product DVD Architect, AC-3 becomes a selection in the final creation of the DVD or can be imported as a separate stream. Vegas Pro does not allow the monitoring of AC-3 files, so be certain that the mix is correct before encoding.

Creating and distributing an AC-3 file technically requires any packaging to contain the Dolby Digital trademark. For more information, visit www.dolby.com.

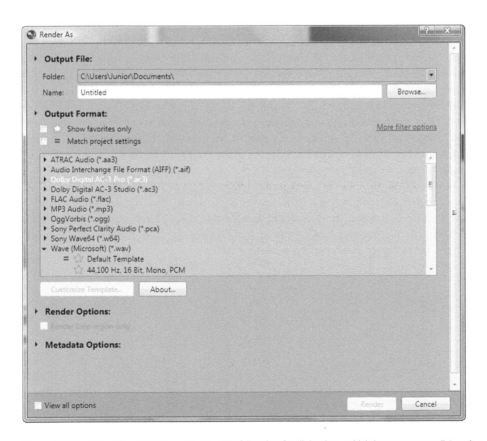

Figure 10.102 Select the AC-3 format in the **File | Render As** dialog box, which has a stereo or 5.1 option.

Figure 10.103   Dolby and the double-D symbol are registered trademarks of Dolby Laboratories.

 Tip_____

Audio levels on your DVD different than on your timeline? When rendering audio to AC-3, consider trying setting the dialog normalization level at **–31** and setting the Preprocessing Line and RF modes to **None**. This will often more closely approximate what's being heard from the Vegas Timeline. Sometimes encoding audio from uncompressed files to AC-3 doesn't have quite the robust sound once encoded, so experiment with audio files to see what most closely approximates what is coming off the timeline. Vegas Movie Studio/DVD Architect Studio do not allow for changing pre-processing modes.

Other Compressed Formats

Vegas Pro offers encoding to virtually every major audio codec available, ranging from a variety of MPEG codecs (including MP3) to high-definition, uncompressed audio. With car audio, iPods, online distribution, embedded audio in web pages, etc., new codecs are constantly becoming available. Vegas Pro offers FLAC, or the Free Lossless Audio Codec, as an encoding option. FLAC is popular across the Internet as a means of sharing full-resolution audio and as an archiving format. FLAC is much like a Zip file for audio; there is no loss when files are compressed to the FLAC format. Be aware that having many FLAC files on a timeline, i.e., a multitrack project of length, can cause an older/slower system to bog down and stutter. FLAC files may be played back in some personal electronics devices and home audio equipment; support is expected to grow as several recording labels and distributors are now beginning to support FLAC as a distribution/download format.

To access the FLAC codec, browse to **File** | **Render As** | **Save As Type** | **FLAC**. Templates ranging from 22 kHz mono to 96 kHz stereo are available.

More information on FLAC may be found at http://flac.sourceforge.net/.

Whew! This is a lengthy chapter, but given that *audio is 70% of what the audience "sees,"* it *should* be lengthy. Be sure to use quality speakers in your editing room, have a quality set of headphones at arm's reach, and learn to pay close attention to audio details in your mixes. The ears love sonic candy, and the more candy available, how sweet it is!

Titling Tools in Vegas

Titling in Sony Vegas

Vegas has titling tools galore. In fact, it's kind of confusing, because out of the box Vegas Pro actually has three titling tools, and Vegas Movie Studio has two, and the choices may become confusing. We'll start with the standard titling tool, new to users of previous versions of Vegas. This is reminiscent of the ProType Titler (which still is installed with Vegas for legacy purposes) yet is much more intuitive, is slightly easier on the CPU, and offers greater flexibility.

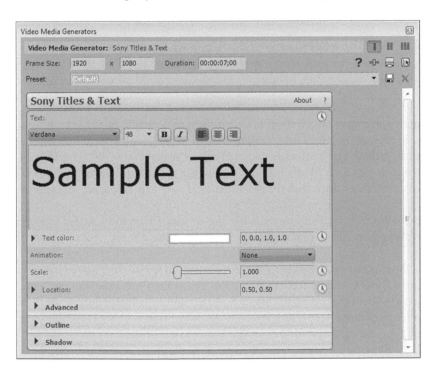

Figure 11.1   This is the Titles and Text generator found in Vegas Pro and Vegas Movie Studio software.

Create a new project in Vegas or Vegas Movie Studio. Vegas Pro users will need to insert a new video track (**Ctrl + Shift + Q**). In a video track, create an empty selection that is seven seconds in length. Right-click inside the blank area and choose **insert Text Media** from the submenu. The length of the selection will determine the length of the title. The Title and Text tool will open.

At the top of the tool, there is a box to set frame size and resolution. Regardless of project resolution, set this to at least **1920 x 1080**.

> Setting the Text Event to a high resolution will be valuable if transitions, motion, pan cropping, or other scaling FX are added to the text later on. This will keep text lines crisp and clean, regardless of final output resolution.

Next to the resolution values are three Column indicators. These offer alternative layouts to the Title/Text tool. Some users may prefer that the Title/Text tool be a vertical column, with all parameters over/under each other. An alternative is to lay out the utility in a horizontal fashion that might fit better in a particular screen layout or configuration. You perhaps already noticed these same Column options are available in all the OFX plug-ins.

The **?** icon is a Help icon and opens a Title/Text help document. The **Replace Plugin** button next to the Help button opens the Generated Media chooser, and a different plug-in may be inserted to replace the Title and Text tool. This doesn't keep any inserted text, it is simply there to allow the title to be replaced with other generated media types (including legacy type).

 Tip_____

Stay away from the **Replace Plugin** button! It will delete your text and an undo will not save it. This button opens up the Generated Media chooser so that the text plug-in may be replaced by any of several other titlers or generated media options. No word to save thee.

The **Match Event Length** button will match the title length to any selected Event length; this button, too, is superfluous. If a selection is created and right-clicked in the blank area as suggested in the beginning of this section, the length is already matched to any selected area. This button does provide functionality when **Insert | Text Media** is selected from the menu bar. However, this is not an efficient method of inserting titles. Stick with the pre-selection if speed and accuracy in length are the objective.

The **Media Properties** button allows users to see what the properties of the text file contain. However, all the properties except the Alpha channel are visible in the plug-in tool on the front dialog box.

The **Preset** drop-down menu is one of two access points for animating text in the Title/Text plug-in tool. This is where the new Title/Text tool acts much like the legacy ProType Title tool but with a more user-friendly approach. Use these presets to control how text enters, behaves during, and exits the scene. As with other plug-ins that offer presets, selecting the **Save Preset** icon will save the values set in the Title/Text tool. Give the current settings a unique name so the preset may be readily identified as a new preset in the Preset drop-down. Deleting a preset is as simple as calling up the preset and selecting the red **X** from the toolbar. The **?** icon in the name bar is another Help icon; two may be better than one, yet they lead to the same Help dialog box.

To the right of each keyframeable value is a lone keyframe/animation toggle (looks like a swirl). Enabling this feature turns on keyframing for the actual text. The new Title/Text tool gives text its own keyframe so that characters on the screen may be keyframed per view. This tool may be used to change out text in a lower third without inserting a new title; I've found it quite useful to create countdowns. Unfortunately, keyframes in the keyframe timeline may not be saved off, but creating a title countdown and saving as a veg file that may be overlaid on any project is very easy.

The Font drop-down provides choices of fonts; you may have Open-Type Format (OTF) fonts that don't show up in the drop-down menu, dependent on the properties of the fonts. Entering text into the text box first, highlighting, and then selecting fonts allows for a preview of the text with the highlighted font. Fonts may be scrolled using the mouse or Up/Down Arrows to test each font. Press the **Enter** key when the desired font is located.

 Tip_____

Avoid using small fonts that contain serifs. Even in HD, these small points are problematic for television and computer display, since the small edges may cause twitter, fringing, and shimmer on some displays. Sans-serif (without serif) fonts are almost always the appropriate choice for video. Sans-serif fonts tend to compact more effectively and fit into tight spaces more eloquently.

Next to the font selection is a font size drop-down menu. Although Vegas allows for scaling the font in the preview window, text will look best at a selected size versus a scaled size. It is preferable to scale down a large font over scaling up a small font. Try to use preset font sizes where possible for best results. The **Bold** and **Italic** buttons will boldface or italicize text selected in the Text box. Individual characters may be selected and stylized. If no word or character is selected, these options do nothing.

Text may be justified right, centered, or justified to the left by selecting text and using one of the three justification buttons in the text toolbar. By default, text is justified to the left.

White is the default color for text. Click the color indicator or the arrow to open the text color picker tool. Note that the text color may be keyframed or animated. This is a great feature for wiping text with color. In earlier versions of Vegas, this could only be done with a text mask over a gradient, so this tool saves not only time but a track and composite control. Render times are also faster.

Below the text color is an **Animation** drop-down. This drop-down offers pre-built animations to fly in and animate text. The animations are not keyframeable and may not be altered.

Text is scalable; this is a keyframeable function. However, use caution in scaling text, because once text becomes 2.5 to 3 times larger than the original, it can become jagged-looking. Different font types will display more "jaggies" than others.

 Tip_____

If you're scaling fonts to fly off screen at the viewer, I recommend creating larger resolutions, such as 4K resolutions (4096 × 3112 or 3656 × 2664) to keep text clean when upscaling. The keyframes make it useful to scale text from small to large or large to small, or merely fast scales to create an effect. Try using closely spaced **Hold** keyframes for some seriously cool effects.

Two different methods may be used to place text in the preview window. The first method is the one I believe most users will want to use. With the text tool open, the text is targeted in the Preview

Figure 11.2   There are many pre-built text animations that will fly in text and control text animation behaviors.

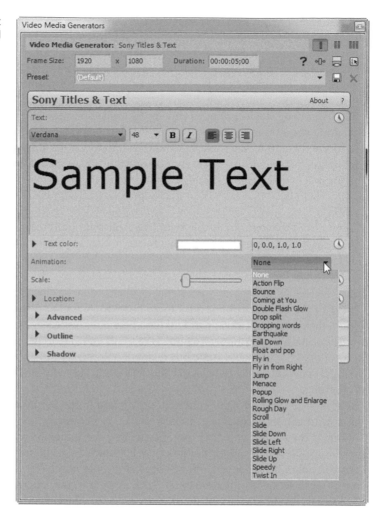

window and may be dragged around for placement. With the Grid tool enabled, precise placement of text is easy and consistent. Text may be placed during timeline looping or playback.

Slower computers or systems running many background operations may find movement of text in the preview window to be slow and kludgy. Vegas may even appear to hang, but it is actually running processes, albeit slowly. Be patient. Be sure to disable as many background applications as possible (editing systems should be clean and optimized, regardless). Setting Preview to **Preview/Auto** is often the best practice for moving text around the preview window. Be aware that text is always 4:4:4 uncompressed media (all generated media is 4:4:4 uncompressed).

The other method of placing text is to expand the **Location** drop-down by clicking the small arrow icon. This opens a window with a target area. The target may be moved around in the representative window, and the text will move in the preview window. Location may be input in the values window as well if the grid coordinates for title placement are specifically known. Personally, I find this method less than ideal, even if just for the latency involved.

The **Advanced** drop-down opens three value fields:

- Background Color
- Tracking (Kerning)
- Linespacing (Leading)

Clicking the background color will open the color picker palette to set a background color. This is good for creating title plates. Colors by default are at 100% transparency; opacity may be controlled in this window. Adjusting the **Hue** slider will shift the hue of the background color from black to a full color palette. The eyedropper tool may be used to click and select a color or range of color in the preview window that may be set as the preferred color. Colors may be set as:

- HSV (Hue, Saturation, Value)
- HSL (Hue, Saturation, Luminance)
- RGB (Red Green Blue)

The default is HSV. By selecting other options in the color palette drop-down, users are presented with different gamuts and means of color selection.

Tracking controls spacing between letters. This feature opens some interesting creative possibilities with keyframes, allowing the spacing of letters to be increased or decreased via keyframes. Tracking is the same as kerning in the print world.

Line spacing controls the amount of space between lines if multiple lines of text are inserted. This feature may be controlled by keyframe, and doing so offers some nice creative opportunities.

If space is a consideration, close the **Advanced** dialog section, and open the **Outline** drop-down. The Outline drop-down has the same

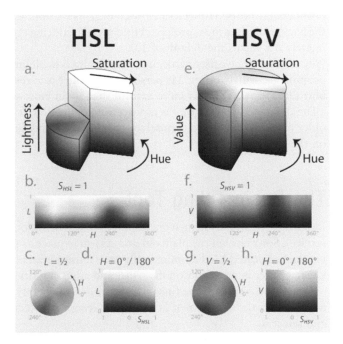

Figure 11.3

color palette options as the background and text color options; the outline is the same as a stroke in the graphics/print world. Although this tool is often used to create contrast color outlines and strokes, another valuable use is to drop on an outline of an identical shade to the text (use the eyedropper to select the text color) and then slightly offset the color. This technique often helps text blend into backgrounds more organically. Both color and width may be independently keyframed.

Close the **Outline** dialog/section by clicking the arrow, and open the **Shadow** drop-down/dialog box. First note the tick box to enable/disable shadows, and see that this feature may be keyframed. This will work with text that is keyframed when one Event is used for multiple titles and shadows *and* needs to be controlled separately from text.

 Tip_____

If titles are to be consistently shadowed and text can live on its own track, it's often more consistent and simple to add a shadow via the track motion tool **Shadow** function. Open **Track Motion** for the track containing text and enable the **Shadow** tick box. One reason I recommend this is that I'm not fond of the default shadow offset in the Title and Text tool and find that correcting it for each title is a time-consuming action. Using the Track Motion shadow, it's a single move, a single placement, and it allows for consistent title shadow from Event to Event. Additionally, if keyframed shadow movement is desired, shadows may be moved off the preview stage across the screen as a separate motion. The Track Glow may be used to compose yet a third image of the shadow. Coupled with the default shadow in the text tool, up to three shadows with motion may be created.

Clicking the shadow color box will open the same color picker as other functions use. The eye-dropper may be used to set a shadow color. This is useful when you're trying to offset shadows from the background. In most projects, I find myself reducing the opacity of the shadow color to approximately .75 versus the default of 1.0.

Shadows may be offset vertically or horizontally with limited range. The defaults for the shadow position are widely offset. My personal preference is to reset the shadow to a setting of .075, and a blur set to .750. This is a more natural shadow in most settings.

The default Title/Text tool is a powerful application; it is also CPU-hungry, so users of slower, older machines may find themselves wishing for something less capable but also less of a weight on the CPU.

The Basic Titling Tool

Much like telephone linemen once referred to Ma Bell's rotary phones as POTS (plain old telephone service), Sony has left the plain old title system in place as part of the install, and it may be accessed via the Generated Media options. If you're a user of an older computer, be grateful it's there. The Legacy Titler is very light on the CPU, and adjusting titles is very fast.

Create a selection on the timeline, right-click the empty selection, and choose **Insert Generated Media** from the drop-down box. In the **Generated Media** window, find the **(Legacy) Text** tool and select it.

Although this is an old title tool, it's quite useful if not powerful. It does offer very basic keyframe capability but does not require much in the way of CPU horsepower.

Figure 11.4   Although this title tool is somewhat clumsy and old, it has served Vegas users very well for years and runs very lightly, requiring few CPU resources.

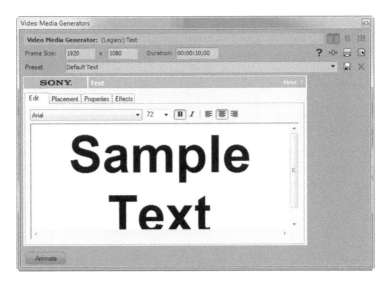

Highlight the words **SAMPLE TEXT** and replace them with text of your own. Click the **Placement** tab to open the Placement dialog box, and drag the text around inside the target window. The indicator in the screen target area is a Title Safe indicator. Click the **Properties** tab. Here is where color of text is set and where any background colors for a title card are to be set up. This is also where text may be tracked (kerned) and leading (line spacing) may be controlled. Text may also be scaled in this window; the same aforementioned cautions regarding scaling apply.

In the **Effects** tab you'll find the Outline, Shadow, and Deformation functions (there is no similar deformation function in the new Title/Text tool).

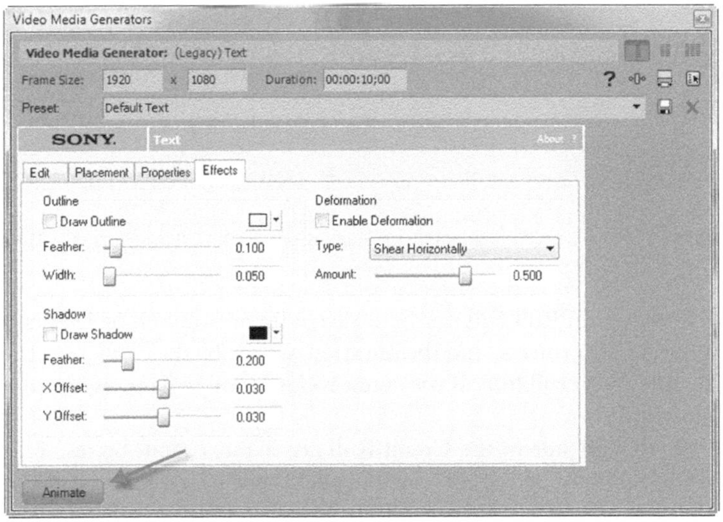

Figure 11.5   Shadows, outlines, and deformations may be performed in this window. The **Animate** button opens up a keyframing timeline.

Select the **Animate** button to open a keyframe timeline. This allows for all parameters of the title to be keyframed, same as in other FX or Media Generators. However, individual parameters may not be keyframed separately. Each parameter needs to be adjusted per keyframe. In other tools, each parameter has its own keyframe. In this tool, each keyframe controls several parameters.

Credit Rolls in Vegas

Vegas offers users the ability to create a credit roll. On an empty track, create a selection matching the length of the desired credit roll and right-click inside the blank selected area. Select **Insert Generated Media** from the submenu. In the **Generated Media** chooser, choose the **Credit Roll** tool. The Credit Roll dialog box will open.

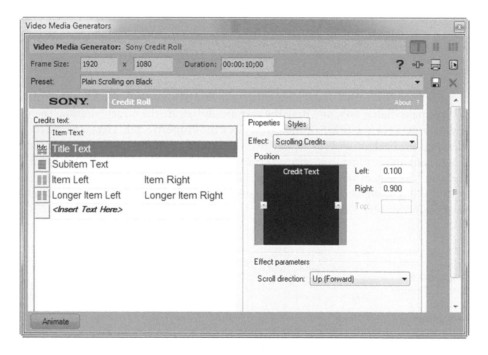

Figure 11.6   The Credit Roll feature in Vegas is very simple but does a what a credit roll tool needs to do.

If the Credit Roll will not be scaled, a text resolution of 1920 x 1080 is likely to be sufficient for HD and SD projects, and the duration was set by the blank selection initially created prior to opening the credit roll tool. If the credit roll is found to be too fast, adjusting the duration is one way to slow it down.

On the left side of the Credit Roll are the text input boxes. Text may be manually entered, and each box may be set for content placement by clicking on the box properties to the left of the text box.

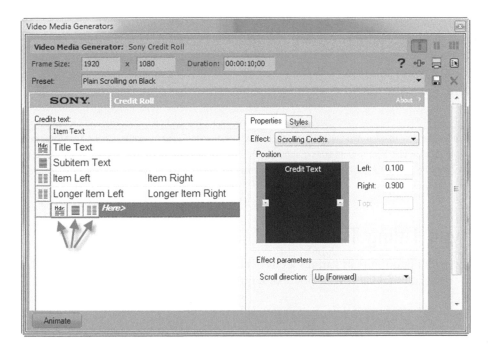

Figure 11.7   Text boxes may be Headers, Single Columns, or Double Columns.

On the right side of the Credit Roll dialog box, find the **Properties** and **Styles** tabs. This is where the behavior of the credit roll is determined. In the **Properties** tab, there is a blue area marked with handles on the sides. Moving the handles side to side controls placement of the credit roll on the screen and controls width of the credit roll. If the area is squeezed too much, the right or left credits will be cut off due to lack of space.

Either rolling and scrolling credits or timed sequences may be preferred. Rolling and scrolling is the common scrolling credit always seen at the end of films. If the **Timed Sequence** option is selected from the drop-down menu, a new set of choices will appear that allow sequences to have a transition before the next element appears, and a choice of speed/number of lines to move up. The credit roll may also be set to roll top-down.

Set the appearance of the credit roll in the **Styles** tab. Each of the column types may have their own font, size, spacing, and color. Click the column to be adjusted, and in the **Style** tab, select the font, size, spacing, and color desired. The speed of the credit roll is determined by the length of the title Event.

 Tip _____

The tool allows for multiple columns of information that may be pasted from outside documents such as Word, Wordpad, or the Windows text tool. Most users will find that this is a more efficient means of working, since it is generally more efficient to type in a text-editing application than in the credit roll tool. For example, text typed as shown here may be copied and pasted from a text or .doc file, and the Vegas credit roll tool will properly place and format the text.

VEGAS PRO EDITING WORKSHOP (HDR)
Including Vegas Movie Studio (single line)
DSE   David McKnight
Randy Stewart   John Rofrano

This is a much easier, faster way to work in my opinion. Then again, your mileage may vary.

 Tip_____

You can also use the standard title tool and the Pan/Crop tool to create credit rolls. Simply type text into the **Text Generator** for its full length (or copy text from a word-editing application), then use the **Pan/Crop** tool to pan up and down the generated text, creating a very controllable credit roll. This method offers more options than the standard credit roll function.

The ProType Titling Tool

This tool is filled with opportunity at various levels of complexity. Simple titles may be created in seconds, or very deep titles taking several hours or days may be created.

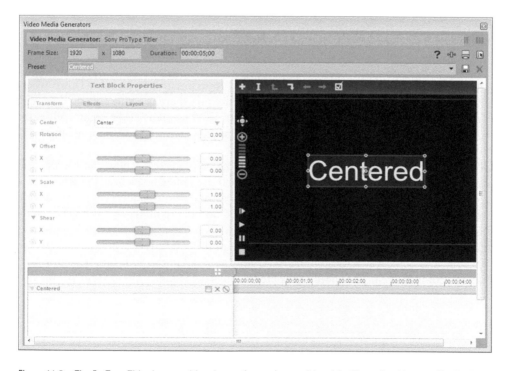

Figure 11.8   The ProType Titler is an exciting, innovative, and powerful tool for Vegas Pro 11 users. The ProType Titler may be opened via the Generated Media menus.

The ProType Titling tool is opened via one of two methods:

- Drag it from the **Generated Media** tab and drop it on a video track.
- Create a selection on a video track, right-click it, and choose **Insert Generated Media | Protype Titler** from the menu.

The second method is my preferred method, since it allows users to set the length of the title prior to the title being inserted. The first method requires that the title length be manually input.

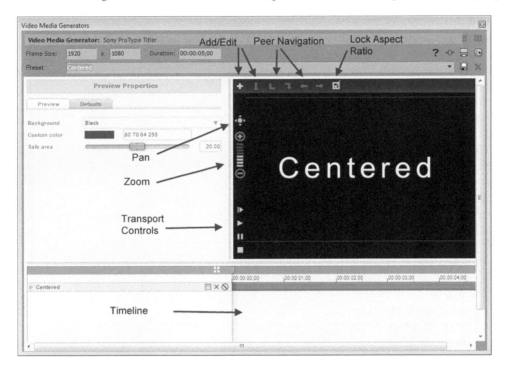

Figure 11.9

Tip_____

Text may also be formatted in a text editor such as WordPad. Copy the text using standard Windows Copy commands, and paste the words into the ProType Titler using **Ctrl + V**. Additionally, right-clicking a title while in **Text Edit** mode allows all punctuation and symbols associated with the selected font to be seen and inserted. This is handy if a trademark symbol, copyright symbol, or other commonly used symbol is needed and you don't know the keystroke associated with the desired symbol.

Let's start by using the titling application at its most basic level. Open the **ProType Titler** using one of the previously mentioned methods. When the Title tool opens, double-click in the workspace. This will insert the words **Sample Text**. (You may need to resize the window to see everything.) The text will be highlighted in blue. For the moment, we'll ignore this text; click the maroon bar at the top of the Title tool, and this will deselect the text. If by chance the text is now surrounded by a sizing boundary, simply click in any blank area surrounding the text. This will also deselect the text.

Notice the tabs to the left of the workspace. The tabs will have changed to a two-tab configuration labeled **Preview** and **Defaults**. In these two tabs, the default fonts, font sizes, safe areas, and background colors in the titling tool are defined.

Select a font that you'd prefer as a default font. Arial may be just fine; many video editors prefer the Verdana variant. Unless you're working with unique colors for title overlay, it's recommended that the background color be left black or neutral gray (RGB values 150, 150, 150). This will help in identifying any aliasing that may take place with serif fonts (it's generally not a good idea to use serif fonts in video titling) or other detailed fonts.

Safe areas should be left to default settings in most instances. This is less an issue when you're creating content for plasma and LCD displays, particularly widescreens, yet care should always be taken to avoid titles or graphics being too close to the bezel or overscan area of any display.

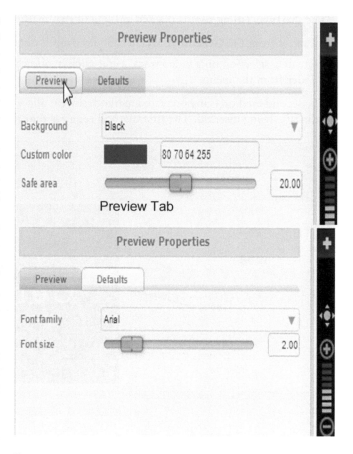

Figure 11.10

 *Tip*_____

The *safe area* is the area of variable edges found particularly wide on cheaper consumer televisions but also on LCD and plasma panels, where portions of the actual signal are not displayed due to bezels, scanning, conversion, or other causes. Titles or graphics placed too near these edges may be fully displayed on some monitors or displays yet cut off on others. For this reason, it's a good practice to be cautious about title and graphic placement. Title safe and Action safe are not the same value. Content destined for HD display needs less than 5% title-safe area, whereas 4:3 television requires approximately 18% safe area.

Once defaults are set, click the words **Sample Text** and a border with sizing handles will appear around the words. These handles can be used to resize the text from its default size. If the **Lock Aspect** checkbox is checked in the titler toolbar (when not in text edit mode), the title will keep its aspect ratio when being sized. Holding the **Shift** key while resizing will disable Lock Aspect temporarily. For this exercise, hold **Shift** while stretching the words **Sample Text** vertically.

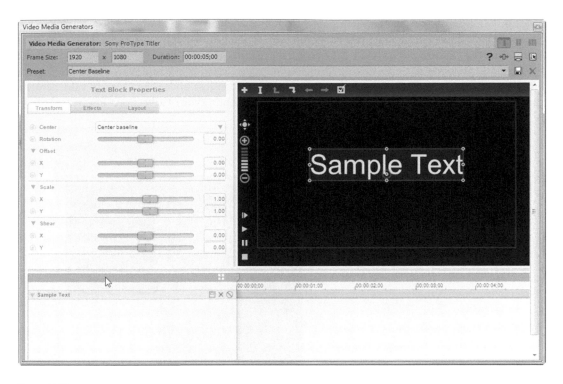

Figure 11.11

This gives an idea of how the text may be stretched; more important, look on the left side of the title tool in the **Transform** tab (by default the first view in the titler) and watch how the parameter controls for **Scaling** are moving as the text is resized. If the **Shift** key is not held, the horizontal and vertical parameters move equally. When you want to scale titles in aspect ratio, dragging the handles is the best way to resize, particularly when setting up automation. (More on that topic later.)

 *Tip*_____

Any control slider in the ProType Title tool window may be reset to its default value by double-clicking the control, just as with any parameter control in Vegas.

Notice the small dot in the center of the title. This indicates the center point around which the text can be rotated. The dot may be moved by click–dragging to any desired point, thus changing the center of rotation. Placing the target in the middle of the first or last letter in a title is a common center point for many titling sequences. For this exercise, click–drag the dot to the middle handle on the left side of the text (should be the middle of the letter **S**).

Now choose the **Effects** tab. In this dialog box, enable **Drop Shadow** and check the **Gradient Fill** checkbox. The title should turn to a white/orange gradient. If you want to change the two shades of the gradient, set the first gradient color by clicking the small diamond on the left side of the gradient selector bar. Set the second color by clicking the small diamond on the right side of the gradient selector bar. Insert additional gradient points by double-clicking in the gradient selector bar and setting the color. Bear in mind that gradient points will combine, and colors may blend. If this happens, click–drag the gradient points while previewing the text in the Vegas Preview window. You can also delete gradient points by right-clicking them and choosing **Delete**. If you find you particularly like the gradient you've created, click the **Save to Collections..**" icon just under the Opacity value, enter a name for your gradient, and press **Enter** to save the gradient to your Collections library.

Figure 11.12

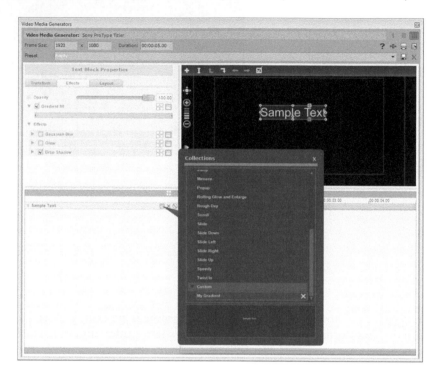

Now that you've created and saved a custom gradient, let's apply a different gradient to the text. Open the **Gradients** library next to the button you clicked to save your custom Gradient. Notice that the previously saved and named gradient appears in the library. To use a gradient from the Gradient library, double-click the gradient name. This will apply the preset gradient to any selected text.

Okay, now we've sized and added a gradient to the text and added a shadow. Let's add a couple more shadows to the text. Select the text and click the **Effects** tab. Click the **Collections** button at the right of any of the Effects parameters, and double-click on **Drop Shadow**. A new drop shadow will appear in the **Effects** menu. Now double-click in the **Collections** window to insert a third Drop Shadow. Three **Drop Shadow** options should now show in the left side of the Effects window. Choose the **Expand** triangle in the left side of the first Shadow dialog box. The **Shadow** dialog will expand to show:

- Blur amount
- Horizontal offset
- Vertical offset
- Shadow color

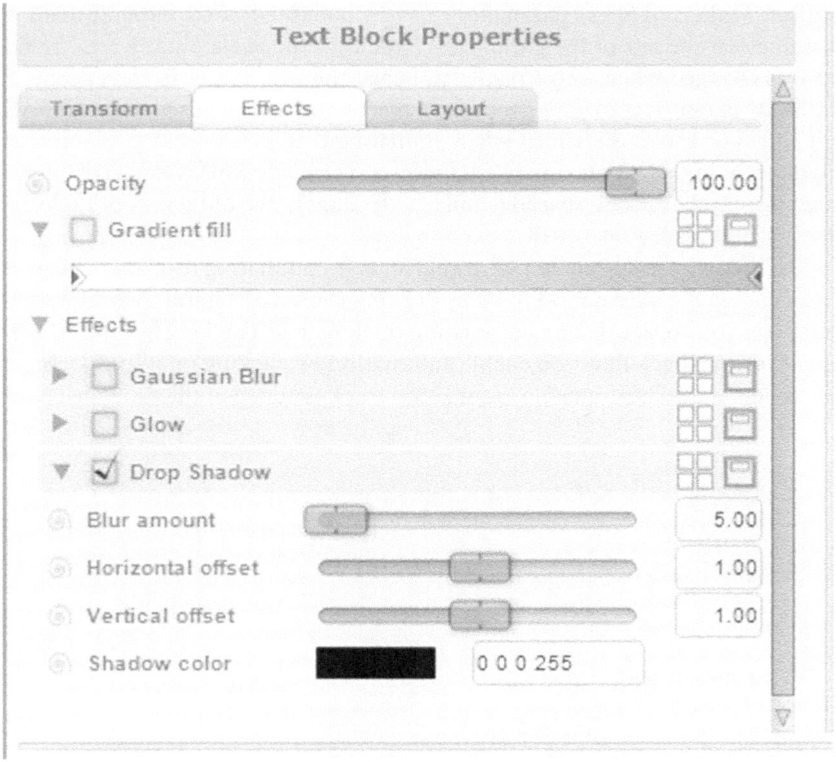

Figure 11.13

In the top shadow, leave the offsets at default, and set **Blur** to a value of **16.00.** You can do this by click–dragging the slider or by clicking in the numeric field that has defaulted to 5.00 and typing **16.00.** Set the shadow color to **255 255 255 80** (a space in between each value). This will increase the transparency of the shadow. Click the **Expand** triangle to collapse the parameters of the first shadow, and then select the **Expand** triangle of the second shadow. In this shadow, set **Blur** to **20.00,** set the **Horizontal** and **Vertical** offsets all the way to the right side for a value of **100** on each parameter, and set the shadow color to **255 255 255 44.** Collapse the parameters for the second shadow.

Expand the third shadow parameters. Set the **Blur** to **10.00, Horizontal** and **Vertical** all the way to the left at **–100,** and the shadow colors to **255 255 255 25.**

There are now three shadows associated with the words *Sample Text.*

Select the first tab in the title tool (**Transform**). In this tab, the angle of the text and related shadows may be set off-center, sheared, or offset to right/left/up/down. Remember earlier when we set the target center? Click and drag the **Rotation** slider to the left or right. The text will rotate but will center around the **S** in *Sample Text.* Notice that in the **Center** dialog box, the preset selected is Custom. To reset our text, double-click in the **Rotation** slider to set it back to 0. This will reset the target point to the center of the title.

At this point, the Offset, Scale, and Shear parameters may be collapsed; if so, expand them by clicking the **Expand** triangle at the left of the parameter. Note that the Scale parameters are not equal; this parameter was changed when we vertically stretched the title earlier in the exercise.

Experiment with the **Shear** parameters to understand how this feature may be used. It can be used to "bounce" text as it enters or leaves the screen when animating text.

Finally, click the **Layout** tab. In this tab, text may be displayed vertically (this is especially useful when setting up rotated displays), tracked, spaced (similar to leading in the old text tool), selected (fades text on/ off screen), and placed on a path.

In this dialog box, we'll discover the automated keyframe tools for animating text on a screen. In the **Tracking** parameter, enable the automation tools by clicking the small "spiral" icon found to the left of the parameter control. Notice that an automation track named Tracking has been added to the titler keyframing timeline. Each time you enable automation by clicking on a spiral icon on the left side in the dialog box, a new keyframable automation track is added in the timeline below.

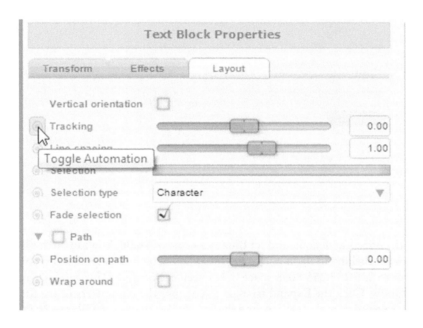

Figure 11.14   This icon is the autokeyframe tool. Enabling it will allow for creation of keyframes in the titler timeline.

With this function enabled, we can now animate the title. We'll be animating several parameters throughout this next section.

By default, the cursor for the titler timeline should be at the beginning/far left of the timeline. If it's not, place it there by clicking and dragging the **Current Time Indicator** (CTI) in the top of the timeline. In the **Tracking** parameter, set the value to **10.00**. This will spread the letters far across the screen. Move the **CTI** to the **3-second** point (third tick in the timeline). Double-click the **Tracking** slider. This will set it to **0**, or default. A new keyframe has been generated and is shown in the titler timeline.

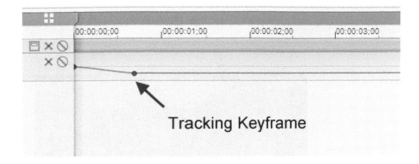

Figure 11.15   Take note of the double triangle in the Tracking level of the titler timeline. Selecting this double triangle will further expand/collapse the keyframe/envelope tools found in the titler timeline. This function is available for all automated timeline parameters. Expanding the timeline is very useful when you're working with Bezier curve controls of fine or tight timeline areas.

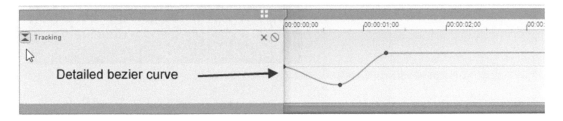

Figure 11.16   Expanding the keyframe timeline will allow very fine control of Bezier curves.

Press the **Play** icon (or **Spacebar**) in the titler preview window, and the title will play. The title should now display a widened start point, narrowing to a normal Tracking setting, illustrating how the automation functions. Setting the resolution of the Vegas Preview window to **Draft | Auto** will give a higher frame-rate playback.

Let's add more animation. Click the **Effects** tab and check the **Gaussian Blur** checkbox. Expand the **Gaussian Blur** parameter set and enable horizontal blur automation by clicking the automation icon found to the left of the Horizontal Blur parameter.

Place the **CTI** at the far left/start point of the keyframe timeline. Slide the **Gaussian Horizontal Blur** parameter control to the far right for a value of **100**. In the keyframe timeline, move the **CTI** to the 3-second point (the same point as the previous keyframe) and then double-click the horizontal slider in the **Gaussian Blur** parameter. This will cause the text to be horizontally blurred at the start of the title, moving to a clean view as the tracking brings the letters in the text together.

In the top of the **Effects** tab is the **Opacity** function. Moving the CTI back to the far left/title start point, enable the **Opacity** automation. Set the **Opacity** value to 0 and then move the CTI to the 2-second point on the timeline, and then set the **Opacity** value to **100**. The title will now begin at full transparency and fade to full opacity.

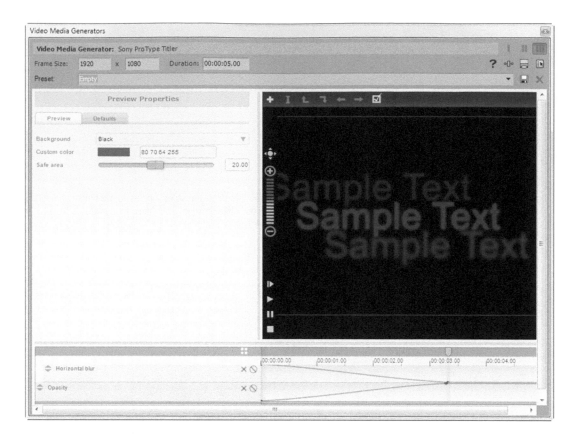

Figure 11.17   Note the tracking, blur, and opacity curves.

Close the title tool by clicking the **X** in the upper right-hand corner; trim the Event to **4–6** seconds in length, and double-click the new title/generated media on the timeline. This will create a selection; use **Shift + B** to generate a RAM render. Preview the title.

Reopen the title tool by either clicking the small green **Generated Media** icon or right-clicking the title and selecting **Edit Generated Media**. This will reopen the ProType Titler.

Inserting a second title in the same title tool is very easy, and this second title may have any of its own behaviors. Double-click in the title tool preview area, and a new text instance will appear. This, too, will say **Sample Text**. The text should already be highlighted; if for some reason it is not, highlight it. For this exercise, change **Sample Text** to read **Flying Letters**. While the text is highlighted, change the font to something different from the *Sample Text* title. If the text has become deselected, double-click to put the text back in Edit mode and rehighlight the text, or click the **Edit Text** I-beam icon on the text toolbar. When in Text Block mode, clicking the I-beam icon puts you in Text Edit mode. When you're in Text Edit mode, clicking the maroon toolbar at the top of the Preview window or pressing the **Esc** key will put you back in Text Block mode.

Once the font is changed and perhaps resized, we'll automate this text. Select the **Layout** tab in the Text Block Properties dialog box. In this tab, enable the following automations:

- Selection
- Fade Selection
- Position on Path

In the **Selection Type** option, click and select **Character** from the drop-down menu.

Underneath Fade Selection, click the checkbox for **Path**. The path should change, causing the letters to be wavy.

Moving down to the titler timeline, place the **CTI** at the far left side and click the **Expand** triangle next to the words *Sample Text* and *Flying Letters*. We want the *Sample Text* keyframed parameters to collapse and the *Flying Letters* keyframed parameters to open.

Moving the **Position on Path** slider to the left (back in the Layout tab) will cause the text to move across the path to the left, just as moving the slider to the right will cause the text to move to the right. It may take a moment or two for your system to redraw this display, so experiment by moving the slider just a little at a time to see the results.

We're now going to move the text around. Start with the text block object **Flying Letters** in the middle of the Preview window. Slide the **Position on Path** slider to the right to a value of **1.4**. This puts it predominantly off-screen. We'll modify the path, but we need to zoom into the Preview screen first.

The titler **Zoom** tool is found on the left of the titler Preview screen. Click–dragging will zoom in/out on the Preview screen/work area. Zoom in deeply enough to see the path associated with **Flying Letters** clearly.

Click and hold the target dot on the left end of the curved path, and drag it farther to the left. Grab the target dot from the associated Bezier curve and extend it, pointing it straight up. This puts a pronounced "hump" at the left side. Click and drag the right target dot (at the base of the **F**), and use the associated Bezier curve to flatten out the title path from the right side.

Move the **CTI** in the title timeline to the 5-second point (five tick marks from the left). Use the **Right/Left Arrow** keys if it seems difficult to achieve precision. Notice that the *Sample Text* title created earlier has now appeared on the screen at its ending position. In the **Layout** tab, set the **Position on Path** value at **.25** (remember that you can click and edit the value directly). This should nearly center the text. On the keyframe timeline, right-click the newly created keyframe and select **Linear** from the menu that opens.

Let's add another keyframe but with the same position value. Place the **CTI** at the 8-second point

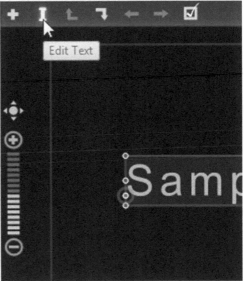

Figure 11.18 Select this icon to edit a selected text object. If only one text object exists in the titler, then that text object will be available for editing.

Zoom Tool

Zoom Out (Click or Press and Hold)

Sentence Parent

ProType Title

Word Child

ProType Title

Character Child

ProType Title

Figure 11.19   Click–drag the **Zoom** tool to increase or decrease the preview size. Alternatively, press and hold the plus and minus keys.

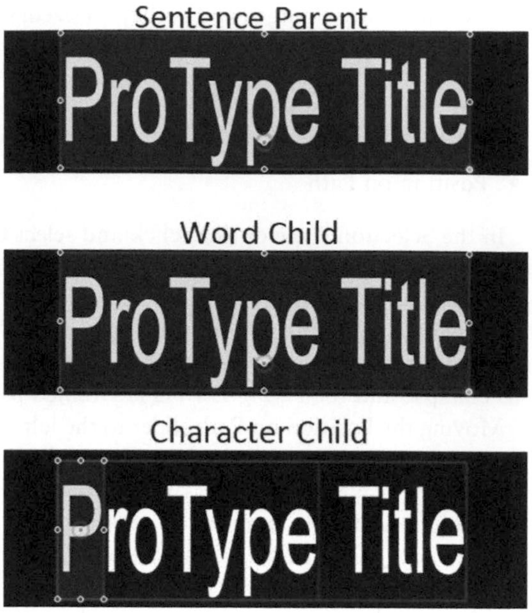

Figure 11.20

on the timeline. Double-click the keyframe envelope in the **Position on Path** envelope to create a new keyframe. Alternatively, move the **Position on Path** slider away and back, being careful to move it back to the same .25 value. Setting two keyframes to the same value provides an amount of time for the animation to remain stationary, in this case for 3 seconds. Right-click the newly created keyframe and set this value to **Linear** in the menu. (These keyframes don't actually need to be set to Linear, a part of this exercise is to become familiar with various keyframe options within the title tool.)

Now move the **CTI** to the **11**-second point and set the **Position on Path** value to –.75. This will take the text to the left and off the screen at the bottom of the Preview window. Return the CTI to the far left of the timeline and hit the **Spacebar** or click the **Play** button in the titler Preview window to preview the title.

Return the CTI to the far left of the timeline. In the **Selection Type** drop-down menu, be sure that Character is displayed. If it's not, click the button and select **Character** from the drop-down. In the **Selection** bar, click on the far-right side of the bar and drag to the left until only the letter F is visible. Notice this creates a fade in the *Flying Letters* object. Place the **CTI** at the 7-second point, and slide the **Selection** bar all the way to the right so that all characters in the *Flying Letters* object are revealed. Play the title from the beginning (**Shift + Spacebar**).

Collection Presets

In the Presets toolbar (upper right in the titler keyframe window), there are four squares. Selecting the **squares** button will open the Collection presets.

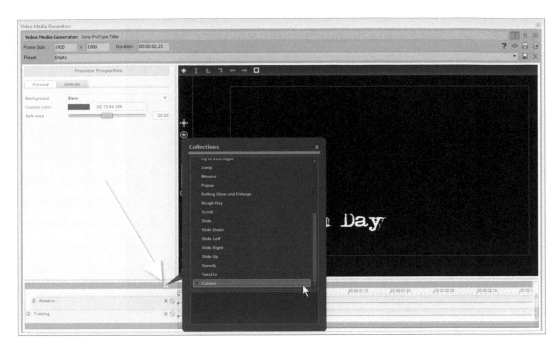

Figure 11.21 There are several prebuilt keyframe curves available in Vegas Pro 11, and you can save your own to the Collections library.

Here is where you can easily add serious life and creative punch to your title objects. In the **Collections** menu, double-click a style, and the name of the style will appear in the preview window as text. Double-click the text and it may be modified to the desired characters. Some of the Collection presets aren't compatible with double-line titles, so be aware that two-line titles may affect keyframes inserted by the collection.

Other Basic Tools

Double-click on a text object in the titler Preview window. This will put the text object into Text Edit mode. On the left side of the title tool, the span properties have changed back to text editing tools such as Font Type, Size, Weight, Centering, Color, Slant, and more. Selecting text by click–dragging over letters allows those letters to be changed.

For example, it is possible to highlight the first letter of each word and change the font or font weight. Perhaps the first letter of each word should be boldfaced, italicized, underlined, or all three. Each character may have its own color, stroke, weight, strikethrough, or underline. Additionally, each character (or all of them) may be backed with a specific color block if desired. Click the **Navigate to Parent** or **Navigate to Child** buttons in the text editor menu bar at the top of the screen.

In the **OpenType** tab, take note of the specialized text options, such as determining whether a fraction should be displayed as a slashed or stacked fraction, or perhaps the number 0 should display with a slash through it.

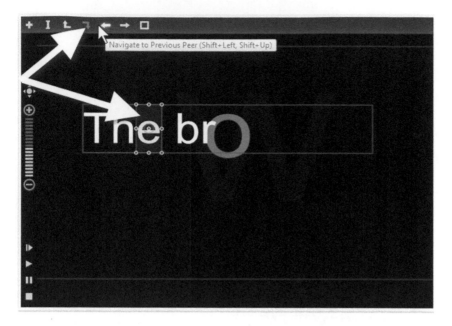

Figure 11.22

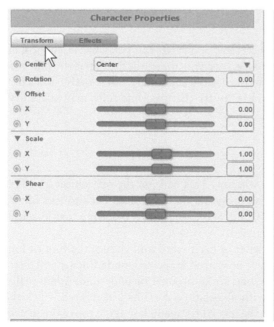
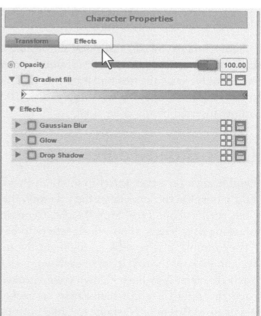

Figure 11.23   In these menus are found controls to affect individual characters or entire text objects. Double-clicking the **Span** properties will also insert a new text object.

Also noteworthy in the OpenType options is the ability to create subscripts, superscripts, or other variants, as well as the ability to specify how capitalized letters are displayed.

The functions found in the Span properties, such as fonts, weights, text color, underlining, and OpenType features, are not keyframe controllable.

Advanced Titling Tools

There are several additional tools found in the ProType Titler that aren't apparent at first glance.

Controlling individual characters is a powerful feature; this is managed through parent/child relationships. Don't confuse the parent/child relationships in the ProType Titler with the Parent/Child tools found in the Track Compositing modes of the timeline.

A full sentence or group of characters may be considered the "parent." Each word in the sentence or group of characters would be one of the "child" levels. Each individual character in a text object would be the smallest "child" in the title object.

| Selected by entire title | Selected by individual word | Selected by individual character |

Figure 11.24   In this example, words and individual characters are selected as children of the larger text (sentence) object.

Navigation between sentences, words, and characters is achieved either using shortcut keys or clicking icons on the titler tool bar. **Shift + Enter** navigates downward until the lowest child level (a character) is achieved. Using the **Esc** key will navigate backward from the child to the parent. When a child is selected, navigating to the next child (called a "peer") is done with the **Shift + Right/Left Arrow** keys.

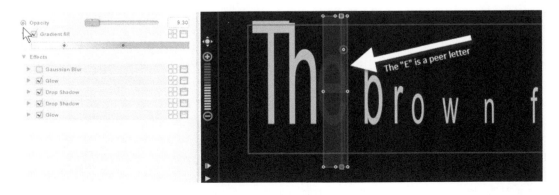

Figure 11.25

Each child may carry its own keyframe attributes in addition to the keyframes assigned to the parent the child belongs to. When a child is selected, note that the Span dialog boxes change to Word dialogs and Character dialogs. These dialogs contain all the keyframable parameters that a selected child may access. Experiment with changing opacity and character sizes for interesting titling effects. These may be made more interesting and creative by adding various Curves presets from the Curves library. Curves may be dragged and edited for individual characters just as they may be added to word or full blocks/spans of text objects.

Here are some exercises that will quickly show the power of the advanced tools found in the titler:

- Keyframe opacity of individual letters, increasing opacity in an odd order, such as last letters first.
- Keyframe a shift in gradients per word.
- Add a stroke to a word, adding blur to the stroke via the Gaussian Blur tools.
- Stroke a different word in the span with a different stroke color and thickness.

Learning to manipulate titles is an introduction to compositing, and titles are one of the most creative and yet difficult aspects of film and video production. In the past, complex applications were required to do in-depth titling, but today Vegas contains many tools that accomplish the same applications as the more complex tools offered in the past. With some creativity and inspiration, Vegas can be used to create Hollywood-level titles. In fact, several Hollywood-level films and television productions contain title work created in Vegas.

Figure 11.26   Inserting a mix of effects can create complex titles.

Flashy Titles

Titling is extremely important in any video production. Some would argue that titling sets up the viewer for what he or she is about to see and therefore makes the difference between a good film and a great film. Titles can take a lot of artistic development time, and a lot of creative energy as well, and therefore titles are often farmed off to editors or artists who specialize in nothing but titling sequences. One of the formats for titling in video is Macromedia's Flash format.

Vegas supports Flash import, and .swf or .flv files may be dropped directly on the Vegas Timeline. Although these files don't always play back at full frame rate, they provide unique opportunities for users to import powerful sequences of images. Flash files containing ActionScripts, audio, or motion video may not be inserted into the timeline, nor may Flash files created in Flash MX. *Only files created in Flash 5 or older may be loaded onto the timeline.*

Vegas does not scale Flash media cleanly when the Pan/Crop tool is used to zoom in on the Flash file, suggesting that the vector information in Flash may be ignored. Create your Flash projects at full size and resolution for best results. Vegas will properly scale them to project resolution. In summary, this is a problem only when zooming in on the Flash file with the Pan/Crop or Track Motion tools.

Importing Static Graphics

When you're importing static images from Photoshop or similar applications, create the title images at the full resolution set for **square** pixels in the graphics editing application. Otherwise, the title may be stretched.

For example, a static graphic for an HD project would be imported to Vegas at a true resolution of 1920 x 1080 or 1280 x 720. Even though an HDV project setting is 1440 x 1080, bear in mind that the pixel aspect ratio is 1.333 for HDV, meaning that the pixels are stretched, and the final display is 1920 x 1080.

Import stills at the following DV resolutions for unstretched results:

- DV 4:3 NTSC = 720 x 480
- DV NTSC widescreen = 873 x 480
- DV 4:3 PAL = 720 x 576
- DV PAL widescreen = 1049 x 576

Note that these are different from when importing still images that are to be pan/cropped.

Track Motion and Pan/Crop

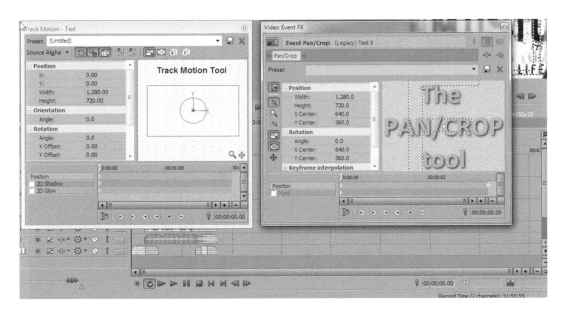

Figure 12.1   Track Motion and Pan/Crop Tools

The Track Motion and Pan/Crop tools in Vegas provide flexibility and speed for Vegas users. Picture in picture, adding motion to graphics, 3D planar effects, and creating split screens are all very easy and fast operations in Vegas. Although these two tools appear to be similar and operate with similar actions, they are quite different from each other. Track Motion will not affect video resolution as long as boundaries are kept within the confines of the Track Motion boundary. Track Motion will not change the number of pixels in a frame, regardless of resizing the image. Pixels may become larger or smaller with the Track Motion tool. In the Pan/Crop tool, portions of the frame may be cropped, therefore decreasing resolution. Pan/Crop must work within the confines of the target area, whereas Track Motion allows users to go beyond the boundaries of the preview.

We examine both tools in depth in this chapter, starting with the Track Motion tool. Video or graphics being controlled by Track Motion are referred to as *objects*.

Open the Track Motion tool by clicking on the **Track Motion** icon in the first video track header.

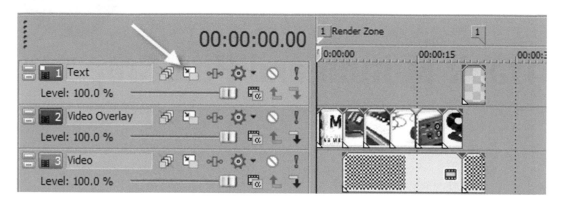

Figure 12.2   Click this icon to open the Track Motion tool.

 Tip_____

The Track Motion tool can be applied to just about any project in some form or fashion, splitting screens, creating multiple screens such as in the opening of the *Brady Bunch* television series, flying titles in or out, or any number of other creative uses.

The Track Motion tool is divided into two distinct parts: the Properties window and the Track Motion Workspace. At the top of the Properties window is the Track Motion toolbar. The first option in the toolbar is the Composite Mode. Vegas Movie Studio provides a Mask Mode and Source Alpha Mode. Vegas Pro offers several compositing modes:

- 3D (3D planes)
- Custom
- Add
- Subtract
- Multiply
- Source Alpha (default)
- Cut
- Screen
- Overlay
- Hard Light
- Dodge
- Burn

- Darken
- Lighten
- Difference
- Difference Squared

See the "Compositing" chapter for more information on these various modes.

The Enable Rotation feature allows Rotation of the image to be locked or unlocked. If this setting is inactive, the Track Motion tool is prevented from rotating the frame.

Snapping provides the option to snap Track Motion boundaries to a grid. The grid may be adjusted in the bottom of the **Properties** window in the **Snap Settings** field. It's generally a good idea to use the Snap feature when you're creating precise PIP or multiframe views/split frame views, so that all corners of the split frames are aligned to the same points. It's generally a good idea to disable snapping for positioning Shadows and Glow (if greater precision than the defaults are desired).

Select the **Edit in Object Space** button if you want to edit in the object's space rather than the camera's space.

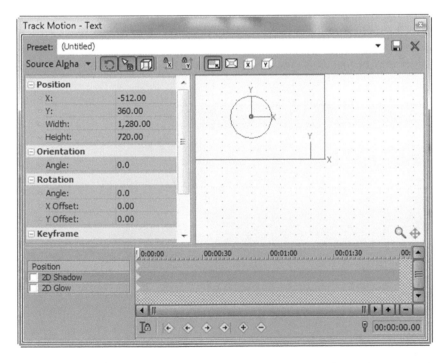

Figure 12.3   With **Edit in Object Space** enabled, the object may be rotated around its own space instead of the camera space defined by the center point of the "camera" that sourced the content.

For example, if a video object is rotated, its X axis may not correspond to the X axis of the of the Video Preview window. Selecting the **Edit in Object Space** button in conjunction with the **Prevent Movement** buttons allows you to move the object along its own X and Y axes rather than the X and Y axes of the video Preview window.

Vegas also allows the X and/or Y axis movement to be limited. This is useful for moving an object straight across the screen (X axis) or up and down the screen (Y axis) and preventing movement in any another direction or diagonal.

Lock Aspect Ratio prevents the Track Motion tool from changing the original aspect ratio of the media. Track Motion may be used to squeeze widescreen into narrow areas or to stretch 4:3 media to fit, or to create any squared dimension that fits the creative process.

Scale About Center locks the TM tool to the center of the frame. Disable this option if you're resizing media to any noncentered position.

The **Prevent Scaling X/Y/Z** (*Vegas Movie Studio does not have a Z feature*) functions as its name implies: Though an object may be moved around the Track Motion workspace, the object cannot be scaled (made larger or smaller).

Track Motion Properties

Click the + icon to expand the Properties Position window. In these fields, precision movements of the object are possible. Although the object may be dragged to position in the Track Motion workspace, these controls provide pixel-accurate placement and sizing of the object. The sliders may be slid back and forth; holding **Ctrl** while adjusting provides for very fine control. Additionally, the value window has a spinner feature. Click and hold the **Up/Down Arrow** to "spin" through the values. Finally, values may be manually entered as numbers.

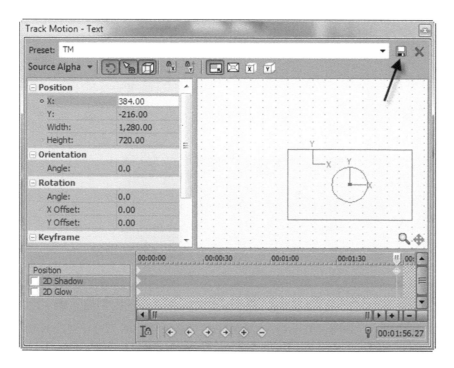

Figure 12.4

The **Orientation** value operates independently of the Enable Rotation. Even if the Enable Rotation feature is not engaged, objects may be rotated via this control. Center offsets may be enabled in this field.

Keyframe smoothness may be set; this is similar to the ramping mentioned elsewhere in the **Lanes/Curves** keyframe tool. Keyframe defaults may be set here, although keyframes may always be right-clicked in the **Keyframe** timeline, and interpolation may be changed there.

The **Workspace Zoom** option is very important, especially for adjusting parameters that go off-screen or out of view boundaries. Use **Zoom out** to enlarge the workspace, or, for precise control of object placement, **Zoom in** deeply.

On the lower right of the workspace is a magnifying glass icon. Click and hold this icon to zoom in or out with the mouse. The workspace may be offset to the left or right for control of off-screen positions. Note the grid/dots. If zoomed out far enough, the 4K maximum resolution area may be recognized.

All values in a Track Motion setting may be saved as a preset for later recall. Give the preset a name in the dialog box at the top of the **Track Motion** dialog box, and select and click the floppy disk icon. This will save the preset. Default presets may not be altered and saved to the same name; a new name is required. I've saved off quarter and thirds windows settings as presets simply because split screens are common workflows for me.

Using Track Motion

In this first track, we're going to create a picture-in-picture effect by making the Event on the first track smaller so that it will lie over the main video. Open the **TrackMotion_PIP.vf** project. Select the **Track Motion** icon on the first track to open the Track Motion tool.

With the **Track Motion** tool open:

1. Disable the **Scale About Center** control.

2. Disable **Sync Cursor**, found below the keyframe timeline. This is very important.

3. Enable the Grid Overlay by selecting the **Overlays** button in the Preview window and selecting **Grid Overlay** from the drop-down menu. This will provide a reference for the Track Motion positions.

4. Enable **Snapping**.

5. Hover the cursor over the bottom-right corner of the Track Motion boundary. A circle will appear in the corner. Click this corner, and drag the right corner upward and to the left. Notice the line of dots that line up with the grid in the overlay. Set the Track Motion boundary so that it fills a quarter of the screen or less.

 Tip_____

> If you're struggling with seeing exactly where the Track Motion-controlled image is aligning with the grid, mute the base video track by selecting the track and pressing the **Z** key (or selecting the **Mute** switch). This will turn the background of the preview window to black (or white or gray, depending on your Preferences setting).

With the PIP in place, there are other functions in the Track Motion tool that are useful. In the Track Motion keyframe timeline, locate the **Shadow** function and enable it. A shadow will immediately appear beneath the PIP image. With the 2D Shadow function selected, the Track Motion Properties will change.

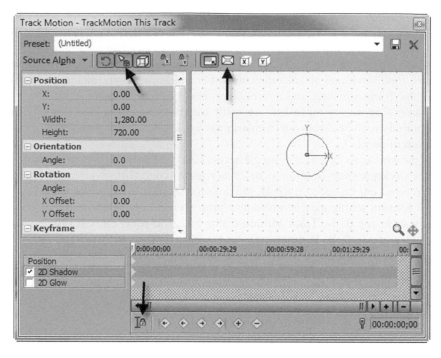

Figure 12.5 Disable the **Scale About Center** feature for this next exercise. When this feature is enabled, all Track Motion functions will center around the target in the Track Motion boundary area. Enable **Snapping**.

Figure 12.6 Your preview window should appear similar to this image.

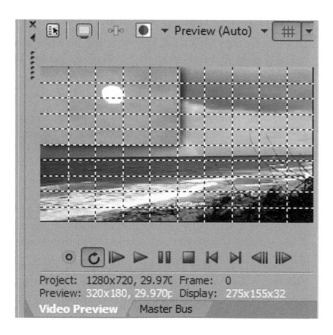

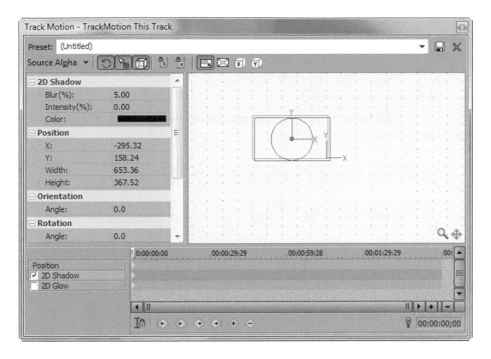

Figure 12.7 This window is called the Track Motion Properties window.

The top value will change, enabling users to modify the position, opacity, and feathering of the shadow. The shadow may be keyframed for motion separate from the PIP. Click and drag on the Track Motion boundary with the 2D Shadow highlighted in the keyframe timeline. The shadow may be dragged around separately from the PIP.

 Tip_____

When you're moving around shadows or glow in the Track Motion dialog box, it's often best to disable Snapping for precise placement of the shadow or glow.

A glow effect may also be inserted. The Glow feature is quite similar to the Shadow feature and may be used as a shadow or second shadow with color to provide greater depth or separation. This is particularly useful for text shadows.

Setting Up a 3D Plane (Not Available in Vegas Movie Studio)

Open the **TrackMotion-Shadow_Glow-Text.vf** file and see how the shadow and glow may be separately keyframed for motion. Pan/Crop has been inserted, providing zoom on the text. Vegas Pro users may want to deconstruct the **TrackMotion3D-Shadow_Glow-Text.veg** file instead. It provides a 3D angle (3D not available in Vegas Movie Studio).

⏱ Speed Tutorial

With this in mind, let's create a new project with a single 3D title in it and a separate 3D graphic. The **3D_Plane.veg** project is the basis for this exercise if you'd prefer to start with a base project.

1. Open a new Vegas Pro project, and create a title on the top track.

2. Place a still or video image on the second track.

3. In the first track, open the **Track Motion** tool and in the **Compositing Modes** drop-down, select **3D Alpha**. The Track Motion tool will open a new view.

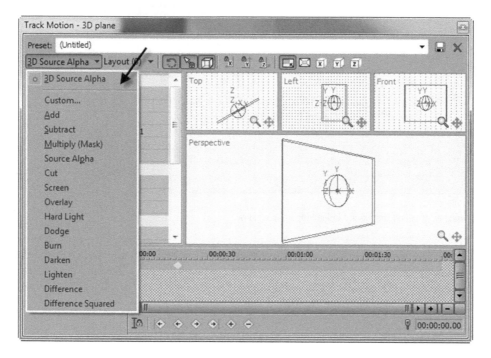

Figure 12.8   The 3D tool offers multiple views for accurate placement of objects in the 3D plane space. The Split Vertical view is my most-used view.

4. In the **Top** view, click/drag the plane forward to give it greater separation from the background object. Pull it forward far enough so that the text is just touching the edges of the preview window.

5. Click on the center of the plane; the cursor will change to a rotation icon. Turn the object toward the front left of the screen, causing the object to be at a diagonal to the background. Don't worry if the left edge of the text disappears off the left side of the screen.

6. In the **Perspective** view, click/drag the object to the right, restoring the left edge of the text object to view. Experiment with dragging corners and enlarging the left side of the text in the perspective window. Notice how the center point of the object provides focus around which any scaling or angles occur.

The image should appear similar to this screenshot.

Once this is set, check the quality of the work by changing the preview window setting from Preview/Auto to **Best/Full**. Depending on the speed of the graphics and CPU, using Best/Full for setting up 3D projects could bog down the system; authoring and editing in Preview/Auto is a common workflow.

 Tip_____

Adding a Gaussian blur set to the **Soften** or **Light Blur** preset to any background image is often very useful when you want to set the viewer focus to the 3D object. It provides an artificial depth of field. In the "Compositing" chapter, we'll delve more deeply into this technique.

Figure 12.9

The **Pan/Crop Tool**

Pan/Crop is a common tool for animating still images, cropping unwanted portions out of a frame, and creating unique angles on a track; yet there is much more that may be accomplished using this tool. Older versions of Vegas placed Pan/Crop as part of the media; Vegas Pro 11 makes Pan/Crop a part of the FX chain and workflow. Pan/Crop is not part of the FX window, yet any time FX are inserted to an Event, Pan/Crop is part of the FX package (*Vegas Movie Studio does not offer this behavior*).

Figure 12.10   Similar to the Track Motion tool, the Pan/Crop tool is broken into two distinct sections, with a slightly less obvious third section/view.

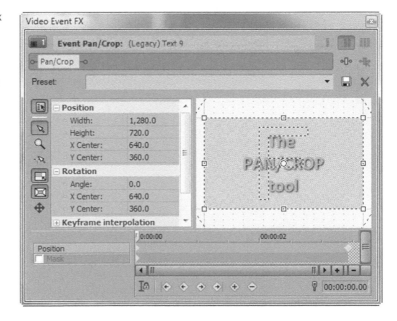

Open the **Pan-Crop.vf** project file. Position the playhead/cursor over the title card/first Event. Right-click the Event and choose **Video Event Pan/Crop** from the submenu.

Pan/Crop presents a Properties window to the left, workspace to the right, and Bezier masking at the bottom (Bezier masking not available in Vegas Movie Studio).

Similar to Track Motion, the Pan/Crop tool has a toolbar. It is found on the left side of the Pan/Crop dialog rather than at the top.

- The top button in the Pan/Crop tool is the **Show Properties** button. This will show/hide the properties window. Hide the properties window when screen real estate is a premium or when you're using drag techniques to set the Pan/Crop position.

- The **Normal Edit** tool is the most common tool for editing points and positions in the Pan/Crop workspace.

- The **Zoom** tool allows users to zoom in/out both with the cursor or with a mouse wheel.

- **Snapping** allows users to snap Pan/Crop boundaries to points in a grid. Grid spacing/number of points is determined in the **Workspace** values of the Properties window.

- **Maintain/Lock aspect ratio** is a default feature; holding down the **Ctrl** key will temporarily override this default command.

- **Scale About Center** keeps all Pan/Crop scaling focused around the center target point in the Pan/Crop window. Holding the **Alt** key will temporarily override this default setting. Both may be disabled by deselecting the option.

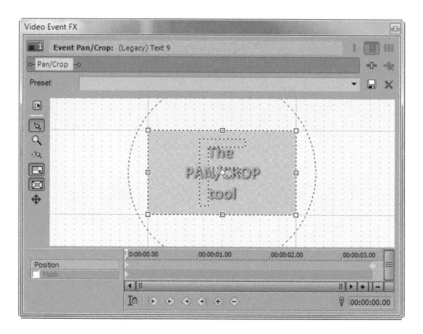

Figure 12.11   Properties may be hidden in the Pan/Crop dialog box, allowing for a larger Pan/Crop workspace. This is useful for precision control or for working on systems where there is minimal screen real estate.

Positioning the Pan/Crop is possible using four methods:

1.   Dragging the Pan/Crop handles in the workspace for manual control

2.   Entering a numeric value in the Position window

3.   Using the position slider (hold **Ctrl** for fine movements)

4.   Using the spinner/Up and Down Arrows in the dialog box (all Property windows may be controlled this way)

Rotation allows not only rotation of a panned/cropped object, it also enables relocation of the center point around which the rotation will occur. Offset rotations, rotating around the object corner, and the like are all possible with this tool. I use the rotation offset on titles to move the titles on a fixed-edge axis point (something the Title tool cannot do).

Keyframe interpolation may be set in this window. **Zero** is the default setting; setting this to higher values will cause a Pan/Crop motion to "settle" into a position. For some types of movement, raising this value may give the motion a more organic feel as it reaches the slope at the end of the keyframe interpolation curve.

The **Source** may be manipulated before it is panned or cropped; if **Maintain Aspect ratio** is disabled in the Source window, the height-to-width ratio does not remain constant as pixels are stretched.

As with the Track Motion tool, the **Workspace** may be zoomed in/out. There is no magnifying zoom in the Pan/Crop tool as the Track Motion tool offers. Use the mouse wheel to zoom in/out or use the slider control in the Zoom parameter.

Grid spacing for snapping may also be increased or decreased in this dialog box.

As with the Track Motion tool, settings for Pan/Crop positions may be stored as presets. Once the settings are complete to satisfaction, enter a unique name in the name dialog box at the top of the window, click and select the disk icon, and the preset will be stored.

Figure 12.12   Save oft-used settings as a preset in the Pan/Crop dialog window for later recall.

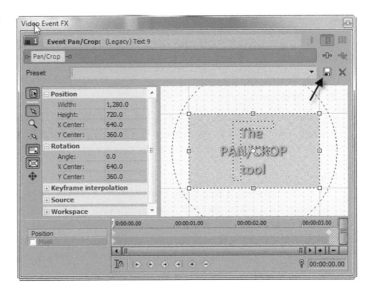

⏱ *Speed Tutorial*

The **Pan-Crop.vf project** file should be open. If it's not, open it now. There are six still images on the timeline; we're going to first make them match the aspect ratio of our project. I've placed a checkerboard pattern beneath the images to display the over-areas.

1. Place the cursor/playhead over the second Event in the project (the guitar). Right-click the Event and choose **Video Event Pan/Crop** from the submenu. The Pan/Crop dialog box will open. Disable **Sync to Cursor**.

2. In the workspace, right-click the image and select **Match output aspect ratio**. This may insert a new keyframe if **Sync to Cursor** was enabled when the Pan/Crop tool opened (this is an annoyance of the Pan/Crop tool; the playhead should auto-return to the first keyframe when Sync is disabled), so you may need to right-click any previous keyframe in the keyframe timeline and select **Delete**.

3. Notice that the guitar image now fills the Preview window. Close the Pan/Crop dialog box. Right-click the guitar Event and choose **Copy** from the submenu that opens.

4. Right-click the next Event (keyboard) and choose **Select Events to End** (or press the **N** key). This will select all downstream Events on the track.

5. Right-click again and choose **Paste Event Attributes**.

6. All of the Events now have the same Pan/Crop applied to them, and all Events should fully fill the Preview window. Play the timeline to assure that all stills have been properly panned/cropped. (This is a good opportunity to play the timeline at 2X speed; press the **L** key twice for 2X playback.)

7. Now we'll add some animation and motion to each still Event. This may be done while looping the timeline, so double-click the first Event to create a selection, press **Q** to enable looping, and begin playback. You might want to mute the audio.

8. Right-click the first Event and select the Pan/Crop tool. Enable **Scale About Center** and **Maintain Aspect ratio**. Grab any corner and slightly zoom into the object. In the Preview window, the zoom will be seen on the graphic.

9. Images may be keyframed to move from side to side, up/down, and zoom in the process. Right-click the guitar Event and choose the **Pan/Crop** tool from the submenu. Click the first keyframe in the Pan/Crop keyframe timeline and zoom in by approximately **40%**, placing the left edge of the crop boundary against the upper-left corner of the workspace.

10. Put the cursor/playhead at the end of the keyframe timeline and move the Pan/Crop to the lower right corner of the workspace.

11. Play the selection/second Event, and the guitar should be panning from the body of the guitar down the neck/fretboard of the guitar.

12. Repeat this exercise with each Event on the timeline until all six Events are moving. Play with different zoom and pan angles. Right-click the keyframes to get a feel for the various interpolation modes, and vary the smoothness of the keyframes to gain a firm understanding of how the smoothness tool functions.

 *Tip*_____

When you're planning to zoom deeply into images, it's a good idea to have images at least 4000 pixels in at least one dimension. Keep in mind that stills from big mega-pixel HDSLRs can bring Vegas to its knees, so use some common sense. Vegas has a maximum resolution space of 4K. A 14k pixel image will require Vegas to do some serious scaling on the image, which consumes CPU cycles. Multiply that 14K image by 100 still images, and now the CPU is brought to its knees. If large quantities of large-pixel images are to be used, rescale the images to no larger than 5K *before* inserting the groups of images to the Vegas Timeline.

In addition to the Match Output Aspect menu in the right-click dialog box, additional choices include the following:

- *Restore.* Restores Pan/Crop boundaries to the edges of the image. No Pan/Crop takes place.

- *Center.* Centers Pan/Crop boundaries around the centering dot found in the middle of the crop boundaries.

- *Flip Horizontal.* Flips images horizontally, making the right side become the left side. (This feature is great for changing a view. Open **multicamera.veg** for more information.)

- *Flip Vertical.* Flips images vertically, causing most images to be upside down.

- *Match Output Aspect.* Matches the image aspect ratio to the settings in the **File | Properties** dialog box, which is usually 720 3 480 for DV editing.

- *Match Source Aspect.* Matches the image aspect to the original aspect ratio. Use this setting when applying full photos over other montages and when it is acceptable for the photo's borders to be seen. This feature will still allow an image to be resized smaller; however, the aspect ratio is that of the original image, not of the project.

Using the Bezier Mask Feature in Pan/Crop (Not Available in Vegas Movie Studio)

The **Bezier Mask** tool enables users to cut holes or masks in media to allow other pieces of media to show through or to overlay other media on top of an Event. One of the easy uses of the Pan/Crop tool is to create a lower third/name bar.

⏱ *Speed Tutorial*

This tutorial may be found as a project on the DVD, labeled **bezier_mask.veg**, for purposes of final comparision.

1. Open a new project and create two video tracks (**Ctrl + Shift + Q**). Insert a video clip on track **Two**.

2. On track **One**, insert a **Generated Media | Color Gradient, Soft Blue Backdrop** preset. When the gradient window opens, the blue is positioned to the bottom/white to the top. Grab and drag the blue (**#1** at the bottom of the color box) to the left side of the gradient window.

3. Click the **#2** target button and the color will change to indicate white. Reduce the opacity of the white by pulling down on the **Color** slider. This will allow some of the underlying image to show through. Don't worry about getting it "right" just yet; we'll tweak it as the lower third is laid in and adjusted.

4. Position the cursor/playhead on the Vegas Timeline so that it is in the middle of the gradient. Open the **Pan/Crop** tool and click the tick box in the **Mask** portion of the keyframe timeline to enable the mask.

5. Select the **Anchor Creation** tool (press **D** until the tool is highlighted).

6. Click on the left side of the gradient to set an anchor point. Moving straight across to the right side, click again. *Do not drag.* You are only clicking individual points. This will create a straight line across the gradient. Directly beneath the right anchor point, create another anchor point, and move to the left directly beneath the first anchor point. Click to create a fourth anchor point. Complete the rectangle by once again clicking on the first anchor point. A rectangle has been created, and a gradient bar should now be sitting above the video on the second track.

Continued

Figure 12.13   Click/drag the target
labeled **1** to position
it to the left side.
This will rotate the
gradient so the blue
is on the left.

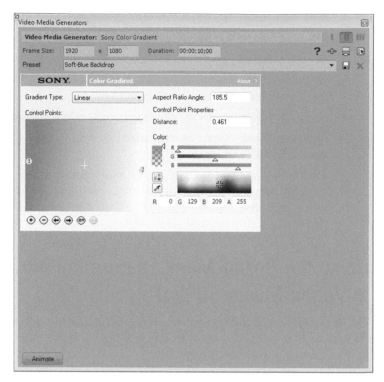

Figure 12.14   When the Bezier
Mask is enabled, the
toolbar on the left
side of the Pan/Crop
tool changes to
masking tools.
Notice that the Sync
Cursor is not enabled
and the Playhead is
at the beginning of
this Bezier Mask
timeline.

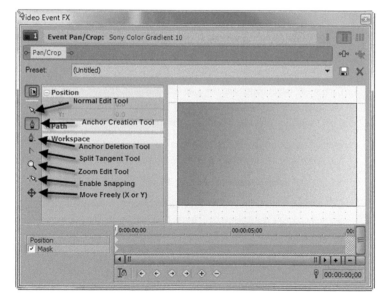

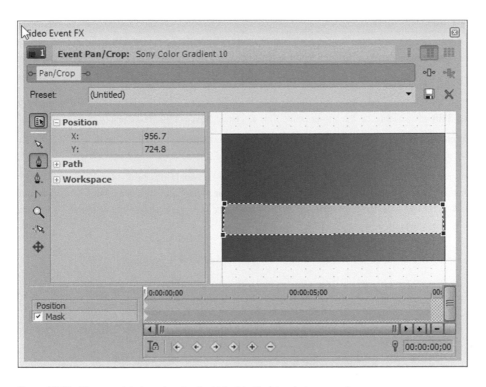

Figure 12.15   The completed mask path should be identical to what you see here.

Figure 12.16   The mask creates a lower third from the generated gradient and area cut out by the Bezier mask.

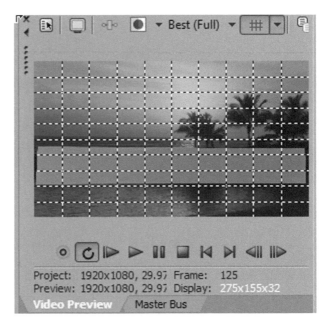

Tip_____

When it's a struggle to create a straight line, enable the **Grid Overlay** in the Preview window. Set the grid line value in the **Options | Preferences | Video | Horizontal/Video Grid lines**. My personal preference is **15** divisions versus the default 10.

7. Select a point further down the Bezier Mask keyframe timeline. The mask may be quickly modified; select the **Normal Edit** tool and hold **Shift** while clicking on the anchor points. This will highlight/select all anchor points.

8. Select the **Anchor Creation** tool (**D** key for shortcut) and click/select any of the anchor points in the Bezier mask. This will automatically create curves on all four points.

9. Grab the tangent handles and drag the ends of the curves inside the frame boundary. Use the grid to align points equally. If all four anchor points are still selected, reclick with the **Anchor Creation** tool to reset to square corners. A new keyframe has been created. The keyframed movement from the first keyframe to the second is a glimpse into what else may be done with the Bezier Mask tool.

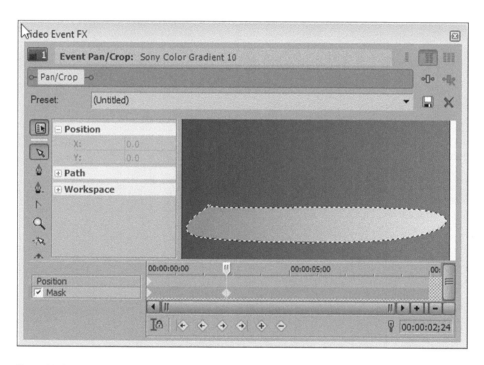

Figure 12.17

Also in this tool set you'll find other controls. In this control set is a setting labeled **Path**. Click on the **Path** label or on the + symbol next to the word *Path*, and a menu appears with several settings. Click on **Mode** and you have the choices Positive, Negative, and Disabled. When **Positive** is chosen, the area inside the curve is visible and the remaining space is transparent. When the **Negative** option is chosen, the area inside the curve is transparent, and the area outside the anchor points and path is visible. This

Figure 12.18 The completed mask should look something like these two images of the Bezier Mask tool and the Preview screen.

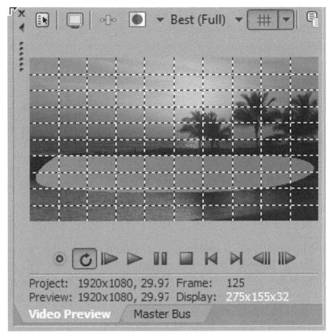

is a great tool for removing a subject from a background, placing it in a new background, or removing a background from a current scene and replacing it. One way to consider this tool is that it's like a chroma key tool that will work regardless of the number of colors found in the background. At many levels, this feature brings some of the tools found in rotoscoping tools to Vegas.

The opacity of the mask may also be controlled via the Pan/Crop Bezier tool. Opacity, like all other aspects of the Bezier tool, is keyframe-controlled. One benefit is that masks may be faded in or out over time by using the keyframe tool to create the type of image needed to complete the composite or overlay.

Open the **Path** dialog box by clicking the + symbol next to the word *Path*. Note the Opacity parameter in the Path dialog box. Opacity may be controlled by entering a value via the keyboard, sliding the **Opacity** slider, or using the spinner controls next to the Slider tool. Use the **Page Up** and **Page Down** keys for coarse control, moving the value in increments of +/–10, and use the **Up** and **Down Arrows** for fine control moving in fractional values. For example, setting the first keyframe in the masking timeline to a value of **0** causes the mask to be transparent, or invisible. Setting the next keyframe to a value of **100** will cause the mask to be completely opaque. This may be used to fade the mask in or out of the image composition.

Next in the list of power tools found in the new Pan/Crop tool is the **Feathering** tool. This tool allows you to blend the masking lines created in the Bezier mask with the background. When you're working with moving media, this is exceptionally helpful because it can assist in blending moving images against a moving backdrop. Feathering can take place either inside the mask or outside the mask or in both directions.

To take advantage of the **Feathering** tool, first create a mask as described previously. Open the **Path** dialog box by clicking the + symbol next to the word *Path*. Note the feathering option beneath Opacity.

Choose how you'd like the path feathered. Experiment with all three feathering modes to determine what works best for the mask. In the pre-built **bezier_mask** project, note that the mask on the vocalist is feathered to soften the transition from altered and unaltered Events. Your final output may be different; check the feathering values on the provided project mask.

As with the Pan/Crop and Track Motion presets, Bezier masks may be remembered and stored as presets. Give the preset a name in the preset field and select the **Save Preset** disk icon.

> Bezier curves were first developed in 1959 and used to design automobile bodies. In vector graphics, Bezier curves are a tool used to model smooth curves that can be scaled indefinitely.

The Bezier Mask tool may also be used to rotoscope a frame; however, this is not what the Bezier Mask is intended for. Rotoscoping a moving object will take tremendous patience and at least 30 keyframes per second of work. There are tools better suited for the job of rotoscoping, such as Boris RED, or even external tools such as After Effects with RotoBrush.

For the popular pulled/stroked effect seen on many network shows, exporting a frame to the clipboard and opening it in a photo-editing application is often the easiest method for frames not shot in front of a plain background.

Figure 12.19 A very practical application of the Bezier Mask tool is masking out hot or dead pixels. This phenomenon occurs less with the newer CMOS camcorders, but it still happens. Make a copy of the Event or clip that needs masking. Using Bezier Mask, mask out the single pixel, shift the lower/underlying frame to the left/right/up/down, and let the "new" pixel show through the mask. This is where the Zoom tool will come in very handy. This same effect may be accomplished with the Cookie Cutter tool, but if there is a larger region that requires shaping and minor movement, the Bezier Mask tool is the way to go.

Track Motion or Pan/Crop?

On the surface, these two functions share a number of properties, so at first, it might be difficult to know which function to use for various tasks.

First and foremost, remember that Track Motion will not crop a frame, so if it's used for resizing a frame (4:3 to widescreen, for example), the viewing aspect will change, usually resulting in stretched or compressed images. Track Motion affects the whole of the frame, generally being inclusive of the frame boundary.

In other words, when the entire frame needs to move and changing resolution is undesirable, Track Motion is usually the best choice.

Pan/Crop is best used when the image needs to be cropped or when the contents inside a frame need to move. Pan/Crop will crop edges and affect the contents inside the frame boundaries, and it may extend beyond the frame boundary. It may act like a camera zoom inside of frame boundaries, and may zoom out beyond frame boundaries. It also may have a significant impact on the resolution of an image as pixels become larger or smaller when it's used for zooming or cropping.

Rendering and Output

Back in the "good ol' days" of broadcasting, editors had to worry about two types of output and one resolution/frame rate: Beta SP for broadcast delivery and VHS replication, or DV for (sometimes) broadcast and VHS replication. Then DVD came along and added a few more challenges. But today we've got to deliver to broadcast, Blu-ray, DVD, intranet, Internet, mobile devices—and all at several different resolutions and a few different frame rates, and it can quickly become confusing.

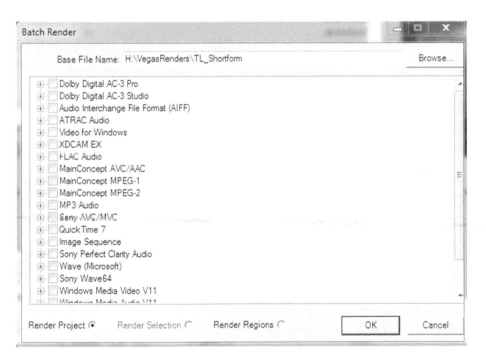

Figure 13.1   Vegas offers many, many choices for output and rendering. The Batch Encoder has all the templates for the various formats.

Let's first look at outputting files for DVD and Blu-ray.

Using Vegas with DVD Architect

DVD Architect (DVDA) will prepare and burn DVD or Blu-ray discs. If a disc is your only deliverable, then you will render the project once for the video stream and once for the audio stream. If you have multiple deliverables, such as web, disc, iDevice, etc., then you would do better to render first as an .AVI file. (More on that technique later.) Our workflow for disc only is to render MPEG-2 for video, render AC-3 for audio (mono, stereo, or 5.1 Surround), then create the disc in DVDA. Prior to rendering to MPEG-2 you can insert markers (M key) as chapter points if desired. DVDA will recognize these markers as chapter points and will insert them as such if instructed to do so in DVDA.

Figure 13.2

Audio for the disc, regardless of whether it is Surround, stereo, or mono, will ultimately be an AC-3 file. If your project is stereo audio you could tick the checkbox to "Include audio stream" (click Custom - Audio) in your MPEG-2 render template and DVDA will automatically convert it to an

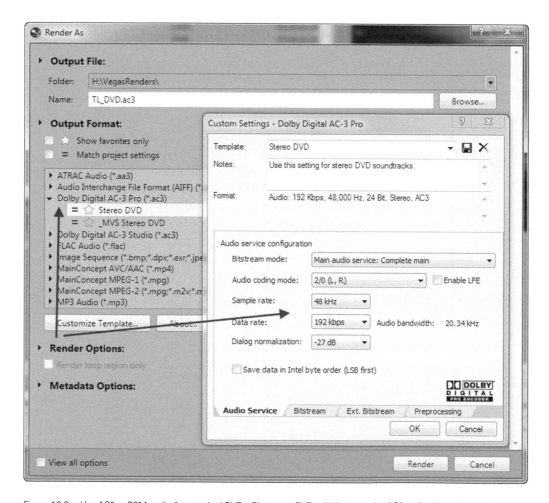

Figure 13.3   Use AC3 or PCM audio for standard DVDs. Blu-ray on DVD will likely require AC3 audio due to the need to save space.

AC-3 file during the DVDA render/burn process. Audio in a 5.1 channel project file cannot be embedded in the MPEG file in any form. My personal workflow is always to create two files, one MPEG-2 and one AC-3 regardless if the audio is stereo or surround.

Video projects that are rendered as 24p files will not be transcoded or recompressed in DVDA; they will stay in their native format. This feature allows 20% more video media to be placed on the DVD, which can be monitored or previewed in DVDA as well. Export of 24p NTSC MPEG-2 for DVD Architect is also supported as an output format in Vegas. Bear in mind that to view 24p media on an external CRT monitor, the frames will have to have pull-down added, creating a 60i or 50i video stream that the external monitor can comprehend. Many LCD/plasma monitors today will properly display 24p in its native format.

The best workflow I've found for rendering files for MPEG-2 and AC-3 files while leaving the system unattended is to use the Batch Render script found in Vegas Pro (not available in Vegas Movie Studio). Go to **Tools | Scripting | Batch Render** and run the script. An interface will open, looking like the one you see here.

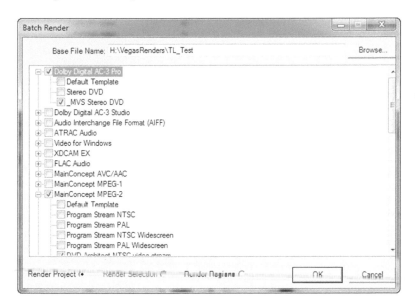

Figure 13.4   The Batch Render script renders multiple forms of media from one timeline and one action.

In this interface, expand the **Main Concept MPEG** option. In the subset, select the format of MPEG you want to use. Do not simply check the MPEG tick box without expanding. During beta testing, I did this for a project containing 11 regions because I hadn't expanded the subset. It rendered all night, and the next morning I had 209 files! Nineteen templates rendered for all 11 regions, and it created a mess. I've accidentally made this mistake for AC-3 as well. If you check only the file format, Vegas will render a version of the file for each template setup in your preferences. Expanding the subsets allows you to select the specific format you'd like files rendered to.

For standard export to DVD Architect, choose the DVD Architect NTSC or PAL video stream and tick the box next to that subset option. Collapse the MPEG set, and choose the **AC-3 subset**. Select either the **Stereo DVD** or the **5.1 Surround DVD** checkbox (or a custom template), depending on the project type. Let the project render, and when it's finished, you'll have both file types of the same name stored in the same folder. DVD Architect will locate the audio with the video, and you'll be set.

You can get better results in both audio and video on your DVDs by creating custom presets that **tweak** the default parameters. To do this, click on **File | Render As**, choose the **MainConcept** MPEG-2 render type, and click the appropriate **DVD Architect XXXX video stream** built-in template to match your basic output settings.

Click on **Customize Template**. Here you will change your bitrate settings based on the length of your program and desired file size. If your program is no more than about 60 minutes in length, I recommend ticking **Constant bit rate** and entering a value of **8,000,000**. Set **Field Order** to **Progressive** if that is the intended output.

Figure 13.5

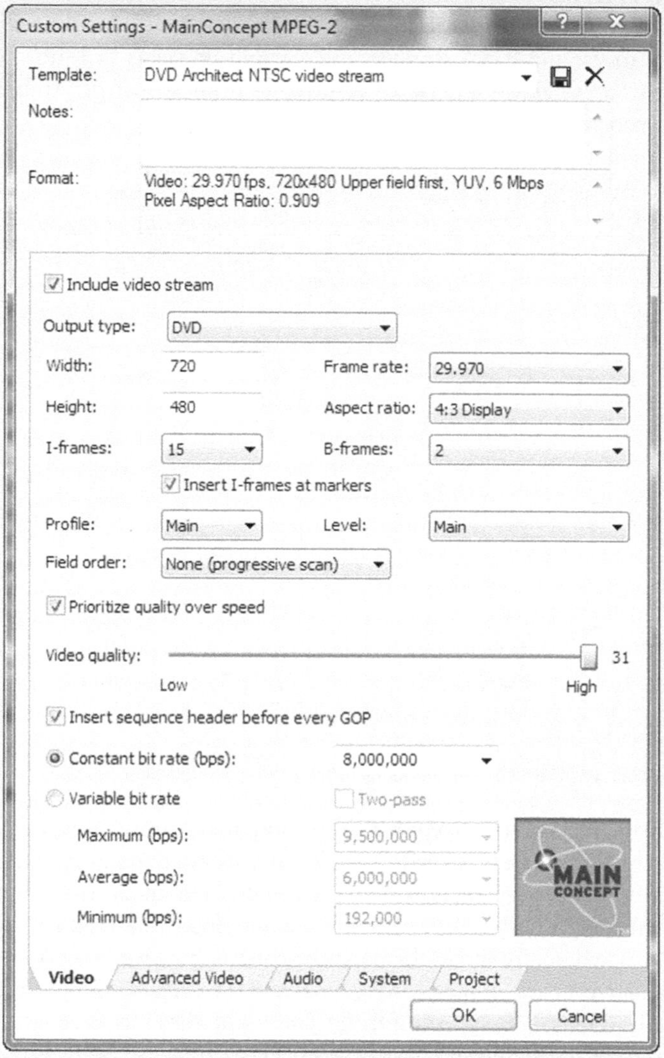

If your program is much longer than 60 minutes, you will need to use a variable bitrate or lower your constant bitrate setting. Why? Because you only have about 4.5 GB available on a standard single-layer DVD, known as a DVD-5. If the bitrate is constant but the program length increases, the file size goes up as well. You can get away with a little more than 60 minutes, but not much. For longer program material, choose variable bitrate and adjust your settings with a bitrate calculator such as the one included with VASST's Ultimate S Pro. You can also find bitrate calculators online.

Is your DVD audio different than what you hear on the Vegas Timeline? Create an AC3 preset based on the default Stereo DVD preset, but set **Dialog Normalization** to **–31** dB, and on the **Preprocessing** tab set **Line Mode** profile and **RF Mode** profile both to **None**.

Tip_____
When using variable bitrate, be sure to tick the **Two-pass** checkbox. Two-pass encoding allows the encoder to scan the media in the project, allocating bits for which sections need more attention in the encoding process, as opposed to single-pass encoding, which merely encodes what is put into the encoder. Two-pass encoding is much slower than single-pass encoding, but for high-motion or high-contrast video projects, it's well worth the end result.

In the two-pass encoding process, Vegas will first scan the project and write a log file containing information about what's in the project media, noting what's found. It then begins the scanning process again, encoding the media based on information contained in the log file. Static media, media that contains little movement or little contrast, will not substantially benefit from two-pass encoding. It's a good idea to render short sections of your project to see if there is a discernable difference between the two-pass and the single-pass process of encoding. In most instances, there should not be a large difference from one to the other. If your project contains a lot of still images, remember to set the video rendering quality to **Best**. This will lengthen the render time but will provide a cleaner encode quality.

Tip_____
DVD-9 media is available (dual-layer DVD) but is generally best for projects that will go out to a replicating house. The compatibility rate of burned dual-layer media with consumer DVD players is lower than the compatibility rate of single-layer DVD media.

The Batch Render script displayed above is great for rendering to .avi, .mpg, and streaming media while you're gone for the night or out to lunch. Long projects don't need as much babysitting. These files do not require DVD Architect for authoring; they may be dropped into any DVD authoring tool and used as source files. DVD Architect simply makes it a smooth, hassle-free process.

Tip_____
Sony Production Assistant has automated tools designed to accomplish this task, and VASST offers the freeware DVD Prep that also does auto-naming and rendering of audio/video files for DVD output.

Outputting for Blu-ray Disc

Blu-ray is all the rage and is the best mechanism for delivering HD on a shiny round disc. One does not need a Blu-ray (BD) burner to export short HD projects to DVD, since existing DVD burners may be used to author BD discs (assuming that the project length is less than 20 minutes). Blu-ray discs are also not required for short projects; a standard DVD-5 may be used.

However, a Blu-ray player is required to play back the Blu-ray disc, whether it is a DVD 5 or an actual BD disc.

Regardless of the disc burning and disc type used, the rendering process is the same.

Finish out the project, and create a render zone/region in case something changes later in the process. Choose **File | Render As | Sony AVC/MVC** in the **Output Format** dialog box. The dialog box opens when the Sony AVC/MVC choice is made. In this dialog box, choose the setting that best works for your source content. Typically, either the AVCHD 1920 x 1080-60i or Blu-ray 1920 x 1080-60i is very common to the U.S. market and 16 Mbps is usually preferred. The Blu-ray 1920 x 1080 may be customized by selecting the **Customize** button at the bottom of the **Render As** dialog box, and the render may be switched from Interlaced to **Progressive Scan** if this project is known to be heading for a progressive scan-only display (most displays have very good deinterlacers built in).

You can also deliver 1280 x 720; this is a very common format in the European Union, although 1920 x 1080 is the standard size for masters.

Create a filename, choose a destination for the rendered file (I recommend rendering to a new folder), and click the **Render** button.

 Tip_____

In general, look for templates labeled with an equals sign (=). These will be more compatible with your project settings right out of the box.

Audio is rendered separately from video in the same way that it should be for SD DVD; the BD disc may contain PCM (uncompressed stereo audio), AC3 stereo audio, or AC3 5.1 surround audio. Be sure that the timeline selection has not shifted (this is one of several reasons I advocate creating render zones and regions). If the file is a Surround file, render using the appropriate Dolby Encoder to a 5.1 Surround file. Vegas Movie Studio users will be most happy with the Surround with AGC (Automatic Gain Control) template. Vegas Pro Users will generally want to use the **Customize** option and set the **Line mode** and **RF mode** Profile to **None** in the **PreProcessing** tab and the **Dialog Normalization** to −31 in the **Audio Services** tab.

Render the audio to the same destination folder as the video stream was stored, using the same filename. This will allow DVD Architect to automatically associate the audio stream with the video stream. Separate names may be used if desired; they merely need to be manually linked in the DVD Architect application. Multiple language files or alternate audio tracks will require manual linking.

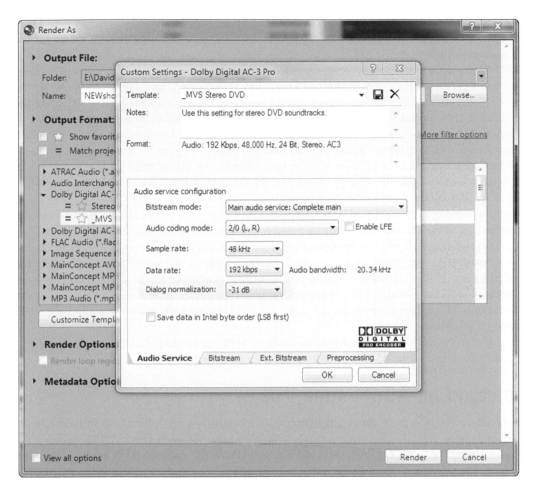

Figure 13.0   Changing some minor settings in the **Dolby** dialog box will yield better results. (Parameters are not adjustable in Vegas Movie Studio.)

What If I'm not Using DVD Architect?

MPEG-2 file types are fairly ubiquitous, and it is the file format of choice for DVD. Vegas uses the MainConcept codec to encode files to the MPEG format, although the Sony version of the Main-Concept codec should not be confused with other applications using this codec. Each group of software engineers from the various NLE manufacturers has written individual interfaces to the codec.

To render to MPEG codecs, select **File | Render As** and choose **MainConcept MPEG-1** or **-2** from the **Save As Type** drop-down menu. Selecting **MPEG-1** renders an MPEG-1 format video that can be placed on a CD or on the Web for download. Selecting the **MPEG-2** option renders the MPEG-2 file for use on CD or for sending to a DVD authoring application. (When using Vegas with DVD Architect, files are not required to render to MPEG until DVD Architect prepares the media for the DVD burn.) Audio files in the MPEG-2 format are rendered to an MPEG-2 audio format.

MPEG files can be rendered as progressive-scan or as interlaced files. MPEG files should be rendered to a progressive-scan output for best appearance if the targeted display is a computer screen or LCD/HD television. If the file will predominantly be played on older-style television sets, leave the file interlaced. If the primary target is for computer viewing, set the file format as progressive scan. In the event that a progressive-scan file is displayed on a television that does not have progressive-scan settings, the television or output device will interlace the video. The settings for progressive scan or interlacing are found under the **Custom** button in the **Render As** dialog box.

The bitrate (encoding depth) can be selected in the **Custom** dialog box as well. This option is found in the **Video** tab.

Bitrate for standard DVDs should be 8 Mbps constant or variable bitrate. Using VBR allows the encoder to determine the quality of frames based on motion in the various frames.

Some DVD authoring applications require separate video and audio streams. Vegas can output separate streams to meet these requirements. To output separate video/audio streams, select the **File | Render As | Mpeg-2 | Custom | System** tab. Place a checkmark in the **Save as separate elementary streams** box in this dialog box. Vegas will create two separate files: one labeled m2v for the video stream and one labeled mpa for the audio stream. Import these two streams into the DVD authoring application.

Unless you are exceptionally well informed about MPEG encoding functions, you shouldn't change anything else in the MPEG output settings.

Outputting an AC-3 Format File

One of the features of Vegas is the ability to output AC-3 audio files. AC-3 is a compression scheme devised and overseen by Dolby Laboratories (www.dolby.com). AC-3 can be output in stereo or 5.1 channel format. The primary benefit of AC-3 is that it allows for audio to be compressed, leaving more space for video on a DVD. AC-3 audio delivers high-quality audio in an encoded format that most consumer and computer DVD players can decode. This option gives viewers the best possible audio experience. Output to AC-3 using the methods described previously.

Output to Intranet or Internet

Corporate intranets (now referred to as *enterprise-level connections*) and the Web once were very disparate delivery destinations. Intranets could manage high bitrate video and the Internet couldn't. With the very efficient codecs and bigger Internet pipelines we have available today, intranets and the Internet are essentially the same delivery vehicle. It's very rare that we have to be concerned about 56 k dialup modem customers any longer; DSL (and faster) has invaded the world landscape.

The question most often asked seems to be, "What bitrate should I be using to push out my video?" The answers are multiple, so the confusion is warranted. The response is, "To where are you delivering your video?" If the answer is YouTube, Vimeo, or the like, then the answer is going to be different than if you'll be streaming the file from one of your own servers. YouTube, Vimeo, and Facebook all convert any video uploaded on their sites to either Flash or HTML 5 so that they can conserve bandwidth as the video is streamed. A few sites convert to Microsoft Silverlight, but unless you've got a specific reason to use Silverlight, it's essentially an also-ran delivery mechanism.

MPEG 4 is a current standard that has all but left Windows Media and REAL in its dust. Very few operating systems cannot open .mp4 streams, either through a QuickTime container or as the unwrapped file. Another benefit to .mp4 is that files sourced from small-format cameras such as AVC and AVCHD camcorders will not have to go through a file conversion (which often means color shift) because the destination file format and colorspace are native to the source format. This generally contributes to faster renders, since format changes can become costly in terms of render time.

To render an mp4 file, browse to **File | Render As**. In this dialog box, there are a couple of .mp4 options. The first is the MainConcept encoder. This is the more commonly used render tool, yet it's not necessarily always the best render tool available.

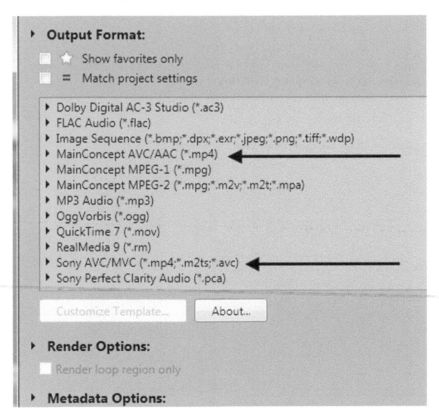

Figure 13.7   Both of these AVC/.mp4 encoders do a great job. My personal rule of thumb is to use MainConcept for lower bitrates and the Sony encoder for higher bitrates and actual AVC encoding.

When the dialog box opens, users are presented with a few choices. This is where having information regarding the destination or display device is very useful.

First, determine the resolution to which the media should be rendered. If it is destined to be played on a television monitor, 1920 x 1080 is a safe bet when the monitor is known to be reasonably new.

If the video is destined to be played over a projection system in a convention center, church, or school, 1280 x 720 is probably a more conservative bet. Not many projectors in the educational, corporate, religious, or convention world have been upgraded beyond SVGA without special request.

If the video is destined for the Web and modern mobile devices, 1280 x 720 is always a good bet.

YouTube and Facebook have no issues taking a 1920 x 1080 stream; they merely dumb down the resolution to other formats so that users have choices. Enterprise YouTube customers are not restricted as to resolution or bitrate.

Once the resolution is determined, the next consideration is bitrate. Vegas enables users to generate constant bitrate (CBR) or variable bitrate (VBR) files. Files destined for Web and mobile devices are generally encoded with VBR. This allows the encoder to use more memory for complex scenes while laying back on memory in static or low estimation scenes. By default, Vegas is set to VBR. To switch from VBR to CBR, check the radio button marked **Constant Bitrate**. The default CBR rate is set to 768 kpbs; this can be set as high as 240 Mbps.

Why super-high bitrates? Check out UHDTV, or Ultra High Definition, slated to hit the residential market somewhere around 2018. At a resolution of 7680 × 4320, it streams between 180 and 600 Mbps, although most certainly VBR will be the standard for UHDTV.

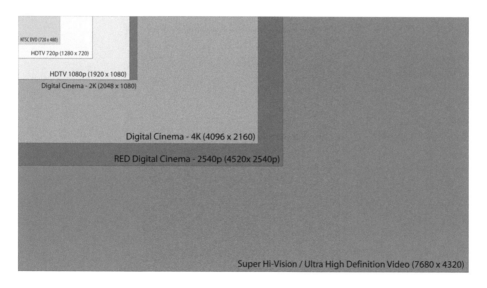

Figure 13.8 UHDTV has a significantly greater resolution than DV, HD, or even 4k Cinema!

Files destined for devices such as the iPhone and Droid can generally be rendered at resolutions of 1280 x 720, VBR not exceeding 2.5 Mbps, and 24, 25, or 30p frame rates. Droid claims that anything above 2 Mbps is going to be problematic; at the time of this writing, I've encoded several 720p files at 4 Mbps that play locally, and they display beautifully when tethered to an HD display. Files destined to play on the iPhone only will look terrific at small resolutions (as they will on the Droid) such as 854 x 480 or even 640 x 360. If the video is to be sent from the phone to AppleTV, 1280 x 720, 2.5 Mbps. Apple recommends a file of 960 x 540 (half full HD size) at 2.5 Mbps.

Notice a couple more options such as number of reference frames and multipasses. Additional reference frames provide more baselines from which the encoder/decoder may work together to create a better picture. Adding reference frames not only slows down the render process, but reference frames are also stored in player memory until they are no longer needed. Depending on the number of reference frames used, this may eat up precious memory on small-memory systems. Most encodes will benefit from 2-pass encoding (excepting iPhones as they do not support Bframes), but this will make the render processing time nearly twice as long.

MPEG-4, MP4, AVC, AVCHD, and MPEG-4 Part 10 are all the same thing.
Or are they?

MPEG-4. A collection of methods defining compression of audio and visual (AV) digital data; introduced in late 1998 and designated a standard for a group of audio and video coding formats and related technology agreed upon by the ISO/IEC Moving Picture Experts Group (MPEG) under the formal standard ISO/IEC 14496; uses of MPEG-4 include compression of AV data for web (streaming media) and CD distribution, voice (telephone, videophone), and broadcast television applications.

H.264. A standard for video compression; known as MPEG-4 Part 10 or MPEG-4 AVC (for Advanced Video Coding); the latest block-oriented motion-compensation-based codec standard developed by the ITU-T Video Coding Experts Group (VCEG) together with the ISO/IEC Moving Picture Experts Group (MPEG).

MP4. Movie or video clip that uses MPEG-4 compression, a standard developed by the Moving Picture Experts Group (MPEG); commonly used for sharing video files on the Internet.

M4V. MPEG-4 file extension used for videos downloaded from the iTunes store; includes music videos, TV episodes, and full-length movies; actually an .MP4 file, but usually copy-protected using Apple's DRM copyright system.

AVCHD. Sony and Panasonic joint dovolopmont that uses H.264 technology but further breaks down macroblocks for greater accuracy.

Output for Youtube, Vimeo, and Facebook (and Other User-Generated Content Sites)

The Web is rapidly becoming our delivery vehicle. With over 2 billion videos watched every day, only a fool would miss the value in using the Web for referencing, approvals, and perhaps final delivery

Figure 13.9

of content. Recently I authored a dual-layer DVD (DVD-9) and the process never went to a mechanical device other than a hard drive until it reached the replicator. The layers (video) were previewed by the client via private view on Vimeo, and the two ISO files were delivered via the Web to the replication house. This saved tremendous time, not to mention cost. We regularly use YouTube, Vimeo, and Facebook as destination/display points for our training videos and have created presets in Vegas Pro and Movie Studio (Vegas Pro presets show up in Vegas Movie Studio when installed on the same machine) that help speed the process.

 Tip_____

YouTube now accepts files up to 4K in resolution. This is a major benefit to those shooting RED cameras, doing time lapse from HDSLRs, or creating motion-action slideshows.

Browse to **File | Render As | MainConcept AVC/AAC** and select an HD template (any template will do, since we'll be customizing the template). Click the **Customize** button, and a new dialog box will be open where specific rendering values may be set.

For Vimeo, Facebook, and YouTube:

Frame size. (Custom frame size) and enter 1280 x 720 or 1920 x 1080, or choose an appropriate frame size such as HD 720p or HD 1080p.

Framerate. If source is 24p, output framerate is 23.976. If source is 60i, 30p, or 60p, output framerate is 29.970. Never, ever convert source 30p, 60p, or 60i to 24p. It's blurry, ghosty, and looks bad in general.

Uncheck **Allow Source to Adjust Frame Size**, even if the destination resolution is the same as the source resolution.

Field order. None (progressive scan).

Bitrate. 720p files are output to 12 Mbps VBR. 1080 files are output to 16 Mbps VBR. YouTube allows for bitrates of up to 50 Mbps. At the time of this writing, Facebook is limited to 24 Mbps, and Vimeo has no restrictions in place. I set Average bitrate to 6 Mbps and Max to 12 Mbps.

I'll generally use a deblocking filter on high-motion videos and none on static/screenshot/training videos. This saves time in the render process.

If the video is very high motion or contains significant detail (such as words on a screenshot), a two-pass encode is usually called for.

If the video has high motion and a lot of scene/color changes, I'll typically insert four reference frames. For training videos, no additional reference frames are inserted.

Check the **Enable progressive download** option. This allows the end user to start playing the video as soon as it begins streaming from the server.

Figure 13.10 My personal settings for rendering HD for UGC sites like YouTube and Facebook.

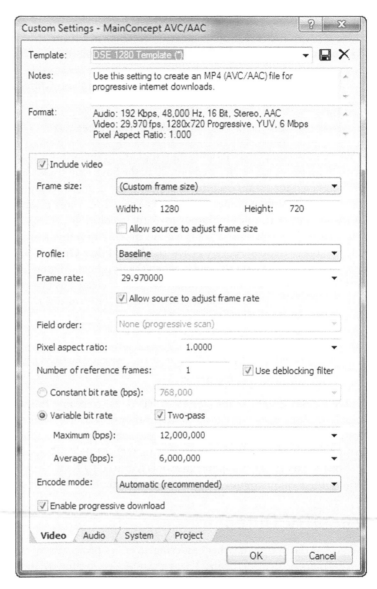

What's in a Frame?

A *reference frame* is a frame that defines a future frame. In older MPEG-2 codecs only one was used (a P-frame, for "Predicted"). In more modern (and more highly compressed) codecs, more interframe (or I-frame) reference frames can be used. However, more reference frames equal a longer encoding time.

Click the **Audio** tab to set audio preferences for the encode. Sample rate should be **48 K** unless there is a specific reason to increase or decrease it. Bitrate should be **384 kbps** in most situations. The bitrate may be set as low as 128 kpbs with good result, and as high as 512 kpbs for Surround Sound projects. The **System** tab allows users to see what GPU (if any) is available to assist in the render. The **Project** tab allows settings that are unique or different from the project settings.

 Tip_____

Enable GPU Assist (if available) in the **Options | Preferences** screen.

We've now completely modified a template. In the top of the template box, rename the template with the settings we've changed out, click the **Save** icon (looks like a floppy disk), and the template will be saved for future use. If you expect to be using the template fairly often, click the small star next to the template name. This allows Vegas to always prioritize this template in future views. With so many variables in output formats, resolutions, frame rates, and bitrates, I've found that "favoriting" templates is a great way to quickly find my go-to settings for almost everything.

In the main **Render As** view, click the **More Filter Options** line, and a new screen opens. Here, filter choices may be set to display when the Render As dialog box is accessed. This does not delete any settings, it merely hides settings that aren't selected as favorites or that don't match the current project. If nothing else, it reduces the potential for error due to so many different options displayed in the Render As dialog box.

 Tip_____

Use the **Favorites** function if only a few render templates are used in a typical workflow. Other templates are always available, yet this reduces the amount of clutter you'll see in the Render As dialog box.

Output may also be sent to WMV or REAL as streaming formats, although these formats are not nearly as efficient by current standards as they once were. Some environments require these formats for legacy purposes, however. All the same settings may be applied to WMV or Real files. Real Networks does support 1080p content, but its Website indicates that the company does not recommend it. Sony Vegas does not support the tools required by Real Networks to author streaming Surround Sound for RealSurround. Microsoft specifies that WMV is designed to deliver 1080p surround.

Tape/DV Output

Vegas has the option of either rendering an entire project or merely doing a print to tape. The difference is that with a print to tape, Vegas temp-renders sections of the project that require recompression. These sections are written as multiple AVI files. A full render writes an entirely new file as one long file. Either method works as well as the other, and the choices are up to the user's workflow and time constraints. A video that needs to be moved off the hard drive and back to tape quickly might be best handled as a print to tape. For final archiving or for multiple file-type outputs, a full render is recommended. If the same media will be output to Windows Media, QuickTime, Web, Blu-ray, and DVD, all these processes will go much faster if working from an AVI file rather than from a project file.

Save the file before rendering, just as a precaution. Writing long video files is taxing on a hard drive and processor, and some older systems cannot handle multiple drives getting very hot and so will shut down.

Rendering to an AVI

Select **File | Render As** to render to an AVI format file. For **Save as type**, choose **Video for Windows** (**.avi*).

Click the **Custom** button. In the **Project** tab of the **Custom Template** dialog box, select **Best** for video rendering quality. This option will slow down the rendering time slightly, yet it ensures that the best rendering options will take place. Under the **Video** tab, the **Create an OpenDML compatible file** checkbox may or may not be checked. Unchecking this option will prevent users from rendering a file larger than 2 GB. You might need to uncheck this box to be compatible with some third-party applications. Leave this box checked if the file contains alpha channels that will need to be accessed later in another editing session, such as when sending video to a compositing application. I generally leave this box checked.

For a standard AVI file to be printed to DV, SD, or HD tape using the Vegas Capture tool, leave the settings under the **Audio** tab, including the codec and aspect settings, at their default positions for a successful print to tape. The video must be 720 x 480 for an NTSC-DV print to tape and 720 x 576 for a PAL DV print to tape (HDV must be rendered to HDV file format using the HDV templates and is not an avi file). HDCAM files must be rendered to an HD 1440 x 1080 file format to be printed to HDCAM over HDSDI. Audio must be 48 kHz/16 bits. Otherwise, the camera, converter, or whatever tool is being used to get the video to a DV tape will not be capable of accepting the media.

To print to tape without rendering the entire project, select **Tools | Print Video to DV Tape** (or **HDV Tape,** depending on your system). This option opens a series of dialog boxes that make sure the project is prepped correctly to print.

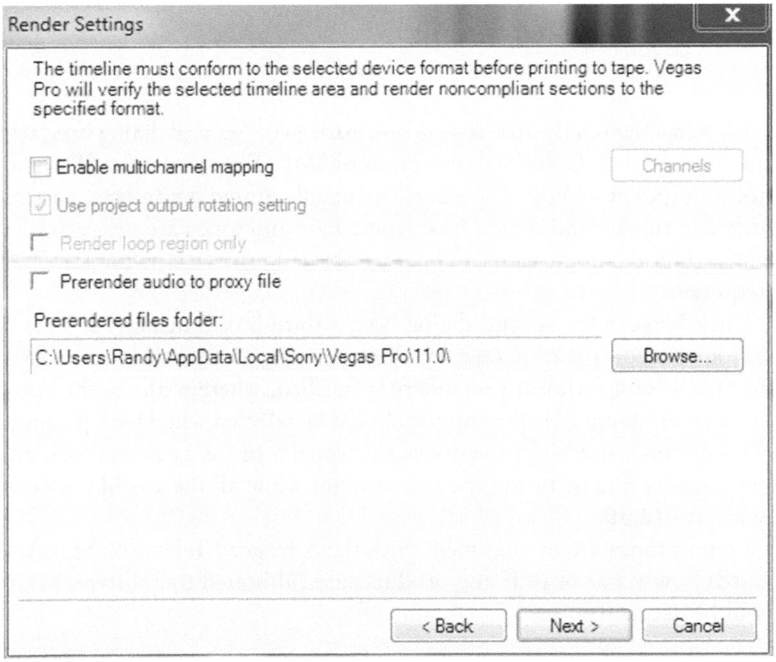

Figure 13.11 First dialog box in the print-to-tape process. Be sure you have the entire region selected if leaving the **Render loop region** box checked.

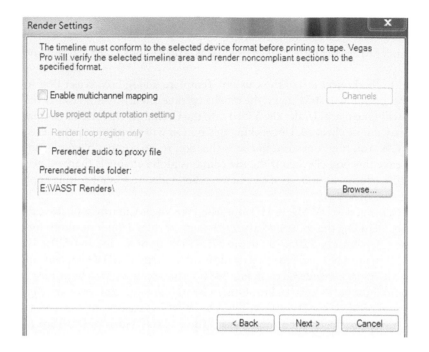

Figure 13.12   Second dialog box in the print-to-tape process. Here is where colorbars and test tones are chosen.

Clicking **Next** in the first dialog box leads to the second dialog box, where test tones and colorbars can be specified. Colorbars are standard SMPTE colorbars for SD, and the test tone is a 1 kHz test tone, output at –20 dB. Colorbars can be substituted for any test pattern by using the choices in the menu in this second dialog box. These bars and tones are necessary, even required by most replication houses and broadcast houses. If this is a print to tape for personal use, tones and bars are not required.

Click **Next** in the second dialog box; a third box is displayed. This box asks whether you want automatic control of a tape machine or manual control. Automatic control will start printing to tape after a series of prerenders is finished, wherein all recompressed media on the timeline is written to a temp file. This option should be selected when long prerendering times are anticipated. This option is useful for the overnight renderer or for users who edit during the day or evening and then render and print to tape late at night while all the world is sleeping. The tones in Vegas 2-7 were at –12 dB.

Output tones are in alignment with the Advanced Television Standards Committee output standards (www.atsc.org). If any products are calibrated to a different output standard, recalibration will be necessary.

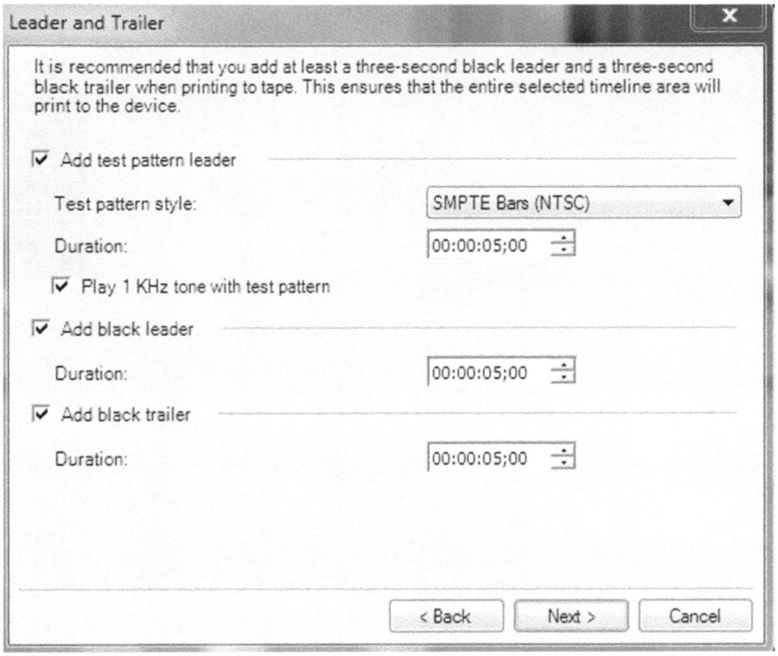

Figure 13.13 Vegas warns users if the render process appears to be a lengthy task.

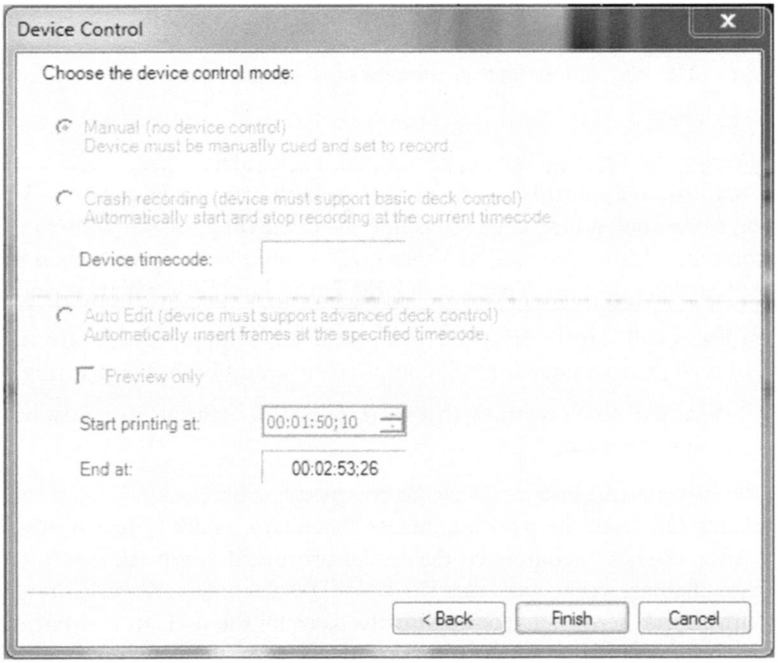

Leader and Trailer

It is recommended that you add at least a three-second black leader and a three-second black trailer when printing to tape. This ensures that the entire selected timeline area will print to the device.

☑ Add test pattern leader

Test pattern style: SMPTE Bars (NTSC) ▼

Duration: 00:00:05;00

☑ Play 1 KHz tone with test pattern

☑ Add black leader

Duration: 00:00:05;00

☑ Add black trailer

Duration: 00:00:05;00

< Back   Next >   Cancel

Figure 13.14 The rendering progress window indicates how long a render will take.

Device Control

Choose the device control mode:

⦿ Manual (no device control)
Device must be manually cued and set to record.

○ Crash recording (device must support basic deck control)
Automatically start and stop recording at the current timecode.

Device timecode:

○ Auto Edit (device must support advanced deck control)
Automatically insert frames at the specified timecode.

☐ Preview only

Start printing at: 00:01:50;10

End at: 00:02:53;26

< Back   Finish   Cancel

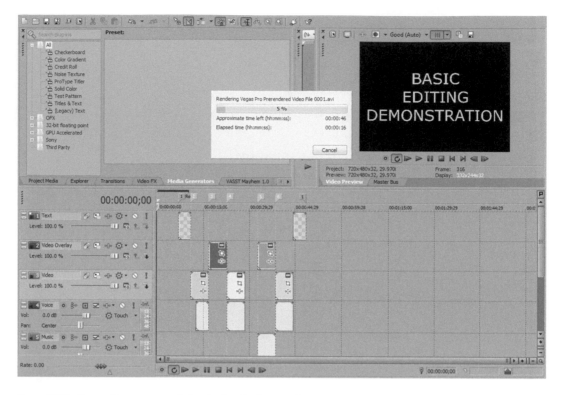

Figure 13.15   Vegas allows users to define the length of a countdown.

Automatic Print to Tape is not available over SDI.

Manual tape control is useful for DV decks that cannot be controlled by the computer or for printing to an analog tape deck. Selecting the manual option still allows users to walk away from the computer during renders, as Vegas gives a countdown option when printing manually.

After this selection is made, click the **Finish** button. Vegas then does one of two things:

- Vegas will start to print to tape immediately if no prerenders are left to complete or if there are very few prerenders, it will complete those and begin the printing or countdown process.

- Vegas will give a warning that more than 80% of the project must be rendered and will ask if you wish to proceed.

In either event, instruct Vegas to complete the process.

Click **OK** from the warning, unless a standard render is determined to be more time-efficient.

After Vegas has completed the render process, if automatic control was selected in the Print to Tape dialogs, Vegas will start the DV/HDV machine automatically and print the project to tape with no further input from or involvement by the user. In a situation in which manual control has been selected in the Print to Tape dialog box, Vegas will prerender the recompressed sections and then wait for a click in a countdown box. Vegas will then count down from 10, providing a beep at each second, until it reaches 3 seconds. It will then start to print to tape. To use this manual feature effectively, allow Vegas to count down and, when the counter reaches 3 and no more beeps are heard, click Record on the tape machine. These steps usually provide enough leader time for various tape machines to get up to speed and begin the recording process.

Exporting Projects to Third-Party Applications

Sometimes it is necessary to export video Events from Vegas to use in a third-party application, for compositing, color grading, or the like. When you're exporting, files should be exported at the best possible resolution, and choices are therefore limited. If DV files (standard def) are exported from Vegas using the standard NTSC-DV settings, most third-party applications can read the files, but until Sony opens its codec up to other applications to use, those third-party applications can't write back to the Sony codec. Using the Microsoft codec really isn't a solution either since it limits quality output too much. Therefore an uncompressed, sequential image file or .mxf codec are the answers.

Uncompressed Files

In the **File | Render As | Video For Windows/AVI** dialog box, an uncompressed setting can be chosen. Understand that using this output method will exponentially increase render times.

Choose a preset such as **NTSC DV** if that matches your project. In the Video Format drop-down, choose **Uncompressed**. Be certain to uncheck the **Create an OpenDML compatible file** option. Most third-party applications cannot read these file types yet.

Another option is to use Quick-Time for output, with its numerous options. Some Vegas users have found great success using either

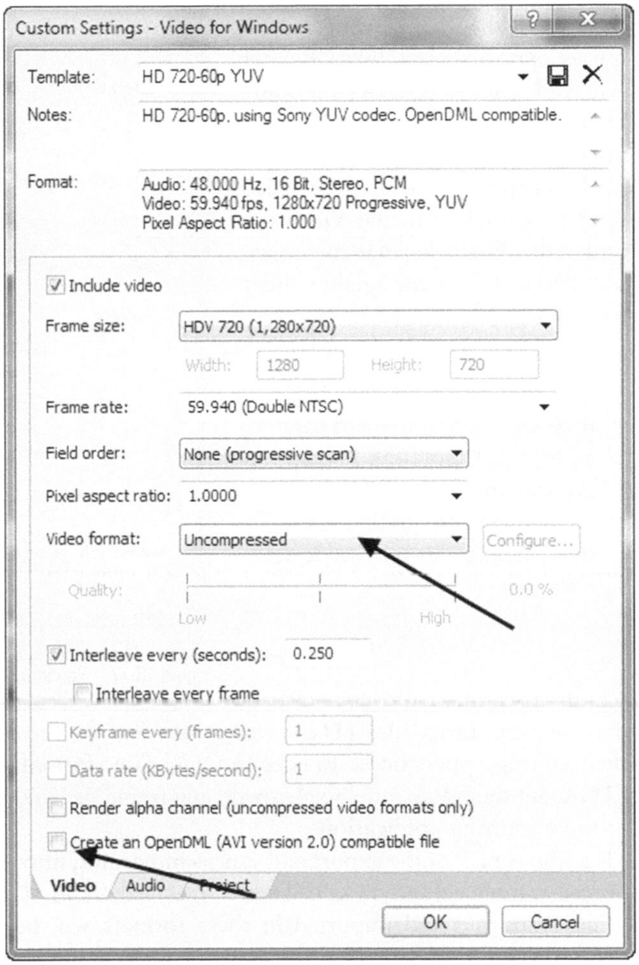

Figure 13.16   Select **Uncompressed** in the **Video** tab in the rendering options. This option also allows the uncompressed file to retain an alpha channel, should one exist or have been created in the editing process.

sequential or base file PNG as an output option that both Vegas and most third-party applications can read. The PNG format is a lossless compression format that keeps file sizes more manageable and render times slightly faster than using a standard uncompressed output.

To render to the QuickTime format and its various codecs, select the part of the file or Event that requires export. Select **File | Render As**, and choose **QuickTime/.mov** from the **Save As** menu. Choose a preset and click the **Custom** button. In the **Project** tab, select **Best** video rendering quality. In the **Video** tab under the **Video Format** menu, select **PNG**. Adjust the quality slider to **100%**.

PNG and TGA sequences packaged in a QuickTime package are known as *contained image sequences* and contain everything needed to play back as a movie.

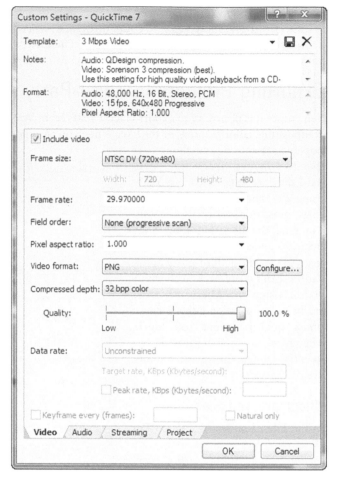

Figure 13.17   Rendering to a PNG/QuickTime format is a high-quality output method for exporting to a third-party application.

Animators and rotoscope artists may require Targa files (TGA) for their editing applications. Render to QuickTime format, select the **Video** tab, and select **Format | TGA**. Set the frame rate, pixel aspect, and frame size in their menus according to the requirements of the importing application.

If audio is part of the export and sync is important, move to the **Audio** tab and change the default output sample rate to **48 kHz/16 bits**, rather than 44.1/16 that QuickTime asks for.

Files exported and imported in these formats will be clean and without quality loss. Using any codec or compressed format between applications runs a risk of loss of quality, so experiment with various outputs to discover what is best for each particular situation. This upsampling/ downsampling is a foolish thing to do, since video always loses some information in the up-/ downsample. Some applications upsample imported DV as 4:2:2 or 4:4:4. Use caution and check files carefully for color accuracy when you're upsampling or downsampling between images.

Figure 13.18 Render a Targa file by using the QuickTime option in the **Render As** dialog box. The QuickTime authoring tools must be installed on the system so that you can access this menu.

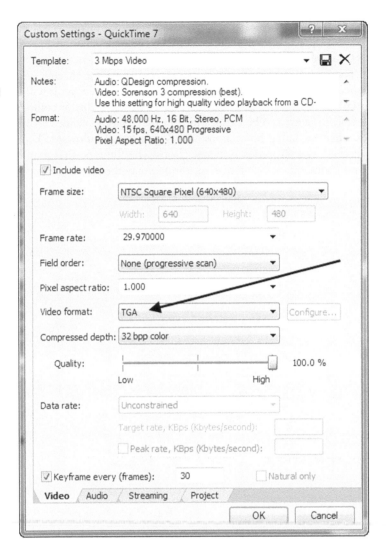

 Tip_____

My personal preference to ship frames from one application to another is to output from Vegas as an XDCAM file. The XDCAM MXF file format may be read by virtually every NLE available. In the **Render As** dialog box, choose **Sony MXF** from the **Save As Type** drop-down. In the **Template** drop-down, select the template that fits your format.

Sometimes files need to be opened in another editing or compositing application. For example, when you're working with tools like Particle Illusion, AfterEffects, or similar compositing tools, a background plate may be needed. In Vegas there are a few options for exporting to other applications.

Most often, composites will need to be exported from Vegas with transparency/alpha channel as part of the workflow. There are limited file types that will support 32 bit file formats that include RGBA information.

The easiest and most common output format for sharing with other applications is to use an uncompressed YUV file. This will be a very large file, yet it will be pristine and should open in virtually any application available today, without codec or compatibility issues.

Select the area to be exported from the Vegas Timeline. Browse to **File | Render As**, and in the **Render As** dialog box, choose the **Video For Windows/AVI** format from the drop-down menu. In the lower drop-down menu, choose the file type that matches the source footage resolution and frame rate. Once rendered, the file may then be sent out to another application for editing.

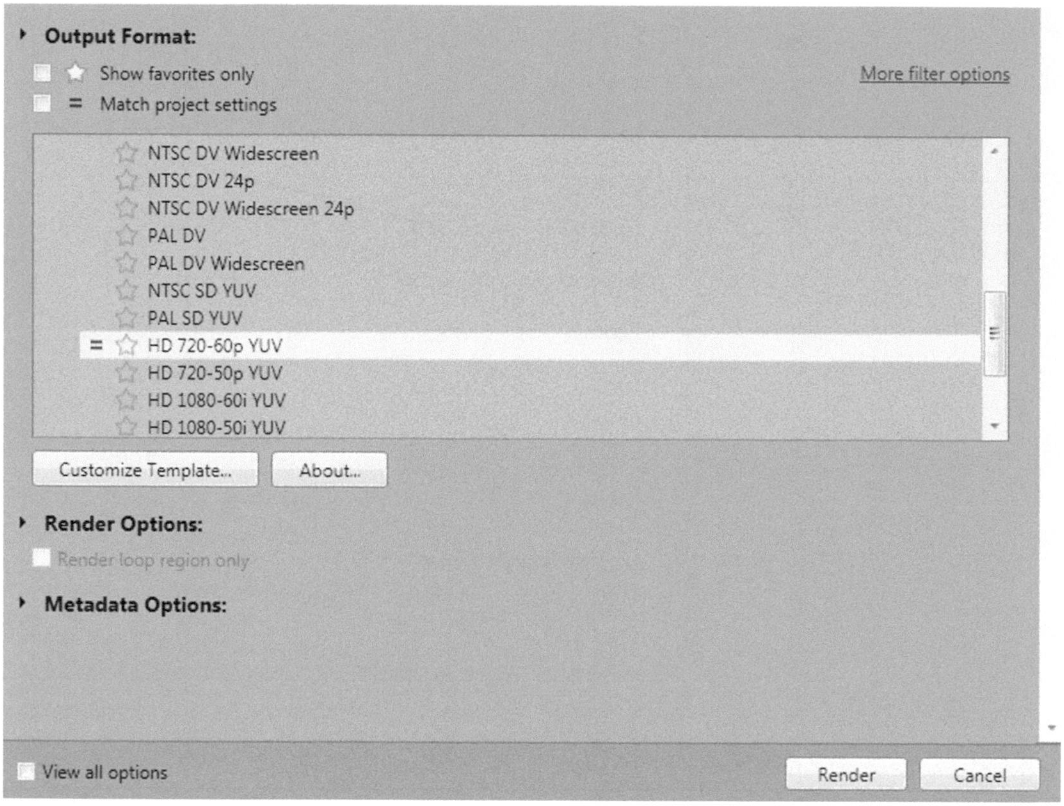

▸ **Output Format:**

☐ ☆ Show favorites only

☐ = Match project settings

More filter options

☆ NTSC DV Widescreen
☆ NTSC DV 24p
☆ NTSC DV Widescreen 24p
☆ PAL DV
☆ PAL DV Widescreen
☆ NTSC SD YUV
☆ PAL SD YUV
= ☆ HD 720-60p YUV
☆ HD 720-50p YUV
☆ HD 1080-60i YUV
☆ HD 1080-50i YUV

Customize Template...   About...

▸ **Render Options:**

☐ Render loop region only

▸ **Metadata Options:**

☐ View all options   Render   Cancel

Figure 13.19

Another option is to render the file as a New Track. This will provide an in/out perfect clip that will match the original source I/O points and may be added as a take to the source clip/Event. Browse to **Tools | Render to New Track** (or use the shortcut **Ctrl + M**). This will open a similar dialog box. Use the **Video For Windows/AVI** and choose the format that matches the source footage.

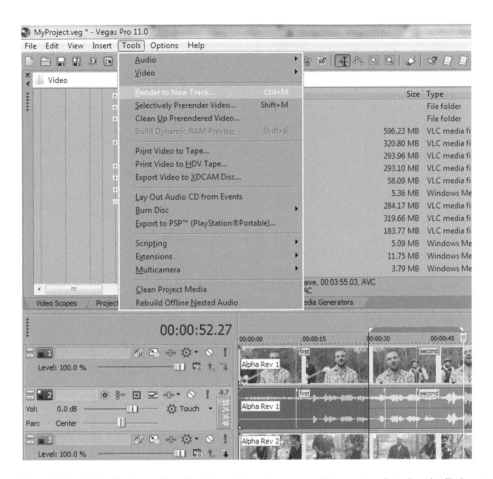

Figure 13.20   Using **Render to New Track** provides a placement-perfect export so that when the file is returned to Vegas after the external application is finished with the file, it will return in place and no movement, import, or further effort are required. Merely save the file to its original name when exporting from the third-party/external application.

Other options include rendering a PNG or TGA sequence; these are great for working in various compositing tools without using as much storage space as the uncompressed YUV file. Browse to **File | Render As | Image Sequence** and choose one of the formats best suited to the external/third-party application. As mentioned previously, PNG and TGA are common formats and may contain an alpha channel. Some applications refer to sequences of individual PNG/TGA files as *base image sequences*. This differentiates them from packaged PNG/TGA files contained in a QuickTime PNG/TGA file, sometimes referred to as a *contained image sequence*.

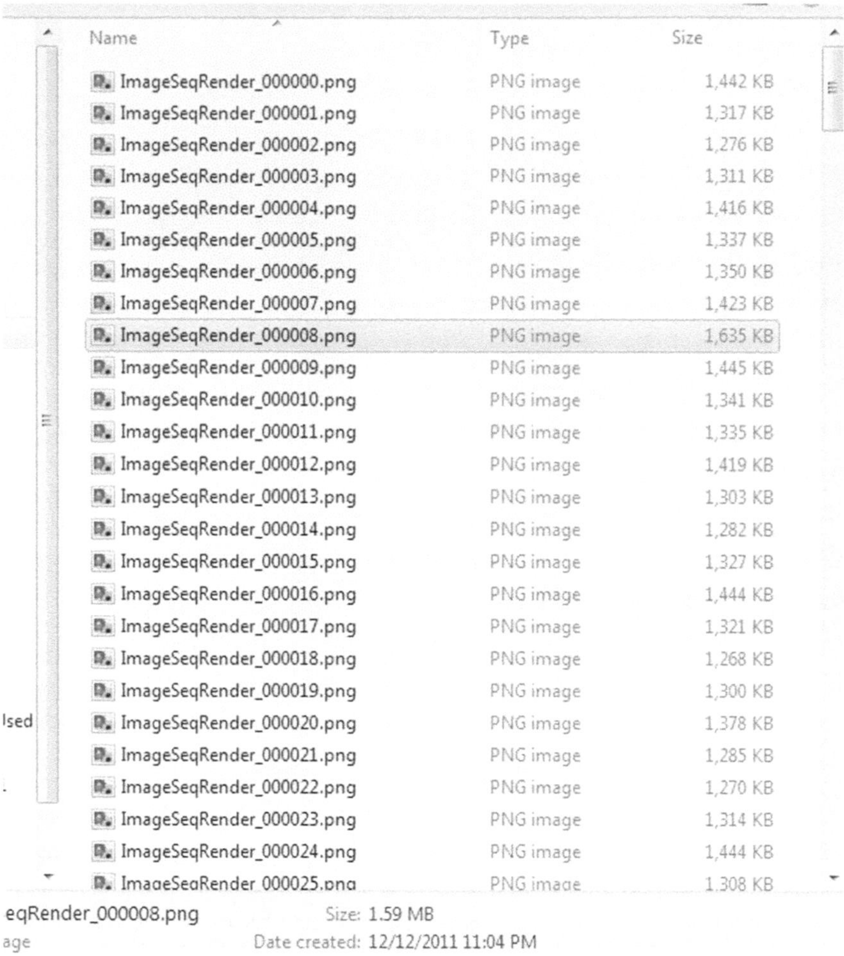

Name	Type	Size
ImageSeqRender_000000.png	PNG image	1,442 KB
ImageSeqRender_000001.png	PNG image	1,317 KB
ImageSeqRender_000002.png	PNG image	1,276 KB
ImageSeqRender_000003.png	PNG image	1,311 KB
ImageSeqRender_000004.png	PNG image	1,416 KB
ImageSeqRender_000005.png	PNG image	1,337 KB
ImageSeqRender_000006.png	PNG image	1,350 KB
ImageSeqRender_000007.png	PNG image	1,423 KB
ImageSeqRender_000008.png	PNG image	1,635 KB
ImageSeqRender_000009.png	PNG image	1,445 KB
ImageSeqRender_000010.png	PNG image	1,341 KB
ImageSeqRender_000011.png	PNG image	1,335 KB
ImageSeqRender_000012.png	PNG image	1,419 KB
ImageSeqRender_000013.png	PNG image	1,303 KB
ImageSeqRender_000014.png	PNG image	1,282 KB
ImageSeqRender_000015.png	PNG image	1,327 KB
ImageSeqRender_000016.png	PNG image	1,444 KB
ImageSeqRender_000017.png	PNG image	1,321 KB
ImageSeqRender_000018.png	PNG image	1,268 KB
ImageSeqRender_000019.png	PNG image	1,300 KB
ImageSeqRender_000020.png	PNG image	1,378 KB
ImageSeqRender_000021.png	PNG image	1,285 KB
ImageSeqRender_000022.png	PNG image	1,270 KB
ImageSeqRender_000023.png	PNG image	1,314 KB
ImageSeqRender_000024.png	PNG image	1,444 KB
ImageSeqRender_000025.png	PNG image	1,308 KB

eqRender_000008.png   Size: 1.59 MB
age   Date created: 12/12/2011 11:04 PM

Figure 13.21 Rendering to a PNG sequence is fast, lossless compression, saves on file space, and is importable to virtually every application in the NLE world. This is one of two methods I commonly use when I'm sharing files with or receiving files from compositors.

A sequential PNG/TGA is a series of PNG or TGA images that the NLE will interpret as individual frames of video. They are imported as a range or series of still images and combined as a clip, creating video from the sequential, individual frames.

 Tip_____

Some editors master from PNG sequences, as rendering the master provides protection against system crashes. If the render fails partway through the process, the render may be restarted where the last frame failed once the system is back up and running.

There is one more option to consider here, a very useful one for exporting for Final Cut or Avid systems to avoid a recompression of the file on the receiving end. The Sony .mxf file format is standard in all professional applications due to the XDCAM HD systems being used in thousands of broadcast houses around the world. Browse to **File | Render As | Save As Type | Sony MXF**. In this dialog box, choose one of the 4:2:2 file formats that best matches the source file. This will render out a .mxf file format in a compression that will save space, be very easy to decode, and have pristine file format quality.

EDLs and Vegas

One of the perceived weak points in Vegas is the lack of OMF and advanced EDL support. Before saying anything else, I'll comment that Vegas is a finishing tool. It's designed to be used as a start-to-finish solution.

That said, Vegas provides scripting tools for CMX 3600-style EDL export and AAF export that will support standard editing functions. Several steps must be taken to have accurate EDL value.

First, make sure your tapes are clearly and cleanly labeled, since the third-party application will likely require recapturing of the media on the tape. Most applications will not be able to read the timecode from the Vegas Vidcap application.

Second, edit the media as a cuts-only project. Most systems will not be able to read wipes and color correction. Set your project up as a drop-frame project rather than nondrop frame.

Third, use the **Tools | Scripting | Export EDL** feature. This will generate an EDL to be provided to whomever will be using the edits to finish their final project.

On the audio side, there are those times that something must be imported or exported from Pro-Tools, Avid, Logic, SADiE, and other applications.

Perhaps someone is sending you a file generated in another application and you want to use their EDL information in Vegas, or perhaps you prefer to work in Vegas but your coworker prefers another application. There is a product from Solid State Logic that will convert most any format of EDL to another format of EDL. This company has perceived the difficulties of all the various studio formats out there and has created a killer product that works for more than just Vegas users, because this is an industry-wide issue.

Pro-Convert is a great application that no professional studio should be without. It's capable of dealing with fades, markers, and in and out points and is basically just a series of clicks. Pro-Convert will examine the project settings of the original EDL and set up the conversion based around those settings. You need to alter these settings only if you are taking the EDL to a project that has different settings, but in most instances, you'll use the default properties.

This tool will work in most any format you can imagine, converting Vegas files to or from Samplitude/Sequoia, Audition/Cool Edit Pro, SAW, Wavelab, SADiE3 and 4, Sonic Studio, Discreet edit, AES31, OpenTL, and OMFI formats. If you are working with a SONAR user, you'll use the OMFI format to import and export for Vegas.

Visit the Solid State Logic Website at http://solidstatelogic.com.

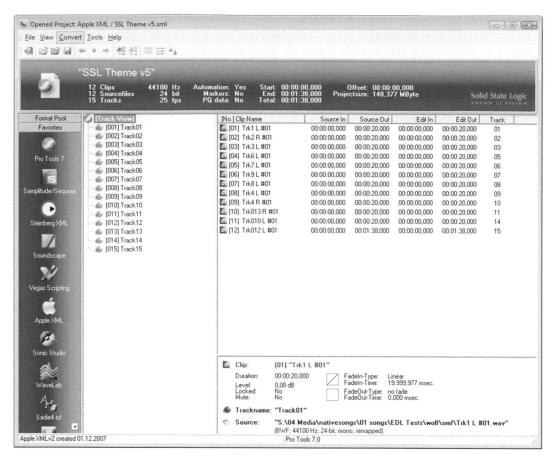

Figure 13.22 Solid State Logic's Pro-Convert will allow you to convert most any audio EDL to a format that Vegas can read or a format that Vegas files can be read in.

AAF Import/Export

No, this isn't related to the band Alien Ant Farm. AAF, or Advanced Authoring Format, is one of a few current standards by which various DAWs and NLEs can share project files. AAF export from Vegas works very well with Adobe Premiere Pro CS4, for example. Using AAF, basic project information may be shared. You can export a project from Vegas and open it in Premiere Pro, Final Cut Pro, Avid products, and a few other NLE systems via AAF, but it's not a perfect transport format protocol. Don't expect things like composites, color-corrected video, or the majority of your transitions to open. It's primarily a means of getting the media onto a new timeline in exact placement with a few additional granules of sugar thrown on top for sweetness, but it's not the total answer.

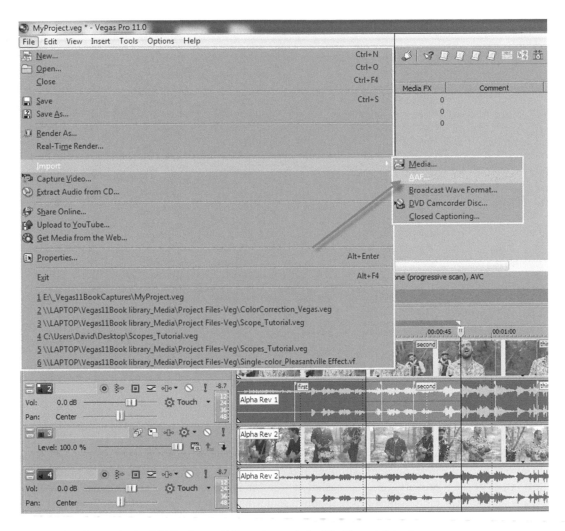

Figure 13.23   Browse for the AAF file that you'd like to import via the **File | Import** dialog box.

To import an AAF project format, choose **File | Import | AAF.** Browse to the location of the AAF file that you'd like to import. This will import all media associated with that project file. Note the word *media.* Any non-media file, such as generated titles or masks that are from a specific application that is not in graphic format, will not be imported. Bars and tones are also not imported if they have been generated by an application-specific process.

Transitions (other than cross-fades), color correction, any special filters, audio processors, and composites will also not be imported, since these are not part of the AAF format. Basically, AAF allows an application to locate assets *outside* the application, along with its relevant in/out points on a timeline.

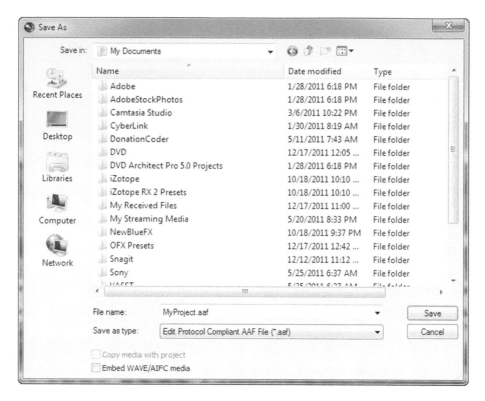

Figure 13.24   Choose **File | Save As** to create the AAF file for export.

This is one of the drawbacks of the AAF format. AAF is a cuts-only transportation format from one application to another. Although more robust than a typical CMX EDL export/import format, it doesn't provide perfect translation from one application to another. Let's hope that Vegas supports the more robust MXF, although somewhat complementary to AAF, in the very near future.

To export an AAF for import into After Effects, SADiE, Final Cut Pro, Avid Express, Cakewalk, or other AAF-supported applications, choose **File | Save As**. From **Save As Type**, choose **Edit Protocol Compliant AAF File**. Use this format for most exports. You'll likely want to check the **Embed Wave/AIFC media** box for audio export in the Wave or AIFC codecs. You'll also note that there is an **Avid Legacy AAF File** option. Use that for exporting to older Avid software tools. The **Embed Wave/AIFC media** checkbox is not available for the Avid Legacy AAF File option.

Another option to check is that the default checkbox for **AAF Export—Use frame unit for audio** in the **Options | Preferences | General** tab is enabled. Otherwise, audio is exported in sample units rather than frame units. Many NLE systems will not be able to read the AAF project file correctly if video is in frame units and audio is in sample units. Therefore, to ensure maximum compatibility, check this box.

Figure 13.25   Find the **AAF Export—Use frame unit for audio** option in the **Options | Preferences | General** tab. Use this as a default for exporting AAF files.

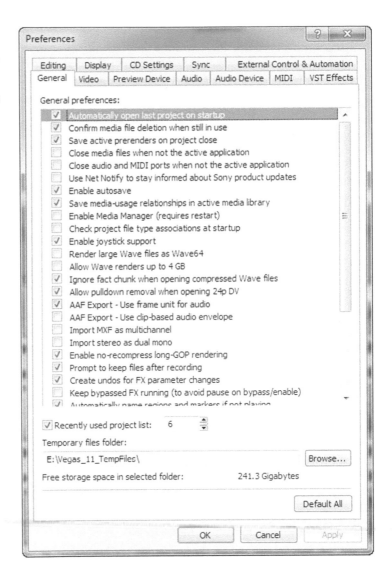

Outputting Other Than AVI Files

Vegas has output capability for nearly every output format, including MPEG-2 and MPEG-4. Although Vegas does a reasonable job of outputting MPEG-1, the primary MPEG format output focus is on MPEG-2, which is used for DVD encoding and authoring. The primary benefit of an MPEG-1 file is that although it's an old codec and not of top quality, MPEG-1 files do indeed play on just about any player in the world.

Burning a Disc from the Timeline

Vegas offers users the ability to burn an SD or HD disc straight from the timeline. This is a useful function for sending out pre-viz for clients where the Internet doesn't fit into the workflow. DVDs from the timeline may be SD (standard DVD) or HD (as a Blu-ray disc burned on either DVD 5 or BD disc). HD discs can't run much longer than 20 minutes, give or take (dependent on the bitrate used to encode video), but they offer a great way to get HD on a disc for playback on PS3 or Blu-ray players.

Browse to **Tools | Burn Disc**. Several options will be shown. DVD and Blu-ray are the two we're working with.

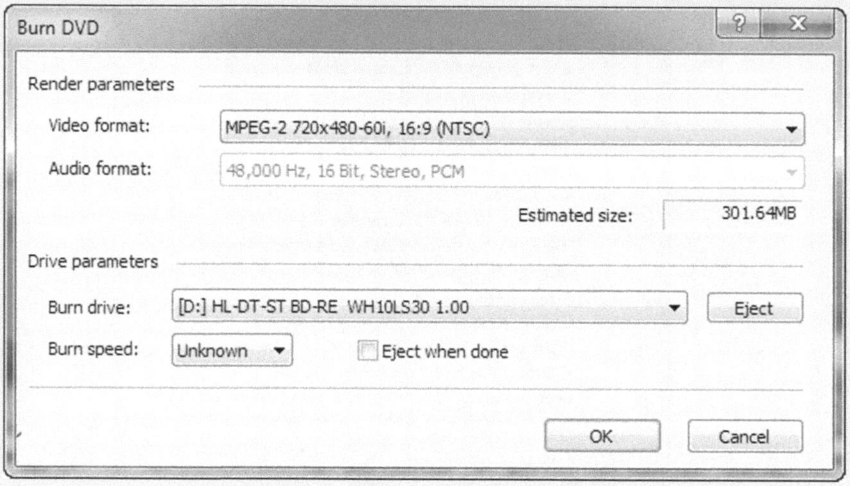

Figure 13.26

If the disc is to be SD, select **DVD**. A few options are presented related to NTSC, PAL, widescreen, or 4:3 display, and choices are found in the drop-down menu. If the disc is to be HD, select **Blu-ray disc** from the menu, and a different dialog box opens. The BD dialog box offers choices for AVC or MPG2 for HD.

If there are markers on the timeline, they may be used as chapter markers in a timeline disc burn. Check the box for timeline chapter markers if this is desired. The video may be stretched to fill the screen, if desired. This option is useful when the desired output format does not match the frame aspect ratio of your project. This generally isn't a useful feature in HD. If the video is derived from a small-format camera that shoots a 1280 x 960 stream, any stretching should have been done either via Pan/Crop or in the Switches mode at the video Event level. If there are stills that don't quite fill the screen and video that does, this too should have been accounted for via either switches or Pan/Crop. However, if there is some potential that a title card or some other Event didn't match the project properties, and speed to disc is important, by all means check this box.

Vegas Pro and Vegas Movie Studio both have a disc size calculator in the **Burn Disc** option. Be sure to not exceed much more than 4 GB for a standard DVD; leave yourself some overhead.

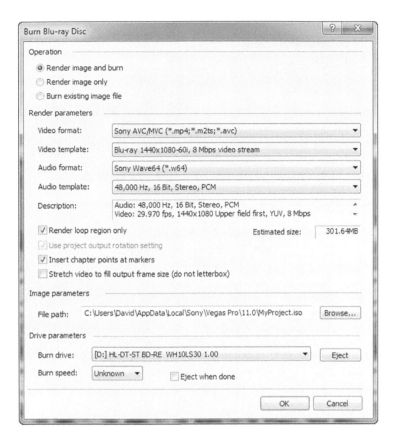

Figure 13.27   In this dialog box, users choose MPG2 or AVC for HD disc burns. AVC is generally the better choice for HD playback on BD devices. AC3 audio is the most common choice. If the audio is a musical performance and pristine quality with wide dynamic range is necessary, choose the WAV 64 option in the audio drop-down. Note the file size change in the disc size estimation.

In the **Image Parameters** box, Vegas will store the rendered file used to burn the disc. Be sure there is enough free space on the disc specified in this dialog box. By default, this burns the image to the C:\Users\XXX\AppData\Local\Sony\Vegas Pro\11.0 folder.

Additional Rendering Options

Vegas has additional rendering options available, giving users a wide variety of choices. For example, a loop region can be defined on the timeline by creating a selection and pressing **Q**, which will turn on the **Looping** tool. In the **Render As** dialog box, rendering only a loop region is an option that is valuable when only selections need to be rendered out.

Another option is to stretch the video to fill the screen. This option prevents black bars from being added to the top, bottom, or sides of a video render that has an aspect ratio different from that of the project. Check this box in the **Render As** options if you want to stretch to fill the aspect ratio. This checkbox is visible after you click **View all options**.

Figure 13.28 Defining a loop region for rendering allows select sections to be rendered for output or export.

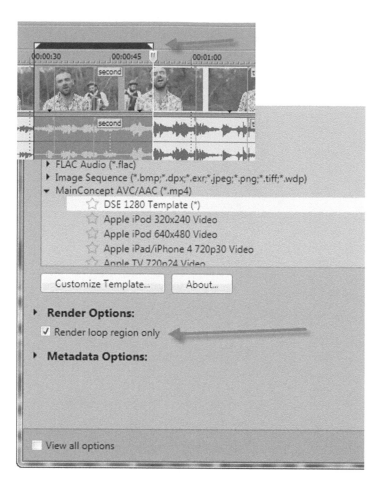

Figure 13.29 Pillar Boxed rendered for RGB output/Windows Media. Avoid delivering files this way to UGC sites; it becomes very ugly when combined with the way the UGC site processes the video.

Figure 13.30   Stretched image, using the **Stretch to Fill Screen** option.

High-Definition Video

Vegas offers the ability to edit and output high-definition media in 720p, 1080i, and 1080p formats. Refer to Chapter 1's "Capturing Video" section for details and specifics on ingesting the various flavors of high-definition media using Vegas Pro and Vegas Movie Studio.

In Vegas, 24p has some very significant benefits and support. Transitions, titles, and filters are optimized in Vegas for 24p. Vegas also has specific support for cameras that shoot in native 24p. Vegas autodetects 2-3 and 2-3-3-2 pull-down at capture and previews and prints to tape in the 24p format when these cameras are used. The 2-3 and 2-3-3-2 pull-downs are performed on the fly in Vegas with no additional hardware required. Vegas also allows for preview on external monitors at 24p.

On the output side, Vegas can output a still image sequence up to 4096 x 4096, is capable of outputting 1080p, 1080i, or 720p at the 24p frame rate, and can print to tape at 24p as well. Windows Media has support for 24p/HD, and streaming file sizes are smaller at 24p than at 29.97. 24p also offers up to 25% additional disk-space savings on a DVD.

The 24p option will continue to exist for many years to come, but the level of 24p accessibility has created more problems than it has created great films.

Vegas edits and prints media at 720p with frame rates of up to 60 fps, at resolutions of 1080p with frame rates of 24 and 29.97 fps, and at 1080i with frame rate of 60 fps (29.97 interlaced). With the output capability of 24 fps/progressive scan, video shot with 24p will stay in its native format with no pull-down.

When you're working with high-definition media, full-frame-rate playback is very difficult to achieve because of the load on the processor. Be aware that playback at full frame rate is unlikely on all but the fastest systems.

With Vegas's ability to recapture media via the Project Media or to work with originally captured media, try to capture using a dual-stream card where possible, so that a low-resolution/compressed capture takes place at the same time as the high-definition media is being captured. Most high-definition cards allow for this to take place. Edit on the timeline using the lower-resolution media and replace media with the high-definition video in the Project Media when you finish editing. This process will allow editing to take place with full motion and full resolution without taxing the processor as heavily as native high-definition media. Rendering to a high-speed HDD system, the media can then be printed to tape either using a high-definition card, capture tool, and high-definition tape machine or using the HDD delivered to a service bureau for final print and replication for distribution. This is a form of offline/online editing but can be done natively with Vegas as both a rough-cutting and a finishing tool. By using the Super Sampling Envelope tool, even DV can be effectively upsampled to HD output. Bear in mind that render times will be fairly slow on longer projects. Upsampling from resolutions of 720 x 480 to 1920 x 1080 will more than double the resolution of DV. Of course, the image will be quite soft. Well-shot DV does upsample to 720 fairly well in Sony Vegas.

When you're working with high-definition media, current IDE and some SATA drive speeds will prove to be unsatisfactory for most users. Use Firewire 800, USB 3, or eSATA drives for best results.

Figure 13.31   Rendering and output settings include high-definition capability in Vegas.

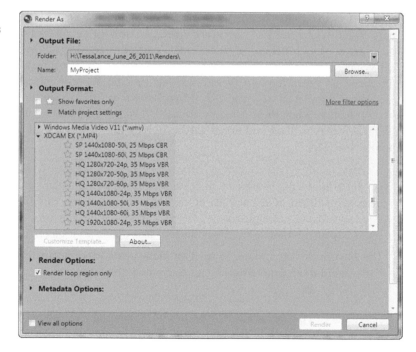

4:2:2 MPEG Capability (Not Available in Sony Vegas Movie Studio)

Vegas is also capable of rendering broadcast streams for delivery to a media server in a broadcast facility such as a Telestream or Matrox Videoserver. This functionality is not for the typical Vegas user but designed exclusively for professional broadcast delivery formats. 4:2:2 broadcast streams have a delivery data rate of up to 80 Mbps, compared to a DVD delivery data rate of up to 15 Mbps. Most DVDs are at a substantially lower bitrate, but the spec allows for a higher than the currently used delivery bitrate.

The 4:2:2 format provides for greater luma and chroma information in the stream, allowing for higher-quality video broadcast display instead of the standard 4:2:0 delivery of consumer-oriented DVD MPEG delivery.

Although it might be tempting to render to this format, there is nothing to be gained by the end user unless it's as an archival or Digital Intermediary (DI) format. No set-top player can play back files at this data rate. If you intend to deliver an MPEG-encoded project for broadcast, check with the broadcast house in advance to learn at what data rate they'd like to see the project finished.

Codecs

Vegas Pro (not available in Sony Vegas Movie Studio) has a 4:2:2 YUV codec. This is of great benefit to users who are rendering files to archive or for multidelivery. Faster than rendering uncompressed and enabling better image quality than 4:2:2 media, this codec benefits HD and SD projects, particularly for archive.

Where this is of value to DV editors is when a project needs to be archived or delivered in multiple formats. Render the project to the 4:2:2 YUV codec, and then use the new master .avi file to render MPEG, streaming media, and any other secondary format. However, using this as an intermediary codec serves little value if delivering to a final MPEG format when sourced from DV. Encoding MPEG from the timeline is always the best proposition if MPEG is the only delivery format.

When DV is dropped on the Vegas Timeline, the source video has already compressed at 4:1:1. When color correction, transitions, and other changes to the media are applied, Vegas upsamples those changes to 4:4:4, or uncompressed media in these processes. The uncompressed sections then become compressed when the final file is rendered. Rendering to 4:2:2 keeps the "new" media at a higher quality than the 4:1:1 render. However, when media is rendered from the timeline to MPEG, it's rendered at 4:2:0, creating yet a third transcode in the process of rendering. Therefore, if you are rendering any sort of project to a single-delivery format, it's always best to render to that format directly from the timeline, saving transcodes and time. However, if there are multiple-delivery formats required, it's a good idea to render to either uncompressed or the higher-quality 4:2:2 format to input to a batch encoder, ensuring that the original source file is of the highest quality available depending on allotment of time in the final rendering process.

There is no benefit of rendering 4:1:1 DV project files to 4:2:2 and then rendering the 4:2:2 to MPEG, unless again, the final source files will be delivered in some format other than DV and in one or more other delivery formats. If you were to render to 4:2:2 and then convert that to

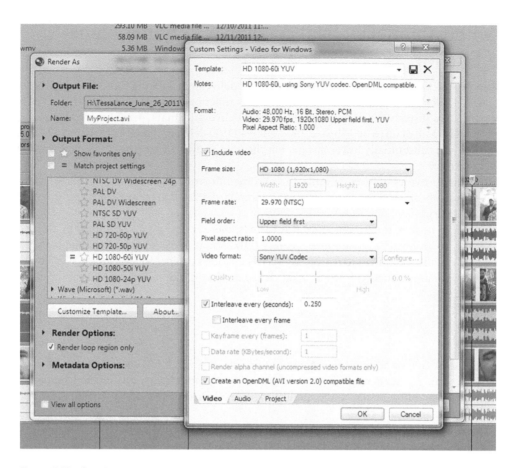

Figure 13.32   Sony has created a 4:2:2 YUV codec, found in Vegas Pro.

4:1:1 again for print to DV tape, information would actually be lost in the process due to transcoding (75% of the original DV color data will be lost).

The YUV codec is of great value if source is AVC, AVCHD, or MJPEG HD from small format cameras or HDSLR cameras. The 4:2:2 colorspace makes compositing (greenscreen in particular) easier and provides for better integrity during color correction where the color needs significant modification. AVC/AVCHD are not designed to be rendered more than once, and the YUV codec protects the relatively frail format when used in a professional workflow. Think of it this way: Pushing color and compositing are like moving dirt. Fine, dry dirt blows around and doesn't hold together well when a bulldozer is used to shove it around. Big heavy clods stay together more easily. The YUV codec will "clump" the fine, lightweight information of the AVC codecs into bigger clumps that hold together better.

Rendering to the 4:2:2 YUV codec is slower than rendering to the 4:1:1 Sony DV codec, as one might expect. Due to various optimizations, rendering to 4:2:0 AVC codecs is actually quite fast.

Scripting

Vegas has a feature that is terrific for users needing customized output and processing options. This feature uses JavaScript to define these behaviors. Vegas can literally be instructed to render several file types, to batch process, to match aspect ratios, even to build a video at random with random transitions from media in the Project Media! Scripts basically provide an open-ended function for Vegas users to implement code to instruct Vegas to provide unique behaviors.

To use scripting, you'll need to have the latest Microsoft .NET framework installed. The .NET framework can be downloaded at no cost from Microsoft. Visit www.microsoft.com/net/ to order a CD or download the framework.

Many scripts are available on the Sony Creative Software peer forum Website as well as on the VASST site, www.vasst.com. Writing scripts is a challenge for those not familiar with Visual Basic or JavaScript authoring. You can write scripts with any plain text editor, even Notepad. The Microsoft developer's Website (msdn.microsoft.com) is probably the most authoritative reference for the .NET scripting languages, but other tutorials are available on the Web. In addition, several books on JavaScript, C# .NET, and Visual Basic .NET are available from Amazon.com and other bookstores.

Figure 13.33   Access the scripts by selecting **Tools | Scripting | Run Script**.

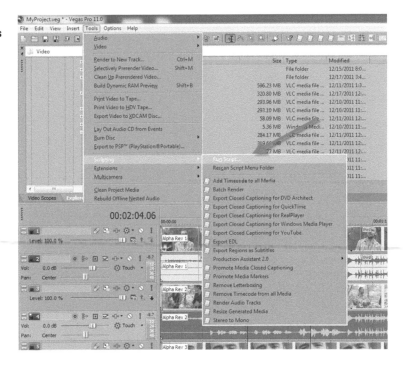

Running scripts can also appear to be intimidating when in truth running scripts is quite straightforward. After locating and downloading scripts, place them in a directory. To run a script, select **Tools | Scripting | Run Script**, which will open a browse dialog box. Browse to where the .vb or .js scripts are stored. After adding scripts to the folder, go to **Tools | Scripting | Rescan Script Menu Folder**. This will place scripts in the **Tools | Scripting** drop-down menu. This will save time in not needing to search out scripts in other folders.

Here is a sample .js script that opens three tracks each of Audio and Video:

```
/**
 * Program: TrackSetup.js
 * Description: This script will create some initial tracks in Vegas for Video,
 * Audio, Video Overlay, and Title. This is for people who don't
 * like the fact that Vegas starts without labeled tracks.
 *
 * Author: Johnny (Roy) Rofrano
 *
 * Date: March 29, 2010
 **/
import Sony.Vegas;
import System.Windows.Forms;
try
{
// Add three video tracks
AddTrack(1, MediaType.Video, "Title");
AddTrack(2, MediaType.Video, "Overlay");
AddTrack(3, MediaType.Video, "Video");
// Add threee Audio tracks
AddTrack(4, MediaType.Audio, "Audio");
AddTrack(5, MediaType.Audio, "Music");
AddTrack(6, MediaType.Audio, "Effects");
}
catch (errorMsg)
{
        MessageBox.Show(errorMsg, "TrackSetup Error", MessageBoxButtons.OK,
        MessageBoxIcon.Error);
}
/*
 * Adds a track to the project with a name and index
 */
function AddTrack(index : int, mediaType : MediaType, name : String)
{
        var track;
        if (mediaType == MediaType.Audio)
        {
        track = new AudioTrack(index, name);    // create audio track
        }
        else
        {
        track = new VideoTrack(index, name);    // create video track
        }
        Vegas.Project.Tracks.Add(track);        // add the track
}
```

Select the script you want to run, which will start the script. Scripts are like baseball cards that are traded among many Vegas users, and a small cottage industry has sprung from this concept of having an open engine. VASST and others offer for-purchase tools that take advantage of scripting operations, potentially saving users inestimable time, depending on the sort of workflow used.

It's easy to become dependent on scripts, since they can perform many mundane tasks with one button. And with key mapping, you can map scripts to any button you'd like, making Vegas a totally personal system. Scripts will continue to add to the power of Vegas and offer users a tremendous number of options.

One aspect of scripting that creates exceptional ease of use is to create a button on the toolbar for the script. This option allows rapid access to commonly run scripts. Up to 10 scripts may be associated with 10 buttons on the toolbar.

To place a button or script on the toolbar, double-click the toolbar, and the **Customize Toolbar** dialog box will open. Select a script button to add to the toolbar. In Figure 13.36, an **Export Closed Captioning** script is selected to be placed in the toolbar. This step places a button on the toolbar that will run the script with one click.

Figure 13.34   The script used in this instance runs the popular and highly useful Batch Render script. This script allows multiple output files from one project and one menu selection.

Figure 13.35   Assign a script to a button on the toolbar in Customize Toolbars. This button runs the Batch Render script from the Vegas Pro toolbar.

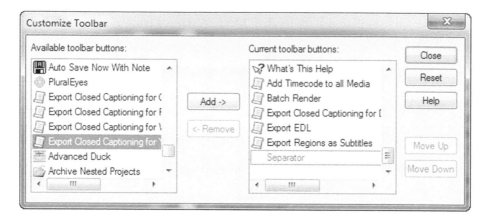

Figure 13.36   Select scripts for use in the Script browser.

Rotated Display Functions (Not Available in Vegas Movie Studio)

It's hard to go through an airport, nightclub, office building, or other high-traffic area without seeing vertically mounted displays. The Rotated Display tools in Vegas Pro make this type of content creation very easy and fast. Media can be rotated 190, 180, or 290° in angle.

Rotated projects begin in the Project Properties settings. Open the **Project Properties** by browsing to **File | Properties | Video**. In the upper portion of the Properties dialog box is a drop-down menu labeled **Output rotation**.

Note that there are three options; the 90° angles are the most common angles for creating display media and the 180° angle is most commonly used for editing footage that has come from footage recorded using a 35 mm adapter on the lens, such as the RedRock Micro adapter (these sorts of adapters turn the video upside-down during the recording process. 3D camera rigs may also have an upside-down image).

Set the rotation to the desired angle in the drop-down box and select **Apply**. This will rotate the display in the Preview window to the desired angle (if 180° was chosen, no visible change will occur).

Figure 13.37   An LCD screen turned 90°, displaying content.

Figure 13.38   Project Property settings for rotated displays.

Producing Rotated Media

The best method for creating vertical content is to shoot at a 90° angle. Many professional tripods allow for a camera to be rotated to a 90° angle. Shooting in this manner allows for stable video recording and will provide for a higher-quality finished product. Handheld shots are much more noticeable in a vertical display than in a horizontal display due to the unique nature of the display and the difference from what the eye is familiar with.

Any media on the timeline will maintain the original aspect ratio; it will simply become smaller in the display.

Nonvertical files placed on the Vegas Timeline will require some additional attention if you want the file to fill the vertical screen. There are two methods of managing the video.

Right-clicking the video Event and selecting **Properties** from the menu displays a **Rotation** option in the **Media** tab. Set the media to rotate and match the Project Properties setting. If the video was created using a rotated camera, this is the method best used.

Another option is to right-click the file and choose **Pan/Crop** (or use the **Pan/Crop** shortcut button found on all video Events). In the **Pan/Crop** dialog box, right-click the open area and choose **Match Output Aspect**. This will crop the video so that it fills the display. Be aware that resolution will be lost in the process and video may become softer.

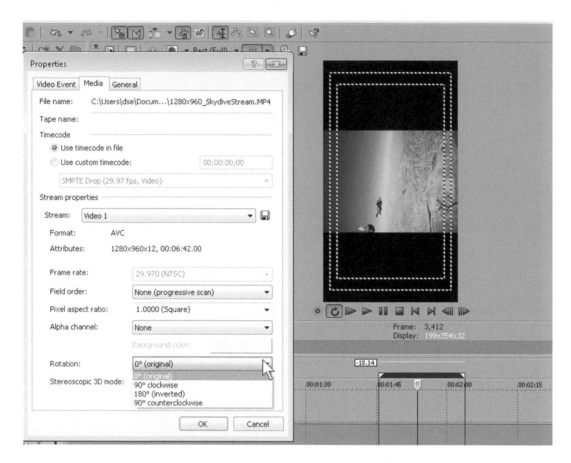

Figure 13.39   Graphics may be created in any image editor; simply change the rotation in the image editor to match the Project Properties after the rotation has been applied. Generally, images will be 480 x 655 or 576 x 702 when working with SD media and 720 x 1280, 1440 x 1080, or 1920 x 1080 when working with HD media.

Titles created in Vegas after Project Properties have been established will *not* be of the correct aspect/rotation angle (unless you're working with the Title/Text tool, the ProType Title tool, or the legacy title tools found in Vegas). Be aware of the narrow restrictions in this mode.

Figure 13.40   Optimal Preview is achieved by tearing the Preview window from the docked area and double-clicking the header bar of the Preview window.

When you're working with Cookie Cutter and other masking FX, the aspect of the mask may need to be changed, as most masks and FX are designed to function horizontally. Either modify the mask in a graphic editor or use Track Motion tools to modify or stretch the mask to fill the vertical display.

Playback of rotated media should be at full frame rate or frame rates identical to similar media playing in horizontal modes.

Figure 13.41   Vegas Preview window in a Rotated Display project.

Summary

This chapter presents so many options for output, some users may be confused about which codec/format to use for finished output. Here is a brief and general summation of outputs:

- Standard Definition Video to DVD
  - Widescreen or 4:3 mpeg2, 29.97fps, 8mbps, audio separate render (same filename) AC3
- Standard Definition DV to DV Tape
  - Widescreen or 4:3 .avi (DV codec), 29.97fps, audio included in render
- HD Video to DROID or iPhone
  - 1280 x 720 .mp4, 15, 24, or 29.97fps, 2.5mbps, audio included in render
- HD Video to YouTube, Vimeo, Facebook, or other UCG sites
  - 1280 x 720 .mp4, 29.97fps, 10mbps OR 1920 x 1080, 29.97fps, 16mbps, audio embedded
- HD Video to HDCAM
  - 1440 x 1080 29.97/23.97 over HD SDI (requires AJA or BlackMagic Design hardware and HDCAM deck such as the JH-3), audio included in render (up to 8 channels)

PART THREE

" ... This One Goes to 11 ... "

Understanding Keyframes

Keyframing is something that seems to vex many NLE users. Keyframing is not used in all editing applications, yet most NLE systems offer some level of keyframing. Users of older versions of Vegas will notice that a new keyframing tool has been implemented in version 11.

Keyframing is merely specifying a specific behavior at a specific point in time or over a period of time. Keyframes may be as simple as moving a title on and off a screen or as intense as hundreds of behavioral points set in a single frame. We all use keyframes in our lives; most of us either wear a wristwatch or use a mobile device to track the time of day.

- Think of a basic keyframe as the alarm clock that wakes you up in the morning.

- A more in-depth keyframe might wake you up, and the next keyframe tells you it's time to go to work.

- A deeper keyframe might tell you that when you go to work, you should wear a red tie, and so on.

Keyframing may be used to animate or transform an object, shift color or exposure as a camera moves across a panorama, create motion on still images, fade in/out an effect, move an effect on a screen, and so very much more. Vegas offers manual and automatic keyframes, and we'll look at various methods of using keyframes in this chapter.

Vegas departs from most NLE systems with regard to keyframes in that Vegas is Event-, track-, or project-based and separate Events may have their own keyframes within tracks that have their own keyframes within a project that has, yet again, its own set of keyframes. (Keyframes are not really useful in the Project Media invocation, since the timeline cannot be accurately played out in the Project Media window.)

Imagine doing a feature-length project and just before picture lock, a 10-frame error is discovered in a set of keyframes related to the entire timeline. In theory, adjusting those keyframes will impact the entire timeline, but with Vegas, not only can the keyframes be adjusted per Event, but the Event may be copied and pasted to another point in the timeline (or to another project timeline) with keyframes intact!

We'll start with a basic keyframe setting that animates motion. Open the **Keyframes.vf** project. A series of regions featuring a sunset and titles will open up. We're going to animate the title using multiple methods to demonstrate the flexibility of Vegas.

In Region 1 **Title Move,** select and click the **Edit Generated Media** button in the title.

Figure 14.1

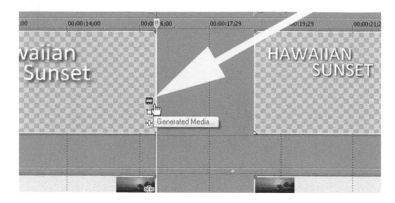

The Title tool will open. In the Title tool, expand the **Location** options by selecting the down arrow next to the word **Location.** This will open up a target. Notice the target in the upper left of the window. To the right of the location window is a small round button; this is the **Enable keyframe/ animate** button. (You might need to open the window wider to see all options.) Selecting this button will open a new timeline inside the Title tool.

Figure 14.2

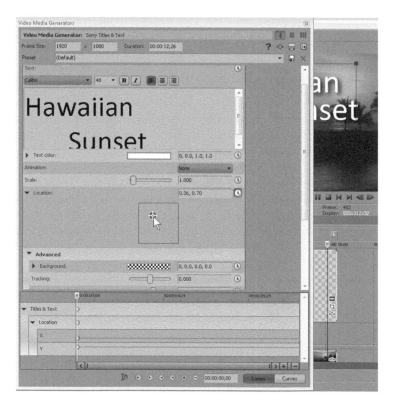

In this timeline, we'll be controlling the position of the title. Select and click the **Sync Cursor to Media Timeline** button in the bottom of the Title tool.

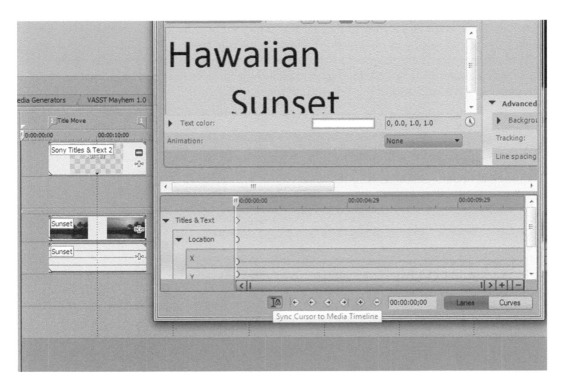

Figure 14.3   Enabling the **Sync** button will allow the keyframe timeline and the Event, track, or project timeline to be in sync. When the playhead is moved around the Event, track, or project, the playhead in the keyframe timeline will also move to match.

Because of the size and number of parameters in the Title tool, the scrollbars at the side may need to be moved down for you to see the entire keyframe timeline. In the keyframe timeline, place the cursor at the end of the timeline (should be at **00:00:12:26**). Now place the cursor over the target in the **Location** window and drag the title target to the lower right of the Location window. The keyframe timeline will move and auto-insert a new keyframe where the playhead is positioned. The keyframe timeline will now display a diagonal line in its X and Y parameters.

 Tip_____

Double-clicking the Event and enabling looping (**Q** key) will allow you to see the movement of the title in real time. This helps visualize what the keyframe is doing.

The title is now moving diagonally from the top left to the bottom right. We can insert more keyframes into the timeline. Position the cursor in the middle of the keyframe timeline. In the bottom of the keyframe timeline is a CTI, or current time indicator. Enter a value of **00:00:05;25** and watch the playhead move on the keyframe and project timelines.

In the **Location** window, move the target to the lower left corner of the window. A new keyframe will be inserted in the Text lane, and two dots will be inserted to the X and Y lanes of the keyframe timeline. These mark the location of the title at that moment in time. If the Project timeline has not been playing in a loop, play the timeline and watch the title move.

As the title moves, it moves smoothly through all three positions. The smoothness of these positions may be controlled as well. In other words, movement does not need to be linear.

Right-click on a keyframe in the Y keyframe lane.

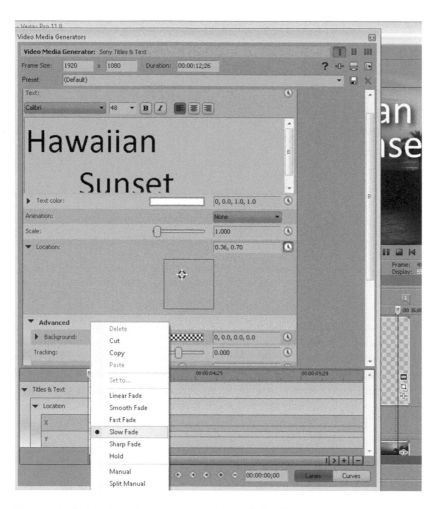

Figure 14.4   Each keyframe has its own ramp or interpolation. Movement from one keyframe to another may be ramped using these different settings.

Select the **Fast Fade** keyframe and watch the title change velocity. Right-click the last keyframe and select **Slow Fade** from the submenu, and the ramp/velocity will change again. These tools help create unique movements to match timing of other Events or to create a more organic feel.

Lanes and Curves

In the bottom of the keyframe timeline, you'll see a pair of buttons labeled **Lanes** and **Curves**. In the preceding project we looked at Lanes. Click on the **Curves** button to see a representation of the way the keyframes are moving the text. This view offers even greater control of how the interpolation curves function. The Curves function is not available on all FX.

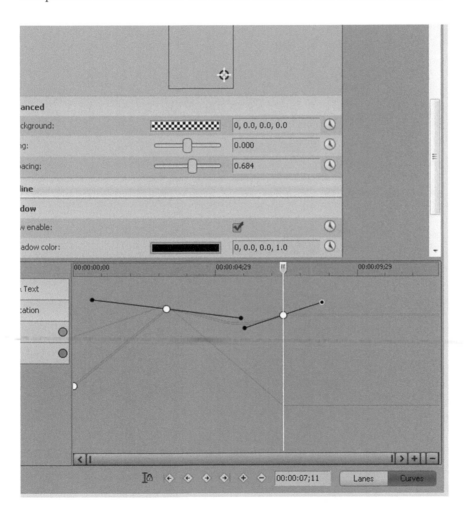

Figure 14.5   In the Curves view, greater control of keyframe interpolation is available. By right-clicking and choosing **Manual** or **Split Manual**, Bezier curve control splines are enabled and provide greater control of keyframe behavior.

In the **Title** tool, click the red **X** location button, and the three keyframes inserted in the **Lanes** view become visible. Right-click the first one in the **Curves** view, and choose **Manual**. A Bezier spline will appear. This allows for manual control of the curve versus the preset control available in the Lanes view. Grab the handle of the spline and move it upward to smooth and accelerate the curve. Right-click the center keyframe and choose **Split Manual** from the submenu. A similar Bezier curve opens; however, each spline may be independently controlled. The Split Manual keyframe empowers extremely precise control of interpolation curves.

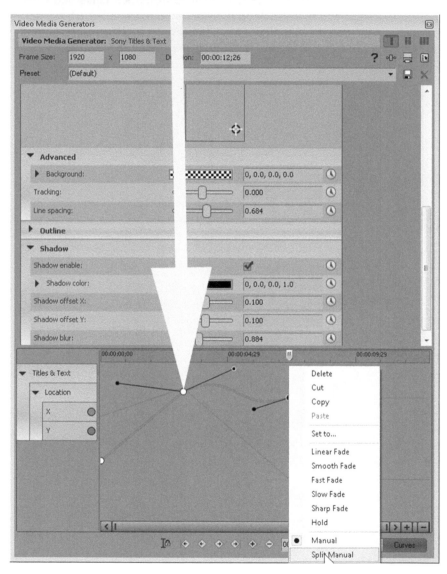

Figure 14.6

Now that you better understand this sort of keyframe, let's look at other uses of keyframes.

The second Event on the timeline is the same sunset with a similar title. The **Legacy Title** tool has been used over this image so that it moves a bit more smoothly. (The Legacy Title tool is much less CPU cycle-hungry.)

Right-click the title and select **Video Event Pan/Crop** from the submenu. The **Pan/Crop** tool may be used to move titles around and may be keyframed.

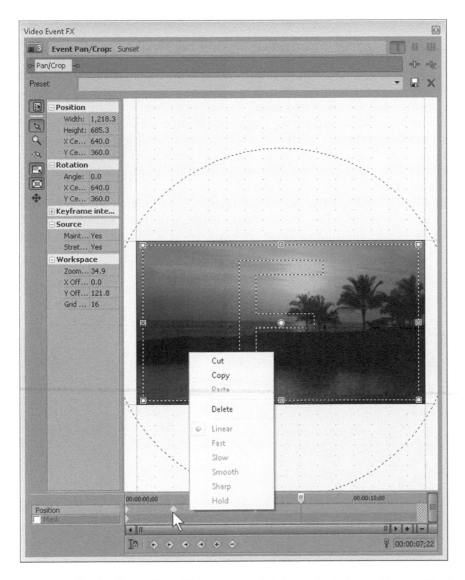

Figure 14.7 The Pan/Crop tool is useful in many ways, including moving text or graphics over video frames.

At the bottom of the **Pan/Crop** tool is a keyframe timeline labeled **Position**. A default keyframe is already inserted. Double-click in the **Cursor/playhead position** time box (lower-right corner), and enter a value of **525**. It will read 00:00:05;25. The cursor will move in the keyframe timeline. If the **Sync Cursor** button is engaged, the cursor/playhead will also move in the timeline.

Click inside the **Pan/Crop** window and move the window to the upper left (another keyframe indicator is inserted at the **05;25** mark). Now play the timeline and watch the title move exactly the same way it did in the other title exercise.

 Tip_____

Use the Legacy Titler for fast projects or on systems that have slower CPUs. The ProType Titler and the Standard title tool are both very CPU intensive.

This is a different keyframing approach and a different approach to moving titles around. Zooming in/out with the Pan/Crop tool will affect the resolution of images; simply moving them across the preview window will not affect resolution.

In the third instance of the sunset scene, there is a wingsuit skydiver; using the Track Motion tool, we're going to make him fly from the upper-left corner of the frame to the lower-right corner, with perspective control.

Place the cursor/playhead at the start of the third region. Both the graphic and the sunset are visible in the preview window.

Open the **Track Motion** tool on **Track Two**, and be sure the **Sync Cursor** button is enabled. Resize the skydiver graphic so that it is almost invisible. Do this by grabbing the lower-right corner of the box (it's highlighted by a circle) and click and drag the box to resize it. Move the Track Motion target to the upper-left corner of the Track Motion boundary.

Figure 14.8

In the Vegas Timeline, place the cursor/playhead in the middle of the sunset Event/clip. In the track motion dialog box, resize the graphic so that it is large, nearly filling the screen, and position the graphic so that it is outside the lower right boundary. Play the Event on the timeline, and the graphic will fly across and off screen.

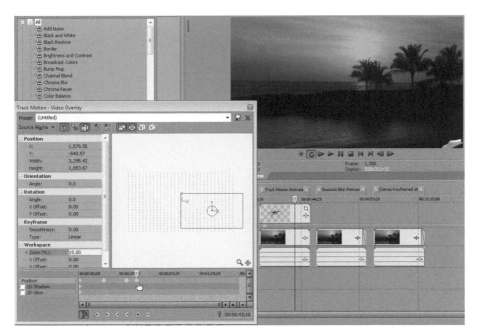

Figure 14.9

Allow the timeline to continuously loop on this Event so that the animation may be fine-tuned in the Track Motion window.

Once movement is from the correct places in the screen, let's modify the curve interpolation of the track motion to give the animation a more organic feel. Right-click the first keyframe in the Track Motion keyframe timeline and set it to **Slow**. Right-click the last keyframe and set it to **Fast**. This should provide a more natural flow/feel to the looping animation.

In Vegas Pro there is a fill light FX that provides the ability to animate a spotlight on the animation, causing light to shift as the fly-by occurs. This lends even more to the natural feel of the animation as it flies by.

The fourth region on the **Keyframes.vf** project timeline has a Gaussian blur inserted and animated. Click the green **FX** button on the Event in the third region to open the **FX properties** dialog box. Remove the FX plug-in; we'll rebuild this effect.

With the FX removed, drag the **Gaussian Blur** to the fourth Event on the timeline. The FX properties dialog box opens. Notice that the keyframe dialog box is not visible. Vegas Pro and Vegas Movie Studio hide the keyframe timeline to keep the view clutter-free. Clicking the **Animate** button at the bottom of the **FX Properties** dialog box will open the keyframe timeline for the Event.

Using the drop-down menu, set the first keyframe to **Soften** or **Medium Blur** (default). Enter the value of **2:00** in the **Cursor/playhead location** box. Move both horizontal and vertical range sliders to 0 in the **Gaussian Blur properties** dialog box and a new keyframe will be inserted.

Enter the value **1100** (Vegas will correctly interpret this as **00:00:11;00**). Select the **Add Keyframe** button.

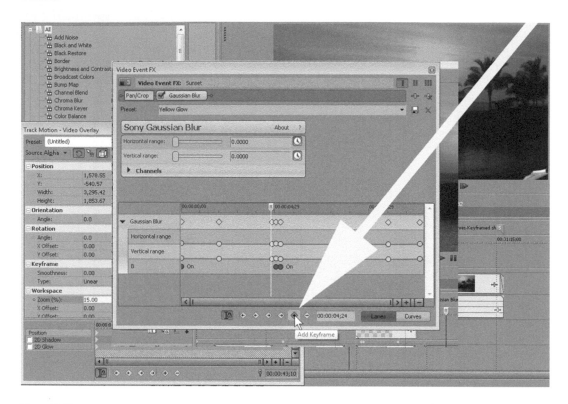

Figure 14.10

This will add another keyframe with the same value as the previous keyframe (parameters set at 0). Place the playhead at the end of the keyframe timeline, and either move the parameter controls to personal taste or select the **Soften** or **Medium Blur** preset. This will create a new keyframe at the end of the Event. Play the Event back to see the changes.

The fifth Event on the timeline has a Color Curves FX added to the Event that animates the sunset colors. Click the green **FX** button on the Event to open the FX Properties. Be certain the FX dialog box is not covering the Preview window and assure that the **Sync Cursor** feature is enabled. Click on the playhead in the keyframe timeline and hold it. Scrub the timeline to the right. The preview window will show the changes; more important, the **FX** dialog box will animate the changes of the **Color Curves** parameters in the dialog box, enabling you to see exactly how the curves are set and how they are being interpolated. Experiment with the keyframe interpolations and watch how the interpolation changes the way the curves ramp during the changes. Since sunsets are fairly linear, the keyframes are set (by default) to **Linear**.

Other Types of Keyframes

There are other kinds of keyframes that are not packaged in an FX filter. Locate and open the **Keyframe_Opacity.vf** file.

Several tracks have various kinds of envelopes inserted. All these envelopes have control points or nodes. Although most applications call these points *nodes* or *rubberband handles*, they are all keyframe points in the master timeline.

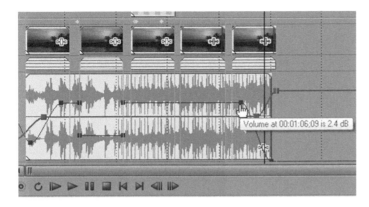

Figure 14.11   If the volume and pan controls are not seen, press the **V** (volume) key and the **P** (pan) key to make them visible. The control points on the various envelopes are keyframes, even if they're known by other names. Right-click any control point to determine interpolation curves. Vegas Pro allows for control of FX envelopes, automation envelopes, master bus/output envelopes, and other kinds of compositing envelopes that are not found in Vegas Movie Studio.

Vegas Pro users should open the **Keyframe_Opacity-VP.veg** file to see other types of envelopes and keyframes on the envelopes.

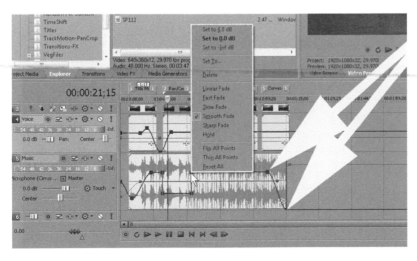

Figure 14.12   These node points are usually referred to as *rubberband handles* but in reality are just another kind of keyframe, controlling a specific behavior over a period of or point in time.

FX and Third-Party Tools

Working with Plug-ins in Vegas

One of the most exciting new features in Vegas Pro 11.0 and 10.0 is the move to OpenFX (OFX) plug-in technology. OFX is an open standard that allows plug-ins to be compatible with any host software that supports the standard. This is exciting for Vegas Pro editors because a whole world of existing high-quality plug-ins is now available for use in Vegas that previously were not. The other reason this is exciting is because OFX allows plug-ins to have tighter integration with Vegas. If you've ever used a plug-in only to find that it gives you a static image of the time-line where you were expecting to see a video preview, this limitation has just been lifted. OFX plug-ins have full access to the video stream so you can preview your video right in the plug-in's interface.

Several software companies have stepped up to Vegas and written plug-ins for the product. The tools that come with Vegas provide a wide variety of additional expressions and emotions for editors in Vegas; however, installing new plug-ins give editors far more arrows for their bows, as well as a feel and capabilities that the standard Vegas filters and effects don't provide. Boris FX, NewBlue, GenArts, ProDad, Pixelan Software, Red Giant, and VASST are just some of the companies that have released powerful tools for Vegas, and demos of some of these products are found on the DVD that accompanies this book.

Sony Production Assistant

Production Assistant is a plug-in for Sony Vegas Pro that was developed by the people at VASST. It is an automation tool that does exactly as its name implies: It assists in speeding up common production tasks and automates most of them. For example, users can insert a memory card from their camera into a card slot connected to the computer, and Production Assistant will sense the card, will begin transferring media to a user-defined location, and will populate a Vegas Pro Timeline (if desired). An edit may be completed almost entirely without touching the keyboard, merely by inserting a memory card (assuming that the cameraperson shot for the edit).

What makes Production Assistant so powerful is that it has a collection of 24 processes that can be chained together in any combination to produce automation workflows in minutes that would normally take hours to complete. Converting 4:3 media to widescreen with pillarboxes or by

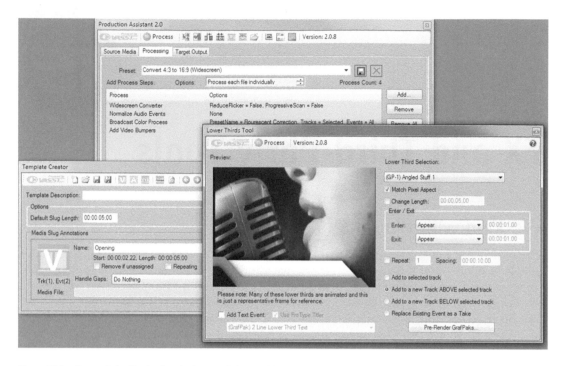

Figure 15.1   Some of the Production Assistant windows within Vegas.

stretching to fit (which involves cropping and loss of resolution) are both common tasks for broadcast or Web display. It's an easy chore, but one that is tedious and time consuming. Production Assistant can do this with its powerful batch-processing mode. Additionally, perhaps a station ID or bug needs to be added to a corner, or perhaps a lower third needs to be added to all those clips at the same time. Perhaps a single timeline needs to be output to multiple formats at once, such as for the Web at various bitrates and formats, high-resolution formats for broadcast, and uncompressed or lightly compressed for archiving. Production Assistant can provide all of these tasks for users in one click. Automatic editing of timelines created around user-built templates, adding pre-established titles at user-defined intervals, and a lot more can be accomplished with this tool.

Production Assistant may be launched without Vegas running; it's so easy to use that a person not familiar with video editing can set up Production Assistant to invoke multiple tasks at once, provided that they can locate and select video files that need processing and understand the processes that need to occur. Several broadcast houses and action-sports production facilities use Sony Production Assistant in places where trained editors are either not available or not financially viable.

Production Assistant accesses the Vegas engine and runs the process in the background. While these out-of-sight processes are taking place, a second (or even a third) instance of Vegas can be open and be used as a typical NLE system by a video editor.

Production Assistant may also be used interactively and accessed from within Vegas, and the Production Assistant process buttons can be placed on the standard Vegas toolbar for even faster access. Photo montages can be set up in seconds with "Ken Burns-style" pan and scan with just a few clicks of the mouse. Motion photo montages can also be set up in seconds that use 3D Track Motion to move images across the screen in several predefined patterns, or you can create your own. Instant ducking of audio, placement of lower thirds, color processing, and more can be controlled through the Production Assistant application. Sony Production Assistant also comes with 50 lower thirds in various themes for users.

> Bonus! Find exclusive video training for Sony Production Assistant on the DVD included with this book.

Boris Continuum Complete

Boris FX makes a series of compositing (RED, BCC), titling (Graffiti), and special effects (Boris FX) tools for a wide variety of NLEs, in addition to providing a standalone product. With the introduction of OFX plug-ins starting with Vegas Pro 10.0 and Vegas Movie Studio HD 11.0, Boris FX has released a new version of Boris Continuum Complete (BCC) and Boris RED for Vegas Pro.

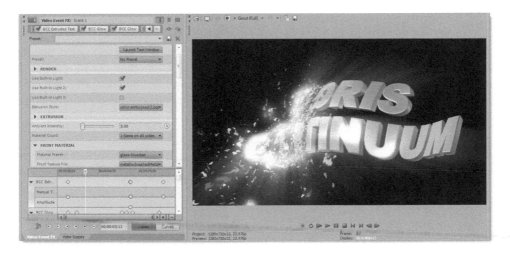

Figure 15.2   The Boris Continuum Complete interface working within Vegas.

Boris Continuum Complete is a comprehensive collection of over 120 filters, transitions, and even a surface generator added for good measure. The collection contains 3D objects, colors and blurs, distortion & perspective, effects, generators, keys and mattes, lights, time based, OpenGL based, and transitions. Boris FX is very aware of the workflow that Vegas offers users and molds its development around this. Within Vegas, users can both apply a Boris effect to the timeline and preview it in the same manner they are accustomed to with other Vegas filters.

As you can see in Figure 15.2, you can combine 3D text with lights, warp, shatter, and glow to make some impressive animated 3D titles. The best part is that the entire chain of effects can be saved in Vegas as a filter package and used in future projects simply by dragging and dropping the filter package onto an empty Event and changing the text. Almost all the parameters are keyframeable, giving you an incredible amount of control over each filter.

Included in Boris Continuum Complete are some of the best keying tools available for Vegas Pro. There is a chroma key, two-way key, linear luma key, motion key, and a variety of matte chokers and matte cleanup tools. There is even a light-wrap tool that uses the light from the background image and wraps it around the foreground keyed image to really help sell the illusion that the foreground subject is in the scene. In addition to the other effects, it is worth noting that among them are a Noise Reduction filter for removing noise artifacts from video, Film Processing effects for getting that Hollywood film look, an Optical Stabilizer for smoothing out shaky footage, and an Optical Flow filter for creating really smooth slow motion without ghosting. This is truly a complete package of video effects that are appropriate for a variety of projects. This is one of my go-to plug-ins when I'm editing, because it has something for almost every situation.

 Tip_____

There are trial versions of Boris Continuum Complete 7 and Boris RED 5.0 software products on the accompanying DVD, along with a Webinar from one of our VASST trainers on how to use them. Watch the Webinars and see what Boris can do for your next project.

Boris RED

Boris RED is a high-end 2D/3D compositing tool that combines effects, titling, rotoscoping, and other aspects of 3D creation and animation. Once installed, it is accessed like every other plug-in available to Vegas. Boris Continuum Complete is a set of individual filters than can be applied to your video, whereas Boris RED is a single plug-in with its own user interface that allows you to perform extremely complex compositing with multiple layers that are all contained within a single Event in Vegas Pro.

Figure 15.3   The Boris RED interface working within Vegas.

As you can see from Figure 15.3, RED has its own timeline, much like Vegas, with keyframing much like Vegas. The best part is that everything you do in RED, no matter how complex, can be saved as an effect preset and applied in future projects with a single click. Like Boris Continuum Complete, Boris RED is both a Vegas transition and a filter, with a surface generator and can be applied to any video Event, track, or the master video bus. After the effect is applied, users can launch the Boris user interface from the native Vegas FX Property page, create their effect, and upon closing, automatically import the Boris effect into the Vegas Timeline. From this point, whenever the Vegas cursor is scrubbed across the Boris effect in the Vegas Timeline, users can view the Boris frames natively in the Vegas Preview window.

Boris RED is a proper superset of Boris Continuum Complete. In addition to containing all the BCC filters, RED also contains a collection of Final Effects Complete (FEC) filters as well as all of the filters contained in Boris FX and Boris Graffiti. It also contains painting tools with which you can animate drawings and logos and other rotoscoping effects. With all this power, RED also has a Library Browser with thousands of presets that can be applied in a single click, so there is no need to have to master the RED interface; you can simply browse to the effect you want and apply it.

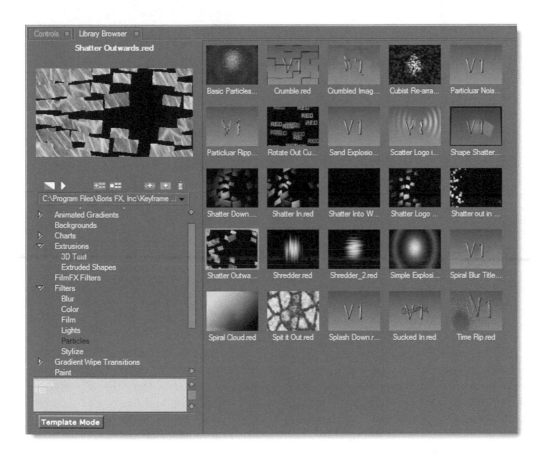

Figure 15.4   The Boris RED Library Browser. All it takes is a double-click to apply them to your project.

GenArts Sapphire/Sapphire Edge

From the people who powered the look of *Iron Man* comes Sapphire and Sapphire Edge. GenArts took a different approach with their Sapphire Edge plug-in. Instead of giving you lots of parameters to learn, Sapphire Edge uses a Preset Explorer/Browser approach where presets may be viewed in real-time as applied to the source footage to get you close to the effect you want, and then they give you control over a small number or important parameters to fine-tune the look. It is a simply brilliant idea that is well executed and the results are... Wow. Just... wow. They are amazing tools, reasonably priced, and huge timesavers for styles and effects.

Figure 15.5   The GenArts Sapphire Edge browser is a huge timesaver and allows direct access to FX Central, a repository for professionally designed looks built by working editors.

Sapphire Edge is a relatively low-cost plug-in for Vegas Pro and Vegas Movie Studio that provides not only great looks and effects but also unique transitions that stem from the very high-end Sapphire product. The transitions are perfect for wiping on/off titles and thirds, and they offer unique transitions that don't have the "amateur flair" that many of the gimmicky transitions in the video world offer. They're inspirational, creative twists on standard broadcast DVEs.

Most of the parameters of Sapphire Edge are keyframeable and offer extreme levels of control.

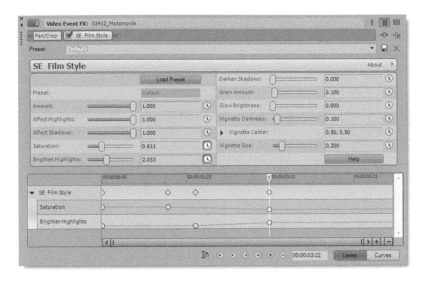

Figure 15.6 Sapphire Edge provides powerful, finite control of inserted FX.

NewBlueFX

NewBlueFX offers several plug-in tools for Sony Vegas Pro and Vegas Movie Studio. The Video Essentials collection of plug-in is one I recommend to all hobbyist editors and one that offers some tremendous and fast "fix it" power for professionals as well. NewBlue tools offer five collections of Video Essentials in addition to Motion Blends, Motion Effects, and others. They all significantly add to any editor's palette of looks and styles.

The Motion Blends transition kit is super-powerful for titles and lower thirds, and I'm a fan of their organic-feeling transitional elements.

Figure 15.7 The New Blue Motion Blends are very organic.

There are trial versions of several New Blue software products on the accompanying DVD. Give 'em a try; you'll likely appreciate the experience.

Another favorite NewBlue plug-in is its Starter Pack. The tools are artistic in nature and are pretty good FX applied directly to an Event. Their real power comes into play when compositing. One of my favorite techniques is to make two copies of an Event, placing one above the other. Adding the Dream Glow, Spotlight, or Colored Pencil to the top Event and using one of the composite modes offers some very cool looks (Overlay, Screen, and Add are all common modes). The Colored Pencil effect can be really useful for sharpening up images that are slightly unfocused when composited this way, giving the illusion of sharp lines.

NewBlue also offers a very powerful titling tool. This application is not only significantly more powerful than the three titlers that come in Vegas Pro and the two that are installed with Vegas Movie Studio, it also offers the ability to generate extruded 3D titles that may be blended with either 2D titles in the NewBlue titler, or with titles created in Sony Vegas Pro or Movie Studio. All the different NewBlue FX plug-ins work in both Vegas Pro and Vegas Movie Studio.

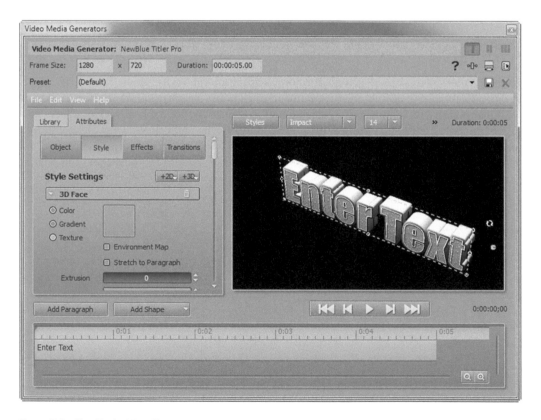

Figure 15.8 NewBlue's titler offers users the ability to create 3D titles.

One aspect I really appreciate in the NewBlue Title Pro tool is the ability to create many 3D layers of text, either as extruded or flat layers. This can be done in Vegas without the titling plug-in; it requires one track per layer. NewBlue's Title Pro plug-in enables many 3D layers on one track. NewBlue Title Pro also gives users the option of putting FX directly on the title from inside the titling application, rather than dropping it on to the title Event. This makes for a totally self-contained file project in one Event. Like the Sony FX, NewBlue gives users the ability to save off presets for future use.

At the time of this writing, the NewBlue Title tool requires a reasonably fast computer and benefits significantly from GPU-accelerated video cards; otherwise, expect some latency.

RE:Vision Effects TWIXTOR

If you want great slow motion, this is the tool. Period. It is the standard of the industry for a reason. There is a short training video on the DVD that accompanies this book. It is much easier to follow than the training video you'll find on the Vision Effects Website (at the time of this writing). No math is needed, just drop on the plug-in and go.

- Slow down clip (general use)
  - Place clip on timeline
  - Trim to start of clip
  - Add Twixtor tool
  - Select slow-down method (speed is default and most common)
  - Set speed you want to use
  - Drag end of clip out to where you want to have it end, regardless of loop points in the clip
- Slow down a segment of a clip and then have it resume normal playback
  - Place clip on timeline
  - Slice section in and out points for the footage you want to convert to slo-mo
  - Create a sub clip so you do not accidentally access additional footage past the end of your desired content

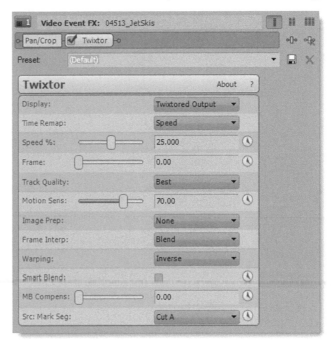

Figure 15.9 For serious slow (or fast) motion with amazing frame interpolation and when a high-speed camera isn't available, Twixtor is the bomb. You gotta have this plug-in.

- Find a rate of slo-mo that you like, and extend the clip until you see it loop
- Set the end of the clip to the last frame, and then butt the resuming clip back up to it

One tip for playing with Twixtor; Be sure to disable **Close Media Files when Vegas not the Active Application** if you see red frames.

Red Giant Magic Bullet

Red Giant Software produces the popular Magic Bullet series of video effects for Vegas users. Magic Bullet provides immediate access to dozens of popular film looks. You've seen "looks" applied to video before if you've seen the movie *Traffic* or the TV drama *CSI: Miami*. "Stylized color" is part of more productions than not these days. There is certainly more to getting your content looking that good than applying a plug-in, but post-production color grading is part of the process of getting a "look." The Magic Bullet plug-ins help facilitate that task, and many users find they don't need to go beyond the software's stock settings.

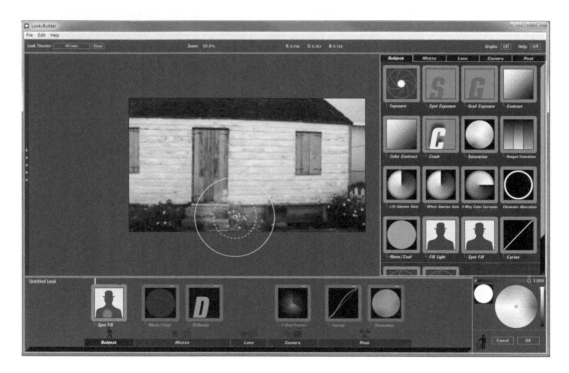

Figure 15.10   The Magic Bullet Looks plug-in for Vegas Pro. This plug-in provides much more control over various parameters and layers than their entry-level Quick Looks plug-in.

What most editors don't realize is that Magic Bullet Looks is a lot more than just film looks. It is an outstanding tool for correcting mistakes in your shot. There are tools for every stage of acquisition and it has one of the most intuitive interfaces I've seen on any plug-in. As you can see in Figure 15.10, along the bottom is a representation of the stages of acquisition from subject, matte box, lens, camera, to post production. Along the right side are effects with names like Exposure, Fill Light, Contrast, and Saturation that should be familiar to any video editor. You can drop effects at any one of the acquisition stages and they behave as they would in the real world. For example, if you have a subject that has his face in shadows, you can drop a Spot Fill on the subject stage and you will be presented with a masking circle to brighten just that area of the image. This would take multiple tracks to accomplish in Vegas alone, but Magic Bullet Looks makes it simple to do. This is another must-have plug-in for advanced color correcting in Vegas.

ProDad

ProDad develops not only FX filters for Vegas but also transitional plug-in tools, adding to the dozens of transitions found in the Vegas application (these plug-in tools also work in Vegas Movie Studio and Movie Studio Platinum). ProDad's Heroglyph is a titling tool that may be added to the titling tools installed with Vegas. An advantage of Heroglyph is that it already has dozens of title presets built in. ProDad also develops Mercalli (to help eliminate shaky-cam footage), as well as Adorage, which generates more than 10,000 effects in Vegas, including particle generators and light rays, and VitaScene transition and filter packages.

I'm a big fan of the Mercalli stabilizer (it's the only ProDad plug-in I use with regularity), which is more powerful and capable than the stabilizer that is stock in Sony Vegas Pro or Movie Studio and is quite flexible by comparison.

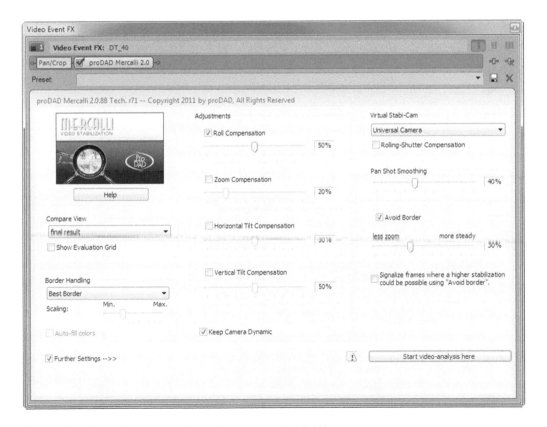

Figure 15.11   Mercalli by ProDad can help to improve shaky handheld footage.

VASST Software (vasst.com)

VASST develops Vegas Pro Command Extensions, Script-based plug-ins, and Direct X-based plug-in tools for Sony Vegas Pro. The VASST UltimateS Pro plug-in productivity tool (not available for Vegas Movie Studio) is one of the most popular plug-in tools available for Sony Vegas, providing tools such as Photo Montage, MotoFoto, Editing Tools, Marker Tools, Film Looks, Audio Tools, Visual Effects, Quad-Cam, Lower Thirds, Special FX, DVD Tools, Render Tools, Auditing Tools, Setup Tools, and Project Tools with features totaling nearly 300 in all. Each of these tools is designed to increase your productivity while editing. Many of the mundane tasks in Vegas have been automated in UltimateS Pro making it a tool that will save you hours during editing.

Figure 15.12   This plug-in brings so many automated features to Vegas that an entire book could be dedicated to what it does for editors. It is a standard in broadcast, action sports, and hobbyist worlds alike.

VASST Mayhem and ScatterShot 3D are also very popular plug-ins for Vegas Pro. Mayhem provides special effects that add action and randomization to your footage for spectacular introductions or as backdrops behind titles. ScatterShot 3D allows you to quickly arrange video or images in 3D space to create video walls, circles, large random areas of videos floating in space, 3D cubes, and so on. Doing these tasks manually in Vegas Pro would take you hours and hours, but ScatterShot 3D and Mayhem perform the task it in only seconds.

Educators, houses of worship, and government institutions will really appreciate Caption Assistant. Federal law states that any publicly funded or general public educational, governmental access to video programming requires closed captioning. Training videos and educational programming both fall into these categories. Many religious institutions require closed captioning, and online broadcast channels such as YouTube and other sites offer captioning for the hearing impaired. Caption Assistant makes this a copy/paste, real-time adjustment of closed captioning in Vegas. Although Vegas offers its own closed-captioning functionality, it is nowhere near as flexible, robust, nor efficient as the Closed Captioning system offered in Caption Assistant.

Figure 15.13   Caption Assistant from VASST makes closed captioning a copy/paste process, with online, real-time adjustment of captions for broadcast over the air, disc, or streamed media. Changing out multiple languages or English subtitles is very easy with Caption Assistant.

There are demos of the VASST tools on the DVD included with this book.

Figure 15.14   Mayhem creates "mayhem edits," which are currently a very popular look. Users of Vegas can create this effect manually, but it is very time-consuming and difficult to do with any degree of consistency or rhythm. Mayhem creates this style in one click.

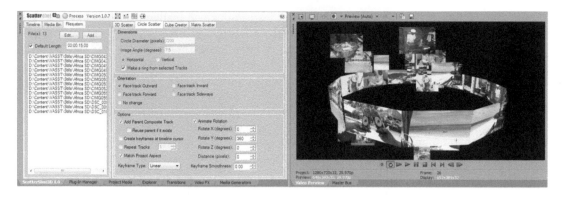

Figure 15.15   Scattershot 3D provides the ability to create stunning 3D rotations, cubes, layers, and more, all with a single click, saving hours of time and providing less difficulty in getting 3D planes "just right." Create projects, save, and put into a new project as a nested video file; render times significantly speed up.

3D Editing, Monitoring, and Output in Vegas Pro and Vegas Movie Studio

Vegas Pro is capable of both handling 3D planes and editing 3D stereoscopic files. Sony Vegas Movie Studio enables video editors to edit 3D stereoscopic files. There are two sources of 3D stereoscopic files:

- Stereo/3D cameras such as the Sony PMWTD 300, the Panasonic AG3D-A1, Sony TDM-10 are all camcorders that record 3D stereoscopic video that may be edited in Sony Vegas Pro and Sony Vegas Movie Studio.

- Two camcorders of identical resolution, frame rate, depth of field, and focal length. These may be large or small format cameras ranging from EX1's to GoPro or similar type cameras.

Three-dimensional output is possible in virtually every 3D format available today, and Vegas will ingest most of the various file formats available in 3D acquisition. Vegas can also function quite well in converting 2D to 3D.

Vegas supports:

- Dual-stream AVI or QuickTime files

- 3D AVC(MVC) .m2ts files created by the HDR-TD10 and 3D Sony Bloggie HD cameras

Figure 16.1

- MPO (multiple picture object) 3D still images
- CineForm Neo3D 5.1 or later (a CineForm product or the free Neo Player is required to read CineForm Neo3D files)

You'll need 3D glasses to check your work. These glasses may be the paper type that are found for free at most 3D film festivals, they may be found at the local big-box stores such as Walmart or Target, or they can be found for free online at many Websites.

> The polarized or shutter glasses used in large movie theaters cannot be used; they use a polarized lens or active switch quartz system designed for projections that does not work with computer monitors.

Setting the 3D Project Properties

Open a new project (**Ctrl + N**) and in the Project Properties window, set the 3D mode to **Anaglyphic Red/Cyan**. There are other options available; we'll be using red/cyan for this exercise because it's visible to the naked eye as well as with the glasses. This may be changed at any point in the editing process.

If a 3D external monitor is being used, browse to **Options | Preferences | Preview Device** and choose the output device to be used.

- If you're using an NVIDIA graphics card that supports 3DVision technology and a 3DVision monitor, choose the **Stereoscopic Graphics Card** setting from the **Device** drop-down list in the Preview Device tab and choose **Left and Right** from the Stereoscopic 3D mode drop-down list.

- If you're using an NVIDIA graphics card that supports 3DVision technology and a 3D-capable HDTV, choose the **Stereoscopic 3D Graphics Card** setting from the **Device** drop-down list in the Preview Device tab and use the **Stereoscopic 3D mode** drop-down list to choose the method your monitor uses to display stereoscopic content—typically Side by side (half) or Line Alternate. Be sure to set the **3D mode** in your television's setup menu and the **Vegas Movie Studio Preview Device** tab.

Choose the **External Display** button in the Preview window to send the video to a secondary/external display device. Use **Alt + Shift + 4** to return to the Vegas Preview window (or click the external monitor and use the **Esc** key).

Importing 3D Media to the Timeline

3D is multicamera work regardless of the source. It's two sources of video whether it was acquired with two cameras splitting beams, two cameras set on a parallax beam, or a single camera with dual lenses. This means that the files will need to be synchronized on the timeline exactly as they are in multicamera workflows. If a single-camera/dual-lens system is used, such as those from the Sony or Panasonic 3D cameras, synchronizing the streams is very easy because timecode (T/C) from the two

Figure 16.2

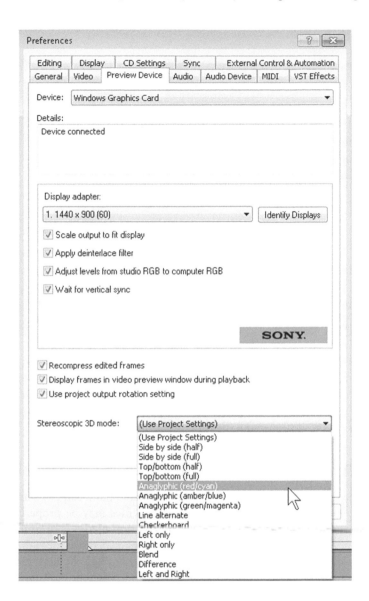

streams is identical. Two-camera systems are rarely turned on at the same time, and even more rarely will they have matching T/C. They will therefore require manual synchronization.

If the media is from a single camera, it may be imported to the timeline directly as one selection. Import the 3D files to the project. Locate them in the **Project Media** window. Hold down **Ctrl** to select the two clips in the Project Media window, and choose **Pair As Stereoscopic 3D SubClip** (not available in Vegas Movie Studio). The two clips will be paired as a subclip, the project media window will show them as a paired subclip, and the subclip may be added to the timeline as a single Event/clip.

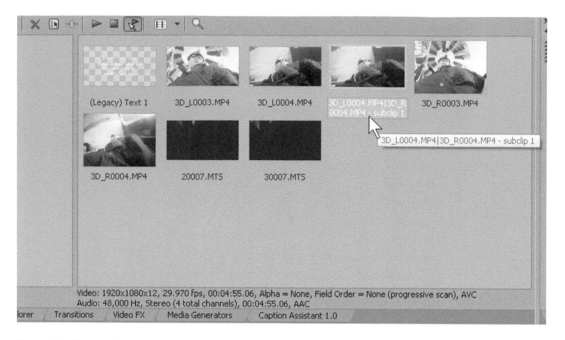

Figure 16.3   Files may be paired in the Project Media window if they are from the same camera source (not available in Vegas Movie Studio) and placed on the timeline as a single clip or Event.

Vegas Movie Studio users will have to manually synchronize clips. If the clips are from a single-source camera, this is easy to do, since the files are identical in length.

Manually Synchronizing Files on the Vegas Timeline

When two cameras are being used, a sync pulse, flash, pet clicker, hand clap, or slateboard should be used to create a spike in the audio signal so that the two files may be properly aligned. It is possible to do this without the spike, but it is more time-consuming and may be less accurate.

Place both files on the timeline. Generally, the left camera is placed above the right camera in the track order, but this is not at all critical, just a standard. Roughly align the files, place the cursor/playhead over the best audio point that may be used for sync, and, using the mousewheel, Up/Down Arrows, or Zoom button, zoom into the start of the timeline. Assure that **Quantize to frames** is enabled. Line up the two files so that the audio waveforms exactly match. Use **Shift** + **Up Arrow** to magnify the waveforms and the 1/3 keys on the 10-key numpad if necessary.

Once the files are aligned, it's a good practice to visually check the files as well. Reduce the opacity of the top file and the two frames will be visible in the Preview window; outlines and action should be identical.

All of the preceding steps have been taken in the 3D-Parachutes.vf file, so from here, you'll be able to follow along and create a 3D project in Vegas. There are two sections from a small-format camera and one section from the Panasonic dual-head 3D camera. Don't forget your 3D glasses!

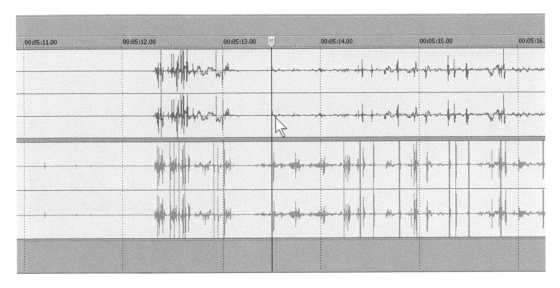

Figure 16.4 Align video using the audio files. This is much faster to accomplish if there are "spikes" in the audio that are inserted from a clap, clicker, or other percussive sound. Be sure **Quantize to Frames** (default) is enabled when you're aligning clips for 3D. It's okay if audio is off by a bit, but frames should be aligned.

With the two files aligned and checked, hold **Ctrl** and select both files. Right-click either file and choose **Pair as Stereoscopic 3D Subclip** from the submenu. One file will disappear and the two files will be overlaid as one clip/Event. This allows us to edit the two Events as though they are one. FX, color correction, track motion, and pan/crop will be identically applied to both clips in the single Event.

These clips will all need white balancing and color correction, and I'd recommend adding some blue via the Color Curves FX or Color Balance FX tools.

If the 3D fields do not appear to be too wide, insert the **StereoScopic 3D Adjust FX** filter to the Event. It's very important that the width of the stereo image not be too wide. Headaches and even nausea may be caused in the audience if these fields are wider than the eye and brain can normally process. This is a deep topic that is best explored by research outside this book. The Vegas Help file offers some information about pixel widths at maximum screen widths.

It is very important that left and right pixels' subject information not be spread too far apart as to be unnatural. Should the separation of distant information be too great, it's possible to cause headaches and nausea for the viewer of your content. It's quite possible for 3D to (improperly) go beyond natural viewing distance. This may cause crossed eyes, ruining the effect of 3D due to the brain trying to decode or see the image. Alternate between 3D glasses and viewing preview with the naked eye to create proper alignment and depth. Be sure to avoid vertical and rotational misalignment; this may cause the viewer to experience imbalance and perhaps nausea.

Tip _____

A great reference source for a better understanding of depth and width *is 3D Movie Making: Stereoscopic Digital Cinema from Script to Screen,* by Bernard Mendiburu.

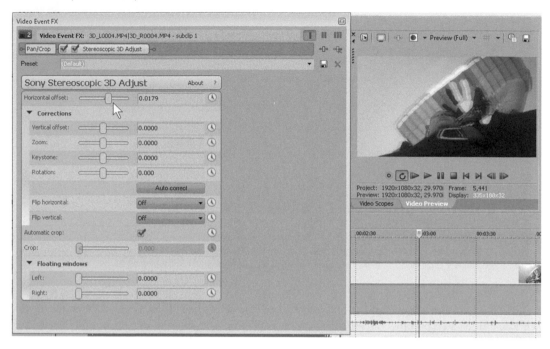

Figure 16.5   The **Stereoscopic 3D Adjust FX** tool is useful for aligning video from two separate cameras. It is very important that vertical alignments be accurate. This function will assist in properly aligning frames from two separate cameras.

Stereoscopic 3D Adjust FX Tool

This powerful FX tool is useful for those shooting two matching cameras on a 3D rig, either with a beam splitter/mirror or on a rail. If the two cameras are not perfectly aligned, the Stereoscopic 3D Adjust FX tool assists in bringing the images into perfect vertical alignment. The vertical offset, zoom, keystone and rotation functions all assist in bringing images into alignment. The Flip Horizontal/Flip Vertical features are used for beam-splitting systems, required for close camera work.

Before applying any manual adjustments for offsets, I recommend letting Vegas attempt to manage the offsets. Click the **auto-correct** option and allow Vegas to attempt an auto-correct. The auto-correct feature is a slow feature, very similar to image stabilization, in that Vegas must analyze all frames and make calculations based on frame content. This is not a fast function and is very dependent on processor capability. However, I've found it does a very good job with footage from small-format cameras such as the GoPro and RePlay and is worth the added time in processing. If the images are too far out of alignment, no plug-in can compensate, so take time in production to try to get it right.

The automatic crop feature allows Vegas to crop the image based on offsets. Cropping may be manually controlled if necessary.

Note that parameters of the Stereoscopic 3D Adjust FX tool may be keyframed over time to compensate for camera movement.

Tip_____

The focal point in a video can be a few feet further back than where we want the viewer to look. The brain then tries to adjust, which strains the eyes, so it's important to ensure that the focus (depth focus or aiming point, not DOF) is aligned correctly on the actual subject. Rough alignment should already be there during the shoot. In post we can do subtle corrections. It's also worth noting that these small-format cameras allow for less post-shifting of the focal point due to the extreme wide angle. It causes a shift on the edge pixels if we move the center of the frame too much.

Applying FX to 3D Video Events

In Vegas Pro, FX are specifically separated for two-channel processing, that is, left/right processes (not available in Vegas Movie Studio). Processing the two channels separately, particularly on still images or non-3D sources, may benefit the illusion of 3D from a two-dimensional image.

When FX are applied to a paired stream in Vegas Pro, two instances of the FX are inserted to the Event. In the top of the FX dialog box are two checked versions of the FX for each FX inserted into the chain. The left checkbox is for the left view/FX, and the right check box is for the right view/FX. Setting different values/parameters for each eye provides for some very interesting effects.

Figure 16.6   These checkboxes enable/disable FX for each eye/view in the 3D stream. Different parameters may be set for each eye, creating interesting and creative effects.

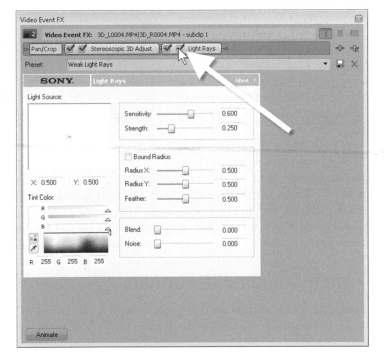

Transitions applied in Vegas Pro function the same way as FX; different values per eye may be set if desired, creating some very interesting effects and transitions. The **Cross Effect** transition is one of my favorites for 3D FX, with the width set to about half again wider than the default. The **Iris** transition is another favorite. Apply edits to the **3D-Parachutes.vf** project to get an idea of how these transitions function.

Vegas Movie Studio users will simply cut and apply FX and transitions as though the project were a 2D project.

Rendering 3D for Output

Vegas will output a 3D or dual stream, depending on the display destination. For delivery to DVD or online distribution, a render to standard formats will apply. For example, the three 3D projects on the 3D-Parachutes.vf project may be rendered to an .mp4 or .mpg for delivery.

In both Vegas Pro and Vegas Movie Studio browse to **File | Render As**. In this menu, choose the file format for delivery. YouTube recommends that you upload video in side-by-side half Left/Right and accepts a variety of video formats such as mp4, avi, wmv, and mov. For YouTube, Facebook, Vimeo, and similar UCG sites, I recommend the MainConcept .mp4 format in a render setting of 1920 x 1080, 16mbps (max), but wmv and QuickTime (.mov) are alternatives.

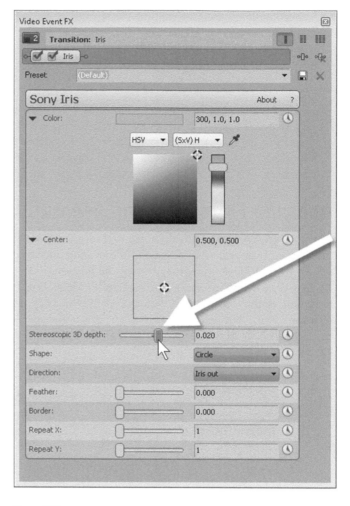

Figure 16.7

Frame Compatible Formats

Sometimes 3D media needs to be moved through an existing 2D process. This is also possible in Vegas by rendering two streams in a frame-compatible format. Set the Vegas project to one of these three modes:

Figure 16.8 YouTube recommends H.264 AVC 1920x1080 Side-by-Side L/R with SEI Frame Packing Arrangement metadata. The Sony manual for Vegas recommends using metatags for processing YouTube video; YouTube no longer supports metatagging. Simply upload the video, select the 3D radio button, and select the placement of the two videos via the various options. Check YouTube.com for the most up-to-date recommendations on 3D authoring for that site because they are certain to continue to change as 3D becomes more popular.

- Side by Side-half
- Top/Bottom-half
- Line Alternate
- If you render side by side and you switch L/R (so right is left, left is right), it allows for viewing without glasses via cross-eyed viewing

and render to standard formats.

Another option is to manually output for projection. Manually set the 3D mode to **Left Only** and render to desired format. Repeat the process setting the 3D mode to **Right Only**.

If this is a common workflow, create a customized template for each of these settings and render using the **Batch Render** script found in Vegas Pro or the batch renderer in Sony Production Assistant software. Each of these templates should be selected for the batching process, and Vegas Pro will automatically create the files using the project filename.

 Tip_____

For archiving, it's a good practice to keep separate streams at full resolution, since this master/archive allows for further editing at full resolution.

It is also possible to render direct to 3D MVC Blu-ray Disc. **Tools | Burn Disc**, create image first, turn off stereoscopic, then burn the prerendered image. This was intended as a tool for pre-imaging commercial discs, but it works great for direct disc authoring!

Rendering for Active Glasses

Active glasses are the kind of glasses that have battery power and active shutters that open and close at double frame rate. 3D televisions that use active shutter technology play alternate-frame sequencing 3D video. This video displays alternating, full-resolution left and right frames. Render to **Side by Side-Full**.

Creating Faux 3D from a Single File

Both versions of Vegas may be used to create faux 3D. This is a very fast and simple process.

Place a clip on the timeline. Make a copy of the video clip and place the copy on a new or empty track above the original track. This may cause a second audio file to be created and layered on the original audio, so be prepared to drag the new audio file to a track beneath the original audio file and then delete the second audio file or track. Zoom in at the head of the clip. Be sure that **Quantize to Frames** is enabled.

Offset the copy by a frame. Pair the two video files together. Depending on the content, adding the **Stereoscopic 3D Adjust FX** to the clip may enhance the 3D effect. Layering 3D titles in front of (and sometimes behind) will help create the illusion of actual 3D.

In Vegas Pro, setting different FX settings may also help deepen the illusion of 3D. Insert the FX twice to the clip, turn off **Left** in one instance, turn off **Right** in the second instance. **Blurs, Light Rays,** and similar FX add a nice touch.

The Stereoscopic 3D Adjust FX cannot make a 2D video become 3D, it merely may enhance the effect. The greater the motion in the clip, the more effective the 3D from 2D becomes. An external tool such as Boris Red for rotoscoping is a faster and more effective method of creating a second layer. Additionally, although this effect can work with still images to a limited extent, I'd recommend using an external rotoscoping application such as Photoshop to create layers for separated depth and controllable depth of field in still images.

3D Titles/Text

Two-dimensional text may be given greater depth by adding the **Stereoscopic 3D Adjust FX** to text Events on the project. Almost all generated media may be given added depth with the Stereoscopic 3D Adjust FX plug-in. Generally, any horizontal alignments should be kept on the conservative side. A slight spherize added to the title provides for an interesting effect, as can light rays applied to clips. Insert the FX twice to the clip, turn off **Left** in one instance, turn off **Right** in the second instance. Be sure to check and compare both with and without 3D glasses. This also may be applied to extruded 3D titles generated by the New Blue Title tool typically included with the Sony bundle.

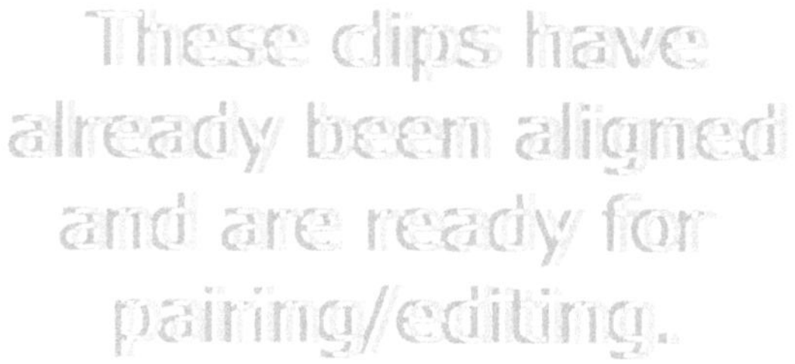

These clips have already been aligned and are ready for pairing/editing.

Figure 16.9   Be sure to check 3D media both with and without 3D glasses; this will help ensure that distances between right and left channels are properly set so that viewers will not get headaches or nausea. Adding too much stereoscopic width to text will confuse the eye and brain. To get an idea of what doesn't work, spend some time on YouTube's 3D channels. There is a lot of great media there, yet the majority of 3D on YouTube leaves a lot to be desired at the time of this writing.

Masks and Compositing in Sony Vegas

What Is Compositing?

Compositing is the combination or interaction of two or more graphic or video images to create a single finished image. Compositing can be as simple as laying a title onto a visual image or as complex as combining hundreds of photographs, video, and animated elements to create complex images.

Compositing in its most complex forms is absolutely an art; there are compositing artists all over Hollywood, Austin, New York, Sydney, and other major cities that do nothing but create complex imagery for major networks, film, and corporate media departments. The fantastic imagery seen on ESPN and CNN lower-third fly-ins and graphics (and in most major motion pictures) is the result of these artists' work. It is most likely that not one major motion picture has been released in the past few years that didn't contain significant compositing, whether it's titling, green- or bluescreen work, or overlaid imagery. *The Matrix* is an amazing example of how greenscreen work is brought to the big screen through the creative use of composited images, as is HBO's *Boardwalk Empire,* the *Harry Potter* films, or Michael Bay's smash-hit *Transformers* series. Most of the full-ship images in *Titanic* were composited together, including CGI animations of people walking, driving, and loading the ship. Most of the scenes including fish were CGI, composited, animated. However, even basic dramas also include composites to fill or reduce skylines. In short, compositing is very much about eye candy and/or illusion.

Picture in Picture

In the chapter on Track Motion and Pan/Crop, we discussed Picture in Picture (PIP) briefly, but we'll look at another aspect of PIP in this brief tutorial.

Open the **PIP_MovieStudio.vf**. In this project, there are two floating PIP images over the top of the band.

The first track contains generated media that creates the frame. The second track is the vocalist laid over the top, with track motion used to resize the picture, just as we did in the Track Motion section of this book. The third track is achieved the same way; track motion is used to reduce the size of the image. Notice that the lower-right image is close to the original aspect ratio, whereas the upper-left image is slightly squeezed. This is due to the Track Motion aspect ratio feature being disabled.

In the third track, the video is the correct aspect ratio, centered over the same image playing beneath. A Border FX has been applied to the track (not the Event; this effect will not work at Event level). Finally, a Gaussian blur has been applied to the lowest image, allowing the same motion to occur in sync with the top level. This is a terrific method of resizing SD to HD footage. Place two copies of the media on two tracks, use Track Motion to reduce the size of the SD media to almost "normal" size while the background is the same SD media stretched to fill the frame, and add blur to offset. If the lower track appears pixelated, add some grain, shift it to grayscale (black and white), or add FX until it looks the way you want it to. It's not common to add a shadow to this sort of floated Event, it would call attention to the float, and generally speaking the video looks better if it appears embedded, not floated.

Creating/Using Masks in Vegas

Masks are exceptionally powerful tools for creating composited media. Masking is the first step in understanding compositing and how to layer composites and is a key element in creating deep comps in Sony Vegas. Remember the overhead projectors we had in elementary school, with the transparent layers of acetate? As more transparencies were added to the projector, more imagery appeared. Being able to animate these transparent layers is the next step in compositing.

Masking helps determine which layer or portion of a transparency is seen at any given time. Masks can be made from just about any photo-editing tool, font, or shape that exists. Vegas auto-senses an alpha channel from most images that contain them and has options to force recognition of an alpha channel if it is not automatically sensed.

To force Vegas to recognize an alpha channel if it is not seeing the channel automatically, right-click the Event containing the alpha channel. Select **Properties** from the submenu that appears. Select the **Media** tab in the Properties window; at the bottom is a menu labeled **Alpha Channel**. Next to this, locate a drop-down list that offers several choices. Select **Pre-multiplied** from the menu.

> An alpha channel defines the areas you want to be transparent. Each image on the video screen comprises four channels: red, green, blue, and alpha. The alpha channel acts as a mask, instructing the other channels on how the pixels should blend or merge. Alpha channels can have gradations, allowing the blending of multiple images on top of one another at various levels of transparency. Another way to understand how an alpha channel functions is to imagine a stencil laid over an object and a can of spray paint. The alpha channel reveals the Events beneath, much as a stencil reveals the object beneath. Alpha channels usually display transparent areas as white space, whereas hidden areas are displayed in black.

Masks can either hide or reveal information or images in a video project, allowing image areas to be defined within an Event. Another name for a mask is a *matte* or a *key*. All these terms mean the same thing: hiding or revealing an area so that another image can show through, or hiding an area so that another image can be composed over the top of it. In any definition, a mask, matte, or key defines the transparent pixels of an image for superimposing or revealing another image.

Just as titles are one of the simplest forms of compositing, they are also one of the most viable uses of masking. Titling is an excellent method of learning exactly how a mask works.

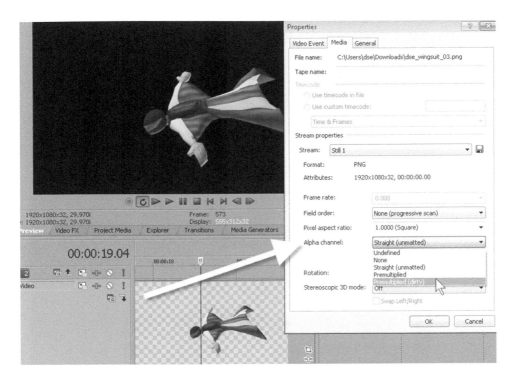

Figure 17.1 Right-clicking and selecting **Properties | Media** allows alpha channel recognition to be forced if an alpha channel is present.

Mask Tutorial #1

1. Open a new project in Vegas. Insert three new video tracks, labeled **1**, **2**, and **3**, starting from the top. Choose a video or still file to serve as a background. To begin, place the video or still image on track **3**.

2. Place a title on track **1**. Do not use fonts that contain serifs or small lines. A font such as Impact or Arial Black will serve best as you learn this technique. Leave the text color set to the default of **white**.

3. On track **2**, place a video file that has high motion with bright colors for the best effect in the learning stage.

4. The text is a mask but is not seen as such just yet. On track **2**, on the extreme right side of the **Track Control** pane just to the right of the Track Header, there is a small arrow pointing upward, which is the **Make Compositing Child (parent/child)** button. Click this button.

5. On the text track, track **1**, click the **Compositing Mode** button and choose **Multiply (Mask)**. Making this selection will cause all areas of track 2 to become transparent. The only portions of track 2 that are seen are inside the letters of track 1.

Figure 17.2   The **Parent/Child** buttons are found on the right side of every video track, beneath the **SOLO! (exclamation point)** button.

Figure 17.3   The video of track 2 (the child) shows through the letters of track 1 (the parent track).

6. Loop and play the timeline. Here's what's happening: The Event on track 2 disappears and becomes visible only inside the title letters. The letters are a mask; the letters become the parent, and the Event beneath becomes the child. This process causes the parent to instruct the child how to be shown. Multiple tracks can be the child, but only one track can be the parent. As many parent and child relationships as necessary can exist across multiple tracks; however, no child track can have more than one parent. If multiple parents are required of a child track, the child track must be duplicated.

To gain a better understanding of the masking process, change the color of the text on track **1** to **black**. It will cause the letters to become invisible (reset the color of the title to white to continue this section).

This process is masking in its most basic form. Any image that contains transparent/alpha information can be used in place of a title. To continue the concept of manipulating the title appearance, however, keep this project on the timeline:

7. In track **1**, right-click the title to edit it or click the **Edit Generated Media** button found on the title Event. The **Title** tool opens. Navigate to the **Effects** tab and enable a shadow on the text. The shadow can't be seen. Changing the color of the shadow will result in the shadow being seen. Disable the shadow in the Text tool before moving on to the next step.

8. To place a shadow on the mask (or to shadow letters/characters in this instance), select the **Parent Motion** tool on track **1**. (Parent Motion is all the way to the left side of the Track Header.) In the Parent Motion tool, check the **2D Shadow** checkbox. A shadow will appear beneath the mask/letters on the Preview screen. This shadow can be keyframed in exactly the same way that a shadow in a normal Track Motion instance would be keyed. Color, size, feathering, transparency, and position can all be user-defined using keyframes.

Shadows inserted at the Title/Text tool level won't display the shadow, since the shadow cannot be part of the mask. The Parent Shadow assigns a shadow to the edges of the mask rather than the contents of the mask.

Mask Tutorial #2

1. Open your favorite photo-editing application. In the application, create a new project/photo image. The image should be **1280 x 720**. Flood the entire work area with **black**.

2. Paint a design or shape in the work area, using **white** as the color. Painting thick, broad lines will best demonstrate this effect. *Save the design as a PNG file for best results.* A GIF, JPEG, TIF, or Targa will also work.

3. Open a new project in Vegas. Create three new video tracks. Place the new image you created on the timeline on track **1**.

4. Also on track **1**, insert a **Mask Generator** FX using the **Track FX** button. This should be set for **Luminance** for this exercise. Set the **Composite Mode** for track **1** to **Multiply (Mask)**. (In versions of Vegas prior to 10 you might not need to do these steps.)

5. Insert the media that should be showing through the mask on track **2**. The length of the Event doesn't matter, since the length of the parent Event determines how long the underlying Event is visible. (Of course, if the child Event is shorter than the parent Event, the child will not be seen for the full length either.) Track 2 Compositing Mode = Source Alpha.

6. On track **3**, insert an Event that contains video or a still image that functions as the background image. Track 3 Compositing Mode = Source Alpha.

7. Now click the **Make Compositing Child** button on track **2**, and the image you created becomes transparent except for the visible mask areas, which now show the Event on track 2.

8. Filters can be applied to the Events on the child track, which will affect how the Events on track 2 are shown. Applying blurs will blend the mask into the underlying Events.

In a gradient mask, white areas are revealed whereas black areas are hidden. When you use other colors as the mask, the closer a color is to white, the more revealed it becomes, whereas just the opposite is true for gradient colors approaching black in value. However, when you use other colors in a mask, those colors reduce the opacity of the underlying image.

Figure 17.4   You can have fun while learning to make masks.

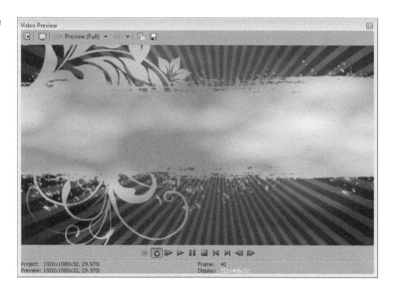

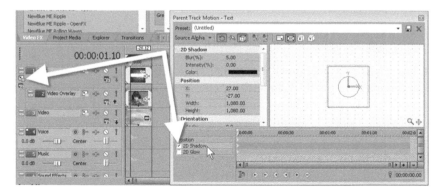

Figure 17.5   Adding a shadow to the mask with the **Track Motion Shadow** tool. Glow can also be added to a mask.

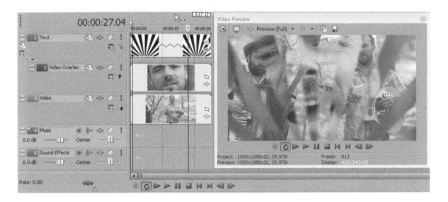

Figure 17.6   Any shape can be used to create a mask as long as it contains a mask and an alpha image.

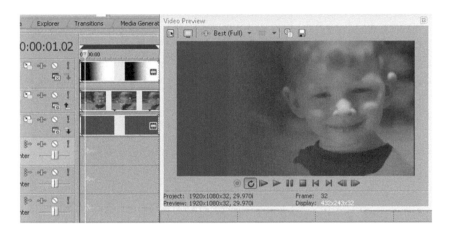

Figure 17.7   Black-to-white gradient changed to solid-blue gradient, reducing the opacity of the image shown through.

Tip_____

Another means of creating a mask in Vegas is to use generated media to define what will be masked out. One useful way to do this process is to create a mask that splits the screen in two or three parts, using blur and mask to create a completely smooth transition from one side to the other.

Mask Tutorial #3

To create a split screen with a seamless transition:

1.   Start a new project. Insert three video tracks. Track 1 is for the mask, track 2 for one-half of the screen, and track 3 for the remaining half of the screen.

2.   Insert the desired Events on tracks **2** and **3**.

3. On track **1,** insert generated media by right-clicking in the track 1 area of the timeline and selecting **Insert Generated Media.** In the **Media Generator** plug-in dialog box, select **Sony Solid Color** and choose **white** as the color.

4. Select the **Pan/Crop** tool on the generated media by right-clicking or by clicking the **Pan/Crop** button found on the media. In the Pan/Crop Preview window, slide the frame to the right until it divides the frame in half, with the left side being all white (in the main preview window). (The Center should be at **720** and **240.**) Close the **Pan/Crop** dialog box.

5. On track **1,** click the **Compositing Mode** and choose **Multiply (Mask).** The white Generated Media panel now shows the video from track 2 on one side, and the other side is black.

6. On track **2,** click the **Make Compositing Child** button on the right side of the track header. This step will cause the screen to split in half, showing track 2 on the left side of the screen and track 3 on the right side. If the images on tracks 2 and 3 are not centered, the **Pan/Crop** tool should be applied to the images to center them.

7. With the screen split, apply a **Gaussian blur** to the Event on track **1,** either by dragging the blur to the Event from the Video FX docking window or by clicking the **Event FX** button on the solid-color Event on track **1.** Apply the blur to the desired setting.

8. This process can also be applied in a series of two transitions as well by adding two more tracks to the project. This step will display three split sections. **Pan/Crop** will need to be applied in opposite directions and in thirds of the screen.

> The project shown here can be found on the DVD that accompanies this book. The filename is **3screen.veg**.

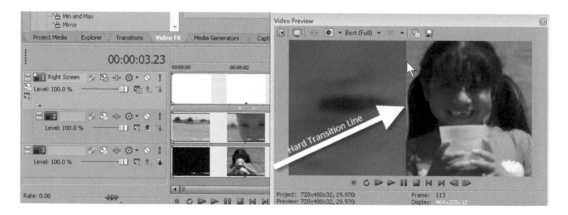

Figure 17.8   Splitting the screen with the Parent/Child feature.

Figure 17.9   Splitting the screen into three parts is fast and simple with masks made from Generated Media.

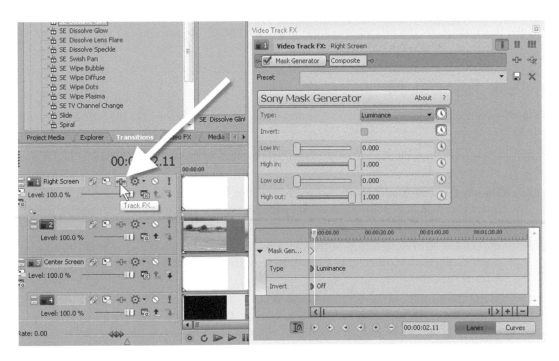

Figure 17.10   Access the Mask Generator by clicking the **Track FX** button found on any parent/child combination. It may also be dragged to the track header from the FX library.

Vegas also has a Mask Generator for every video track parented to another.

Five different mask modes are available in the Mask Generator dialog box. Each mode blends or masks media differently based on color or luminance found within the parent image:

- *Luminance*. Uses luminance in the image to determine transparency.
- *Alpha*. Uses an alpha channel to determine transparency.
- *Red channel*. Uses the color red to determine transparency.
- *Blue channel*. Uses the color blue to determine transparency.
- *Green channel*. Uses the color green to determine transparency.

Open the **colorchannel.veg** file on the DVD included with this book. Use the **Low in/High in** sliders to limit or delimit the information in the child Events in the parent/child relationship. These attributes are keyframable and can be used to limit/delimit transparency of a channel over time. Use this tool as one alternative to animate lines on a map, create handwriting on an image, or mask out a color channel over time.

There are many creative ways to use masks in Vegas. Using masks, a reflection of text can be quickly composited.

For this tutorial, set the project properties to equal NTSC DV Widescreen.

Mask Tutorial #4

Open a new project. Insert six video tracks numbered from top to bottom. Do the following steps in order:

1. On track **6**, insert a background image. For purposes of this exercise, use generated media, preferably a color gradient.

2. Double-click the media on track **6** to create a timeline selection. On track **5**, right-click to insert text media. For this exercise, keep the text to one single line. Use a creative font for best results.

3. On track **4**, with the selection still active from double-clicking track **6**, right-click and select **Insert Generated Media | Sony Color Gradient**. (If the selection is not active, double-click track **6** again.)

4. In the **Gradient** dialog box, select **Linear White to Black** from the Preset drop-down. In the **Aspect Ratio Angle** dialog box, enter a value of **37**. Click the **Animate** button to display keyframes. In the keyframe timeline of the **Color Gradient** dialog box, click the **Last Keyframe** button (**Ctrl + End**) to move the cursor in the dialog box to the end of the selection/Event.

5. At this last keyframe, change the **Aspect Ratio Angle** value to **2180.0**, which will cause the gradient to rotate in the project. Close this **Generated Media** dialog box.

6. Select the **Make Compositing Child** button on the right of track 5. Reduce the opacity of this Event to **50%**.

7. Right-click the text on track **5** and select **Copy**. Right-click in track **3** and select **Paste**. Vegas will ask if you want to create a reference to existing media or if you want to create a new copy. Select **New Copy**.

8. On track **5**, select the **Track Motion** button. In the **Track Motion** dialog box, right-click in the Track Motion Preview window and select **Flip Vertical**. Now resize the track position as follows: X = 0, Y = **–136.61**, Width = **947.10**, and Height = **–631.40**. Close this **Track Motion** dialog box; this positions the reflected text.

9. Now let's position the regular text. Select **Track Motion** for Track **3**.

10. Resize the track position for Track **3** as follows: X = 0, Y = **–35.80**, Width = **765**, and Height = **510**. Close this **Track Motion** dialog box.

11. Now working on the Event on track **5**, insert the following Event FX: **Sony Add Noise**, **Sony Gaussian Blur**, **Sony Deform**, and **Sony Light Rays**. These plug-ins will create the illusion of a reflected surface. Set the **Add Noise** plug-in to **0.168**, with **MonoChromatic** and **Gaussian Noise** boxes checked. In the **Gaussian Blur** dialog box, set the Horizontal value at **0.023** and Vertical at **0**. In the **Deform** dialog box, set the Amount to **1.00**. Check the **Center Image** box. Leaving the Left and Right sliders set at 0, set the Top slider value to **–0.209** and the Bottom slider value to **0.510**. Leave the Shear values set at 0. Finally, set the Light Rays to the values shown in Figure 17.11.

12. Click the **Animate** button. Place the cursor in the center of the **Light Rays** keyframe timeline. Set the Strength value to **.550** and move the **Light Source** indicator to the center of the Preview box. Notice that a new keyframe is created. Move the cursor to the end of the keyframe timeline in the **Light Rays** keyframe timeline. Set the Strength value to **.250** and move the **Light Source** indicator to the far right of the Preview box. A final keyframe is created at the end of the keyframes timeline. Close the **FX** dialog box.

13. Right-click the Event on track **4** and select **Copy**. Paste this copy on track **2**. Once again, Vegas will ask whether

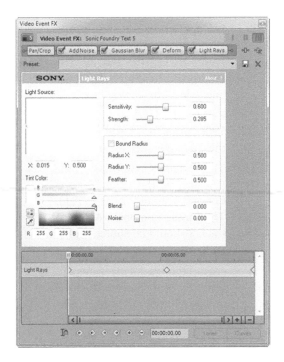

Figure 17.11   Light ray values.

a new copy should be created or a reference to the original file should be made. Create a new copy.

14. Click the **Generated Media** button found on the generated media on track **2**. In the **Aspect Ratio Angle** dialog box, select the first keyframe and enter a value of **0.0**. Now click the last Keyframe button in the keyframe timeline and enter a value of **2180.0** (it may already be present). Close this dialog box.

15. On track **3**, click the **Make Compositing Child** button to cause track 2 to be a parent to the text Event found on track 3.

16. Create a timeline selection again by double-clicking any Event on the timeline. On track **1**, right-click and select **Insert Generated Media | Sony Color Gradient**. In the **Gradient** dialog box, set the values to the settings shown in Figure 17.12. Position the + near the lower left, position the two control points as shown, and use the eyedropper to select a **dark blue** hue. Close this dialog box.

17. Reduce the level of track **1** to **19%**, using the Level slider in the Track Header for track **1**.

18. The **Parent Composite Mode** (left edge of the Track Header) of track **4** should be set to **Add**. The **Parent Composite Mode** of track **2** should be **Source Alpha**.

19. Set the **Composite Modes** (right edge of the Track Header) as follows: track 1, **Screen**; tracks 2 and 4, **Multiply (Mask)**; tracks 3, 5, and 6, **Source Alpha**.

20. Use the **RAM Preview Render** setting by creating a selection of all the media and pressing

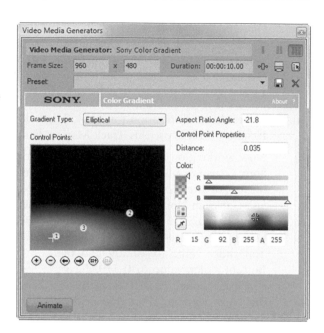

Figure 17.12   Setting values.

Figure 17.13   Creating a reflective surface is very fast and requires no additional plug-ins.

Shift + B. Vegas will take a moment to render the project to RAM. Be sure that RAM preview is set to the maximum available amount in the **Options | Preferences | Video** dialog. The default setting is 16 MB of RAM. I recommend setting your RAM preview to half of your installed RAM. This project is on the DVD, titled **reflection.veg.**

Empty Events

Empty Events are generally used as slug points or blank points in a project. However, empty Events may also be used for compositing. Open the **AlphaRev_Multicam.vf** project. Insert a new track via shortcut keys (**Ctrl + Shift + Q**). In the new track, create a timeline selection that is the same length as the video Events on the lower three tracks. The easiest way is to double-click one of the Events, which will create a selection of the correct length. Right-click in the blank area and choose **Insert Empty Event.** A transparent Event will load into the timeline. Drag the **Vegas Timecode FX** to the track, and timecode will indicate on the track. Use the timecode FX tools to position the timecode. The timecode display is white with a black bar background. We want to get rid of this black bar. Drag the **Mask Generator FX** to the empty Event. By default, the **Mask Generator** is set to **Luminance.** This will allow the white parts of the timecode reader to pass and will hold the dark parts of the timecode reader. The timecode display is now white only.

Figure 17.14

Compositing Modes in Vegas

Vegas Pro has 14 different compositing modes. Vegas Movie Studio has two. Source Alpha is the default mode, whereas additional modes can be used for a number of image manipulation and creative settings.

Compositing modes define the manner in which a higher track combines with a lower track. As higher-level tracks dominate, for purposes of reference, the higher-level tracks are referred to as *foreground*, and lower-level tracks are referred to as *background*.

Compositing Mode tools allow for rapid access to creating multilayered images quickly. Compositing Mode parameters are not adjustable. Using compositing envelopes allows you to adjust compositing level, or color management plug-ins can be used to provide opacity, chroma (color),

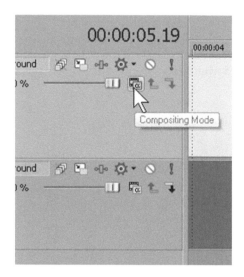

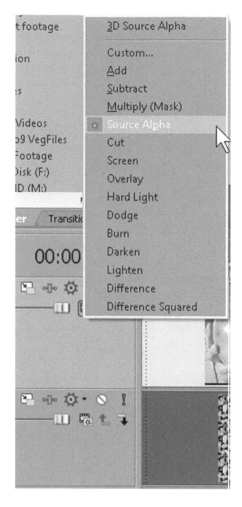

Figure 17.15   Compositing Mode button on each video track.

Figure 17.16   Various compositing modes in Vegas.

Figure 17.17   Original foreground and
background Events.

and transparency control over all Events. For instance, in the Add mode, using the Color Correction Secondary plug-in, combined with blur, creates a moving sonic wave. Using the Screen mode creates a more organic property in the sonic wave, almost as if it were a moving cloud.

Out-of-focus video is sometimes an issue with even the most experienced videographers. Using the Hard Light composite mode and a plug-in or two, marginally out-of-focus video can be brought to a faked focus or, at the least, a more sharpened image.

Place the problem footage on a track and duplicate the track. On the upper track, apply the **Convolution** filter and the **Sharpen** preset in the Convolution filter. Reduce the opacity of the upper track to approximately **50%**. Various settings will apply to individual Events. On the lower track, apply a **Hard Light** compositing mode.

Some Events with good color balance can also benefit by applying a Hard Light overlay mode in the compositing modes selection.

When tracks become parented to one or more lower tracks, a new icon will appear in the Track Control pane of the uppermost track of the parent/child set. This is the **Parent Composite Mode** button.

The **Parent Track Overlay Mode** button provides options to manage masked Events above other Events.

When you select this button, there are two menu choices. The first is the default Multiply mode, and the second is Custom. Selecting **Custom** opens a dialog box offering three compositing overlay modes: Displacement Map, Height Map, and Bump Map.

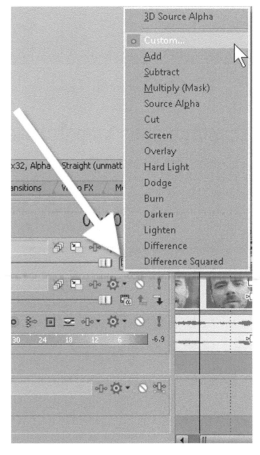

Figure 17.19   Parent Composite Mode button.

Figure 17.18   Before and after applying Hard Light and Convolution Kernel filter.

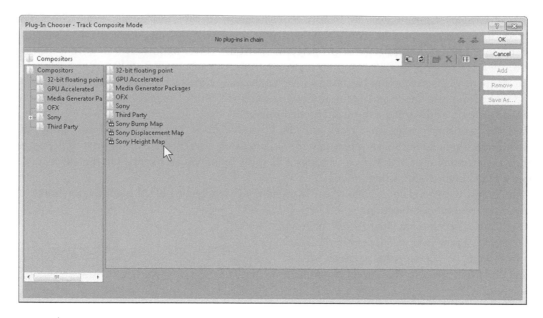

Figure 17.20   Parent Composite Overlay Mode.

Displacement Map Tutorial

This mode uses the parent image as a controller to offset the pixels in the composited child tracks along the X and Y axes. This process uses a two-channel displacement. In other words, pixels are displaced to the left, to the right, up, or down, depending on their relationship to colors in the mask. The displacement map is also useful for following contours of shapes.

To learn more about the displacement map:

1. Create two video tracks and place the **stone.png** image (from the Media directory of the DVD) on track **2**.

2. Create a title using a bold font on track **1**. Duplicate track **2** and slide the new track so that it is track **1**, the text is on track **2**, and the original image is on track **3**.

3. Make track **1** parent to track **2**, which will cause the text to be masked.

4. Check the **Composite Mode** button on track **1** and choose **Custom | Sony Displacement Map** from the plug-in chooser that opens.

5. In the dialog box, change channels of both the X and Y axes to **red**. In the Horizontal axis, set the value to **–0.018**, and set the Vertical axis to **0.027**.

6. The appearance of the text in the Preview window will vary depending on the font used. Experiment with the slider values to find the appropriate setting. Notice how the lettering conforms to the rocks in the photo. Using a text color slightly lighter in hue over the rocks completes the effect.

Figure 17.21   This plug-in can be challenging to control. Working with solid colors or gradients as masks will yield the best results, particularly when you're learning how to use this tool.

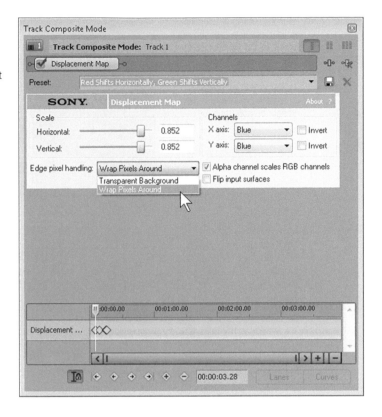

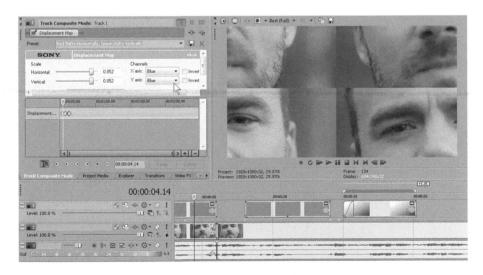

Figure 17.22   Using a red mask causes the image to shift in a clean four-way split.

Figure 17.23   Using a blue-to-green mask causes the image to shift all pixels to the right, creating an extremely wide-angle appearance around the center of the screen without the associated rounding of the image, or vignetting.

Figure 17.24   Three tracks are required to create the project illustrated in Figure 17.25.

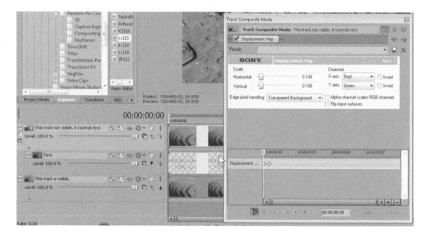

Figure 17.25   Three tracks were used to create this effect.

Height Map Tutorial

This mode uses the parent image as a controller to cause pixels in the composited child tracks to appear closer to or farther away from the viewer. Adding a height map is a great tool for creating the appearance of moving water or viewing an image through glass or water, creating shimmers, fire, or smoke over another image. This mode can be added to gradients, masks, or other images above lower images.

To learn more about the height map, create a new project.

1. Insert two video tracks. Place the image **rings.png** from the DVD that accompanies this book onto track **1** and place a video or generated media Event on track **2**.

2. Make track **1** the parent to track **2** by selecting the **Make Compositing Child** button of track **2**, on the right side of the Track Control pane.

3. On track **1**, click the **Compositing Mode** button. From the menu, select **Custom | Sony Height Map** in the plug-in chooser.

4. Enter the following settings in the dialog box:
   - Amplitude: 0.023
   - Elevation: 0.319
   - Height Scale: 0.320
   - Smoothness: 11
   - Source Channel: Intensity (menu selection)
   - Edge Pixel Handling: Wrap pixels around (menu selection)

5. Click on the Pan/Crop icon of the Event on track **1**; create a keyframe at the end of the Event and zoom in by **40%**.

6. Experiment with the **Amplitude** and **Elevation** settings in the **Height Displacement** dialog box to understand better how this plug-in functions.

Any track-level keyframes can be viewed, moved, and edited directly from the timeline. By expanding the keyframes in the track view, keyframes can be slid forward or backward in time and double-clicked to open the Track Motion or Compositing keyframes This feature provides a visual reference at all times when there is track motion or compositing information on a track, which allows for cursor placement on musical beats or specific musical or dialogue points or simply provides a reference to what is being seen in the Preview screen.

Figure 17.26   The **Expand Track Keyframes** button opens a key frame pane directly on the timeline.

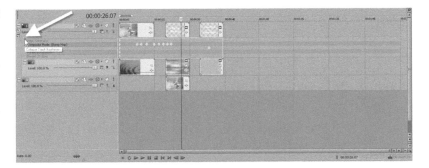

In nearly all of the previous projects, a gradient mask is used. Gradients and other generated media forms are very useful as masks. As an example, try this method of creating a mask:

1. Create a new video track (**Ctrl + Shift + Q**). Insert a gradient mask.

2. For mask shape, select **rectangular**.

3. In the **Gradient Preview** window, slide the color placement control points so that they are lying over the top of each other with very little overlap.

This process takes some attention because if the control points are not placed correctly, the mask will reverse itself and change from an outer mask to an inner mask. This element can also be used as a valuable tool. A color with reduced opacity can also be added to the mask's outer area, acting as an overlay, if desired. This type of mask is similar to the way the Cookie Cutter filter functions; however, this method has greater flexibility in many instances. At VASST, we use this feature to mask out or highlight sections of software interfaces in our training videos.

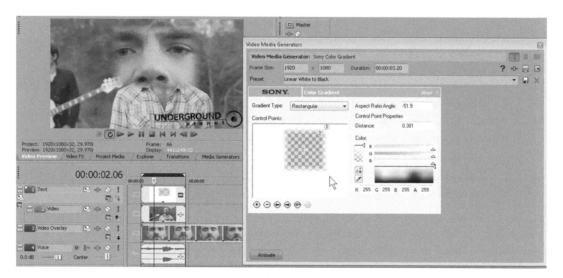

Figure 17.27   Masks can be any shape at all. They can be created with the **Masking** tool found in Pan/Crop or created using **Gradient Maps**. Of course, outside images may be used to create masks as well.

 Tip_____

Practice using the black-to-white gradient as a mask in projects because it is one of the most powerful masking tools Vegas offers.

Open the file called **jellyfishswim.veg** from the DVD that accompanies this book. It is a fairly complex project and contains many attributes found in Vegas. Let's look at each track individually:

*   Track 1. Contains generated media and height map and is at 20%. The generated media acts as a guide to shift pixels generated on track 2.

- Track 2. Contains generated media from the new Noise Texture generator. The Noise Generator is shifting in bias, causing it to create ripples on the "water."

- Track 3. A gradient mask over track 4. It's composited in an Add mode, which brightens the image and adds contrast to allow the jellyfish to stand out over the other elements.

- Track 4. Another noise-generated Event, with color shift and Pan/Crop to create motion in the water.

- Track 5. A simple blue generated media overlay at 50% opacity.

- Track 6. Another gradient, in Subtract compositing mode, acting as a mask for track 7. This feature helps bring out the colors in the jellyfish by masking brighter color values. With some work, a similar effect can be had with a secondary color corrector.

- Track 7. A noise-generated Event, shifting across the Frequency, Noise, Offset, and Amplitude settings. Masked by the gradient on track 6, this color sets the shimmer over the jellyfish.

- Track 8. The still image of the jellyfish, using Pan/Crop to move the fish, whereas two instances of the Spherize plug-in create the motion in the jellyfish. There is also a minor adjustment to the color of the still, reducing the exposure of the flash in the original shot. It also contains a height map to give the jellyfish texture and shine and is mapped to the Event on track insert 9.

- Track 9. A noise-generated Event, creating a texture of movement under the water, beneath the jellyfish.

Underneath all these layers is a motion blur added only to the jellyfish and noise-generated layer found on track 9. Motion blur is applied at a value of 15%.

With this project open, change the compositing modes, opacities, and generated media gradients or colors. See how these changes affect the jellyfish appearance. This demonstration provides a visual overview of the function of each aspect of the tools.

Bump Map Parent (Not Available in Vegas Movie Studio)

Open the **bumpmap.veg** file on the DVD that accompanies this book to see the results of the bump map examples in the following images.

Bump maps use the texture of the parent image to create a map of light and dark information. This tool is very handy for creating 3D titles, creating textures over an Event, and mapping a texture to an underlying Event.

Lighting angles are definable with the **Lighting Type** menu. Use the **Intensity** slider to increase or decrease the presence of a light. The X, Y, and Z parameters can be controlled by inputting values to the input field or by moving the target dot in the **Bump Placement** window. Reset the X–Y parameter by double-clicking the yellow dot or by right-clicking in the **Bump Placement** window and selecting **Reset**.

The Z slider (vertical) controls the height of the light on the mapped image. When **Spotlight** is selected from the menu, the distances of X and Y are controllable, and the Focus slider is enabled

Figure 17.28 In this image, the stone creates a texture, laid over the scuba diver, creating a hand-drawn effect with water ripples.

Figure 17.29 In this image, a simple text Event takes on 3D attributes with definable lighting, depth, and bump height.

as well. **Focus** controls the tightness or breadth of the light image. **Omni-directional** and **Directional** menu options automatically disable the Focus and X–Y distance controls. The **Destination** of X–Y can be adjusted by moving the X in the Bump Placement window.

The **Shininess** slider controls the reflective surface of the map, and the **Ambience** slider controls the amount of light seen in the mapped image.

The **White is high** checkbox causes the bump map to view white areas as the highest areas of the bump texture. Leaving this box unchecked causes the black areas to define the high areas of the texture.

Finally, flipping the input surface reverses the two images, causing the upper and lower tracks to flip images.

Learning to work with these tools helps build titles, scene atmospheres, and magical shots quickly and powerfully. Compositing itself is an art form and requires a great deal of time and experimenting. Vegas has some of the most powerful compositing tools in its class of editing systems and, overall, has more compositing tools than any NLE system that doubles as a finishing editor. On the DVD in this book, several compositing projects are available, although not described in this chapter.

Using Chroma-Key Tools in Vegas

Chroma key, also referred to as *greenscreening* or *bluescreening*, is an art form that must first be practiced at the camera and shooting stage of a production. Even fairly weak footage, however, can be usable in Vegas when filtered with the color-correction tools and chroma-key tools.

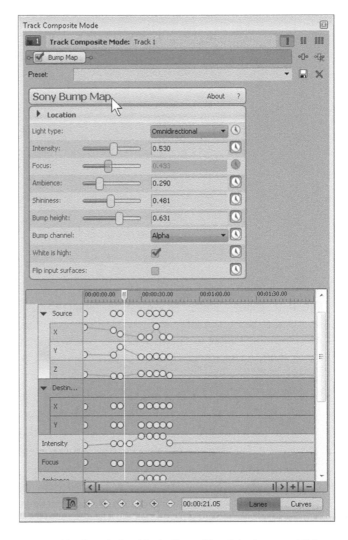

Figure 17.30   Controls found in the **Bump Map** dialog box control light, focus, depth of mapping, and light displacement.

Chroma (color) and key (mask) come together to create a mask from a selected color(s). A quality mask or key can also be made from nearly any color or reasonable gradient of color. Selectable colors/chroma can be keyed or masked out so that other Events can show through those sections. Although industry tradition uses a screen of blue or green, any color can be keyed. Due to the luminance and chroma sensitivity of the bright green used in screens, however, in most situations green is the best choice when shooting in digital formats.

Figure 17.31 A reasonably clean keyable shot with no spill on the face of subject. This is not an easy scene to key without specialty software.

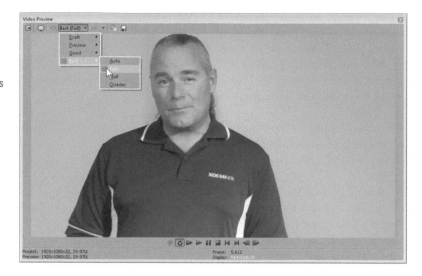

Shooting a clean screen is critical to having a relatively smooth experience with keying. Many tutorials are available on how to shoot a clean screen, and the Sundance Media Group VASST training course teaches this as well (www.vasst.com). Some basics to know are presented here to assist the inexperienced cameraperson or editor in creating a clean shot to be keyed in the editing stage.

- Use Rosco green paint or a commercially produced greenscreen. I recommend the Photoflex dual-color screens that have flex hoops in them for easy storage.

- When shooting on DV, green is a safe choice, especially for highly compressed formats. Blue can be used for shooting as well, but due to the way green is derived in most digital video workflows, green is highly recommended.

- Good lighting is critical. To shoot a clean screen requires at least three lights: a key light for the talent and two lights for the screen itself. A reflector for the key light to light the opposite side of the subject is valuable too, as are flags (masks) to keep the key light from spilling onto the screen.

- There should be a minimum of six feet between the subject and the screen. Essentially we want the height of the subject to set the distance from the key. This practice is necessary to prevent reflection from spilling onto the subject. This kind of reflective spill is very difficult to remove in editing, regardless of the application used for creating a key or matte. The image seen in this section is shot with a backlight and a key light, no fill or rim lighting used. It is a challenging scene, which is why it is good for this tutorial.

Vegas has excellent chroma-key tools that allow for rapid and clean keying of colors. A successful key, however, is also dependent on practice and experience on the part of the user.

From the DVD, open the **chromakey.mp4** file on the timeline in Vegas. Select the **Event FX** on the file and open the **Sony Chroma Keyer** tool.

In the **Chroma Key** dialog box, uncheck the checkbox in the upper-left corner. The **Chroma Key** dialog box defaults to blue, and unchecking this box allows Vegas to sample an accurate replacement color. Select the eyedropper tool, found in the left center of the Chroma Key dialog. With the eyedropper enabled, click the color to be removed from the Event in the Preview window.

Enable the **Chroma Key** tool by placing a checkmark in the checkbox in the upper left of the Chroma Key dialog box. A portion of the selected color will immediately change in the Preview window. Now the Chroma Key tool must be adjusted to create a clean key.

Start by placing the Event to be seen beneath the keyed Event. This process helps adjust the key for best matting. Generated media is great for this task, especially generated media that is a color similar to that of the replacement Event. Of course, the replacement Event can also be used. If it's a fairly busy Event with lots of detail, however, it is sometimes difficult to create clean lines, since the detail in the background Event hides lines during the key process.

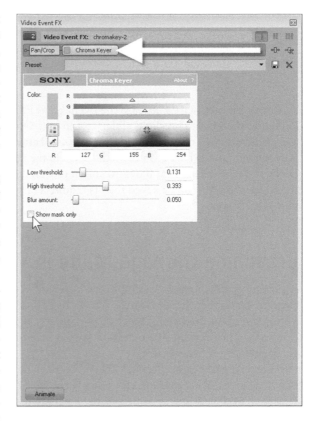

Figure 17.32 **Chroma Key** tool at default setting. Uncheck the **Chroma Keyer** box in the upper-left corner.

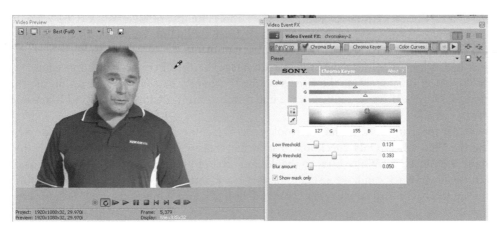

Figure 17.33 Draw or click in the Preview window to select color for removal.

Viewing the key process on an external monitor is helpful to ensure a clean key process. During the color selection, however, the preview must be on the computer screen. After the key color is selected, video can be sent to an external NTSC or PAL monitor.

After an Event is placed beneath the Event being keyed, slide the **Low Threshold** slider to the right and slide the **High Threshold** slider to the left. On the **greenscreen.avi** file, a clean key will be achieved with the Low Threshold slider at **0.400** and the High Threshold at **0.800**. The Blur setting is dependent on the background media used. In the instance of the greenscreen.veg file found on the DVD, the Blur setting is at **0.015** to soften the harsh transition between the background color and the edges of the key. Some keyed Events require a fair amount of blur, whereas others can require no blur whatsoever.

Creating a Garbage Matte in Vegas

A *garbage matte* or *mask* is a simple mask created from an Event or image in Vegas that isolates one element from other elements on the screen. By definition it gets the "garbage" out of the image. This option assists in the keying process, particularly where more than one color must be keyed out. The earlier project did not require a garbage matte; however, many instances exist in which a garbage matte is beneficial.

To create a garbage matte, click the **Show mask only** box in the Chroma Key tool. This step displays the areas being masked and quickly shows a clean or unclean key. This matte/mask can be rendered to a new track, which is then parented to the original Event, saving processor time and allowing multiple masks to take place on the timeline or project. If your computer has enough horsepower, rendering the garbage matte to a new track is not necessary, yet doing so certainly saves on CPU cycles.

To render the matte to a new track, solo the track containing the mask. Double-click the Event to be rendered to a new track, creating a selection. Select **Tools | Render to New Track (Ctrl + M)**. In the dialog box, select **Custom** and select the **Audio** tab. Uncheck **Include Audio**. A popular effect is to create an image that is entirely black and white except for one or two colors. This is part of a color pass, which allows a color to pass through an image that is otherwise black and white.

To create this effect quickly, place the Events on the timeline to be color passed. Duplicate the track so that two identical tracks exist. On the upper track, insert a **Chroma Key** and **Black and White** filter in order.

Using the eyedropper in the **Chroma Key** tool, select the color to be passed, or allowed to be shown. Use the **View Mask Only** checkbox to see what areas will be knocked out in black and white. Adjust the **Black and White** filter to the desired level of black-and-white blend. For maximum effect, the lower track can have a slight blend of black and white with the color. This option reduces the amount of contrast between the color and the black-and-white areas if this is the desired effect.

This is one method of color passing in Vegas; also see the "Color Correction" chapter, which discusses alternative methods.

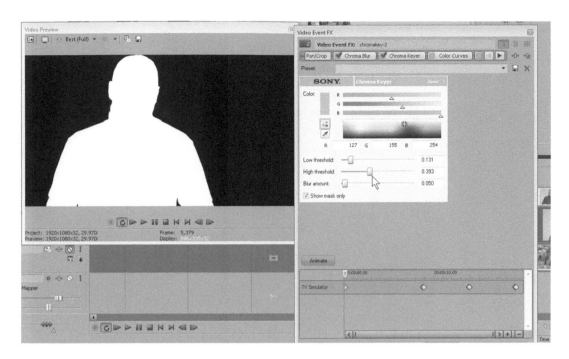

Figure 17.34   A clean and simple garbage matte/mask.

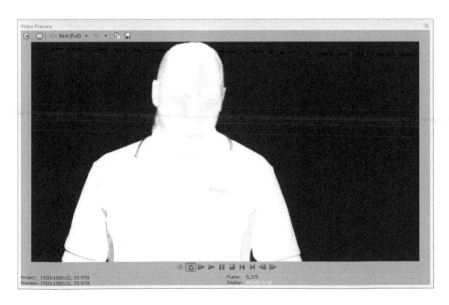

Figure 17.35   An improper mask/matte.

Figure 17.36   Click the **Show Mask Only** tickbox to see only the mask, which will allow the lower track to pass through the area seen in white.

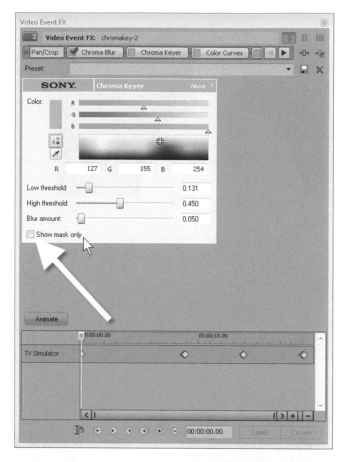

Figure 17.37   Track 1 soloed and with **Show mask only** enabled in the Chroma Key tool. This process is done to render a matte/mask to a new track. Notice that **Best/Full** is enabled; always view masks in this mode, and periodically check all composites in Best/Full mode so that fringing or other problems may be seen.

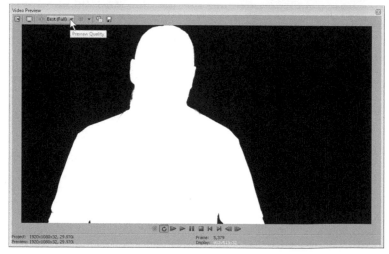

After the new track is rendered, it should be parented to the original track. Click the **Event FX** button on the original track and disable the **Chroma Key** tool by unchecking the checkbox in the upper left of the tool. Parent the mask Event to the original Event by clicking the **Make Compositing Child** button to the right of the original track.

Figure 17.38   Parent track 1 to track 2 by using the **Make Compositing Child** button on track 2.

Figure 17.39   A clean composite.

The two Events over the third track, which contains the background information, create a clean composite over the background image or gray plate if all parameters are adjusted correctly, as illustrated in Figure 17.39. The original image can be color corrected, blurred, or otherwise filtered for creative presentation if desired. Figure 17.40 shows three problem areas in the screen:

- The corners of the screen are visible. These areas will not mask cleanly.

- Split in the glass background shows across screen. This will not mask cleanly.

- Fine hairs are part of the subject. This will not mask cleanly without specialty software.

Figure 17.40 Identifying problem areas in a screen isn't always easy or obvious. Putting a gray plate/gray generated media beneath the keyed image helps identify problem areas.

These problems can be overcome, but the time involved, coupled with the loss of resolution, quickly demonstrate the necessity and time savings of having media shot correctly in the production stage.

To see how to correct the poorly shot footage, open the **badscreen.veg** file on the DVD in this book. A clean mask has been rendered to track 1. This garbage matte is required to create a clean composite. Track 2 is parented to the mask/garbage matte, which is similar to the way the first greenscreen project was done. To be able to create a clean mask, however, a secondary color corrector and black restore were used to cause the mask to render cleanly. The Event is also panned/cropped to remove the corners from the scene and to create a clean masking area. Still, the original Event requires color correction to blend into the background with a believable presentation. The original settings for the color correction and chroma key have been left in place on the original Event in region 1. Click the **Event FX** to enable these two FX, allowing you to see how the mask was created. Color correction has been added to the Event as well. Disable this by unchecking the checkbox in the upper-left corner of the **FX** dialog box. A very small amount of blur has been added to the mask to smooth over the transition from the masked area to the background area.

These are two examples of how a chroma key can be used to repair a background image or to insert new media. There are other instances in which a screen is valuable, however.

Open the **tvscreen.veg** file on the DVD that accompanies this book. The tvscreen.veg file contains a still image: **tvshot.png**. This image is an old photograph of a child watching television.

The television screen has been replaced with green, allowing for a motion picture to be placed in the television screen. This method can also be used to replace screens in television studio-type shots or military establishment-type shots to create a sense of realism. There are more examples of this sort of masking on the tvscreen.veg file. Play with them and notice how the Track Motion tool is used to fill in the masked sections.

Never be afraid to experiment using various FX, Track Motion, Pan/Crop, and other tools on composited media. Turn lots of knobs, slide the sliders, and check the checkboxes. Various combinations turn up lots of artistic possibilities, and, as mentioned at the front of this chapter, compositing is an art form. Be creative!

Create a Holograph in Vegas!

Remember the beamed holographs seen in *Star Wars* episodes? At the time the first *Star Wars* movie came out, this was an exceptionally cool thing, never seen nor conceived before. *Star Trek* had a simple transporter beam effect that used masks to create the look of being transported, but the holograph was a method of communication and projection never before seen on film. Playing around in Vegas on a VASST tour, I was working with a piece of footage and realized how simple this would be in Vegas. To accomplish this look you'll need to shoot against a solid backdrop, preferably green if you are shooting in digital formats.

This project file is on the DVD that accompanies the book; it is named **holograph.vf**.

Shoot your footage with your actor dressed in imaginative clothing that works with the concept of the hologram. The color of the clothing won't matter much because we'll be applying a blue filter over the original footage to mask most color detail. Just be sure the clothing doesn't contain colors that are the same or fairly similar to the background color. You'll have the most effective look if your actor is shot full-body, but even half or three-quarters works acceptably well. However, to mimic the

Star Wars look, you'll want to do a full-body shot. Remember, if this is to look like a communication transmission, your actor should look at the camera just as though he or she can see a video or holographic representation of the person he or she is speaking to.

Figure 17.41   The original image is shot against a blue background. Green is generally preferred, but I've used a poorly balanced glass wall to demonstrate that virtually any color *can* be used.

1.   First, I used the secondary color corrector to pop my blues, allowing for better extraction from the background, which has a few gradients, since we didn't use the cyclorama's full lighting system.

2. I then added a Chroma Key tool, and using the **Show mask only** checkbox, I cleaned up my output. The project .veg file has left these two tools in place, merely turned off, so you can work with the demo media to see how I popped the blue and cleaned up the output.

3. I used the Pan/Crop tool to create a 16:9 letterbox and used the Track Motion tool to stretch the body and create a thinner and off-aspect appearance to the shot. After getting the mask setup, I found a background .jpeg that I wanted to insert the original image into. In this case, it's a shot of a living room.

4. Next, I rendered a new track with the **Show mask only** box still checked. I unchecked **Include Audio** from the **Render | Custom** options, since I wanted the new mask track to lie directly above the original track with no audio, and the audio from the original track was used in the project, removing the need to have a second, duplicate audio track. This allowed me to create a garbage mask or matte to be used as a parent to the original image.

5. Don't create the mask or matte until the Pan/Crop and Track Motion attributes have been determined. Be sure Ripple is disabled before rendering to a new track.

6. On the original track, remove the Secondary Color Corrector and Chroma Key from the original. With the matte above the original track, parent the matte to the original by pressing the Make Compositing Child button on the original track. This will allow the original track to show through.

7. At this point, you should see a fairly clean image over top of the selected background. Set the opacity of your matte to 75% for starters. This will allow the background to be seen through the hologram.

8. Using selected filters, we'll now create the image of the hologram. Drag the Gaussian Blur filter to the matte. Set the values for both horizontal and vertical blur to approximately .025 for starters. This will likely be tweaked later. The blur helps create a soft edge on the original media. It also washes out the screened edges and blends the image into the background a little more smoothly.

9. Drop the Secondary Color Corrector onto the original video track. Choose the Desaturate All But Red preset for starters. Slide the Saturation slider to the right, to a value of 3.000. Now slide the Limit Hue value to the full right, to a value of 360. Slide the corrector target dot to the lower left in the color wheel, setting the track to a blue color. Set this to the desired level. This should blow out the edges of the original media. This step is not necessary for creating this particular look. I simply wanted to blow out my edges.

10. Now drop the TV Simulator on the original media. Select the TV Look preset. Slide Line Sync, Scan Phasing, and Phosphorescence all to the right to create a fast scan image. Add a tiny value of Static if you'd like to distort the image a little further. If you want less interlacing (the horizontal lines in the image) reduce the Interlacing value to 0. For a unique look, keyframe Line Sync and Scan Phasing value movements to make the picture break up every now and then. Notice there are no keyframes in the project. I left these blank so you could experiment with these values on your own.

11. Now drop the Brightness and Contrast filter on the original image, setting the Brightness value to .22. That's all there is to it. The project is ready to be rendered.

Figure 17.42 Match the sliders in this screenshot to create fast, pulsing sync lines.

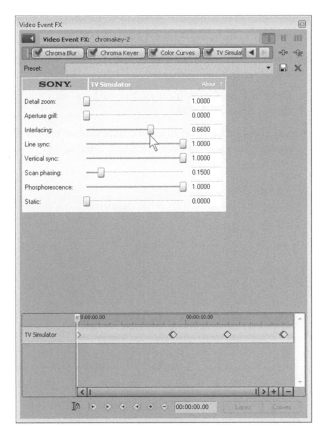

Figure 17.43 Here is the look of the final product.

Some options you might want to try, depending on source footage if other than the media used in the training file:

- Drop the Glow filter on the footage and apply sparingly. This can help smooth out the highlights.

- Drop a Film Grain filter on the original along with the TV Simulator to create noise in the file.

- Use the Convolution filter to create unique effects. This won't work for all looks but is a great look for some effects.

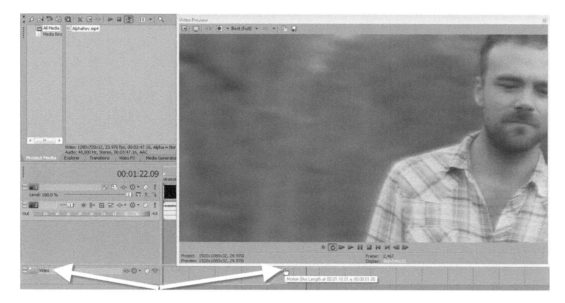

Figure 17.44 Motion blurred at full value with the **Motion Blur** tool. In this image, the singer isn't moving much, so he is in reasonably clear focus. The camera is moving, so the background is blurred. Using a static subject and a moving background can create a very cool effect!

Motion Blur

Vegas has a feature called Motion Blur that allows you to apply an envelope controlling the duration and shape of the blur applied to the motion of video. What makes Motion Blur unique is that it applies blur at the frame level, creating a blur over time (temporal) as the video shows movement. This option makes zooms, pans, and motion in the image blur smoothly. A standard blur applies a blur in 2D space or a spatial blur. A motion blur acts more like a wide-open shutter, allowing for a greater exposure time.

Applying the envelope is performed by selecting **View | Video Bus Tracks** (**Shift + Ctrl + B**) and then right-clicking the video control pane and inserting a **Motion Blur** envelope. Double-clicking the envelope and adding handles/nodes controls the amount of blur.

Applying this filter to sequences of still images, fast- or slow-motion video, and animations can add a sense of realism to the media. It can also be inserted with great intensity to generate a dream-like quality.

One really great effect to try with Motion Blur is to render an Event with lots of motion to a new track and to add a motion blur to suit the eye. In that new track/Event, right-click and select **Undersample**. Undersample the Event by at least **.750**, which will create a unique and stuttered look with blur shifting. The most unusual effect comes from using an extremely low undersampling/frame rate in which the frames skip enough to cut the blurred frames to the point at which they are almost unrelated in motion.

Another terrific use of this tool is to blur a camera pan when transitioning from one scene to another. A motion blur, coupled with a velocity filter and transition, is a good combination for the popular effect of stuttered motion or stopped-motion blurring during a pan into another scene or shot sequence. Motion blur does add considerable time to a rendered section, so make sure the envelope is completely off when not being used.

Every track will be blurred when this envelope is up, unless the **Bypass Motion Blur** button is chosen. This option allows you to blur tracks selectively. The button is next to the Scribble Strip on each video track in the Track Control pane. Leaving it enabled causes the video track to be blurred.

Supersampling

Supersampling resamples each pixel of video information in Vegas and significantly improves the smoothness of the pixel edges and matches to adjoining pixels. This feature is primarily valuable when used in conjunction with the Motion Blur envelope but is also beneficial when used in upsampling smaller resolutions to DV or higher levels, where the PAR changes. Supersampling will not be as noticeable with video containing high motion or with video that is not being changed in output size or resolution. Use supersampling in connection with Motion Blur, when upsampling small-resolution video, or when working with extremely low-resolution stills. It works reasonably well for shifting the aspect ratio from one size to another, such as converting video that is 160 x 160 to 720 x 480. Don't expect it to be fast.

A Kiss Composite

Figures 17.45 and 17.46   On the left is the original image from Thomas Edison's 1900 film *The Kiss*. Notice black edges to be cropped out, bringing the image to correct aspect ratio. Next to it is the same image after cropping and supersampling at a value of 2x frames.

Continued

The way this works is that Vegas creates interpretive frames based on the difference between the project frame rate and the frame rate of the media or the computer-generated imagery. This process also creates smoother flow and edges for generated behaviors, such as Pan/Crop, Track Motion, Transitions, and other new media created in the timeline during the editing stages.

Insert a **Supersampling** envelope in the same manner as inserting a Motion Blur envelope by selecting **View | Video Bus Tracks (Shift + Ctrl + B)** and inserting a Supersampling envelope. Use the envelope to control how many interpolative frames are created. For instance, by using an envelope setting of **4**, four times as many frames are rendered as existed in the original Event. This means that render times are significantly slowed, so don't plan on doing a supersample while you are answering a phone call or grabbing a quick bite to eat. Supersampling, however, is a fantastic tool when shifting resolution, frame rate, or both. It often is beneficial to add a small amount of Gaussian blur as well, to shift the image spatially. Supersampling *won't* benefit media that isn't changing aspect ratio or frame rate; if it merely is being employed to go from one format to another format of matching dimension, you'll spend a lot of time for zero benefit.

Nesting Composites

Another great feature found in Vegas is the nested compositing tools. In earlier versions of Vegas, the compositing tools were powerful but were limited in creating in-depth composites. Vegas can have multiple tracks entirely controlled by one parent track. Individual tracks may have their own motion in space using 3D or 2D tools, with a master composite track controlling all tracks beneath it that are assigned to it. This is great for building monster composites and having one final track control them. In the audio world, this is similar to a mixdown, with a master volume, pan, and effects. The tracks of video are all controlled by the master. In the case of nested tracks, even the master track may have its own 3D properties as well that affect all tracks nested or acting as children to the parent or master.

Figure 17.47   For users familiar with earlier versions of Vegas, parent/child switching is slightly different due to the nested compositing modes.

Follow these steps to understand the basics of parent/child tracks:

Click **File | New** to start a new project. Insert four new video tracks (**Ctrl + Shift + Q**) and name them 1–4, top to bottom.

Track 1 will be the parent track. It's easiest to think of parent tracks as being on top, with their children underneath. Let's start with the child tracks. In tracks 2, 3, and 4, place either video or generated media.

> Notice that the Parent track has an "arm" around the Child track? This is one way to quickly identify the Parent/Child relationship. Look to the left side of the track headers and the Parent/Child relationship is immediately apparent. A parent track may also be a "grandparent" in the family of compositing.

On each of these three tracks, open the **Track Motion** dialog box, turn on **3D Alpha** mode, and create 3D motion in each track so that all three tracks reveal themselves at some point in the project.

In each track header, there is a **Make Compositing Child** switch. Press the switch in tracks **2, 3,** and **4** to cause all tracks to act as child tracks beneath the parent.

In Track 1, open the *Parent* Track Motion dialog box, found on the left edge of the track header, and enable the **3D Alpha** mode on this parent track. Remember that there is no media on track 1 at this time.

Create movements on that track using X, Y, and Z planes as well as orientation and rotation. All three tracks beneath the parent will respond to the parent track motion, regardless of their own motion.

In the parent track (track 1), insert text or other form of media.

In the track header of the parent track, click the **Track Motion** button. Enable **3D Alpha Channel** mode in this dialog box. Assign 3D motion in this dialog box as well, creating keyframes to animate the track. This track animation is independent of the other three tracks that are children to the parent track, yet the parent track controls this track's motion as well.

In the composite created here, there are five track motion elements occurring at one time. Each of the four tracks has its own track motion element, with the parent track controlling each of these tracks in a separate motion path. You also may need to move the parent position by a few pixels to see the shadow or glow beneath the child tracks.

As you are working on individual tracks, notice that the track header number contains a small blinking indicator signifying which track is being affected by whatever process is being applied. This is particularly helpful when working on parent/child comps because it makes it clear which track is currently selected. Even when multiple tracks are selected, only the number of the track for which the properties are going to be affected will blink.

Parental Guidance/Shadows and Glow

Another benefit of a master parent track is that all child tracks may be assigned a master shadow or glow. This allows for a more cohesive composite as opposed to creating separate shadows and glows individually.

In the composition created earlier, open the **Parent Track Motion** and disable the **3D Alpha Channel** mode.

To the left of the keyframing timeline in the **Track Motion** dialog box is a checkbox for Shadow and for Glow. Enable the **Shadow,** and you'll see that the child tracks have shadow showing where the background allows it to be seen. You may need to create a non-child track at the bottom of the timeline that contains a white generated media slug to see the shadow, depending on the color of your shadow and media content.

You can also insert a white slug on the parent track and insert a compositing envelope on the parent track. This will allow the parent track to control opacity of all nested media. Open the **ringopacity.veg** file on the disk in that accompanies this book. Notice how the parent tracks control opacity of tracks nested as child tracks. Move the handles on the composite envelopes on the tracks to get a feel for how this works.

To insert a composite envelope to control nested tracks:

1. Create the composite as you'd like it to appear.

2. Insert a new video track above the composition.

3. Parent the new video track to the tracks beneath.

4. In the new parent track, choose the compositing mode tool in the header, and select **Multiply/ Mask** mode.

5. Choose the **Parent Track Motion** button in the parent track. In this track, you'll assign 3D motion (or any other motion) to the child tracks. Assign any motion you would like, if any. Otherwise, right-click the track header and insert a compositing envelope.

6. Double-click the compositing envelope to assign handles to the envelope, allowing the opacity or transparency of the track to be adjusted.

Glows and shadows will be cleaner in the 32-bit modes available in Vegas, but beware of the hit on render times.

Ten-Bit Color and 32-Bit (Floating) Processing (Not Available in Vegas Movie Studio)

Vegas Pro users will enjoy the addition of 10-bit color sampling and 32-bit float processing. Ten-bit color sampling adds an additional 2 bits per color channel when ingesting video. This represents the number of levels per color channel. The default color sampling is 8 bits per channel (the same as most cameras shoot), which equates to 256 levels of color per channel; 10-bit offers 1024 levels per channel, or four times more brightness levels than 8-bit offers.

However, the availability of 10-bit video doesn't necessarily mean that your video quality will increase.

Where 10-bit video offers some significant benefit is when video is captured as 10-bit and is to be color corrected, composited, or worked within a serial digital interface (SDI) workflow for broadcasting or higher-end postproduction workflows. Ten-bit is the standard in all mid-level to highlevel postproduction houses and in all broadcast facilities.

To benefit from 10-bit video sampling, a hardware card that supports 10-bit video is required. Currently, the AJA Kona LH and Black Magic Design Decklink and Intensity series are the only fully supported cards. Video shot on an 8-bit format such as DV, HDV, AVCHD, AVC, XDCAM, and HDCAM will still benefit when captured as 10-bit video due to the way the codec will work with the video and the way the codec will respond to color correction and other processing.

At the end of the day, this can be said: 10-bit video simply looks better than 8-bit video. The question of whether to go 10-bit isn't about the quality but about the associated costs of building a 10-bit workflow. Ten-bit video will require more hard drive space, faster hard drives, an HD/SD SDI card, and perhaps an HD/SD SDI monitor, depending on workflow. All of these additional requirements may easily increase the cost of an editing system by a factor of 5.

One of the immediately visible benefits of the 32-bit floating-point process is seen if you're shooting sky, water, or any other large area that contains a single graduated color. In 8-bit processing, the image will display banding at some point, but with a 32-bit float, the banding disappears.

The 32-bit floating point is a different feature; no hardware card is needed for users of Vegas Pro to benefit. The 32-bit floating point is a processing function. The primary benefit of 32-bit floating point is a far more precise processing of frame information. What this means in layman's terms is that gradients will be smoother, edges of blurred edges or motion information will be softer, and fades will be smoother. Transitions that blend information will also be better overall. The 32-bit processing will use significantly more system resources than 8-bit processing, so be prepared for longer renders and slower previews.

Vegas Pro offers three modes of working with media (these processing bits should not be confused with color bits):

- 8-bit processing (this is the standard of previous versions of Vegas)
- 32-bit processing with 1.00 gamma
- 32-bit processing with 2.222 gamma

The 32-bit mode with 1.00 gamma may decode video differently, depending on the source media. XDCAM, HDV, and AVCHD format media will all decode differently. This may create problems if you're not sure exactly what the footage should look like. Additionally, the footage is decoded to computer RGB vs. studio RGB. This means that rather than being confined to the broadcast standard of 16–235 RGB, the video will be decoded to 0–255 RGB. This isn't going to be a problem for media destined for DVD or the web, but it could potentially create problems for media heading for broadcast. Bear in mind that previewing on an external broadcast monitor will not deliver accurate results, as the media is being converted back to 16–235 (IRE standards) on output.

Additionally, some of the FX in Vegas will not function accurately when working with 1.00 mode; experiment with various FX to get an idea of how they may function. Dissolves, cross-fades, and similar transitions will be smoother and more cinema-like. Titles will be richer and deeper in color and may blend better with underlaid video, but the transparency level of the titles may behave differently as well.

Some of the FX that ship with Vegas, and most of the third-party FX available for Sony Vegas, are 8-bit only. The 8-bit FX are indicated by a small blue square next to the FX in the FX window. Using these FX will always force the video stream to be processed in 8 bits.

HDV, AVCHD, MXF IMX and HD, Sony YUV (8- and 10-bit), and uncompressed RGB floating point formats read directly into 32-bit floating point without going through 8-bit first. HDV, AVCHD,

MXF IMX and HD, and Sony YUV (8- and 10-bit) formats may render without passing through 8-bit. Video FX and transitions with blue squares appearing next to the FX/Transition name are not floating-point capable, and the image will be reduced to 8-bit before using these plug-ins.

The decision to work in 32-bit modes in Vegas Pro is one that should best be made prior to beginning a project. FX and some transitions may display different results between the 1.00 and the 2.222 gamma modes. To get an idea of how this may affect you, create a timeline and place a couple of HDV, AVCHD, or XDCAM files on the timeline. Create cross-fades with them, and add color correction to the files or track. Switch between the gamma modes in the Project Properties and observe the changes. Choose one mode or the other prior to beginning the project for consistent results. A good rule of thumb when choosing 32-bit is to start with 2.222 gamma, as this has a color profile similar to that of standard 8-bit. But, try alternate settings for the most appropriate look.

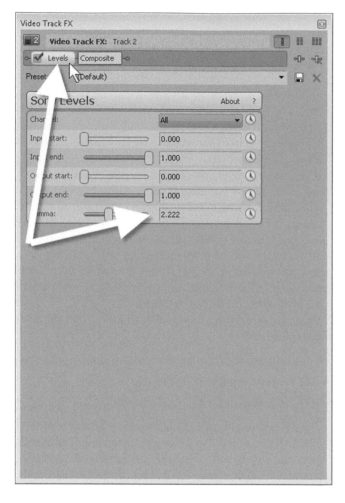

Figure 17.48 The Levels filter set to 2.222.

The Levels filter may be used to correct media that isn't correct in a 1.00 gamma project.

 Tip_____

Need to process FX before a composite or after a composite? Drag the FX in the FX window so that it appears before or after the composite as seen in Figure 17.48. Old versions of Vegas had a Pre/Post toggle in the dialog box; this has been replaced by moving FX before or after the composite in the top of the dialog box. When you're using Levels, make sure it's in the "Pre" mode, or at the front of the composite chain.

There are some workarounds to working with 1.00 gamma in projects that may be creating problems. If the 1.00 gamma project offers the desired results in compositing, creating blurs, diffusion, or effects that benefit from the linear light processing found in the 1.00 mode, build those segments in a 1.00 gamma timeline and nest this timeline in a 2.222 gamma project. Another option is to work in a 1.00 gamma project but apply the Levels filter with a gamma setting of 2.22 at the track level. Place media that should receive linear light processing on one track, and create another track for media that, when processed, doesn't meet the desired appearance with the 1.00 gamma setting. When you drop the Levels filter on the track, you'll want it to process first in any chain or spatial change made to the media (such as Pan/Crop) so select the Pre/Post switch in the plug-in chain.

When will you see absolute benefit from 32-bit floating point processing? As mentioned before, HDV, AVCHD, and XDCAM projects become richer as a result of the difference in decoding. Additionally, media from AVCHD and HDV camcorders that offer XV color will also be significantly more rich and saturated. If the 10-bit YUV codec is used via an AJA Kona or Black Magic Design cards, this media too, will benefit from the 32-bit floating-point process. These formats will benefit when you color correct and push color; the banding normally associated with pushed 8-bit disappears.

Generated Media

Vegas has the ability to create or generate media using nothing but plug-ins (no physical file is required) that can generate titles, solid colors, noise, gradients, checkerboards, and other graphic elements. You can quickly and easily generate colors for inserted media, masks, filling backgrounds under titles that don't have associated video or graphic Events, and many other uses.

Generated Media Tutorial

To learn how to create generated media, let's whip up a generic star field from scratch.

Figure 17.49 The **Gradient Color** dialog box is used to define Gradient colors on the timeline.

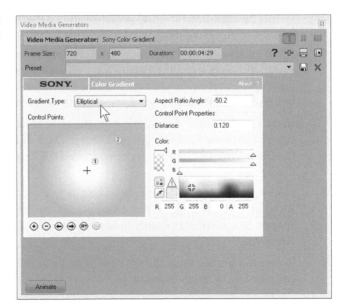

1. Insert a new video track in a new project by right-clicking the **Track Control** pane and choosing **Insert New Video Track** or by pressing **Ctrl + Shift + Q**.

2. Right-click in the timeline area of the new track and choose **Insert Generated Media** from the menu. The Generated Media dialog box opens.

3. Select **Sony Solid Color**. The Solid Color dialog box opens, and you can select the color of choice. For this exercise, choose **black**.

4. After setting the color, set the length of time that the Event should last and close the dialog by clicking the **X** in the upper-right corner. A black Event now appears on the screen.

5. Click the **Event FX** button found on the Event, or right-click and choose **Event FX**.

6. From the **FX** dialog box, select two plug-ins: **Sony Add Noise** and **Sony Black Restore**. Both can be selected at the same time by pressing and holding **Ctrl** down while selecting the second FX plug-in. On the top/header of the plug-ins dialog box, you should see both FX names displayed.

7. Click the **Add Noise** box. In the Add Noise plug-in dialog box, uncheck the **Animate** checkbox, and slide the **Noise Level** slider to **1.0**. In the **Black Restore** dialog box, set the threshold for **0.475**.

You have just created a star field from nothing more than computer-generated media.

To add more media to the star field to make it more realistic or interesting, insert a new video track above the existing track. Right-click in the timeline area and choose **Insert Generated Media**, just as you did before. Now follow these additional steps:

1. Choose **Sony Color Gradient**.

2. Select **Sunburst** from the preset menu. Notice that by moving the target marker around in the **Gradient Preview** screen, the curve of the gradient can be adjusted.

3. Define the length of time that the Event should occur. This length of time should be the same length of time as the previous Event created. Now close the dialog box.

4. The new gradient now covers the entire Preview screen. To show only the portions that are to be actually seen, select the **Video FX** tab on the bottom left of the Docking windows (depending on preferences, the tab may be at the top of the Docking windows) or click the **Event FX** button found on the new gradient. Choose the **Sony Cookie Cutter FX** plug-in.

5. In the Cookie Cutter dialog, select the **Arrowhead** in the **Shapes** menu. The screen can still be covered with the Sunburst image. Using the **Size** slider, size the arrowhead so it is not filling the entire Preview window. A size of around **0.050** is a good choice. Close the **Cookie Cutter** dialog box.

6. Now open the **Track Motion** dialog box on track 1. With the circle displayed, indicating that rotation is possible, place the cursor where the circle and the Y intersect. The cursor will change into a circular shape, indicating that the Track Motion tool is prepared to rotate the frame.

7. Rotate the frame so that the arrowhead in the Preview window is pointing at the lower-right corner of the Preview window.

8. Click and hold in the middle of the **Track Motion** frame and slide the frame to the upper-left corner of the frame window. The arrowhead in the Preview window will move to the same location and should remain pointed at the lower-right corner.

9. Enable the sync cursor in the **Track Motion Keyframe** section. In the main timeline, place the cursor on the right edge of the generated media Event. In the **Track Motion** tool, move the frame to the lower-right corner. A new keyframe will be inserted in the timeline as a result of the sync cursor being enabled.

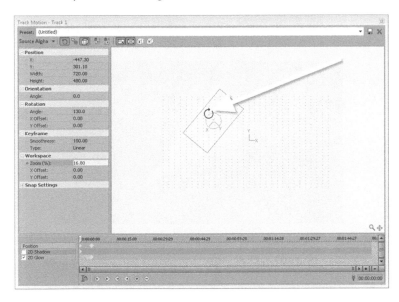

Figure 17.50   The cursor changed to a rotating cursor, used for rotating the frame inside the Track Motion tool.

Now press the **Spacebar** or click **Play** on the Transport control. You should see the arrowhead flying across the star field, and if the loop is enabled (press **Q**), the arrowhead/starship will fly across the screen from the upper left to the lower right.

Figure 17.51   Flames created with glow give a realistic edge to the starship.

Adding an orange glow and sizing it to cover only the back of the arrowhead will create a flame coming out of the back of the arrowhead/starship. By animating the feather, opacity, and intensity of the glow, the flames can come to life, moving at different depths and opacity, giving a realistic sense of video to an otherwise static image.

This project can be found on the DVD included with this book and is labeled **compositerocket .veg**. The keyframes animating the flame are also found on the veg file.

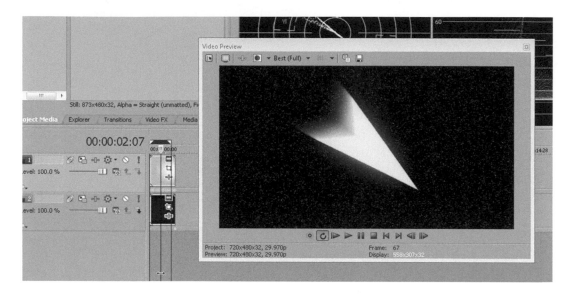

Figure 17.52   The CompositeRocket.veg file shows the finished project described above.

Nested Projects (Not Available in Vegas Movie Studio)

Not to be confused with Nested Composites, Vegas Pro allows for the nesting of projects. This feature is similar to Nested Sequences in other applications. What this does is allow Vegas users to drop veg or .vf files directly on the Vegas Timeline, and Vegas Pro treats the veg as though it were a media file, regardless of how many stacked tracks are contained in the .veg or .vf dropped on the timeline.

To insert a nested project, locate a .veg file in the Windows or Vegas Explorer, and drag it to the Vegas Pro Timeline.

The nested project may be trimmed, color corrected, FX added, and so on. There are many uses for this feature, but there are a few specific instances where I find it extremely useful:

- When building 3D planar projects such as those created using VASST Scattershot, the sheer number of tracks can eat up a lot of CPU cycles, and invoking the 3D mode in the project sets the CPU cycling for the entire project. Creating a 3D project in one instance of Vegas, saving as a .veg file, and dropping on a new timeline as an element to be mixed with other less

CPU-intensive media will speed renders. It also allows for messy projects to be easily cleaned up and treated as a single piece of media.

- Another valuable use of the nested .veg feature is that users may create their timeline based on scenes, then drop scenes into a master timeline to be finished out as a final master.

- Yet another use is to drop .veg files as header/footer files on episodic or repetitive works, allowing for speed of render and consistency in projects.

The "single" piece of media is still a project that may be edited, even though the nested veg function will treat the media as though it has been rendered. Right-clicking a nested file will open a submenu, and in this menu, users may select **Edit Source Project**. This will open the source project in another instance of Vegas so that it may be edited.

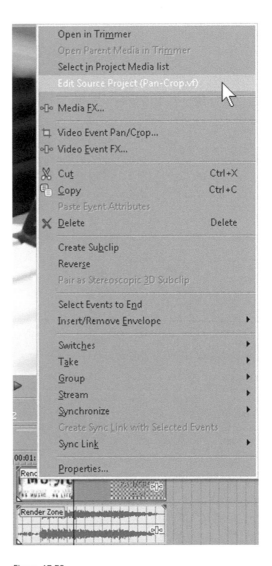

Figure 17.53

Media Manager

The Media Manager is a powerful search and retrieval tool for organizing and finding media quickly. It provides a way to catalog all the video, audio, and still images used in your projects or anywhere on your hard drives and organize them into multiple categories for instant identification. It also provides three ways to search for your media and find it quickly. If you have lots of stock footage, image libraries, or music libraries, the Media Manager will get you organized quickly and keep you organized and productive when you're looking for particular images.

Overview and Concepts

Before we start is it important to understand that the Media Manager does not contain any media. The media is still on your hard drive even after you add it to the Media Manager. The Media Manager is simply cataloging where the media is located and showing it to you all in one place, much the way your phone book catalogs people's phone numbers and shows them all in one place. Similarly to the way the phone number in a phone book is a pointer to a person, the Media Manager maintains pointers to all your media, wherever it may be.

There are two ways in which you can use the Media Manager. You can use it to catalog stock footage, motion backgrounds, royalty free music, ACID loops, and the like and use it as a library. Or you can allow it to dynamically catalog every piece of media that you have ever used in a project. In the first case you add media manually and deliberately, and only the media that you add gets into the Media Manager. In the second case, media is added by Vegas when you simply place it on the timeline of a project. Each use has its benefits, and you should think about how you want to use the Media Manager as you read this chapter.

It is also important to understand that you can have multiple Media Manager databases. This means that you can have some that are libraries of stock media and others that are collections of media you have used in your projects. You can also decide to make several smaller databases that are good for particular kinds of projects. For example, you might have a Media Manager database with documentary media, another with news media, and another with wedding media. The possibilities are endless.

User Interface Layout

The layout of the Media Manager interface is shown in Figure 18.1.

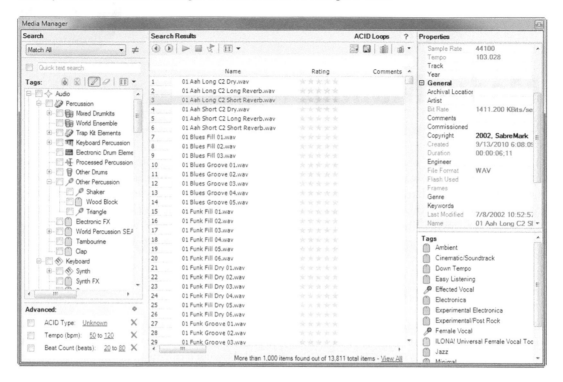

Figure 18.1   The Media Manager interface.

On the left from top to bottom is the quick text search (keyword search) on top, the tag tree (the organizational heart of the interface) in the middle, and the advanced search on the bottom. The center of the interface shows the main interface toolbar at the top and the search results in the middle. Notice at the bottom it says, "More than 1,000 items found out of 13,811 total." It would be difficult to browse through 13,811 pieces of media, so this view is limited to a subset that you can control in the preferences. Normally you would see fewer files because a query would restrict the view to only those files that match the search criteria. On the right top are the properties of the currently selected file; the right bottom shows any tags associated with that file. Tags are discussed in the "Organizing Your Media with Tags" section of this chapter.

At the top of the center search results area is the Media Manager toolbar.

Figure 18.2   The Media Manager toolbar.

The icons on the left allow you to cycle through the previous and next queries, play, stop, and auto-play the selected media, and change the search view from a grid to a list or thumbnail view. The icons on the right allow you to add media, save the tags to the media, open the reference library, and create and load new libraries and change the options.

Setup and Preferences

The Media Manager is an optional installation. Make sure that you have it installed from the Vegas Pro 11.0 CD or you can download it from the Sony Website. You also want to be sure that it is enabled in Vegas Pro.

To enable the Media Manager:

1. Select **Options | Preferences | General** tab.

2. Check **Enable Media Manager** *(requires restart)*.

If this option was not checked, you will have to restart Vegas to make the Media Manager active.

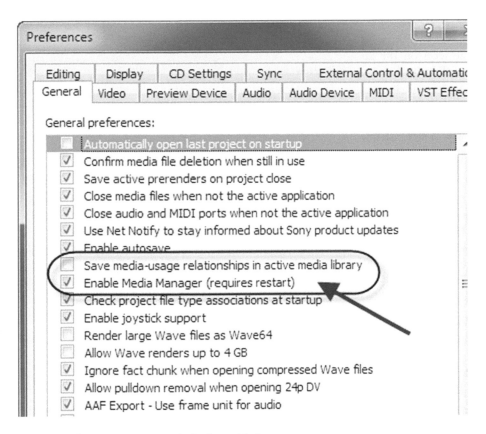

Figure 18.3 Enable Media Manager in the General Preferences.

Another important option on the General Preferences tab is "Save media-usage relationships in active media library." If you would like to use the Media Manager to catalog stock media and not have your project media added, you should *uncheck* this option. If you don't have this option unchecked, every piece of media that you drop on the timeline or into a media bin, whether you use it or not in the final project, will get cataloged. This is not desirable if you are creating a stock media library. However, if you want Vegas to dynamically add the media that you use in projects to the library, keep this option checked.

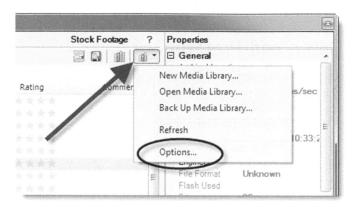

Figure 18.4   Menu options.

Changing Options

The Options dialog box is accessed by the icon on the far right of the toolbar called the **Media Library Actions** button. Selecting this toolbar button will give you a number of choices. For now we will select the one marked **Options**.

If you plan to add any Sony media like ACID loops to your library, make sure that you have the **Sony Sound Series Loops and Samples** reference library enabled. This is an optional download and install from the Sony Website.

Create a New Library

The Media Manager creates a library called **Default** when it is first installed. You can add all your media to this library or you can create a new library.

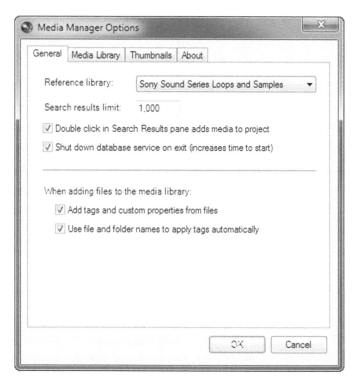

Figure 18.5   General options for the Media Manager.

To create a new media library:

1.   Select **Media Library Actions | New Media Library**.

You will be prompted to give this new library a name. Name it something meaningful so that you will know what's in it. In this example we will create a library with motion backgrounds and royalty-free music suitable for titles and DVD menus.

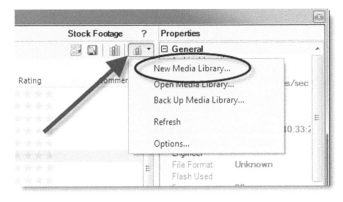

Figure 18.6

You can have as many Media Manager libraries as you want and easily switch between them. The default folder to hold them is in your **.\Documents\Sony Media Libraries** folder, but you can place them anywhere you'd like on your hard drive or even on a network drive to be shared among editors.

If you want to know which media library you have open, just look at the top of the Media Manager interface and you will see the name above the toolbar to the right.

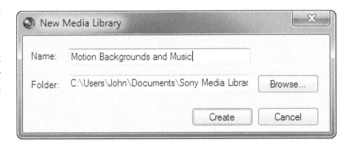

Figure 18.7   Name your new media library something meaningful.

Adding Media to the Media Manager

Once you have your options set and a new library created, it's time to add your media to the library. The term **Add** is a bit of a misnomer because the media does not go into the library; rather, it is *cataloged* by the library. This means that a pointer to the media is added to the library so it can be found later, much like a card catalog at the library points to books on the shelves.

To add media to the library:

1.   Press the **Add Files To Media Library** button.

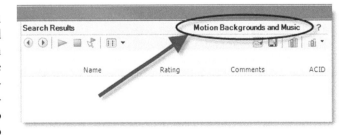

Figure 18.8   The library name is displayed on top.

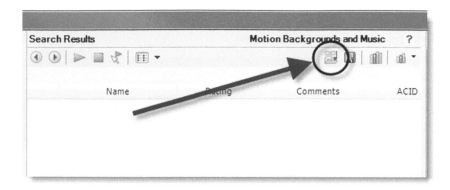

Figure 18.9   Use the **Add Files to Media Library Button** to add media.

You will be prompted to browse for the folder that you would like to start searching for the media. If your media is in multiple folders, you want to start one level above. If your media is all in one folder, just select that folder.

This brings up the Add Files to Media Library window.

If you have selected a starting folder that has subfolders and you want those subfolders to be searched for media, make sure you have the *Include subfolders* option checked (this is the default). It is also important that you select the file types to search for if your folders have more than one type of media and you only want certain types to be found. In the example, each folder may contain audio or the video media and a still image thumbnail of the video. Since the Media Manager will automatically show us thumbnails of the video, we do not want these still images imported, so only the **Video** and **Audio** types have been selected.

In the **Advanced** options, you can elect to have only new files added or to rescan all files, which

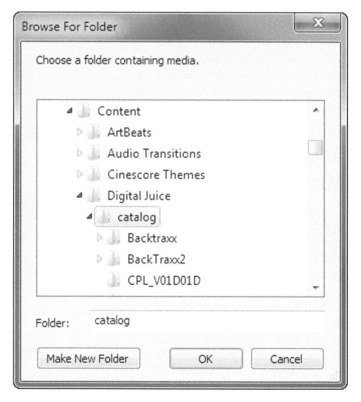

Figure 18.10   Select the folder to start scanning for media.

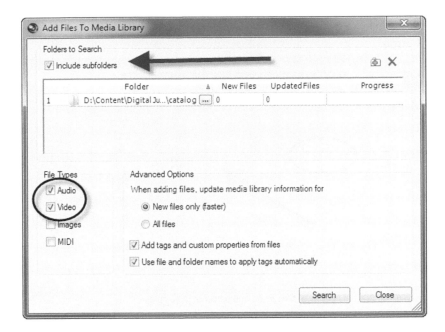

Figure 18.11   Add Files to Media Library window.

will take considerably longer. The first time you are adding files from a folder, it doesn't matter which you select because all the files will be new. On subsequent runs, you would only want to scan for all of the files if you changed the existing files and want the new changes to be picked up. Otherwise use **New files only**.

The **Add tags and custom properties from files** option will import any tags that were saved with the files and will save you hours of tagging the media manually. You will learn how to save your tags with the media later in this chapter. You also might want to check the **Use files and folder names to apply tags automatically** option. This will match file folder names to any tags in the library with the same name, and it will tag the files as being part of that category. For example, if you have a tag called **Backgrounds** and the scan finds a file in a folder called .\Backgrounds it will automatically

add the Backgrounds tag to the file in the library.

You can have the Media Manager search more than one location on your hard drive.

To do this press the **Add Folder** icon at the top right of the **Add Files to Media Library** window. This will bring up the **Browse Folder** window again and you can add more folder locations to search.

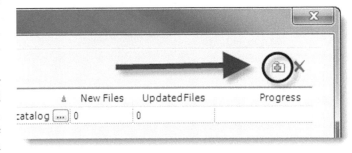

Figure 18.12   Add a folder to search.

To start adding media:

1.   Press the **Search** button.

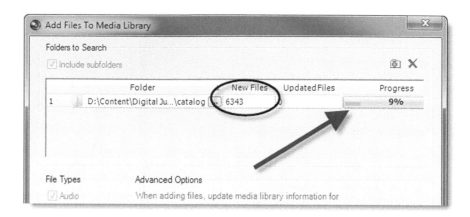

Figure 18.13   While searching you will see the number of files found and percentage complete.

Once the search is complete, press the **Close** button and you will see all of the media listed in the center window of the user interface. To make this view more interesting, you can change it from a list view to a thumbnail view:

1.   Select **Change Search Results View** icon | **Thumbnail**.

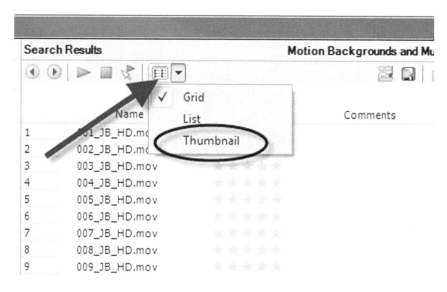

Figure 18.14   Change to **Thumbnail** view for video or image media viewing.

The Thumbnail view is great for video files and images because it allows you to see the contents of your media easily. If you hover your mouse over a thumbnail it will magnify the image so that you can see it better.

Figure 18.15   Magnify thumbnails by hovering over them.

Once the magnifier is active, you can move your mouse over the other thumbnails and they will each magnify in turn without delay. You can also display the filenames under the thumbnail by checking the **Details** checkbox.

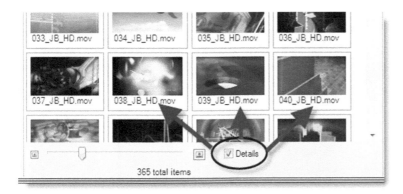

Figure 18.16   Add filenames to thumbnails with the **Details** checkbox.

Organizing Your Media with Tags

Organizing your media is the key to finding individual pieces easily. You can organize before you add media or after you've added media, it's up to you. In this example we are going to organize before we add media to a new library called **Stock Footage** so that we can take advantage of the option to **Use files and folder names to apply tags automatically.** We will build a tag tree that matches the folder names of the files we are going to import. This will allow the Media Manager to automatically tag the files as they are added to the media library.

You can add new tags to the existing Audio and Video tree, or you can create new top-level tags. To add a new tag:

1.   Right-click any tag and select **New** from the popup menu.

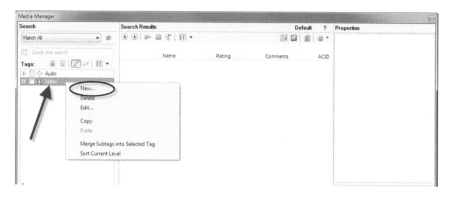

Figure 18.17   Right-click any tag to add a new tag.

You can name this tag anything you want. In this example we will call it **Stock Footage.** You can also assign a new icon to it to distinguish it from other tags easily. To do this:

2.   Right-click on the tag you want to edit and select **Edit** from the popup menu.

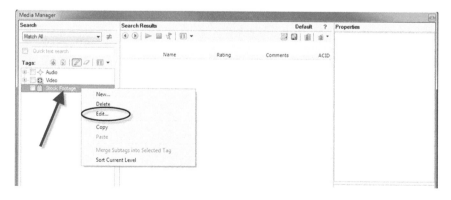

Figure 18.18   Change the tag icon by right-clicking and selecting **Edit**.

The Tag Editor window will appear where you can change the name and select a new icon.

3.   Click on the new icon and press **OK.**

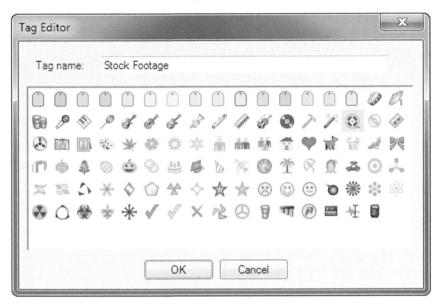

Figure 18.19   Select a new icon from the Tag Editor.

Continue to add tags by right-clicking and selecting **New.** You can drag and drop a tag under another tag to make a hierarchy of tags so that Stock Footage is the parent tag and all others are the child tags.

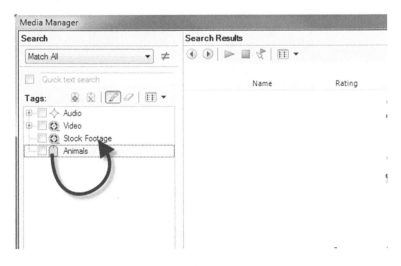

Figure 18.20   Drag tags to form a hierarchy.

Continue to add tags until you have made categories for all your footage.

In this example, when we add media to the library, the Media Manager will assign all the media from the Animals folder to the Animals tag and all the media from the Backgrounds folder to the Background tag, and so on. This allows you to click on a tag and see only the media that is assigned it. In the example in Figure 18.22, the **Clouds** tag is checked, and only media that has been assigned to the Clouds tag is shown.

Once you have your media library organized and all your data tagged, it is very important to save the tags with the media.

The reason it is important to save the tags with the media is so that you can create a new media library and not have to retag the data. Once you save the tags with the media, you can re-import that media into a new media library and the tags will return, leaving all your media automatically organized the way you want.

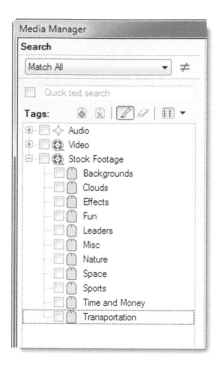

Figure 18.21   Create a hierarchy by adding tags and dragging and dropping into place.

Figure 18.22   Click on a tag to find media quickly.

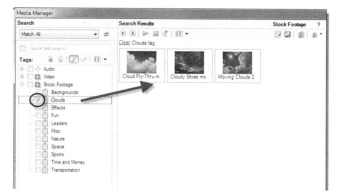

Figure 18.23   Save tags with the media so you can reuse them.

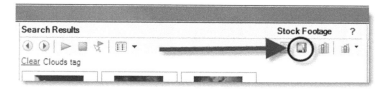

The Power of Search

The real power of the Media Manager is in its search capabilities. You have seen how you can use tags to perform a search simply by clicking on the tag. In this section we will learn two more powerful ways to search.

At the top of the search pane is an option that affects all searching (quick text, tag, and advanced). They are **Match All**, **Match Any**, and **Not Equal** ($\neq$).

When you select:

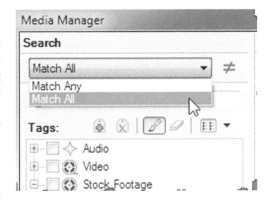

Figure 18.24   The **Match** option affects all searches.

- **Match All.** The search will return the media that matches all the search criteria. For example, if you select two tags, only the media that is associated with both tags will be returned.

- **Match Any.** The search will return the media that matches any of the criteria selected. For example, if you selected two tags, the media returned can be associated to either one of the tags.

- **Not Equal** ($\neq$). The search will return the opposite of the search criteria. In other words, it returns all the media that does not match.

It is important to understand how Not Equal will affect the match criteria:

- **Match All + Not Equal.** The search will contain none of the criteria. For example, if you selected the tag **Cloud** and the keyword **Fly**, you will get media that does not have the Cloud tag and also does not contain the keyword Fly.

- **Match Any + Not Equal.** The search will contain some of the search criteria. For example, if you selected the tag **Cloud** and the keyword **Fly**, you will get media that either does not have the Cloud tag or does not contain the keyword **Fly**. This means that some of the media that has the Cloud tag but does not contain the keyword Fly will be returned because Match Any says that it can match any of the criteria.

Before doing any search, press the **Clear** link to clear any previous search.

Figure 18.25   Press the **Clear** link before doing a new search.

Quick Text or Keyword Search

The quick text search, or as it's sometimes called, the keyword search, will search all the fields in a library. When you use the Grid view you will notice that there are several columns that have information in them, such as Filename, File Format, Size, Bit Depth, Path, Copyright, Tags, and Comments. The keyword search looks in all of these columns. Be mindful of this when you do your search. If you only want to search a specific column or set of columns, use the Advanced search.

To use the keyword search:

1. Type the keywords to search for into the keyword entry field (you can use the words *and* and *or* in your search).

2. Check the checkbox to make the search active.

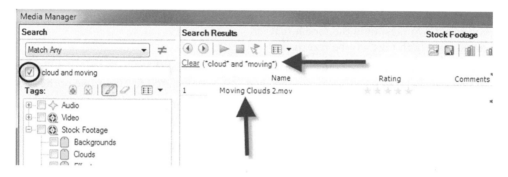

Figure 18.26   Use the **Keyword** search checkbox to turn the search on and off.

In the example, we used the keywords *cloud and moving* and the search returned one file with *Moving Clouds* in the name. Notice that the media matched even though the words in the filename were reversed. This is because it looked for each keyword individually, regardless of the order in which they were found. If you really wanted to find media with the words *clouds moving*, you would leave out the *and* and add quotes around the keywords. If you are ever unsure of what the search criteria is, just look next to the Clear link. The search is always displayed there when active.

Advanced Search

The Advanced search looks in individual fields. You can enable and disable the criteria using the checkboxes to the left of each field, just as you did with the keyword search. You can also remove criteria entirely and add new criteria. Let's start by removing any existing criteria:

To remove advanced search criteria:

1. Click the red **X** in the Advanced search section.

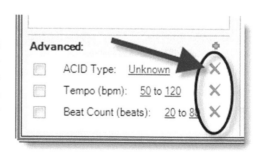

Figure 18.27   Click the red **X** to remove criteria.

To add a field to search:

1.   Click the *green* + (plus sign) to add a field to search.

This will bring up the Search Criteria Chooser, where you can select any of the available fields and add them to the search.

2.   Double-click or drag and drop the field you want to search on.

3.   Click on the value to select a new one.

4.   Check the checkbox to activate the search.

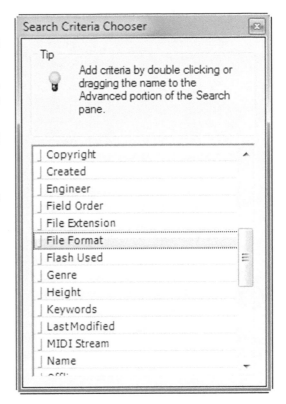

Figure 18.29   Drag and drop a field into the **Advanced** search.

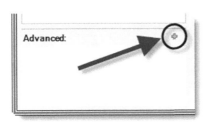

Figure 18.28   Click the green + to add a field to the Advanced search.

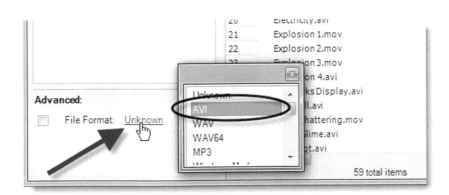

Figure 18.30   Select a value to search by and check the checkbox to activate.

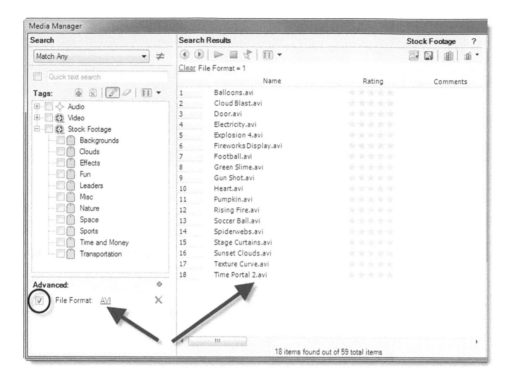

Figure 18.31   Search results from File Format AVI.

It is important to understand that all three searches can be active at the same time. This means that you can select a tag, add a keyword, and use the Advanced search to fine-tune the criteria by which media is returned. You use the checkboxes to control which search is active and use the Clear link to uncheck them all.

Previewing the Media in Vegas Pro

Once you have used a query to narrow down the video clips returned by a search, you might want to preview them in full details on the Vegas preview monitor. This will give you a better view of the footage than the thumbnail view can.

To preview the media in the Vegas preview window:

1.   Click the **Play** button at the top of the search results.

You can also use the **Auto-play** button to have media automatically play as you click on it. This is the same behavior as exhibited in the Vegas Explorer window.

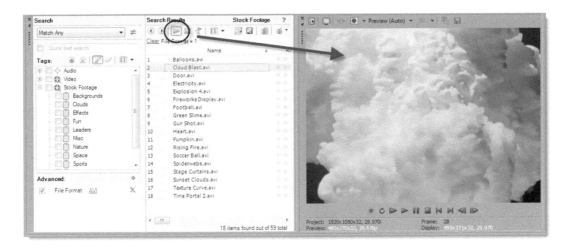

Figure 18.32   Preview media in Vegas Pro.

Placing the Media on the Timeline

Once you have found the piece of media you'd like to use in your project, you can double-click on it to place it on the timeline at the current cursor position, or you can drag and drop it from the Media Manager onto the timeline at any position.

Using Usage Relationships

Earlier in the chapter we mentioned that on the **General Preferences** tab is an option called **Save media-usage relationships in active media library.** If you would like to use the Media Manager to keep track of all the media added to your project, you would enable this option. This will tell the Media Manager to catalog every piece of media that you drop on the timeline or into a media bin, whether you use it or not in the final project. What this allows you to do is then look for media that was used along with this media in any of your projects. For example, if you are using a particular piece of video media in a project and you know that in a previous project you used a sound bite that went well with it but you can't remember which sound file it was, the Media Manager can tell you.

To see media relationships in the Media Manager:

1.   Right-click any piece of media and select **Find Related Items.**

The **Related Items** menu has a submenu that will allow you to find media that was **Used with, Previewed with, Rendered to or from,** and so on. It's a quite powerful relationship mechanism for quickly finding pieces of media that you often use together in projects.

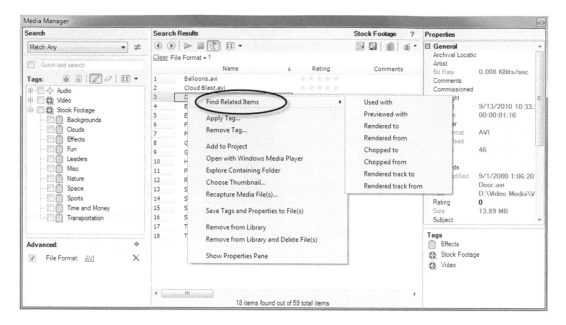

Figure 18.33   Find Related Items.

Conclusion

The Media Manager can be a real timesaver when you're searching for a particular piece of media. It does take some time to set up the way you want it, but once you are organized you will more than make up that time in productivity gain. Don't forget to save the tags with your media, and always press the Clear link before starting a new query so that you get back the media you intended.

4K Resolutions and Vegas Pro
Not Available in Vegas Movie Studio

As camcorders, imagers, and display systems progress, it's only natural that resolutions increase. The RED camcorder, for example, offers a 4K image that is 4096 x 2304 pixels in output image size. Vegas Pro supports the RED and RED EPIC camera file format natively and does so with a rather unusual grace. Even on a mid-level laptop with some optimizations to the computer system (reducing the load on RAM due to number of programs running in the background), RED files can be edited directly off the RED Compact Flash (CF) cards, RED drive, or transferred files on a hard drive while maintaining a full-frame-rate playback. In other words, with a proper computer system, Vegas Pro can manage RED files much the way it manages DV files. Vegas has been 4K-prepared for nearly a decade.

Although it is entirely possible to edit RED files directly from the CF cards and a USB reader, it's not advisable unless you're merely previewing data from the shoot. This can be accomplished while copying and transferring data from the CF card to an external USB, SATA, or Firewire drive. I'd recommend a Firewire 800, USB 3, or external SATA drive for best results.

Editing directly from a REDMag, a RED Drive, or a RED Ram is perfect if dailies

Figure 19.1   Notice that the frame attributes of a RED file in Vegas Pro are square pixel, progressive scan, 23.976, and the format is the raw R3D video.

or rushes are needed, and transfers can be accomplished later in the day. Use the Firewire or ESATA ports on the REDMag for best experiences.

RED files will show up in the Vegas Explorer with the extension r3d. This is the native file extension and is the only file format you'll need to see to open up the RED files on the Vegas Timeline or in the Trimmer tool. In fact, if Auto Preview is enabled, the .r3d file will immediately begin playing in the Preview window (or the Trimmer window, depending on the way your particular Vegas preferences are set up). These files should nearly always play back at full frame rate when you view them via the Auto-preview setting, since these files are unbuffered.

Using the Auto-Preview function is a great way to review shots, mark timecode, or check for any problems in the frame prior to actual shooting.

Figure 19.2

Figure 19.3   Note the RED .r3d files in the Explorer; there may be small QuickTime .mov files that won't apply to the Vegas Pro workflow, but they are applicable in some other NLE applications.

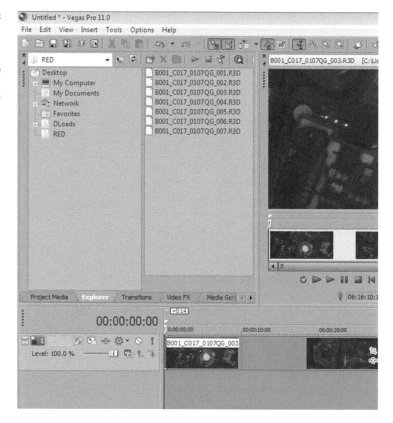

Right-click the **.r3d** files to open them in the Vegas Trimmer, or drag the files to the Vegas Pro Timeline to begin editing. In **Options | Preferences**, Vegas Pro allows users to set a preference that a double-click in Explorer will either open a file on the Vegas Timeline from the cursor point or open a file in the Vegas Trimmer.

That's all there is to it. Simple, fast, easy. No file conversion, no conforming, no rendering to a nonnative format.

Accessing RED Decode/Raw Data

RED shoots in a RAW format, not terribly unlike the way high-end DSLR camcorders shoot. If you're familiar with working with RAW photo files in Photoshop or other graphics editing systems, then you're going to be very comfortable working with the RED Decode files in Vegas Pro.

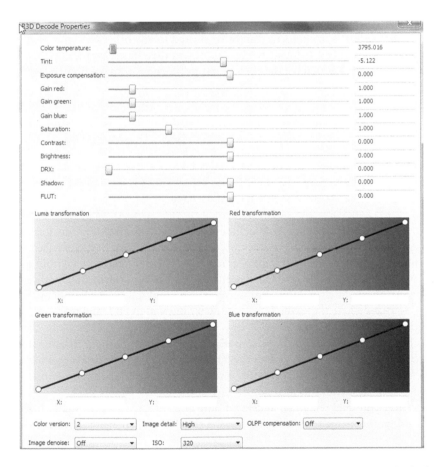

Figure 19.4   The RAW **Decode** dialog box offers a number of image manipulation opportunities for the metadata embedded in the RED media without requiring recompression for preview and without adding noise or processing time to the media.

Access to the Decode properties is fairly straightforward and will immediately show modifications in the Vegas Pro Preview window.

To access the raw file and metadata, open the **Vegas Project Media** tab (**Alt + 5** if the tab isn't already visible) and any RED files that are on the Vegas Timeline or have been imported to the Vegas project will be visible with either a thumbnail or filename.

Right-click an **.r3d** file and in the submenu, choose **File Format Properties** (do not confuse this with the Properties option found just beneath the File Format Properties option). This will open the RED **Decode** properties dialog box.

Most of the options are self-explanatory: color temperature (allowing the frame to be warmed or cooled), color tinting, exposure compensation, and individual color channel gain. Some features are less self-evident, such as the DRX value/slider. The DRX information allows RED to auto-detect blown highlights on individual channels and correct any odd colors that may result from blown highlights. The best way to observe exactly what DRX is doing to an image is to first open a Histogram window in Vegas Pro (**Ctrl + Alt + 2**) and then open the RED **Decode** properties dialog box. (Once the RED dialog box is open, focus cannot be shifted to any other option in Vegas Pro. Yes, this is annoying.) In fact, it is best to locate the best representative frame for the clip that is anticipating changes at the RAW level by placing the cursor on that frame prior to opening the RED Decode properties dialog box.

 Tip_____

Before you open the RED Decode properties dialog box in the Project Media window, place the cursor/playhead on the frame that provides the best representative information for the clip. Once the Decode properties dialog box is open, you cannot move the cursor on the timeline, nor can playback be started. A workaround to this issue is to set up a loop of the clip to be adjusted, start playback, and, while the file is looping, open the RED Decode properties dialog box. At this point, you can see changes to the raw file in real time, with motion media versus a simple still frame.

Other options in the Decode properties dialog box include the ability to control the transformation curves along five unique points. The Gamma curve can be kept in the RED space, converted to the HD Red709 space, linear gamma, or the RED logarithmic space. The same can be set within the Colorspace options; Camera RGB, Rec 709, or RED space. Image detailing offers Low, Medium, and High. It's tempting to set this to High and forget it, since we're all looking for the best detailing we can achieve, yet in most cases where the media is being downconverted to HD (and particularly SD), the highest setting may cause twittering.

The Optical Low Pass Filtering (OLPF) option is an anti-aliasing feature. Be cautious in using this feature; it's easy to remove the "smooth, silky" look of the RED camera if it's overused. Use a high-quality external monitor and set Preview to BEST/FULL for best results. It'll take the computer a moment or two to render each frame, but in the end, it's worth the wait.

With the image denoise, use caution. I recommend using it only when it's obvious the image has a lot of noise. It's easy to soften the image too much when using this feature, so again, have a good monitor handy.

The ISO feature allows compensation for what the ISO of the camera may have been set to. RED sets its ISO at 320. There is some debate in the film-moving-to-digital community about light meters and how RED sets the camera ISO. This option allows for compensation after the shoot (although this may increase noise in the media).

Previewing a 4K Project

Few users will have a 4K resolution monitor capable of displaying the raw media. Most users will require a downconvert to 2K, which Vegas will properly manage on its own. Setting the Vegas Preview window to **Draft/Auto** will provide full frame-rate playback on most systems while still providing quality resolution for editing. Putting the **Preview Window** mode to **Good/Auto** will provide a resolution suitable for color correction that will still provide a reasonable framerate, although **Best/Full** should generally be used for color correction. As always, use a calibrated monitor and use bars from the camcorder to set up the monitor.

Outputting a RED File

As of this writing, Vegas offers limited options for previewing outputting a 4K file. Image sequencing (ideal for a film transfer) or uncompressed AVI options are currently the only means of maintaining a 4K resolution file. Be aware that outputting an uncompressed AVI file at 4K resolution is going to be huge; have a RAID and a very cool, stable computer system before you attempt to output a feature-length project. Check with your film transfer house to learn which format they'd prefer. Some will want image sequence files in one format or another; others might prefer an uncompressed video file. Expect more output options for 4K files as the larger-resolution formats standardize and mature.

Other 4K cameras besides the RED include the Sony F65, the Dalsa Origin, and new models coming from Canon. Vegas is already prepared for these new formats; they will not have the same RAW access module that RED offers, but it is anticipated that Vegas will have identical access to the RAW data from these newer model 4K cameras, just as Vegas was already prepared for the Epic and Scarlet media.

Other Benefits of 4K Resolution Support in Vegas Pro

In the past, users of DLSR cameras have put large photo format files on the Vegas timeline. Due to the 2K restriction of Vegas prior to version 9, photos were significantly downsampled and on some systems the application would simply crash due to available system memory and buffering ability. Consider the weight of putting a couple hundred 4-megapixel images on an NLE's Timeline without a lot of RAM or cache ability; crashing or other hiccups were inevitable.

Vegas Pro makes this a much smaller issue now that it supports higher resolutions. A major benefit to the 4K resolution option is that in doing the "Ken Burns effect" on still images (deep zooms or pans on still photos to give the illusion of movement), the photo can be zoomed more deeply while maintaining great detail.

Additionally, DSLRs used to shoot still image sequences for time lapse may be zoomed into and panned for greater effect, which provides the illusion of motion tracking.

However, keep in mind that as DSLR resolutions grow, too many photos at super-resolutions (greater than 8 megapixels) can still bring some Vegas systems to their knees. In this regard, consider using JPEG, PNG, and

TGA image formats, and if possible reduce high-resolution images to no greater than 4000 pixels in either dimension. Vegas works best with PNG and JPG files. Batch processing tools for Photoshop, PhotoTools, IrfanView, and other image processors are available for no to little cost and will greatly contribute to the stable operation of any NLE system, not to mention savings in file sizes.

Index

Page numbers followed by *b* indicate boxes and *f* indicate figures.

T - #0600 - 071024 - C0 - 235/191/24 - PB - 9780240823690 - Gloss Lamination